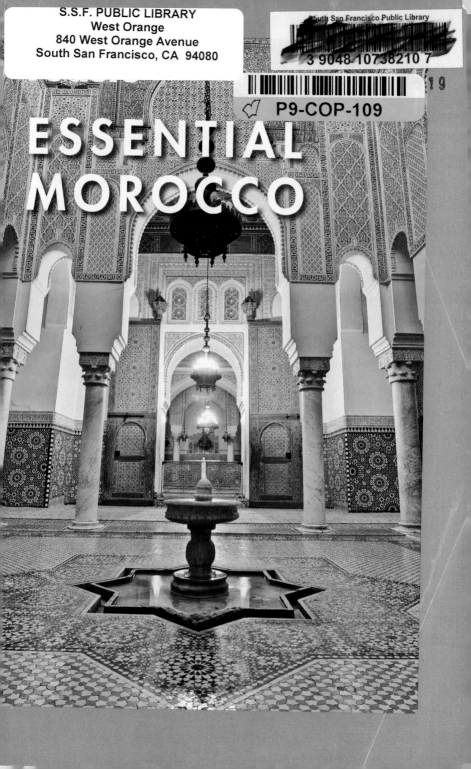

ESSENTIAL
MOROCCO

WELCOME TO MOROCCO

For centuries, Morocco has inspired travelers with its colorful energy, fascinating history, and dazzling combination of Arab, European, and African influence. From vibrant and bustling medinas to the sparse but breathtaking Sahara, the country packs a remarkable variety of adventures into its corner of North Africa. Surfers catch waves at windswept Atlantic coast beaches and hikers trek the scenic Atlas Mountains. Kasbahs and mosques offer a glimpse of a more mystical time, while hip cafés and high-design riads reflect Moroccans' modern, cosmopolitan side.

TOP REASONS TO GO

★ **Exotic Cities:** Sultry Marrakesh, market-filled Fez, historic Rabat.

★ **History:** Ancient ruins, mosques, and Berber villages invite discovery.

★ **Beaches:** From Agadir to Essaouira, surfing and sunbathing abound.

★ **Souks:** Traditional crafts, leather, rugs, and more are for sale in bright markets.

★ **Food and Drink:** Stewed tagines, saffron couscous, smoked zaalouk, mint tea.

★ **Trekking:** The rugged High Atlas and vast Sahara await exploration by camel or on foot.

18 ULTIMATE EXPERIENCES

Morocco offers terrific experiences that should be on every traveler's list. Here are Fodor's top picks for a memorable trip.

1 Camel Trekking

Camel treks are a unique way to explore the rolling sand dunes and abandoned kasbahs of the Moroccan desert, one of the most gorgeous regions on earth. *(Ch. 7)*

2 Mint Tea

Enter any shop, café, or home and you'll be greeted with a cup of refreshing mint tea, the quintessential sign of hospitality in Morocco. *(Ch. 1)*

3 Ben Youssef Medersa, Marrakesh

One of the best-preserved historic sites in Marrakesh, this 16th-century Koranic school and its expansive courtyard is a breathtaking work of architecture. *(Ch. 2)*

4 Kasbah des Oudayas, Rabat

Originally built by Muslim refugees from Spain, Rabat's imposing 12th-century fortress and its quaint walled garden offer a glimpse into the city's long history. *(Ch. 4)*

5 Berber Villages

The semi-nomadic Berber tribes still live in mountain and desert villages, where they continue ancient traditions and you can experience their famed hospitality. *(Ch. 6)*

6 Sahara Desert Camping

The windswept Saharan sand dunes make for the ultimate camping experience. Settle into a simple Bedouin tent for unforgettable stargazing and spectacular sunsets. *(Ch. 7)*

7 Marrakesh Souks

Wind your way through the narrow and colorful labyrinths of the city's medina to haggle for handcrafted rugs, clothing, jewelry, pottery, and more. *(Ch. 2)*

8 Hiking the High Atlas

From North Africa's tallest peak to the epic Cascades d'Ouzoud waterfalls, a trek through the High Atlas Mountains is the perfect respite from urban Morocco. *(Ch. 6)*

9 The Old City of Fez

Fondouks, medersas, mosques, and palaces dating back a thousand years fill the 9,500 alleyways of Fez's medina, making it the world's most active medieval city. *(Ch. 5)*

10 Surfing the Atlantic Coast

The magnificent coastline between Agadir and Essaouira draws surfers and other water-sport fanatics, thanks to its huge waves and extreme winds. *(Ch. 8)*

11 The Goat Trees

Argan oil, a luxury beauty product, comes from trees that grow only in Morocco. Goats are also found in these trees, feasting on nuts, making for a strange photo-op. *(Ch. 8)*

12 Moroccan Music Festivals

Morocco's rich musical heritage is best experienced through its festivals, from the Gnaoua World Music Festival in Essaouria to the World Sacred Music Festival in Fez. *(Ch. 1)*

13 Hammams

An important part of Moroccan culture, hammams are a mixture between a sauna and a Turkish bath. You can choose from inexpensive public ones to luxurious private ones. *(Ch. 2)*

14 Cooking Classes

Shop for groceries at a souk, then learn to make wonderfully aromatic tagines in a cone-hatted pot of the same name. Café Clock offers great classes in Marrakesh and Fez. *(Ch. 2)*

15 Chefchaouen

Founded in the 15th century in the foothills of the Rif Mountains, the blue village of Chefchaouen is considered one of Morocco's most picturesque places. *(Ch. 3)*

16 Hassan II Mosque, Casablanca

One of the few mosques in Morocco non-Muslims can enter, Casablanca's huge Hassan II Mosque is known as the country's most exceptional representation of Moroccan artistry. *(Ch. 4)*

17 Roman Ruins at Volubilis

The well-preserved Volubilis was once the capital of the Roman province of Mauritania and still contains intricate mosaics and majestic columns from the time. *(Ch. 5)*

18 Renting a Riad

While found throughout the country, Marrakesh in particular has a superb collection of restored 16th-century palaces that have been turned into charming guesthouses. *(Ch. 2)*

Fodor's ESSENTIAL MOROCCO

Editorial: Douglas Stallings, *Editorial Director*; Margaret Kelly, *Senior Editor*; Alexis Kelly, Jacinta O'Halloran, and Amanda Sadlowski, *Editors*; Teddy Minford, *Content Editor*; Rachael Roth, *Content Manager*

Design: Tina Malaney, *Design and Production Director*; Jessica Gonzalez, *Production Designer*

Photography: Jennifer Arnow, *Senior Photo Editor*

Maps: Rebecca Baer, *Senior Map Editor*; David Lindroth, Mark Stroud (Moon Street Cartography), *Cartographers*

Production: Jennifer DePrima, *Editorial Production Manager*; Carrie Parker, *Senior Production Editor*; Elyse Rozelle, *Production Editor*; David Satz, *Director of Content Production*

Business & Operations: Chuck Hoover, *Chief Marketing Officer*; Joy Lai, *Vice President and General Manager*; Stephen Horowitz, *Director of Business Development and Revenue Operations*; Tara McCrillis, *Director of Publishing Operations*; Eliza D. Aceves, *Content Operations Manager and Strategist*

Public Relations and Marketing: Joe Ewaskiw, *Manager*; Esther Su, *Marketing Manager*

Writers: Rachel Blech, Jane Folliot, Olivia Gunning Bennani, Sarah Gilbert, Alice Morrison, Lynn Sheppard

Editors: Amanda Sadlowski, Alexis Kelly, Jacinta O'Halloran

Production Editor: Jennifer DePrima

Production Design: Liliana Guia

1st Edition

ISBN 978-1-64097-008-3

ISSN 2574–0652

PRINTED IN THE UNITED STATES OF AMERICA

10 9 8 7 6 5 4 3 2

CONTENTS

Fodor's Features

CONTENTS

MAPS

ABOUT
THIS GUIDE

Fodor's Recommendations

Everything in this guide is worth doing—we don't cover what isn't—but exceptional sights, hotels, and restaurants are recognized with additional accolades. Fodor'sChoice★ indicates our top recommendations. Care to nominate a new place? Visit Fodors.com/contact-us.

Trip Costs

We list prices wherever possible to help you budget well. Hotel and restaurant price categories from $ to $$$$ are noted alongside each recommendation. For hotels, we include the lowest cost of a standard double room in high season. For restaurants, we cite the average price of a main course at dinner or, if dinner isn't served, at lunch. For attractions, we always list adult admission fees; discounts are usually available for children, students, and senior citizens.

Hotels

Our local writers vet every hotel to recommend the best overnights in each price category, from budget to expensive. Unless otherwise specified, you can expect private bath, phone, and TV in your room. For expanded hotel reviews visit Fodors.com.

Top Picks	Hotels &
★ Fodor'sChoice	Restaurants
	🖭 Hotel
Listings	↵ Number of
✉ Address	rooms
✉ Branch address	⦿ Meal plans
☎ Telephone	✕ Restaurant
🖷 Fax	⌂ Reservations
⊕ Website	🏛 Dress code
✉ E-mail	⊟ No credit cards
🎫 Admission fee	$ Price
⊙ Open/closed times	**Other**
Ⓜ Subway	⇨ See also
⊹ Directions or Map coordinates	☞ Take note
	⅀ Golf facilities

Restaurants

Unless we state otherwise, restaurants are open for lunch and dinner daily. We mention dress code only when there's a specific requirement and reservations only when they're essential or not accepted.

Credit Cards

The hotels and restaurants in this guide typically accept credit cards. If not, we'll say so.

EUGENE FODOR

Hungarian-born Eugene Fodor (1905–91) began his travel career as an interpreter on a French cruise ship. The experience inspired him to write *On the Continent* (1936), the first guidebook to receive annual updates and discuss a country's way of life as well as its sights. Fodor later joined the U.S. Army and worked for the OSS in World War II. After the war, he kept up his intelligence work while expanding his guidebook series. During the Cold War, many guides were written by fellow agents who understood the value of insider information. Today's guides continue Fodor's legacy by providing travelers with timely coverage, insider tips, and cultural context.

EXPERIENCE MOROCCO

WHAT'S WHERE

Numbers refer to chapters.

2 Marrakesh. Marrakesh is the meeting point between Morocco's north and south, Arab and Berber, big city and small town. If you see only one city in Morocco, make it Marrakesh.

3 Tangier and the Mediterranean. Many of Morocco's most dramatic social and economic contrasts are painfully evident in Tangier and vicinity. Both the mountain stronghold at the blue city of Chefchaouen and the coastal city of Tetouan are also worth visiting.

4 Rabat and Casablanca. Morocco's economic capital, Casablanca, and political capital, Rabat, are the country's most Europeanized cities. Meanwhile, the Atlantic beaches offer miles and miles of wild surf, sand, and sea.

5 Fez and the Middle Atlas. The Arab-Islamic and Berber chapters in Morocco's history are most evident in the cities of Fez and Meknès. Side trips to the Roman ruins at Volubilis and the holy town of Moulay Idriss are musts, while the Middle Atlas is an underrated mountain range of great natural beauty.

6 The High Atlas. Although parts of the High Atlas can be mobbed with hikers at certain

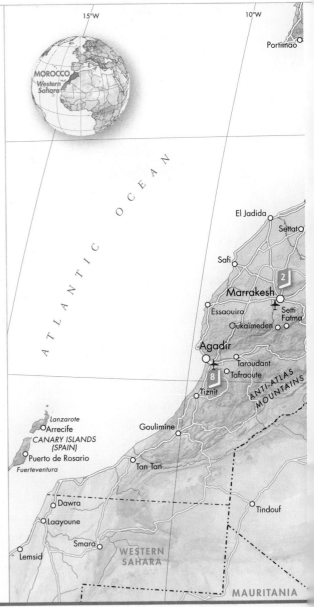

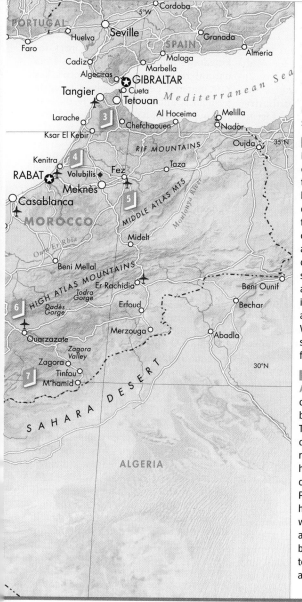

times of year, you can still get away from the package tours on foot or mule and taste rural Morocco at its most colorful and hospitable. Decent roads offer pleasant rides to Setti Fatma and the ski resort Oukaïmeden.

7 The Great Oasis Valleys. No trip to Morocco is complete without a taste of the desert. Some of Morocco's best scenery is on the way out to Merzouga or M'hamid in the southeast, where crumbling kasbahs, arid hills, and winding date palm oases cling to the few rivers that sustain this region. The Dadès and Todra gorges seem impossibly sculpted in the late afternoon light. The Zagora Valley along the river Drâa south of Ouarzazate is known for its green-glazed pottery.

8 Agadir and the Southern Atlantic Coast. Busy Agadir contrasts with Essaouira's breezy bohemian vibe. Agadir, Tafraoute, and Tiznit are connected by curvy mountain roads studded with deserted hilltop kasbahs, villages, and centuries-old granaries. People-watching is interesting here, as women's wraps vary widely within the region, from austere black or navy full-body coverings in Taroudant to brightly flowered garments along the southern coast.

MOROCCO TODAY

Politics

Following the fall of regimes in Tunisia, Libya, Egypt, and Yemen, and unrest in neighboring Algeria during the Arab Spring, the world's gaze shifted nervously to Morocco. Widely regarded as the most moderate and stable of North African nations, the kingdom acted fast to appease dissenters. Although a cautious modernizer in the past, King Mohammed VI, who had already introduced some economic and social liberalization, revised the constitution and brought forward elections in 2011 in response to protests. His ability to calm his populace, many of whom remember the far fiercer reign of his father, Hassan II, ensured the stability of his kingdom and won him the trust of Western nations. Encouraged by Mohammed VI's popularity with his people, Washington granted Morocco the status of non-NATO ally. However, after the gruesome death of a fishmonger in late 2016, ongoing protests in the northern province of Rif have showed there is still a desire for better governance throughout Morocco, especially for the country's Berber minority.

Despite the close proximity of the kingdom to Europe, Morocco remains friendly with the continent, but staunchly independent. Long-term efforts by the UN have tried to end the political deadlock that continues in the Western Sahara, which Morocco seized after Mauritania and Spain withdrew in the 1970s, with little success.

Economy

Morocco is lucky to enjoy a vibrant and expanding tourist trade, and a good annual supply of exports in the form of handicrafts, fruits, vegetables, nuts, and oils. The country is also investing in new industries in global value chains such as textiles, automobiles, and the aeronautical industries in order to diversify its economy. As with other African countries, the kingdom's principal wealth comes from natural resources, with Morocco's key raw material being phosphate (used in pesticides, animal feed, and fertilizers). Although a poor harvest dragged Moroccan GDP growth down to 1.1% in 2016, it is expected to bounce back to 3.8% soon. The country has found it difficult to tackle youth unemployment, which stood for 20% of total unemployment in 2016 and continues to cause concern, due to the vulnerability of the nation's young men to radicalization. In a bid to disperse dissent, there has been a push in recent years to clear shantytowns in major cities and move squatters into specially constructed residences out of town.

Women's Rights

In recent years, King Mohammed VI has had to balance the demands of feminist organizations, calling for an expansion of women's rights, with resistance from the country's Islamic political parties, who fiercely oppose change. In the beginning of the century, Morocco made sweeping reforms to its family-law code, the Moudawana, creating one of the most progressive family codes in the Arab world. The new Moudawana gave women significantly more rights and protections. They now have the right to request a divorce, the legal age of marriage has leapt from 15 to 18, and polygamy is now severely restricted. Women also now have the right to child support and shared custody. In 2011, the country passed a new constitution guaranteeing gender equality. That said, incongruities concerning women's rights remain; generations of customary practices are hard to reverse and the application of the new laws is patchy, especially in more rural areas. To help with this transition, Morocco has introduced female Islamic preachers and guidance counselors called Morchidat, whose role is to help women and girls distinguish between customs, Islam, and the law in asserting their rights.

Religion

An estimated 99% of Moroccans are Muslim, with the king being able to trace his lineage to the Prophet Mohammed. The second most practiced religion is Christianity, which predates Islam; only a few Jewish Moroccans remain today, although they were a significant part of the population pre–World War II. Moroccans are, on the whole, tolerant of other people's beliefs. As in most Islamic countries, a faith of any sort is easier to understand than no faith at all. Muslim prayers are said five times a day, with men tending to gather in mosques upon hearing the call to prayer. It is common to see men praying elsewhere, such as by the side of the road, in fields, or even corners of the office. Women tend to pray in the home and seldom stop work to pray in public throughout the day. It is considered highly impolite to interrupt a person who is praying and advisable not to cross in front of them. Fasting takes place during the holy month of Ramadan, which falls in the ninth month of the lunar cycle.

Despite a close regard for Islam, Moroccans tend to interpret its laws in a less conservative way than many Muslim countries. Travelers familiar with other Islamic nations, such as Pakistan or Saudi Arabia, may be surprised by the fact that modesty in women's dress emphasizes covering the skin rather than disguising the female form. It is not uncommon to see young girls wearing skin-tight jeans with long-sleeve T-shirts and headscarves, rather than the voluminous coverings commonly seen in other Muslim regions. Female visitors find it useful to carry a long scarf or sarong to cover their shoulders or hair upon occasion. There are times when bare arms and low necklines attract unwelcome attention. Similarly, beachwear, shorts, and skirts above the knee are best restricted to the beach. Men are not expected to wear shorts in formal or mixed company and should never go bare-chested anywhere but the beach.

Music

Music is integral to daily and ritual life in Morocco, both for enjoyment and as social commentary. It emanates from homes, stores, markets, and public squares everywhere. In the Rif you hear men singing poetry accompanied by guitar and high-pitched women's choruses; in Casablanca, *rai* (opinion) music, born of social protest, keeps young men company on the streets; cobblers in the Meknès medina may work to the sound of violin-based Andalusian classical music or the more folksy Arabic *melhoum,* or "sung poetry." You know you've reached the south when you hear the banjo strum of Marrakesh's roving storytellers. *Gnaoua* music is best known for its use in trance rituals but has become a popular form of street entertainment; the performers' brass *qraqeb* hand cymbals and cowrie-shell-adorned hats betray the music's sub-Saharan origins. This rich culture of sound has been modernized in recent years with fusions of Western-influenced pop music and traditional Moroccan beats. Morocco's music festivals are growing every year in size, quality, and recognition.

NEED TO KNOW

Rabat

MOROCCO

AT A GLANCE

Capital: Rabat

Population: 34,817, 000

Currency: Moroccan dirham

Money: ATMs common; credit cards accepted, but cash is better for souks

Language: Arabic, Berber, French

Country Code: 212

Emergencies: 19 or 15

Driving: On the right

Electricity: 127v or 220v/50 cycles; plugs have two round prongs

Time: Five hours ahead of New York

Documents: Up to 90 days with valid passport

Mobile Phones: GSM (900 band), UMTS (2100 band)

Major Mobile Companies: Maroc Telecom, Inwi, Orange

WEBSITES

Morocco Travel:
🌐 www.visitmorocco.com

Much Morocco:
🌐 www.morocco.com

GETTING AROUND

✈ **Air Travel:** Casablanca's Mohammed V is the largest airport. Flights from Europe use regional airports like Marrakesh and Agadir.

🚌 **Bus Travel:** For cities not served by trains, buses are relatively frequent, and seats are usually available.

🚗 **Car Travel:** A car is not necessary in major cities, but sometimes it's the best and only way to explore Morocco's mountainous areas, small coastal towns, and rural areas like the High Atlas.

🚆 **Train Travel:** Morocco's punctual rail system serves mostly the north; fares are relatively inexpensive compared to Europe.

PLAN YOUR BUDGET

	HOTEL ROOM	MEAL	ATTRACTIONS
Low Budget	700 DH	120 DH	Dar Si Saïd entrance and most public monuments, 10 DH
Mid Budget	1,500 DH	200 DH	Jardin Majorelle Gardens, 70 DH
High Budget	2,500 DH	500 DH	Hot-air balloon rides, from 2,000 DH

WAYS TO SAVE

Risk the stalls. Dining at a souk food stall can be cheap and delicious, but risky; be sure to eat at popular stalls where food is freshly cooked right in front of you.

Head to the roof. Some budget hotels, especially in the center and south of the country, will let you stay cheaply on a mattress on the rooftop.

Settle in advance. If your taxi doesn't have a meter, it's imperative that you settle on the fare in advance, or you'll risk being severely overcharged.

Bargain. Never, under any circumstances, pay the asking price at a souk; with good bargaining, you can usually take home the item for half or less.

PLAN YOUR TIME

Hassle Factor	Medium. A few direct flights operate from North America, and connections are plentiful. Public transport and taxis are decent, although less reliable in more remote areas.
3 days	Base yourself in Fez, and soak up the culture of its many sights and souks. Take a side trip to the beautiful city of Meknès, Morocco's one-time capital or the Roman ruins at Volubilis.
1 week	Arrive in Casablanca, then hit the road to Rabat, Meknès, and Volubilis. Spend a few days exploring Fez, then catch a flight to Marrakesh.
2 weeks	Continue onward from Marrakesh to the picturesque port city of Essaouira, the beautiful beaches at Agadir, the Berber market town of Tiznit, and the red ocher-walled city of Taroudant.

WHEN TO GO

High Season: July and August are Morocco's high season on the coasts, when crowds are large and prices are high. But inland temperatures soar and only the foolish visit Marrakesh or the desert in summer. Easter and June are also a busy time.

Low Season: November to March is the low season for Morocco, when temperatures are much cooler, but still quite bearable. In fact, this is the perfect time to visit the southern desert areas, or to ski in the High Atlas Mountains. Airfares and big city hotel prices are generally much lower than at other times.

Value Season: The late spring months of April and May and early fall months of September and October are perhaps the best times to visit Morocco, when prices, crowds, and the heat are all more bearable than at their summer highs.

BIG EVENTS

May: Folk music, dancing, and rose products of every kind highlight the two-day Rose Festival at Kelaat-M'Gouna. ⊕ en.kasbahdesroses.com

May/June: The enchanting nine-day Fes Festival of World Sacred Music highlights spiritual music from across the globe. ⊕ www.fesfestival.com

September: Some 30,000 Berbers converge in the High Atlas for the ancient and lively spouse-picking Imilchil Marriage Festival.

READ THIS

- **The Caliph's House: A Year in Casablanca,** Tahir Shah. An English travel writer moves his family to Morocco.

- **Dreams of Trespass: Tales of a Harem Girlhood,** Fatema Mernissi. A leading Moroccan feminist recounts her early life as part of a traditional household.

- **The Sand Child,** Tahar Ben Jelloun. Raised as a boy so she can receive inheritance, a young Moroccan woman sexually awakens.

WATCH THIS

- **Casablanca.** An American expat bumps into a former lover in free-wheeling North Africa in the early days of World War II.

- **The Man Who Knew Too Much.** An American family vacationing in Morocco stumbles upon a murder plot.

EAT THIS

- **Couscous**: steamed semolina topped with meat or vegetable stew

- **Harissa**: hot paste of chilis, garlic, and olive oil

- **Tagine**: spicy stew charcoal-cooked in a pot of the same name

- **Pastilla**: sweet and salty pie of chicken or fish with almonds, cinnamon, and sugar

FLAVORS OF MOROCCO

Close your eyes, inhale, and breathe the spices of North Africa. Situated on ancient trade routes, the kingdom benefits from a vibrant import trade from all corners of the world and an agreeable climate. Despite the summer heat, the fertile red earth, expansive coasts, and cooler mountains produce a bountiful harvest from field, orchard, and ocean. Arab, African, Jewish, Persian, and French influences fuse with ancient Berber culinary skills in the kitchen.

Drinks

Mint tea is at the very heart of Moroccan cuisine and culture. Whether in cosmopolitan Casablanca or a rural Berber village in the Atlas Mountains, there is one universal truth: *thé* is served (that's the French word for it; it's called *atay* in Arabic). Recipes vary from region to region—and even from family to family—but all contain a mix of green tea, fresh mint leaves, and sugar. **Coffee** is served black (*café noir*), with a little milk (*café crème*), or half milk–half coffee (*nuss nuss* in the Moroccan dialect). **Orange juice,** freshly squeezed, is abundantly available in cafés and restaurants as well as from street vendors.

Bread

There is no foodstuff more important to this nation than bread. Seen as God-given, bread is used for mopping up the juices of thick stews, or in place of a fork, in a country where food is traditionally eaten with the fingers. Due to its cultural and religious significance, bread is never placed directly on the ground or thrown away, and it is common to see great piles of stale crusts drying in public areas, ready for collection by the poor or those wanting to feed animals. Bread comes in a variety of shapes and sizes, from the crumbly *harcha* (a popular, yellow, semolina-rich teatime snack) to the easy-to-eat, puffy *batbout*, which resembles a pita pocket and is best stuffed with fish, salad, or meat. The daily bread of the nation is *khobz,* which is a common round loaf of whole-meal or white flour.

Seasonings

Several notable spices and herbs are common in Moroccan cuisine: cumin, paprika, garlic, salt, pepper, ginger, cinnamon, coriander, saffron, turmeric, sesame seeds, fresh parsley, cilantro, *harissa* (red-chili-and-garlic paste), olive oil, and olives. Preserved lemons are another key ingredient in many tagine recipes and some salads. It is common to find cumin on the table as well as salt and pepper.

Breakfast

With Muslims rising at dawn to pray, breakfast is an important and often hearty meal, consisting of a variety of dishes and beverages. There's mint tea and freshly squeezed orange juice, bread, olive oil, honey, nuts, and omelets fried with preserved meat (*khlea*). There are the usual French croissants, *pain au chocolat,* and crepes, plus two delicious traditional Moroccan alternatives. The first is *msemn,* a layered pastry–pancake oozing melted butter and honey. The second is a small holed pancake called a *baghir* that is similar to a drop scone or crumpet. This is equally delicious eaten with honey or jam. Those on-the-go often enjoy a steaming bowl of *beysara,* a thick soup made of fava beans laced with olive oil and cumin.

Moroccan Salads

No meal is complete in Morocco without a salad (*salade marocaine*), a simple dish of chopped tomatoes, cucumber, parsley, and onion, quite often brought to the table whether ordered or not. Dressed with a dash of lemon juice and good amount of olive oil, this tangy, refreshing salad goes well with all manner of main courses. Other popular salads are made with cooked vegetables, such as roasted eggplant pureed with tomatoes and spices, boiled carrots with cinammon and orange juice, and roasted bell peppers in a spicy tomato sauce.

Tagines

A *tagine* is the name for both the stew served in most Moroccan homes at lunch and dinner and the name of the traditional clay pot with a tall, cone-shaped lid in which it is generally cooked. Moroccan tagines use chicken, beef, or lamb as the base along with vegetables like carrots, peas, green beans, and a variety of other ingredients, including chickpeas, olives, apricots, prunes, and nuts. Typical tagines are chicken and preserved lemon, lentils with meat and prunes, chicken and almonds, and *kefta* (meatballs) and egg.

Couscous

Couscous is probably the most famous Moroccan dish, combining tiny balls of steamed wheat pasta with a meat-and-vegetable stew poured on top. The meat base for the stew can be chicken, beef, or lamb, and vegetables usually include a combination of turnip, carrot, sweet potato, pumpkin, and zucchini, with chickpeas and raisins sprinkled throughout. Couscous is typically a Friday-lunch meal but is served at other times as well.

Pastilla

Pastilla is an elaborate meat pie combining sweet and salty flavors. Traditionally filled with pigeon, it is often prepared with shredded chicken. The meat is slow-cooked with spices and then combined with cinnamon, ground almonds, and crisp, thin layers of a phyllo-like dough. Pastilla is reserved for special occasions due to the complexity of its preparation. In urban areas, it is common to find a phyllo chef hard at work preparing the sheets for sale to women without the space, time, or skill to prepare the pastry at home.

Vegetarians

The idea of vegetarianism is foreign to Moroccans, as offering meat is seen as the ultimate in hospitality and an indicator of status. Vegetarians should be wary of "vegetarian" dishes on the menu, because they may simply be the tagine or couscous of the day with the meat chunks removed. Having said that, fresh produce abounds and salads, bread, and eggs are reliable alternatives. Try the Berber omelet, an omelet on a base of stewed tomatoes, onions, and spices available at even the most primitive and meat-heavy roadside cafés.

Dessert

After a meal, Moroccan desserts are often limited to fresh seasonal fruit. Many types of Moroccan pastries and cookies exist, almost always made with almond paste. These pastries are often reserved for special occasions or served to guests with afternoon tea. One common pastry is *kaab el-ghzal* ("gazelle's horns"), which is filled with almond paste and topped with sugar.

Prohibited Items

Both pork and alcohol are forbidden by Islam. Pork is difficult to find in the country except in larger cities with hypermarkets and hotels catering to foreigners. However, alcohol is drunk (discreetly) all over the country and sold openly in bars and hotels catering to foreigners. Both beer and wine are produced domestically.

KIDS AND FAMILIES

Traveling in Morocco with children is great fun, especially because Moroccans adore kids. Locals usually warm to and greet travelers with kids more enthusiastically than they would the average tourist. However, at the same time, expect a few practical challenges along the way.

Choosing a Place to Stay

Choosing the right place depends largely on the ages of your children, the type of holiday you want, the regions you wish to visit, and your budget.

For a beach holiday with on-site kid's activities, a modern resort destination like Agadir is ideal. Here, there is **Club Med** or **ClubHotel Riu Tikida Dunas.** Farther up the coast, the beach at Essaouira offers lots of water sports, and **Sofitel** has a private beach and pool. There is a pretty coastal lagoon resort at Oualidia, too—popular with Moroccan vacationers—and the hotel **La Sultana Oualidia** is luxurious.

For rural activity holidays and trekking, most places are fairly simple mountain *gîtes* (self-catering apartments or homes), *auberges* (hostels), and *maisons d'hôtes* (essentially bed-and-breakfasts in private homes). For deluxe accommodation accessible by road try **Kasbah Tamadot** in Asni near Mt. Toubkal National Park, or **La Pause Marrakech,** a luxe desert-style camp near Marrakesh with outdoor activities including donkey and camel rides. The **Xaluca** hotel group also has family-friendly five-star hotels convenient for hiking trips to the Dadès Gorge and Sahara Desert in Erfoud and Merzouga.

Cities such as Fez, Meknès, and Marrakesh have the widest variety of accommodations. Although a traditional Moroccan riad or riad-style boutique hotel (traditional Moroccan homes or former palaces turned into guesthouses) offers atmosphere in the old medinas, it may be a less attractive option for families with younger kids. You may prefer a more modern hotel, but realize that not all have elevators, even newer ones. If you don't fancy a hotel in the new town, and a riad doesn't suit you, consider renting a villa or apartment, some of which provide a maid, cook, and babysitting services.

Top Experiences for Families

Morocco does not have many ready-made attractions such as zoos or theme parks, but if you like spectacular natural beauty, your family will be well served.

Sahara Desert. You can see the desert by foot, camel, or four-wheel-drive vehicle on short, hour-long rides into the dunes or on full-day treks through an oasis. You can also pack for a multiday trip deep into the Sahara with a nomad guide. Visit Erg Chebbi or Erg Chigaga to climb the highest sand dunes in Morocco, and then glide down on a sand board. Many hotels have their own desert camps, and there are countless agencies in Marrakesh, Ouarzazate, Zagora, Merzouga, and M'hamid, which can fix you up.

Water Sports and Beaches. Agadir has a large concentration of all-inclusive resorts, though few people would go all the way to Morocco for a beach vacation. Families with older children and teenagers should check out the coast between Sidi Ifni and Essaouira for some of the best spots for **kite-surfing, windsurfing,** and **surf schools.** In Marrakesh, **Oasiria** has two pools, waterslides, gardens, and restaurants for hungry kids and parents.

Mountain Trips. Mule trekking or hiking in the **High Atlas Mountains** near Mt. Toubkal is easily achievable for younger children, while toddlers can hop up in front of mom or dad on a mule. Families with smaller kids can stay in one place and take day hikes; if you have older children, you can travel with a guide, staying in mountain gîtes as you pass through neighboring valleys—or even attempt the summit. In the foothills near Marrakesh, **Terres d'Amanar** is an outdoor activity center with archery, climbing, zip lines, and crafts workshops. Near the **Dadès Gorge**, with the help of a guide, you can visit nomad families living in caves and old salt mines.

Film Studios. The **Atlas Film Studios** in Ouarzazate is an interesting stop on the way south. You can see some of the film sets used in major movies such as *Kundun, Kingdom of Heaven,* and *The Mummy.*

Markets and Bazaars. The ancient medinas of Fez and Marrakesh are full of exotic delights—the intricate architecture of palaces and mosques, colorful chaos of the souks, intoxicating smell of sizzling street food, and labyrinthine alleyways where tourists, shoppers, and traders intertwine. In Marrakesh, the bustling main square, **place Djemâa el Fna**, fascinates all ages with its daily cornucopia of musicians, snake charmers, henna artists, storytellers, and acrobats. At night, it is transformed into the biggest outdoor barbecue in the world.

History. Explore one of Morocco's most famous historic sights, the ruined Roman city of **Volubilis** near Meknès, and the **Rabat Archaeological Museum**, which houses many relics from this site. In the Valley of a Thousand Kasbahs, along the Drâa and Dadès valleys, be sure to see the kasbahs of **Telouet**, **Aït Ben Haddou**, and **Taourirt**. The museum at **Ksar Tissergate** near Zagora is also well worth visiting.

Wildlife. Walk in the beautiful cedar forests near **Azrou** and visit an 800-year-old tree as Barbary apes swoop overhead. See apes in the wild and take a boat trip under the waterfall at the **Cascades d'Ouzoud.**

Classes. Learning to shop for produce in the souks and cooking your own tagine is a great family activity. Cooking classes at **Souk Cuisine** in Marrakesh and **Café Clock** in Fez are good starting points.

Practical Considerations

Baby Care. There are almost no public changing facilities or high chairs in Morocco. You can buy disposable diapers in city supermarkets and they are often available individually in corner shops. The quality, however, despite the same branding, is often not the same as in Western countries, so you may want to bring your own. In rural areas you may struggle to find diapers, so stock up if touring. The same goes for formula, though any café or restaurant is happy to boil you water for mixing. The choice of foods for babies who are weaned, but not yet on adult food, is limited and often over-sweetened, so packing baby food might be a good idea. Breast-feeding should be done discreetly.

Traveling with Smaller Kids. Most car-rental agencies and tourist transport providers are able to supply a child seat (car seats are now a legal requirement, but check in advance). In taxis and buses there is rarely even a seat belt and car seats are not obligatory. If a child is small enough to sit on your lap, he or she usually travels for free on buses and taxis.

Walking. Sidewalks are rare, or else broken and narrow, which makes pushing a stroller difficult. It's easier to carry small children.

Sun Care. Children are very prone to sunburn, dehydration, and sunstroke, so always have plenty of drinking water, strong sunscreen, and sun hats.

RECOMMENDED TOUR OPERATORS

Morocco's infrastructure has improved in recent years, making traveling around the country by train or even by car easier. But there are two key areas where it may be more helpful to have a local guide, even if you don't choose to do a fully guided trip to Morocco. Despite some development in rural Morocco's infrastructure, the High Atlas remains relatively undiscovered: hence its unspoiled charm. In order to reap the rewards of such an area, suitable transport (whether organized in advance or upon arrival in the region) and an experienced driver are keys to a successful trip. The same is said for the desert, where arranging camels, four-wheel-drive transportation, and tented camps is best done through a well-connected local guide.

Even the smallest one-man-band tour operators in Morocco now have an Internet presence, and it is possible to book tours and excursions online through internationally renowned or local outfits. For both the High Atlas and Sahara regions, local guides are easily found in Marrakesh or, for the High Atlas, in the small hill stations, most notably Imlil. A homegrown guide personalizes your traveling experience, often suggesting unknown restaurants and small riads, or organizing (with your permission) a visit to his or her own home. The plus side here is the authentic cultural experience; the downside may be a lack of reliability, possibly poor vehicle maintenance, and limited English. All the good hotels in Marrakesh can make these arrangements, even with little prior notice. Prices vary greatly, but you should expect to pay around $150 a day for a vehicle and driver-guide (and you should tip around $10 per day). If recruiting locally, expect to pay in dirhams—in cash, rather than

credit card. If making these arrangements in advance, check how experienced a tour operator or guide is.

You tend to get what you pay for in Morocco, and almost anything is possible, with operators capable of arranging all manner of tours. High-end travel, for example, might include air-conditioned luxury transport, five-star accommodations, spa treatments, and lavish meals. Another option might be experience-based: with quad biking, ballooning, cooking classes, a trip to a local *moussem* (festival), or skiing in Oukaïmeden. Very popular these days are ecotours, which typically arrange stays in unspoiled Berber hamlets or eco-lodges; visit local cooperatives, such as argan oil or carpet-weaver co-ops; and shower under breathtaking waterfalls.

Luxury Tours

Many large international tour companies offer ultraluxurious tours. On the plus side, you have the backing of an established and respected operator and are able to pay by credit card prior to travel. On the minus, the choice of luxury in rural parts of Morocco is limited, and you may miss out on some of the simple charms of the country.

Abercrombie and Kent. Pioneers for years in the luxury travel market, this hugely respected outfitter offers a number of tailor-made, high-end packages to Morocco. ☎ 800/554–7016 ⊕ *www.abercrombiekent.com* ✉ *From $2995.*

Travel Exploration. This upmarket, female-owned company guarantees in-depth, authentic travel experiences that are curated to deliver an insider's view of the country. Private tours include a combination of architecture, culture, arts and crafts, gastronomy, rural adventure, special workshops, food tours, and Jewish heritage, all led by expert local guides. ☎ *800/787–8806* ⊕ *www.kensingtontours.com* ✉ *From $1850.*

Experiential Tours

Plan-it Morocco. Plan-It Morocco promises a new world of sensory experiences in the old world of Fez and throughout the country. Hugely experienced company founders (Australian Michele Reeves and Briton Gail Leonard) are passionate about sharing their discoveries in and around this ancient city and Morocco-wide. They create experiences that let you taste, smell, feel, and hear Morocco rather than merely seeing it. Immensely popular are their culinary adventures, which incorporate tastings, cooking classes, and supplier tours. ☎ *0535/63–87–08* ⊕ *www.plan-it-fez.com* ✉ *From $80.*

High Atlas Tours

Moroccan Mountain Guides. This team of young, passionate Berber and Spanish guides specializes in the High Atlas. They offer homestays and hotels with a family atmosphere as well as cultural tours in more remote areas. There's a strong slant to ecotours, including mountain biking, horseriding, Toubkal ascents, and bivouacs. English, Spanish, French, Arabic, and Berber speakers are available. Half-day and full-day treks typically start in the High Atlas or excursions can be organized from Marrakesh. ☎ *0657/71–10–53 in Morocco* ⊕ *www.moroccomountainguides.co.uk* ✉ *From $120.*

Moroccan Gates. This young company, established by graduates of Morocco's only mountain guide school in the Ait Bougemez Valley, combines in-depth mountain knowledge with years of experience of working for larger tour operators. The "Toubkal Express" tour promises to take you to the highest summit in North Africa in three days. ☎ *0670/39–85–27 in Morocco* ⊕ *www.xaluca.com* ✉ *From $45 for 2 people on a half-day trek.*

Sahara Tours

Desert Majesty. Based in Ouarzazate, this company offers budget 4x4 tours using local drivers who know the region inside and out. One of their tours combines the desert with the Anti-Atlas region around Taroudant. ⊕ *www.desertmajesty.com* ✉ *From $200.*

SheherazadVentures. This English–Moroccan boutique tour company offers tailored private travel throughout Morocco, specializing in the Sahara Desert and the Great South. It's good for families and couples who want hands-on cultural activities, an authentic desert experience, and top–notch service. ☎ *0615/64–79–18 in Morocco* ⊕ *www.saharaexpe.ma* ✉ *From $300 a day for 2 people.*

GREAT ITINERARIES

THE IMPERIAL CITIES: THE CLASSIC TOUR OF MOROCCO

For longer stays in Morocco, tailor your tour around more exhaustive exploring of regions and adventurous diversions. If time is limited, focus on the major experiences and sights. This weeklong holiday gives you enough time to sample the best of Morocco. Remember to add a day on each end for travel time (a direct flight from New York to Casablanca takes approximately eight hours), and pace yourself to see the most important places.

Day 1: Arrival in Casablanca

Flights generally arrive in Casablanca in the early morning. The city doesn't have that many sights and only requires a few hours to see them all. As your starting point, visit the **Hassan II Mosque** and the Mohammed V Square designed in French colonial, Art Deco style. You're going to be exhausted anyway after a transatlantic flight, so spend your first night in Casablanca; however, if you want to make an early start in the morning, travel one hour along the coast to Rabat.

Day 2: Rabat

Explore the capital city of Rabat. The best sights in the city are the **Hassan Tower** and **Mohammed V Mausoleum, Chellah Gardens and Necropolis,** and **Oudayas Kasbah** overlooking the Atlantic Ocean. In the late afternoon, drive to Meknès to spend the night.

Day 3: Meknès and Volubilis

Begin your tour by passing the **Bab Mansour** and visiting the holy **Mausoleum of Moulay Ismail,** which is open to non-Muslims. Walk toward the lively place el-Hedime, which leads to the medina. Tour the open bazaars of the medina streets; enjoy an inexpensive classic Moroccan lunch; and visit the food souk near the row of pottery stands. The **Museum of Moroccan Art** in the 19th-century Dar Jamai palace and **Heri el Souani** (Royal Granaries) are recommended stops. In the afternoon, drive 30 minutes to the ancient Roman archeological ruins of **Volubilis.** When you approach, the Triumphal Arch rises in the open field. Count on 90 minutes for a thorough visit. The Tangier Gate, House of Orpheus, House of Columns, and House of Ephebus are must-sees. You can spend the night near Volubilis at Moulay Idriss, or head back to Meknès.

Days 4 and 5: Fez

Try to arrive in Fez as early as possible so you can spend two full days exploring everything the **Fez el-Bali, Fez el-Djedid,** and **Ville Nouvelle** have to offer: medieval monuments, artisan workshops, public squares, ancient tombs, cultural museums, chaotic souks, atmospheric cafés, and palatial gardens. The blue-tiled gate of **Bab Boujeloud** is the gateway to the main alley of Talaa Kebira. The most important sites include the **Bou Inania medersa, Attarine madrassa, Mausoleum of Zaouia Moulay Idriss II** (peek in from the doorway—it's not open to non-Muslims). and **Karaouine Mosque and University** (the latter generally considered the oldest academic institution in the world, with a recently renovated library that welcomes visitors). Visit the restored **Nejjarine fondouk** for the best examples of woodworking craftsmanship. Watch the full fabrication process of the leather tanneries from a rooftop terrace. Shop for the famous blue-and-white Fassi pottery. Discover the area of the **Royal Palace** (Dar el-Makhzen) that leads to the active Mellah quarter beyond the Fez el-Djedid. Watch the sunset over the entire medina from the **Merenid tombs**

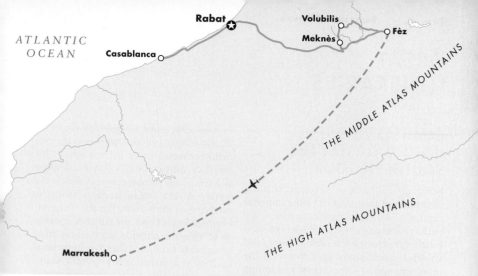

or **Musée des Armes** atop the hills of the Borj Nord, or from the **Borj Sud**, south of the walled city. Indulge in an authentic Fassi dinner in a riad courtyard. Spend two nights here.

Days 6 and 7: Marrakesh

The quickest way to travel the 398-km (242-mile) distance between Fez and Marrakesh is by plane; but be warned, most flights stop off in Casablanca. After dropping your bags at your hotel in Marrakesh, hit the ground running. The best place to start is the famed **Djemâa el Fna**, the perfect gateway into the labyrinth of medina streets filled with hundreds of souks, including the **Souk des Teinturiers** for leather, **Souk Addadine** for metalwork, and **Souk Zarbia**, the main carpet market. The **Ali ben Youssef Medersa, Dar Si Saïd** museum, **Palais Bahia**, and **Koutoubia Mosque** are important sites (though non-Muslims cannot enter the mosque). Walk south of the Palais Bahia to explore the bustling streets of the **Mellah**, the former Jewish quarter and largest in Morocco. In the evening, splurge on a Moroccan feast, or head to the open grills in back on the busy main square. On your second day in Marrakesh, take a petit taxi for a relaxing promenade through the **Ville Nouvelle** and lush **Majorelle Gardens and Museum**, where

TIPS

■ One of only two mosques in Morocco non-Muslims can enter is the Hassan II Mosque in Casablanca (the other is the Tin Mal mosque in the High Atlas mountains). Visits are allowed only between prayer times (with official on-site guides) at 10 am, 11 am, and 2 pm. The 2 pm tour tends to be quieter, as bus groups visit in the morning.

■ During Ramadan, check for special hours; while many sites are open on holy days, some local restaurants and cafés close for the day or entire month.

■ Make your visit more special by attending an annual outdoor event, such as the World Sacred Music Festival held in Fez or the Marrakesh Popular Arts Festival, which hosts traditional musicians and dancers from all over Morocco.

you can do some bird-watching and see an extraordinary collection of Berber ceramics, textiles, jewelry, and art. After, head back toward the medina and visit the 16th-century **Saadian Tombs** for one of the country's finest representations of Islamic *zellij* (tile) work. Plan a relaxing hammam treatment to rejuvenate after a week of touring.

GREAT ITINERARIES

COASTAL AND INLAND OASES: THE SOUTHERN TOUR

For those who want to escape the bustling medinas and touristy feel of the imperial cities, the Southern Atlantic coastline is the perfect alternative, with miles of deserted beaches, enchanting seaside villages, and colorful exotic landscapes to enrich the mind and spirit. The scenery is stunning and varied with rocky wilderness, vast seascapes, and fertile plains. Much of the area (except for Agadir) remains pristine and gets relatively few visitors. Swim, surf, sunbathe, bird-watch, and breathe in fresh ocean air. Laid-back towns, surfer havens, coastal resorts, and unexpected oases offer a holistic way to learn about local culture, food, language, and history.

Day 1: Marrakesh

Fly directly to Marrakesh Menara International Airport. Rent a car in the airport terminal, and check in to a hotel in Guéliz. Take a taxi to enjoy a delectable Moroccan dinner and experience the exotic activity of the **Djemâa el Fna,** the city's main square. Don't miss the city's excellent nightlife, with live street entertainment, local clubs, bars, and theater performances showcasing the fusion of Berber, Arab, African, and Andalusian influences in music and dance.

Day 2: Essaouira

Rise early to drive west to the relaxing, picturesque port city of Essaouira. After you check in to your hotel, take a walking tour of the harbor and town of whitewashed houses, and then stop to have lunch near the port. Don't miss the fresh charcoal-grilled sardines and shrimp in seaside food stalls. The town is a hub for contemporary Moroccan

artists—check out **art galleries** showcasing Gnaoua expressionism. Shop the colorful pedestrian-only medina streets for ceramics, thuya wood, *babouches* (leather slippers), and woven fabrics. Watch the sunset on the ocean horizon atop the ramparts of the **kasbah.** For the best panoramic view, access the fortress at **Skala de la Ville,** the cliffside sea bastion lined with brass cannons. Dine on fresh local seafood at a casual open grill or in one of many restaurants around the medina and along the beachfront.

Day 3: Agadir

Head south to Agadir, stopping off for magnificent sea views on the undisturbed sand dunes of Morocco's most beautiful beaches. **Sidi Kaouki, Tafedna,** and **Taghazout** are the most well-known beaches to sunbathe and dip your toes into the Atlantic waters. **Taghazout** attracts surfers and offers brisk ocean breezes. When you finally arrive in Agadir, visit the hilltop **kasbah** and **fish stalls** by the harbor. Enjoy dinner and one night here.

Day 4: Tiznit

Continue your journey to Tiznit, famous for its silver and wool blankets. Stay one night in Tiznit to experience local Berber living and hit its wonderful market, especially if you are looking for jewelry.

Day 5: Tafraoute

On Day 5, discover the natural beauty of the Anti-Atlas region, passing palm groves, almond orchards, rocky landscapes, fertile valleys, and fortified towns. Pass through the small villages **Igherm** and **Oumnast** before enjoying the beauty of Tafraoute. Explore the **Ameln Valley** region, then return to town in the late afternoon. Spend the night at the Auberge Kasbah Chez Amaliya, under hillsides scattered with pisé villages.

Day 6: Taroudant

Take a relaxing drive toward Taroudant, where the atmosphere is very low-key and you can enjoy the walk around the open markets and historic ramparts. The red-ocher-walled city is well known for hand-crafted leather items and aromatic spices. There are two main souks in the town. In the medina, don't miss the jewelry souk, fish market, kasbah, and pretty gardens. Listen for Tashelheit, the Berber dialect of the southern Souss region. On Sunday, locals from surrounding areas sell produce, livestock, and various wares near the main gate. A short loop drive east, about 10 km (6 miles) from Taroudant, takes you through the fertile Souss valley plains and barren terrain leading toward the ruins of the Kasbah de Frieja. Spend the night in Taroudant.

Day 7: Return to Marrakesh

Count on at least four hours to return to your starting point. If you plan to depart on the same day, head straight to the Menara airport. If you decide to stay one more evening, head back to the famed Djemâa el Fna, and shop for last-minute souvenirs in the **Souk des Teinturiers** for leather, **Souk Addadine** for metalwork, and **Souk Zarbia** for carpets. The **Ali ben Youssef Medersa, Dar Si Saïd** museum, **Palais**

Bahia, and **Saadian Tombs** are important sites. If time and energy permit, walk south of the Palais Bahia to explore the bustling streets of the Mellah, the largest former Jewish quarter in Morocco. Another option is to book a hammam treatment in your hotel for a final hedonistic treat.

TIPS

■ Go off the beaten track—head to coastal destinations of Oualidia and Mirleft, a small village fast becoming a trendy spot for surfers and sun worshippers.

■ For an outdoor adventure, arrange a horse ride on the beach or rent ATVs through several stables or quad-trek companies.

■ To avoid serious problems, buy and carry a supply of bottled water to beat the heat on beaches and while walking through the villages and open terrain of the Anti-Atlas. Bring sunscreen. Both are difficult to find on the road.

■ Carry a Moroccan-Arabic phrase book. Neither English nor the standard Arabic of the Middle East are widely spoken in rural regions.

GREAT ITINERARIES

QUINTESSENTIAL MOROCCO: THE GRAND TOUR

In two weeks you can experience most of Morocco: coastal havens on the Atlantic coast, the High Atlas Mountains, pre-Saharan palmeries, Berber and Moorish architecture, rural hillside towns, and exquisite imperial cities.

Days 1 and 2: Tangier, Tetouan, and Chefchaouen

The best way to enjoy Tangier is by taking a walking tour along the beachfront. Enter the medina and see the **Grand Mosque** and large market at the **Grand Socco.** Head to the north side of the mosque to enter the beautiful **Mendoubia Gardens** before meandering through the smaller alleyways to the **Petit Socco.** From here, reach the 15th-century **kasbah** and sultanate palace of **Dar el-Makhzen,** which houses the **Museum of Moroccan Arts** and **Museum of Antiquities.** Visit the historic **American Legation Cultural Center and Museum** commemorating the first diplomatic relations between the United States and Morocco. Enjoy a leisurely dinner by the water. On Day 2, pick up a rental car and drive southeast through the Rif Mountains to visit **Tetouan,** the historic town and UNESCO World Heritage Site dating from the 8th century. Continue onto the stunning blue-washed hillside city of **Chefchaouen;** stay in Casa Hassan-Dar Baibou, which is nestled in the heart of the medina.

Day 3: Meknès and Volubilis

Start early on Day 3. Drive through **Ouazzane** en route to Fez, stopping off at the Roman ruins of **Volubilis.** Spend at least 90 minutes walking the grounds. The Tangier Gate, Diana and the Bathing Nymphs mosaic, House of Orpheus, House of Columns, and House of Ephebus are must-sees. Then continue onto Meknès, arriving by midday. Pass the **Bab Mansour** and visit the holy **Mausoleum of Moulay Ismail,** which is open to non-Muslims. Walk toward the lively place el-Hedime, which leads into the medina. Tour the open bazaars of the medina streets and have some lunch. Near the row of pottery stands, visit the food souk. The **Museum of Moroccan Art** in the 19th-century Dar Jamai palace and **Heri el-Souani** (Royal Granaries) are recommended stops. Late in the afternoon, get back in the car and continue to Fez, arriving by nightfall, and splurge on a sumptuous Fassi meal in a riad or former palace.

Days 4 and 5: Fez and the Middle/High Atlas

Spend Day 4 and the morning of Day 5 exploring the Fez **medina,** absorbing the view from one of many rooftop terraces overlooking this ancient labyrinth or atop the hill of the **Musée des Armes** for an incredible panorama of the whole city. Tour the Fez el-Bali and Fez el-Djedid. Don't miss the blue-tiled gate of **Bab Boujeloud, Bou Inania medersa, Attarine madrassa, Zaouia Moulay Idriss II, Nejjarine fondouk,** and **Karaouine Mosque and University.** Visit the tanneries to find leather bargains, and explore the souks for famous blue-and-white Fassi pottery and carved cedar wood. On the afternoon of Day 5 head south through olive groves and small villages before reaching the indigenous macaques playing in their natural habitat of the serene **Azrou Cedar Forest** en route to **Erfoud,** where you can spend the night.

Days 6 and 7: Merzouga Dunes and Ouarzazate

Rise very early on Day 6 to catch the sunrise over the **Merzouga dunes,** and then get on the road to **Tinerhir.** Visit the spectacular **Todra Gorge** and stay overnight in this dramatic region. On Day 7 explore the rugged landscape on the **kasbah** route in the Dadès Valley, passing stunning cliffs and canyons and palm-lined oases on the road to **Ouarzazate.** Treat yourself to a night at the wow-factor Hotel Sultana, where you can stargaze surrounded by flickering lanterns.

Days 8–11: Marrakesh and Essaouira

Devote Day 8 to driving the Tizi-n-Tichka pass to Marrakesh, stopping off at the *ksour* (fortified villages) of **Aït Ben Haddou** and **Telouet.** Settle into a Marrakesh hotel by nightfall, and spend days 9 and 10 storming the medina, architectural monuments, and **Djemâa el Fna.** On Day 11, escape the crowds and head west to the calm coastal town of **Essaouira** for a relaxing afternoon and evening by the Atlantic shores.

Days 12–14: Oualidia, Casablanca, and Rabat

Day 12 takes you north along the coast to **Oualidia,** where you should try some of the famous oysters, then on to the former Portuguese port town of **El Jadida.**

TIPS

■ If you'd rather stick mainly to the four imperial cities, take the train instead of a rental car. It's inexpensive, reliable, and fast.

■ A car is the best and sometimes only way to reach Morocco's mountainous area, small coastal villages, and rural regions, where roads are often rough and dirt.

■ Avoid driving at night. Roads are not well lighted, if at all.

■ Consider an adventure tour like camel riding in the Sahara, white-water rafting on the Ahansal River, or hot-air ballooning over the Ourika Valley.

■ Avoid faux guides and unlicensed tour drivers.

Spend the night here at the charming Hotel L'Iglesia. On Day 13, check out the stunning ocean-side **Hassan II Mosque** in Casablanca before heading up to Rabat for your last day. Wander through Rabat's **rue des Consuls** for last-minute purchases on your way to the 12th-century **Kasbah des Oudayas,** savoring your final taste of imperial Morocco. Casablanca is about an hour away by train.

THE DYNASTIES OF MOROCCO

For centuries, Morocco, whose essence lies in a culturally rich mosaic of Arabic, European, and African influences, has lured and intrigued foreigners. With a complex and tumultuous history dating back more than 5,000 years, Morocco today is as unique and exotic as the diverse ethnic civilizations that have shaped everything here from language, music, art, and architecture to politics, education, and the economy.

 At the crossroads between East and West, Africa and Europe, Morocco has attracted invading conquerors seeking a strategic foothold in fertile valleys, desert oases, and coveted coastal outposts on the Atlantic and Mediterranean. Excavations from the 12th century BC show the remains of Phoenician settlements in ancient times. It was not until the 7th century, when Arabian invaders introduced Islam, that the Moroccan political landscape became more spectacular, often extreme, with radical religious reformers founding Muslim kingdoms in the midst of Christian encroachments and nomadic Berber tribal rule. Rural Berber tribes engaged in lawless conflict, battling it out with bloody family feuds in the harsh Sahara and unforgiving cliffs of the Atlas mountains. Successive invasions by Arab, French, and Spanish civilizations ensued, but the indigenous Berbers survived, remaining an integral component of today's Morocco. European colonization ultimately gave way to Morocco's independent state and a centralized constitutional government, still ruled today by monarchs, descended from the Alaouite Dynasty.

(left) Casablanca's Hassan II Mosque (top) Tomb of Moulay Ismail, Méknes

(left) A mosaic in the Roman ruins at Volubilis (above) an aerial view of the city of Moulay Idriss (right) a Roman coin excavated near Essaouira, on Morocco's Atlantic coast

1200 BC – AD 700

Predynastic Morocco

As Phoenician trading settlements expanded along the Mediterranean, the Romans also began to spread west through North Africa, declaring Volubilis its capital, whose ruins stand outside of Meknès. In the 2nd century BC, the Romans annexed Volubilis, Lixus, Chellah, and Mogador. Volubilis, orginally a Berber settlement, expanded dramatically under the Romans. The first Arab invasions occurred circa AD 682, collapsing the Roman Empire.

682 – 1000

Idrissid Dynasty

Under the regime of Oqba Ibn Nafi, Arabs spread the religion of Islam and its holy language, Arabic, both of which took hold (to varying degrees) throughout Morocco. In 788, exiled from Baghdad, Moulay Idriss I established the first Islamic and Arab dynasty that lasted almost 200 years. He set out to transform the village of Fez into the principal city of western Morocco. In 807, Idriss II, his son, founded Fez el-Bali (literally, Fez the Old) as the new intellectual capital in the Fez River's fertile basin—the Oued Fez, also known as Oued el-Yawahir, the River of Pearls. Attracted by its importance, Andalu-

sian and Tunisian Muslims arrived and established one of the most significant places of learning during its time—the Kairaouine University. The Fez medina is divided into two quarters on either side of the Fez River. The Andalusian Quarter originally housed refugees from Moorish Spain, who had begun to flee the *Reconquista* (the Christian re-conquest of Spain); the Kairaouine Quarter originally housed refugees from the Kairaouine. By the 10th and 11th centuries, the Bedouin tribe known as the Benu Hilal descended upon rural regions, destroying farmlands and villages.

Rome annexes
Morocco

Moulay Idriss I establishes first
Arab-Islamic dynasty in Morocco

Berber Merinid Dynasty
established

400   800   1200   1600

1

IN FOCUS THE DYNASTIES OF MOROCCO

(top left) Aït Ben Hadou, a ksar near Ouarzazate (near right) the entrance gates to Chellah, Rabat (far right) the towering minaret for the Koutoubia Mosque in Marrakesh

Almoravid Dynasty

1060 – 1150

From the south, one of the major Berber tribes emerged to create the Almoravid Dynasty, which led conquests to control desert trade routes to the north. By 1062, the Almoravids controlled what is now Morocco, Western Sahara, and Mauritania. Youssef Tashfin established Marrakesh as his capital, building fortressed walls and underground irrigation channels, and conquered Tlemcen—what is today Algeria. He eventually extended his kingdom north into Spain by 1090.

Almohad Dynasty

1150 – 1248

The Almohad Dynasty, started by radical reformer Ibn Toumert (the Torch) in the High Atlas village of Tinmal, gave rise to an empire stretching across Spain, Tunisia, and Algeria. The Almohads built the current capital of Rabat and its famous landmarks, Marrakesh's iconic Koutoubia mosque, and the Giralda Tower in Seville. After 100 years of rule, the Almohad empire collapsed because of civil warfare, causing Berbers to return to local tribes.

The Merinid Dynasty

1248 – 1472

The nomadic Banu Merin Berber tribe from the Sahara established the Merinid Dynasty, pushing westward into northeastern Morocco and ousting the Almohads, who were once their masters. As Merinid tribesmen waged holy wars, they seized control of the Fez el-Jdid, constructing numerous Islamic mosques and madrassas (colleges). Tribal in-fighting served to weaken the dynastic rule while invaders from Portugal captured coastal cities.

(far left) Asilah, a city in
northern Morocco (near left)
the Saadian Tombs in the
Marrakesh medina (above) the
fortified walls of Taroudant

The Wattisid Dynasty
1472 – 1554

Facing mounting territorial occupation by the Portuguese in what are now Tangier, Essaouira, and Agadir, the Merinids lost control to the Wattisids, due to the rising perception that a ruler was only legitimate if they descended from the Prophet Mohammed. The Wattisids reigned between 1472 and 1554 from Fez, relinquishing rule because of Moorish conquests on the Moroccan side of the Straits of Gibraltar. By 1492, Muslims had lost control of Spain and sought refuge back in the Maghreb.

The Saadian Dynasty
1554 – 1669

As the first Arab kingdom since the Idrissids, the Saadian Dynasty drove out the Christians. Lacking any loyalty to Berber tribes, they also proclaimed their superiority as direct descendants of the prophet Mohammed. The Saadi family originally settled in the Drâa Valley near Zagora in the 12th century and later in the Sous near Taroudant, which became the Saadian capital until they declared Marrakesh their sultanate in 1524. The greatest of the eleven Saadian sultans, Ahmed el Mansour, reigned for more than 25 years, building ties with England's monarchy against Spain. He commanded an army to conquer the West African Songhai empire and led a gold rush on the Niger River. His impact on Morocco as "The Victorious" ended when he died in 1603, leaving his vast kingdom to his sons, who continued to reign for the next 60 years in both Marrakesh and Souss but failed to keep order and peace. General anarchy swept the country as Jewish and Muslim refugees from Catholic Spain arrived on chaotic shores while bands of pirates (the notorious Barbary pirates) sailed from Rabat and Salé.

Moulay Rashid captures Marrakesh from Saadiens	Morocco signs a treaty with Spain	Morocco becomes a French protectorate	Moroccan independence
1700	**1800**	**1900**	**2000**

1

IN FOCUS THE DYNASTIES OF MOROCCO

(far left) Moulay Ismail, who united and liberated Morocco from European powers in 1672 (near left) the gardens of the Museum of Moroccan Arts, Fez (bottom right) Tangier's waterfront promenade

The Alaouite Dynasty

1669 – 1894

The Alaouite Dynasty, led by Moulay Rashid, captured Marrakesh in 1669. By 1672, the ruler Moulay Ismail seized Meknès, launching years of brutal holy wars while effectively liberating the country from European powers and laying the foundation for European trade relations. In 1767, Morocco signed a peace treaty with Spain and a trading agreement with France. In 1787, a U.S. peace treaty was signed. But the 19th century saw losses of territory to France.

European Conquest

1906 – 1956

By 1906, the majority of Africa was under European rule. Morocco, though still independent, was on the verge of bankruptcy after years of borrowing from European powers, in particular France. The Treaty of Fez in 1912 distributed Morocco's regions between Spain and (mostly) France, declaring the country as a French protectorate with Rabat as its capital. It was during this time that the Glaoui, who controlled one of the High Atlas passes from their kasbah at Telouet, became allies with the French. Uprisings took place in the 1920s, and by the 1930s and 1940s,

violent protests across the country heightened as the independence movement of the Istiqulal Party gained strength in Fez. Writers including Paul Bowles settled in Tangier, an international zone since 1923, and began an artistic counter-culture there. By 1955, the situation had reached a boiling point; France granted Morocco independence in 1956.

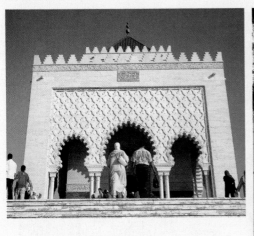

(above) The Mohammed V
Mausoleum, Rabat (right)
Agadir's popular beachfront

Return of the Alaouite Dynasty

1956 – 1961

In 1956, Mohammed V returned from exile to regain the Moroccan throne. The Glaoui-French alliance was broken, and the Glaoui Dynasty went into an immediate decline. When Mohammed V died unexpectedly in 1961, his son, Hassan II, inherited the responsibility to continue social and political reforms, building up the country and maintaining his position as the country's spiritual leader. Hassan II was instrumental during the 1970s and 1980s in developing foreign relations between North Africa and the world.

A New Morocco

1961 – 1987

The ascension of King Hassan II reflected the dynamic yet insecure spirit of a country in transition. Radical left-wing supporters emerged as serious threats to the monarchy. The Socialist Union of Popular Forces campaigned for radical reforms, a view shared by newly-independent Algeria, which briefly engaged in a territorial war with Morocco over disputed frontiers. Militants tried but failed to assassinate King Hassan II five times between 1963 and 1977. Rioting leftists took to the streets in violent protest against what they considered autocratic, absolute rule. At the same time, beach resorts were being built in Agadir in the 1970s and early 1980s, creating an influx of European beach-goers.

The desolate Western Sahara region in the deep south became one of Africa's most controversial and longest-running territorial conflicts beginning with the Green March of 1975, when Morocco exerted its control over the territory. The area remained a powder keg for explosive behavior throughout the 1980s, as stakes remain high to own the area's valuable natural resources, including phosphate deposits, fish reserves, and oil.

On Nov. 6 1975, Hassan II orders "Green March" into Western Sahara	Mohammed VI becomes King	New family code gives women more power	Political reforms after "Arab Spring" uprisings
1980	**2000**	**2010**	**2020**

1

IN FOCUS THE DYNASTIES OF MOROCCO

(above) Moroccan women can be both modern and traditional (right) Quartier des Habous, Casablanca

The Progressive Years

1987 – 1999

Morocco granted more local control and even elected a house of representatives. Infrastructure began to improve. The Casablanca Stock Exchange installed an electronic trading system in the early 1990s. A busy film economy, which had begun in the early 1960s, began to develop in Ouarzazate. With the death of King Hassan II in 1999, his son, Mohammed Bin al Hassan, was immediately enthroned as Mohammed VI at the age of 36 in a peaceful transition.

Modern Morocco

1999 – 2011

When King Mohammed VI married engineer Salma Bennani in 2002, she became the first wife of a Moroccan ruler to be publicly acknowledged and given a royal title. Following many years of hard work by activists, women's rights have since improved. The minimum age for matrimony has risen to 18, and women have more freedom of choice in marriage and divorce. Women have also won seats in parliamentary elections. Terrorist bombings in 2003 and 2011 have raised fears of radical Islamic extremists, but King Mohammed VI has tried to expand constitutional reforms to create more free-

dom and limit the powers of the monarchy. Morocco has sought membership in the European Union, but the stalemate in Western Sahara remains unresolved, something that has hindered the region's stability and prosperity. Significant investments have been made in tourism, infrastructure, and renewable energy, including the world's largest solar power plant near Ouarzazate. The king continues to implement reforms and retain the affection of his people despite the 2011 Arab Spring, which toppled the regimes of many of Morocco's neighbors.

RENTING A RIAD

For an authentic Moroccan lodging experience, venture into the medinas of Fez, Meknès, Marrakesh, or Essaouira and stay at a traditional riad.

What is a riad?

These beautiful, cloistered dwellings are usually tucked away discreetly behind heavy wooden doors set into high, featureless walls on blind alleys, called *derbs*. Traditional riad-style houses were (and still are) the domain of wealthier families and pass down from one generation to the next. They contain many of the same decorative and structural elements as their more palatial counterparts, including hand-cut, colorful tiles (zellij), silky *tadelakt* walls of finely pressed and waxed plaster, painted cedarwood ceilings, arched colonnades, living rooms on the ground floor, and sleeping quarters on the upper floors. At the center of a riad is an ornamental garden with a central fountain or water feature and rooms that peer inward through windows of wrought iron or wooden latticework.

In more recent times, with changing fashions and the development of modern *nouvelle villes* by colonial rulers, many Moroccans relinquished their old houses for more comfortable dwellings with 20th-century sanitation and modern household amenities. However, the faded charm and beauty of these traditional structures have captured the imagination of foreign investors, who often snap them up as holiday retreats; many have been restored lovingly to their former glory with sumptuous attention to detail and the addition of state-of-the art facilities. Now, hundreds of riads offer boutique accommodations in Morocco's older cities, usually with about three to six bedrooms over two levels.

What is included?

Riads that operate year-round as guesthouses have an on-site manager who attends to daily housekeeping and security and performs concierge services. Of course, some people want complete privacy, so ask if the manager is on duty during your stay. Quoted prices usually include daily cleaning, breakfast, bed linen and towels, Wi-Fi, satellite TV, a DVD player, hair dryers, and access to the kitchen for cooking your own meals. Ask at the time of booking if there's an extra charge for electricity or firewood. Additional meals, private transport, guides, special activities, and excursions can normally be arranged for an additional cost.

How much does it cost?

Riads come in all sizes and levels of luxury, so prices range anywhere from 300 DH to 3,000 DH per room per night. A midrange, well-equipped, and stylishly furnished riad costs approximately 700 to 1,000 DH per night per room; for a typical riad with four bedrooms, expect to pay around 2,500 DH to 3,500 DH per night, including a discount for stays of more than one night.

How do you find a riad to rent?

A simple Internet search turns up dozens of riads, and if booking far ahead, you should be able to rent a full riad. Good sources for privately owned riads that can be rented directly from the owner include ⊕ *www.ownersdirect.co.uk*. There are also agencies such as ⊕ *www.riadsmorocco.com*, which represent various properties. Finally, for the high end of the market, companies such as ⊕ *www.boutiquesouk.com* organize stays at premier properties with full concierge service.

MARRAKESH

WELCOME TO MARRAKESH

TOP REASONS TO GO

★ **Djemâa el Fna:** Wander amid the sizzle and smoke of the world's most exuberant marketplace.

★ **Souk shopping:** Lose yourself (literally) in the alluring lanes of the bazaars and souks of the "red city "labyrinth.

★ **Authentic accommodations:** Stay in a riad and sip mint tea in the airy confines of your bougainvillea-filled courtyard haven.

★ **Historic sights:** Step back in time to bygone dynasties by exploring elaborate tombs and palaces of sultans, and the tranquil beauty of the intricate medersa.

★ **Dance till dawn:** From intimate clubs with belly dancers and hookah pipes to full-on techno raves with international DJs, Marrakesh is the hedonistic capital of Morocco.

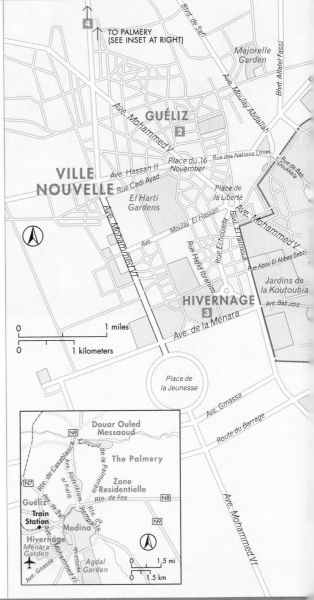

2

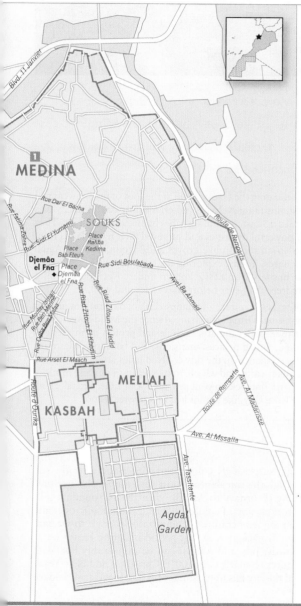

1 Medina. The old walled city contains the bulk of the attractions, the *souks*, and *riads*. It's a warren of narrow *derbs*, where it's easy to get lost.

2 Guéliz. Northwest of the medina, Guéliz is the modern administrative center, home to the tourist information office, fashionable boutiques, art galleries, cafés, restaurants, and banks; Avenue Mohammed V runs down its spine.

3 Hivernage. Outside the ramparts, south of avenues Hassan II and Mohammed V, Hivernage is populated largely with chic private residences, large hotels, and nightclubs. Its long, leafy boulevards stretch out to the Menara gardens.

4 The Palmery. The Palmery is a 30,000-acre oasis, 7 km (4½ miles) north of the medina between the roads to Casablanca and Fez. Once a series of date plantations, it's now a hideaway for the rich and famous, with a crop of luxury hotels and secluded villas springing up among the palms.

Updated by
Rachel Blech

Marrakesh is Morocco's most intoxicating city. Ever since Morocco's "Jewel of the South" became a trading and resting place on the ancient caravan routes from Timbuktu, the city has barely paused for breath.

Lying low and dominating the Haouz Plain at the foot of the snowcapped High Atlas Mountains (a marvelous sight on a sunny day), the city was stubbornly defended against marauding tribes by successive sultans. They maintained their powerful dynasties and surveyed their fertile lands from the Menara Garden's tranquil olive groves and lagoon, and the Agdal Gardens' vast orchards. Today, exploring the city has never been easier. A crackdown on hustlers who hassle and an undercover Tourist Police mean that you're freer than ever before to wander and wonder.

The medina is Marrakesh's miracle—a happy clash of old and new, in turn beguiling and confusing. Virtually unchanged since the Middle Ages, Marrakesh's solid, salmon-pink ramparts encircle and protect its mysterious labyrinthine medina, hiding palaces, mansions, and bazaars. Pedestrians struggle to find their balance on the tiny cobbled lanes among an endless run of mopeds, donkey carts, and wheelbarrows selling a mixture of sticky sweets and saucepans. But pick up your jaw, take your time, and take it all in, stewing in the Rose City like a mint leaf in a pewter teapot.

PLANNING

WHEN TO GO

Marrakesh can get surprisingly cold in the winter and after the sun goes down. Although the sun shines almost year-round, the best time to visit is in spring (February to April), when the surrounding hills and valleys are an explosion of colorful flowers, and fall (October and November), when the temperature is comfortable enough to warrant sunbathing. The only exception in that period is during Easter week, which brings crowds. July and August can be unbearably hot, with daytime temperatures regularly over 100°F. Christmas and New Year's is peak season and the city fills to bursting, with hotels and riads booked up months in advance.

PLANNING YOUR TIME

To get a true feel for the charm and chaos of Marrakesh, a stay of at least five full days is recommended. Deciding exactly where to stay depends largely on personal taste and budget. Inside the ancient walled **medina**, cozied up in a traditional riad, you'll never be far from the souks and historic sights. Most are reached on foot through a muddle of alleys with a taxi stand usually no more than a short walk from the front door. Small taxis and horse-drawn carriages can navigate to other points in the medina or into the *nouvelle ville* neighborhood. Families may prefer to opt for modern hotels in **Hivernage** or **Guéliz** where the vibe is more European. The streets here are safe (though the paving often broken and hazardous) and taxis are plentiful for the short hop to the medina. Farther afield is the luscious **Palmery**, oozing exclusivity and offering boutique hotels for idyllic days of total relaxation to a soundtrack of birdsong. The drawback here is that transport into town gets costly, at around 150 DH for a taxi each way.

GETTING HERE AND AROUND

AIR TRAVEL

Menara Airport in Marrakesh receives domestic flights from Casablanca and direct international flights from the United Kingdom, Europe, and Scandinavia. Flights from the United States, Canada, Brazil, and the Middle East pass through Casablanca.

The trip from the airport to town is only 15 minutes by car, taxi, or bus. On first arriving in Marrakesh, it's wise to ask your hotel or riad to arrange a private transfer direct from the airport. It may cost around 200 DH (for four people) but makes for a far less stressful arrival.

BIKE TRAVEL

A new initiative in the city of Marrakesh inspired by hosting the prestigious COP22 UN Climate Change Conference in 2016 means that there are now banks of bicycles for hire at key touristic hubs like Theatre Royal, Palais de Congrès, Koutoubia mosque, and Jardin Majorelle. Payment is made through a mobile phone app in order to unlock the bike and you get charged by the hour or by the day. Look for the racks of orange and gray bicycles called **Medina Bike.**

Bike Contacts Medina Bike. ☎ *0612/64–47–34* ⊕ *www.medinabike.ma.*

BUS TRAVEL

Intercity buses all leave from Marrakesh. Use the *gare routière* at Bab Doukkala for national public buses, or the Supratours or Compagnie du Transports au Maroc (CTM) bus stations in Guéliz. Buses arrive at the gare routière from Casablanca, Rabat, Fez, Agadir, Ouarzazate, and other cities. CTM and Supratours buses have their own terminals, but also stop at the gare routière. They are quicker, safer, and more comfortable than public buses to most key destinations. Supratours, which has its office next door to the train station on Avenue Hassan II, links up with Morocco's train network, with bus routes to destinations south and west of Marrakesh. Visit the ONCF (national rail network) website for information and timetables for Supratours. Ticket reservations must be done in person.

Public Bus No. 19 departs the airport every 30 minutes from 6:30 am to 9:30 pm daily. It stops at Place Djemâa el Fna and continues through to Guéliz, serving most of the main hotels along avenues Mohammed V and Mohammed VI (cost 30 DH).

Within Marrakesh, the public Alsa City Bus runs all over town; fares are a standard 4 DH.

Bus Contacts ALSA City Bus. ☎ *0524/33–52–70* ⊕ *www.alsa.ma.* **Compagnie de Transports au Maroc.** ✉ *Gare Routière, Bab Doukkala* ☎ *0800/09–00–30 call center* ⊕ *www.ctm.ma* ✉ *Rue Abou Bakr Seddiq, near Theatre Royal, Guéliz* ☎ *0800/09–00–30 call center* ⊕ *www.ctm.ma.* **Supratours.** ✉ *Av. Hassan II, next to train station, Guéliz* ☎ *0890/20–30–40* ⊕ *www.oncf.ma.*

CALÈCHE TRAVEL

Calèches are green, canopied, horse-drawn carriages that hold four to five people. Even if they do scream "tourist," they're a great way to reach your evening meal, and children love riding up front beside the driver. They're also picture-perfect for trips out to enjoy the Majorelle, Menara, and Agdal gardens. You should always agree on a price beforehand, but keep in mind that rides generally cost a minimum of 150 DH per hour; trips to the Palmery might cost 500 DH, and round-trip excursions (circling the ramparts, say) might cost 300 DH. There are two main pickup stops: one is in the medina, along the left side of the street stretching from the Djemâa el Fna to the Koutoubia Mosque; the other is in Guéliz, just south of Place de la Liberté and west of Bab Nkob. You can also try flagging one down.

CAR TRAVEL

Marrakesh is in Morocco's center, so it connects well by road with all other major destinations. Most of these roads are good, two-lane highways with hard, sandy shoulders for passing. There is a freeway connecting Marrakesh to Casablanca and Rabat in the north and Agadir to the southwest.

Within the Marrakesh medina, driving is not recommended. Cars can pass through some of the medina's narrow alleys, but not all, and unless you know the lay of the land you risk getting stuck and being hard-pressed to perform a U-turn. Outside the medina, in the nouvelle ville and suburbs, traffic is frenetic and locals freely admit that stoplights and lane markings are purely decorative and rarely observed. It can be hazardous to drive here as well. Leave your car at a guarded parking lot and walk.

Rental Cars Avis. ✉ *Marrakech Menara Airport, Hivernage* ☎ *0524/43–31–69* ⊕ *www.avis.com.* **Europcar.** ✉ *63, bd. Zerktouni, in the Afriqui gas station forecourt, Guéliz* ☎ *0524/43–12–28* ⊕ *www.europcar.com.* **Hertz.** ✉ *154, av. Mohammed V, Guéliz* ☎ *0524/43–99–84* ⊕ *www.hertz.ma.* **Label Voiture.** ✉ *Appt. 20, Immeuble 90, bd. Zerktouni, 1st fl., Guéliz* ☎ *0524/42–15–19* ⊕ *www.labelvoiture.com.* **Medloc Maroc.** ✉ *1st fl., no. 3, 75, rue Ibn Aicha, Guéliz* ☎ *0524/43–57–57* ⊕ *www.medloc-maroc.com.*

2

TAXI TRAVEL

Petits taxis in Marrakesh are small, beige, metered cabs permitted to transport three passengers within the city limits only. A petit taxi ride from one end of Marrakesh to the other should cost around 20 DH (50% extra from 8 pm to 6 am). The journey is sometimes shared with other passengers if plans coincide. When getting into the taxi, make sure the driver sets the meter (*le compteur*) on the dashboard for your journey. Taxi Vert is a dial-a-cab service that allows you to preorder a petit taxi for a specific pickup for 15 DH on top of the metered charge, very useful for late at night.

Grands taxis are either old four-door Mercedes or newer minivans. Most often they simply take a load of up to six passengers on short hauls to suburbs and nearby towns, forming a reliable, inexpensive network throughout each region of Morocco. They can also be chartered for private hire for excursions and airport transfers. ■ TIP➜ **Negotiate a price directly with the driver or through your hotel if chartering a special trip.**

The standard charge for a run from the airport into the medina in petits taxis starts at about 100 DH during the daytime and 150 DH after 8 pm, but you will have to negotiate. Grand taxis cost 100 DH to 150 DH during the day, 150 DH to 200 DH after 8 pm.

Taxi Contacts Taxi Vert. ☎ *0524/40–94–94.*

TRAIN TRAVEL

Marrakesh is connected by good train service to Tangier, Rabat, Casablanca, and Fez. The train station is located on Avenue Mohammed VI at the junction with Avenue Hassan II in Guéliz and is Morocco's main southern terminus. Advance reservations can be made for first class only. Per day there are six trains to Tangier, eight to Fez, and nine to Casablanca.

Train Contact ONCF. ✉ *Av. Mohammed VI, at Av. Hassan II, Guéliz* ☎ *2255 call center (from local phones only)* ⊕ *www.oncf.ma.*

GUIDES AND TOURS

Guides can be helpful when navigating the medina's serpentine streets. They can point out little-known landmarks and help you understand the city's complicated history. You are best off booking a licensed guide through a tour company or your hotel's staff should be able to suggest one to suit your interests. Although guides can be very knowledgeable about the city, don't rely on them for shopping. Store owners will inflate prices in order to give the guides kickbacks. The going rate for a city guide is 300 DH for a half day, 600 DH for a full day.

A number of companies offer full-day excursions (or longer) departing from Marrakesh by bus, 4WD, or motorbike and side-car.

There are numerous smartphone apps available for unguided walking tours like ⊕ *www.gpsmycity.com*; if you go this route, be aware of phone-snatchers.

TOUR COMPANIES AND GUIDES

Legendes Evasions. This highly respected local agency runs chauffeured vehicle tours to some of the Berber villages around Marrakesh. Day trips start at around 2,200 DH for up to six people per car. ✉ *Galerie Elite, 212, av. Mohammed V, 1st fl., Guéliz* ☎ *0524/33–24–83* ⊕ *www. legendesevasions.com.*

Marrakech Insiders. Established in 2015, Marrakech Insiders has a small fleet of super-cool vintage bikes and experienced local riders that offer a different perspective on the city—discover the medina, the nouvelle ville, the outlying Palmery, or the Agafay desert of Marrakesh. Tours start at 1,400 DH (per bike) and you can be picked up at your hotel. ✉ *Guéliz* ☎ *0669/69–93–74* ⊕ *www.marrakechinsiders.com.*

Mohammed Lahcen. If you want a top-notch private guide for Marrakesh, you can't beat English-speaking Mohammed Lahcen. His going rate for a guided tour is 300 DH for a half day, 600 DH for a full day (depending on number of people). ✉ *Medina* ☎ *0661/20–06–39* ✐ *bab_adrar@ hotmail.com.*

Sahara Expedition. This budget agency runs daily group excursions and tours throughout the region, including Ourika Valley and Essaouira. Three-day sprints via minibus to the Sahara desert at Merzouga start from 1,000 DH per person with very basic hotels. ✉ *22, bd. Mohammed Zerktouni, Guéliz* ☎ *0524/42–97–47* ⊕ *www.saharaexpe.ma.*

Said el-Fagousse. The amiable Said el-Fagousse has encyclopedic knowledge of Marrakesh's secret treasures and Moroccan history. Originating from the desert village of M'Haimd el Ghizalne, he is a qualified guide for both city and nationwide destinations. His rates are 400 DH for a half day, 700 DH for a full day. ✉ *Medina* ☎ *0661/78–32–98* ✐ *moroccotourguide@gmail.com.*

SheherazadVentures. This Marrakesh-based English-Moroccan company organizes private tailored tours for families and small groups, with a cultural focus. They're specialists in Southern Morocco and Sahara offering active day excursions from Marrakesh, as well as nationwide tours. Rates start around 1,500 DH per person per day for two people. ✉ *Appt. 55, Residence Ali (C), Av. Mohammed VI, near Café Cesar, Guéliz* ☎ *0615/64–79–18* ⊕ *www.sheherazadventures.com.*

SAFETY

Like other Moroccan cities, Marrakesh is quite safe. While women—particularly those traveling alone or in pairs—are likely to suffer from catcalls and whistles, there is generally little physical risk. The city does have its fair share of pickpockets, especially in markets and other crowded areas; handbags should be zippered and held closely, and wallets placed in inside pockets. The old city shuts down relatively early, so don't wander its dark alleys late at night. The Moroccan Tourist Police take their jobs very seriously, so don't hesitate to call on them. They operate undercover so are hard to identify, but in the medina they are never far away; ask any guide or shopkeeper to alert them if you're in trouble. Their office is on the northern side of the place Djemâa el Fna. Additional armed foot patrols are visible and vigilant at key locations in the city and throughout the popular tourist areas.

Contacts Brigade Touristique (Tourist Police). ✉ *Pl. Djemâa el Fna* ☎ *0524/38–46–01.*

VISITOR INFO

The Delegation Regionale du Tourisme office in Gueliz is the only Tourist Information office; it has maps, brochures, and general tourist information for Marrakesh and the surrounding area. The office is closed on weekends. **Delegation Regionale du Tourisme de Marrakech.** ✉ *Pl. Abdel Moumen Ben Ali, Av. Mohammed V and Rue Yougoslavie, opposite Les Negoçiants café, Guéliz* ☎ *0524/43–61–79.*

EXPLORING MARRAKESH

Most of the medina is navigable only on foot, and you may opt to engage one of the official city guides to steer you through the maze. Most of the medina's monuments charge an entry fee of 10 DH to 50 DH and have permanent but unsalaried on-site guides; if you use one, tip him about 30 DH to 50 DH.

MEDINA

If you can see the ramparts, you're either just inside or just outside the medina. In some respects not much has changed here since the Middle Ages. The medina is still a warren of narrow cobblestone streets lined with thick-walled, interlocked houses; designed to confuse invaders, the layout now serves much the same purpose for visitors. Donkeys and mules still deliver produce, wood, and wool to their destinations, and age-old crafts workshops still flourish as retail endeavors. ■ TIP→ When walking the narrow streets of the medina, keep to the right-hand side (and keep your shoulder-bag to the right also) as mopeds often zip through at great speed with little respect for window-shopping pedestrians.

TOP ATTRACTIONS

Fodor'sChoice ★ **Ali ben Youssef Medersa.** If you want a little breath taken out of you, don't pass up the chance to see this extraordinarily well-preserved 16th-century Koranic school, North Africa's largest such institution. The delicate intricacy of the *gibs* (stucco plasterwork), carved cedar, and *zellij* (mosaic) on display in the central courtyard makes the building seem to loom taller than it really does. As many as 900 students from Muslim countries all over the world once studied here, and arranged around the courtyard are their former sleeping quarters—a network of tiny upper-level rooms that resemble monks' cells. The building was erected in the 14th century by the Merenids in a somewhat different style from that of other medersas; later, in the 16th century, Sultan Abdullah el Ghallib rebuilt it almost completely, adding the Andalusian details. The large main courtyard, framed by two columned arcades, opens into a prayer hall elaborately decorated with rare palm motifs as well as the more-customary Islamic calligraphy. The Koranic school closed in 1960, but the building was restored and opened to the public in 1982. ✉ *Off Rue Souk el Khemis, Medina* ☎ *0524/44–18–93* 💰 *20 DH for medersa, 60 DH combination ticket with Musée de Marrakech.*

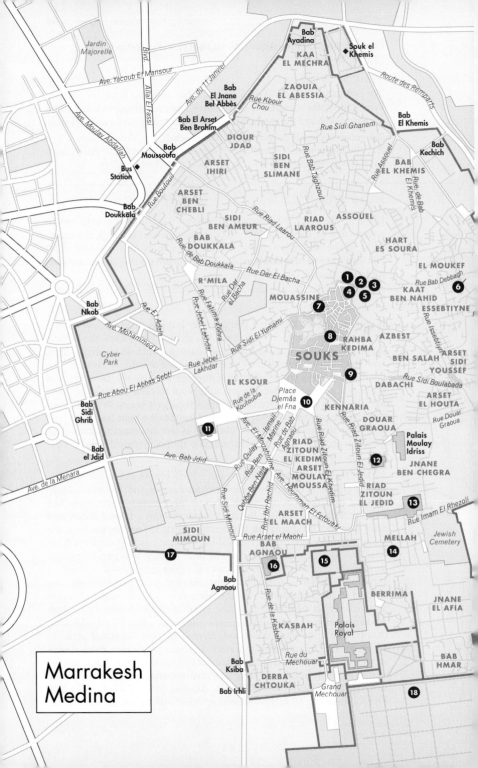

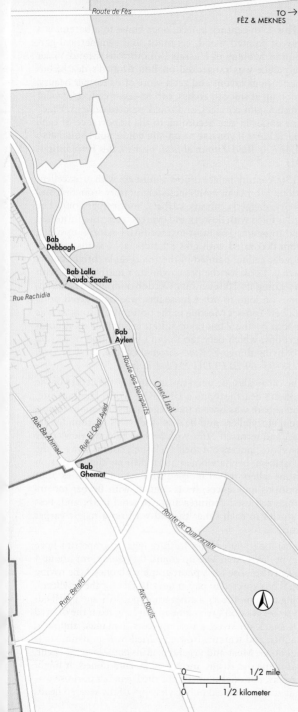

Route de Fès

TO →
FÈZ & MEKNES

Bab
Debbagh

Bab Lalla
Aouda Saadia

Rue Rachidia

Bab
Aylen

Route des Remparts

Oued Issil

Rue El Qadi Ayad

Rue Ba Ahmad

Bab
Ghemat

Route de Ouarzazate

Rue Belaid

Ave. Rouis

0   1/2 mile

0   1/2 kilometer

Fodor's Choice ★ **La Bahia Palace.** This 19th-century palace, once home to a harem, is a marvelous display of painted wood, ceramics, and symmetrical gardens. Built by Sultan Moulay el Hassan I's notorious Grand Vizier Bou Ahmed, the palace was ransacked on Bou Ahmed's death, but you can still experience its layout and get a sense of its former beauty. Don't forget to look up at smooth arches, carved-cedar ceilings, *tadlak* (shiny marble) finishes, gibs cornices, and zouak painted ceilings. Fancy a room? Each one varies in size according to the importance of each wife or concubine. ■ TIP→ **If you use an on-site guide, you should also tip 30 DH–50 DH.** ✉ *Rue Riad Zitoun el Jdid, near Pl. des Ferblantiers, Medina* 🎫 *10 DH.*

Dar Si Saïd. This 19th-century palace is now a museum with an excellent collection of antique Moroccan crafts including pottery from Safi and Tamegroute, jewelry, daggers, caftans, carpets, and leatherwork. The palace's courtyard is filled with flowers and cypress trees, and furnished with a gazebo and fountain. The most extraordinary salon is upstairs; it's a somber room decorated with gibs cornices, zellij walls, and an amazing carved-cedar ceiling painted in the *zouak* style (bright colors in intricate patterns). Look for the prize exhibit, a marble basin with an inscription indicating its 10th-century Córdoban origin. The basin, which is sometimes on loan to other museums, was once given pride of place in the Ali ben Youssef Mosque in the north of the souk. It was brought to Morocco by the Almoravid sultan in spite of its decorative eagles and griffins, which defy the Koran's prohibition of artistic representations of living things. ✉ *Riad Zitoune El Jdid, Derb Si Saïd, Medina* ☎ *0524/38–95–64* 🎫 *10 DH* ⏲ *Closed Tues.*

Fodor's Choice ★ **Djemâa el Fna.** The carnivalesque open square right at the center of the medina is Marrakesh's heartbeat and a UNESCO World Heritage site. This centuries-old square was once a meeting point for regional farmers and tradesmen, storytellers and healers; today it's surrounded by bazaars, mosques, and terraced cafés with perfect balcony views over the action. Transvestite dancers bat their eyelashes; cobras sway to the tones of snake charmers; henna women make their swirling marks on your hands; fortune-tellers reveal mottled futures; apothecaries offer bright powder potions and spices; bush dentists with Berber molars piled high on tables sell used dentures and extracted teeth; and, best of all, men tell stories to each other the old way, on a magic carpet around a gas lamp.

All day (and night) long you can get fresh orange or grapefruit juice from the green gypsy carts that line up round the square, for about 4 DH a glass. You can also pose for a photograph with one of the roving water sellers (you'll be expected to pay at least 10 DH for the privilege), whose eye-popping costumes carry leather water pouches and polished-brass drinking bowls—we don't recommend drinking from the offered cup of water. Or snack on sweet dates, apricots, bananas, almonds, sugar-coated peanuts, and walnuts from the dried fruit–and–nut stalls in the northwest corner. Meat and vegetable grills cook into the night, when Marrakshis come out to eat, meet, and be entertained. It might be a fun bazaar today, but once upon a time the Djemâa's purpose was more gruesome; it accommodated public viewings of the severed heads of sinners, criminals, and Christians. *Djemâa* actually means "meeting place" and *el Fna* means "the end" or "death," so as a whole it means something along the lines of "assembly of death" or "meeting place at the end of the world." △ Beware of pickpockets! ✉ *Medina*.

El Badi Palace. This 16th-century palace was once a playground for Saadian princes and visiting diplomats—a mammoth showpiece for opulent entertaining. Today it's a romantic set of sandstone ruins, policed by nesting storks. Sultan Ahmed el Mansour's lavish creation was ransacked by Moulay Ismail in the 17th century to help him complete his own palace at Meknès. But it's not hard to see why the palace, whose name translates as "The Marvel," was once among the world's most impressive monuments. A huge swimming pool in the center (still there today, but empty) is flanked by four others, along with four sunken orange orchards. The main hall was named the Koubba el Khamsiniyya, referring to its 50 grand marble columns. Along the southern wall is a series of belowground corridors and underground dungeons. It's a vast, calm, and mystical place. Also on display is a collection of goods from the Minbar (pulpit from which the Imam gives services) of the Koutoubia Mosque. If you use an on-site guide (otherwise unpaid), who can bring the place to life, you should also tip 30 DH to 50 DH. ✉ *Kasbah* ✛ *Enter ramparts and enormous gateway near Pl. des Ferblantiers* ☎ *0524/37–81–63* ✆ *10 DH for palace, 20 DH for palace and Koutoubia Mosque Minbar.*

Fodor'sChoice   **Koutoubia Mosque.** Yacoub el Mansour built Marrakesh's towering
★   Moorish mosque on the site of the original 11th-century Almoravid mosque. Dating from the early 12th century, it became a model for the Hassan Tower in Rabat and the Giralda in Seville. The mosque takes its name from the Arabic word for book, *koutoub,* because there was once a large booksellers' market nearby. The minaret is topped by three golden orbs, which, according to one local legend, were offered by the mother of the Saadian sultan Ahmed el Mansour Edhabi in penance for fasting days she missed during Ramadan. The mosque has a large plaza, walkways, and gardens, as well as floodlights to illuminate its curved windows, a band of ceramic inlay, pointed *merlons* (ornamental edgings), and various decorative arches. Although non-Muslims may not enter, anyone within earshot will be moved by the power of the evening muezzin call. ✉ *South end of Av. Mohammed V, Medina*.

Musée de Marrakech. The main reason to come to this small, privately owned museum next door to the Ali ben Youssef Medersa is not the exhibitions of regional pottery, ceremonial daggers, and traditional costume, but rather the stunning central atrium, a tiled courtyard containing a huge lampshade that resembles a descending UFO. Set within the restored 19th-century Menebhi Palace, this is a perfect place to relax while enjoying Moroccan architecture and gentle music piped through speakers. There are occasional exhibitions in the courtyard of beautiful artifacts or paintings, but they're poorly displayed and lack English translations. The museum also has a bookstore and a café. ✉ *Pl. ben Youssef, Medina* ☎ *0524/44–18–93* ⊕ *www.museedemarrakech. ma* ✆ *50 DH.*

The El Badi Palace, built by the Saadian sultans, is one of the largest structures in Marrakesh's medina.

Saadian Tombs. This small, beautiful, 16th-century burial ground is the permanent resting place of 166 Saadians, including its creator, Sultan Ahmed el Mansour, the Golden One. True to his name, he did it in style—even those not in the lavish mausoleum have their own colorful zellij graves, laid out for all to see, among the palm trees and flowers. Because the infamous Moulay Ismail chose not to destroy them (he was apparently superstitious about plundering the dead), these tombs are one of the few Saadian relics left. He simply sealed them up, leaving only a small section open for use. The complex was rediscovered only in 1917 by General Hubert Lyautey during the French protectorate. Passionate about every aspect of Morocco's history, the general undertook the restoration of the tombs.

The central mausoleum, the **Hall of Twelve Columns,** contains the tombs of Ahmed el Mansour and his family. It's dark, lavish, and ornate, with a huge vaulted roof, carved cedar doors and *moucharabia* (carved wooden screens traditionally used to separate the sexes), and gray Italian marble columns. In a smaller inner mausoleum, on the site of an earlier structure containing the decapitated body of the Saadian dynasty's founder, Mohammed esh Sheikh, is the tomb of El Mansour's mother. ■ TIP→ Get here either early or late to avoid the crowds and to see the monuments swathed in soft golden sunlight. If you use one of the on-site guides (who are unpaid), you should tip 30 DH to 50 DH. ✉ *Rue de la Kasbah, next to mosque, Kasbah* 🎟 *10 DH.*

Fodor's Choice
★

Souks. The vast labyrinth of narrow streets and derbs at the center of the medina is the souk—Marrakesh's marketplace and a wonder of arts, crafts, and workshops. Every step brings you face-to-face with the

2

colorful handicrafts and bazaars for which Marrakesh is famous. In the past, every craft had a special zone within the market—a souk within the souk. Today savvy vendors have pushed south to tap trading opportunities as early as possible, but the deeper in you venture, you will be rewarded by cheaper prices and by seeing authentic artisans—metalworkers, the carpenters, the tailors, and the cobblers—at work. Look for incongruities born of the modern era. Beside handcrafted wooden pots for kohl eye makeup are modern perfume stores; where there is a world of hand-sewn djellabas at one turn, you'll find soccer jerseys after the next; fake Gucci caps sit beside handmade Berber carpets.

■ TIP→ As you wander through the souk, take note of landmarks so that you can retrace your steps without too much trouble. Once the shops' shutters close, they're often unrecognizable. The farther north you go the more the lanes twist, turn, and entwine. Should you lose your way, retrace your steps to the busiest thoroughfare and then look for the brown painted signs (usually found at key intersections) indicating the direction of Place Jemaa el Fna. But mostly you'll rely on people in the souk to point the way. If you ask a shopkeeper rather than a loitering local, you'll be less likely to fall into the clutches of a "faux guide." ⊠ *Medina* ✛ *North of Pl. Djemmaâ el Fna.*

NEED A BREAK

Chez Lamine Hadj Mustapha. Although the row of severed lambs' heads out front may not be everyone's idea of culinary heaven, Marrakshis love Chez Lamine Hadj Mustapha, and you'd be missing out not to try it. English TV chef Jamie Oliver chose this spit-and-sawdust street restaurant in a filming trip for a gutsy example of Moroccan roast lamb specialty, *mechoui*—and it's not every day you walk past a whole lamb being cooked underground. Follow a tiny alley that leads off the Djemâa el Fna (running behind The Zeitoun Cafe) and you'll see exactly that. Ask to see the oven—a hole in the ground where the entire animal is cooked over hot wood ash. The meat is then hauled up and cut in front of you. Served as a simple sandwich, or as a laden plateful priced by weight, it is best paired with a pot of mint tea and enjoyed upon a rooftop terrace. ■ TIP→ Cash only. ⊠ *18–26, Souk Ablouh, Medina.*

WORTH NOTING

Agdal Garden. Stretching a full 3 km (2 miles) south of the Royal Palace, the Jardin de l'Aguedal comprises vast orchards, a large lagoon, and other small pools, all fed by an impressive, ancient system of underground irrigation channels from the Ourika Valley in the High Atlas. Until the French protectorate's advent, it was the sultans' retreat of choice for lavish picnics and boating parties. Sadly the Agdal Gardens have suffered from neglect in recent years and now have little charm for visitors. The largest basin, the 12th-century "Tank of Health," and the small pavilion next to it are still accessible on Friday and Sunday, but the vast orchards and olive groves, where Moroccans once strolled, are now closed to the public. ⊠ *Medina* ✛ *Approach via Méchouar; or from outside the ramparts, walk left on Rte. d'Agdal and main garden entrance is on right* ☉ *Closed Mon.–Thurs. and Sat.*

Ali ben Youssef Mosque. After the Koutoubia, this is the medina's largest mosque and Marrakesh's oldest. The building was first constructed in the second half of the 12th century by the Almoravid sultan Ali ben Youssef, around the time of the Qoubba Almoravid. In succeeding centuries it was destroyed and rebuilt several times by the Almohads and the Saadians, who changed its size and architecture accordingly; it was last overhauled in the 19th century, in the then-popular Merenid style. Non-Muslims may not enter. ⊠ *Just off Rue Souk el Khemis, Rue Assouel, next to Ali ben Youssef Medersa, Medina.*

◼ NEED A BREAK

✕ **Kasbah Café.** Perfectly positioned just opposite the entrance to the Saadian tombs, this Spanish-owned café is a welcome retreat for those who find themselves "kasbahed-out" at the end of a trek through the monuments of Marrakesh. The menu features Moroccan standards, as well as pizza, salads, and a cool gazpacho. Known for: lovely rooftop terrace. ⊠ *Rue de la Kasbah, opposite Saadian tombs, Kasbah* ☎ *0524/38–26–25* ⊕ *www.kasbahcafemarrakech.com.*

Heritage Museum. This family-owned and operated museum displays an impressive collection of ancient pottery, Islamic manuscripts, Jewish ceremonial items, tribal jewelry, and costumes that portray the city's rich Berber, Arab, and Jewish heritage. The private collection is housed in a traditional riad that the owner's family once occupied; rooms are decorated in typical Moorish style. ⊠ *25 Znikat Rahba, near Riad Enija, Medina* ☎ *0524/39–02–80* ⊕ *www.heritagemuseummarrakech. com* 🖼 *30 DH.*

Maison de la Photographie. This restored riad, in the heart of the medina, houses a rare collection of original black-and-white photos and glass negatives that depict life in Moroccan communities between 1862 and 1960. The archive, which was established in 2009, is constantly growing and there are regular thematic exhibitions. There is also a very pleasant roof terrace café. ⊠ *46, rue Souk Ahel Fes, near Medersa Ben Youssef, Medina* ☎ *0524/38–57–21* ⊕ *www.maisondelaphotographie.ma* 🖼 *40 DH.*

Mellah. As in other Moroccan cities, the Mellah is the old Jewish quarter, once a small, walled-off city within the city. Although it was once home to a thriving community of native and Spanish Jews, along with rabbinical schools and scholars, today it's home to only a few Jewish inhabitants. You can visit the remains of a couple of synagogues with the help of an official guide, or local kids will be happy to point the way in return for a few dirhams. The Lazama Synagogue is open daily and is still used for weddings and bar mitzvahs of foreign visitors. It has a pretty, blue-tiled inner courtyard. The Mellah gets its name from the Arabic word for salt, and some say that the Jewish residents who lived here acquired their wealth through the salt trade. ◼ TIP➜ The Mellah district underwent many renovations in 2016 and the main Place des Ferblantiers now offers a wide range of cafés and shops for tourists. ⊠ *Medina.*

Qoubba Almoravid. This is the city's oldest monument and the only intact example of Almoravid architecture in all of Morocco (the few other ruins include some walls here in Marrakesh and a minaret in El Jadida). Dating from the 12th century, this masterpiece of mechanical waterworks somehow escaped destruction by the Almohads. It was once used for ablutions before prayer in the next-door Ali ben Youssef Mosque (relying on the revolutionary hydraulics of *khatteras,* drainage systems dug down into the water table), and also had a system of toilets, showers, and faucets for drinking water. It was only excavated from the rubble of the original Ali ben Youssef Mosque and Medersa in 1948. ■TIP→ **The monument is in an advanced state of disrepair and in 2014 was closed to the public for safety reasons. You can view it from the exterior perimeter.** ⊠ *Pl. Ben Youssef, Medina.*

Ramparts. The medina's amazingly well-preserved walls measure about 33 feet high and 7 feet thick, and are 15 km (9 miles) in circumference. The walls are fashioned from local reddish ocher clay laid in huge blocks. The holes that are visible on the exterior surface are typical of this style of construction, marking where wooden scaffold supports have been inserted as each level is added. Until the early 20th century, before the French protectorate, the gates were closed at night to prevent anyone who didn't live in Marrakesh from entering. Eight of the 14 original babs (arched entry gates) leading in and out of the medina are still in use. Bab Agnaou, in the Kasbah, is the loveliest and best preserved of the arches. ■TIP→ **The best time to visit the walls is just before sunset, when the swallows that nest in the ramparts' holes come out to take their evening meal. A leisurely calèche drive around the perimeter takes about an hour.** ⊠ *Marrakesh.*

Fodor'sChoice
★ **The Secret Garden.** The Secret Garden, or *Le Jardin Secret,* opened to the public in 2016 after three years of intensive excavation, restoration, and planting. Once one of the largest private riads in the medina, the 16th-century site is home to beautiful Islamic architecture, the lush Exotic and Islamic gardens, an ancient, but still operational, water management and irrigation system, and the original watchtower that has commanding views over the whole medina. The restored Pavilions, which were once formal reception rooms, now house a small café and an exhibit of photographs that show the property's excavation and reconstruction. There are areas to sit and relax, a bookshop, café, and exhibition rooms. Well-informed guides are on-site and provide free tours of the gardens. Entry to the Tower is an extra 30 DH and includes a guide. ⊠ *121, rue Mouassine, Medina* ☎ *0524/39–00–40* ⊕ *www. lejardinsecretmarrakech.com* ⊠ *50 DH.*

Tanneries. For a whiff of Marrakesh life the old way, the tanneries are a real eye-waterer, not least because of the smell of acrid pigeon excrement, which provides the ammonia that is vital to the tanning process. Six hundred skins sit in a vat at any one time, resting there for up to two months amid constant soaping, scrubbing, and polishing to get the leather strong, supple, clean, and ready for use. Goat and sheep skins are popular among Berbers, while Arabs prefer camels and cows and tend to use more machine processes and chemical agents. Once the hides have been stripped of fur, washed, and made supple through this six-week process, the final stage involves soaking and rubbing in a mix of ground mimosa bark and water, which eventually turns the grayish-green hides into the natural reddish-brown or "tan" shade that we always expect in our natural leather goods. The tanned skins are dried in the sun and then sold direct to the artisans near Ben Youssef Mosque. Additional color dyeing takes place after the skins have been purchased by the artisans in another part of the souk.

Thirteen tanneries, mixing both Berber and Arab elements, are still in operation in the Bab Debbagh area in the northeast of the medina. Simply turn up Rue de Bab Debbagh and look for the tannery signs above several open doorways to both the right and left of the street. To visit one of them, just pop in and the local manager will offer you mint leaves to cover the smell, explain the process, and guide you around the vats of dyes. In return he'll hope for a healthy tip to share with his workers; this is a dying art in a poor dyeing area, so the more you can tip, the better. ■ TIP➔ **Finding the Tanneries can be frustrating. It's best to arrive via taxi and ask for Bab Debbagh (the tanneries are straight ahead through the gate) or the Place el Mokf (Avenue Bab Debbagh is at the top on the left). Alternatively task an official guide to include the visit as part of a city walking tour, but beware of false guides and do not visit after dark.** ⊠ *Av. Bab Debbagh, Medina.*

GUÉLIZ AND HIVERNAGE

In addition to office buildings, contemporary shops, and malls—none of which may exceed the nearest mosque's height—Guéliz has plenty of sidewalk cafés, snack bars, restaurants, art galleries, upscale boutiques, and antiques stores. Connecting the two sectors, between avenues Mohammed VI and Hassan II, are the delightful public El Harti Gardens.

Hivernage is a leafy suburb by comparison, with olive trees, roses, and orange trees lining its boulevards. It's the most expensive urban residential district within the city boundaries, with gated private residences interspersed with resort hotels, casinos, nightclubs, restaurants, and chic cafés. It was also one of the first districts to be built outside the medina during the French Protectorate in the 1920s.

TOP ATTRACTIONS

FAMILY **El Harti Gardens.** This delightfully mature and beautifully maintained
Fodor's Choice public garden does not receive the attention it deserves. Paved pathways
★ wind through cactus plantations, rose gardens, and exotic flowerbeds, past ornamental fountains, and through striking cascades of bougainvillea. For those in search of a moment's peace under the lofty eucalyptus trees, it's the perfect escape from the city mayhem. There's also a rather neglected children's play area with a sandpit and concrete dinosaur. ⊠ *Rue El Qadi Ayad, Guéliz* ✛ *Entrance behind fountain on Place Novembre 16 (opposite main post office).*

Fodor's Choice **Majorelle Garden.** The Jardin Majorelle was created by the French painter
★ Louis Majorelle, who lived in Marrakesh between 1922 and 1962. It then passed into the hands of another Marrakesh lover, the late fashion designer Yves Saint Laurent. If you've just come from the desert, it's a sight for sore eyes, with green bamboo thickets, lily ponds, and an electric-blue gazebo. There's also a fascinating Berber Museum housed within the painter's former studio, with a permanent exhibit of tribal jewelry, costumes, weapons, ceramics, and rustic household tools and implements. There is also a museum shop, and a delightful café. The

The Majorelle Gardens were most famously owned by the French designer Yves Saint Laurent.

Yves Saint Laurent Museum, which opened in late 2017, is next door. ■ **TIP →** Try to visit the gardens in the early morning before the tour groups—you'll hear the chirruping of sparrows rather than the chatter of humans. ⊠ *Av. Yacoub el Mansour, main entrance on Rue Yves Saint Laurent, Guéliz* ☎ *0524/31–30–47* ⊕ *www.jardinmajorelle.com* ⊠ *Garden 70 DH, museum 30 DH.*

Musée Yves Saint Laurent Marrakech. Opened in late 2017, the Yves Saint Laurent Museum is next to the Jardin Majorelle and the Villa Oasis where the designer lived. It houses a vast collection of fashion and haute-couture accessories as well as a reference library of botany, fashion, and Berber culture. ⊠ *Rue Yves Saint Laurent, Guéliz* ⊕ *www.museeyslmarrakech.com.*

WORTH NOTING

FAMILY **Menara Garden.** The Menara's vast water *bassin* and villa-style pavilion are ensconced in an immense royal olive grove, where pruners and pickers putter and local women fetch water from the nearby stream, said to give *baraka* (good luck). A popular rendezvous for Marrakshis, the garden is a peaceful retreat. The elegant pavilion—or *minzah*, meaning "beautiful view"—was created in the early 19th century by Sultan Abd er Rahman, but it's believed to occupy the site of a 16th-century Saadian structure. In winter and spring snowcapped Atlas peaks in the background appear closer than they are; and, if you are lucky, you might see green or black olives gathered from the trees from October through January. Moroccan families swarm here during the holidays and weekends to picnic in the olive groves. Children can ride camels and ponies outside the garden gate. ⊠ *Hivernage* ✛ *From Bab el Djedid, garden is about 2 km (1 mile) down Av. de la Menara.*

THE PALMERY

The expanse of palm groves to the north of the medina is dubbed the "Beverly Hills" of Marrakesh, a place of manicured golf courses, private villas hidden behind high walls, upmarket boutique hotels, and luxurious secret gardens. Though there are no real tourist attractions here, the area is well worth visiting to enjoy a camel ride in the oasis, a quad-bike ride along dusty tracks, or a lavish cabaret dinner. Also worth a visit is the Museum of the Palmery, showcasing contemporary Moroccan art.

Fodor's Choice ★ **Museum of the Palmery.** Signposted on the Route de Fes as you head out to the Palmery, this cultural oasis is well worth a detour for an hour or two—it's an art gallery, exotic garden, and sculpture park all rolled into one. Marrakesh-born Abderrazzak Benchaabane—ethnobotanist, perfume maker, garden designer, and local legend—has created an enchanting walled garden and, within it, a contemporary art museum. The garden adjoins his home and exhibits his own collection of contemporary Moroccan art, paintings, and sculptures. Benchaabane was responsible for the restoration of the Majorelle Gardens at the request of Yves Saint Laurent in 1998, and the garden designs here clearly reflect his passion for creating beautiful natural spaces. The indoor gallery and arcades open out to a water garden with pergolas and pavilions, an Andalusian garden, rose beds, and cactus gardens. ⊠ *Dar Tounssi, Rte. de Fes, Palmery* ☎ *0661/09–53–52* ☏ *40 DH.*

WHERE TO EAT

Marrakesh has arguably the largest selection of restaurants in Morocco, which serve equal parts Moroccan and international cuisine at varying price points. Restaurant dining, once reserved mainly for the wealthy or very special occasions, is now part of the norm for virtually all Marrakshis. Options vary from inexpensive snack bars, cafés, and fast-food restaurants to the more pricey French bistros, sushi bars, and sophisticated Moroccan fine-dining options. In restaurants where alcohol is served, meal prices tend to be high as licenses are expensive. Home entertaining, however, with lavish meals to impress visitors, is still very much part and parcel of the old Marrakshi way of life. To get an idea (albeit a rather expensive one) of traditional yet sumptuous Moroccan entertaining, treat yourself to an evening at one of Marrakesh's popular riad gastronomique restaurants in the medina. ■TIP→ **Morocco is a Muslim country, so don't assume that all restaurants will serve alcohol. Licenses are expensive and, inside the medina especially, are very hard to come by.**

You can also eat well at inexpensive sidewalk cafés in both the medina and Guéliz. Here, don't miss out on a famous local dish called *tanjia,* made popular by workers who slow-cook lamb or beef in an earthenware pot left in hot ashes for the whole day. Food is cooked and served from an outdoor street-kitchen with shared tables, but it's a hearty meal with locals for around 30 DH.

Most restaurants in Marrakesh tend to fall into two categories. They're either fashionable, flashy affairs, mostly in Guéliz and the outlying areas of Marrakesh, which serve à la carte European, Asian, and Moroccan cuisine, or they're more traditional places, often tucked inconspicuously into riads and old palaces in the medina. Both types can be fairly pricey, and, to avoid disappointment, are best booked in advance. They also tend to open quite late, usually not before 7:30 in Guéliz and 8 in the medina, although most people don't sit down to eat until 9 or 9:30. In recent years a third dining category, the dinner-cabaret, has become a popular format, attracting tourists, expats, and well-heeled Moroccans for their entertainment value, if not necessarily for their cuisine.

There's no set system for tipping. Your check will indicate that service has been included in the charge; if not, tip 10% or 15% for excellent service.

Restaurants are listed alphabetically within neighborhood. Use the coordinate (⊕ D2) at the end of each listing to locate a site on the Where to Eat and Stay in the Medina map. Dining reviews have been shortened. For full information, visit Fodors.com.

WHAT IT COSTS IN DIRHAMS			
$	$$	$$$	$$$$
under 80 DH	80 DH–150 DH	151 DH–300 DH	over 300 DH

Restaurant prices are the average cost of a main course at dinner, or if dinner is not served, at lunch.

COOKING SCHOOLS

With so many chic riads serving up a culinary storm, it's no surprise that cooking schools in Marrakesh are in demand. Tagines, couscous, and briouates are all on the menu for the Maghrebian master chef in the making. Many hotels and riads now arrange their own cooking classes in-house, too.

Café Clock Marrakech. The all-day course starts with a shopping trip to the local market before returning to the kitchen on the terrace of Café Clock in the Kasbah neighborhood. The group chooses from a menu of tagines or couscous, cooked salads, harira soup, Moroccan pastries, dessert, and flat breads. Sometimes the day involves visiting a local community oven to bake bread. Classes are 600 DH per person (cash only) and must be reserved in advance. ⊠ *224, Derb Chtouka, Kasbah* ☎ *0524/37–83–67* ⊕ *www.cafeclock.com.*

Jnane Tamsna. All-day cooking classes are offered upon request in this delightful boutique guesthouse, surrounded by a thriving organic garden in the middle of the Palmery. An English-speaking chef gives instruction in the preparation of exquisite Moroccan recipes that are easy to replicate back home. You are invited to cook, eat lunch, and then relax by the swimming pool for the afternoon. Classes are 650 DH per person for a minimum of two people. ⊠ *Douar Abiad, Circuit de la Palmeraie, Palmery* ☎ *0524/32–84–84* ⊕ *www.jnane.com.*

Fodor's Choice ★ **La Maison Arabe.** Originally a fine Moroccan restaurant run by two revered French ladies in 1946—frequented by the pasha and visiting royals and a favorite of Sir Winston Churchill—La Maison Arabe is now a luxury boutique hotel. It continues to enjoy a reputation for great Moroccan cuisine, and was in fact one of the first establishments in Marrakesh to offer cooking courses. Nowadays the classes are open to guests and nonguests in groups of up to eight people at a time, instructed by a *mada* (female head cook). Courses are run daily in the upstairs modern kitchen with a translator on hand (Arabic, English, French). Participants learn about the key spices and how to prepare signature Moroccan dishes such as tagines, couscous, pastilla, pastries, and Moroccan cooked salads. The class is about four hours long, and at the end you eat the meal you have prepared. **TIP→ La Maison Arabe has extended their cooking school (600 DH pp) to include their private garden property in the countryside just outside Marrakesh.** ✉ *1, Derb Assehbe, Bab Doukkala, Medina* ☎ *0524/38–70–10* 🌐 *www.lamaisonarabe.com.*

Souk Cuisine. The very popular daylong cooking classes run by Dutch cook Gemma van de Burgt will have you mastering the art of tagine preparation before you know it. Classes meet at Café de France to shop for spices and ingredients in the medina, then prepare a meal together; small groups cook at Gemma's home, larger groups cook at Riad Safa in the north of the medina. The price (550 DH; cash only) includes recipes to take home, lunch, and a glass of wine. Children eight years and up are welcome, too. ✉ *, Derb Tahtah 5, Zniquat Rahba, Medina* ☎ *0673/80–49–55* 🌐 *www.soukcuisine.com.*

MEDINA

$$
ITALIAN

🍴 **Café Arabe.** This three-story restaurant in the heart of the medina is a happening place by day and by night, serving both Moroccan and Italian food. Homemade pastas are on offer at this Italian-owned establishment, but main courses also include grilled swordfish, lamb, and beef. **Known for:** cocktails on the terrace; laid-back lounge atmosphere. [$] *Average main: 150DH* ✉ *184, rue el Mouassine, Medina* ☎ *0524/42–97–28* 🌐 *www.cafearabe.com* ✣ *E2.*

$
MOROCCAN
FAMILY

🍴 **Café Clock Marrakech.** Mike Richardson's cross-cultural café project, first established in Fez, is rocking the Kasbah area of Marrakesh. A youthful, funky vibe combined with tasty contemporary Moroccan cuisine at reasonable prices is a sure winner, and locals as well as tourists and ex-pats intermingle easily. **Known for:** camel burgers; cultural activities and live music. [$] *Average main: 70DH* ✉ *224, Derb Chtouka, Kasbah* ☎ *0524/37–83–67* 🌐 *www.cafeclock.com* ✣ *D6.*

$
CAFÉ
FAMILY

🍴 **Café des Épices.** In the medina's "spice square," this little Moroccan-owned café has set the trend and copycat cafés with burnt sienna walls, woven stools, and rustic tables have sprung up all over the medina. In keeping with its name, the café offers spiced teas and coffees along with a range of freshly squeezed fruit juices, smoothies, and light snacks, salads, and sandwiches. **Known for:** well-priced tasty snacks and juices; great location. [$] *Average main: 60DH* ✉ *75, Rahba Lakdima, Medina* ☎ *0524/39–17–70* 🌐 *www.cafedesepices.ma* ✣ *F2.*

$ ✕ **Chez el Bahia.** It won't win prizes for design, but this cheap joint is
MOROCCAN   perfect for a lunchtime or evening pit stop. Locals and visitors alike frequent this friendly little canteen just on the right before the road opens into Djemâa el Fna. **Known for:** unconventional range of tagines; authentic local street food. $ *Average main: 55DH* ✉ *206, Riad Zitoune el Kdim, Medina* ▬ *No credit cards* ✢ *F4.*

$$ ✕ **Dar Moha.** This isn't the most stylish riad setting and service can
MOROCCAN   be patchy, but it has an established reputation for *nouvelle cuisine marocaine.* Head to the outside tables that are arranged around a small pool and shaded by lush banana palms to try delicious adaptations of traditional dishes such as tiny melt-in-the-mouth *pastilla* (sweet pigeon pie) filled with a vegetable puree. **Known for:** modern Moroccan gastronomy; serves alcohol. $ *Average main: 120DH* ✉ *81, rue Dar el Bacha, Medina* ☎ *0524/38–64–00* ⊕ *www.darmoha.ma* ✢ *D1.*

$$$$ ✕ **Dar Yacout.** One of Marrakesh's luxurious five-course *gastronomique*
MOROCCAN   experiences, the palatial Dar Yacout is in a house designed by Bill Wil-
Fodor's Choice   lis as a *One Thousand and One Nights* restaurant. It has become an
★   institution serving a traditional Moroccan feast, with huge servings, so come hungry to make the most of it. **Known for:** magical fairy-tale setting; sumptuous Moroccan dining. $ *Average main: 700DH* ✉ *79, Sidi Ahmed Soussi, Bab Doukkala* ☎ *0524/38–29–29* ⊕ *www.daryacout. com* ☾ *Closed Mon. No lunch* ✢ *D1.*

$ ✕ **Earth Café.** Vegetarians, vegans, and gluten-free diners may feel
VEGETARIAN   unloved in Marrakesh until they get to Earth Café, where they rule the roost. Generous portions are served all day at this wholesome little eatery that's tucked into a side alley near the main square. **Known for:** the only place for vegetarians and vegans. $ *Average main: 90DH* ✉ *2, Derb Zouak, off Riad Zitoune Lkdim, Medina* ☎ *0661/28–94–02* ⊕ *www.earthcafemarrakech.com* ▬ *No credit cards* ✢ *F5.*

$ ✕ **La Famille.** Rustic whitewashed walls, long wooden tables, and woven
VEGETARIAN   chairs shaded from the harsh sun by bougainvillea and fruit trees will
FAMILY   make you feel like you've stepped right into the heart of the local countryside. In this tiny *beldi* garden, off one of the medina's main shopping streets, the French owner serves a constantly changing menu derived from fresh local ingredients; think enormous main-course salads or pizettas topped with anything from carrots and apples to raspberries, mint, and beetroot. **Known for:** charming garden space; fresh local produce; vegetarian food. $ *Average main: 80DH* ✉ *42, Riad Zitoun Jdid, Medina* ✢ *Near Bahia Palace* ☎ *0524/38–52–95* ☾ *Closed Mon.* ✢ *G5.*

$$ ✕ **Le Foundouk.** This French-run place hidden at the souk's northern tip
MOROCCAN   is regularly booked with upscale tourists and expats, and the candlelit roof terrace is a popular spot for balmy summer nights or predinner cocktails. The menu features traditional Moroccan fare as well as lighter international dishes such as sea-bass fillet served in a clam sauce, or vegetarian risotto. **Known for:** filled with character in a historic setting; intriguing international cuisine; romantic rooftop terrace. $ *Average main: 150DH* ✉ *55, Souk Hal Fassi, Kat Bennahid, near Medersa Ben Youssef, Medina* ☎ *0524/37–81–90* ⊕ *www.foundouk.com* ☾ *Closed Mon.* ✢ *G1.*

$$$$ ✕ **Gastro MK.** The menu at the English-owned Gastro MK features
MOROCCAN   exceptionally fine modern-Moroccan cuisine. The menu is a balance
of Moroccan and European influences aiming to be light and subtle
to tempt those who are "tagined out'"; dishes include cauliflower
couscous with raisins and capers or a deconstructed tagine of beef
fillet with herb mash and zucchini. **Known for:** Moroccan fine dining;
boutique experience; alcohol is served. Ⓢ *Average main: 650DH* ✉ *14,*
Derb Lafkih Sebaii, Bab L'Ksour, Medina ☎ *0524/37–61–73* ⊕ *www.*
maisonmk.com ☉ *Closed Wed.* ✛ *D3.*

$$ ✕ **Le Jardin.** Building on the success of his Café des Épices, Moroccan
MOROCCAN   entrepreneur Kamal Laftimi has sprouted another high-quality culinary
pit stop in the heart of the souks. Fresh local produce is displayed in
a market stall at the entrance to this renovated 16th-century building.
Known for: cool and tranquil setting in the souks; excellent desserts.
Ⓢ *Average main: 120DH* ✉ *32, Souk el Jeld, Sidi Abdelaziz, Medina*
☎ *0524/37–82–95* ⊕ *www.lejardinmarrakech.com* ✛ *F1.*

$$ ✕ **Latitude 31.** Owner Ali Lamsouber has opened up his ancestral family
MOROCCAN   home in the Bab Doukkala neighborhood to create a welcoming open-
Fodor's Choice   air restaurant in an enclosed garden courtyard. The innovative menu
★   takes classic Moroccan dishes and adds an element of surprise, for
example a succulent lamb tagine is loaded with wild mushrooms from
the Middle Atlas Mountains, or the traditional *pastilla* (pastry) is filled
with dates, apples, and ginger. **Known for:** Moroccan nouvelle cuisine;
friendly and welcoming atmosphere. Ⓢ *Average main: 140DH* ✉ *186,*
rue el Gza, Bab Doukkala ☎ *0524/38–49–34* ⊕ *www.latitude31mar-*
rakech.com ☉ *Closed Sun.* ✛ *E1.*

$$ ✕ **Le Marrakchi.** With zellij walls, painted cedar ceilings, and white tile
MOROCCAN   floors, this old palace serves up reliable Moroccan cuisine to mostly a
non-Moroccan clientele. You can choose from the à la carte menu or
one of the set menus, which begin at 280 DH. **Known for:** belly dancers;
dining with a view of Djemâa el Fna. Ⓢ *Average main: 150DH* ✉ *52,*
rue des Banques, just off Djemâa el Fna, Medina ☎ *0524/44–33–77*
⊕ *www.lemarrakchi.com* ✛ *F3.*

$$ ✕ **Nomad.** Tucked into a side street off "the Spice Square" in the souks,
MOROCCAN   Nomad has quickly become a local favorite for those seeking modern
Moroccan cuisine in a fresh and funky outdoor setting. It's the latest restaurant project of Kamal Laftimi, who established his reputation with
the nearby Terrasse des Épices and then Le Jardin. **Known for:** trendy
location; modern Moroccan food; delicious desserts. Ⓢ *Average main:*
120DH ✉ *1, Derb Aarjan, off Rahba Lkdima, Medina* ✛ *Near Café*
des Epices ☎ *0524/38–16–09* ⊕ *www.nomadmarrakech.com* ☉ *Closed*
for lunch during Ramadan ✛ *F2.*

$$$$ ✕ **Royal Mansour.** The prestigious Royal Mansour, led by the Michelin-
MOROCCAN   starred chef Yannick Alléno, is home to four restaurants: La Grande
Table Marocaine, La Grande Table Francaise, La Table, and Le Jardin.
La Grande Table Marocaine serves classic Moroccan dishes with a
modern twist, while La Grande Table Francaise is a lavish all-white
romantic affair with a French menu and specially crafted tableware
that compliments the food's artistry. **Known for:** the finest Moroccan
cuisine; exclusive and elaborate setting; strict dress code. Ⓢ *Average*

main: 700DH ✉ Rue Abou Abbas el Sebti, Medina ☎ 0529/80–82–82 🌐 www.royalmansour.com ✥ A3.

$ SEAFOOD 🍴 **Snack Grand Atlas.** Serving simple, old-school Moroccan street-eats, Snack Grand Atlas is reeling in the pescetarians with its wide menu of grilled, fried, skewered, or baked fresh fish and seafood. Menu offerings depend on the recent catches from Agadir, but may include fish pastilla, swordfish kebab, fish tagine, seafood pastas, or grilled sea bass. **Known for:** fresh fish and seafood; old-school Moroccan street-eats. [$] *Average main: 50DH ✉ Rue Bani Marine, Medina ✥ Opposite Hotel Ali ☎ 0668/33–36–55 ▭ No credit cards ✥ E4.*

$$ MOROCCAN 🍴 **Le Tanjia.** This stylish restaurant is a good bet for a special night out with traditional Moroccan cuisine, live acoustic North African and Arabian music, and slick service. The three-tiered restaurant is centered on a rose-filled fountain of the inner patio where the musicians play from early evening. **Known for:** Marrakshi specialty "tanjia"; lively atmosphere. [$] *Average main: 150DH ✉ 14, Derb J'did, next to Pl. des Ferblantiers, Medina ☎ 0524/38–38–36 ✥ G6.*

$$ INTERNATIONAL FAMILY 🍴 **La Terrasse des Épices.** Hidden on a rooftop deep within the northern quarter of the souks, this all-day (and evening) restaurant is a popular spot for expats, tourists, and trendy locals. The menu mixes Moroccan and international cuisine from fish tagine and tanjia (beef or lamb cooked slowly for several hours over charcoal in an earthenware jug) to pasta dishes, goat cheese salad, and tenderloin steaks. **Known for:** contemporary ambience; one of few informal medina restaurants serving alcohol. [$] *Average main: 120DH ✉ 15, souk Cherifia, Sidi Abdelaziz, Medina ☎ 0524/37–59–04 🌐 www.terrassedesepices.com ✥ F1.*

$$$$ MOROCCAN 🍴 **Le Tobsil.** A perfect setting for a romantic gastronomic feast, Le Tobsil serves copious amounts of classic Moroccan food inside an old riad. The name may be Arabic for "dish," but get ready for several, a procession of flavors served in crescendo at this fine-dining restaurant. **Known for:** elegant and romantic setting; fine Moroccan cuisine. [$] *Average main: 700DH ✉ 22, Derb Abdellah ben Hessaien, R'mila Bab L'Ksour, Medina ☎ 0524/44–15–23 ⏲ Closed Tues. and July and Aug. ✥ D3.*

GUÉLIZ

Marrakesh's restaurant scene changes faster than a belly dancer at quitting time, and today's hot tagine can quickly become tomorrow's soggy couscous. This is especially true in trendy, finicky Guéliz. Some of the most celebrated restaurants have built their reputations around stunning decor rather than stunning food, but they're still worth going to as long as you know this. Sound out local opinion, and don't be afraid to take a chance.

$$ MOROCCAN Fodor's Choice ★ 🍴 **Al Fassia Guéliz.** Serving some of the best à la carte Moroccan food in the city and also with an extensive choice of Moroccan wines, Al Fassia has a long-standing reputation for high-quality traditional food without the obligation to participate in a five-course gastronomic feast. Run by women, it brings classic cooking to Guéliz with an affordable menu that includes tasty tagines, tender brochettes with saffron rice, couscous topped with caramelized onions, succulent tangia, and sweet-savory

pigeon pastilla. **Known for:** delicious and varied Moroccan dishes; traditional recipes from Fez; all-female family-run business. [$] *Average main: 150DH* ✉ *55, bd. Zerktouni, Guéliz* ☎ *0524/43–40–60* 🌐 *www.alfassia.com* ⏲ *Closed Tues. and 3 wks in June and July.*

$ MOROCCAN FAMILY 🍴 **Amal Women's Association Restaurant.** This pretty little restaurant-cum-social project near the public hospital ticks all the boxes: great food, great prices, great ethics, great service. A nonprofit center established the restaurant to help women from troubled backgrounds learn culinary skills to earn an independent living. **Known for:** great value; community ethics. [$] *Average main: 40DH* ✉ *Av. Ben Ahmed and Rue Ibn Sina, Guéliz* ☎ *0524/44–68–96* 💳 *No credit cards* ⏲ *Closed daytime during Ramadan.*

$$ FRENCH 🍴 **L'Annexe.** Bistro meets resto in this popular, affordable French eatery at the edge of Guéliz where service is warm and welcoming. The three-course set lunch menus are an exceptional value at 120 DH. **Known for:** good value; bistro-style menu. [$] *Average main: 140DH* ✉ *14, rue Moulay Ali, Guéliz* ☎ *0524/43–40–10* 🌐 *www.lannexemarrakech.com* ⏲ *Closed Sat. lunch and Sun. dinner.*

$$ INTERNATIONAL 🍴 **Café du Livre.** A contemporary café, restaurant, and bar serving beer on tap, the Café du Livre is a welcome relief for those suffering from 'tagine fatigue,' and it's a popular meeting place for young Marrakshis and English-speaking expats alike. Peruse a quirky collection of secondhand books, participate in the English-speaking Monday quiz nights, come for dinner, or just have a light salad lunch or tapas. **Known for:** English-speaking quiz nights; beer on tap. [$] *Average main: 90DH* ✉ *44, rue Tarik ben Ziad, Guéliz* ☎ *0524/44–69–21* ⏲ *Closed Sun.*

$$ INTERNATIONAL FAMILY 🍴 **Café 16.** This modern terrace café with lime-green parasols sits at the edge of the Marrakesh Plaza in the heart of Guéliz. At the indoor restaurant you can enjoy a glass of wine or cold beer until 1 am and food until 11 pm. **Known for:** hand-made pastries and cakes; big outdoor terrace on the Marrakesh Plaza. [$] *Average main: 130DH* ✉ *Marrakesh Plaza, Pl. du 16 Novembre, Guéliz* ☎ *0524/33–96–70.*

$$ BISTRO 🍴 **La Cantine Parisienne.** Parisian Michael Gabbay has been in the bistro business since he was 17 years old. He's brought this expertise and hands-on approach to Marrakesh creating a distinctly urban-styled, modern restaurant that attracts crowds of young Marrakshis as well as tourists and expats. **Known for:** T-bone steaks and halal "bacon" burgers; live music Friday and Saturday evenings; lively atmosphere. [$] *Average main: 150DH* ✉ *Residence Maha, Rue Ibn Hanbal, Guéliz* ☎ *0524/45–85–65* 🌐 *www.lacantineparisienne.com* ⏲ *No lunch weekends.*

$$ SPANISH Fodor's Choice ★ 🍴 **Casa Jose.** The Spanish-Moroccan chain, which has restaurants in Casablanca and Rabat, opened this location in 2016. Fresh fish is shipped in from Agadir or Casablanca each morning, and the authentic tapas selection includes classics such as tortillas, shrimp with garlic, patatas bravas, and the more adventurous Galician octopus. **Known for:** authentic Spanish tapas; good wine list; pleasant outdoor terrace. [$] *Average main: 100DH* ✉ *8, av. Oued el Makhazine, Guéliz* ✣ *Near Royal Tennis Club* ☎ *0524/42–37–72.*

$$ ✗ **Catanzaro.** One of Marrakesh's most popular restaurants for locals
ITALIAN   and expats, this homey Italian spot offers dining on two floors, bright-
FAMILY   ened by red-chintz tablecloths. The menu has a good selection of Italian
salads, pastas, and pizzas at prices that make them a fabulous value.
Known for: reasonably priced pasta and pizzas; often fully booked
on weekends. $ *Average main: 80DH* ✉ *Rue Tariq Ibn Ziad, Guéliz*
☎ *0524/43–37–31* ☽ *Closed Sun.*

$ ✗ **Chez Lamine.** Slightly more elegant than its hole-in-the-wall branch in
MOROCCAN   the souks, Chez Lamine has a reputation for the best mechoui (whole
roasted lamb) in town and couscous on Friday. Its street-side tables
in Guéliz are regularly filled with Moroccan families on Friday and
weekends; there's also inside seating. **Known for:** traditional mechoui
(roasted lamb); popular with Moroccan families. $ *Average main:*
60DH ✉ *Rue Ibn Aicha, opposite Montecristo, Guéliz* ☎ *0524/43–*
11–64 ▭ *No credit cards* ☽ *Closed during Ramadan.*

$ ✗ **Le Comptoir de Charlotte.** This family-run and family-friendly eatery
INTERNATIONAL   at the edge of Guéliz serves up tasty homemade French-style tarts and
FAMILY   quiches, along with daily specials such as moussaka with salad. On
Thursday the house special is English-style fish-and-chips, which are
possibly the best in town. **Known for:** homemade quiches and tarts;
friendly service; family-friendly. $ *Average main: 60DH* ✉ *Residence*
Assala 1, 50, bd. Mohammed VI, Guéliz ✛ *Near Lycée Victor Hugo*
☎ *0524/43–87–41* ☽ *Closed Sun., no dinner* ▭ *No credit cards.*

$$ ✗ **La Cuisine de Mona.** Just beyond the fringes of Guéliz, this tiny Lebanese
LEBANESE   restaurant is a winner on all counts—fresh, tasty, authentic Lebanese
food; a warm welcome; and quirky decor. The big, cheerful personality of Lebanese-born restaurateur Mona is evident as you step into this
tiny restaurant. **Known for:** cheerful ambience; fresh Lebanese cuisine.
$ *Average main: 90DH* ✉ *Residence Mamoune 5, 115b, Quartier el*
Ghoul, off Rte. de Targa, Guéliz ☎ *0618/13–79–59* ⊕ *lacuisinedemona.*
eresto.net ☽ *Closed Sun.*

$$$ ✗ **Grand Café de la Poste.** The French colonial atmosphere provides a
FRENCH   fabulous backdrop for salads, pastas, steaks, and fish specials including
Fodor'sChoice   oysters from Oualidia. A long-standing favorite for expats and well-
★   heeled Moroccans, expect cold beer or a glass of Moroccan wine on the
covered veranda. **Known for:** colonial vibe; elegant service; French cui-
sine. $ *Average main: 170DH* ✉ *Bd. el Mansour Eddahbi at Av. Imam*
Malik, just off Av. Mohammed V, Guéliz ☎ *0524/43–30–38* ⊕ *www.*
grandcafedelaposte.restaurant.

$ ✗ **India.** This tiny restaurant on a side street of central Guéliz is run by
INDIAN   India-native John Jinendrom, who imports spices, like masala, directly
from Europe. This means authentic-tasting Indian halal cuisine at local
prices, which is a rarity in Marrakesh. **Known for:** authentic Indian
cuisine; good value;. $ *Average main: 80DH* ✉ *66, rue Tarik Ibn Ziad,*
Guéliz ☎ *0524/44–84–11* ▭ *No credit cards.*

$$ ✗ **Kechmara.** This is one of the trendy places to hang out in the new
EUROPEAN   city, with ice-cool midcentury design, contemporary art on display,
FAMILY   and some of the best salads in town. The menu pitches itself between
French brasserie and Americana; during the day it's a lovely family-
friendly spot. **Known for:** live music and DJs on the weekend; great

In the Djemâa el Fna, you'll find plenty of food vendors as well as tradititional Moroccan dancers.

range of salads. $ *Average main: 120DH* ⊠ *3, rue de la Liberté, Guéliz* ☎ *0524/42-25-32* ⊕ *www.kechmara.com* ☉ *Closed Sun.*

$$ ✕ **Les Jardins de Guéliz.** Hidden at the edge of the Harti Gardens, this
FRENCH   French-owned restaurant is a great value, with an excellent fixed-price
FAMILY   menu, as well as an à la carte menu and self-serve buffet. The buffet
has lots of vegetarian choices, including tortillas, stuffed vine leaves, and pasta salads, but it does runs out quickly. **Known for:** pretty garden setting; great value. $ *Average main: 100DH* ⊠ *Av. Oued el Makhazine, next to Royal Tennis Club, Guéliz* ☎ *0524/42-21-22* ☉ *Closed Sun. and July.*

$$$ ✕ **Le Loft.** This is where expats and many young Marrakshis come for
INTERNATIONAL   a touch of New York style in a bistro setting, and there's alcohol.
Le Loft is popular for its menu of beautifully presented steaks: fillet, entrecôte, and tartare. **Known for:** trendy and lively ambience; French and international menu using local produce. $ *Average main: 160DH* ⊠ *18, rue de la Liberté, Guéliz* ☎ *0524/43-42-16* ⊕ *www. restaurant-loft.com.*

$ ✕ **Panna Gelato Italiano.** This ice-cream parlor and café is at the very far
CAFÉ   end of Guéliz, but well worth the journey. The ice cream and sorbet
FAMILY   (possibly the best in Morocco) are made with all-natural ingredients
and no additives, and flavors vary every month. **Known for:** fantastic homemade ice cream; late hours. $ *Average main: 25DH* ⊠ *89, rte. de Targa, at Rue du Capitaine Arrigui, Guéliz* ☎ *0524/43-65-65* ⊕ *www. pannagelatoitaliano.it.*

$ ✕ **Restaurant Al Bahriya.** Cheap and cheerful, this restaurant is possibly
SEAFOOD   the best catch in town. The no-frills Moroccan street restaurant in the
heart of Guéliz (near La Grande Poste) is packed at night with locals

CLOSE UP

Marrakesh Street Food

Marrakshis have perfected the art of cooked street food, traditionally the province of the working class. There are hundreds of sidewalk grills scattered throughout both the medina and Guéliz. Step up for a tasty, satisfying meal at one of these institutions; it's a priceless experience that costs next to nothing. From midday to midnight, choose from grilled minced beef, sausage, lamb chops, brochettes, Moroccan salads, and french fries, supplemented by bread, olives, and hot sauce. (No credit cards, clearly.)

DJEMÂA EL FNA

For the ultimate grilling experience, there's only one place. By dusk, more than a hundred stalls sizzle and smoke their way through mountains of fresh meat and vegetables. Step up to the stall of your choice and order from the wild array of perfectly done veggies, salads, *kefta* (beef patties), merguez sausages, beef brochettes, couscous, and even french fries. In cooler months or during Ramadan, try a bowl of hearty *harira* (chickpea, lentil, and meat soup) or country eggs in homemade bread. The meal starts with free bread (to weigh down your paper place setting) and a hot dipping sauce called *harissa.* The mint tea at the end should be free, too. There's little continuity of quality, even at the same stall, so it's luck and instinct all the way for each sitting. However, since leftovers are given to the poor every night, the food is always freshly made. Vendors will do anything to attract your attention, from dragging you to a seat, chasing you down the lanes, and best of all, performing the occasional comic rundown of classic English phrases ("It's bloody marvelous!") with matching Cockney accent. **■ TIP→ Eat where the Moroccans eat: they know what to order, how much to pay, and they really get into their food.**

STREET FOOD TOURS

If you find the idea of dining at one of the stalls on the square, or even eating alone, a little bit daunting, there are organized evening food tours with a local Moroccan guide and a resident English-speaking expat to show you the ropes, sample the flavors, and guide you through the street entertainment. To join a mixed group try **Marrakech Food Tours** (🌐 *www.marrakechfoodtours.com*) or for a more bespoke, private tour try **Tasting Marrakech** (🌐 *www.tasting-marrakech.com*).

getting their fishy fix. **Known for:** always packed with locals; fresh fish daily. [$] *Average main: 60DH* ✉ *75 bis, av. Moulay Rachid, Guéliz* ☎ *0524/84–61–86* 💳 *No credit cards* ⏲ *Closed during Ramadan.*

$$$ ITALIAN 🍴 **La Trattoria.** Due partly to the pizzazz of its late owner, Giancarlo, La Trattoria has long held a place among Marrakesh's top restaurants and, unlike others, has kept up a consistently high standard. Tables are tightly packed around the pool area and advance reservations are recommended to try the hallmark Italian homemade ravioli and seafood pasta variations. **Known for:** homemade pasta; beautiful inner garden. [$] *Average main: 180DH* ✉ *179, rue Mohammed el Béqal, Guéliz* ☎ *0524/43–26–41* 🌐 *www.latrattoriamarrakech.com.*

HIVERNAGE

Hivernage is known for its large upmarket chain hotels and some very exclusive apartment buildings. Among them are also a scattering of decent restaurants and cafés—some independent, some located within hotels, and some even attached to the outlying nightclubs. On Avenue Mohammed VI (opposite the Palais de Congrès) are a number of pizzerias and a few upscale restaurants. Toward the Guéliz end of Avenue Moulay el-Hassan, near the old football stadium, is a cluster of international restaurants and cafés.

$$ MOROCCAN

🍴 **Al Fassia Aguedal.** The Al Fassia name has become synonymous with fine Moroccan cuisine in Marrakesh, and with tables hard to come by in Guéliz, this branch at the boutique Hotel Al Fassia near the Agdal Gardens lives up to the same high standards set by the older sister restaurant. The atmosphere is elegant though casual, and the restaurant is more spacious and tranquil than its city-center counterpart. **Known for:** fine Moroccan cuisine; outdoor garden restaurant; excellent Moroccan wine list. [$] *Average main: 150DH* ✉ *Hotel Al Fassia, 9 bis, rte. de Ourika, Zone Touristique de l'Aguedal, Hivernage* ☎ *0524/38–11–38* 🌐 *www.alfassia.com* 🕓 *Closed 3 wks in June and July.*

$$$ INTERNATIONAL

🍴 **Comptoir Darna.** Snazzy, jazzy, and a little razamatazzy, Le Comptoir is a fusion of bar, club, and restaurant that's been a nighttime draw for hip Marrakshis and visitors since the turn of the 21st century. The restaurant serves Moroccan, international, and Asian dishes; it's expensive, but the main attraction isn't the food, it's the trendy atmosphere and free entertainment—live musicians, belly-dance cabaret (starting at 10:30 pm), and an upstairs DJ spinning chilled-out world-music vibes until 3 am. **Known for:** hip and trendy venue; live entertainment. [$] *Average main: 200DH* ✉ *Av. Echouhada, Hivernage* ☎ *0524/43–77–02* 🌐 *www.uk.comptoirmarrakech.com.*

THE PALMERY

$$$$ CANTONESE Fodor's Choice ★

🍴 **Ling Ling.** Just south of the Palmery, 7 km (4½ miles) east of the city on Route de Ouarzazate, the Mandarin Oriental is home to Ling Ling Cantonese, one of the finest dining experiences in Marrakesh. The Moroccan-inspired decor may lead diners to believe they have stepped into an emporium of Moroccan gastronomy, but the menu actually features mouth-watering Cantonese cuisine prepared in the open kitchen. **Known for:** delicious dishes; fabulous cocktails; beautiful setting. [$] *Average main: 350DH* ✉ *Rte. de Royal Golf, Palmery* ✣ *Near Royal Golf Club, Rte. de Ouarzazate* ☎ *0524/29–88–88* 🌐 *www.mandarinoriental.com/marrakech* 🕓 *Closed during Ramadan.*

WHERE TO STAY

Marrakesh has exceptional hotels. Five stars are dropped at every turn, the spas are superb, and the loving attention to detail is overwhelming. If, however, you'd prefer not to spend a fortune sleeping in the bed where a movie star once slumbered, solid budget riads and midrange boutique options abound. They're small, clean, and suitably Moroccan in style to satisfy adventurous penny-pinchers.

To take on the historic heart of Marrakesh and live like a pasha of old, head to one of the medina's riads. Riad restorations, many by ultrafashionable European expats, have taken over the city; you'd trip over them, if only you knew where they were. Anonymous doors in the narrow, twisting derbs of the medina, and especially the souks, transport you to hidden worlds of pleasure. There are cheap ones, expensive ones, chic ones, funky ones, plain ones. Riads normally have around four to six rooms arranged around a courtyard and each room can be rented individually on a nightly basis. For special events and larger gatherings, it's worth considering booking the whole property.

Marrakesh is something of a Shangri-la for designers who, intoxicated by the colors, shapes, and patterns of the city, feel free to indulge themselves in wildly opulent and ambitious designs. Although it isn't all tasteful, much of the decor and style in Marrakesh hotels and riads is fascinating and easy on the eye.

Most of the larger hotels (classified with three, four, or five stars by the Moroccan government) are in Guéliz, Hivernage, and in the zone touristique located beyond the Agdal Gardens heading out of town on Route de Ourika. There are also many superb guesthouses just a few miles out of town in the surrounding countryside. If you prefer something authentic and inexpensive near the action, choose one of the numerous budget-friendly riads in the medina, near Djemâa el Fna. ■ TIP→ Anybody with mobility issues or physical limitations should note that staying in a traditional riad usually involves a walk from the nearest parking area through narrow streets to reach the front door and climbing stairs to access the bedrooms and terrace. There are rarely elevators in all except very few of the larger luxury riads or boutique hotels.

Hotels and riads vary their prices wildly between high and low season. This means that if you time your trip right you can find some great deals. High season runs from March to May and from October to December, with spikes at Christmas, New Year's, and Easter.

Use the coordinate (✛ D2) at the end of each listing to locate a site on the Where to Eat and Stay in the Medina map. Hotel reviews have been shortened. For full information, visit Fodors.com. Lodgings are listed alphabetically within neighborhood.

WHAT IT COSTS IN DIRHAMS			
$	$$	$$$	$$$$
under 700 DH	700 DH–1,500 DH	1,501 DH–3,500 DH	over 3,500 DH

Hotel prices are the lowest cost of a standard double room in high season.

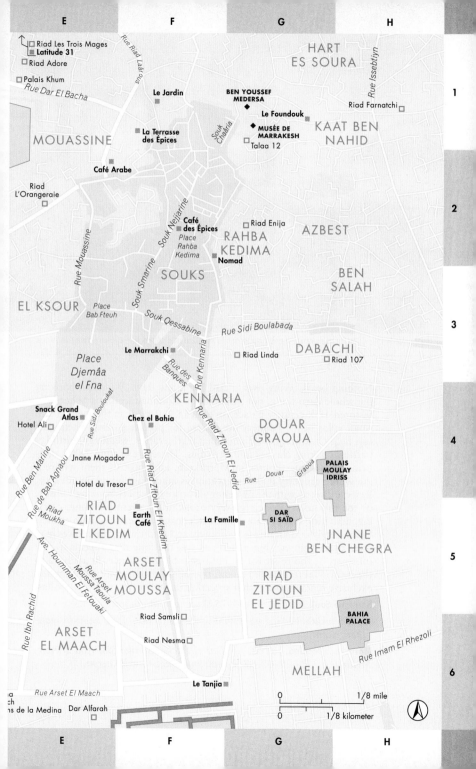

La Mamounia is one of Morocco's grande dame hotels, not to mention one of the finest luxury hotels in Africa.

RENTING A RIAD

Nothing beats taking over a riad for a few days. We mean booking the whole darn thing, not just a room. Commandeering a beautifully restored 16th-century palace isn't cheap, but riads in the medina and small villas in the Palmery are geared for private parties. Their staff can help organize meal plans, special itineraries, weddings, birthday parties, cooking classes, and activities. There are around 2,000 riads being run as guesthouses in Marrakesh, and most of them will rent the whole property if the reservation is made far enough in advance. Reserve directly with the owner or via an intermediary booking website, or for full luxury concierge service including event planning, catering, activities, and private transport, engage the services of an agency. From trendy and luxurious to homely and traditional, the choices may seem overwhelming, but as long as you find one that appeals to you (not hard!), you're set for an unforgettable experience. In addition to the individual riads listed below, try the following event planners and exclusive rental agencies that specialize in both riads and private villas.

Boutique Souk. ☎ *0661/32–44–75* ⊕ *www.boutiquesouk.com.*

Hip Marrakech. ✉ *Medina* ☎ *0207/570–0336 in U.K.* ⊕ *www.hipmarrakech.com.*

Marrakech Medina. ✉ *102, rue Dar el Bacha, Souika Sidi Abd al Aziz, Medina* ☎ *0524/29–07–07* ⊕ *www.marrakech-medina.com.*

MEDINA

$$ ⌂ **Dar Alfarah.** This authentic riad near the Badi Palace in the Mellah
B&B/INN   quarter was renovated and restyled in 2015 by new French own-
FAMILY   ers. **Pros:** good location; plenty of atmosphere; family-friendly. **Cons:**
small pool; bathrooms and showers need maintenance; service some-
times slow. $ *Rooms from: 1000DH* ✉ *58, Derb Touareg, Ksibat
N'Hass, Kasbah* ☎ *0524/38–42–69* ⊕ *www.daralfarah.com* ⟿ *10
rooms* ⦿ *Breakfast* ✛ *E6.*

$$$$ ⌂ **L'Hotel.** Celebrated British designer, Jasper Conran, opened this hotel,
B&B/INN   his first in Marrakesh, in 2016. **Pros:** easy car access; idyllic roof ter-
race; free transfer to and from airport. **Cons:** no children allowed;
restaurant menu is limited; no twin rooms. $ *Rooms from: 4800* ✉ *41,
Derb Sidi Lahcen ou Ali, Bab Doukkala* ☎ *0524/38–78–80* ⊕ *www.l-
hotelmarrakech.com* ⟿ *5 rooms* ⦿ *Breakfast* ✛ *D1.*

$ ⌂ **Hotel Ali.** A long-standing favorite among budget travelers and back-
B&B/INN   packers, Hotel Ali is right at the edge of the main square and is con-
stantly abuzz with activity, but don't expect many creature comforts.
Pros: great place to meet fellow travelers; right on the main square;
great value. **Cons:** noisy; beds and room furnishings are worn; heating/air-con
not reliable. $ *Rooms from: 400DH* ✉ *Rue Moulay Ismail, Medina*
✛ *55 yards from Dejmâa el Fna* ☎ *0524/44–49–79* ⊕ *www.hotel-ali.
com* ⊟ *No credit cards* ⟿ *39 rooms* ⦿ *Breakfast* ✛ *E4.*

$ ⌂ **Hotel du Tresor.** A haven for artists and design lovers, this beautifully
B&B/INN   converted hotel near the Djemâa el Fna has been featured in interior design
magazines. **Pros:** fantastic location; retro-modern interior design; helpful
management. **Cons:** pool is tiny and overlooked in small courtyard; cash
only; small rooms. $ *Rooms from: 600DH* ✉ *77, Sidi Boulokat, Riad
Zitoun Kdim, Medina* ☎ *0524/37–51–13* ⊕ *hotel-du-tresor.hotelsmar-
rakech.net/en* ⊟ *No credit cards* ⟿ *13 rooms* ⦿ *Breakfast* ✛ *F4.*

$$$ ⌂ **Les Jardins de la Koutoubia.** Despite its location on an unprepossessing
HOTEL   street, this hotel is in the heart of the action and has a rather grand and
opulent interior that cannot fail to impress. **Pros:** central location; great
pool areas; wheelchair accessible. **Cons:** expensive; decor is tired; rooms
in the medina side can be noisy. $ *Rooms from: 2700DH* ✉ *26, rue de
la Koutoubia, Medina* ☎ *0524/38–88–00* ⊕ *www.lesjardinsdelakout-
oubia.com* ⟿ *108 rooms* ⦿ *Breakfast* ✛ *D3.*

$$$ ⌂ **Les Jardins de la Medina.** This 18th-century palace once belonging to
HOTEL   the cousin of King Hassan II is now a luxurious boutique hotel with
FAMILY   lush gardens hidden in the Kasbah area of the medina. **Pros:** fabulous
gardens; stylish decor; excellent restaurant. **Cons:** 20-minute walk to
reach main square; pool area rather cramped; slow service. $ *Rooms
from: 2500DH* ✉ *21, Derb Chtouka, Kasbah, Medina* ☎ *0524/38–18–
51* ⊕ *www.lesjardinsdelamedina.com* ⟿ *36 rooms* ⦿ *Breakfast* ✛ *D6.*

$ ⌂ **Jnane Mogador.** This well-managed, budget riad is a cut above the rest
B&B/INN   with an ideal location just a stone's throw from Place Djemâa el Fna.
The decor is simple with Moroccan textiles, rugs, and lamps adding
a splash of color to each of the bedrooms, which are clean and well-
appointed. **Pros:** near the main square; very good value; good service
and amenities. **Cons:** bathrooms and plumbing need updating; rooms
are cramped; books up months in advance. $ *Rooms from: 580DH*

✉ *116, riad Zitoun Kedim, Derb Sidi Bouloukate, Medina* ☎ *0524/42–63–24* 🌐 *www.jnanemogador.com* 🛏 *18 rooms* 🍴 *Breakfast* ✥ *F4.*

$$$ HOTEL 🏨 **La Maison Arabe.** Situated at the edge of the medina with easy access to parking, taxis, and the main Djemâa el Fna square, La Maison Arabe is a stylish and sought-after address for those seeking exceptional Moroccan hospitality. **Pros:** lots of little nooks; renowned cooking school; exemplary service. **Cons:** some rooms are small; the outdoor restaurant overlooks the pool; often fully booked. [$] *Rooms from: 2800DH* ✉ *1, Derb Assehbe, Bab Doukkala, Medina* ☎ *0524/38–70–10* 🌐 *www.lamaisonarabe.com* 🛏 *26 rooms* 🍴 *Breakfast* ✥ *C1.*

$$$$ HOTEL Fodor's Choice ★ 🏨 **La Mamounia.** Since 1923, Morocco's most prestigious hotel has achieved legendary status for its opulence, grandeur, celebrity guest list, and hefty price tag. **Pros:** one of the finest hotels in the world; exquisite restaurants; stunning architecture and interiors. **Cons:** some standard classic rooms; ground-floor rooms have no view of garden; exorbitant bar/restaurant prices. [$] *Rooms from: 6200DH* ✉ *Bab Jdid, Medina* ☎ *0524/38–86–00* 🌐 *www.mamounia.com* 🛏 *208 rooms* 🍴 *Breakfast* ✥ *B5.*

$$$ RESORT FAMILY 🏨 **Le Naoura Marrakech.** The first venture onto African soil from this well-respected French luxury hotel chain, the Naoura Marrakech is ideally situated on the edge of the medina but an easy walk from the main sights. **Pros:** spacious standard rooms; central location; the private villas are exceptional. **Cons:** noisy pool area; lack of outdoor garden spaces; hotel rooms lack character. [$] *Rooms from: 2400DH* ✉ *Rue Djbel Alakhdar, Bab Doukkala* ☎ *0524/45–90–00* 🌐 *www.hotelsbarriere.com/en/marrakech/le-naoura.html* 🛏 *115 rooms* 🍴 *Breakfast* ✥ *C2.*

$$ B&B/INN Fodor's Choice ★ 🏨 **Palais Khum.** This exquisite, Italian-owned boutique riad opened in 2014 just near the Dar el Bacha Royal residence on a street filled with antique dealers and quality boutiques. **Pros:** fabulous design; quiet location; easy accessibility. **Cons:** no outdoor pool; some rooms have no external window or view; pool is too close to restaurant. [$] *Rooms from: 1500DH* ✉ *2, Derb el Henaria, off Rue Dar el Bacha, Medina* ✥ *Enter through gardens of its very own patisserie, Kremm Café, and there's an elevator to access all levels and terrace* ☎ *0524/39–03–89* 🌐 *www.palaiskhum.com* 🛏 *11 rooms* 🍴 *Breakfast* ✥ *E1.*

$ B&B/INN 🏨 **Riad 107.** This budget-friendly riad with great amenities (including air-conditioning) is located in a quiet, safe alley not far from Place Jemâa el Fna. Its simple decorations and traditional architecture give the property a peaceful vibe that's fresh and modern as well as cozy Moroccan—think colorful throws and cushions set against pale walls, a small tiled central courtyard, and a small plunge pool. **Pros:** safe and convenient location; splash pool; stylish modern decor. **Cons:** small rooms; street noise can affect ground-floor rooms; narrow stairs to terrace. [$] *Rooms from: 600DH* ✉ *107, Derb Jdid, Douar Graoua, Medina* ☎ *0524/38–64–57* 🌐 *www.riad107.com* 🛏 *6 rooms* 🍴 *Breakfast* ✥ *G3.*

$$$ B&B/INN 🏨 **Riad Adore.** The jewel in the crown of the English-owned Pure Riads collection, Riad Adore is decorated in cool, pale shades of white, beige, and gray, with tadelakt walls and subtle lighting—an elegant and sophisticated guesthouse close to the main medina action. **Pros:** elegant design; great location; beautiful roof terrace. **Cons:**

small splash pool; three-night minimum stay; children under 12 not accepted. *Rooms from: 1900DH* *97, Derb Tizouagrine, off Rue Dar el Bacha, Medina* *0524/37–77–37* *www.riadadore.com* *10 rooms* *Breakfast* *E1.*

$$$ HOTEL **Riad el Fenn.** Vanessa Branson (sister of the British entrepreneur, Richard Branson) created this riad "adventure" in 2002, and since then it has been reworked and extended to create a palace of individually conceived rooms designed with a stylish modern aesthetic. **Pros:** dripping with good taste; loads of communal spaces for relaxation; accessible to travelers with disabilities. **Cons:** 7.5% compulsory service charge added; cheapest small rooms are very dark; bar and restaurant open to public. *Rooms from: 3000DH* *2, Derb Moulay Abdellah ben Hessaien, Bab Ksour, Medina* *0524/44–12–10* *www.el-fenn.com* *20 rooms* *Breakfast* *D3.*

$$$ B&B/INN **Riad Enija.** Walking through the heavy door that opens into Riad Enija is like stepping into a fairy tale: sculptures, Italian lamps, carved doors, and unique handmade furnishings make this home more of an art gallery than a guesthouse. **Pros:** high-quality services; breakfast served until 1 pm; beautiful interiors and spaces. **Cons:** not all bathrooms are en suite; no nearby car access; property is hard to find. *Rooms from: 3000DH* *9, Derb Mesfioui, Rahba Lakdima, Medina* *0524/44–09–26* *www.riadenija.com* *15 rooms* *Breakfast* *G2.*

$$$$ B&B/INN **Riad Farnatchi.** On the souk's northern tip is this lavish, deluxe riad spread across five adjoining properties; hidden among artisans at work are wide white walls with carved stucco, enormous mosaicked suites with marble baths, an overflowing tiled courtyard pool, and elite clientele (Angelina Jolie and Russell Crowe have stayed here). **Pros:** excellent service; royal treatment; vast private suites. **Cons:** expensive; edgy neighborhood; steep stairs to access some rooms. *Rooms from: 3500DH* *2, Derb el Farnatchi, Qa'at Benahid, Medina* *0524/38–49–12* *www.riadfarnatchi.com* *Closed Aug.* *10 suites* *Breakfast* *H1.*

$$ B&B/INN FAMILY **Riad Les Trois Mages.** Tucked in a derb in the Riad Laarouss neighborhood, Les Trois Mages is a delightful small riad with English-speaking staff and spacious, tastefully furnished rooms. **Pros:** rooftop pool; great service; easy access to parking and taxis. **Cons:** quite far from the main square; can be noisy in rooms if riad is full; prices are set in GB sterling so can fluctuate. *Rooms from: 1100DH* *11, Derb Jemaa, off Rue el Gza, Riad Laarouss, Medina* *0524/38–92–97* *www.lestroismages.com* *7 rooms* *Breakfast* *E1.*

$ B&B/INN **Riad Linda.** A Scottish-owned riad with English-speaking staff on-site, Riad Linda is an unpretentious and welcoming little guesthouse that gives excellent value for the price. **Pros:** excellent value; in the heart of the medina; English-speaking staff. **Cons:** no pool; far from nearest taxi drop-off point; rooms are small. *Rooms from: 650DH* *93, Derb Jemaa, Derb Dabbachi, Medina* *0524/39–09–27* *www.riadlinda.com* *6 rooms* *Breakfast* *G3.*

$$$ B&B/INN Fodor's Choice ★ **Riad l'Orangeraie.** With easy access from Bab Laksour and just five minutes' walk to Djemâa el Fna, this luxurious riad is a great base for exploring the medina. **Pros:** English-speaking staff; great location; cozy fireplace in winter. **Cons:** rooms next to the pool can be noisy;

30% surcharge at Christmas and New Year; in-house meals expensive. [$] *Rooms from: 1600DH* ✉ *61, rue Sidi el Yemani, Mouassine, Medina* ☎ *0661/23–87–89* 🌐 *www.riadorangeraie.com* 🛏 *7 rooms* 🍴 *Breakfast* ✣ *E2.*

$$ B&B/INN **Riad Malika.** The rambling Riad Malika occupies three old houses and was one of the first riads to become a guesthouse back in the 1990s. **Pros:** plenty of character; parking nearby; large bedrooms. **Cons:** far from main square; furnishings and finishes looking worn; lots of stairs. [$] *Rooms from: 1100DH* ✉ *29, Arsat Aouzal, Bab Doukkala, Medina* ☎ *0524/38–54–51* 🌐 *www.riadmalika.com* 🛏 *9 rooms* 🍴 *Breakfast* ✣ *D1.*

$ B&B/INN FAMILY **Riad Nesma.** Proof that staying in a beautiful riad with elegant rooms does not have to break the bank, this Moroccan-run guesthouse is a real treasure, newly extended to add a second tier of rooms and a delightful roof terrace for sunbathing and dipping in the pool or Jacuzzi. **Pros:** excellent value; great location; roof terrace with pool and Jacuzzi. **Cons:** rooms are small; no ground-floor access; rooms opening onto patio are noisy. [$] *Rooms from: 700DH* ✉ *128, Riad Zitouen Lakdim, Medina* ☎ *0524/44–44–42* 🌐 *www.riadnesma.com* 🛏 *24 rooms* 🍴 *Breakfast* ✣ *F6.*

$$ B&B/INN **Riad Samsli.** Made up of two adjoining houses around separate courtyards, Riad Samsli has 10 charming rooms at very good prices. **Pros:** excellent location; lovely communal salons; English-speaking staff. **Cons:** no ground-floor rooms; some rooms are small; no doors between bathroom and bedroom. [$] *Rooms from: 1050DH* ✉ *24, Derb Jdid, Riad Zitoun Lkdim, Medina* ☎ *0524/42–77–49* 🌐 *www.riadsamsli.com* 🛏 *10 rooms* 🍴 *Breakfast* ✣ *F6.*

$$$$ HOTEL Fodor's Choice ★ **Royal Mansour.** Built and owned by King Mohammed VI of Morocco, the Royal Mansour opened in 2010 and is an ultraluxurious private medina within the medina. **Pros:** complete privacy and luxury; fabulous spa treatments; finest Moroccan craftsmanship. **Cons:** entire riads only can be booked (not individual rooms); very strict dress code; no ground-floor bedrooms. [$] *Rooms from: 17000DH* ✉ *Rue Abbou Abbas el Sebti, Medina* ☎ *0529/80–80–80* 🌐 *www.royalmansour.com* 🛏 *53 rooms* 🍴 *Breakfast* ✣ *A3.*

$$$$ HOTEL **La Sultana Marrakech.** There's a certain over-the-top charm to this series of five luxurious interconnected riads of palatial proportions, each with a different decorative theme inspired by previous ruling dynasties. **Pros:** fireplaces in every room; impeccable service; stunning interiors. **Cons:** standard of cuisine is only average; small pool; cheapest rooms are small. [$] *Rooms from: 4200DH* ✉ *403, rue de la Kasbah, Kasbah* ✣ *On tiny alley heading left just behind Saadian tombs* ☎ *0524/38–80–08* 🌐 *www.lasultanamarrakech.com* 🛏 *28 rooms* 🍴 *Breakfast* ✣ *D6.*

$$$ B&B/INN **Talaa 12.** This modernist, minimalist riad—almost next door to the Museum of Marrakech in the heart of the medina—has rooms drenched in natural creams and beiges and beds low and draped with just enough color to make them inviting (though a few more comfy chairs in the bedrooms would not go amiss). **Pros:** central location; elegant design. **Cons:** no pool; expensive. [$] *Rooms from: 2000DH* ✉ *12, Talaa ben Youssef, on way to Ali ben Youssef Medersa, Medina* ☎ *0524/42–90–45* 🌐 *www.talaa12.com* 🛏 *8 rooms* 🍴 *Breakfast* ✣ *G1.*

$$$$ HOTEL **Villa des Orangers.** Formerly the private residence of a Marrakesh judge, this exquisite 1930s property has all the understated glamour and class you'd expect from a Relais & Chateaux hotel, with unobtrusive service, libraries to hide away in, and bedrooms with enormous bathrooms. **Pros:** unsurpassed luxury; plenty of privacy; excellent restaurant. **Cons:** very expensive; wood-paneled rooms rather gloomy; lots of stairs to climb. [$] *Rooms from: 4400DH* ✉ *6, rue Sidi Mimoun, Medina* ☎ *0524/38–46–38* 🌐 *www.villadesorangers.com* 🛏 *27 rooms* 🍴 *Breakfast* ✣ *D5.*

GUÉLIZ

The hotels in Guéliz mostly cater to package holiday groups, so unless you're with a family in need of a big hotel to drown out the noise you make, they may not appeal to you. They overflow with facilities but lack the character or personal service you find in an old riad. Still, we've found a few that buck the trend and are all in lively, city center locations.

$$ HOTEL **Bab Hotel.** This boutique hotel in the heart of Guéliz is chic and hypermodern in style, with trendy designer furniture, a space-age lounge bar, and minimalist bedrooms furnished in pale shades. **Pros:** funky interior design; great location; spacious rooms. **Cons:** small pool; noisy neighborhood; patchy service. [$] *Rooms from: 900DH* ✉ *Rue Mohammed el Beqqal, at Bd. Mansour Eddahbi, Guéliz* ☎ *0524/43–52–50* 🌐 *www.babhotelmarrakech.ma* 🛏 *45 rooms* 🍴 *Breakfast.*

$ HOTEL **Le Caspien Hotel.** A modern three-star hotel with small pool, Spanish tapas restaurant, bar area, and clean, spacious rooms and suites (many have twin beds), Le Caspien is a convenient local base in the heart of Guéliz with some traditional decorative touches such as stucco cornices, carved wooden doors, and *beldi* (a traditional, handmade, mosaic tile) floors. **Pros:** central location; good value for money; friendly and helpful staff. **Cons:** Wi-Fi/Internet connection is unreliable; hot water not always reliable; noisy neighborhood. [$] *Rooms from: 600DH* ✉ *12, rue Loubnane, Guéliz* ☎ *0524/42–22–82* 🌐 *www.lecaspien-hotel.com* 🛏 *38 rooms* 🍴 *Breakfast.*

$ HOTEL FAMILY **Diwane Hotel.** This city-center hotel has a huge, riad-style atrium, giving it some sense of Moroccan charm along with standard hotel amenities such as restaurant, bar, gym, spa, and pool. **Pros:** great location; good-sized pool; great value. **Cons:** the bars are shabby and smoky; standard of buffet restaurant is inconsistent; decor needs updating. [$] *Rooms from: 600DH* ✉ *24, rue de Yougoslavie, corner of Av. Mohammed V, Guéliz* ☎ *0524/43–22–16* 🌐 🛏 *125 rooms* 🍴 *Breakfast.*

$$ HOTEL **Opera Plaza Hotel.** Next to the train station and opposite the Theatre Royal, this modern four-star hotel makes a convenient and well-priced base in the nouvelle ville—even though it's not the most glamorous location—as taxis are on the doorstep for the short skip to the old medina and it's walking distance to the rest of Guéliz. **Pros:** lovely pool area; central location; spacious and clean. **Cons:** building lacks charm; air-conditioning not always working; service can be slack. [$] *Rooms from: 1000DH* ✉ *Av. Mohammed VI and Av. Hassan II, Guéliz* ☎ *0524/35–15–15* 🌐 *www.operaplazahotel.com* 🛏 *115 rooms* 🍴 *Breakfast.*

$$
HOTEL

2Ciels Hotel. This Spanish-Moroccan owned boutique hotel opened in 2016 and it's a great city-center base—downtown Guéliz is on the doorstep and it's close to modern restaurants, cafés, and nightlife—but it's also on a quiet corner close to the El Harti Gardens and Royal Tennis Club. **Pros:** great location; trendy design; lovely rooftop bar; underground spa. **Cons:** small pool; rooms are cramped; service is slack. $ *Rooms from: 1300DH ⊠ Av. Oued el Makhzine, Guéliz ☎ 0524/25–95–70 ⊕ www.2ciels.com ⇨ 85 rooms ⎮⊚⎮ Breakfast.*

HIVERNAGE

Wide, shaded streets lined with orange and olive trees, and a few secluded villas with palm trees towering above the garden walls, create a sense of tranquillity and affluence in this neighborhood just to the west of the ramparts. However, Hivernage also houses a number of large hotels that are ideal for families that want plenty of amenities, exotic garden space, swimming pools, and even wheelchair access. It's a great location not too far from the old medina. After dark, Hivernage is abuzz, as many of the smartest nightclubs are in this area. A calèche ride along the avenues makes for a pleasant afternoon jaunt as part of a city tour.

$$$
HOTEL

Dar Rhizlane. Hidden in the wealthy residential neighborhood of Hivernage, Dar Rhizlane is a luxury boutique hotel that was designed to look like the capacious villas built during the French Protectorate in the 1920s. **Pros:** peaceful location yet near to medina; excellent service; excellent Moroccan restaurant. **Cons:** pool sunbathing area is small; breakfasts need improving; cheapest rooms are very cramped. $ *Rooms from: 2100DH ⊠ Rue Jnane el Harti, Hivernage ☎ 0524/42–13–03 ⊕ www.dar-rhizlane.com ⇨ 20 rooms ⎮⊚⎮ Breakfast.*

$$$
HOTEL
FAMILY

Es Saadi Marrakech Resort. The 1950s design of this former casino does little to inspire, but this family-run hotel with every amenity does the job and offers four different types of accommodation from classic luxury hotel to private minikasbahs. **Pros:** family-friendly; spacious grounds; three swimming pools. **Cons:** dated design; impersonal; large pool/garden not open to all guests. $ *Rooms from: 1700DH ⊠ Rue Ibrahim el Mazini, Hivernage ☎ 0524/44–88–11 ⊕ www.essaadi.com ⇨ 267 rooms ⎮⊚⎮ Breakfast.*

$$$$
RESORT
FAMILY

Four Seasons Resort Marrakech. Opened in 2012, Four Seasons has created a luxurious minimedina outside the walls of the old city: avenues of palm trees, arcades, and patios connect the low-rise pavilions, all surrounded by acres of exotic gardens, terraces, pools, and fountains. **Pros:** pure luxury; family-friendly; restaurants and bar on-site. **Cons:** far from medina; hefty price tag on any extras arranged through the hotel; patchy customer service. $ *Rooms from: 7000DH ⊠ 1, bd. de la Menara, Hivernage ☎ 0524/35–92–00 ⊕ www.fourseasons.com ⇨ 141 rooms ⎮⊚⎮ Breakfast.*

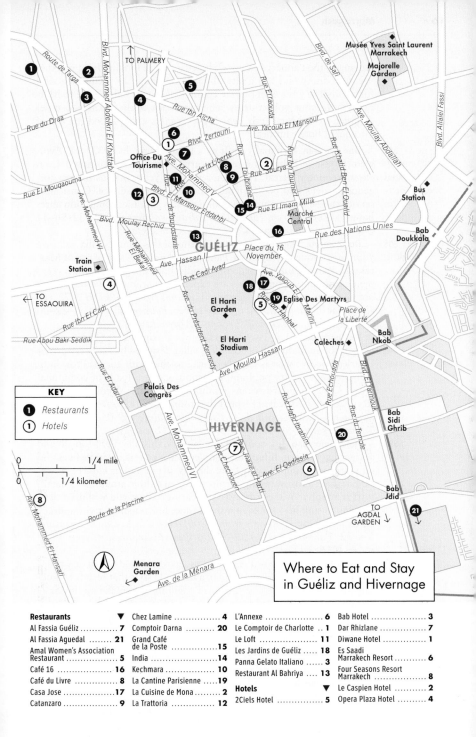

Where to Eat and Stay in Guéliz and Hivernage

THE PALMERY

Staying in the Palmery is a good choice if you're looking for a relaxing vacation and won't feel guilty about exchanging the medina's action for an idyll in your own private country palace. It's also close to Marrakesh's famous golf courses. The drawback is the 7-km (4½-mile) distance from Marrakesh, which necessitates a car, a taxi, or use of infrequent hotel shuttles.

$$$
HOTEL
FAMILY
Fodor's Choice
★

Dar Ayniwen. Originally built as a family home in 1982, Dar Ayniwen (House of Palms) is now a luxurious small hotel disguised as an elegant country retreat. **Pros:** unpretentious yet luxurious rooms; gorgeous gardens and pool; friendly and welcoming service. **Cons:** meal service can be slow; minimum two-night stay; Internet connection unreliable. $ *Rooms from: 2500DH* ⊠ *Tafrata, Palmery* ☎ *0524/32–96–84* ⊕ *www.dar-ayniwen.com* ⟿ *10 rooms* ⊙| *Breakfast.*

$$$
HOTEL

Dar Zemora. The unpretentious charms of this country villa will ease your guilt about staying in the Palmery and possibly seeing less of Marrakesh. **Pros:** beautiful gardens; friendly English-speaking staff; complete tranquillity. **Cons:** meals are expensive; minimum two-night stay; not all rooms have private terrace. $ *Rooms from: 2400DH* ⊠ *72, rue el Aandalib, Ennakhil, just off road to Fez, Palmery* ☎ *0524/32–82–00* ⊕ *www.darzemora.com* ⟿ *7 rooms* ⊙| *Breakfast.*

$$$
HOTEL
FAMILY

Les Deux Tours. The Two Towers enjoys a magnificent garden setting with accommodation in neoclassical villas designed by architect-owner Charles Boccara who is usually on-site to chat with guests. **Pros:** individual design; pretty pool and enormous garden; loads of communal areas. **Cons:** standard rooms cramped and stuffy; decor and upholstery is tired; noise carries from other rooms. $ *Rooms from: 2500DH* ⊠ *Douar Abiad, Circuit de la Palmeraie, Palmery* ☎ *0524/32–95–27* ⊕ *www.les-deux-tours.com* ⟿ *37 rooms* ⊙| *Breakfast.*

$$$$
RESORT

Hotel Amanjena. Just south of the Palmery, this blend of Moorish and ancient Egyptian architecture, completed in a palette of subtle hues and set in its own grounds away from the city, lives up to its name: a peaceful paradise. **Pros:** stunning architecture; incredible attention to detail; staff is attentive without being overbearing. **Cons:** you will need deep pockets to stay here for even a short time; few on-site activities; decor needs refreshing. $ *Rooms from: 8800DH* ⊠ *Old Rte. de Ouarzazate, Km 12, Palmery* ☎ *0524/39–90–00* ⊕ *www.amanresorts.com* ⟿ *39 rooms* ⊙| *Breakfast.*

$$$
HOTEL

Jnane Tamsna. The word *jnane* means "garden," and this luxury property lives up to its name: modeled in a hacienda style that blends Moroccan with Mexican, the five villas and pavilions that make up this oasis complex are surrounded by palms, olive trees, cactus gardens, herbs, and rose beds. **Pros:** plenty of pampering; charitable projects supported; exceptional gardens. **Cons:** swimming pools not heated year-round; meals expensive; service can be sluggish. $ *Rooms from: 2750DH* ⊠ *Douar Abiad, Circuit de la Palmeraie, Palmery* ☎ *0524/32–84–84* ⊕ *www.jnane.com* ⟿ *26 rooms* ⊙| *Breakfast.*

$$$$
HOTEL

Ksar Char-Bagh. Rising like a Byzantine, 14th-century kasbah from the Palmery and surrounded by 10 acres of manicured grounds, this Relais & Chateaux hotel is the last word in sumptuous, escape-it-all luxury.

Pros: beautiful decor; huge heated pool; exclusive and private. **Cons:** service sometimes falls short; restaurant more French than Moroccan; extra services very expensive. $ *Rooms from: 4800DH* ✉ *Djnan Abiad, Circuit de la Palmeraie, Palmery* ☎ *0524/32–92–44* ⊕ *www.ksarcharbagh.fr* ⊘ *Closed Aug.* ⇘ *13 rooms* ⦿ *Breakfast.*

$$$$
HOTEL
🏨 **Palais Namaskar.** You'll feel like a celebrity when you arrive at this dreamy resort, which opened to great acclaim in 2012 in Marrakesh's Palmery. **Pros:** romantic setting; excellent service; pampering spa. **Cons:** water features and harmony pools not kept clean; main pool is rather small and overlooked by the restaurant; lacks personality and warmth. $ *Rooms from: 6000DH* ✉ *Rte. de Bab Atlas, No. 88/69, Province Syba, Palmery* ☎ *0524/29–98–00* ⊕ *www.palaisnamaskar.com* ⇘ *41 rooms* ⦿ *Breakfast.*

$$$
HOTEL
🏨 **Palais Rhoul.** This flashy, horseshoe-shaped mansion is the height of bohemian boutique chic, if a bit Beverley Hills. **Pros:** the height of luxury; fabulous gardens; family-run with owners on-site. **Cons:** restaurant overrated; little English spoken; only main pool is heated. $ *Rooms from: 3300DH* ✉ *Rte. de Fès, Circuit de la Palmeraie, Km 5 Dar Tounsi, Palmery* ☎ *0524/32–94–94* ⊕ *www.palais-rhoul.com* ⇘ *23 rooms* ⦿ *Breakfast.*

$$$
RESORT
FAMILY
🏨 **Palmeraie Palace.** Tasteful it isn't, but this giant, gaudy, self-contained bubble in the middle of the Palmery offers every kind of distraction, and plenty to keep children amused. **Pros:** great for golfers; plenty of pampering; family-friendly. **Cons:** lacks charm; poor customer service; poor restaurant/buffet meals. $ *Rooms from: 1800DH* ✉ *Circuit de la Palmeraie, Palmery* ☎ *0524/33–43–43* ⊕ *www.palmeraieresorts.com* ⇘ *325 rooms* ⦿ *Breakfast.*

NIGHTLIFE

Without a doubt, Marrakesh is Morocco's nightlife capital. Options include everything from the free but fascinating goings-on at Djemâa el Fna square to the hedonistic cocktail scene of Hivernage, with its cluster of casinos, cabarets, and nightclubs.

MEDINA

BARS

Alcohol was once frowned upon in the medina, and while it's still unthinkable to swig liquor on the streets or even on outdoor plazas or terraces, there are a few good places to go for a drink within the city walls. However, alcohol licenses are still hard to come by and as a result the drinks are expensive.

Café Arabe. One of the most elegant settings is Café Arabe, a galleried, bougainvillea-strewn riad with a sleek rooftop bar, two relaxed dining salons, and a resident lounge DJ. Enjoy cocktails, Moroccan wine, or champagne. The pasta dishes are all homemade, so come for dinner and make an evening of it. ✉ *184, rue el Mouassine, Medina* ☎ *0524/42–97–28* ⊕ *www.cafearabe.com.*

Fodor's Choice **El Fenn.** Luxury riad El Fenn is a hub for designers, artists, and photog-
★ raphers (the name El Fenn means art in the local dialect). It's also open
to nonguests who want to find a fashionable spot in the medina with an
indoor Art Deco lounge bar or a boho-chic roof terrace bar. Wine, beer,
spirits, and a vast selection of cocktails are available and can be sipped
fireside in winter, or under the rooftop Berber tent with views across to
the Koutoubia mosque. ⊠ *Derb Moulay Abdellah ben Hessaien, Bab
L'Ksour, Medina* ☎ *0524/44–12–10* ⊕ *www.el-fenn.com.*

Les Jardins de la Koutoubia. The attractive Art Deco stylings and extensive
cigar rack of the piano bar at hotel Les Jardins de la Koutoubia are
decadent, but there's nothing better than grabbing a cocktail and heading to the salons and terraces in the open-air courtyard. A pianist plays
7 to midnight. ⊠ *26, rue de la Koutoubia, Medina* ☎ *0524/38–88–00*
⊕ *www.lesjardinsdelakoutoubia.com.*

Kosybar. The Kosybar and restaurant is a long-standing favorite in Marrakesh for a late-night drink in the medina, served with live jazz entertainment every night, and a platter of sushi if you wish. Enjoy classic
cocktails on the large roof terrace, which has great views of the storks
nesting in the nearby ramparts of the Badii Palace and into the "lantern-
making" square (Place des Ferblantiers) below. The interior restaurant and bar, with mosaic-tiled floors, wrought-iron balustrades, and
fireplaces, are truly cozy. ⊠ *47, pl. des Ferblantiers, Kzadria, Medina*
☎ *0524/38–03–24* ⊕ *www.kosybar.com.*

La Maison Arabe. The intimate surroundings of the jazz bar at hotel
La Maison Arabe provide a cozy fireside setting for cocktails and a
tasty menu of light savory snacks. A resident pianist tickles the ivories
every evening from 7 to 9. ⊠ *1, Derb Assehbe, Bab Doukkala, Medina*
☎ *0524/38–70–10* ⊕ *www.lamaisonarabe.com.*

Le Salama. A stone's throw from the Djemâa el Fna and up a narrow
staircase, Le Salama is one of the few places in the medina where you
can grab a cold beer or an aperitif without having to eat dinner. Drinks
are served either at the bar area in the elegant, colonial-style restaurant
or on the top terrace Sky Bar with views across to the Koutoubia.
⊠ *40, rue des Banques, Kennaria, Medina* ☎ *0524/39–13–00* ⊕ *www.
le-salama.com.*

CAFÉS

Nowhere is café culture busier than on Djemâa el Fna, where several
terraces compete for the award for best view of the square.

Café Argana. Following a terrorist incident in April 2011 that destroyed
much of the building, the Café Argana is back on top. Moroccan
authorities and local people have restored the famous landmark to its
former glory, and then some. The terraces have been extended to three
floors and now have comfortable seating and some of the best sunset
views across Place Djemâa el Fna. Ice cream and main meals are also
served. ⊠ *1–2, pl. Djemâa el Fna, Medina* ☎ *0524/44–27–57.*

Café de France. Though it's a bit past its prime, Café de France is a local
cultural institution and a great place for people-watching from morning
till night. It's also the perfect spot for a late-night glass of mint tea with
a good view. On the ground floor there's a tiny snack restaurant with

bright plastic tables, serving sandwiches and quick bites until closing time. Head to the top floor for a ringside view of the square. ⊠ *Pl. Djemâa el Fna, on northeastern corner, Medina* ☎ *0524/44–23–19* ⊕ *www.cafe-france-marrakech.com.*

Grand Balcon du Café Glacier. To catch the sunset and the beginnings of the alluring smoke and sizzle of the grills, the rightly named Grand Balcon du Café Glacier, to the south of the square, is a top choice. It shuts relatively early, though (around 10 pm), and you'll have to compete for elbow room with all the amateur photographers who throng the best spot. Service is slow and soft drinks overpriced—but that's not unexpected for this bird's-eye view. ⊠ *Pl. Djemâa el Fna, Medina.*

CASINOS

La Grand Casino de La Mamounia. The casino at La Mamounia has a large room for roulette, poker, and blackjack; a slot-machine hall; and is open until 6 am. You'll need to dress up to gain entrance to this exclusive establishment. ⊠ *Av. Bab Jdid, Medina* ☎ *0524/33–82–00* ⊕ *www.grandcasinomamounia.com.*

GUÉLIZ

BARS

For evening drinks in elegant surroundings, dress the part and head to one of Marrakesh's prestigious hotels such as **La Maison Arabe** or **La Mamounia** in the Medina. In Guéliz, nearly all the modern tourist hotels in the new town have a bar that serves alcohol to varying degrees of respectability. A handful of hotels also feature a rooftop bar with views over the city; some are better than others. There are also a few other late-night drinking dens scattered in the side streets south of Place du 16 Novembre along Avenue Mohammed V, but, and we hate to say this, women might not be welcome. Night owls in search of something livelier should head to the trendy hangouts of Hivernage for upmarket nightclubs. Some restaurants also have a small bar counter, but usually patrons are obliged to order food.

Lola Sky Lounge. The rooftop bar of the 2Ciels Hotel has sixth-floor views over the Royal Tennis Club, the old Marrakesh soccer stadium, and the Hivernage area of the city. The bar serves tapas, beer, wine, cocktails, and coffee throughout the day and has pleasant shaded seating areas with tables and reasonable prices. ⊠ *2Ciels Hotel, Av. Oued el Makhazine, Guéliz* ☎ *0524/35–95–50* ⊕ *www.2ciels.com.*

Le 68. This tiny little wine-bar, which resembles a black box from outside, is the place where locals and ex-pats meet up for post work drinks and snacks. A decent wine list is available and there's a small restaurant on the upstairs mezzanine that serves French cuisine at reasonable prices. Le 68 is popular and as such the place can get very smoky. ■TIP→ **It's closed during Ramadan.** ⊠ *68, rue de la Liberté, Guéliz* ☎ *0524/44–97–42* ⊕ *www.le-68.com.*

Festivals in Marrakesh

Since 2000, the high-profile **Marrakesh International Film Festival** has attracted the glitterati of the international movie world for screenings of Moroccan and international films throughout the city; previous special guests have included Susan Sarandon, Leonardo DiCaprio, and Martin Scorsese. Held in early December, it's the biggest, brightest, and glitziest event of the Marrakesh cultural calendar and attracts movie fans from near and far. Free public screenings are held at the Palais de Congrès, the Cinema Colisée, and Place Djemâa el Fna. For more information, visit the festival's website (⊕ *en.festivalmarrakech.info*).

The brainchild of Vanessa Branson (sister of Richard), the **Marrakech Biennale** strives to address social issues using the contemporary arts and features talks, exhibitions, and installations throughout the city by Moroccan and international artists. It usually takes place in March, and the next event is anticipated for 2018. See the website (⊕ *www.marrakechbiennale.org*) for details of future events.

Street art and site-specific performance art are the raison-d'être for the annual **Awaln'Art Festival** (⊕ *www.awalnart.com*), which brings together international artists every April or May to create shows that combine elements of circus, dance, and theater. Events usually take place in public areas such as gardens and streets and all are free.

Ramadan is the holy month of fasting, which lasts approximately 30 days, though the dates vary annually and each year start about 12 days earlier than the previous year; it's the ninth month of the Islamic lunar calendar. Muslims abstain from eating, drinking, and other worldly pleasures between sunrise and sunset. Each evening, the breaking of fast is marked by the *l'ftour* meal. Occasionally there are special musical concerts arranged in the late evenings to coincide with Ramadan. Visitors can experience *l'ftour* at several small street cafés in the medina and in Guéliz. **Aïd el-Seghrir** celebrates the end of Ramadan and is felt largely as a citywide sigh of relief. There are no big festivities, but families get together to share a meal. **Aïd el-Kebir**, the Day of Sacrifice, is the biggest of the religious celebrations, but has a somber tone; approximately 2½ months after the end of Ramadan, Muslims everywhere observe the last ritual of the pilgrimage to Mecca by slaughtering a sheep. Vegetarians and animal-lovers might want to avoid looking too closely.

NIGHTCLUBS

Montecristo. Housed in a beautiful Art Deco villa on the edge of Guéliz, Montecristo is a nonstop party destination every night of the week—on weekends it attracts crowds from Rabat and Casablanca—as it has a far more intimate, eclectic vibe than the large cavernous clubs farther out of town. You can smoke *sheesha* on the roof terrace, dine downstairs, watch live bands in the lounge bar, or dance the night away to an ever-changing program of music in the first-floor club, but be aware of the omnipresent "working girls." ■ **TIP➔ Closed during Ramadan.** ✉ *20, rue Ibn Aicha, Guéliz* ☎ *0524/43–90–31* ⊕ *www.montecristomarrakech.com.*

HIVERNAGE

BARS

Comptoir Darna. A lively crowd gathers regularly in the darkened corners of popular Comptoir Darna to dance to the tunes of the resident DJs, take in the nightly cabaret show, or chill out by candlelight with cocktails on the plant-filled patio. ☒ *Av. Echouhada, Hivernage* ☏ *0524/43–77–02* ⊕ *www.uk.comptoirmarrakech.com.*

Pearl Hotel Sky Lounge. This sky lounge, on the hotel's fourth-floor terrace, has the most impressive views over the ramparts to La Mamounia and the Koutoubia mosque, as well as the Menara Gardens and beyond. It's the perfect spot for sunset drinks (or tea, coffee, or snacks). Added bonus: there's a doughnut-shaped pool in the middle if you want to sunbathe and take a dip (for an extra 300 DH). ☒ *The Pearl Hotel, Angle av. Echouhada and rue des Temples, Hivernage* ☏ *0524/42–42–42* ⊕ *www.thepearlmarrakech.com.*

CASINOS

Es Saadi. Apart from La Mamounia, the only casino of note in Marrakesh is the one in the gardens of the Es Saadi hotel, set apart from the main building. Established in 1952, it was the town's first casino, and it has undergone a revamp and contains a mixture of one-armed bandits and tables for roulette and blackjack. There are also regular poker tournaments and poker games every night from 6 pm to 8 am. ☒ *Hotel Es Saadi, Rue Ibrahim El Mazini, Hivernage* ☏ *0524/33–74–00* ⊕ *www.essaadi.com.*

DINNER SHOWS

Fodor'sChoice **Lotus Club.** The cabaret entertainment at Lotus Club is its raison d'être—
★ and clearly built into the prices for drinks and food, which includes Mediterranean, Moroccan, and Japanese dishes. The show, entitled Oh La La!, features a burlesque-style revue of samba, Oriental, and Egyptian-inspired vignettes performed by corseted dancers flaunting feather boas, and live music from Moroccan guitar virtuoso Mahmoud "Mood" Chouki. Come around 9 pm to see the show. ☒ *Rue Ahmed Chawki, Hivernage* ☏ *0524/42–17–36* ⊕ *www.lotusclubmarrakech.com.*

NIGHTCLUBS

Fodor'sChoice **Buddha Bar.** An impressive Buddha statue greets partygoers upon arrival
★ at one of Marrakesh's newest and hippest night spots. An Asian vibe mixes with modern decor in the various corner salons, while the restaurant offers a "Pacific Rim" fusion of Asian, Thai, Japanese, and Chinese cuisine. In the signature style of the Buddha Bar "eatertainment" concept that originated in Paris, the music is an eclectic, ethnic world fusion with guest DJs, bellydancers, and even a Bollywood set. An added bonus: No entry fee. ☒ *Av. Prince Moulay Rachid, Hivernage* ⊹ *Within Menara Mall complex* ☏ *0524/45–93–00* ⊕ *www.buddhabar.ma.*

Palais Jad Mahal. Once one of Hivernage's hippest nightspots, the Indian-tinged Palais Jad Mahal continues to satisfy those in search of an exotic night on the town. Prices are steep and service is iffy, but the atmosphere, excellent house band, belly dancers, and cabaret entertainment make it more than worthwhile. ■ TIP→ When the flavored vodka kicks in after midnight, head next door to the Russian-themed Raspoutine nightclub. ⊠ *10, rue Haroun Errachid, Hivernage* ☎ *0524/43–69–84* ⊕ *www.palaisjadmahal.net.*

Raspoutine. This legendary Parisian nightclub opened in Marrakesh in 2016 attracting a beautiful crowd who dance the night away as DJs spin deep-house until the wee hours of the night. There are plenty of red velour furnishings, drapes, and gilded mirrors hinting back to the original Champs-Elysée Russian-cabaret venue of the 1960s. There is no entry fee, but do expect to pay top dollar for drinks at the elaborately decorated bar. Make sure to dress the part. ⊠ *10, rue Haroun Errachid, Hivernage* ✛ *Next to Palais Jad Mahal* ☎ *0616/60–94–70* ⊕ *www.raspoutine.com/raspoutine-marrakech.*

SO Night Lounge. A stylish nightspot with contemporary decor and furnishings, attracting an upmarket crowd of tourists, Moroccans, and expats alike, SO has live music starting around 9 pm and resident DJs, a Moroccan restaurant, licensed bar, chill-out spaces, and a relaxed garden terrace area to enjoy sheesha and alcohol-free cocktails. Sofitel guests and diners at SO Food restaurant avoid the hefty 200 DH cover. ⊠ *Sofitel, Rue Haroun Errachid, Hivernage* ☎ *0524/42–56–00* ⊕ *www.so-nightlounge.com.*

Le Théâtro. Hip, loud, and gregarious, Le Théâtro draws locals and tourists for its festive vibe. On the menu are house music, hard-core Dutch house, live DJs, candy girls, and circus cabaret acts. ■ TIP→ **To reserve a table, you must purchase a minimum drinks package of 10,000 DH.** ⊠ *Hotel Es Saadi, Rue Ibrahim El Mazini, Hivernage* ☎ *0664/86–03–39* ⊕ *www.theatromarrakech.com* ⊠ *200 DH weekdays, 300 DH weekends.*

PALMERY

DINNER SHOWS

Le Blokk. Located in the Palmery, outside of town, Le Blokk is a dinner-cabaret venue well worth the taxi ride. The kitchen serves up Japanese and International cuisine with reasonably priced fixed menu options (starting at 270 DH); Moroccan dishes can be ordered by special arrangement. The live music and entertainment, however, take center stage. Tap your feet while talented singers perform songs from the last 50 years, followed by acrobatic performers who start to twirl from the ceilings around midnight. Top off the night with DJs spinning Oriental and Western dance music until around 1 am. Reservations are a must and children are welcome, too. ⊠ *Circuit de la Palmeraie, next to Mehdi Palace, Palmery* ☎ *0674/33–43–34* ⊕ *www.leblokk.com* ☽ *Closed Mon. Closed during Ramadan.*

Chez Ali. The long-standing nightly spectacle that takes place at Chez Ali is a Disney World-meets-Marrakesh experience, catering to the mass tourism market. After a multicourse dinner of couscous, pastilla, and tagine in breezy tents, the *fantasia* begins in the outdoor arena. Featuring hundreds of performers and dozens of horses, this singing-and-dancing pageant is a celebration of traditional culture. It's all very

tacky and you'll feel pressured into tipping the lackluster performers that snag you at every possible opportunity. Taxis will take you
there, or your hotel can organize an all-inclusive price that includes
round-trip transportation. Expect to pay around 450 DH per person
including return transport. ⊠ *Circuit Jaafaria, Douar Belguid, Palmery*
☏ *0524/30–77–30* ⬙ *450 DH.*

Fuego Latino. A high-octane performance of samba drummers, musicians, and carnival dancers shimmying their way among the crowd
and dancing on the tabletops, Fuego Latino includes an all-you-can-eat
extravaganza of grilled meats and fish in the Brazilian *churrascaria* style.
You can also enjoy the show from the bar (with hefty drinks prices).
The show starts around 10 pm. Tickets start at 420 DH; ringside tables
are 600 DH with fixed menu. ⊠ *Palmeraie Palace Hotel, Circuit de
la Palmeraie, Palmery* ☏ *0619/27–29–45* ⊙ *Closed during Ramadan.*

SHOPPING

Marrakesh is a shopper's bonanza, full of the very rugs, handicrafts, and
clothing you see in the pages of magazines back home. Most bazaars
are in the souk, just north of Djemâa el Fna and spread through a seem-
ingly never-ending maze of alleys. Together, they sell almost everything
imaginable and are highly competitive. Bargaining here is hard, and you
can get up to 80% discounts. So on your first exploration, it's often a
better idea to simply wander and take in the atmosphere than to buy.
You can check guideline prices in some of the more well-to-do parts of
town, which display fixed price tags for every object.

There are a number of crafts and souvenir shops on Avenue Mohammed
V in Guéliz, as well as some very good Moroccan antiques stores and
designer shops that offer a distinctly modern take on Moroccan clothing, footwear, and interior decoration. These allow buyers to browse
at their leisure, free of the souk's intense pressures. Many have fixed
prices, with only 10% discounts after haggling. Most of these stores are
happy to ship your purchases overseas. Bazaars generally open between
8 and 9 am and close between 8 and 9 pm; stores in Guéliz open a bit
later and close a bit earlier, some breaking for lunch. Some bazaars in
the medina close on Friday, the Muslim holy day. In Guéliz, most shops
are closed on Sunday.

**OFF THE
BEATEN
PATH**
Away from the medina and beyond Guéliz, the gritty, nontouristy
industrial zone of **Sidi Ghanem** has recently become a hot shopping
destination, with local designers and artisans setting up workshops and
showrooms targeting the wholesale and export market. Riad owners,
restaurateurs, hoteliers, expats, and tourists scour the outlets to buy
superior-quality, contemporary-style housewares, furnishings, ceramics,
fashion, jewelry, and perfumes. About 5 km (3 miles) out of town on
Route de Safi, it requires hiring a taxi for a few hours to take you there,
wait while you shop, and then bring you back downtown.

BARGAINING

Bargaining is part of the fun of shopping in the medina's souks. Go back and forth with the vendor until you agree on an acceptable price. If you are not sure if the vendor's "lowest price" is really the lowest, slowly leave the store—if the vendor follows you, then you can negotiate further. If bargaining is just not your thing and you don't mind paying a little extra, consider the shops of Guéliz. Although these shops are not as colorful as the souks, a reasonable variety of high-quality goods are on offer.

SHOPPING GUIDES

Many guides have (undeclared) affiliations with certain shops, and taking on a guide may mean you'll be delivered to the boutique of their choice, rather than your own discovery. You should be fine on your own, as long as you keep your eyes peeled for mini-adventures and overly aggressive sellers. Small boutique shopkeepers who can't afford to tip guides will thank you for it.

There are also a few personal shopping guides working in Marrakesh (mostly expats), trying to strike the best deal for the customer and take the pain out of seeking, finding, and haggling for those "must-have" items.

FONDOUKS

If you tire of the haggling in the souk but still want to pick up a bargain, try visiting a *fondouk*. These were originally storehouses, workshops, and inns frequented by merchants and artisans on their journeys across the Sahara (known as *caravanserai* in the Middle East), and are still in use today, particularly by Berber merchants bringing carpets and other goods from surrounding villages; others are staffed by artisans at work on goods destined for the market. They're easily recognized by courtyards full of junk, usually with galleries on upper levels. Fondouks always keep their doors open, so feel free to look around. Because you deal with the artisans directly, there's less of a markup on prices. There are a couple of fondouks on Dar el Bacha as you head toward the souk, and on Rue Bab Taghzout by the fountain known as Shrob ou Shouf ("Drink and Look").

Patrizia Bell-Banner. Personal shopper Patrizia Bell-Banner is an interior decorator living between London and Marrakesh. She knows her way through the best boutiques of the souks and out to the designer showrooms of the Sidi Ghanem industrial zone, and can point you in the direction of those special items you may be seeking. For around €300 per day it's great retail therapy. ⊠ *Marrakesh* ☏ *0661/42–43–82* ✍ *patbanner@onesourcehomesearch.com.*

MEDINA

THE SOUKS

From dried fruit to handbags, carpets to candlesticks, the jumbled labyrinth of merchants and artisan workshops to be found in the souks of the Marrakesh medina is one of the wonders of the city, where all manner of curious exotic items can be found. It stretches north from Place Djemâa el Fna to Ali ben Youssef Medersa. Each souk has a name that defines its specialty and that relates to the crafts guilds that used to control each area.

2

Heading north from Bab Fteuh square, near Place Djemâa el Fna, the souks are laid out roughly as follows:

Souk Semmarine: textiles and souvenirs; Souk Rahba Kdima: spices, herbs, apothecaries, woolen hats, baskets; Souk el-Kebir: carpets, leather goods, and wood wares; Souk Zarbia: carpets; Souk des Bijoutiers/Souk Tagmoutyime: jewelry; Souk el-Attarine: polished copper and brass and mirrors; Souk des Babouches/Souk Smata: leather slippers; Souk des Teinturiers/Souk Sebbaghine: fabric and wool. Several other souks—including Souk Chouari: wood-carpenters; Souk Haddadine: black-smiths; and Souk Cherratine: leatherworkers—are at the northern end.

Generally, credit cards are not accepted here, except at the more upmarket bazaars and shops. Most places are open daily from 9 to 9, though some places close on Friday. A small side market called Souk Cherifia is located at the northern end of the souks beyond Souk Haddadine. The ground floor sells standard touristic items, but go up to the second floor near the entrance to La Terrasse des Épices restaurant and you'll find several fascinating little boutique outlets by up-and-coming young Marrakesh-based designers.

Carpet Souk. The site of the old slave auctions held up until the French occupied the city in 1912, the main carpet souk—called the Souk Zrabia or *Le Criée Berbère*—has a flat, shiny floor in the middle of the surrounding boutiques used to roll out the rugs to display to potential buyers. To get there head north on Rue Semarine, and just after the Souk el Attarine branches off left, take the next right turn off the street (which is now more properly named Rue Souk el-Kebir—the Big Souk Street). The carpet souk can also be reached from a passage in Rahba Qdima's northeast corner (to the right of Le Café des Épices). ⊠ *Rahba Qdima, Medina.*

Leather Souks. At the northeastern edges of the souk (just beyond the northern end of the main Rue Souk el Kebir) are the leatherwork-ers—busy cutting out templates for babouches, hammering and pol-ishing, and making up bags and satchels from several types of animal skins. Look for signs to the Souk des Sachochiers (bag makers), Souk Chairia, and Souk Cherratine, all leather-working areas. The tanner-ies, where the raw hides have been prepared and dyed, are some 20 minutes walk farther northeast from Souk Cherratine along Rue Bab Debbagh. Also in the northeast are a range of instruments, especially drums (Souk Moulay aii) and woven baskets (Souk Serrajine). ⊠ *Rue Souk Chairia, Medina.*

Rue Mouassine. One of the easiest ways to head back to Djemâa el Fna from a day of souk shopping is to find Rue Mouassine, the souk's westernmost main north–south artery (the other main artery is Rue Souk Semarine, on the eastern side of the souks). Rue Mouassine is quite easy to find, and it's almost impossible to veer away from the correct path once you're on it; the simplest route is to take a coun-terclockwise loop from behind the Ben Medersa Mosque—when you hit the big mosque, you've hit Rue Mouassine. This is heavy souvenir territory, with the whole gamut of goods on display—lanterns, teapots, scarves, babouches, djellabas. It's an easy trip south. ■TIP→ **Look for**

Colorful spices are sold in the Marrakesh souks.

Fnac Berbère, the Berber bookshop, on the southern section of Rue Mouassine (the southern section from the fountain to Bab Fteuh square is sometimes known as Rue Fehl Chidmi). It's a good landmark. The street spits you out into the northeast corner of Bab Fteuh square, and from there it's a short hop down to Djemâa el Fna. ⊠ *Medina*.

NEED A BREAK

Dar Cherifa. Wind down at Dar Cherifa, an airy 16th-century riad turned café turned library turned art gallery. It puts on the occasional cultural evening, including poetry readings, traditional music, and storytelling. It also styles itself as a literary café, so you can take a book on Morocco down from the shelves, sit on the low-slung cushions at the foot of the four pillars, and sip mint tea. Alternatively, peruse the art exhibitions and enjoy a light lunch in the elegant alcoves: magical. ⊠ *8, Derb Cherfa Lakbir, Mouassine, Medina* ☎ *0524/42–65–50* ⊕ *www.dar-cherifa.com* ⊗ *Closed Wed. dinner.*

Souk des Babouches. Best approached by taking the main left fork onto Souk el-Attarine where it branches off from Rue Souk el Kebir and then continuing north for about 150 yards, the Souk Principal des Babouches—also called Souk Smata—is on the right-hand side and is filled with the pointed leather slippers so beloved of Moroccans. The small doorway opens up to an enormous emporium with examples in every color imaginable.

It can be hard to judge the proper value of these fairy-tale leather slippers, because price depends on so many things, such as the thickness of the sole, the number of layers, the presence or absence of a stepped heel, and of course the decoration. Use your nose, but be warned that a fair price can vary from 60 DH to 400 DH, depending on quality.

Look for the tiny wool boutique on the left as you come to the arch before the right turn for the babouches market. It's on the way to the Souk des Teinturiers (Dyers' Souk). You can see men rolling out wool to make into fetching striped handbags, and, best of all, into small balls, and looping them up into the most unusual necklaces going. ⊠ *Rue Souk Smata, Medina.*

Souk des Bijoutiers. North of the carpet souk on Rue Souk El-Kebir you'll see an overhead sign for the Souk des Bijoutiers (also labeled Souk Tagmoutyime). Follow that just off to the right into a thin mall, full of jewelry stores displaying their wares behind glass. It is by no means the only place in Marrakesh to buy jewelry, however, especially the bulky kind. ⊠ *Rue Souk Tagnaoutuyime, Medina.*

Fodor's Choice ★ **Souk des Teinturiers.** Using the Mouassine Mosque as a landmark, keep the Mouassine fountain on your right and continue until the street widens out with shops on either side. At the point where it branches into two alleys running either side of a shop selling handmade lamps and textiles, take an immediate sharp left turn. You can follow that derb and look for the helpfully daubed word "teintuties" in spray paint and then head right. Souk des Teinturiers is also called Souk Sebbaghine. The main square for fabric dyeing is hidden down a little shimmy to the right and then immediately left, but anyone can direct you. Here you'll see men dipping fabrics into vats full of hot dye. Don't forget to look up—there are scarves and trains of wool hanging all over, in individual sets of the same bright colors.

For the best view, head into the dyers' square and ask to be led into the boutique. A dyer can show you the powders that the colors come from. A lovely bit of magic involves the fact that green powder dyes fabric red; red powder dyes things blue; and yellow powder dyes things purple. Head up the steep stairs and onto the roof if you are allowed— a spectacular view of industry unfolds, with head scarves and threads of every color hanging up to dry in separate color blocks all over the rooftops. ⊠ *Rue Souk Sebbaghine, Medina.*

Souk el Attarine. Traditionally the market street for perfumes, essential oils, and spices, Souk el Attarine is one of the main left turns from Souk Semarine (as you head north), leaving the road at a "10 o'clock" angle. If this is as deep as you wish to explore in the souks, then you can make an interesting loop by walking as far as the entrance to the Souk des Babouches (on the right) and then soon after take a turn off left, passing through the wool-dyers' souk and heading to the Mouassine mosque. Turning left after the mosque you head back south eventually, down Rue Mouassine to rejoin Bab Fteuh square. ⊠ *Rue Souk el Attarine, Medina.*

Souk Haddadine. From Rue Souk el-Attarine, follow that main souk street as faithfully as possible and it will take you north, looping clockwise to the east, and through the ironmongers' souk, where you'll see blacksmiths at work, hammering out lanterns and wrought-iron chairs. ⊠ *Medina.*

FAMILY   **Souk Lghzal.** North of Djemâa el Fna on Souk Semarine, you pass a fairly prominent derb that turns off to the left (Rue R'mila Bab Ksour, also called Rue el Ksour). Take the next right turn and wander down a few yards (toward the Spice Square or Rahba Qdima) and on the right you will find the small square of Souk Lghzal, the Wool Souk. Today women sell second-hand clothes in the square, and the odd djellaba. A real treat can be found in the apothecary stalls leading up to the entrance to the square, and immediately to the right on entering it. There are spices and potions galore, as well as animal skins (zebra, snake, leopard), used by women for magic: mostly in their desire for marriage and pregnancy. ⊠ *La Criée Berbère, Medina.*

FAMILY   **Souk Rahba Qdima.** Just a quick turn right and then left out of the Souk
Fodor'sChoice   Lghzal (via Rue Souk Semarine) is the large square called Souk Rahba
★   Qdima. Pushier and more mass-market than the spice street, this is the souk's main spice center. There are also lots of woven baskets and hats for sale here. If you are feeling peckish or just tired, pause for a pleasant pit stop at the. ⊠ *Souk Rahba Qdima, Medina.*

Souk Semarine. From Djemâa el Fna take the street just to the left of Café Argana, which leads into the small Bab Fteuh square, and then keep bearing right. To the left there is a *kissaria* (covered market), with dried fruits, herbs and spices, essential oils, and traditional colored eye kohls. Veer right into the covered market, past a couple of stands selling teapots and mint tea glasses, and take a left onto Rue Souk Semarine. It's signposted and lined with fabrics and inexpensive souvenirs. ⊠ *Rue Souk Semarine, Medina.*

▮ **NEED A BREAK**   ✕ **Souk Kafé.** After a hectic few hours in the souks, this café is a welcome respite for the frazzled traveler. Just beyond the Souk Cherifa and Souk Semmarine, you can relax in the stylish lounge of this converted old family house and admire your purchases. Colorful textiles, leather pouffes, African artifacts, and old photos adorn the walls; from the small terrace you can gaze over the surrounding rooftops. **Known for:** friendly service; views from the terrace; open late. ⊠ *11, Derb Souk Jdid, Sidi Abdelaziz, Medina* ☎ *0524/39-08-31.*

SPECIALTY STORES
ANTIQUES

Fodor'sChoice   **Khalid Art Gallery.** Popular with the international jet set, the reputa-
★   ble Khalid Art Gallery is a gorgeous riad full to the brim of the most sought-after Moroccan antiques, Jewish-Moroccan treasures, and Berber pieces. Owner Khalid speaks excellent English and is an authority on most of the art coming out of Marrakesh. ⊠ *14, rue Dar el Basha, Mouassine, Medina* ☎ *0524/44-24-10* ⊙ *Closed Aug.*

Fodor'sChoice   **Le Trésor des Nomades / Mustapha Blaoui.** The highly respected Le Trésor
★   des Nomades—often referred to just by the name of its owner, Mustapha Blaoui—extends over several floors and two adjacent properties. Here you'll find antique doors, lanterns, vintage tribal carpets, mats from Mauritania, Berber jewelry, and all kinds of crafted furniture, homewares, and textiles. It's so well known that there is no sign over the door. ▮**TIP→** Shipping can be arranged for large purchases. ⊠ *142, rue Bab Doukkala, Medina* ☎ *0524/38-52-40.*

Twizra. Prices are high at this general antiques and jewelry store in the Kasbah—so haggle hard! They can (reliably) organize international shipping and also accept credit cards. ⊠ *361, Bab Agnaou, Medina* ☎ *0524/37–65–65.*

ART

Galerie Dawiya. At this small gallery, owners Dominique and Mohammed aim to create awareness of lesser-known Moroccan painters. There's a variety of styles, sizes, and prices from small watercolors to larger oil-paintings and sculptural pieces. Credit cards are accepted. ⊠ *129, rue Dar el Bacha, Medina* ✛ *Next to Bureau de Change* ☎ *0524/39–05–52.*

Ministero del Gusto. For something a bit more cutting edge, Ministero del Gusto combines boutique and gallery and shows off gorgeous items in both. Vintage clothing is also for sale. ■ **TIP→ The shop is only open weekday morning unless you make an appointment.** ⊠ *22, Derb Azzouz el Mouassine, off Rue Sidi El-Yamami, Medina* ☎ *0524/42–64–55* ⊕ *www. ministerodelgusto.com* ⊗ *Closed weekday afternoons and weekends.*

Fodor'sChoice
★

Riad Yima. This riad turned art gallery and tearoom is filled with original artwork by owner Hassan Hajjaj who's known as Morocco's Andy Warhol. True to the artist's pop aesthetic, expect to find colorful portraits blending pop culture and the artist's own fashions. Smaller items include upcycled lanterns made from sardine tins, notebooks, and posters. ⊠ *52, Derb Aarjane, Rahba Lkdima, Medina* ☎ *0524/39–19–87* ⊕ *www.riadyima.com.*

BOOKS

Fnac Berbère. This shop is renowned for its range of books on Berber life and culture. The little *café littéraire* up the stairs immediately to the left of the bookstore also has a small selection of books, though not the same owner. ⊠ *Rue Mouassine, Medina.*

Librairie Dar el Bacha. Here you'll find a good selection of guidebooks, maps, cookbooks, art books, novels, and postcards. ⊠ *2, rue Dar el Bacha, Medina* ☎ *0524/39–19–73.*

Librarie el Ghazali Ahmed Ben Omar. This shop just off Place Djemâa el Fna has a range of guidebooks, cookbooks, novels by Moroccan authors, and maps. Most publications are in French. ⊠ *51, rue Bab Aganou (also known as Av. Prince Moulay Rachid), off Pl. Djemâa el Fna, Medina* ☎ *0524/44–23–43* ⊗ *Closed Sun.*

CARPETS

Bazar de Sud. Run by the Lamdaghri family in Marrakesh since 1940, this shop works with more than 200 artisans and has a huge collection of old and new tribal carpets as well as antique Berber textiles. ■ **TIP→ Worldwide shipping can be arranged and credit cards are accepted.** ⊠ *117 and 14, souk des Tapis, Rahba Lakdima, Medina* ☎ *0524/44–30–04* ⊕ *www.bazardusud.com.*

Palais Saâdiens. This shop has an enormous selection of Berber, Bedouin, and tribal carpets. ⊠ *16, rue Moulay Taib, L'Ksour, Medina* ☎ *0524/44–51–76.*

CLOTHING

Aya's. This shop sells bespoke caftans and tunics made with the highest quality fabrics—cashmeres, linens, silks—all hand-embroidered. Celebrity clients include Julia Roberts, Tom Hanks, and Hugh Jackman.

✉ *Derb Jdid, Bab Mellah, 11 bis, near Le Tanjia restaurant, Medina* ☎ *0524/38–34–28* ⊕ *www.ayasmarrakech.com* ☺ *Closed Sun.*

Max & Jan. The flagship store for this contemporary fashion label has a selection of Moroccan designer accessories, fashion items for men and women, and a pricey collection of designs by the Swiss-Belgian duo Max & Jan. They also have a constantly changing showcase for other up-and-coming local designers. ✉ *14, rue Amsefa, Sidi Abdelaziz, Medina* ✛ *Near to Kui-Zin Café* ☎ *0524/37–55–70* ⊕ *www.maxandjan.ma.*

Warda La Mouche. This boutique stocks handmade clothing for women in great fabrics and colors embellished with Moroccan traditional elements such as embroidery and tassels. The tunics are especially wearable and figure-flattering. Prices are reasonable for the quality of workmanship. Credit cards are accepted. ✉ *127, rue Kennaria, Medina* ☎ *0524/38–90–63.*

CRAFTS

Antiquités du Sahara. Handcrafted jewelry from southern Morocco of Berber, Touareg, and Blue Men traditions is for sale here. Camel-skin decorated dromedary carry-packs and ornamentally carved wooden Touareg tent pegs reminiscent of tribal caravans or bygone times also line the shelves. ✉ *176, Rahba Lakdima, next to carpet market, Medina* ☎ *0524/44–23–73.*

Chabi Chic. Some of the trendiest riads serve guests using the *beldi* (traditional) pottery with modern designs that are the hallmark of Chabi Chic. Product lines from serving ware, tea sets, and coasters to spices, carpets, and beauty products. Their medina outlet is housed within Nomad restaurant and they have a new store in the Sidi Ghanem Industrial zone in the Marrakesh outskirts. ✉ *1, Derb Aarjane, Rahba L'Kdima, Medina* ✛ *Within Nomad restaurant* ☎ *0524/38–15–46* ⊕ *www.chabi-chic.com.*

Ensemble Artisanal. It may be rather touristy, but this is a great way to see all the wares of the souk under one hassle-free umbrella. Several boutiques in modern confines display fixed prices (which are high) for handicrafts including babouches, embroidery, lanterns, bags, jewelry, carpets, and paintings. You can see baskets being woven, carpets on the loom, and other artisans at work. There's even a snack bar. ■TIP→ **Make a note of prices here and then aim to pay around 25% less in the souks.** ✉ *Av. Mohammed V, Medina* ☎ *0524/38–66–74* ☺ *Closed Sun.*

HEALTH AND BEAUTY

Aachab Atlas. This apothecary is stuffed from floor to ceiling with spices, perfumes, argan oil, and traditional medicines for ailments such as rheumatism and back pain. The helpful staff speak fluent English, and credit cards are accepted. ✉ *Rue sidi el Yamani, Bab Laksour, Medina* ☎ *0524/42–67–28.*

GUÉLIZ

SPECIALTY STORES

ANTIQUES

Galerie Le Pacha. This sprawling showroom is filled with inlaid furniture, antique doors, and an impressive carpet collection on the first floor. Credit cards are accepted. ✉ *79, bd. Moulay Rachid, Guéliz* ✛ *Next to Hotel Almas* ☎ *0524/43–04–76.*

L'Orientaliste. This charming mixed bag of a place specializes in exotic perfumes bottled in Marrakesh. Downstairs there are housewares including copper bowls, candlesticks, early 20th-century engravings, Fez pottery, furniture, and all sorts of antiques. There are two locations on the same street. ⊠ *11 and 15, rue de la Liberté, Guéliz* ☎ *0524/43–40–74* ⊘ *Closed Sun.*

La Porte d'Orient. This sibling of the medina's Porte d'Or sells Moroccan and Asian antiques. It's geared toward those who prefer to browse before buying. ■ TIP→ **Shipping can be arranged.** ⊠ *9, bd. Mansour Eddahbi, near Hotel Agdal, Guéliz* ☎ *0524/43–89–67* ⊘ *Closed Sun.*

TinMel. The gallery TinMel has a vast stock of high-quality artwork, Berber jewelry, ceramics, antique carpets, and beautifully crafted furniture from Morocco and Syria. ⊠ *38, rue Ibn Aisha, Guéliz* ☎ *0524/43–22–71* ⊘ *Closed Sun.*

ART GALLERIES

BCK Gallery. Exhibitions of contemporary art and sculpture from new and emerging Moroccan and international artists are on display here, and Marrakshi trendsetters can be spotted at the gallery openings. ⊠ *Résidence Al Hadika El Koubra, Rue Ibnou Aïcha Imm C, Guéliz* ☎ *0524/44–93–31* ⊕ *www.bck.ma* ⊘ *Closed Sun.*

David Bloch Gallery. This small modern gallery showcases up-and-coming contemporary Moroccan artists that lean toward graphic and urban styles. ⊠ *8 bis, rue des Vieux Marrakchi, Guéliz* ☎ *0524/45–75–95* ⊕ *www.davidblochgallery.com* ⊘ *Closed Sun.*

Matisse Gallery. This gallery has an interesting collection of works by young Moroccan artists, Moroccan masters, and the Orientalists. ⊠ *No. 43 Passage Ghandouri, 61, rue de Yougoslavie, Guéliz* ☎ *0524/44–83–26* ⊕ *www.matisseartgallery.com* ⊘ *Closed Sun.*

Fodor's Choice ★ **Tindouf Gallery.** This gallery houses a permanent exhibit of orientalist paintings, ornate inlaid furniture, and antique ceramics. There is a constantly changing program of exhibitions and works for sale by top-notch Moroccan artists and foreign painters living in the kingdom. ⊠ *22, bd. Mohammed VI, Guéliz* ☎ *0524/43–09–08* ⊕ *www.gallerytindouf.com* ⊘ *Closed Sun.*

BOOKS

Librairie Papeterie Ahmed Chatr. Greetings cards, schoolbooks in Arabic and French, and some English-language books—including novels, maps, and coffee-table books on Moroccan culture—are sold here. It also has office stationery supplies and a new outlet just around the corner with a huge range of art materials. ⊠ *19–21, av. Mohammed V, Guéliz* ☎ *0524/44–79–97* ⊘ *Closed Sun.*

CLOTHING

Atika Boutique. This boutique is best known for its shoes, especially its soft leather moccasins in every shade of the rainbow. They rarely accept credit cards. ⊠ *34, rue de la Liberté, Guéliz* ☎ *0524/43–64–09* ⊘ *Closed Sun.*

Hadaya. This designer boutique sells T-shirts, sundresses, sandals, handmade shoes, funky bags, and accessories. ⊠ *31, rue Majorelle (also known as Rue Yves Saint Laurent), opposite Majorelle Garden, Guéliz* ☎ *0524/29–28–84.*

Intensité Nomade. Browse chic and rather expensive Moroccan-inspired clothing for men and women, designed by Frédérique Birkemeyer. ⊠ *139, av. Mohammed V, Guéliz* ☎ *0524/43–13–33* ⊙ *Closed Sun.*

Kaftan Queen. Using locally sourced materials and traditional Moroccan dressmaking techniques, the collection at Kaftan Queen is modern and Bohemian. Model-turned-fashion designer Sarah Buchan creates most of the styles on-site. ⊠ *61, rue Yugoslavie, Passage Ghandouri, Guéliz* ✛ *Opposite Cinema Coliée* ☎ *0524/42–07–97* ⊕ *www.kaftanqueen. store* ⊙ *Closed Sun.*

Michele Baconnier. This French designer boutique sells colorful high-end clothing, jewelry, babouches, and bags that offer a hip twist on contemporary design. ⊠ *12, rue des Vieux Marrakchis, Guéliz* ☎ *0524/44–91–78* ⊕ *www.michele-baconnier.net* ⊙ *Closed Sun.*

Place Vendome. Come here to find gorgeous leather goods of much better quality than what is offered in the souks. ⊠ *141, av. Mohammed V, corner of Rue de la Liberté, Guéliz* ☎ *0524/43–52–63* ⊙ *Closed Sun.*

Simostyle. Tucked in an alley leading to Al Fassia restaurant, designer Mohamed Bensaida's little boutique features unique designs that use local fabrics and upcycled items such as tablecloths, blue jeans, curtains, and upholstery materials. Fashion items are affordable, unique, and fun to wear. There are shirts and tunics for men as well as women's fashion, shoes, and casual bags. ⊠ *Residence Tayeb, 55, bd. Zerktouni, Guéliz* ✛ *Next to Al Fassia restaurant* ☎ *0671/43–80–57* ⊙ *Closed Sun.*

CRAFTS

Fodor's Choice
★
Ben Rahal Art. No longer in the Medina's Souk des Tapis, but rather in a shop in Guéliz, Ben Rahal Art has a magnificent array of Berber tribal rugs and antique carpets. Owner Mohamed Taieb Sarmi can also show you more examples from his stockroom upstairs or from his house in Bab Doukkala, where he will painstakingly explain their origins and value. Sarmi sends rugs and carpets anywhere in the world; for packages to the United States, the import tax is paid in Morocco. English is spoken. ⊠ *28, rue de la Liberté, Guéliz* ☎ *0524/43–32–73* ⊕ *www. benrahalart.com* ⊙ *Closed Sun.*

Moor. The Guéliz sister shop to Akbar Delights in the medina, Moor sells a high-quality range of locally crafted items for the home as well as fashion items and accessories. You'll find handmade embroidered tunics and jackets, throws, cushions, and painted lanterns. ⊠ *7, rue des Vieux Marrakchis, Guéliz* ✛ *Near Carré Eden Shopping Mall* ☎ *0671/66–13–07* ⊕ *www.akbardelightscollections.com* ⊙ *Closed Sun.*

Fodor's Choice
★
33 Rue Majorelle. Slap-bang opposite the gates to the Majorelle Garden, this bright and funky concept store stocks a range of fashions and quirky crafts, jewelry, and souvenirs from hip young Moroccan and European designers all working in and inspired by Marrakesh. ⊠ *33, rue Majorelle (also known as Rue Yves Saint Laurent), Guéliz* ☎ *0524/31–41–95* ⊕ *www.33ruemajorelle.com.*

JEWELRY

Brins d'Orient. Crafter on-site, this contemporary silver jewelry incorporates traditional Moroccan motifs and semiprecious stones, as well as an unusual modern slant on classic pendants, rings, and necklaces. ✉ *10, rue Majorelle, Guéliz* ☎ *0679/92–98–37 mobile.*

HAMMAMS

The *hammam* (bath) ritual is part of Moroccan culture. The following public hammams are of an acceptable standard for tourists, but the private hammams and spas are a treat open to all (even nonguests, if in a hotel).

PUBLIC HAMMAMS

Hammam el Basha. As far as public hammams go, this is one of the largest and most accessible (it's 10 minutes north of Djemâa el Fna). Even in its current rundown condition you get a good sense of how impressive this hammam must have been in its heyday. Instead of the typical series of small low rooms, here you bathe in large, white-tiled chambers that give a pleasant sense of space. After your bath, dry and dress in a huge domed hall skirted with inset stone benches. There are segregated hours for men (morning) and women (afternoon). ■**TIP**➔ Cash only. ✉ *20, rue Fatima Zohra, Medina* 🖼 *20 DH.*

Semlalia Hammam. The oldest public hammam in Guéliz opened in 1965 and is still thriving. For the uninitiated, you can ask for somebody to help you through the process and they'll scrub you down with black soap made from olives. For the basic use of the hammam you'll pay 20 DH; for the use of the hammam, black soap, exfoliation, and a *kaçal* (male or female attendant) to scrub you down, the cost is 100 DH. ✉ *48, bd. Mohammed El Khattabi Abdelkrim, Rte. de Casablanca, Guéliz* 🖼 *12 DH.*

PRIVATE HAMMAMS

Les Bains de l'Alhambra. This candlelit marble hammam has sunken baths filled with floating oranges and bath oils and a colonnaded patio for relaxing. Hammam with scrub starts at 150 DH. Massages and other beauty treatments are on the menu, too. ✉ *9, Derb Rahala, Kasbah, Medina* ☎ *0524/38–63–46* ⊕ *www.lesbainsdelalhambra-marrakech.com.*

Les Bains de Marrakech. A temple to exotic beauty treatments and therapies, Les Bains de Marrakech will bathe you in milk with orange water and rose petals, massage you with argan oil, and rub you down with mint-steamed towels. Basic hammam and scrub start at 200 DH. Reservations are required. ✉ *2, Derb Sedra, Bab Agnaou, Kasbah* ☎ *0524/38–14–28* ⊕ *www.lesbainsdemarrakech.com* 🖼 *170 DH.*

Hammam de la Rose. As you step into the cool blue relaxation room with subtle lighting and chic decor, you might mistake this city-center hammam for a nightclub; but the gentle music, perfume, and whispering staff are pure spa. The two hammams are steaming hot all day, and a traditional, or *beldi,* hammam with exfoliation and spice-infused cleanse costs 250 DH. Massages and other treatments are available,

Guide to Hammams

To escape the bustling souks and crowded cities—or simply to recover from hours of trekking and touring—a hammam is the perfect retreat to soothe both body and soul in a uniquely Moroccan way. Essential to Moroccan life, hammams are hydro-therapeutic rooms best described as something between a Turkish bath and a Finnish sauna. Like the tagines used to cook the national dish, hammams provide a mixture of baking and steaming. Water pipes run beneath marble-tiled floors, which are heated by wood fires below ground. For public hammams, at least, these fires are the same ones used for the neighborhood's bread-baking ovens, which is why you'll usually find them in the medina of any Moroccan town. Water arrives through taps and creates a constant, light steam before being removed by drains at the center of the room.

Walking into a public hammam for the first time can be daunting or disenchanting if you're imagining a luxurious bathing chamber. It isn't a full-service spa—like those now offered in many upscale riads and hotels—but rather a basic, unadorned public bath, with no signs for the uninitiated. Most public hammams are a popular weekend stop for a family scrub-down since many private homes are without bathrooms. It's perfectly safe, but perhaps not the most hygienic environment. If you know what to expect, there is nothing like it to make you feel you are truly in Morocco.

ORIGINS
Islamic public baths were originally cold, and only men were permitted to use them. When the prophet Mohammed came to believe that hot water could promote fertility, the heated hammam (meaning "spreader of warmth") was inaugurated, and its use was extended to women. It soon became central to Muslim life, with several in each city, town, and village annexed to the mosque, to make hygiene available to everyone in accordance with the laws of Islam. The hammam's popularity also increased because the heat was thought to cure many types of diseases. The price of entry was—and still is—kept low so that even the poorest could afford it. Unlike the Roman baths, which were large, open, and designed for socializing, Moroccan hammams are mostly small, enclosed, and dimly lighted to inspire piety and reflection. In time the hammams drew people to socialize, especially women, whose weekly visits became so important to them—the only time they were allowed to leave the confines of their house—that eventually it was viewed as a right.

CHOOSING A HAMMAM
If you're looking for an authentic experience, head to a public hammam. If you're shy, have a higher budget, or seek a more luxurious experience, head to a private one. But realize that all hammams are sex-segregated. When looking for a public hammam, ask at your hotel about public hammams that are welcoming to foreigners. Entry to a public hammam is usually 20 DH; private hammams cost 200 to 500 DH depending on treatment package. Upscale spa treatments can add 600 to 1,000 DH.

WHAT TO BRING
In a public hammam, take basic toiletries: soap, shampoo, comb and/

2

or hairbrush, razor, a towel (women should bring an extra towel to wear as a turban when you leave, as hair dryers are not permitted), and a spare pair of underwear. You may also want to bring a pair of flip-flops, as the hammam's tiled floors are slippery and hot. Buy a small plastic water jug, scrubbing glove called a kessel (or kees, or kis), the dark olive soap called *savon noir*, and mineral-laden clay for conditioning hair and skin called rhassoul from a local grocer or pharmacy.

Don't bring any valuables; you'll leave your belongings in an open cubby (the attendants watch diligently over these, so bring 5 to 10 DH for a tip). If you hire a tayeba, an assistant, who will basically do everything from start to finish for you, tip 20 to 50 DH. Private hammams usually provide individual bags containing everything you need.

ETIQUETTE

The hammam is generally relaxed, with the echo of voices and splashing water resounding from each room. As a tourist, you may be stared at, but a big smile will ease anxiety. A warm "salaam" when you arrive will help break the ice. Once you have stripped down to your underwear and stored your bagged belongings in a cubby, take two buckets from the entry room and enter the hammam. Most hammams consist of three intercon-nected rooms, usually dimly lit from tiny windows in a small, domed roof. The floors are often white marble tiles—both hot and slippery—so tread carefully. The first room is warm, the next hot, and the last is the hottest.

Choose a spot in the hot room first. Then go to the taps and fill your

buckets, one with hot water, the other with cold for mixing. Go back and rinse your sitting area, and sit on a mat (which is usually provided). You can either stay here to let your pores open or go to the hottest room for 15 minutes or so.

Apply the olive soap over your body. Sit for a while before rinsing it off, then begin scrubbing your skin with the kessel mitt. Particularly in women's hammams, one of the other bathers may offer to scrub your back; it's polite to allow her to scrub yours and offer to scrub hers in return. Now rinse off with jugs of water mixed from the hot and cold buckets. You may refill your buckets at any time. Apply the rhassoul over your hair, and comb or brush until it's silky smooth, then repeat.

Finally, lather your body with regular soap, followed by a final all-over rinse, including rinsing your sitting area clean before leaving. Wrapped in your towel, you can relax back in the changing room before dressing and going outside. If you hired a tayeba, pay him or her now, and tip the attendant who looks after the belong-ings. (Moroccan women never leave a hammam with exposed wet hair, and you may want to wrap yours with a towel or scarf as well; this isn't such a big deal for men.)

Private hammams follow the same ritual. Towels are usually supplied or rented. Specialized products are available for purchase. In hotels and upscale spas, you won't need to take anything with you, as attendants, towels, and all products are included in the fee. Tayebas in private hammams should be tipped 40 to 60 DH.

too, and a couple's hammam can be booked as well. ⊠ *130, Dar el Bacha, Medina* 📞 *0524/44–47–69* ⊕ *www.hammamdelarose.com* 🔳 *From 250 DH.*

Hammam Ziani. Sister to Casablanca's Ziani, this hammam not far from Bahia Palace in the medina is highly recommended. Both men and women are welcome. It's traditional without being in the slightest bit down-at-the-heels. The full hammam and *gommage* (exfoliation) works cost 120 DH, while packages priced between 300 DH and 350 DH include hammam, scrubbing, massage, and a seaweed wrap. English is spoken. ⊠ *14, Riad Zitoune Jdid, near Bahia Palace, Medina* 📞 *0662/71–55–71* ⊕ *www.hammamziani.ma* 🔳 *100 DH.*

HOTEL HAMMAMS

La Maison Arabe. A morning or afternoon spent in this sumptuous hotel's hammam will make you feel like royalty. The staff may not scrub you quite as hard as you like, but the hammam room is beautiful, and the small pool filled with roses is just for you. It's popular, so reservations are essential. ⊠ *La Maison Arabe, 1, Derb Assehbe, Bab Doukkala, Medina* 📞 *0524/38–70–10* ⊕ *www.lamaisonarabe.com* 🔳 *650 DH for hammam and 30-min massage.*

La Mamounia. A day pass to the Mamounia's hammam or spa and swimming pool is an extravagance fit for special celebrations and allows you to spend some downtime at this famously exclusive establishment. The hammam and spa is open by reservation only, required for both hotel guests and nonguests. ⊠ *Av. Bab el Djedid, Medina* 📞 *0524/44–44–09* ⊕ *www.mamounia.com* 🔳 *500 DH day pass, 1,000 DH hammam.*

FAMILY **Spa Diane Barrière.** Underground at the Naoura Barrière hotel, this state-of-the-art spa offers not just hammams, scrubs, and scented beauty treatments, but a heated hydrotherapy pool with water jets, aqua-bikes, bubble seats, and a walk-against-the current area. It's fully accessible to disabled clients and open to nonguests. A basic hammam with body scrub starts at 400 DH for 30 minutes and includes access to the hydro pool. Treatments for children are also available. ⊠ *Le Naoura Marrakech Hotel, Rue Djbel Alakhdar, Bab Doukkala, Medina* 📞 *0524/45–90–00* ⊕ *www.hotelsbarriere.com* 🔳 *400 DH.*

La Sultana Marrakech. In the Kasbah district, close to the Royal Palace, the hammam at hotel La Sultana Marrakech offers bath therapy, affusion showers (showers with lukewarm water combined with hand massage), hammam, Jacuzzi, and sauna. ⊠ *403, rue de la Kasbah, Kasbah* 📞 *0524/37–54–64* ⊕ *www.lasultanamarrakech.com* 🔳 *400 DH for Royal hammam, 1,100 DH with 50-min. massage.*

SPORTS AND THE OUTDOORS

With more than 300 days of sunshine a year, Marrakesh residents pretty much live outdoors. Beat the heat poolside at one of many upscale country retreats just outside of the city such as **Beldi Country Club** or find a shady spot in one of the city's gardens. Whatever you do, don't forget the sunscreen for outdoor activities. But also realize that in winter the weather can be unpredictable and sometimes rainy, which makes it the perfect time to plan a trip to a hammam or take a cooking class.

CAMEL TREKKING

Dunes & Desert Exploration. This reliable outfitter organizes all kinds of adventure activities including 90-minute camel rides in the Palmery. If you don't have time to get to the Sahara to experience the real desert, then a quick jaunt in the Marrakesh oasis is the next best thing. Prices start at 275 DH per person including return transfer from your hotel. ⊠ *Marrakesh* ☎ *0524/35–41–47* ⊕ *www.dunesdeserts.com.*

CYCLING

Marrakech City Bike Tours. Take a two- or four-hour guided bike tour through the city's old quarters, via the ramparts or out to the Palmery. Prices start at 450 DH per person (based on two people minimum). ⊠ *44, rue Tarik Ibn Ziad, Medina* ✛ *Next to Café du Livre* ☎ *0661/24–01–45* ⊕ *www.marrakech-city-bike-tour.com.*

GOLF

Marrakesh's popularity as a golfing destination is booming and there are now more than 20 golf courses in and around town, with even more luxury resorts under construction.

Golf Amelkis Club. The 27-hole Golf Amelkis Club, designed by Cabell B. Robison, offers plenty of challenges with water features and bunkers. Unwind afterward with a drink at the bar in the kasbah-style clubhouse with the Atlas Mountains as a backdrop. ⊠ *Km 12, Rte. de Ouarzazate, Palmery* ☎ *0524/40–44–14* ⊕ *www.golfamelkis.com* 🖼 *600 DH* ⅄ *27 holes (three 9-hole courses), 11600 yards, par 72.*

Royal Golf Club. The long-established Royal Golf Club is one of the oldest in Morocco, founded in 1933. It is a tree-filled haven, with the original 18-hole course and another more challenging 9-hole Menara course added in 2007. The casual Club House restaurant is open to nongolfers and has a delightful shaded terrace for a light and inexpensive lunch. ⊠ *Km 7, Rte. de Ouarzazate, Palmery* ✛ *7 km (4½ miles) south of Marrakesh on old Ouarzazate road* ☎ *0524/40–98–28* ⊕ *www.royalgolfmarrakech.com* 🖼 *600 DH* ⅄ *18 holes, 5937 yards, par 72.*

HORSEBACK RIDING

Les Cavaliers de l'Atlas. Half-day and full-day trekking excursions on horseback are offered from this ranch in the Palmery from 500 DH for two people, for a half-day. Both novices and experienced riders are catered to. Horseback riding out into the countryside at Lake Lalla Takerkoust and the Agafay Desert can also be arranged, with transportation included. ⊠ *Palmery, Palmery* ✛ *Near Ksar Char-Bagh luxury hotel* ☎ *0672/84–55–79* ⊕ *www.lescavaliersdelatlas.com.*

HOT-AIR BALLOONING

Ciel d'Afrique. For a bird's-eye view of Marrakesh and the outlying plateaux, desert, and High Atlas Mountains, the French company Ciel d'Afrique is the most reliable and experienced. Balloon flights start at around 2,200 DH per person, including transfer to and from your hotel, with breakfast before the launch. ⊠ *Guéliz* ☎ *0524/43–28–43* ⊕ *www.ciel-dafrique.com.*

QUAD BIKING

Quad bikes and sand buggies are available for hire on the outskirts of Marrakesh, with most of the outfitters taking advantage of the sandy tracks of the Palmery for a half-day or so of fun, but some can organize treks that range farther afield, to the Agafay desert or Lalla Takerkoust.

Dunes & Desert Exploration. For those who like the more-adrenaline-pumping entertainment of quad bikes, this outfitter is a one-stop shop that can also arrange camel rides in the Palmery, hot-air-balloon rides, mountain biking, or even stand-up paddle boarding on Lake Takerkoust. Multiday rafting in the Atlas Mountains depends on the season. ⊠ *Marrakesh* ☎ *0524/35–41–47* ⊕ *www.dunesdeserts.com.*

FAMILY **Kech Motor Bike.** Outside the city, this outfitter organizes quad-biking excursions from one hour to four days in the Agafay desert region or around Lalla Takerkoust, 30 minutes from Marrakesh. Prices start from 400 DH per hour and include transport to the site from your hotel. Children from five years old can participate in a learning session on miniquads. Cash only. ⊠ *Km 25, Rte. d'Amizmiz* ✛ *Oumnass* ☎ *0679/20–46–62* ⊕ *www.quads-marrakech.com.*

ROCK CLIMBING

Climb Morocco. For beginners and experienced climbers, this professional outfit have AMGA trained instructors that small groups for day-climbs in the crags and crevices of the High Atlas Mountains, which are a two- to three-hour drive from Marrakesh. ■TIP➜ **Advance booking through the website is required.** ⊠ *Guéliz* ⊕ *www.climbmorocco.com.*

SWIMMING

If your riad or hotel lacks a pool, you may find that a nearby hotel will let you use their facilities for a small fee.

Beldi Country Club. For a tranquil and elegant afternoon by the pool and away from the throngs in town, consider the vast, manicured gardens of Beldi Country Club, 6 km (4 miles) outside the city. A day pass, including lunch on the shaded terrace, use of sunbeds, and use of the pool is 370 DH; use of the pool alone is 200 DH. Charter a taxi to take you there. ⊠ *Km 6, Rte. de Barrage* ☎ *0524/38–39–50* ⊕ *www. beldicountryclub.com* ☉ *Closed Jan.–Mar.*

TANGIER AND THE MEDITERRANEAN

WELCOME TO TANGIER AND THE MEDITERRANEAN

TOP REASONS TO GO

★ **Tangier:** As the capital of the Tangier-Tetouan-Al Hoceima region in Morocco's industrial heartland, Tangier has been at the center of Moroccan culture since the 5th century BC. Today, it continues to draw visitors with its breathtaking views and friendly locals.

★ **The Rif Mountains:** Running parallel to the Mediterranean coast for 200 km (125 miles), the Rif Mountains span from Cap Spartel and the Strait of Gibraltar to northern Morocco's most scenic areas.

★ **Tamuda Bay:** With miles of golden beaches lapped by the Mediterranean, the area known as the Moroccan Riviera features upscale resorts, fine dining, water sports, and a world-class golf course.

★ **Chefchaouen:** This charming blue-and-white mountain stronghold is one of Morocco's fairy-tale towns offering some of the most beautiful views in the country.

Tangier's long and varied history, as well as its location directly across from mainland Europe, has produced a unique and diverse culture filled with traces of the past. Founded by the Carthaginians in the 5th century BC and colonized by the Romans, Arabs, Portuguese, Spanish, and French over the following centuries, the city has combined the architecture, cultures, and culinary traditions from each civilization that has sought to capture it. The fertile lands throughout the Rif Valley and deep-sea fishing around Tangier have produced successful commercial industry, contributing to the wealth of the local economy.

1 Tangier. The sights, sounds, and aromas of Morocco are never better highlighted than in this tumultuous collision of Rifi Berber, Arabic, and European cultures. Tangier conveniently and uniquely offers within its small borders lively souks, laid-back cafés and bars, access to both the Atlantic and the Mediterranean, and plenty of flora and fauna for nature lovers to explore.

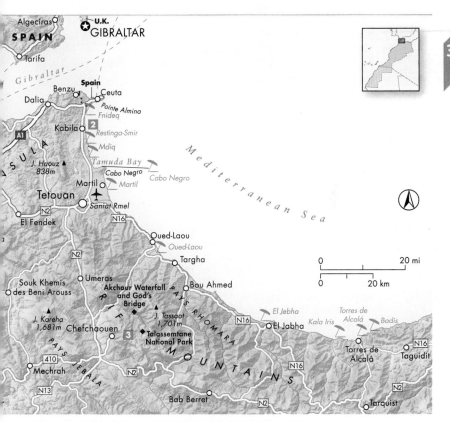

2 **The Atlantic and Mediterranean Coasts.** Morocco's northwest tip is home to glorious beaches, historic seaside towns, and luxurious resorts, both along the country's Atlantic coast and at Tamuda Bay, south of Ceuta on the Mediterranean. The Cap Spartel lighthouse marks the meeting place of the Mediterranean and Atlantic.

3 **Chefchaouen and the Rif.** Chefchaouen only opened to Christians in the 20th century and has since become a favorite of locals and tourists alike. The pure mountain air, the cool, blue-and-white medina, and the slow pace of life encapsulate another era.

Updated by
Sarah Gilbert

Nestled between the Mediterranean Sea and the backbone of the Rif Mountains, Tangier, and the surrounding Tangier-Tetouan-Al Hoceima region hold all the *Arabian Nights* allure that many people associate with the country—as well as an energy unparalleled in the rest of Morocco.

The ancient cities of Tangier and Tetouan offer a glimpse of evolving urban Morocco with their Arab-inspired sophistication, European dress and languages, palm-lined boulevards, and extensive infrastructure for travelers. Here the vast majority of the population is under 25, and the streets are full of children until late in the evening, especially in the summer months. Tangier is in sharp contrast to the villages and small towns along the Rif Mountains routes, where regional dress and a traditional, agricultural way of life persist. As you travel farther east, the language shifts from Arabic to Rifi Berber (Tarifit), spotted with Spanish and French.

PLANNING

WHEN TO GO
The region has a temperate, coastal climate throughout the year, with the traditional high season lasting from late July to the end of August. In Tangier and along the Mediterranean Coast, winter brings rain and surprisingly cold temperatures, whereas the summer months of June through September see hot and sunny days. The Rif Mountains are perfect for skiing in the winter, when thick snow covers the entire range. Spring and summer bring an influx of tourists to the region, during which time the airports and seaports get busier, rooms are hard to find, and the medina, cafés, and beaches overflow with visitors.

PLANNING YOUR TIME
First-time visitors to the region would best use their time by basing themselves in Tangier. The city's bustling medina and abundance of accommodations ensure a good starting point for exploring all that the surrounding area has to offer. Traveling to Tetouan and Chefchaouen is possible by taking CTM buses; however taking a taxi directly from

Tangier is much easier (fares should be decided before departing). It's possible to see the major points of the region in a week, but it's best to spend at least four days in Tangier and two days in any other town or city visited to truly get a sense of this unique corner of Morocco.

GETTING HERE AND AROUND

AIR TRAVEL

Tangier Ibn Battouta Airport is becoming more popular for both full-service and low-cost airlines, offering domestic and international connections. Tetouan's smaller regional Sania Ramel Airport connects to a small number of domestic destinations and European cities in the summer.

BOAT AND FERRY TRAVEL

Ferry travel is a popular way to get to the Tangier region, especially from Europe. The Tanger-Med cargo port is now being used more as a passenger terminal, with connections to and from Algeciras and Barcelona in Spain, Gibraltar, Genoa and Savona in Italy, and Sete in France. Tanger Ville is a passenger port with regular ferries to and from Tarifa in Spain; it's also a stop for several major cruise lines.

BUS TRAVEL

CTM buses offer intercity transportation between Tangier and regional towns and villages.

CAR TRAVEL

Renting a car in Tangier to explore the region is possible and manageable (though automatics are still very scarce and roads tend to get very busy during the summer months), as is hiring local drivers (and their cars) for varying lengths of time through local travel agencies. You can also haggle with taxi drivers who may allow you to hire their services for the day to travel to areas directly surrounding Tangier. The latter may work best for those looking to explore the region immediately surrounding Tangier.

TAXI TRAVEL

Grands taxis (taxis that travel fixed routes indicated by their parking stations and leave only when full, meaning with six people) are a good way to get from point to point. They travel between cities as well as along fixed routes within Tangier. To avoid a squeeze or unpredictable delay, offer to pay for more than one spot. There are also *petits taxis* (these are either yellow or blue with a horizontal yellow stripe) that can be flagged down on the roadside and will transport passengers between Tangier and Tetouan; meters should be used for fair pricing.

TRAIN TRAVEL

Frequent intercity train connections can be found between the Tanger Ville train station and Marrakesh, Rabat, Fez, and Casablanca; prices are very cheap, often even for first-class tickets. The Tangier-Casablanca high-speed rail line (LGV) is currently due to start running in summer 2018, but this may change as the date approaches. Trains also depart from Tangier to the popular seaside resort of Asilah and the Algerian border at Oujda.

GUIDES AND TOURS

In the port area there are still plenty of unlicensed guides wanting to show you around; give them a firm "no thanks/non merci/la shukran." Most licensed guides sport a badge and work for tour companies; you can also find them in any tourist office or book one online in advance.

RESTAURANTS

As much of a mosaic as the region itself, northern Moroccan cuisine combines influences from several other cultures with added spices and native ingredients—and notably features Spanish tapas (sans ham, though there is a cured turkey variety that is mischievously called *jambon de dinde*, or "turkey ham"). Tapas are one way to roll here, as you can eat a filling meal for free with the purchase of a few beers at many of the bars. Tagines are made with particular flair in the north, where olives and spices are local. The abundance of fresh seafood makes it a natural choice in coastal areas. Fresh grilled sardines, shrimp, and calamari are standard fare here, as are larger more-gourmet Mediterranean catches such as *pageot* (red sea bream), swordfish, sole, St. Pierre (John Dory), and *dorado* (mahimahi). A local delicacy that can be purchased on almost every street corner within the medina is the *brouchette,*a kebab filled with swordfish, vegetables, and spices. There is no shortage of restaurants and cafés in Tangier and the major regional towns, but they tend to get quite busy in the summer months, and the most popular restaurants require reservations. *Dining reviews have been shortened. For full information, visit Fodors.com.*

HOTELS

Accommodations in the north range from opulent to downright spare, with everything in between. Other than at the height of the summer tourism season, you'll have a range of options in most areas. Hotels in Tangier can be on a par with those of Europe, especially those at the heart of the medina, but the farther you venture off the beaten path, the farther you might feel from Tangier's five-star welcome. Particularly in some of the smaller cities east of Chefchaouen and Tetouan, hotels lack the amenities to call themselves "top-tier." Look a bit closer, though—what they lack in luxury these hotels often make up in charm, character, and, most of all, location.

Many hotels and B&Bs in the region don't take debit or credit cards, so it's always advisable to pay online in advance or be prepared to pay with cash. During high season, prices tend to rise quite drastically, but booking ahead can secure some superb rooms. *Hotel reviews have been shortened. For full information, visit Fodors.com.*

WHAT IT COSTS IN DIRHAMS			
$	**$$**	**$$$**	**$$$$**
Restaurants	under 100 DH	100 DH–150 DH	151 DH–200 DH	over 200 DH
Hotels	under 500 DH	500 DH–1,000 DH	1,001 DH–1,500 DH	over 1,500 DH

Restaurant prices are the average cost of a main course at dinner, or if dinner is not served, at lunch. Hotel prices are the lowest cost of a standard double room in high season.

TANGIER

15 km (9 miles) across Strait of Gibraltar from Algeciras, Spain; 350 km (220 miles) north of Casablanca; 278 km (172 miles) north of Rabat.

A refreshing alternative to more popular Moroccan tourist hubs like Marrakesh and Agadir, the city of Tangier makes for a great weekend trip from Europe, especially during the spring and autumn months, when the summer crowds have abated. Giddy from the rush provided by crossing the Strait of Gibraltar from the European continent to Africa, first-time visitors may find Tangier such a rude awakening that they fail to see the beauty of the place. Mobs of faux guides and bona fide hustlers greet the arriving ferries, hungry for greenhorns to fleece in any way they can. Once you hit your stride and start going places with confidence, Tangier has a charm that this raucous undercurrent only enhances: crumbling kasbah walls, intimate corners in the serpentine medina, piles of bougainvillea, French balconies, Spanish cafés, and other remnants of times gone by. Newer additions to the cityscape include a glamorous marina, lined with super-yachts; a second, neighboring marina is due to open in 2021, alongside a new state-of-the-art fishing port.

Grab a seat at a sidewalk café and you'll begin to see how dramatically the urban brouhaha is set against the backdrop of the turquoise Mediterranean. Tangier is a melting pot—a place where it's not uncommon to see sophisticated Moroccans sharing sidewalks with rural Rifi Berbers wrapped in traditional striped *mehndis* (brightly striped blankets women wear tied around their waists) and eccentric expatriates, as well as the new generation of fashion-conscious teenagers. This is also Hercules's city, and recently rudimentary graffiti tags in the empty lots have sported this name. Musclemen advertise fitness clubs and burgeoning gymnasts and acrobats, many of whom then join the world's foremost circuses and shows, can be spotted practicing on the beaches and in the parks.

GETTING HERE AND AROUND

AIR TRAVEL

Tangier Ibn Battouta Airport is just 15 km (9 miles) from Tangier's city center and is accessible by taxis located outside of the airport terminal. Several airlines fly to Tangier through European gateways, including Air Arabia (from London Gatwick and Amsterdam), Iberia (from Madrid), Royal Air Maroc (from several European cities); Ryanair (from Brussels, Paris, and others), and Vueling (from Barcelona). Many of the airlines have local offices.

BOAT AND FERRY TRAVEL

Ferry travel is a popular option for tourists and locals alike, with frequent connections from Algeciras and Tarifa. A number of ferry companies operate routes across the Strait of Gibraltar.

The Spanish ferry company FRS operates a regular 60-minute service between Tarifa and Tanger Ville (the city's port; 395 DH per passenger, 1,450 DH per car); a 90-minute service between Algeciras and Tanger-Med (250 DH per passenger, 1,295 DH per car); and a once-weekly 90-minute service between Gibraltar and Tanger-Med (520 DH per passenger, 1,845 DH per car). Trasmediterranea and Balearia also operate services from Algeciras, while Grandi Navi Veloci and Grimaldi Lines offer ferries from Barcelona. Cruise ships regularly dock in Tanger Ville.

While Tanger Ville is the main ferry port at the heart of Tangier, Tanger-Med (which is about two hours away along the cost) is equally viable thanks to its complimentary coach service to Petit Socco (a main square) in Tangier.

Many ferry companies also offer hydrofoil trips, which are the most comfortable modes of transport across the Strait. Be aware that on very windy days, the sea can get choppy and it's not uncommon for ferries to turn around; if this happens, be sure to ask for a refund.

Contacts Balearia. ☎ *0539/93–44–63 in Tanger-Med* ⊕ *www.balearia.com.* **FRS.** ☎ *0539/94–26–12 in Port Tanger Ville* ⊕ *www.frs.es.* **Grandi Navi Veloci.** ☎ *010/209–4591 in Italy* ⊕ *www.gnv.it.* **Grimaldi Lines.** ☎ *0531/11–11–11 in Tanger-Med* ⊕ *www.grimaldi-lines.com.* **Port Tanger-Ville.** ☎ *0539/33–23–32* ⊕ *www.sapt.ma.* **Tanger-Med Port.** ☎ *0539/33–70–00* ⊕ *www.tmsa.ma.* **Trasmediterranea.** ☎ *801/00–35–36* ⊕ *www.trasmediterranea.es.*

BUS TRAVEL

Tangier-Tetouan-Al Hoceima's regional bus operator is CTM. Several buses run daily between Tangier, Tetouan, Chefchaouen, Al Hoceima, Nador, and many other cities within the region. The company even has an overnight 10-hour bus to Marrakesh, as well as a 5½-hour bus to Casablanca.

Contacts CTM. ✉ *Av. Moulay Idriss* ☎ *0539/32–03–83 539, 0522/54–10–10 countrywide* ⊕ *www.ctm.ma.*

CAR TRAVEL

If you want to rent a car to explore this region of Morocco on your own time, there are several major car-rental companies operating in Tangier. Cars can be rented out of the airport, city center, and at ferry ports.

TAXI TRAVEL

In the new part of the city, abundant petits taxis are the safest and most efficient way to get around. Petits taxis have a meter, so make sure to insist that the driver turns it on. You can wave one down by indicating the general direction you wish to travel. If the driver is going your way, he'll stop. For longer distances, or if you are among a group of four or more, you'll need the larger grand taxi, which can be called from most major hotels. A 10-minute petit taxi ride should cost about 9 DH to 11 DH; in a grand taxi (by yourself), the same journey would be about 30 DH. At night the fare increases by half. From the port and airport to the city center or Kasbah, daytime prices should be 20 DH to 30 DH and 100 DH to 150 DH, respectively. Make sure to agree on a price before departing.

TRAIN TRAVEL

Tangier is served by ONCF, the Moroccan rail service, with connections to Casablanca (6 hours—the upcoming LGV rail will cut this to just over 2 hours), Marrakesh (10½ hours), and Fez (8½ hours). Tangier

Ville train station is 3 km (2 miles) outside of the city, a short taxi ride from the medina. First-class accommodations or sleeper cars are recommended for longer journeys, especially overnight ones. Regional trains also link to the seaside town of Asilah.

Train Contacts Office National des Chemins de Fer (*ONCF*). ⊠ *Tanger Ville Railway Station* ☎ *0890/20–30–40* ⊕ *www.oncf.ma.*

SAFETY

Tangier has become a much safer place since it became the favorite city of the current Moroccan king, who recognized its potential to be a great tourist destination and subsequently increased police presence. Using common sense when exploring by day and staying out of dark alleys at night will help keep you out of harm's way. When in doubt about walking through dimly lighted areas, take a taxi. Tangerines are known as late sleepers, so don't be surprised that the streets are usually empty and stores shut until 10 am. Tourists should keep a photocopy of their passports with them at all times in case the police ask to see it.

VISITOR INFORMATION

Tangier's tourist information center is open weekdays and can usually supply information about local events as well as brochures and some rudimentary maps, but if you need or want a good city map, you'll have to buy one.

Contacts Conseil Régional du Tourisme Tanger-Tétouan-Alhoceima. ⊠ *Rabii 3, Appt 15, Rue Jamal Eddine Afghani* ☎ *0539/34–11–33* ⊕ *www.visit-tanger.com.*

EXPLORING

MEDINA

TOP ATTRACTIONS

Cinémathèque de Tanger (*Cinema Rif*). This popular cinema and cultural center, the Cinémathèque de Tanger, is housed in a renovated, whitewashed 1938 theater and offers retrospective screenings and cutting-edge films across two screens. Old Spanish film flyers dazzle from under the glass at the café, where there is a full menu of curious, ciné-inspired cocktails, as well as light bites. The colorful, comfy chairs spill out onto the legendary Grand Socco, perfect for people-watching. ⊠ *Pl. du 9 Avril (aka Grand Socco), Medina* ☎ *0539/93–46–83* ⊕ *www.cinemathequedetanger.com* ☒ *20 DH.*

Fodor's Choice ★ **Kasbah.** Sprawling across the ancient medina's highest point, Tangier's Kasbah can be blinding at midday as the infamous Mediterranean sun bounces off the pristine white walls, but the narrow streets give ample shade and breeze later in the afternoon, and it is a pleasant place to spend some time. Modified since the Roman era, its impressive wall is a relic of the Portuguese in the 16th century. During early Arab rule it was the traditional residence of the sultan and his harem. The Kasbah has always been shared by Moroccans and foreign residents alike—and particularly in the International Zone era. It is currently the site of some of the best hotels in the city. At one end of Place de la Kasbah, step through iconic Bab el Bhar for glorious views of the fishing port and across the Atlantic to Spain (only 20 miles away). There is also Bab el-As'aa (Door of the Rod), a beautiful worn zellij gate that used to be the site of punishments, and Bab Haha, another ancient gate. You can reach the Kasbah by passing through Bab el Fahs ("Checkpoint Gate" in Arabic) into the medina from the Grand Socco and climbing Rue d'Italie, which turns into the steep Rue de la Kasbah, and entering through the Kasbah gate, Bab el Kasbah, at the top. ⊠ *Medina*.

Fodor's Choice ★ **Kasbah Museum of Mediterranean Cultures.** Occupied since the 12th century, the current Kasbah Palace was reconstructed in the 18th century by Ahmed Ben Ali. This former seat of power now houses a beautiful museum with mosaic floors, carpets, jewelry, ceramics, leather, daggers, illuminated manuscripts, textiles, and finely crafted examples of carved and painted cedar ceilings. The marble columns in the courtyard were taken from the ancient Roman city of Volubilis. Don't miss the mosaic *Voyage of Venus* or the life-size Carthaginian tomb. There's also a lovely Moroccan-Andalusian garden to stroll through and a rooftop café with stunning views. Exit the palace via the former treasury of Moulay Ismail, the Bit el Mal; look for the giant knobby wooden boxes that once held gold and precious gems. ⊠ *Pl. de la Kasbah, Rue Ibn Abbou, Medina* ☎ *0539/93–44–81* ⊕ *www.fnm.ma/musee-de-la-kasbah-de-tanger* ⊠ *20 DH* ۞ *Closed Tues.*

Petit Socco. Tennessee Williams based his play *Camino Real* on this square—and it is indeed dramatic, with a cast of characters passing through at any time of the day who are bound to give you a taste of Moroccan daily life. It has a theatrical range of seating, which is split among the three main cafés—parterre (Tingis), orchestra (Centrale), or balcony (Fuentes). The Fuentes used to be the German post office in the International Zone period—supposedly the most reliable one before the Germans fled during WWII. It's a great place to take a break before plunging back into the souks that surround it, or let gravity take you down past the Grand Mosque to the viewing platform looking out onto the port. ⊠ *Medina*.

Fodor's Choice ★ **Tangier American Legation.** As the first American public property outside of the United States, the Tangier American Legation pays testament to the long-standing relationship between Morocco and the United States. Since the building was donated to the U.S. government by Sultan Moulay Suliman in 1821, the museum has amassed a large collection of paintings, books, maps, and portraits. In the adjoining Forbes Museum, not-to-be-missed miniature depictions of famous battles take place daily. Other displays showcase the original correspondence between George Washington and the sultan, honoring the 1777 recognition of the United States by the Moroccan head of state. There's also an amusing letter home from a panicked ambassador who was given an unusual goodwill gift of friendship by the Moroccan people: a now-extinct Barbary lion. ⊠ *8, Zankat d'Amérique, Medina* ☎ *0539/93–53–17* ⊕ *www.legation.org* ⊠ *20 DH; guided tours 50 DH per person* ۞ *Closed Sun.*

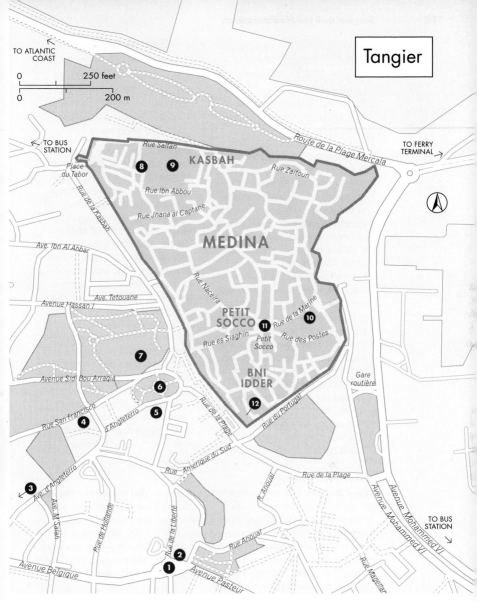

Tangier

TO ATLANTIC
COAST

TO BUS
STATION

TO FERRY
TERMINAL

Route de la Plage Mercala

Rue Saltan

KASBAH

Place
du Tabor

Rue Zaitoun

Rue Ibn Abbou

Rue de la Kasbah

Rue Jnana al Captane

Ave. Ibn Al Abbar

MEDINA

Ave. Tetouane

Avenue Hassan I

Rue Naceira

**PETIT
SOCCO**

Rue de la Marine

Rue es Siaghin

Petit
Socco

Rue des Postes

Avenue Sidi Bou Arraqia

**BNI
IDDER**

Gare
routière

Rue San Francisco

d'Angleterro

Rue de la Plage

Rue du Portugal

Ave. d'Angleterro

Ave. M. Salah

Rue de Hollande

Rue Amérique du Sud

Rue de la Plage

TO BUS
STATION

Avenue Mohammed VI

Rue de la Liberté

Rue Anoual

R. Anoual

Avenue Belgique

Avenue Pasteur

Rue Magellan

TANGIER HISTORY

Tangier's strategic position at the juncture of the Mediterranean Sea and Atlantic Ocean has long been hotly contested. Following ancient Carthaginian, Roman, and then Arab conquerors, Portugal seized Tangier in the 15th century, only to hand it over to Britain in the 17th century as part of Catherine of Braganza's dowry on her marriage to King Charles II (a dowry that also included Bombay). England's control of Tangier was short-lived; in 1685 it fell into the hands of the Arab sultan Moulay Ismail. The French came to Tangier in 1912, but not without disputes from England and continuous scurries for control, so that by 1923 Tangier was declared an international zone administered by France, Spain, Great Britain, and Italy; it even had its own flag. The city's international status, complete with special tax laws and loose governance, attracted a cosmopolitan crowd. In the first half of the 20th century, Tangier was a sumptuous, rather anarchic sensory feast that drew artists, writers, diplomats, heiresses, and free spirits from all over the world. Rumor has it that Allied secret agents from across the world used Tangier as a meeting base during World War II.

After Moroccan independence from French rule in 1956, Tangier was incorporated into the kingdom of Morocco. The international population—and investors—dwindled, and the city's magnificence began to retreat into the realm of myth. Now, with the support of the king, this gritty port city is sweeping away decades of neglect with major civic and cultural renewal, including a new marina, ferry terminal, fishing port, and a high-speed train service to Casablanca. Modern-day Tangier may be more subdued than the sybaritic haven of its past, yet it still has a distinct chiaroscuro appeal. Like Morocco's distinctive *zellij* tiles, the city is an amalgam—in this case of various periods and nationalities—that appears to change shape depending on the angle from which it's viewed.

WORTH NOTING

Grand Mosque. The towering white-and-green-tiled minaret of the largest mosque in the city make it one of the most recognizable attractions in Tangier's medina. Built in 1685 (on the ruins of a destroyed European-built church) under the orders of the Sultan Moulay Ismail, it was a tribute to and celebration of Morocco's return to Arab control. While only Muslims are allowed to enter the mosque, its vibrant exterior make it a great spot for photos as you wander through the medina. ⊠ *Rue Siaghine, Medina.*

VILLE NOUVELLE

TOP ATTRACTIONS

Fodor'sChoice
★ **Grand Socco** (*Place du 9 Avril 1947*). Tangier's chief market area in times past, the Grand Socco (a combination of French and Spanish meaning "great souk")—and otherwise known as Place du 9 Avril (which corresponds to the date of a famous speech made by King Mohammed V on the occasion of independence) now serves as a local transportation hub. Bab el Fahs, the main door to the medina,

Fishing trawlers dot the landscape of Tangier's harbor.

stands at the bottom. As late as the 1940s, when the new city was just beginning, the door was locked at night to seal off outsiders, thus its name, literally meaning "Inspection Gate." You'll find plenty of cafés around Grand Socco, perfect for people-watching. ⊠ *Rue de la Liberté, Ville Nouvelle.*

Mendoubia Gardens. Directly opposite Cinema Rif stands the former residence of the Mendoub—the sultan's representative on the governing commission during the international years—now a flourishing park. Flanked by a row of French colonial–era buildings, it's popular with young couples and local families on weekends. On a peak of the central hill, surrounded by historic cannons, an engraved stone monument displays the speech King Mohammed V gave to the French asking for Moroccan independence in 1947. ⊠ *Av. Sidi Bou Araqia, Ville Nouvelle.*

Place de France. Famous for its café scene in the first half of the 20th century, Place de France is one of Tangier's main squares and is named for the French consulate located in one corner of the square. The square fills up after about 6 pm for a nightly promenade. During World War II, legend has it that the square was a popular haunt for European secret agents and shady deals. More recently it was the star of a thrilling chase scene in the 2007 blockbuster film, *The Bourne Ultimatum.* ⊠ *Ville Nouvelle.*

Fodor's Choice ★ **St. Andrew's Church.** While Morocco is now a Muslim country, this towering Anglican church still stands as a vestige of Tangier's international days. Consecrated in 1905, on land granted by Queen Victoria, you'll get a sense of the flourishing interfaith relations that Tangier was once

Tangier's Grand Socco is a popular destination both day and night.

famous for in the church's interior; the Lord's Prayer is engraved in Arabic behind the altar and quotes from the Koran appear across the Moorish-style walls. A cemetery surrounds the church and holds graves of British and Commonwealth soldiers who died fighting in North Africa during World War II. The caretaker is almost always on-site, and for a small donation to the church (around 20 DH), he will astound you with his knowledge about the church and those buried here. ⊠ *50, rue d'Angleterre, Ville Nouvelle* ☉ *Closed Fri.*

WORTH NOTING

Mohamed Drissi Gallery of Contemporary Art. Located in the stately former British Consulate building built in 1890 and surrounded by a lovely garden, this gallery, run by Morocco's ministry of culture, shows mostly traveling exhibitions. ⊠ *52, rue d'Angleterre, Ville Nouvelle* ☎ *0539/94–99–72.*

Place des Canons. Located in Place de France, the so-called Wall of Lazies is where you'll find three cannons standing on a viewing plat-fom, pointed in the direction of Spain; some say this is meant to stop Spanish invaders, or perhaps the French, the British, or the Portu-guese. Popular with locals, on a clear day it's possible to see the outline of Spain on the horizon; freshly roasted nuts from the many vendors make for a tasty snack as you take in the view. ⊠ *Ville Nouvelle.*

WHERE TO EAT

Tangier's cuisine is a unique mishmash unlike anywhere else in North Africa, where Moroccan, French, Spanish, and even British flavors combine to create a wonderfully diverse culinary scene. Thanks to the proximity of the Mediterranean, very fresh seafood is prominent on menus, while traditional dishes like tagine, couscous, and *bissara,* a bean soup, are available nearly everywhere. The city's top hotels house restaurants that serve unique and sometimes opulent dishes, while you can buy brouchettes or mouthwatering *harira* soup at street vendors for very cheap.

MEDINA

$ MOROCCAN 🍴 **Café a la Anglaise.** The decor of this cute café reflects Tangier's mix of cultures. The chef only makes three main dishes a day depending on market finds—perhaps *briouates*, kebabs, and her unique artichoke tagine—and when she runs out, they close for the day. **Known for:** fresh, seasonal dishes; vegetarian and vegan-friendly options; lovely roof terrace. [$] *Average main: 70DH* ✉ *37, rue de la Kasbah, Medina* ☎ *0635/18–67–66.*

$$$ MOROCCAN 🍴 **El Korsan.** Located within the Minzah Hotel, El Korsan serves traditional Moroccan cuisine in sumptuous style. Specialties include succulent *mechoui* (roasted lamb or mutton) and slow-cooked tagines, often served to a soundtrack of Andalusian music. **Known for:** authentic Moroccan cuisine; opulent setting; belly-dancing performances. [$] *Average main: 160DH* ✉ *Hotel el Minzah, 85, rue de la Liberté, Medina* ☎ *0539/93–58–85* 🌐 *www.leroyal.com/morocco* 🕘 *No lunch.*

$$$ FRENCH Fodor's Choice ★ 🍴 **El Morocco Club.** In 1931, an American architect renovated a Tangerine mansion and turned it into El Morocco Club. Today it's three venues in one: a sophisticated restaurant serving a fusion of Mediterranean and Moroccan cuisine, a seductively lit piano bar, and a pretty café terrace. **Known for:** relaxing café terrace; affordable lunches; seafood couscous. [$] *Average main: 200DH* ✉ *Pl. du Tabor, Medina* ☎ *0539/94–81–39* 🌐 *www.elmoroccoclub.ma* 🕘 *Closed Mon.*

$ MOROCCAN 🍴 **Hammadi.** Decorated in an over-the-top Moroccan style, with banquettes covered with sumptuous pillows and rich brocades, Hammadi (named after the affable owner) is never dull. Try the house pastilla, chicken tagine, or *kefta* (beef patties), along with a steaming cup of freshly brewed mint tea. **Known for:** excellent kefta; live Andalusian music daily; alcohol menu available. [$] *Average main: 60DH* ✉ *2, rue de la Kasbah, Medina* ☎ *0539/93–45–14.*

$$$$ MOROCCAN Fodor's Choice ★ 🍴 **Hotel & Restaurant Nord-Pinus.** Boasting an unforgettably romantic ambience, this restaurant serves traditional Moroccan dishes with a creative twist. The catch-of-the-day features heavily, along with dishes like chicken and olive tagine (cooked on a traditional open fire), and tempting desserts. **Known for:** gorgeous terrace with awesome views of the sea; romantic setting; tagines cooked over an open fire. [$] *Average main: 390DH* ✉ *11, rue Riad Sultan, Medina* ☎ *0539/22–81–40* 🌐 *www.nord-pinus-tanger.com.*

$ MOROCCAN 🍴 **Salon Bleu.** Decked out in dazzling blues and whites, this seaside house behind Place de la Kasbah has been turned into a tea salon and restaurant. Tuck into delicious Moroccan dishes in the intimate salons or on the terrace with views across to Spain. **Known for:** stunning views; three-course, fixed-price menus; uniquely flavored mint tea. [$] *Average main: 60DH* ✉ *71, rue Amrah, Medina.*

VILLE NOUVELLE

$ MOROCCAN 🍴 **DARNA.** Stop for lunch at this community center, whose name means "Our House," and you won't just enjoy a scrumptious home-style meal, you'll also be supporting women in need. The traditional couscous served on Friday shouldn't be missed, especially when served on the sun-drenched patio. **Known for:** homemade Moroccan meals; role as a center for the city's women and children in need; on-site shop that sells products made by the community. [$] *Average main: 60DH* ✉ *Rue Jules Cot, off Pl. du 9 Avril, Ville Nouvelle* ☎ *0539/94–70–65* 🌐 *www.darnamaroc.com.*

$$ FRENCH 🍴 **Eric Kayser.** The sleek café-restaurant of renowned French pastry chef Eric Kayser serves up an array of French goodies such as baguettes, melt-in-your-mouth croissants, *pain au chocolat*, *mille-feuille*, and *choux* buns. Marvel at the elaborate displays, then grab a decadent cake and a coffee, relax, and people-watch. **Known for:** delicious cakes and pastries; contemporary setting; excellent people-watching. [$] *Average main: 100DH* ✉ *Corner of Rue des Amoureux and Rue Casablanca, Ville Nouvelle* ☎ *0539/33–160–83* 🌐 *www.maison-kayser.com/en.*

$$$ MOROCCAN 🍴 **Saveurs de Poisson.** At this iconic restaurant, the menu and the price are fixed, so just sit down and be prepared to enjoy several fish-focused courses designed to be shared by the table. The main course is always the catch of the day—it's usually St. Pierre, dorado, or sole. **Known for:** fresh and tasty catch of the day; no frills but full of atmosphere; fruit juice from a secret recipe. [$] *Average main: 165DH* ✉ *2, Escalier Waller, down from El Minzah Hotel, Ville Nouvelle* ☎ *0539/33–63–26* 💳 *No credit cards* 🕒 *Closed Fri.*

WHERE TO STAY

Whether the style is sparse modernism or over-the-top opulence, Tangier is all about leisure and luxury, sometimes with a vintage or old-world feel. Add Morocco's famous hospitality and Tangier's plethora of gorgeous views (it's almost impossible to find a place to stay that doesn't offer breathtaking views of the sea or over the medina) and you have an unforgettable experience.

MEDINA

$$ HOTEL Fodor'sChoice ★ 🏨 **Dar Nour.** In the heart of the medina and boasting a 360-degree view over the city, the Atlantic, the Strait of Gibraltar, the Bay of Tangier, and even Spain on a clear day, this "House of Light" is partly built right on the Kasbah's western ramparts. **Pros:** personal service; cozy atmosphere; stylish decor. **Cons:** steep stairs; can be a difficult to find; no access for cars. [$] *Rooms from: 650DH* ✉ *20, rue Gourna, Medina* ☎ *0662/11–27–24, 0654/32–76–18* 🌐 *www.darnour.com* 🛏 *10 rooms* 🍽 *Breakfast.*

$$ 🔲**Hotel Continental.** One of Tangier's first hotels, Hotel Continental was
HOTEL   built in 1870 to house a British diplomat, but it has made some changes
since then, adding Moroccan arches and other decorative flourishes,
and while its heyday has long since past, it's still imbued with a cer-
tain nostalgic charm. **Pros:** great views; good location; historic appeal.
Cons: not all rooms are air-conditioned; some renovated rooms are
impersonal; decor is tired. Ⓢ *Rooms from: 650DH* ✉ *36, Dar Baroud,
Medina* ☎ *0539/93–10–24* ⊕ *www.hotel-tanger.com/lhotel-continental-
tanger-034* ⤶ *53 rooms* ⦿ *No meals.*

$$$$ 🔲**Hotel & Restaurant Nord-Pinus.** At the highest point of Tangier's Kas-
HOTEL   bah, the terraces of Hotel & Restaurant Nord-Pinus offer 360-degree
views of the mountains and Straits of Gibraltar afar and the bustling
crowds below. **Pros:** chic decor; in the heart of the medina; spectacular
views. **Cons:** expensive rates; steep stairs to upper floors; might be too
intimate for some. Ⓢ *Rooms from: 2220DH* ✉ *11, rue Riad Sultan,
Kasbah* ☎ *0593/22–81–40* ⊕ *www.nord-pinus-tanger.com* ⤶ *5 rooms*
⦿ *Breakfast.*

$$$ 🔲**La Maison Blanche.** This elegant townhouse has been sensitively trans-
B&B/INN   formed into a tranquil haven amid the mayhem of the medina. **Pros:**
Fodor'sChoice   beautifully decorated riad; extremely helpful staff and owner; delicious
★   breakfasts with a view. **Cons:** steep stairs to upper floors (there is one
ground-floor room); pedestrian-only access but very close to parking;
small property. Ⓢ *Rooms from: 1100DH* ✉ *2, rue Cheikh Ahmed Ben
Ajiba, Kasbah* ☎ *5393/37–51–88* ⊕ *www.lamaisonblanchetanger.com*
⤶ *9 rooms* ⦿ *Breakfast.*

$$ 🔲**La Maison de Tanger.** Every room in this traditional hotel is completely
HOTEL   unique, each individually decorated and with balconies looking out
to the hotel gardens and the sea in the distance. **Pros:** intimate and
relaxed atmosphere; great staff; lovely garden. **Cons:** can be difficult
to find; steep stairs to upper floors; pedestrian-only access. Ⓢ *Rooms
from: 850DH* ✉ *9, rue Al Mabara, Medina* ☎ *0539/93–66–37* ⊕ *www.
lamaisondetanger.com* ⤶ *12 rooms* ⦿ *Breakfast.*

$$ 🔲**La Tangerina.** At the highest point of the Kasbah, this light, bright
B&B/INN   riad is stylishly decorated in Belle Epoque-meets-Moroccan style, with
Fodor'sChoice   vintage finds, large parlor palms, black-and-white checkered floors,
★   atmospheric lanterns, and colorful carpets. **Pros:** stunning views from
terrace; friendly, helpful staff; lovely decor. **Cons:** steep stairs to upper
floors; rooms facing street can be noisy in summer; no restaurant.
Ⓢ *Rooms from: 550DH* ✉ *19, rue Riad Sultan, Medina* ☎ *0539/94–
77–31* ⊕ *www.latangerina.com* ⤶ *10 rooms* ⦿ *Breakfast.*

VILLE NOUVELLE

$$ 🔲**El Minzah.** Built in 1930, one of Tangier's most iconic hotels has
HOTEL   faded somewhat but still offers beautiful gardens, an elegant patio, the
constant sound of falling water from the capacious courtyard, and fine
views over the Strait of Gibraltar. **Pros:** historic hotel; good facilities;
can be reached by vehicle. **Cons:** outside the medina; expensive rates;
standards have fallen. Ⓢ *Rooms from: 1,000DH* ✉ *85, rue de la Liberté,
Ville Nouvelle* ☎ *0539/93–58–85, 0539/33–34–44* ⊕ *www.leroyal.com/
morocco* ⤶ *140 rooms* ⦿ *Breakfast.*

$$$ HOTEL FAMILY Fodor's Choice ★ **Hilton Tanger City Center Hotel & Residences.** Morocco's only five-star Hilton, this hotel just a few blocks from the Mediterranean shows a whole other side to Tangier. **Pros:** excellent service; stylish design; rooftop pool and bar. **Cons:** outside the medina; no spa; rates can be expensive. [$] *Rooms from: 1200DH* ✉ *Pl. du Maghreb Arabe, Ville Nouvelle* ☎ *0539/30–97–00* 🌐 *www3.hilton.com/en/hotels/morocco/hilton-tanger-city-center-hotel-and-residences-TNGCCHI/index.html* 🛏 *180 rooms* 🍴 *Breakfast.*

NIGHTLIFE

Tangier's nightlife begins with the early-evening promenade and café hour, from about 6 to 9, when the streets teem with locals and expats alike. While in the winter the nightlife scene can be lacking, in spring and summer many beachfront cafés are full well into the night. Late dining is another mainstay of Tangerine nightlife, with many restaurants open past 10 pm—rare in Morocco and, along with tapas, another example of Spanish influence in the region.

Tangier has plenty of vibrant cafés, where writers and other creative types go to talk and mingle. Due to its Islamic roots, the nightlife scene tends to be dominated by men, with women typically patronizing the *salons de thé* instead. Major hotels have piano bars where much of the city's business is undertaken as cigar smoke drifts through the air.

There is also an abundance of discos throughout the main areas of Tangier, which are open well into the early hours of the morning; be aware that the common assumption is that women who attend these discos are "working."

MEDINA

CAFÉS

Café Centrale. Ringside seating at the greatest show on Earth can be had from the pavement tables of the Café Centrale, which sits smack bang in the middle of the Petit Socco. It's a good place to catch your breath with a coffee or freshly squeezed orange juice and a croque-monsieur as you watch the strange cast of characters wander past. ✉ *Petit Socco, Medina* ☎ *0539/07–92–83.*

Les Fils du Detroit. Aging Andalusian musicians hold jam sessions here every evening around 6 in the closet-sized but wonderfully atmospheric Les Fils du Detroit (the Sons of the Strait). Sometimes your presence is enough to get the band going. You'll pay just the price of a mint tea, but it's nice to leave a tip for the musicians. ✉ *Pl. du Méchouar, off Pl. de la Kasbah, Medina.*

Gran Café de Paris. With its tufted brown leather seats, wood paneling, mirrors galore, and a wall covered with fading photographs of Volubilis and wood-carvings of astrological creatures, Gran Café de Paris will make you feel like you're back in the 1950s with Burroughs (he wrote here), or in *The Bourne Ultimatum* (it was filmed here, as well as on the rooftops of Tangier). This is a perfect place to watch the *paseo* (evening stroll) on the boulevard or the Wall of the Lazies. Have an orange juice or a Nescafé with milk (café au lait). ✉ *Pl. de France, Medina.*

VILLE NOUVELLE
BARS

Atlas Bar. Although it has a speakeasy exterior and sometimes a burly security guard at the front door, Atlas Bar is cute and mild-mannered on the inside. The place has barely changed since it opened in 1928; at the center is an island bar surrounded by high bar stools. The best part, however, is the generous selections of tapas served with every drink. ✉ *30, rue Prince Heritier, Ville Nouvelle.*

El Tangerino. Facing the beach, this contemporary restaurant-bar-lounge channels a marine theme, complete with a wooden fishing boat and nets hanging from the ceilings. Enjoy delicious tapas at the bar or a huge dish of paella in the dining room—you'll be getting some of the freshest seafood around. There's a well-stocked bar, too. ✉ *186, av. Mohamed VI, Corniche de Tanger, Ville Nouvelle* ☎ *0539/94–39–73.*

Number One. This renovated apartment turned bar-cum-restaurant with pink walls and an impressive collection of memorabilia from the last 20-odd years gives you the feeling that you are behind the scenes of the myth of the city. Karim, the bar's owner, has great taste in blues and jazz and lived in America for ten years. The low-lit outpost occupies the building on the corner across from the Rembrandt hotel, where Boulevard Pasteur ends. Though the tapas can be a bit pricey, an adjoining restaurant is also a decent option for dinner. ✉ *1, bd. Mohammed V, Ville Nouvelle* ☎ *0539/94–16–74.*

Tanger Inn. A vestige of the former International Zone, a late-night libation at the Tanger Inn is the opportunity for literary nostalgia. Knowing that your bar stool may have supported the likes of William Burroughs, Allen Ginsberg, Jack Kerouac, Paul Bowles, Jean Genet, Tennessee Williams, or Federico García Lorca always adds a dash of erudition to your cocktail. Approaching from Boulevard Mohammed V with a friend is advisable, as the area can be sketchy by night. On weekends the place is unmanageably packed with young locals and is anything but smoke-free. ✉ *Hotel El Muniria, 1, rue Magellan, Ville Nouvelle.*

CAFÉS

Café Hafa. West of the Kasbah overlooking the Strait of Gibraltar and set up on seven levels plunging toward the sea, this laid-back cliff café dates back to 1921, and soon became the favorite sunset-watching haunt of locals and bohemian visitors. Waiters impressively deliver 16 steaming cups of sweet tea at a time, along with bowls of *bissara* (traditional pea soup). People will often test if you've been to Tangier by whether you have been here. ✉ *Av. Mohammed Tazi, Ville Nouvelle.*

DANCE CLUBS

Regine Club Tanger. A favorite of weekending Spaniards, local professionals, and hip twentysomethings, the dance floor here gets steamier and steamier as the night goes on. The music is typical, somewhat bland Mediterranean House with some flashbacks to the 1980s, whose pop stars line the walls after your descent down a funhouse-like mirrored entrance and stairway. There's a happy hour every Monday night from 11 pm to 1 am. ✉ *8, rue el Mansour Dahbi, Ville Nouvelle* ☎ *0606/73–20–26* ⊕ *www.regineclubtanger.com.*

SHOPPING

Shopping in Tangier can be just as mystifying and thrilling as it is in Marrakesh. Be ready to haggle for better prices; learning a few numbers in Arabic helps to earn the respect of vendors and makes it more likely you'll get a good deal. Ville Nouvelle boutiques offer standard Moroccan items, such as carpets, brass, leather, ceramics, and clothing at higher—but fixed—prices. The more unusual and creative high-quality items, however, are mostly in the specialty shops throughout the medina. Don't be afraid to stop at small, unnamed stores, as these often stock real off-the-beaten-path treasures.

MEDINA
ANTIQUES
Boutique Majid. One of the finest antiques shops in Morocco, Boutique Majid has a wide collection of antique textiles, silks, rich embroideries, vintage rugs, and Berber jewelry (often silver with coral and amber), as well as wooden boxes, household items, copper, and brass collected from all over Africa on the owner's regular scouting trips. Prices are high, but the quality is indisputable, and it's worth a visit just to hear tales from Majid himself. International shipping is also available. ⊠ *66, rue des Chrétiens, Medina* ☏ *0539/93–88–92* ⊕ *www.boutiquemajid.com.*

CRAFTS
Fodor'sChoice ★ **Las Chicas.** Just outside the Bab el Kasbah, Tangier's first concept store is a delight. Putting a contemporary spin on traditional Moroccan style, the eclectic stock includes clothing, accessories, original art, housewares, and cosmetics. They promote Moroccan design, from Hassan Hajaj lampshades to couture clothing from Noureddine Amir and Fadila El Gadi, as well as Las Chicas' own designs. There's also a lovely café on the roof terrace serving delicious cakes, quiche, and other light bites, and a ground-floor gallery space. ⊠ *Pl. du Tabor, Medina* ☏ *0539/37–45–10.*

Topolina. Topolina is the eponymous store of French designer Isabelle Topolina (she also has two stores in Marrakesh). She creates a unique clothing and accessories collection by upcycling vintage finds and turning vibrantly colored printed fabric from Morocco and sub-Saharan Africa into covetable one-of-a-kind items. ⊠ *Pl. du Tabor, Kasbah.*

Volubilis Boutique. Opposite the Café Centrale, the colorful Volubilis Boutique has been in business for over 45 years. It stocks handmade leather boots, shoes and bags for both men and women, as well as traditional clothes with a Western twist. Ask the friendly owner, artist Mohamed Raiss el Fenni, to show you his delicate watercolor and highly original ice-cream stick paintings. ⊠ *15, Petit Socco, Medina* ☏ *0539/93–13–62.*

PERFUMES
Parfumerie Madini. Founded in 1919, this famous perfume house produces some of the world's longest-lasting and most highly regarded oud fragrances. The parfumerie is owned by Sidi Madini and has been passed down through his family for more than 500 years. Copies of some of the most recognizable scents, like Chanel and Dior, are available here, alongside secret recipe perfumes. ⊠ *14, rue Sebou* ☏ *0539/93–43–88* ⊕ *madini.com.*

VILLE NOUVELLE

ANTIQUES

Galerie Tindouf. Across from the Hotel Minzah is this pricey antiques shop specializing in home furnishings and period pieces from old Tangier, with an especially large inventory of older rugs. The owners also run the Bazaar Tindouf right down the street, where Moroccan ceramics, wood, iron, brass, and silver, plus embroidery and rugs, are piled floor to ceiling. ⊠ *72, rue de la Liberté, Ville Nouvelle* ☎ *0539/93–86–00* ⊕ *www.gallerytindouf.com.*

CRAFTS

Ensemble Artisanal. The fixed-price, government-regulated Ensemble Artisanal offers handicrafts from all over Morocco. The store is a little pricey, but it's a good place to develop an eye for quality items and their market prices before you hit the medina. You can also custom emboss or cover bound books in leather. ⊠ *Rue de Belgique at Rue Ensallah, 3 blocks west of Pl. de la France, Ville Nouvelle* ☎ *0539/93–78–41.*

Fondouk Chejra (*Weaver's Market*). This weaving cooperative is housed on the second floor of an old stable and inn whose name translates to "tree hotel" and overlooks what used to be the large courtyard where visitors parked horses. Weavers and their looms are tightly packed into nooks that are also shops, with walls lined in naturally dyed blankets, throws, curtains, linens, thick wool djellebahs, and synthetic silk scarves all hot off the looms. As the cooperative is unmarked from the outside, ask a local to show you the portal that leads into the complex, which is below the Waller steps. ⊠ *Rue el Oualili, below and to right of Waller steps and Rue de la Liberté, Ville Nouvelle.*

SPORTS AND THE OUTDOORS

Taking a nature walk through the surrounding hills, cliffs, and beaches is a perfect way to see the diverse fauna of the region, especially in the summer months when flowers are in bloom. Jet-skiing along the coast and golfing on the ever-increasing number of courses are also becoming more popular.

BEACHES

The one constant across Tangier and northern Morocco is outstanding beaches. From crowded city beaches to miles of empty space, from fine sand to high cliffs, you'll find whatever combination of leisure, civilization, and scenery you have in mind on these shores.

GOLF

Golf, the favorite sport of the late King Hassan II, has quickly spread throughout Morocco.

Royal Golf de Tanger. The 18-hole Royal Golf de Tanger, founded in 1914, is one of two premier courses in the north and is located 3 km (2 miles) outside of the city center. The course measures 6605 yards and is par 70. The greens fee is 400 DH for 18 holes and 50 DH for practice. ⊠ *Rte. de Boubana* ☎ *0539/93–89–25* ⊕ *www.royalgolftanger.com* 🖂 *400 DH* 🏌 *18 holes, 6605 yards, par 70.*

THE ATLANTIC AND MEDITERRANEAN COASTS

The northwest coast of Morocco offers such splendid views and gentle breezes that it is difficult not to recommend it if you have the time and curiosity to spend a day there. The N16 coast road east from Tangier hugs the edge of the Strait of Gibraltar all the way to the Djebel Musa promontory and Cap Spartel.

CAP SPARTEL

16 km (10 miles) west of Tangier.

Minutes from Tangier is the jutting Cap Spartel, the African continent's extreme northwest corner. Known to Romans as Ampelusium ("cape of the vines"), this fertile area sits high above the rocky coast. A shady, tree-lined road leads up to the summit, where a large lighthouse has wonderful sweeping views out over the Mediterranean at the very point where it meets the Atlantic.

GETTING HERE AND AROUND

Cap Spartel is most easily reached by grand taxi from Tangier.

EXPLORING

Fodor's Choice ★ **Cap Spartel Lighthouse.** Built by Sultan Mohammed III in 1864, this lighthouse was maintained by Britain, France, Spain, and Italy until Morocco's independence from France in 1956. From atop a cliff at the northernmost point of the African continent, the area around the lighthouse offers amazing views of the Strait of Gibraltar. On a clear day, it is possible to look out on the horizon and see the meeting point of the dark blue Atlantic and the turquoise Mediterranean. ■TIP→ **The terrace of the Cap Spartel Café & Restaurant opposite the lighthouse is a good place to take in the stunning sunsets.** ⊠ *Cap Spartel.*

FAMILY **Caves of Hercules.** Five kilometers (3 miles) south of the cape are the so-called Caves of Hercules, a popular tourist attraction tied to the region's relationship with the mythical hero, who was said to rest here after his famous labors. Inhabited since prehistoric times, the caves were used more recently to cut millstones, hence the hundreds of round indentations on their walls and ceiling otherwise attributed to Hercules' clawing fingers. The caves are known for their window-like opening in the shape of the African continent, through which the surf comes crashing into the lagoon and lower cave. Legend has it that the cave leads to a tunnel that crosses through the Strait of Gibraltar, leading you to the other side of the Mediterranean. There are plenty of cafés by the entrance to the caves, where you can sit on the terrace under a parasol and take in the sea views over a cold drink. ⊠ *Cap Spartel.*

Cotta. Approximately 7 km (4½ miles) south of Cap Spartel, look down toward the beach and you'll see the ruins of the 3rd century BC Roman town of Cotta. It was known for its production of garum, an anchovy paste that was exported throughout the Roman Empire. All that remains of the town now are the foundations of buildings, baths, and villas. You can walk to the site from the road or, more

Cap Spartel's lighthouse looks out over the Mediterranean and the Atlantic.

easily, from the expanisve beach that runs south from the lighthouse, known locally as Robinson Plage. ✉ *Cap Spartel.*

Parc de Perdicaris. Halfway to Cap Spartel, Rmilet is a park popular with local families on weekends. It has shady pine, mimosa, and eucalyptus groves, as well as camel-riding and humble kebab huts at the end of the path in a parking lot with incredible views. Here you can also see the restored house of Ion Perdicarus and imagine his kidnapping by the Rifi bandit El Raissouni, with whom he later became friends. It's a great stop-off or day-trip for a few hours with the family. The stylish café across from the main entrance offers yet another stunning and unusual view of Tangier. ✉ *Cap Spartel.*

WHERE TO EAT AND STAY

$ MOROCCAN 🍴 **Chez Abdou.** Open for lunch and dinner, this laid-back restaurant is difficult to find but well worth the search. Abdou himself, a rare and well-loved Tangier personality, serves up some of the freshest fish, simplest salads, and most perfect paella in the area. **Known for:** fresh fish and seafood; beach views; friendly owner. [$] *Average main: 90DH* ✉ *Foret Diplomatique Km 17, Rte. de Larache* ☎ *0658/11–06–66* 💳 *No credit cards.*

$$$$ HOTEL 🏨 **Le Mirage.** Located above the Caves of Hercules, this luxury resort is popular with the Moroccan elite and visiting dignitaries. **Pros:** luxurious retreat; excellent facilities; beautiful setting. **Cons:** 20 minutes from the city; expensive rates; service can be indifferent. [$] *Rooms from: 2400DH* ✉ *Grotte de Hercules, Rte. de Cap Spartel* ☎ *0539/33–33–31* 🌐 *www.lemirage-tanger.com* 🛏 *40 rooms* 🍽 *No meals.*

SPORTS AND THE OUTDOORS

BEACHES

Cap Spartel's beaches vary widely from wide inlets to long stretches of sand. Ashakar is a public beach with three parts: the first is level with the road while the following two, more highly recommended, are accessed by descending steep steps down cliffs and sometimes flowering dunes, and eventually becomes Robinson Beach.

FAMILY **Robinson Plage.** Just west of Tangier, and running south from Cap Spartel lighthouse, the area's most famous beach on the far Atlantic coast offers several uninterrupted miles of fine, silky sand, and good waves ideal for families and surfers alike. Like its counterpart at Tarifa across the Strait of Gibraltar, there is generally a lot of wind around Robinson, making it also ideal for windsurfing. This is the last beach on the Atlantic before its waters merge with those of the Mediterranean at Cap Spartel, so the winds and current can be tricky. Staying close to shore is recommended for safety. **Amenities:** food and drink; water sports. **Best for:** snorkeling; walking; windsurfing. ✉ *Plage Municipale, off Av. Mohamed VI, Tangier.*

ASILAH

40 km (25 miles) southwest of Tangier.

Straddling the cliffs of the north Atlantic coast, Asilah was founded by the Phoenicians around 1500 BC. A prosperous trading town, it was invaded by the Carthaginians, Romans, Normans, and Portuguese, among others; it was officially Spanish territory before being returned to Morocco in 1956.

Today this sleepy fishing village heaves with Moroccan and Spanish tourists during summer. It's also known as one of the country's most artistic communities, hosting an annual arts festival, where artists from all over the world are invited to paint vibrant murals on the picturesque medina's whitewashed walls. There are also several relaxing beaches here, and restaurants that offer some of the area's best fresh fish and seafood dishes.

GETTING HERE AND AROUND

Asilah can be reached from Tangier by either a grand taxi, CTM bus (which leaves from Tangier's central bus station near Petit Socco), or a train from Tanger Ville Railway Station.

WHERE TO EAT

$ SPANISH Fodor's Choice ★ 🍴 **Casa Garcia.** People flock to this relaxed seafood restaurant for no-nonsense fresh fish, langoustines, paella, and seafood tagines. The terrace is a nice place to linger over a bottle of Moroccan wine. **Known for:** Moroccan wine list; fantastic seafood tagines; large weekend crowds. [$] *Average main: 75DH* ✉ *Corner of Av. Prince Heritier and Melilia* ☎ *0539/41–74–65* 💳 *No credit cards.*

$ MOROCCAN 🍴 **Oceano Casa Pépé.** Reliable and friendly, this small restaurant is located outside Bab al-Kasaba, the Old Town's main gate. The anchovy appetizer is not to be missed, and neither is the simply fried fish. **Known for:** fish and seafood tapas; popular with groups. [$] *Average main: 90DH* ✉ *8, pl. Zellaka* ☎ *0539/41–73–95.*

$ 🍴 **La Perle d'Asilah.** The sophisticated menu here is largely French, with
FRENCH FUSION a dash of Asian and Moroccan, and a focus on fish and seafood. Daily
Fodor's Choice ★ chalkboard specials highlight the catch of the day—perhaps John Dory or crab. **Known for:** creative fish and seafood dishes; excellent service; terrace dining. [$] *Average main: 75DH* ✉ *Rue Allal Ben Abd Allah and Av. Melilla* ☎ *0539/41–87–58.*

WHERE TO STAY

$$ 🏨 **Dar Manara.** This Spanish-owned riad has been nicely restored and
B&B/INN converted into an intimate B&B. **Pros:** in the heart of the medina; helpful staff; intimate feel. **Cons:** small property, so need to book ahead; pedestrian-only access; steep stairs to the rooms. [$] *Rooms from: 772DH* ✉ *23, rue M'Jimaa* ☎ *0677/39–82–67* 🌐 *www.asilah-darmanara.com* 🛏 *5 rooms* 🍽 *Breakfast.*

$$ 🏨 **Hotel Al Alba.** With bright, traditional-style rooms, this hotel reflects
HOTEL the medina and sky with its fresh blue-and-white color scheme, stained-
Fodor's Choice ★ glass skylights, and plant-filled patios. **Pros:** friendly multilingual staff; on-site hammam and spa; generous breakfast. **Cons:** outside the medina; small property. [$] *Rooms from: 814DH* ✉ *35, Lot. Nakhil* ☎ *0539/41–69–23* 🌐 *www.asilahalalba.com* 🛏 *10 rooms* 🍽 *Some meals.*

LARACHE

80 km (50 miles) southwest of Tangier.

Known primarily for its proximity to the ruins of the ancient town of Lixus, Larache is worth a stop for a stroll along the Balcon Atlantico, a seaside promenade that runs along the rocky shore. There are numerous cafés on the promenade where you can enjoy a fruit drink. Another enjoyable walk is to French writer Jean Genet's grave in the Catholic Cemetery just south of the medina. It's near the Muslim graveyard, which boasts decorative tile graves and dramatic views.

Larache's sleepy plaza feels like Spain all over again. Many of the people in this town grew up speaking Spanish as their first language and even attending Spanish Catholic schools—a few nuns still live here. Visible from afar, the 16th-century Geubibat Fort sits atop the highest cliff in Larache. The mouth of the snaking Loukos River is the fabled site of the Garden of Hesperides where Hercules picked his golden apples.

GETTING HERE AND AROUND

Larache can be reached from Tangier by either a grand taxi or a CTM bus, which leaves from Tangier's central bus station.

EXPLORING

Fodor's Choice ★ **Lixus BC.** You may have heard of Volubilis, Morocco's most famous Roman ruins in Meknès, but on the Loukkos River, Lixus BC is a lesser-known but still interesting site just 45 minutes away from Tangier. Only a small proportion of the site has been excavated, but the main attractions are an amphitheater, a column-lined road, a mosaic of a sea-god (half man, half crab), and the religious center of the town, high on the hill, which retains the foundations for the places of worship of each civilization to have settled there. The hill held great importance to a series of seafaring civilizations, starting with the Phoenicians in the

7th century until the time of the Arabs. The guides at the entrance are official and informative. They are paid by the government to do their job, but appreciate a tip. ✉ *Asilah* 🎫 *Free (tips appreciated).*

WHERE TO STAY

$ HOTEL 🏨 **La Maison Haute.** Located in the Kasbah, and offering great rooftop views of the city and ocean, this little gem of a hotel is hidden behind an unassuming exterior. **Pros:** friendly staff; great location; lots of character. **Cons:** steep steps; basic amenities and not all rooms are en suite; cash only. [$] *Rooms from: 400DH* ✉ *6, Derb Ben Thami, Asilah* ☎ 🌐 *lamaisonhaute.free.fr/en* 💳 *No credit cards* 🛏 *7 rooms* 🍴 *Breakfast.*

CEUTA

94 km (58 miles) northeast of Tangier.

Set on a rocky peninsula protruding into the Mediterranean, Ceuta—known as Sebta in Morocco—was once one of the finest cities in the north. Originally thriving under its Arab conquerors, the city was extolled in 14th-century documents for its busy harbors, fine educational institutions, ornate mosques, and sprawling villas. Smelling prosperity, the Portuguese seized Ceuta in 1415; the city passed to Spain when Portugal itself became part of Spain in 1580, and it remained under Spanish rule after Moroccan independence.

Since 1995, Ceuta has been an autonomous city and a military base, with an economy boosted by its duty-free status. However, its strategic position on the frontier between Europe and Africa means that it's become a hotspot for the trafficking of drugs and migrants from sub-Saharan Africa. This is demonstrated by the high security around its small border. Issues aside, with its relaxed air, golden beaches, imposing buildings, pretty plazas, and buzzy tapas bars, it makes for a pleasant stopover if you're en route to or from Algeciras in Spain.

GETTING HERE AND AROUND

Ceuta can be reached from Tangier by either a grand taxi or a CTM bus, which leaves from Tangier's central bus station.

Trasmediterranea operates five ferries a day from Algeciras, Spain to Ceuta, a trip that takes approximately 70 minutes (€34).

Upon arrival in Ceuta by road you will be greeted with a lengthy customs and immigration process (sometimes taking up to several hours) while passing through several checkpoints. Note that euros are the standard currency here, with dirhams rarely accepted. Cash machines are available downtown and usually give the best exchange rate. Ceuta also uses Spanish as the official language, and when calling Ceuta from Morocco or from overseas, you must use the Spanish country code (34).

ESSENTIALS

Visitor Information Ceuta Tourist Information. ✉ *Edificio Baluarte de los Mallorquines* ☎ *0856/20–05–60, 0956/50–62–75 Estación Marítima* 🌐 *www.ceuta.es.*

EXPLORING

Castillo del Desnarigado. Located just under Ceuta's lighthouse, and named for a flat-nosed Berber pirate who made the cove his home in 1417 after escaping from an Algerian mining prison, the fort was built here in the 19th century. It now houses a military museum showcasing the evolution of weapons from the 16th to 19th centuries. You can look out across Ceuta's port and, on clear days, take in a stunning view of Gibraltar from the ramparts. ✉ *Carretera Del Hacho* ☎ *956/51–40–66 in Spain* 🎫 *Free* ☼ *Closed Sun.*

Foso de San Felipe. St. Philip's Moat was built in 1530 by Portuguese crusaders to strengthen the town's fortifications. Crossing the moat gives you grand views of the ramparts, including their inner walls and structures. ✉ *Calle del la Independencia.*

Plaza de África. A lovely Andalusian-style space, the plaza is the heart of the old city. Check out the noteworthy war memorial, honoring those who took part in the Spanish invasion of Morocco in 1859. Flanking the main plaza is a pair of impressive churches, both built on the sites of former mosques. To the north is the church of Nuestra Señora de África (Our Lady of Africa), an ornate baroque structure much frequented by Ceutíes (residents of Ceuta) looking for peace and quiet. On the southern end of Plaza de África, look for the city's cathedral. Constructed in an 18th-century baroque style—much like Nuestra Señora de África—it is larger and lushly ornate. ✉ *Ceuta.*

WHERE TO EAT AND STAY

Much like Ceuta itself, the city's cuisine is a hybrid of Spanish and Moroccan influences. With the Mediterranean at its doorstep, Ceuta's culinary expertise lies in seafood. From shrimp sautéed in a spicy pepper sauce to creamy baked whitefish dishes and enormous grilled sardines to Spanish-style cold anchovy, garlic, and olive-oil tapas, Ceutan seafood is an experience not to be missed. Moroccan influences are present in the form of couscous, as well as sweet-salty combinations such as prunes with roast lamb. A favorite pastime here is eating jamón serrano and drinking wine (both difficult to do just a few minutes away in Islamic Morocco).

$ ✕ **Meson La Esquinita Iberica.** For a quick snack, head to this no-nonsense
SPANISH tapas bar near La Plaza Nuestra Señora de Africa. Try the *insalata russo* (a Spanish take on the Russian Salade Olivier), a Spanish tortilla (a mix between an omelet and potato pancake), or some Serrano ham with bread. **Known for:** Spanish tapas; popular with locals. [$] *Average main: €8* ✉ *4, Calle Jaudenes* ☎ *0956/51-61–04 in Spain.*

$$ ✕ **Parador de Ceuta Restaurant.** Generally considered Ceuta's best res-
SPANISH taurant, this charming dining room with exposed beams and tropical plants serves classic Andalusian dishes such as seafood paella, stuffed shrimp, shellfish in sauce, and creative daily specials. Dramatic lighting is provided by Andalusian lanterns hanging from the high ceiling in a romantic constellation. **Known for:** excellent Spanish cuisine; high prices; romantic setting. [$] *Average main: €15* ✉ *Gran Hotel Parador– La Muralla, 15, pl. de África* ☎ *956/51–49–40 in Spain.*

$$ 🏨 **Parador de Ceuta.** This aging grande dame is still one of the best

HOTEL   options in Ceuta. **Pros:** central location; good restaurant; relaxing. **Cons:** dated decor; service is slow; food and drink can be expensive. $ *Rooms from: €120* ✉ *15 Plaza nr. Sra. de África* 🕾 *956/51–49–40 in Spain* ⊕ *www.parador.es* ⇆ *106 rooms* ⦿ *No meals.*

SPORTS AND THE OUTDOORS

BEACHES

El Chorrillo Beach. Ceuta's most frequented beach both day and night, El Chorrillo offers perfect sun rays in the morning and a calm Mediterranean atmosphere after dark. The sand is nothing special, but the water is relatively calm all year-round, and the undertow is unthreatening. It can get very crowded in summer. **Amenities:** parking; toilets; water sports. **Best for:** sunrise; sunset; swimming; windsurfing. ✉ *Just off Av. Martinez Catena.*

SAILING

Estación Náutica. At the Estación Náutica, you can find companies offering all manner of water-based activities, including diving, snorkeling, deep-sea fishing, sailboat rentals, and sea kayaking. ✉ *Puerto de Ceuta* 🕾 *628/ 86–74–97.*

TETOUAN

40 km (24 miles) south of Ceuta, 57 km (35 miles) southeast of Tangier.

Andalusian flavor mingles with the strong Rifi Berber and traditional Arab identities of the majority of the populace to make Tetouan a uniquely Moroccan fusion of sights and sounds. Tetouan's medina, a UNESCO World Heritage Site, remains largely untouched by tourism and retains its quotidian life and authenticity. The name Tetouan itself comes from the Tarifi (Rifi) Berber word for "the springs," to which the city owes its numerous fountains and gardens.

Nestled in a valley between the Mediterranean Sea and the back bone of the Rif Mountains, the city of Tetouan was founded in the 3rd century BC by Berbers, who called it Tamuda. Romans destroyed the city in the 1st century AD and built their own city in its place, the ruins of which you can still see on the town's edge. The Merenids built another city in the 13th century, which flourished for a century and was then destroyed by Spanish forces, which ruled intermittently from the 14th to the 17th century. The medina and kasbah that you see today were built in the 15th and 16th centuries and improved upon thereafter: Moulay Ismail took Tetouan back in the 17th century, and the city traded with the Spanish throughout the 1700s. Tetouan's proximity to Spain, and especially to the enclave of Ceuta, kept its Moroccan population in close contact with the Spanish throughout the 20th century. As the capital of the Spanish protectorate from 1913 to 1956, Tetouan harbored Spanish religious orders that set up schools here and established trading links between Tetouan, Ceuta, and mainland Spain. Their presence infused the city with Spanish architecture and culture. Peek into the vintage cinemas you see along the way, such as the Spanish-built Cinéma Espagnol just off of Place Hassan II, for a hint at the opulence of a bygone era.

Tetouan was the capital of Spanish Morocco in the early 20th century.

GETTING HERE AND AROUND

Tetouan has a small airport, the Sania Ramel Airport, that's just 5 km (3 miles) outside town, with flight connections to Casablanca and Al Hoceima with Royal Air Maroc.

CTM is the region's main bus company and runs several buses daily to Tangier, Chefchaouen, Al Hoceima, and Nador.

Bus Contacts CTM Tetouan. ⊠ *Av. Hassan II* ☎ *0539/96–16–88* ⊕ *www.ctm.ma.*

ESSENTIALS

Visitor Information Tetouan Tourism Office. ⊠ *30, av. Mohammed V* ☎ *0539/96–19–15.*

EXPLORING

TOP ATTRACTIONS

Medina. Tetouan's UNESCO-protected medina is one of Morocco's most compact and interesting spaces, and was particularly important in the 8th century, when it served as a connection point between Morocco and Andalusia. Surrounded by a wall and accessed by seven gates, it includes a rectilinear Jewish quarter, the Mellah, as well as exceptional 19th-century Spanish architecture from the period of the protectorate. Note the constantly flowing fountains, such as the one in the corner of Souk el Fouki; they are supplied by underground springs that have never stopped working and whose origins have never been explained. Crafts, second-hand clothing, food, and housewares markets are scattered through the medina in charming little squares such as Souk el Houts el Kadim (the old fish market) and L'Wusaa.

Kharrazin is where animal hides are hung to dry in the sun, and through a door to the north you'll find *debbagh*, or the traditional leather treatment baths. Tetouan's medina is relatively straightforward, so don't hesitate to deviate from the main path and explore; it's hard to get lost. ⊠ *Rue Terrafin at Bab er-Rouah.*

Place Hassan II (*Place Feddane*). If you follow the pedestrian Boulevard Mohammed V past Spanish houses with wrought-iron balconies and tilework, you will eventually flow into Place Hassan II, the open square near the Royal Palace, unusually located in the very center city and a central gathering place in the evening. On the east side look up to see Dar Tair (the "House of the Bird"), an old Spanish apartment building crowned with a majestic bronze statue of a man sitting atop an eagle. The square is also the entrance point to Bab er-Rouah, the historical covered market on the north side, the Mellah and M'sala on the east and south, and Rue Zawiya, where you'll find a few nice dining options. ⊠ *East end, Av. Mohammed V.*

Place Moulay El Mehdi. A leisurely stroll through Tetouan begins most naturally in Place Moulay El Mehdi, a large plaza ringed with cafés, a post office, and the Spanish Eglise Nuestra Señora de Las Victorias, aglow with strings of lights in the evening. It is often the site of outdoor concerts and evening snack vendors and strollers. ⊠ *Bd. al-Moukaouama, near Bd. Mohammed V.*

Fodor'sChoice **School of Arts and Crafts** (*Escuela y Artes y Oficios / Dar San'aa*).
★ Located across from Bab el Okla, this living museum founded by the monarchy has been considered the premier school in Morocco for the creation and preservation of traditional Andalusian, Berber, and Arab-influenced crafts and interior design since 1919. The school has resided in its current, architecturally significant Moorish-Andalusian home since 1928. The architectural splendor includes a colonnade inscribed with Kufic inscriptions, stained-glass details, and a green-tiled exterior in the style of Fez. You can also buy directly from the artisans here. ⊠ *Tetouan* ✛ *Opposite Bab el Okla* ☎ *0539/97–27–21* ⌑ *10 DH* ⊗ *Closed weekends.*

Tetouan Museum of Modern Art (*Centro de Arte Moderno de Tetouan*). The north's most prominent showcase of Moroccan art, this gallery, located in a beautiful, castle-like former train station, is a mecca in the region for art lovers. The dazzlingly white minimalist interiors boast paintings by Moroccan contemporary artists, including Mohammed Drissi, Mohammed Hamri (of the Jajouka musicians and Rolling Stones fame), and Hassan Echair, as well as sculpture, photography, and temporary exhibitions. ⊠ *Av. Al Massira* ☎ *0539/71–89–46* ⌑ *20 DH* ⊗ *Closed Sun. and Mon.*

WORTH NOTING
Archaeological Museum. Off Place Al Jala, this three-room museum holds a large collection of Roman mosaics and statuettes, coins, bronzes, and pottery found at various sites in northern Morocco such as Lixus and Cotta, as well as pictures of the archaeological site of Tamuda (which resembles Stonehenge), where Anteus is fabled to have been buried after his battle with Hercules. The garden paths are rimmed with Jewish

tombstones marked with pre-Columbian motifs brought back from South America and elaborate calligraphic Muslim tombstones. ⊠ *2, av. Ben Hassan* ☎ *0539/93–20–97* ⬛ *10 DH* ⊙ *Closed Sun.*

Ethnographic Museum. Created in 1928, the Ethnographic Museum was moved to its current home in 1948; the building is the former fortress of the sultan Moulay Abderrahman, built around 1830 and surrounded by an Andalusian garden. The museum has a wonderful collection of traditional Moroccan costumes, jewelry, embroidery, weapons, musical instruments, and other handcrafted objects. The most elaborate displays are of the accoutrements of Tetouani wedding ceremonies, which are among the most elaborate of Moroccan wedding attires. ⊠ *Av. Skala Bab El Oukla* ☎ *0539/97–05–05* ⬛ *10 DH* ⊙ *Closed Tues.*

WHERE TO EAT

In recent years the town has seen an expanding number of good restaurants; though a fair percentage of them are foreign-owned, they still retain local charm. Otherwise, street delicacies are best here. Local specialties, found especially in the Mellah, for example at the corner of Rue al-Quds, are not to be missed. You may wish to sample *z'az'a* (a shake), flan *beldi* (meaning it is made with fresh country milk and eggs), and a pastry soaked in honey called *aslia.*

$ ✕ **Restaurant Blanco Riad.** Set within a jasmine-scented courtyard, this is
MOROCCAN   one of the prettiest dining spots in the city. The food is equally as good
Fodor's Choice   as the setting, thanks to a menu of modern Moroccan cuisine featuring
★   dishes such as orange, carrot, and saffron salad, seafood cannelloni, and to-die-for nougat ice cream. **Known for:** modern Moroccan cuisine; beautiful setting; tasty ice cream for dessert. $ *Average main: 80DH* ⊠ *5, rue Zawiya Kadiria* ☎ *0539/70–42–02* ⊕ *www.blancoriad.com/en.*

$ ✕ **Restaurant El Reducto.** The restaurant in this Spanish-run hotel is one
MOROCCAN   of best options for a great homemade meal short of being invited into a Tetouani home. Fine Moroccan and Spanish dishes include chicken pastilla, fish skewers, delicious nut-based pastries, and Spanish *croquetas.* **Known for:** delicious local cuisine; alcohol menu available; straightforward options for unadventurous diners. $ *Average main: 80DH* ⊠ *38, Zanqat Zawya* ☎ *0539/96–81–20* ⊕ *www.elreducto.com.*

$ ✕ **Restaurant Restinga.** A small alleyway leads off a pedestrian street
MOROCCAN   to a small courtyard with a large fig tree as its centerpiece. Try one of the traditional meat tagines or the platter of fried fish, which usually includes sole, calamari, rouget, and shrimp. **Known for:** fresh fish dishes; alcohol menu with complimentary tapas for each drink; lovely courtyard setting. $ *Average main: 40DH* ⊠ *21, bd. Mohammed V* ☎ *0539/96–35–76* ▭ *No credit cards.*

WHERE TO STAY

$$$$ 🏨 **Banyan Tree Tamouda Bay.** Morocco's first Banyan Tree is an all-pool
RESORT   villa resort, just a pebble's throw from a sweep of shell-strewn beach.
FAMILY   **Pros:** gorgeous villas; excellent facilities; right on the beach. **Cons:** rates
Fodor's Choice   can be expensive; main pool and villa pools aren't heated; spa is pricey.
★ $ *Rooms from: 4345DH* ⊠ *Oued Negro, Fnideq* ☎ *0539/66–99–99* ⊕ *www.banyantree.com/en/em-morocco-tamouda-bay* ⤳ *92 villas* 🍽 *Breakfast.*

3

$$ HOTEL Fodor's Choice ★ [H] **Blanco Riad.** This beautiful, Spanish-run riad once served as the city's Spanish consulate. **Pros:** tranquil atmosphere; beautifully designed; excellent restaurant. **Cons:** pedestrian-only access; steep stairs to the upper floors. [$] *Rooms from: 650DH* ✉ *25, rue Zawiya* ☎ *0539/70–42–02* 🌐 *www.blancoriad.com* 🛏 *8 rooms* 🍴 *Breakfast.*

$$ HOTEL [H] **Riad El Reducto.** One of the best options in Tetouan, the riad was built for the Moroccan prime minister during the Spanish protectorate in 1810 and retiled in 1940 thanks to a gift from the Spanish governor. **Pros:** friendly staff; great views; wonderful restaurant. **Cons:** the busy courtyard restaurant means the surrounding rooms can be noisy; steep stairs to the terrace; pedestrian-only access. [$] *Rooms from: 600DH* ✉ *Mechwar, Essaid Zanqat Zawya Kadiriya 38* ☎ *0539/96–81–20* 🛏 *10 rooms* 🍴 *Breakfast.*

$$$$ RESORT [H] **Sofitel Tamuda Bay Beach and Spa.** With its striking architecture, ultra-contemporary design, and vibrant colors, the Sofitel Tamuda Bay pays homage to the Riviera lifestyle, fusing the atmospheres of the Mediterranean and the Rif to create a unique resort. **Pros:** location right on the beach; arty, contemporary design; cool vibe. **Cons:** rates can be expensive; breakfast not included; service can be less than five stars. [$] *Rooms from: 3450DH* ✉ *Rte. de Sebta M'Diq* ☎ *0539/71–62–00* 🌐 *www.sofitel.com/gb/hotel-8216-sofitel-tamuda-bay-beach-and-spa/index.shtml* 🛏 *104 rooms* 🍴 *No meals.*

SHOPPING

The most interesting shopping is found in the medina where *mendils,* the bright, multicolor cloth used by farmers from the Rif for all-purpose protection from the elements, are made and sold in a little square northeast of Bab er-Rouah. Wood and leather are other artisanal products to look for in the medina.

Ensemble Artisanal. At this government-sponsored crafts center, rug weavers, leather workers, woodworkers, and jewelry designers manufacture and sell their wares. Prices are not negotiable here, but the quality is excellent, and there can be a certain value in not having to haggle. ✉ *Av. Hassan I* ☎ *0539/99–20–85.*

CHEFCHAOUEN AND THE RIF

The trip south from Tetouan to Chefchaouen takes you through fertile valleys where locals sell produce along the road, sheep graze in golden sunshine, and the pace of life slows remarkably from that of the regions just to the north. The route from Chefchaouen to Al Hoceima winds through the spectacular scenery of the Rif, northern Morocco's highest mountains.

CHEFCHAOUEN

64 km (38 miles) south of Tetouan, 98 km (61 miles) southeast of Tangier.

Nestled high in the Rif Mountains, Chefchaouen, known as the "Blue City," is built on a hillside, and is a world apart from its larger, Spanish-style neighbors. The pace of life here seems somehow in tune with the abundant natural springs, wildflowers, and low-lying clouds hovering above the surrounding mountains. From Rifi Berbers dressed in earth-tone wool *djellabas* (long, hooded robes) and sweaters (ideal for cold, wet Rif winters) to the signature blue-washed houses lining its narrow streets, Chefchaouen has maintained its unique identity throughout the years.

Founded in 1471 by Moulay Ali ben Rachid as a mountain base camp for launching attacks against the Portuguese at Ceuta, Chefchaouen was historically off-limits to Christians until recently, and had been visited by only three Europeans when Spanish troops arrived in 1920. Vicomte Charles de Foucauld—French military officer, explorer, and missionary—managed to make it inside the walls disguised as a rabbi in 1883. In 1889 British journalist Walter Harris, intrigued by the thought of a city closed to Westerners a mere 97 km (60 miles) from Tangier, used a similar strategy to gain access to Chefchaouen while researching his book *Land of an African Sultan*. The third visitor, American William Summers, was less lucky and was caught and poisoned in 1892.

Chefchaouen's isolationism had increased with the arrival of Muslims expelled from Spain at the end of the 15th century and again at the start of the 17th. Jews expelled from Spain with the Muslims chose various shades of blue for the facades of their houses, while the Muslim houses remained green or mauve. When the Spanish arrived in 1920 they were stunned to find Chefchaouen's Sephardic Jews speaking and writing a medieval Spanish dialect that had been extinct in Spain for four centuries. The medina has been walled since its earliest days, and is still off-limits to cars.

Somehow, even the burgeoning souvenir shops don't make much of a dent in the town's mystique. Chaouen, as it's sometimes called, is an ideal place to wander through a tiny medina, walk up into the looming mountains above the valley, and sip mint tea in an open square. No other place in Morocco has Chefchaouen's otherworldly, bohemian appeal—a place that ranks as a consistent favorite among travelers to the region.

GETTING HERE AND AROUND

CTM is the region's bus company with several buses daily between Tangier, Tetouan, Al Hoceima, and Nador. Grands taxis can be taken from Tangier (around 60 DH per person) or from Tetouan directly to Chefchaouen.

Bus Contacts CTM - Gare Routière. ☏ *0539/98–76–69* ⊕ *www.ctm.ma.*

EXPLORING

OFF THE BEATEN PATH

Akchour Waterfall and God's Bridge. Located a short walk from the village of Akchour and a five-minute drive by grand taxi from Chefchaouen to Talassemtane National Park, these two waterfalls and a natural bridge are the highlights of any trip into the heart of the Rif mountains. The path to the first waterfall is an easy 45-minute walk. From there, you have the option of continuing on a four-to-five-hour round-trip hike to a second, much larger waterfall. On the other side of the river, you can either head up on a very steep path to the so-called God's Bridge itself, a natural bridge, or follow the canyon to a view from below. Be prepared to wade a little if the water is high. Several small cafés offering vegetable tagines and mint tea sprinkle the path, as do wildflowers and small wildlife. Be aware that some locals will try to sell you things, some of them illegal. ✉ *Akchour.*

Fodor's Choice ★ **Medina and Kasbah.** Chefchaouen boasts one of the most picturesque medinas in Morocco. Compact and crowd-free, it's a delight to explore, with almost every building along its tangle of alleyways painted in a dazzling blue hue, with photo opportunities at every turn. At its heart is the cobbled main square, Place Outa el Hammam. Looming over it are the dusky red walls of the 13th-century Kasbah, now home to a lovely Andalusian garden and a small ethnographic museum. Climb the tower for incredible views of the medina and the mountains beyond. ✉ *Chefchaouen* 🎫 *Kasbah, 10 DH.*

Talassemtane National Park. Established in 1989, the Talassemtane National Park is a beautiful 45-minute drive from Chefchaouen. The 145,000-acre expanse boasts a Mediterranean ecosystem that hosts a unique variety of Moroccan pine as well as more than 239 plant species, many of which are endangered, such as the black pine and the Atlas cedar. There are many hiking options, including the popular hike to the Akchour Waterfall and God's Bridge. It's recommended to use a guide on longer hikes, especially overnight ones. ✉ *3, rue Machichi* ☎ *039/98–72–67.*

WHERE TO EAT

$ MOROCCAN 🍴 **Café Clock Chefchaouen.** The hugely popular Café Clock company has arrived in a cool blue riad in Chefchaouen. It comes with the same relaxed vibe as its counterparts in Fez and Marrakesh, as well as menu favorites like camel burger and a wide variety of fish dishes. **Known for:** great range of activities, including cooking classes; vegetarian and vegan-friendly; unique camel burger. [$] *Average main: 95DH* ✉ *Derb Tijani* 🌐 *www.cafeclock.com.*

$ MOROCCAN 🍴 **Casa Aladdin.** It's all about the bird's-eye views over the main square from the three-story riad's terraces here, as the food can be hit or miss. Tagines are the best bet, or stick to a mint tea and pastries. **Known for:** views over the main square; popular with groups; classic tagines. [$] *Average main: 50DH* ✉ *17, rue Targui* ☎ *0539/98–90–71* 💳 *No credit cards.*

$ ITALIAN 🍴 **Pizzeria Mandala.** For a break from the standard Moroccan fare, head to this popular pizzeria just outside the medina. Pizza and pasta are the mainstays of the menu, but they also serve meat dishes and good-size salads. **Known for:** great pizza and pasta; delivery to area hotels; chocolate fondant for dessert. [$] *Average main: 60DH* ✉ *Av. Hassan II* ☎ *539/88–28–08* 🌐 *www.pizzeriamandala.com.*

$ MOROCCAN 🍴 **Restaurant Beldi Bab Ssour.** A great value and an always-busy restaurant, Beldi Bab Ssour is the best choice for Moroccan dishes full of home-cooked flavor. House specialties include regional favorites such as bisarra, goat tagines, and offal, as well as plenty of options for vegetarians. **Known for:** traditional and homecooked Moroccan cuisine; regional specialties like goat tagines; family-style shared dishes. [$] *Average main: 40DH* ✉ *5, rue Elkharrazin* ☎ *660/26–11–28.*

WHERE TO STAY

$$ HOTEL
Dar Baibou and Casa Hassan. With two separate locations run by the same owner, these two riad complexes offer gorgeous decor and true Moroccan hospitality. **Pros:** traditional Moroccan decor; plenty of public spaces; central location. **Cons:** pedestrian-only access; some rooms are small and dark; steep stairs to upper floors. [$] *Rooms from: 850DH* ✉ *22, rue Targui* ☎ *0539/98–61–53* 🌐 *www.casahassan.com* 🛏 *24 rooms* 🍴 *Some meals.*

$ HOTEL
Hotel Dar Mounir. This traditionally decorated B&B was designed by local painter Karim Al-Haoulani, whose paintings also decorate the walls. **Pros:** close to the main square; friendly staff; good restaurant. **Cons:** steep stairs to upper floors; pedestrian-only access; the neighborhood can be noisy at night. [$] *Rooms from: 425DH* ✉ *Pl. Uta Hammam, Kadi Alami Hay Souika* ☎ *0539/98–82–53* 🛏 *18 rooms* 🍴 *Breakfast.*

$$ B&B/INN Fodor's Choice ★
La Petite Chefchaouen. Restoring this riad was a labor of love for the well-traveled Moroccan owner, and he's met his own high standards with the clean, contemporary look here. **Pros:** extremely helpful staff; stunning views from the terrace; delicious dinners on request. **Cons:** pedestrian-only access (but they'll help with your luggage); steep stairs; not for those wanting traditional Moroccan decor. [$] *Rooms from: 800DH* ✉ *169, av. Hassan Ier* ☎ *0661/57–22–72* 🌐 *www.lapetitechefchaouen.ma/en* 🛏 *5 rooms* 🍴 *Breakfast.*

SPORTS AND THE OUTDOORS

Less visited than the High Atlas range mountain, the Rif Mountains around Chefchaouen still offer all manner of walking opportunities, from easy rambles along the banks of the Ras el-Maa River to more ambitious full-day hikes, such as scaling Jebel al-Kalaa, which looms over the town, as well as multiday hikes.

SHOPPING

Chefchaouen is one of the north's best places to shop for quality traditional crafts. Wool items and leather goods are the main local export: look in small medina stores for thick blankets, rugs, bags, and shoes.

Abdellah Alami. This shop sells nothing but bronze products, made by a family of bronze workers who produce some of this region's finest handmade plates, bowls, and trays. Prices are reasonable, and the selection is vast. ✉ *257, Onsar Rasselma* ☎ *0539/98–73–03.*

Artisanal Chefchaouen. The small cooperative workshop Artisanal Chefchaouen produces beautiful, inexpensive, and high-quality goods, including hand-painted wood boxes, weavings, original art, and leatherwork. ✉ *Pl. el Makhzen, just outside medina walls.*

La Botica de la Abuela Aladdin. This small and sweet-smelling store is a riot of color and awash with the fragrance of rose, amber, sandalwood, vanilla, Damascus jasmine, and more. The owner creates around 20 different types of handmade soaps, body oils, lotions, and solid perfumes made from all-natural ingredients. Beautifully packaged, they make perfect gifts to take back home. ✉ *17, rue Targi* ☎ *0631/86–43–86.*

Chefchaouen is known as the "blue city" because of its blue-washed walls.

AL HOCEIMA

215 km (133 miles) east of Chefchaouen.

Surrounded on three sides by the foothills of the Rif Mountains and rimmed on the fourth by turquoise Mediterranean waters, Al Hoceima is a dominating town atop rolling hills. The town perches directly over a stunning turquoise bay and, while it isn't nearly as developed as Tangier and Tetouan, its natural sights and exquisite coastline make it the perfect place to relax for a day or two.

Established by the Spanish in 1925 as Villa Sanjuro, Al Hoceima was built as a stronghold against Rifi Berber rebellions. Al Hoceima is now proudly Berber, and Berber flags and signs are becoming more and more prominent. The king has even recognized *Tamazight*—a general term that encompasses six different Berber dialects, four of which are in use by Morocco's Berber population—as Morocco's second official language, alongside Arabic. Tarifit (Rifi Berber) is spoken by about 4 million people in the Rif Valley, sometimes exclusively of any other language, though there are many Spanish words interspersed with Tarifit.

The finest Spanish edifice in the town is the beautifully tiled **Spanish College** (Instituto Español Melchor de Jovellanos de Alhucemas) at the end of Boulevard Mohammed V. The Old Town is centered on the pretty, Art Deco **Place du Rif.** There are few sights here, but you can wander the town's markets, kick back at a café, and just enjoy the relative quietude. In the Ville Nouvelle, the clifftop **Place Mohammed VI,** just above the main beach, is the focal point of the evening *paseo* (promenade) and has a fun sidewalk punctuated by fountains. Festivals and citywide events are held here in the summer months, when many expatriate Al Hoceimans residing in Europe return home on vacation.

GETTING HERE AND AROUND

Al Hociema's Cherif Al Idrissi Airport, located just 17 km (11 miles) southeast of the town, connects to Casablanca and Tetouan with Royal Air Maroc. There are some seasonal flights from Europe.

CTM buses operate several daily services to Tangier, Tetouan, Chefcha-ouen, and Nador. If you're driving yourself, the N2 cuts east toward Nador and Melilla, and there is also a scenic coastal road from Tetouan to Al Hoceima.

Bus Contacts CTM. ✉ *Junction of Av. Mohammed V and Rue General Meziane* ☎ *039/98–22–73* ⊕ *www.ctm.ma.*

ESSENTIALS

Visitor Information Al Hoceima Tourism Office. ✉ *Blvd. Al Hamra, Cala Bonita* ☎ *0539/98–11–85.*

EXPLORING

The real reasons to come to Al Hoceima are the many beaches. The main city beach, **Plage Quemado,** sits in a natural bay formed by moun-tains on each side. The water is crystal clear, perfect for snorkeling and scuba diving, and you can rent equipment from a hut on the beach. (Be sure to check the equipment carefully before use.) Near Quemado Beach is Al Hoceima's port, where several restaurants cook up wonderfully fresh seafood. The coastline outside of town is equally as scenic; the beach at **Asfiha,** located 1 km (½ mile) west of the city, stretches around the bay with miles of uninterrupted, fine, ash-color sand. It is a popular family resort and is usually very crowded in sum-mer, with many beachside cafés in which to hide from the sun and have tea or lunch. The beach is very much worth a trip, for from here you can see the tiny Spanish rock fortress **Peñon de Alhuceimas,** meaning "Lavendar Rock." **Souani Beach** is a nice small bay backed by a pine forest, a perfect place for a picnic.

The remote Al Hoceima National Park, about 20 km (12 miles) east of Al Hoceima, is a great spot for hiking and mountain-biking. Its little-visited canyons and forests are home to several rare species of birds, reptiles, and mammals. Well-marked trails traverse the park, as do Berber settlements, where you can watch villagers making pots and weaving baskets. It's best visited on an organized tour unless you have your own vehicle with four-wheel drive.

WHERE TO EAT AND STAY

$
SEAFOOD
Fodor'sChoice
★

✕ **Club Nautique.** Fresh, simply grilled fish and other seafood reign supreme here, along with several resort-style bars placed strategically around the two terraces and captain's cabin–style interior. There is a large selection of Moroccan wines on offer, with Guerrouane being a good bet. **Known for:** fish dishes straight off the boat; gorgeous outdoor seating with views of the bay; impressive wine list. $ *Average main: 100DH* ✉ *Port d'Al Hoceima* ☎ *0539/98–14–61.*

$$ ⬚ **Suites Hotel Mohammed V by Accor.** Al Hoceima's grand old hotel has
HOTEL contemporary rooms and bungalows for guests to choose from. **Pros:**
away from the hubbub; near the beach. **Cons:** rooms a bit utilitarian;
a bit pricey for what you get. $ *Rooms from: 940DH* ✉ *Pl. de la
Marche Verte* ☎ *0539/98–22–33* ⊕ *www.accorhotels.com* ⤳ *21 rooms*
○ *Breakfast.*

SPORTS AND THE OUTDOORS
BEACHES
The area around Al Hoceima has some of North Africa's finest Medi-
terranean beaches. Quemado Beach, a busy urban strip in Al Hoceima
proper, is a cove tucked between large hills, with fine sand and crystal-
line water; during a simple swim you can see coral and schools of fish
below. There are plenty of beaches to explore just outside—for instance,
Tala Youssef, just west of Al Hoceima, where King Mohammed VI
spends his summer holidays.

To the east, the beaches beyond Nador such as Kariet Arkmane, Ras
Kebdana, and Saïdia are quieter and less well equipped for family activi-
ties, but excellent for relaxing and communing with nature.

RABAT AND
CASABLANCA

WELCOME TO RABAT AND CASABLANCA

TOP REASONS TO GO

★ **Rabat's Kasbah des Oudayas:** Rabat's medieval kasbah has evocative architecture and a glorious garden overlooking the mouth of the Oued Bou Regreg River and the city of Salé beyond.

★ **Casablanca's Tour Hassan II:** The largest mosque in Africa and one of the largest in the world, this modern extravaganza makes elaborate use of traditional Moroccan craftsmanship.

★ **Colonial France's southern Riviera:** Developed during the Protectorate, Casablanca's Quartier des Habous and La Corniche are a memorable mix of vintage French and Moroccan styles.

★ **Casablanca's southern beaches:** The splendid coastline between Casablanca and El Oualidia features sublime beaches with famously surfable waves crashing in from the Atlantic.

You can easily drive to Rabat from the northern cities of Tangier and Tetouan on the newer highway, although the older, slower coastal road is still open. From there, you can go on to Casablanca, Azemmour, and El Jadida, where the highway ends. The coastal road will lead you farther south from this point—a good idea if you wish to explore the southern beaches, Essaouira, Marrakesh, or the Atlas Mountains. Either way you'll absorb plenty of coastal scenery. If you only have limited time to spend in the region, you may want to fly straight into Rabat as it's richer in traditional sights.

1 **Rabat.** Visitors are enticed by the tranquillity of Rabat, where beautiful Moorish gardens are bordered by charming cafés. They marvel at the Hassan Tower, which has overlooked the city for eight centuries, and the adjacent Mohammed V Mausoleum. The Museum of History and Civilisation, home to an extensive collection of archaeological artifacts, lures history buffs, while the Royal Golf Dar Es-Salamg and Rabat's south shore draw golfers and beach bums respectively.

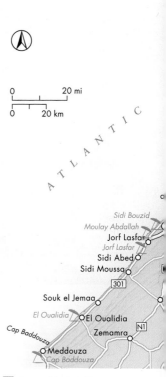

2 **Around Rabat.** For those captivated by Morocco's medinas, the nearby city of Salé promises one notable for its traditional architecture and pottery shops. Bird lovers should consider a day trip to Lake Sidi Bourhaba, near Mehdiya Plage, known for its 200-odd species of birds. The sandy beaches in the direction of Skhirat are equally breathtaking and much-loved by locals.

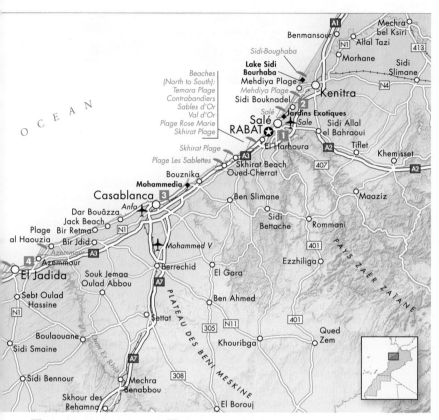

O C E A N

Beaches
(North to South):
Temara Plage
Contrabandiers
Sables d'Or
Val d'Or
Plage Rose Marie
Skhirat Plage

Sidi-Boughaba

**Lake Sidi
Bourhaba**
Mehdiya Plage

Mehdiya Plage
Sidi Bouknadel

Mechra
bel Ksiri
Benmansour
Allal Tazi
Morhane
Sidi
Slimane

Kenitra

Salé
Jardins Exotiques
Salé
Salé
Sidi Allal
el Bahraoui
RABAT

El Harhoura
Tiflet
Khemisset

Skhirat Plage
Skhirat Beach
Oued-Cherrat

Plage Les Sablettes
Bouznika

Mohammedia
Casablanca

Ben Slimane
Maaziz

Dar Bouâzza
Anfa
Jack Beach
Plage Bir Retma
al Haouzia Bir Jdid

Sidi
Bettache
Rommani

Azemmour
Mohammed V
Ezzhiliga

El Jadida
Berrechid
El Gara

Souk Jemaa
Oulad Abbou

Sebt Oulad
Hassine
Ben Ahmed

Boulaouane
Settat
Khouribga
Oued
Zem

Sidi Smaine

Sidi Bennour
Mechra
Benabbou

Skhour des
Rehamna
El Borouj

P A Y S   Z A E R   Z A I A N E

P L A T E A U   D E S   B E N I   M E S K I N E

4

3 Casablanca. Featuring broad avenues lined with contemporary and Hispano-Moorish structures, plus Art Deco edifices, public fountains, and a spacious shoreline, Casablanca is an appealing blend of East and West. The massive Hassan II Mosque—an architectural marvel completed in 1993—flashes its laser beams to Mecca, underscoring the city's eclectic spirit.

4 Around Casablanca. Dar Bouazza, a fishing community and growing resort town, has great beaches and oceanfront restaurants. Oualidia is a haven centered on a splendid lagoon, while Azemmour offers a white-washed medina and artsy atmosphere. El Jadida, built by the Portuguese, feels quite different from other Moroccan towns and offers more dining and lodging options.

Updated
by Olivia
Gunning
Bennani

Rabat and Casablanca, two of Morocco's most modern and elegant cities, straddle the North Atlantic coast, welcoming visitors with their varied histories and blossoming cultures.

As the political capital of Morocco, Rabat is a surprisingly sedate urban center that brims with historical interest and splendid architecture from both Arab and Art Deco periods. The royal city boasts many monuments from successive Arab dynasties as well as a simple unmarked cave on the coast that is thought to be one of the first sites ever inhabited by humans. Rabat and her more traditional twin city, Salé, watch one another over the River Bou Regreg, where they both offer traditional medinas full of market bustle as well as some of the most important historical sights in the country.

No more than 100 km (62 miles) southwest of Rabat is Casablanca, once a Berber town and now a thoroughly modern city, developed by the French from 1912 until Moroccan independence. The country's main industrial and commercial axis stretches from Casablanca to Kenitra, making the city the undisputed commercial capital with rich strata of history piled everywhere.

Despite the historical riches, Rabat, Casablanca, and their surrounding towns are somewhat removed from the pressures of the larger tourist centers like Marrakesh, Fez, and Agadir. Quite apart from the more gentle climate, you'll generally find yourself—unlike in, say, Fez—free to wander around relatively unhassled.

Breakers roll in all along the rest of Morocco's North Atlantic coast, contrasting markedly with the placid waters of Morocco's Mediterranean shore. From here, the ocean stretches due west to the United States. Much of this coast is lined with sandy beaches, and dotted with simple white *koubbas,* the buildings that house a Muslim saint's tomb.

What you can really sample when visiting this region is the urban side of North Africa, which overflows with modern structures in industrial, commercial, and leisure terms. Yet the old has been by no means ousted, so expect conspicuous contrasts: traditional dress alongside contemporary European designs and ancient Moorish edifices not far from trendy restaurants bubbling over with international tourists and young locals.

PLANNING

WHEN TO GO

During July, August, and the first part of September, temperatures are hot, beach towns are crowded, and hotels are typically more packed and expensive. April through June and October, the weather is delightful—easily warm enough to enjoy the beaches (although, depending on your tolerence level, it may be too cold to swim)—and most coastal resorts are pleasantly empty. If you don't want to swim or sunbathe, you can sightsee from November to March (and even then the weather can be quite warm). The relatively cool period lasts from around early December through the end of February, when temperatures on the coast can drop to 4°C–6°C (39°F–43°F).

PLANNING YOUR TIME

Rabat's airport is developing fast, but more flights to this region still land in Casablanca, so it may be best to start there. After a few days exploring the city that constitutes Morocco's economic heart, you'll probably be in search of some peace, so head north toward Rabat, stopping at Mohammedia for an afternoon. While in Rabat, spend a few days admiring the magnificent architecture, elegant restaurants, and lively medina. For an even more peaceful atmosphere, skip farther north to Moulay Bousselham, a bird-lover's paradise. To explore the southern parts of the area, stop by Azemmour and El Jadida on your way to Oualidia. You need a good two weeks to complete this tour fully, although some visitors prefer to focus on just the two cities and make brief day trips to some surrounding beach towns.

GETTING HERE AND AROUND

AIR TRAVEL

The major airport in this region is Casablanca's Mohammed V International Airport, which is located about 25 km (16 miles) south of the city. While the airport in Rabat is increasingly well-served, Casablanca's remains the most common international gateway for Americans traveling to Morocco, and many airlines fly there direct from North America, the Middle East, and Europe. Train, shuttle, or taxi services located outside the arrivals terminal can easily get you to the city proper, as well as to Rabat and other regional destinations.

BUS TRAVEL

You can reach some outlying destinations by bus if you don't wish to drive, but the trips can be long and less than comfortable. Always make sure you use a reputable company—the roads here are dangerous.

CAR TRAVEL

If your stay in this region is limited to Casablanca and Rabat, you won't need a car at all. If, however, your aim is to relax in small coastal towns like Moulay Bousselham and El Oualidia, a car is far more useful than the often slow and complicated public transportation to those places.

TRAIN TRAVEL

There is excellent nonstop train service every 30 minutes between Casablanca and Rabat (even more frequently at the beginning and end of the day). This is the best way to move between the cities. You can also travel onward to Tangier, Fez, Meknès, Marrakesh, and a few other destinations by train. This can be a comfortable and reasonably priced way to travel within the country.

SAFETY

Official guides in Morocco are identified by large, brass badges. Be wary of the numerous unofficial guides who will offer to find you a hotel, take you on a tour, or, in some cases, supply hashish, or *kif*, for you. Some will falsely claim to be students who merely wish to practice their English. To avoid these hustlers, you should appear confident and aware of where you are going. If you feel bullied or harassed, do not hesitate to summon police. As in any large city, pickpockets exist, and you should be alert and aware of your surroundings while walking around. Be careful to keep essential documents out of reach—an inside pocket is the most sensible, since bag-grabbing (often by motorcyclists) is quite common. If you have access to a reliable safe, it's smart to carry copies.

RESTAURANTS

Morocco's northern Atlantic coast is the national center of seafood par excellence. Along the length of it the menus are remarkably similar: *crevettes* (prawns), *friture de poisson* (fried fish and octopus), *calamar* (squid), and various kinds of fish. *Fruits de mer* are always shellfish and prawns, not fish. In addition to seafood, Casablanca and Rabat offer many types of international cuisine—you'll find Italian and other Mediterranean restaurants, as well as Asian and even American eateries—and, of course, ones serving traditional Moroccan fare and French cuisine. Although it's tempting to think you can find good examples of the former anywhere, the best ones on this stretch of the coast are really limited to Casablanca and Rabat. (Locals eat Moroccan cuisine at home, so they tend to choose alternatives when dining out.) Vegetarians should note that Moroccan salads—cooked and raw, such as *zallouk* (eggplant puree) and *felfla mataisha* (grilled pepper and fresh tomato)—are truly delicious. *Dining reviews have been shortened. For full information, visit Fodors.com.*

HOTELS

It's always a good idea to book ahead in this part of the country, as Rabat and Casablanca fill up with business travelers, and the beach resorts are packed during the summer months. Casablanca has branches of the familiar brand-name business hotels, and business hotels in both that city and Rabat may discount their published rates by applying corporate ones at the drop of a company's name. In the smaller coastal resorts you'll typically find midrange sea-view hotels with pools, but increasingly these towns also offer smaller, more personalized, bed-and-breakfast-type lodgings and traditional riads. *Hotel reviews have been shortened. For full information, visit Fodors.com.*

WHAT IT COSTS IN DIRHAMS			
	$	$$	$$$	$$$$
Restaurants	under 80 DH	80 DH–120 DH	121 DH–160 DH	over 160 DH
Hotels	under 900 DH	900 DH–1,500 DH	1,501 DH–2,000 DH	over 2,000 DH

Restaurant prices are the average cost of a main course at dinner, or if dinner is not served, at lunch. Hotel prices are the lowest cost of a standard double room in high season.

FESTIVALS

There is a good sprinkling of festivals in the region. L'Boulevard, which takes place in Casablanca in early or late summer, is an annual competition among local and foreign artists that is popular with the younger crowd. Rabat's Mawazine festival, usually staged between May and June, has achieved international recognition, bringing high-quality performers to Morocco. Note that exact festival dates vary according to Ramadan; many festivals are not held during their typical period due to the holiday, so scheduling can be unpredictable.

RABAT

40 km (25 miles) southwest of Kenitra, 91 km (57 miles) northeast of Casablanca.

Rabat, a diplomatic center with a large community of foreign residents, boasts a medina and an array of historical sites and museums; yet it exerts significantly less of the pressure that most travelers experience in a place like Fez. You'll generally find yourself free to wander and browse without being hassled to buy local wares or engage a guide, so it's an excellent place to get acquainted with Morocco. Attractive and well kept, with several gardens, it's arguably the country's most pleasant and easygoing city as far as tourists are concerned.

Rabat was founded in the 12th century as a fortified town—now the Kasbah des Oudayas—on a rocky outcrop overlooking the River Bou Regreg by Abd al-Mu'min of the Almohad dynasty. Abd al-Mu'min's grandson, Yaqoub al-Mansour, extended the city to encompass the present-day medina, surrounded it with ramparts (some of which still stand), and erected a mosque, from which the unfinished Hassan Tower protrudes as Rabat's principal landmark. Chellah, a neighboring Roman town now within Rabat, was developed as a necropolis in the 13th century.

In the early 1600s, Rabat itself was revived with the arrival of the Muslims, who populated the present-day medina upon their expulsion from Spain. Over the course of the 17th century the Kasbah des Oudayas grew notorious for its pirates, and an independent republic of the Bou Regreg was established, based in the kasbah; the piracy continued when the republic was integrated into the Alaouite kingdom and lasted until the 19th century. Rabat was named the administrative capital of the country at the beginning of the French protectorate in 1912, and it remained the capital of the Alaouite kingdom when independence was restored in 1956. The Royal Palace continues to be the King's principal residence.

The city has grown considerably over the last 20 years, and today it has many important districts outside the kasbah, the medina, and the original French Ville Nouvelle. These include L'Océan, the seaside area that was once Spanish and Portuguese (during the French protectorate); Hassan, the environs of the Hassan tower; Agdal, a fashionable residential and business district; Ryad, an upscale residential district; and Souissi, an affluent enclave of wealthy folks and diplomats. Take a ride in a taxi, a tram, or your own car around the various neighborhoods to get a real understanding of the city as a whole.

GETTING HERE AND AROUND

AIR TRAVEL
Although most flyers still choose Casablanca as their arrival or departure point, Rabat does have its own growing airport—Rabat-Salé, located 10 km (6 miles) northeast of the capital—which offers domestic and international service. Getting into town costs about 200 DH by taxi or 20 DH by bus.

Airport Contacts Rabat-Salé Airport. ✉ *Rte. de Meknes* ☎ *0537/80–80–90* ⊕ *www.onda.ma/en/Our-Airports/Rabat-Sale-Airport.*

BUS TRAVEL
The bus station in Rabat is on the outskirts of the city in a neighborhood known as Kamara; from there you can take a taxi or a city bus into town. Service providers include CTM, Morocco's most reliable coach company.

Bus Information CTM. ✉ *2, Av. Hassan II* ☎ *0800/09–00–30* ⊕ *www.ctm.ma.*

CAR TRAVEL
You may prefer not to bother with a car if you're only visiting Rabat and Casablanca, but having one can be helpful if you want to explore further. Major international agencies have rental outlets in Rabat itself or at the airport.

Rental Cars Avis. ✉ *9, rue Abou Faris el Marini* ☎ *0537/72–18–18* ⊕ *www.avis. ma.* **Hertz.** ✉ *Rabat-Salé Airport* ☎ *0537/82–97–00* ⊕ *www.hertz.ma.*

TAXI TRAVEL
Rabat's *petits taxis,* which are blue, can get you easily from Point A to Point B, and you'll find them just about everywhere in town. A typical metered fare will cost about 15 to 20 DH (after 9 pm there is a 50% surcharge).

TRAIN TRAVEL
Rabat has two train stations: Rabat-Agdal, on the outskirts of town toward Casablanca, and Rabat-Ville, closer to most hotels and attractions. Rabat is three hours by train from Meknès, four hours from Fez, and four hours from Marrakesh. All these trains also call at Casablanca. In addition, there are overnight trains from Rabat to Oujda, and three direct trains daily to Tangier, which also have bus connections from an intermediate stop (just before Asilah) to Tetouan.

Casablanca's tramway costs 6 DH per ride and is an excellent way to get around the city.

Train Contacts Office National des Chemins de Fer - Gare de Rabat Ville (O.N.C.F). ⊠ *Av. Mohammed V* ☎ *2255* ⊕ *www.oncf.ma.*

GUIDES AND TOURS

Guided tours of several cities in this region are best reserved in your home country. Generally speaking, you can't book a spot on a local guided tour upon arrival the way you can in many other countries.

Atlas Voyages. This professional agency offers almost any kind of tour or break you could desire, from a Rif mountain escape to an urban exploration of one of the Kingdom's regal cities. It caters to all budgets and group sizes and is flexible in terms of trip type. ⊠ *Mahaj ryad n°22, Hay Riad Rabat* ☎ *0802/00–20–20* ⊕ *www.atlasvoyages.com.*

SAFETY

Rabat is considered one of the safest, least harried cities in Morocco. Travelers can generally expect minimal harassment from vendors and fake tour guides. Nonetheless, streets can be somewhat desolate after sundown, so visitors may prefer to use taxis then.

EXPLORING

TOP ATTRACTIONS

Fodor's Choice
★
Chellah Ruins and Gardens. Chellah was an independent city before Rabat ever existed. Presumably founded by Phoenicians, it dates from the 7th or 8th century BC. You'll see the remains of the subsequent Roman city, Sala Colonia, on your left as you walk down the path. Though these remnants are limited to broken stone foundations and column bases (with lots of resident storks), descriptive markers point to the likely location of the forum, baths, and market. Sultan Abu Saïd and his son Abu al Hassan, of the Merenid dynasty, were responsible for the ramparts, the entrance gate, and the majestic portals. The Merenids used Chellah as a spiritual retreat, and at quiet times the *baraka* (blessing) of the place is still tangible.

The entrance to the Merenid sanctuary is at the bottom of the path, just past some tombs. To the right is a pool with eels in it, which is said to produce miracles—women are known to toss eggs to the eels for fertility. The ruins of the mosque are just inside the sanctuary; you can still see the beautiful arches and the *mihrab* (prayer niche). Birds nest on the impressive minaret. On the far side of the mosque is a beautiful wall decorated with Kufi script, a type of Arabic calligraphy characterized by right angles. To the left of the mosque is the *zaouia* (sanctuary), where you can see the ruins of individual cells surrounding a basin and some ancient mosaic work. Beyond the mosque and zaouia are some beautiful, well-maintained walled gardens. Spring water runs through them at one point, and they give Chellah a serenity that's quite extraordinary considering that it's less than a mile from the center of a nation's capital. From the walled gardens you can look out over the River Bou Regreg: you'll see cultivated fields below and cliffs across the river. On the right is a hill with a small white koubba. ⊠ *Chellah* ☎ *10 DH.*

Hassan Tower. At the end of the 12th century, Yaqoub al Mansour—fourth monarch of the Almohad dynasty and grandson of Abd al Mu'min, who founded Rabat—planned a great mosque. Intended to be the largest in the Muslim world, the project was abandoned with the death of al Mansour in 1199. A further blow to the site occurred with the strong tremors of the 1755 Lisbon earthquake, and this tower is the only significant remnant of al Mansour's dream. A few columns remain in the mosque's great rectangular courtyard, but the great tower was never even completed (which is why it looks too short for its base). Note the quality of the craftsmanship in the carved-stone and mosaic decorations at the top of the tower. From the base there is a fine view over the river. Locals come here at dawn to have their wedding photos taken. ⊠ *Hassan* ☒ *Free.*

Fodor'sChoice

★

Kasbah des Oudayas. Rabat's early history is based around this Kasbah. Built strategically on high ground over the mouth of the Bou Regreg River and the Atlantic, it was originally constructed for defensive purposes. Still inhabited, it once comprised the whole of the city, including the castle of Yaqoub al Mansour.

Walk up the steps to the huge, imposing ornamental gate, built, like Bab Rouah, by the Almohads. The gate's interior is now used for art exhibits. Enter the Kasbah and turn right into Rue Jama (Mosque Street). The **mosque,** which dates from Almohad times (it was built in the mid-12th century), is on the left; it was supposedly reconstructed in the late 18th century by an English Muslim—Ahmed el Inglizi. Continue to the end of the road past a house called Dar Baraka, and you'll emerge onto a large platform overlooking the Bou Regreg estuary. Here there is the magnificent view across the river to the old quarter of Salé, and you can walk down to the water's edge. Go back along Rue Jama until you come to Rue Bazo on the left; this winds down the Kasbah and past picturesque houses. Turn left, walk to the bottom of the street, and proceed down to the banks of the Bou Regreg to see the beautiful **Jardin des Oudayas** (Oudayas Garden), a walled retreat that you can explore at your leisure. The garden (which is now wheelchair accessible) was laid out in the early 20th century, but its enclosure dates from the beginning of the present Alaouite dynasty in the 17th century. ⊠ *Medina.*

Fodor'sChoice

★

Musée Mohammed VI d'Art Moderne et Contemporain (*Museum of Modern and Contemporary Art*). Inaugurated in 2014, this striking must-see museum is an exquisite showcase of contemporary pieces from across the nation. The permanent collection charts the evolution of Moroccan artwork from the 20th century onward, while the skillfully curated temporary exhibitions focus on fascinating themes. ⊠ *Av. Moulay Hassan, Hassan* ☎ *0537/76–90–47* ⊕ *www.museemohammed6.ma* ☒ *40 DH* ☉ *Closed Tues.*

Musée de l'Histoire et des Civilisations (*Museum of History and Civilization*). Formerly known as the Musée Archéologique, this museum originally opened in 1931 and displays prehistoric, Roman, and Islamic-period artifacts discovered throughout the country. Roman pieces include many inscribed tablets; the Chellah and Volubilis sites

DID YOU KNOW?

Chellah is far older than Rabat, but the magnificent ramparts and entry gate were built by the Merenid sultan Abu Al Hassan in the mid-14th century.

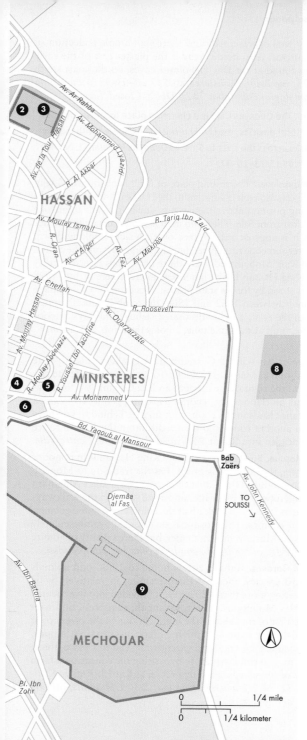

HASSAN

Av. Ar-Rahba

Av. Mohammed Lyazidi

Av. de la Tour Hassan

R. Al Akbar

Av. Moulay Ismaïl

R. Tariq Ibn Zaïd

R. Oran

Av. d'Alger

Av. Fez

Av. Meknès

Av. Chellah

R. Roosevelt

Av. Moulay Hassan

Av. Ouarzazate

R. Youssef Ibn Tachfine

R. Moulay Abdelaziz

MINISTÈRES

Av. Mohammed V

Bd. Yaqoub al Mansour

Bab Zaërs

Av. John Kennedy

TO SOUISSI

Djemâa al Fas

Av. Ibn Batota

MECHOUAR

Pl. Ibn Zohr

0   1/4 mile

0   1/4 kilometer

are particularly well represented, and there's an ample collection of Roman bronze items. Also noteworthy is the plaster cast of the early human remains found at the Dar Es-Soltane caves, on the coast south of the city. ⊠ *23, rue Brihi, Ministères* ☎ *0537/20–03–98* ⊕ *www.fnm. ma/musee-archeologique-de-rabat* 🖅 *20 DH* ⊘ *Closed Tues.*

**NEED A
BREAK**

✕ **Oudayas Café.** The Oudayas Café is a charming place to pause for a glass of tea and local pastries; the shady terrace is decorated with mosaic tilework and looks across the river to Salé. ⊠ *Oudayas Museum, 1, bd. Al Marsa, Medina* ☎ *0537/73–15–37.*

Mohammed V Mausoleum. The resting place of King Mohammed V, who died in 1961, this mausoleum is adjacent to the Hassan Tower and, thanks to a commanding position above the river, is similarly visible to anyone approaching Rabat from Salé. The tomb itself is subterranean; the terrace that overlooks it is approached by steps on each side. Looking down, you're likely to see someone ritually reading the Koran. Beyond the central sarcophagus of King Mohammed V are those of his sons Prince Moulay Abdallah and King Hassan II; the latter was interred here in July 1999 as world leaders stood by for his state funeral. Designed by a Vietnamese architect and built between 1962 and 1966, the tomb is cubical, with a pyramidal green-tile roof, a richly decorated ceiling, and onyx interior walls. A mosque, built at the same time, adjoins the tomb. ⊠ *Hassan.*

WORTH NOTING

Bab Rouah (*Gate of the Winds*). Currently an art gallery, this city gate was built by Yaqoub al Mansour in 1197. To see it, go outside the city walls and look to the right of the modern arches. Originally a fortification, the gate has an elaborately decorated arch topped by two carved shells. The entrance leads into a room with no gate behind it; you have to turn left into another room and then right into a third room to see the door that once led into Rabat. ⊠ *1, av. de la Victoire, Centre Ville.*

Lalla Soukaina Mosque. Built in the 1980s by King Hassan II in honor of his granddaughter, this mosque is proof that the tradition of Moorish architecture that produced the Court of Lions in Granada's Alhambra is alive and well. Notice the exquisite sandstone work on the walkways surrounding the mosque, and look up at the colorfully painted geometric designs on the ceilings. The mosque is surrounded by immaculately kept gardens. Non-Muslims may not enter, but there's plenty to admire from outside. ⊠ *Edge of Souissi, beyond Ibn Sina Hospital, Souissi.*

FAMILY **Rabat Zoological Gardens.** Rabat's zoo is home to 1,800-odd animals representing 150 species, most of them residing in relatively wide enclosures. Covering more than 120 acres, it's divided into five themed ecosystems—Atlas Mountains, desert, savannah, rainforest, and wetlands—with the first of these being the highlight due to the presence of Atlas lions, which only exist in captivity. Elephants, giraffes, hippos, and hordes of magnificent oryx and gazelles also call this place home. After ogling them, you can learn more by visiting the educational farm or catching one of the scheduled daily events. ⊠ *Km 13, Rte. de Kenitra* ☎ *0537/29–37–94* ⊕ *www.rabatzoo.ma* 🖅 *50 DH adults, 30 DH children, free 3 and under.*

Royal Palace (*Mechouar*). Built in the early 20th century, Morocco's Royal Palace is a large, cream-color building set back behind lawns. Its ornamental gate is accented by ceremonial guards dressed in white and red. The complex houses the offices of the cabinet, the prime minister, and other administrative officials. Don't stray from the road down the middle of the complex; the palace is occupied by the royal family and closed to the public. ✉ *Mechouar.*

Sunna Mosque. Rabat's most important mosque was originally erected in the 18th century. Since then it's undergone various rebuildings but has nonetheless been sheltered from architectural anarchy, retaining its beauty and dignity to this day. The French had wanted to extend Avenue Mohammed V through the site; however, Moroccans resisted. Thanks to the martyrs of that confrontation, the mosque still stands on its sacred ground. Non-Muslims may not enter. ✉ *At top of Av. Mohammed V, Centre Ville.*

WHERE TO EAT

$ MOROCCAN 🍴 **Dar Naji.** Loved by locals and visitors alike, Dar Naji is one of the city's most authentically Moroccan, medina-based restaurants. Prices are reasonable, but attention to the quality of the salads, tagines, and couscous dishes is unrelenting. **Known for:** truly authentic menu; excellent value; friendly service; open nonstop midday to midnight. [$] *Average main: 60DH* ✉ *Bab Al Had, Rue Jazirat Al Arab, Medina* ☎ *0537/26–25–28* 💳 *No credit cards.*

$$$$ MOROCCAN Fodor's Choice ★ 🍴 **Dinarjat.** Occupying a palatial medina house, this atmospheric restaurant serves gourmet versions of traditional Moroccan cuisine. Live Andalusian music creates a charming backdrop for the dishes, which include irresistible salads as well as classic tagines and couscous. **Known for:** gourmet Moroccan menu; impeccable service; romantic environment. [$] *Average main: 200DH* ✉ *6, rue Belgnaoui, Medina* ☎ *0537/70–42–39.*

$$$$ FRENCH 🍴 **Le Goéland.** Located near the flower market on Place Petri, Le Goéland is a convivial place that specializes in French-style cuisine, with lots of fresh fish and a good selection of tapas. On weekends, DJs spin into the early hours and a party atmosphere prevails. **Known for:** genuine French cuisine; high-quality fish dishes; high-spirited atmosphere. [$] *Average main: 280DH* ✉ *9, rue Moulay Ali Cherif, Hassan* ☎ *0537/76–88–85.*

$$ ITALIAN 🍴 **La Mamma.** Rabat's original Italian restaurant serves pastas, pizzas, grilled meats, and other classic Italian fare. Expect a pretty cheap and cheerful place with a central brick oven and a homey *cucina* vibe. **Known for:** inexpensive Italian classics; speedy service; extensive menu offers something for everyone. [$] *Average main: 100DH* ✉ *6, Zankat Tanta, Centre Ville* ☎ *0537/70–73–29.*

$$$$ JAPANESE 🍴 **Matsuri.** This Japanese franchise has restaurants in various Moroccan cities and is known throughout the country for its high-quality food. The selection of fish is always fresh, and the staff are helpful. **Known for:** genuine Japanese menu; accommodating service; peaceful setting; nonstop service midday to midnight. [$] *Average main: 220DH* ✉ *151, av. Mohamed VI, Rte. de Zaers, Souissi* ☎ *0537/75–75–72* 🌐 *matsuri-rabat.ma.*

$$$ ✕ **Paul.** A café, bakery, and French restaurant all rolled into one, Paul
FRENCH is a popular spot in the Agdal district. The salads, fish, and meat dishes
are reliably good, while the delicious desserts and patisseries provide
a touch of decadence. **Known for:** unrivaled French pastries; beautiful
terrace; refined, efficient service. Ⓢ *Average main: 150DH* ✉ *82, av.
Nations Unies, Agdal* ☎ *0537/67–20–00* ⊕ *www.paul.fr.*

$$$ ✕ **Le Petit Beur.** If you're looking for genuine local food, Le Petit Beur
MOROCCAN (aka Dar Tagine) has it all: couscous, brochettes, tagines, and *harira* (a
bean-based soup with vegetables and meat) served in a friendly, casual
setting. The pretty tiled walls and painted ceilings add a further level of
authenticity. **Known for:** high-caliber Moroccan menu; bustling atmosphere; affordable prices. Ⓢ *Average main: 140DH* ✉ *8, rue Damas,
Centre Ville* ☎ *0537/73–13–22* ⊕ *www.lepetitbeur.ma.*

$$$$ ✕ **Picolo's.** This friendly Mediterranean-style restaurant serves a broad
MEDITERRANEAN selection of fish, meat, and pasta dishes in a charming setting. White
linens top the tables in the cheery dining room; and the beautiful airy
garden, where intimate tables snuggle amid the greenery, is a delight.
Known for: discerning staff; lovely tapas; great for outside dining. Ⓢ *Average main: 250DH* ✉ *149, rte. des Zaers, Souissi* ☎ *0537/63–69–69.*

$$$$ ✕ **Restaurant Cosmopolitan.** Set in an exquisite Art Deco villa, this restau-
FRENCH rant focuses on refined French cuisine. Al fresco diners can choose a seat
on the swish yet sunny garden patio; inside, the dining rooms stretch
out with French poise. **Known for:** fantastic 1930s-style dining areas;
decadent dessert menu; sophisticated atmsophere. Ⓢ *Average main:
180DH* ✉ *Av. Ibn Toumart, Centre Ville* ☎ *0537/20–00–28.*

$ ✕ **Tajine wa Tanjia.** This is the place to discover a delicacy from Mar-
MOROCCAN rakesh—the *tanjia* (a type of casserole cooked in a large earthen
jar)—along with other authentic Moroccan dishes. It's cozy and
friendly, with very reasonable prices. **Known for:** bustling atmosphere; friendly, unpretentious service; Moroccan music. Ⓢ *Average
main: 80DH* ✉ *9, rue Baghdad, Hassan* ☎ *0537/72–97–97* ▭ *No
credit cards* ⊗ *Closed Sun.*

$$ ✕ **T'y Potes.** Set among verdant gardens, this enchanting eatery offers
FRENCH a menu that encapsulates the Brittany region of France: think luscious
Fodor's Choice salads and buckwheat crepes oozing with all you can imagine, as long
★ as it's (mostly) French. You can also try another regional specialty,
tartines—open sandwiches with fancy spreads. **Known for:** Breton-
style ingredients; great daily specials; good wine list. Ⓢ *Average main:
90DH* ✉ *11, rue Ghafsa, Hassan* ☎ *0537/70–79–65* ⊕ *www.typotes.
com* ⊗ *No dinner Sun.–Wed.*

WHERE TO STAY

$$ ⌂ **Riad Azhara.** This exceptionally original riad has only four rooms
HOTEL spread over an enormous and incredibly stylish space. **Pros:** attractive
old-meets-new look; intimate atmosphere; lovely terraces. **Cons:** some
might find contemporary accents jarring; open stairwells hazardous for
small children; parts of the terrace don't have barriers. Ⓢ *Rooms from:
970DH* ✉ *11, rue Skaia Belmekki, Medina* ☎ *0537/20–20–28* ⊕ *www.
riadazahra.com* ⇥ *4 rooms* ⫟⊖| *Breakfast.*

$$
HOTEL
Fodor's Choice
★
⊞ Riad Kalaa. A gorgeous interior courtyard plus a relaxing terrace with a small plunge pool and views of Rabat's rooftops help make this 17th-century medina house one of the most beautiful riads in town. **Pros:** an idyllic haven; very stylish; great service. **Cons:** may be difficult to find (the riad will send someone to meet you on request); if there's a party on the terrace, it can be noisy; watch your head if your sleeping area is in a mezzanine. $ *Rooms from: 1180DH* ⊠ *3–5, rue Zebdi, Medina* ☎ *0537/20–20–28* ⊕ *www.riadkalaa.com* ⟿ *15 rooms* ❑ *Breakfast.*

$
B&B/INN
⊞ Riad Marhaba. This comfy, recently refurbished spot has a welcoming atmosphere and attractive rooms that retain their medina-esque architectual features. **Pros:** friendly atmosphere; comfortable rooms with a local look; pleasant rooftop terrace. **Cons:** a little tricky to find; as with all medina houses, rooms can be somewhat dark; medinas are pedestrianized, so arrange a porter if your bags are too heavy. $ *Rooms from: 450DH* ⊠ *Rue Açam, Medina* ☎ *0537/70–65–54* ⊕ *www.riadmarhaba. com* ▭ *No credit cards* ⟿ *4 roooms* ❑ *Breakfast.*

$$$$
HOTEL
⊞ Sofitel Rabat Jardin des Roses. Right near the Royal Palace, this large yet peaceful luxury lodging allows guests to escape the city's bustle because it's surrounded by 17 gorgeous acres that include parkland, eucalyptus forest, and, of course, the rose gardens for which the hotel is named. **Pros:** a true luxury hotel; beautiful grounds; tranquil atmosphere. **Cons:** expensive; won't appeal to those looking for smaller, more intimate lodgings; relatively far from public transport. $ *Rooms from: 2080DH* ⊠ *Quartier Aviation, Souissi* ☎ *0537/67–56–56* ⊕ *www. sofitel.com* ⟿ *229 rooms* ❑ *No meals.*

$$$$
HOTEL
⊞ La Tour Hassan. If you want a luxury hotel that reflects classic Moroccan style, the Tour Hassan is ideal. **Pros:** near the city center; authentic decor; soothing gardens. **Cons:** rather expensive; rooms in north wing are near a bar and can be loud; some rooms are a little small. $ *Rooms from: 2100DH* ⊠ *26, rue Chellah, Hassan* ☎ *0537/23–90–00* ⊕ *www. latourhassan.com* ⟿ *140 rooms* ❑ *No meals.*

$$$$
HOTEL
Fodor's Choice
★
⊞ Villa Diyafa Boutique Hotel. Pampering is the name of the game at this modern boutique hotel, located in a tranquil area not far from the Royal Palace. **Pros:** fantastic facilities; comfortable, well-appointed rooms; great service. **Cons:** rather pricey; a little far the town center; only 10 suites, so may book up fast. $ *Rooms from: 5500DH* ⊠ *Rue Bani Yadder* ☎ *0538/05–08–00* ⊕ *www.villadiyafa.com* ⟿ *10* ❑ *Breakfast.*

$$$$
HOTEL
Fodor's Choice
★
⊞ Villa Mandarine. Located in a residential neighborhood, this spectacular villa offers all you need to be truly at ease: smart hosts, savvy fellow guests, and outstanding classic-meets-contemporary French and Moroccan cuisine. **Pros:** romantic setting; good on-site facilities, including a relaxing hammam; beautiful gardens. **Cons:** expensive rates; away from the town center, so not ideal for those wanting proximity to nightlife or shopping; limited public transportation. $ *Rooms from: 2141DH* ⊠ *19, rue Ouled Bousbaa, Souissi* ☎ *0537/75–20–77* ⊕ *www.villaman-darine.com* ⟿ *36 rooms* ❑ *Breakfast.*

Rabat's Kasbah des Oudayas is visible behind fishing boats overturned on the banks of the Oued Bou Regreg.

NIGHTLIFE

BARS AND CLUBS

Amnesia. Drawing a party-loving crowd, the city's original nightclub has been going strong for well over 25 years and shows no sign of stopping. If you're after something lively, look no further. ⊠ *18, rue Monastire, Centre Ville* ☎ *0671/14–42–55* ⊕ *www.amnesiarabat.com.*

Fodor'sChoice ★ **Le Bistrot du Pietri.** Inside the Pietri Urban Hotel, Rabat's most popular jazz restaurant features superb musicians every Friday and Saturday night. Expect anything from bebop and Latin to jazz fusion. The food is excellent, too, with the menu embodying a good deal of Mediterranean taste and some genuine inventiveness from the chef. ⊠ *4, rue Tobrouk, Centre Ville* ☎ *0537/73–71–44* ⊕ *lepietri.com/restaurant.*

Le Dhow. Permanently moored on the Bou Regreg River, this boat has several decks on which you can eat, drink, and people-watch. Naturally, the nautical theme is distinct. At night, the nearby Oudayas Kasbah illuminates the twinkling lights of the walled medina across the street. ⊠ *Quai de Bou Regreg, Av. Al Marsa, Medina* ☎ *0537/70–23–02* ⊕ *www.ledhow.com.*

5ème Avenue. Complete with wannabe models and DJs spinning tunes into the early hours, this perennial favorite attracts Rabat's see-and-be-seen set. ⊠ *4, av. Bin Al Ouidane, Centre Ville* ☎ *0679/72–16–03.*

O'Goethe 2.0. Part of the Goethe Institute, this combination bar-restaurant-cultural hub is packed every night. Drinks and food are reasonably priced, and the interior is charming. Head over when there's live music for extra conviviality. ⊠ *26, rue Oqba Ibn Nafiq* ☎ *0537/68–21–84.*

Upstairs Bar. Always a high-spirited place, this English pub-style bar gets even livelier when live musical events are staged. ✉ *8, av. Michliffen, Agdal* ☎ *0537/67–41–11.*

SHOPPING

In addition to offering Moroccan furniture, clothing, artwork, and locally made crafts, Rabat, like other major cities here, is becoming more and more European in terms of shopping options. The Agdal neighborhood has a high concentration of furniture and antiques stores, while the lower part of **Avenue Mohammed V** is a good place to buy traditional Moroccan garments.

CRAFTS

Ensemble Artisanal. Near the River Bou Regreg is a series of small workshops where you can see artisans create Morocco's various handicrafts. You'll find everything from traditional mosaic tilework, embroidery, leatherwork, and painted wood to brass, pottery, and carpets. Items can be purchased hassle-free at fixed prices, which are a little higher than the well-negotiated ones in nearby Rue des Consuls. ✉ *6, Tarik el Marsa, Espace les Oudayas, Medina* ☎ *0537/73–05–07* 💰 *Free.*

Fenyadi. This high-end boutique sells exquisite household creations—both traditional and contemporary—that encapsulate refined and inventive Moroccan design. From ceramics to candles, expect incomparably stylish objects of desire. ✉ *34, rue du 16 Novembre, Agdal* ☎ *0537/67–14–64* ⊕ *www.fenyadi.com* ☙ *Closed Sun.*

Rue des Consuls. The medina's Rue des Consuls is the place to shop for handicrafts and souvenirs in Rabat: it's pedestrian-only, has a pleasant atmosphere, and imposes no real pressure to buy, aside from the typical encouragements. Among the treasures here are Berber jewelry, leather goods, wooden items, brass work, traditional clothing, and slippers. You can also peruse Zemour carpets (striped in white and burgundy) from Khémisset, near Meknès; deep-pile Rabati carpets, in predominantly blue-and-white designs; and orange, black, and white Glaoui rugs. Some of the larger shops take credit cards. ■ TIP→ **Try to visit on a Monday or Thursday morning when the entire street turns into a carpet market.** ✉ *Medina.*

HAMMAMS

Hammam & Spa Dar El Kebira. Lodged amid a cluster of medina houses, this spa offers an authentic hammam experience along with a host of other pampering treatments, including ones that utilize henna and traditional ghassoul clay. ✉ *1, rue des consuls, Impasse Belghazi* ☎ *0537/72–49–06* ⊕ *www.darelkebira.com/en/luxury-riad-rabat-services/hammam-spa.*

SHOPPING CENTERS AND MALLS

Mega Mall. If you're looking for a more familiar type of retail therapy, Rabat's Mega Mall will do the trick. Following the design of a typical American mall, it contains dozens of mid- to high-end stores, plus a food court, bowling alley, and ice-skating rink. ✉ *Km 4.2, Av. Mohamed VI, Souissi* ☎ *0537/75–75–75* ⊕ *www.megamall.ma.*

SPORTS AND THE OUTDOORS

GOLF

Fodor's Choice ★ **Royal Golf Dar es Salam.** Morocco's most famous golf club is on the road toward Romani, at the far edge of the Souissi area. Designed by Robert Trent Jones and ranked among the best in the world, it includes two 18-hole courses and one 9-hole course in 162 verdant acres. ⊠ *Km 9, Av. Mohamed VI – Rte. des Zaers, Souissi* ☎ *0537/75–58–64* ⊕ *www. royalgolfdaressalam.com.*

AROUND RABAT

Rabat is an easy city to be in; however, it's still a busy hub, with all the noise and bustle that entails. So you may find yourself wanting to take a break nearby. Crossing the river to the twin city of Salé—where you can absorb Morocco's history and living traditions with little hassle—is an obvious choice. What's more, within minutes of it lie the Jardins Exotiques, a veritable botanical paradise. For ocean lovers, splendid beaches aren't far away either; head north or south and in no time you'll find fine stretches of golden sand and wild Atlantic waters.

SKHIRAT BEACH

20 km (12 miles) southwest of Rabat.

Southwest of Rabat, toward Casablanca, is lovely Skhirat Beach. Because it's close to the capital, Skhirat is perfect for either an afternoon by the sea or a weekend away. Home to the luxurious L'Amphitrite Palace Hotel, it's also the site of the 1971 attempt to assassinate the former King Hassan II during his birthday gala at the Royal Palace of Skhirat.

While it's easiest to reach Skhirat by car, you can take the train from Rabat Ville station to Bouznika station. From there, grab a cab to the Plage Bouznika (5 DH). Grands taxis also run from Rabat to Skhirat (9 DH).

EXPLORING

Contrabandiers Beach. Connected to Temara Plage by a walkway across the rocks, pretty Contrabandiers Beach draws throngs of sunbathers, swimmers, and surfers in summer. As is always the case on this coastline, currents can be extremely dangerous, so don't plan to take a dip unless you're a strong swimmer. Locals will rent you a beach umbrella, and there are usually several vendors who walk up and down the sand selling ice cream and other snacks. **Amenities:** food and drink; lifeguards (in summer); parking. **Best for:** swimming; surfing; walking. ⊠ *Skhirat.*

Dar Es-Soltane Cave (*Les Grôttes de Harhoura*). On the coastal road, across from Contrabandiers Beach, is a cave with iron railings in front. This spot, known as El Harhoura or Dar Es-Soltane, is one of the earliest identified sites of human habitation. Casts of the prehistoric human skeletons discovered here in the 1930s by Armand Ruhlmann are on display in the Museum of History and Civilisation. ⊠ *Av. Moustapha Assayeh, Temara.*

Skhirat Plage. To say that Skhirat Plage is loved by Moroccans during the summer months—and by some faithful souls year-round—is quite the understatement. The long stretch of fine, golden sand lying just beyond the Royal Palace of Skhiratis is perfect for strolls but also a known a surfing spot, as the plethora of boards reveals. Swimmers love it, too, but beware of dangerous currents—lifeguards are not always present. **Amenities:** food and drink; lifeguards (in summer); parking. **Best for:** swimming; surfing; walking. ⊠ *Skhirat.*

FAMILY **Temara Plage.** This cute little beach can be empty during colder months, but it's very much the opposite in summer. Aside from near-perfect sand, Temara Plage has a bank of rocks for those into rockpooling. It can be reached by car from the R322 from Rabat, or from the highway. Otherwise, take the train from Rabat and get off at Temara station; the beach is a short walk away. **Amenities:** food and drink; lifeguards (in summer); parking. **Best for:** sunsets; swimming; walking. ⊠ *Rabat.*

WHERE TO STAY

$$ **L'Amphitrite Palace.** This sleek luxury hotel is tantamount to a palace
HOTEL on a splendid beach—one where you can watch surfers, chat with fishermen, and soak in the crashing Atlantic before retiring to a tasteful room that is well-appointed and well-equipped. **Pros:** modern building; fresh decor; beautiful beach. **Cons:** an expensive option; service isn't always the best; very large so lacks the personal atmosphere of cozier places. $ *Rooms from: 1500DH* ⊠ *Skhirat Plage, Skhirat* ☎ *0537/62–10–00* ⊕ *www.lamphitrite-palace.com* ➳ *192 rooms* ⦿ *Breakfast.*

OUED CHERRAT

36 km (22 miles) from Rabat.

Oued Cherrat is a small beach area with superb ocean views and excellent surf conditions. Once a wild and relatively unfrequented stretch of sand, it's now a lot more popular and development is truly underway, although it's still less crowded than other North Atlantic beaches during the summer months.

GETTING HERE AND AROUND

Coming by car, take the highway from Rabat toward Casablanca, taking the Bouznika exit and then the coastal road toward Oued Cherrat. You can also take a train from Rabat Ville station; they leave each hour, on the hour, to Bouznika station. From there, taxis to the Plage Oued Cherrat are around 7 DH. Grands taxis also go from Rabat to Bouznika (15 DH).

EXPLORING

Bouznika Bay. This bay is one of the prettiest in the region and much loved by both Rabat and Casablanca locals. For this reason, it gets exceptionally crowded when the weather is hot and everyone hits the golden sands and surfers stream into the waves. It's a lovely place out of season too—perfect for picnicking and rockpooling (exploring the tide pools). During summer, there is a good selection of restaurants and cafés. **Amenities:** food and drink; lifeguards; parking. **Best for:** surfing; swimming; walking. ⊠ *Plage de Bouznika, Rabat.*

SALÉ

37 km (23 miles) southwest of Kenitra, 13 km (8 miles) northeast of Rabat across river.

Salé, the country's second-most-populated city, is a great place to experience unspoiled, hassle-free Moroccan culture. It was probably founded around the 11th century, and in medieval times became the premier trading harbor on this part of the Atlantic coast. At the beginning of the 17th century, it joined Rabat in welcoming Muslims expelled from Spain. The two were rivals for more than 100 years following this, but Rabat eventually gained the upper hand. Today Salé is rather shabby, but still an important cradle of Moroccan history. The medina alone is worth the journey both for its monuments and its authenticity. Expect to see more people in traditional dress or practicing traditional crafts than you would in most other Moroccan large-city medinas.

GETTING HERE AND AROUND
The Rabat–Salé tramway provides the ideal option for traveling between the two cities, costing just 6 DH per ride. Buses and taxis are also options.

TIMING AND PRECAUTIONS
Most travelers visit Salé just for the day. It's a relatively safe city, with very little harassment; however, if you do feel threatened, don't hesitate to summon police.

EXPLORING
Salé's most interesting sights are located in and around the medina—and there are plenty of them. A good place to start your tour is at the entrance to the medina, near the Great Mosque, which you can access from the road along the southwest city wall. Don't worry if you lose track of where you are within the medina; many a shop will distract you, but you're never far from an entry gate. If you feel like traveling a little farther afield, the Jardins Exotiques to the north of the city are well worth a visit.

Abou el Hassan Merenid Medersa. Turn left around the corner of the Great Mosque, and you'll see on your right the Abou el Hassan Medersa. Built by the Merenid sultan of that name in the 14th century, it's a fine example of the traditional Koranic school. Like the Bou Inania in Fez or the Ben Youssef in Marrakesh, this medersa has beautiful intricate plasterwork around its central courtyard, and a fine *mihrab* (prayer niche) with a ceiling carved in an interlocking geometrical pattern representing the cosmos. Upstairs, on the second and third floors, you can visit the little cells where the students used to sleep, and from the roof you can see the entire city. ⌧ *Rue Ash al Shaiara* 🖃 *10 DH.*

Battlements and Fortresses of Salé. A heavily fortified town for centuries, Salé still has many traces of its eventful history preserved within the old medina walls. Many landmarks in the area have been named as national heritage sites or monuments. **Borj Bab Sebta** is an 11th-century, square-shaped fortress situated at the Sebta gate into the old medina. **Borj Adoumoue,** also called the Old Sqala, is an 18th-century bastion, where cannons gaze over the waters to this day. **Borj Roukni,** also called Borj Kbira, or the large fortress, is a semicircular, 19th-century edifice built to counter attacks by the French. **Borj al-Mellah** is at the entrance to the old Jewish quarter. There's also a fantastic kasbah (although in need of preservation) known as the **Gnawa Kasbah,** built by Moulay Ismail in the 1700s. ✉ *Medina.*

Fodor's Choice ★ **Complexe des Potiers.** Salé has long been known throughout the country, and beyond, for its local pottery. At this particular complex (just off the road toward Fez, to the right after the river from Rabat) visitors can browse through a whole series of pottery shops, each with its own style; you might also get the chance to chat with a potter or maybe even try your own hand at clay work. Other crafts have been added as well, notably bamboo and straw work and mosaic-tile furnishings. ✉ *Oulja, Rte. Ain Houalla.*

Djemâa Kabir (*Great Mosque*). A few steps from the tomb of Sidi Abdellah ben Hassoun is the great mosque known as Djemâa Kabir. Built by the Almohad dynasty in the 12th century, this beautiful structure is the third-largest mosque in Morocco after the Hassan II in Casablanca and the Kairaouine in Fez. Non-Muslims cannot enter. ✉ *Zanqat Sidi Abdellah ben Hassoun.*

FAMILY Fodor's Choice ★ **Jardins Exotiques.** Near Sidi-Bouknadel, 9 km (5½ miles) north of Salé, you'll find the extraordinary Jardins Exotiques, which were created in the mid-20th century by a Frenchman named Marcel François, who used to play classical music to his plants. Planned to represent different regions (like Polynesia, Brazil, or Japan), the gardens are a haven for birds and frogs. The profusion of walkways and bridges makes them a wonderful playground for children, too. Since François's death in 1999, the property has been maintained by the government, and a touching autobiographical poem forms his epitaph at the entrance. ✉ *Km 13, Rte. de Kenitra, Sidi-Bouknadel* ☎ *0537/82–27–56* 🌐 *www.jardinsexotiques.com* 🎟 *15 DH.*

Sidi Abdellah ben Hassoun Tomb. One of the streets in Salé's medina is Zanqat Sidi Abdellah ben Hassoun—named after the town's patron saint. His magnificent tomb is situated here. He died in Salé in 1604. ✉ *Zanqat Sidi Abdellah ben Hassoun.*

Zaouia Tijania. Just before the tomb of Sidi Abdellah ben Hassoun is the *zaouia* (an Islamic school) of the Tijani order, a mystical Sufi Islamic sect founded by Shaykh Ahmad al-Tijani (1739–1815). ✉ *Zanqat Sidi Abdellah ben Hassoun.*

WHERE TO EAT AND STAY

$$$$ MEDITERRANEAN 🍴 **Al Marsa.** When Salé's marina was built, it brought with it a couple of swanky restaurants including Al Marsa—meaning "port" in Arabic—which serves Spanish food in a glass-encased dining room overlooking the River Bou Regreg. The menu is based on fish and seafood, the produce is fresh, and the dishes imaginative. **Known for:** stunning views; buzzy, European-style atmosphere; great paella. [$] *Average main: 220DH* ✉ *Port de Plaisance, Marina de Bou Regreg* ☎ *0537/84–58–18.*

$ HOTEL FAMILY Fodor's Choice ★ **The Repose.** This outstanding riad is a veritable sanctuary set over three floors and run by a lovely Anglo-Moroccan couple. **Pros:** exceptional food; beautiful, restful environment; excellent service. **Cons:** can be hard to find; only four rooms, so fills up fast; in a pedestrianized area, so no transport right to the door. [$] *Rooms from: 495DH* ✉ *17, Zankat Talaâ, Ras Chejra, Medina* ☎ *0537/88–29–58* 🌐 *www.therepose.com* 🛏 *4 rooms* 🍴 *Some meals.*

SHOPPING

Souk Laghzal. A couple of times a week, usually Tuesday and Thursday, an auction is held in the wool market square. At this quirky event, a crowd sits in a circle around the auctioneer, who sells off an unpredictable array of items that might include an old kaftan, a plastic chandelier, or a beautiful pottery piece—you never can guess. A jumble sale with heaps of low-priced clothing takes place nearby. As the square's name would suggest, this is also a wool area; you can buy dyed wool on one side of the square and wool products (carpets and the like) on the other. ✉ *Medina.*

SIDI-BOUKNADEL

18 km (11 miles) northeast of Rabat.

Sidi-Bouknadel (also known as Bouknadel) isn't accessible from the autoroute, but its attractions lie to the north, halfway between Kenitra and Rabat, and are accessible via the coastal road from either of the two.

GETTING HERE AND AROUND

Taxis run regularly from Salé to Sidi-Bouknadel in summer. If traveling from Rabat by bus, board Bus No. 13 at Avenue Moulay Hassan in Rabat. You can take the same bus back to Rabat from Sidi-Bouknadel. Taxis can be chartered to and from Rabat, Salé, and Kenitra throughout the year.

TIMING AND PRECAUTIONS

Most travelers visit Sidi-Bouknadel for the day en route to Rabat or on their way north. Sidi-Bouknadel is generally safe, with minimal hassling of visitors. The beach, however, is rather secluded after sundown, so caution is advised for those desiring an evening walk on the shore.

EXPLORING

FAMILY Fodor's Choice ★ **Jardins Exotiques.** Near Sidi-Bouknadel, 9 km (5½ miles) north of Salé, you'll find the extraordinary Jardins Exotiques, which were created in the mid-20th century by a Frenchman named Marcel François, who used to play classical music to his plants. Planned to represent different regions (like Polynesia, Brazil, or Japan), the gardens are a haven for birds and frogs. The profusion of walkways and bridges makes them a wonderful playground for children, too. Since François's death in 1999, the property has been maintained by the government, and a touching autobiographical poem forms his epitaph at the entrance. ✉ *Km 13, Rte. de Kenitra* ☎ *0537/82–27–56* 🌐 *www.jardinsexotiques.com* 🎟 *15 DH.*

MOULAY BOUSSELHAM

46 km (29 miles) southwest of Larache, 82 km (51 miles) northeast of Kenitra, 150 km (93 miles) northeast of Rabat.

Made up of little more than a single street with a smattering of cafés and souvenir shops, the laid-back fishing village of Moulay Bousselham is virtually empty in the cooler months but very popular with Moroccans in summer. Its lagoon and beach are breathtaking, and its sandbar (a potential hazard for swimmers) creates a continual crash of breaking waves. This is also one of northern Morocco's prime bird-watching locations, with boat trips organized to see thousands of herons, pink flamingos, sheldrakes, and gannets. The whole area is considered a wetland protected by the Ramsar Convention (an international treaty working for the conservation of wetlands) as well as by the village's two patron saints.

4

GETTING HERE AND AROUND

Moulay Bousselham has a train station with daily service from Larache and Rabat. There are frequent buses and taxis to Moulay Bousselham from Souk el-Arba du Rharb, which is accessible from Rabat and Larache by grand taxi.

TIMING AND PRECAUTIONS

Most travelers stay in Moulay Bousselham for a couple of nights. It's generally considered safe, with most annoyances stemming from vendors hawking their wares. But the village becomes desolate after sundown, so it's wise to take the usual precautions.

EXPLORING

Merdja Zerga (*Blue Lagoon*). Moulay Bousselham is at the head of Merdja Zerga (the Blue Lagoon), which gives its name to the surrounding 17,000-acre national park. This region is a major stopover for countless birds migrating from Norway, Sweden, and the United Kingdom to Africa: the birds fly south at the end of summer and stop at Merdja Zerga in September, October, and November before continuing on to West Africa and even South Africa. They stop off again on their way back to Europe in spring, so spring and fall are the times for bird-watching. The pink flamingos on their way to and from Mauritania are particularly spectacular. ✉ *Moulay Bousselham.*

Moulay Bousselham's Tomb. At the foot of the village, near the sea, you'll find the tomb of Moulay Bousselham. Like Sidi Abdel Jalil's somewhat smaller one, it is a white building capped with a dome. ✉ *Moulay Bousselham.*

WHERE TO STAY

$ B&B/INN 🏨 **La Maison des Oiseaux.** Notable for having a beautiful garden right opposite the lagoon, the cute but rather faded "Bird House" is a low-key B&B with a few basic rooms, a library, and an artist's studio upstairs. **Pros:** friendly atmosphere; unpretentious accommodations; very genuine welcome. **Cons:** can be difficult to find; basic but presentable rooms; little to do in the area after nightfall. [$] *Rooms from: 350DH* ✉ *BP 66* ☎ *0537/43–25–43* 🌐 *moulay.bousselham.free.fr/la_maison_des_oiseaux.html* 💳 *No credit cards* 🛏 *8 rooms (6 with bath)* 🍴 *Breakfast.*

$$ **Vila Bea.** Offering staggering lagoon views and a bright retro-esque
HOTEL style, this bewitching hotel has all the requisite elements of a relaxing
retreat. **Pros:** stylish decor; excellent service; incomparable views. **Cons:**
expensive for the area; little to do in the way of social life; few din-
ing options outside the hotel. $ *Rooms from: 1180DH* ✉ *41, front de
mer, Moulay Bousselham* ☎ *0537/43–20–87* ⊕ *www.vilabea.com* ⇔ *7
rooms* ⍟ *Breakfast.*

CASABLANCA

91 km (57 miles) southwest of Rabat.

Casablanca is Morocco's most modern city, and diverse groups of peo-
ple call it home: hardworking Berbers who came north from the Souss
Valley to make their fortune; older folks raised on French customs
during the Protectorate; wealthy business executives in the prestigious
neighborhoods of California and Anfa; new and poor arrivals from the
countryside, living in conspicuous shantytowns; and thousands of oth-
ers from all over the kingdom who have found jobs here. There is also
a large community of expats—most of them French. The city has its
own stock exchange, and working hours tend to transcend the relaxed
pace kept by the rest of Morocco.

True to its name—*casa blanca* in Spanish (white house), which, in
turn, is Dar el-Beida in Arabic—the city is a conglomeration of white
buildings. Present-day Casablanca, known colloquially as "Casa" or
"El Beida," was only founded in 1912, so it lacks the abundance of
ancient monuments that resonate in Morocco's other major urban
centers; however, there are still some landmarks, including the famous
Hassan II Mosque.

GETTING HERE AND AROUND

AIR TRAVEL

From overseas, Casablanca's Mohammed V Airport is the busiest gate-
way to Morocco itself: you'll find a modern arrivals hall, relatively
efficient and usually courteous staffers, and a not-so-complicated con-
tinuation of your journey by train or car. Passport control can be very
slow, however. Trains connect the airport to the national network from
7:35 am to 10:30 pm (although you should always check online for
changes); taxis are available to the city of Casablanca at comparatively
expensive but fixed rates (250 DH–300 DH).

Airport Contacts Mohammed V Airport. ✉ *Nouasseur* ☎ *0522/53–90–40*
⊕ *www.onda.ma/en/Our-Airports/Casablanca-Mohammed-V-Airport.*

BUS TRAVEL

Buses are fine for short trips, like Casablanca to El Jadida or Safi, but
trips longer than a couple of hours can be interminable, hot, and dusty.
Inquire at the station for schedule and fare information. In Casablanca
the Compagnie de Transports au Maroc (CTM) bus station is by far the
most convenient, because the other stations are on the outskirts of town.

Bus Contacts CTM Casablanca. ✉ *23, rue Léon l'Africain, Centre Ville*
☎ *0800/09–00–30* ⊕ *www.ctm.ma.*

The Legend of the Blue Lagoon

The legend of the Blue Lagoon and Moulay Bousselham dates from the 10th century, when the saint Saïd ben Saïd immigrated to the Maghreb from Egypt, following a revelation instructing him to pray where the sun sets over the ocean. He had a disciple called Sidi Abdel Jalil who, according to the story, saw Saïd ben Saïd fishing with a hook and asked him why a man with such great powers needed one. To show that he required no aids himself, Sidi Abdel Jalil put his hands into the water and pulled out fish as numerous as the hairs on his hand. Provoked by this act, Saïd ben Saïd took off his *selham* (cloak), swept it along the ground, called out, "Sea, follow me," and proceeded to walk inland. He did not stop until he had walked 10 km (6 miles). The sea followed him, and so the lagoon was formed. After this, Saïd ben Saïd was called Moulay Bousselham—"Lord, Owner of the Cloak." Both Moulay Bousselham and Sidi Abdel Jalil are buried in the town.

CAR TRAVEL

You may not want a car if you are staying in Casablanca, as driving here is almost a hazardous sport. However, it is possible to rent one if you are planning to explore the country. Others may prefer moving onto their next destination, such as Fez or Marrakesh, before picking up a vehicle.

Rental Cars Avis. ⊠ *19, av. des Forces Armées Royales, Centre Ville* ☎ *0522/31–24–24* ⊕ *www.avis.com.*

TRAIN TRAVEL

Casablanca has three train stations: Casablanca Port, Casablanca, and Casablanca l'Oasis (the former two both downtown, the latter in the Oasis neighborhood). By train you can travel quickly and pleasantly to Marrakesh, Fez, Rabat, Tangier, and smaller towns like El Jadida and Azemmour. Direct trains from the airport go to both Casa Voyageurs and l'Oasis. Trains to Rabat depart every half-hour (the train is by far the best way to move between Casablanca and the capital). Casablanca is less than three hours by train from Marrakesh (nine trains daily), 3½ hours from Meknès (eight trains daily), and 4½ hours from Fez (nine trains daily). In addition, there are overnight trains from Casablanca to Oujda (three daily, 10 hours) and direct trains daily to Tangier (three daily, six hours). However, you should always check online for changes to timetables.

Contacts Office National des Chemins de Fer, Casa-Oasis (*O.N.C.F.*). ⊠ *Rte. de l'Oasis* ☎ *22–55* ⊕ *www.oncf.ma.* **Office National des Chemins de Fer, Casa-Port** (*O.N.C.F.*). ⊠ *Bd. Houphouet Boigny, Medina* ☎ *22–55* ⊕ *www.oncf. ma.* **Office National des Chemins de Fer, Casa-Voyageurs** (*O.N.C.F.*). ⊠ *Bd. Ba Hmad, Centre Ville* ☎ *22–55* ⊕ *www.oncf.ma.*

TRAM TRAVEL

The tramway has given this city something to be very proud of: it's safe, clean, affordable, and runs on time, which is no mean feat here. With the tram, you can easily navigate from some of Casablanca's major locations, such as the Ain Diab beach area, the old pedestrianized town center around boulevard Mohammed V, and the old medina. It also makes a link between some of the city's more affluent areas and the less salubrious suburbs. For now, the tram comprises 48 stations that run along one major line that forks at one end, meaning there are three possible termini. The website includes a route finder and downloadable plan.

Tickets cost 6 DH. The tram runs from 5:30 am to 10:30 pm on weekdays and until 11:30 pm on weekends. ⊕ *www.casatramway.ma.*

GUIDES AND TOURS

Contacts Visit Morocco. ⊠ *3, rue Ahmed Ben Bouchta, Val d'Anfa* ☎ *0522/36–16–32* ⊕ *www.visitmorocco.ma.*

TIMING AND PRECAUTIONS

Many visitors spend at least a couple of nights in Casablanca, often using it as a base to visit other places in the area. As in any large city, travelers should be cautious after dark when walking in the center and around the old medina. It is best to use a taxi late at night when returning from restaurants, bars, or nightclubs.

EXPLORING

TOP ATTRACTIONS

Fodor'sChoice   **Abderrahman Slaoui Museum.** One of the city's few museums, the Abderrahman Slaoui is hidden away in a splendid Art Deco villa. Permanent exhibits feature a collection of the nation's treasures, including delicate crystal perfume bottles, vintage prints, and 300-year-old jewelry from Fez. The museum also has a small café with lovely bay windows. Guided visits are available for 100 DH. ⊠ *12, rue du Parc, Centre Ville* ☎ *0522/20–62–17* ⊕ *www.musee-as.ma* ☜ *30 DH* ☉ *Closed Sun. and Mon.*

Habous. At the edge of the new medina, the Quartier des Habous is a curiously attractive mixture of French colonial architecture with Moroccan details built by the French at the beginning of the 20th century. Capped by arches, its shops surround a pretty square with trees and flowers. As you enter the Habous, you'll pass a building resembling a castle; this is the Pasha's Mahkama, or court, completed in 1952. The Mahkama formerly housed the reception halls of the Pasha of Casablanca, as well as a Muslim courthouse; it's currently used for district government administration. On the opposite side of the square is the Mohammed V Mosque—although not ancient, this and the 1938 Moulay Youssef Mosque, in the adjacent square, are among the finest examples of traditional Maghrebi (western North African) architecture in Casablanca. Look up at the minarets and you might recognize a style used in Marrakesh's Koutoubia Mosque and Seville's Giralda. Note also the fine wood carving over the door of the Mohammed V. The Habous is well known as a center for Arabic books; most of the other shops here are devoted to rich displays of traditional handicrafts aimed at locals and tourists. ■ TIP→ **This is the best place in Casabalanca to buy Moroccan handicrafts.** You can also purchase traditional Moroccan clothes such as kaftans and *djellabas* (long, hooded outer garments). Immediately north of the Habous is Casablanca's Royal Palace. You can't go inside, but the outer walls are pleasing; their sandstone blocks fit neatly together and blend well with the little streets at the edge of the Habous. ⊠ *Habous.*

DID YOU KNOW?

Casablanca's Hassan II Mosque, which was finished in 1993, is one of the largest mosques in the world and is graced by the tallest minaret.

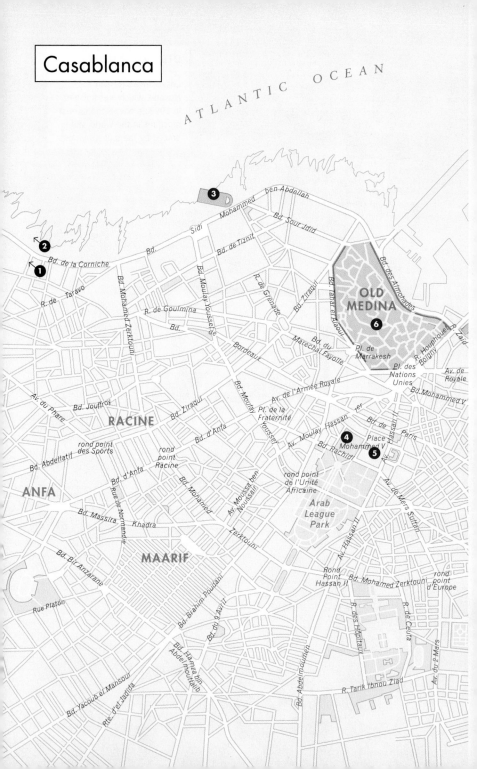

Port

0   1/4 mile

0   1/4 kilometer

Gare de
Casa Port

Bd. Moulay Abderrahmane
ou Hmad
l'Armée
Pl.
Zellaga

Bd. du Forbin

Pl.
Mirabeau

Av. Pasteur

CENTRE
VILLE

R. Karatch

Bd. Émile Zola

R. Mohammed Diouri

Bd. Mohammed V

Rte. Guelta
Zemmour

R. Mohammed
Smiha

Bd. Émile Zola

Bd. Mohammed V

Bd. Abdellah Ben Yacine

Av. Lalla
Yacout

Place
de la
Victoire

Bd. de Khouribga

R. Khattabi

Bd. Ibn Tachfine

Gare des
Voyageurs

Bd. de la Résistance

Bd. du 11 Janvier

R. Hadj
Amar Riffi

Pl.
Résistance

Bd. de la
Dubreuil
Lemalgre

Rte. des Oulad Ziane

Rte. de la Gironde

Rte. de Médiouna

R. de Rome

R. Ahmed el Figuigui

Royal
Palace

7
HABOUS

Hassan II Mosque. Casablanca's skyline is dominated by this massive edifice. No matter where you are, you're bound to see it thanks to its attention-grabbing green-tile roof. The building's foundations lie partly on land and partly in the sea, and at one point you can see the water through a glass floor. The main hall holds an astonishing 25,000 people and has a retractable roof so that it can be turned into a courtyard. The minaret is more than 650 feet high, and the mezzanine floor (which holds the women's section, about 6 feet above the main floor) seems dwarfed by the nearly 200-foot-high ceiling. Still, the ceiling's enormous painted decorations appear small and delicate from below.

Funded through public subscription, designed by a French architect, and built by a team of 35,000, the mosque went up between 1987 and 1993 and is one of the largest in the world, its minaret being the tallest. It was set in Casablanca primarily so that the largest city in the kingdom would have a monument worthy of its size. Except for Tin Maland, this is the only mosque in Morocco that non-Muslims are allowed to enter. ■TIP→ **If you fly out of Casablanca, try to get a window seat on the left for a good view of the mosque in relation to the city as a whole.** Right next to the mosque is the "mediatheque," which contains a fantastic public library and occasionally hosts talks and workshops. ⊠ *Bd. de la Corniche, Medina* ☎ *0522/48–28–86* ⊕ *www. mosquee-hassan2.com* ✉ *120 DH.*

Place Mohammed V. Casablanca's version of London's Trafalgar Square has illuminated fountains, plenty of pigeons, and a series of grand buildings. Coming from the port, you'll pass the main post office on your right, and on your left as you enter the square is its most impressive building, the courthouse, built in the 1920s. On the other side of Avenue Hassan II from the post office is the ornate Bank Al Maghrib; the structure opposite, with the clock tower, is the Wilaya, the governor's office. The more modest buildings on the right side of the square house the notorious customs directorate (where importers appeal punitive taxes). To avoid confusion, note that Place Mohammed V was formerly called Place des Nations Unies and vice versa, and the old names still appear on some maps. Now that the tram serves this area, it's easy to get here from nearly anywhere else in the city. ⊠ *Centre Ville.*

WORTH NOTING

Corniche. Get a feel for Casa's Atlantic setting by stopping at a Corniche café to relish the sun and breeze. On weekends, this area is bursting with people settling in the seafront line of cafés and restaurants, basking in the beach resorts, and walking up and down the wide pavement. In the evenings, nightclubs and bars open their doors for all kinds of partygoers. ⊠ *Ain Diab.*

NEED A
BREAK
✕ **La Sqala Cafe Maure.** Situated within an 18th-century Portuguese fortress, La Sqala enchants with its beautiful gardens, patio, greenery, and fountains. It may serve the best Moroccan breakfast in town, and if you want a quick snack while sightseeing, the pastries and mint tea are a great bet. ⊠ *Bd. des Almohades, Medina* ☎ *0522/26–09–60* ⊕ *resto-pro.ma/sqala.*

🍴 Venezia Ice. After strolling along the Corniche, take a break on trendy Venezia's terrace and enjoy one of their 60 flavors of ice creams and sorbets. There are several other branches in town, and the quality of frosty treats is faultless at all. ✉ *Above Tahiti Beach Club, La Corniche, Ain Diab* ☎ *0522/79–83–64.*

Old Medina. The simple whitewashed houses of the medina, particularly those closest to the harbor, form an extraordinary contrast to Morocco's economic and commercial nerve center just a few hundred yards away. European consuls lived here in the 19th century during the early trading days, and there is still a youth hostel and a few cheap hotels within. Today it boils over with busy Moroccan shoppers, vendors, and beggers. The medina has its own personality and charm, due in part to the fact that many Casa residents living in more affluent areas never set foot here. Near Place des Nations Unies a large conglomeration of shops sells watches, leather goods, crafted wood, and clothes. It's best avoided at night unless you're accompanied by a local you know well. ✉ *Medina.*

Sidi Abderrahman. If you follow the Corniche to its southwestern edge, you will see the tomb of Sidi Abderrahman, a Sufi saint, just off the coast on a tiny island. Moroccans come to this shrine if they are sick or if they feel they need to rid themselves of evil spirits. Before the bridge was built in 2013, it was accessible only at low tide, at which point you would simply walk to the small collection of white houses, built practically one on top of the other. Non-Muslims are allowed to visit and have their futures told by a resident fortune-teller, although access to the shrine itself is prohibited. The other side of the island is one of the most exciting places in Casablanca to sit and watch the wild Atlantic swell. Be sensitive to the people who live here, as they will not appreciate being taken for museum exhibits and may object to having their pictures taken. **■ TIP→ On the sands, just in front of the tomb, you can enjoy some snails, or pancakes if you prefer, and Moroccan mint tea along with the locals.** ✉ *Ain Diab.*

WHERE TO EAT

$$$$ FRENCH
🍴 A Ma Bretagne. This restaurant is along the Corniche, past Sidi Abderrahman, and serves French provincial cuisine. The setting is modern and elegant, with hardwood floors, sleek columns, and wall-to-wall sea-view windows. **Known for:** refined French ambience; stylish dining room; waterside setting. [$] *Average main: 215DH* ✉ *Bd. de la Corniche, Sidi Abderrahman, Ain Diab* ☎ *0522/36–21–12.*

$$$ MOROCCAN FAMILY
🍴 Al-Mounia. Casablanca's first and most cherished Moroccan restaurant has a lovely patio with a centuries-old tree. The excellent cooking is all local but with a refined touch. **Known for:** warm, convival service; traditional decor; a rare Moroccan restaurant in contemporary Casa. [$] *Average main: 130DH* ✉ *95, rue Prince Moulay Abdallah, Centre Ville* ☎ *0522/22–26–69* ⌚ *Closed Sun.*

$$ ITALIAN
🍴 Bacco e Venere. Priding itself on the use of authentic ingredients, this excellent Italian restaurant focuses on classic fare—namely perfect pizzas, fresh pasta, and, for bigger appetites, mouthwatering meat and

fish dishes. The antipasti and desserts are quintessentially Italian, too. **Known for:** lively atmosphere; clean, modern look; pizza cooked in a wood-burning oven. $ *Average main: 95DH* ⊠ *50, av. Hassan Souktani, Gauthier* ☎ *0522 /27–41–73* ⊕ *www.baccoevenere.com.*

$$$$ ✕ **Le Bistrot Chic.** This place prides itself on fine wines, treating customers
BISTRO to a fantastic range of options from France and beyond. There's a proper bistro ambience in the restaurant area, which offers reasonable prix-fixe menus for both lunch and dinner; the mezzanine bar, meanwhile, serves French-style tapas including a very respectable cheese board. **Known for:** informative staff; intimate atmosphere; elegant crowd. $ *Average main: 180DH* ⊠ *8, rue Taha Houcine, Gautier* ☎ *0522/29–78–78* ⊕ *www.bistrot-chic.com* ☾ *Closed Sun.*

$$$ ✕ **La Bodega.** Every night is fiesta night at La Bodega. Opposite the
TAPAS central market, this restaurant offers a warm and colorful atmosphere with a fun Latin flavor. **Known for:** high-quality Latin fare; tempting fixed-price menu at lunch; very lively atmosphere in the evenings. $ *Average main: 145DH* ⊠ *129, rue Allal ben Abdellah, Centre Ville* ☎ *0522/54–18–42* ⊕ *www.bodega.ma* ☾ *No lunch Sun.*

$$$$ ✕ **Brasserie la Bavaroise.** For a supreme culinary experience, head to
FRENCH Brasserie la Bavaroise where the menu is awash with delectable French
Fodor's Choice favorites, sumptuous steaks, sophisticated fish dishes, and beguiling
★ desserts. The restaurant has a contemporary look that's elegant without being stuffy and an atmosphere to match. **Known for:** exceptional French menu; handsome dining room; efficient yet unobtrusive service. $ *Average main: 220DH* ⊠ *133, rue Allal Ben Abdellah, Centre Ville* ☎ *0522/31–17–60* ⊕ *restopro.ma/bavaroise* ☾ *Closed Sun. dinner.*

$$$$ ✕ **Le Cabestan Ocean View.** Located right near the Corniche lighthouse,
FRENCH this restaurant focuses on fine Mediterranean cuisine. Its ocean views are spectacular, and you can look down from a window seat onto blue rock pools as you savor delicious fish dishes. **Known for:** stellar ocean views; glittering clientele; late-night music and dancing. $ *Average main: 220DH* ⊠ *90, bd. de la Corniche, Phare d'el Hank, Ain Diab* ☎ *0522/39–11–90* ⊕ *www.le-cabestan.com.*

$$$ ✕ **La Cantine de Charlotte.** A top choice in the well-heeled Gautier district,
MODERN FRENCH little Cantine de Charlotte showcases Chef Richard Meyniel's culinary
Fodor's Choice skills. The frequently changing menu is always a fabulous mix of refined
★ and innovative; and while there's a penchant for luxurious components (like lobster, asparagus, and oysters), there's also a good helping of fresh local ingredients. **Known for:** chic, laid-back ambience; intimate setting; fantastic wine list. $ *Average main: 160DH* ⊠ *3, rue Abou Adil El Allaf, Gautier* ☎ *0522/27–23–00* ☾ *Closed Sun.*

$$$ ✕ **Casa José.** This upscale Spanish tapas restaurant is a favorite among
SPANISH residents and always abuzz with diners and drinkers (which makes it a great place to meet true Casablancans). Products are local and fish is supplied daily, with typical options including calamari and patatas bravas; for those missing pork, there's even real chorizo. **Known for:** lively atmosphere; extensive menu; opens early for an afterwork crowd. $ *Average main: 130DH* ⊠ *Bd. Felix Houfouet Boigny, Centre Ville* ☎ *0522/29–70–12.*

$$
JAPANESE

✕ **Kayzen.** One of the city's best-loved Japanese restaurants serves a broad, reasonably priced array of options ranging from sushi to bento to tempura. While all of the classics are available, there's a little imagination injected into certain dishes, so you can be adventurous if the mood strikes. **Known for:** affordable prices; broad choice of dishes; good take-away and delivery menu. $ *Average main: 110DH* ✉ *Résidence Palais JJ, Rue Ahmed Charci* ☎ *0522/94–40–78.*

$$$$
THAI

✕ **Mai Thai.** Casablanca's adored Thai restaurant is frequented by a rather affluent clientele. Set in a renovated villa, it's booked up most nights thanks to its authentic Asian menu. **Known for:** imaginative Thai-fusion menu; stylish backdrop; congenial service. $ *Average main: 180DH* ✉ *408, bd. Driss Slaoui* ☎ *0522/95–02–34.*

$$
FRENCH FUSION

✕ **Paul.** An outpost of the popular French café, bakery, and restaurant group, Paul is housed in the beautiful Art Deco Villa Zevaco. Whether for breakfast, lunch, or afternoon tea, Paul's terrace is always full of customers who come to enjoy its fabulous garden and baked goods. **Known for:** extravagant breakfasts; friendly, efficient service; well-heeled clientele. $ *Average main: 90DH* ✉ *Angle Bd. d'Anfa at Bd. Moulay Rachid, Anfa* ☎ *0522/36–60–00* ⊕ *www.boulangeries-paul.com.*

$$$$
MEDITERRANEAN

✕ **Le Petit Rocher.** For fine dining or drinks with a fantastic view, the superelegant Petit Rocher is just the ticket: its unrivaled position lets you gaze over the sublime Atlantic waves and the Hassan II Mosque. Sample delicious, decidedly Mediterranean cuisine and good wine in the restaurant area, or settle down at the bar where fabulous cocktails are poured and a DJ often plays. **Known for:** exceptional ocean-side setting; well-crafted menu; after-dinner party atmosphere in the bar. $ *Average main: 220DH* ✉ *Complexe au Petit Rocher, Bd. de la Corniche, Ain Diab* ☎ *0522/36–26–26* ⊘ *Closed Sun. dinner.*

$$
SEAFOOD
FAMILY

✕ **Restaurant du Port de Peche.** Tucked away inside the port, this family-friendly spot is one of Casablanca's oldest fish restaurants and always draws a crowd at lunchtime. What to choose depends on what's been caught that day, so be sure to ask the waiters for advice. **Known for:** canteen-style ambience; no-nonsense service; reasonable prices. $ *Average main: 120DH* ✉ *Port de Pêche, Medina* ☎ *0522/31–85–61.*

$$$$
FRENCH
Fodor'sChoice
★

✕ **Le Rouget de l'Isle.** This exceptional French restaurant occupies an Art Deco villa set amid beautiful gardens. The menu lists elegant dishes, each edged with an element of luxury; the wine pairings are as refined as the food and the staff discrete yet congenial. **Known for:** peerless French dishes; exquisite vintage environment; sophisticated atmosphere. $ *Average main: 220DH* ✉ *16, rue Rouget de l'Isle, Centre Ville* ☎ *0522 /29–47–40* ⊘ *Closed Sun. No lunch Sat.*

$$
SEAFOOD

✕ **Taverne du Dauphin.** One of the city's most established fish-and-seafood restaurants, the Dauphin is a convivial alternative to more expensive eateries offering a similar menu. The prices—coupled with its placement in the town center, near the port and on the edge of the old medina—make it a bustling spot. **Known for:** yesteryear atmosphere and decor; fresh ingredients; unpretentious service. $ *Average main: 110DH* ✉ *115, bd. Félix Houphouet Boigny, Medina* ☎ *0522/22–12–00* ⊕ *www.taverne-du-dauphin.com* ⊘ *Closed Sun.*

4

Casablanca has lively nightlife and dining scenes.

$$ 🍴 **Tulik.** Conveniently positioned near one of the main shopping districts, Casablanca's original salad bar offers a breath of fresh air for travelers seeking a healthy lunch option. You can put your own together from fresh vegetables, proteins, and homemade dressings—vegetarians will have a field day. **Known for:** wholesome food; homemade options; take-out available. [$] *Average main: 80DH* ✉ *Rue Assilme, Racine* ☎ *0526/92–21–31* 💳 *No credit cards* 🕒 *Closed Sun. No dinner.*
CAFÉ

WHERE TO STAY

$$ 🏨 **Barceló Casablanca.** Ideally located on Casablanca's Boulevard Anfa, this hotel is perfect for business travelers, and several features (including meeting facilities) cater to them. **Pros:** very convenient location; business facilities on-site; upper-floor rooms have great city views. **Cons:** no spa, gym, or pool; can feel a little impersonal; off-site restaurants generally have more character. [$] *Rooms from: 1100DH* ✉ *139, bd. Anfa, Racine* ☎ *0522/20–80–00* 🌐 *www.barcelo.com* 🛏 *85 rooms* 🍴 *Breakfast.*
HOTEL

$$$ 🏨 **Hotel & Spa Le Doge.** A refuge amid the cacophony of Casablanca, this Relais & Chateaux boutique hotel is an Art Deco delight that offers high-quality accommodations and personalized services consistent with brand standards. **Pros:** faultless service; high-quality restaurant; sublime decor. **Cons:** difficult to find; can be expensive; 1930s-inspired style won't suit all tastes. [$] *Rooms from: 1610DH* ✉ *9, rue du Docteur Veyre* ☎ *0522/46–78–00* 🌐 *www.hotelledoge.com* 🛏 *16 rooms* 🍴 *Breakfast.*
HOTEL
Fodor's Choice ★

$$ **Hotel Gauthier.** Named for the chic district it's located in, the Gauthier
HOTEL is a stunning boutique property with a cool contemporary look. **Pros:**
cool contemporary decor; comfortable yet stylish rooms; lovely terrace.
Cons: food and drinks a little expensive; service can be slow at busy
times; certain rooms are rather dark. $ *Rooms from: 1400DH* ⊠ *2 bis,
rue Ilya Abou Madi, Quartier Gauthier* ☏ *0522/22–32–24* ⊕ *www.
hotelgauthier.com* ↝ *35 rooms* ❍❘ *Breakfast.*

$$$$ **Hyatt Regency Casablanca.** Casablanca's most conspicuous hotel occu-
HOTEL pies a large site next to Place des Nations Unies. **Pros:** conveniently
located in the old town center; some fantastic views; excellent service
and facilities. **Cons:** the exterior is a little kitschy for some tastes; lacks
the intimacy of smaller lodgings; rather expensive. $ *Rooms from:
2100DH* ⊠ *Pl. des Nations Unies, Centre Ville* ☏ *0522/43–12–34*
⊕ *www.casablanca.regency.hyatt.com* ↝ *255 rooms* ❍❘ *No meals.*

$$ **Kenzi Tower.** Located in one of Casablanca's Twin Center towers, this
HOTEL sophisticated spot offers all the comforts and amenities you'd expect
from a modern luxury hotel—including a fitness center, indoor pool,
and full-service spa; plus it delivers panoramic views of the Hassan II
Mosque and the ocean beyond. **Pros:** fantastic views; central location;
great facilities. **Cons:** not every room has a city view; some rooms
look a bit tired; based on a busy road. $ *Rooms from: 1475DH* ⊠ *Bd.
Zerktouni, Maarif* ☏ *0522/97–80–00* ⊕ *www.kenzi-hotels.com* ↝ *237
rooms* ❍❘ *No meals.*

NIGHTLIFE

Most Casablanca nightlife for the young and wired develops out along
Boulevard de la Corniche, a 30 DH to 35 DH taxi fare from the center
of town. Exceptions are the major hotel discos, such as the Black House
in the Hyatt Regency.

BARS AND PUBS

Fodor'sChoice **Le Cabestan Ocean View Bar.** The bar area inside Le Cabestan Ocean View
★ restaurant heats up after dark, drawing the glitterati of the city who
drink, dance, and gossip the night away beneath the DJ's watchful eye.
Spectacular coastal views and briny air add to the unforgettable experience. ⊠ *Cabestan, 90, bd. de la Corniche, Ain Diab* ☏ *0522/39–11–90*
⊕ *www.le-cabestan.com.*

Le Chester's. Pop into this popular watering hole to have a drink at the long
bar, sample tapas (or a meal if you prefer), then dance while the DJ spins.
Soccer fans should note that if there's a big game on, Chester's will be
showing it. ⊠ *3, rue Abou Faraj Al Asbahani, Racine* ☏ *0522/94–12–82.*

Rick's Café. Within the walls of a restored medina riad, Rick's Café
evokes, of course, the romantic Casablanca from the classic Humphrey
Bogart film—which wasn't actually shot here. The pianist, Issam, plays
jazz nightly and also organizes jazz jams next to the bar. Service is efficient and the menu blends American, French, and local cuisines. You
can dine while sitting atop a high stool at the bar or settle in at one
of the intimate tables. The cocktails are perfectly crafted and there's
a comprehensive wine list. ⊠ *248, bd. Sour Jdid, Pl. du Jardin Public,
Medina* ☏ *0522/27–42–07* ⊕ *www.rickscafe.ma.*

Fodor's Choice
★
Le Wynn. Take a stool at the bar or squeeze around a table and enjoy fantastic wine along with excellent cheese and charcuterie at this chic French brasserie. ⊠ *7, rue Omar Ben Abi Radia* ☎ *0522/26–37–12.*

DANCE CLUBS

Fodor's Choice
★
Bao Night-Club. Any night out at Bao, with its inimitable African atmosphere, is memorable. The 100 DH entry charge includes a drink—but you'll likely want more than one because this place is pretty wild until the early hours. ⊠ *Complexe Miami Beach, La corniche, Ain Diab* ☎ *0693/75–85–69.*

Brooklyn Bar. In you're looking for a place to drink and dance, head to Brooklyn Bar, which blends the scenes of New York City and Casablanca nightlife. ⊠ *56, bd. de la Corniche, Ain Diab* ☎ *0661/25–96–98.*

Vertigo. Set in the old town center, Vertigo offers a great mix of entertainment from DJs to live music to quirky theater. It's a small place pulling in a cultured crowd of all origins and ages. Drinks are reasonably priced as is the simple but appetizing menu. Entrance fees vary according to what's on. ⊠ *110, rue Chaouia* ✛ *Opposite Hotel Transatlantique* ☎ *0664/09–45–25.*

SHOPPING

Every year, Casablanca becomes more and more a cosmopolitan city that prides itself on the availability of fashionable Western garments. The greatest concentration of clothing boutiques by far is in the **Maarif area,** where you'll find the Twin Center shopping mall, assorted European high-street retailers, and all manner of specialty stores. The top place to shop for traditional souvenirs and handicrafts is the **Quartier des Habous.** It offers the best variety and prices, but you should still try to get an idea of market prices before starting to bargain. In close proximity to Casa's luxury hotels, the shops lining **Boulevard Houphouet Boigny** offer few deals, and their business is mostly geared to tourists. They do present a broad sampling of all things Moroccan, however, and are convenient for last minute, one-stop shopping.

ANTIQUES

Maarif. Casablanca's main shopping area is the Maarif, just south of Boulevard Zerktouni. The maarif market is famous among Casablancans, stocking fruits, vegetables, fish, spices, and olives, as well as flowers and argan products. On the other side of Boulevard Massira al Khadra, you'll find a good number of European stores such as Zara, Pimkie, Mango, and Massimo Dutti. Maarif also hosts specialty shops devoted to everything from chocolate to porcelain. Built on a grid, you'll find that the lower part, nearer Boulevard Bir Anzarane, is more traditional, with lots of hole-in-the-wall places selling local products. ⊠ *Maarif.*

CRAFTS

Coco Corner. You'll discover a chic collection of desirable home decor objects, furnishings, and accessories at this inspiring spot. The keyword here is design, and nothing is conceived without elegance. ⊠ *89, av. Stendhal, Val Fleuri, Cité Plateau* ☎ *0522/99–00–10* ⊕ *www.cococorner.com* ☉ *Closed Sun.*

Exposition Nationale d'Artisanat. This expo offers three floors of authentic crafts from all over Morocco at various prices. Those prices are generally fixed, so bargaining isn't necessary—a plus for anyone who prefers low-hassle shopping. ⊠ *3, av. Hassan II, Centre Ville* ☎ *0522/26–70–64.*

HAMMAMS

The following hammams are open to all.

PUBLIC HAMMAMS

Hammam Le Pacha. Popular with locals, these private baths stick to tradition without forgetting the pampering principle. Use of the hammam with combo exfoliation/soaping costs 100 DH and towels are 30 DH. You can also reserve a massage—prices vary according to duration and type. ⊠ *484, bd. Gandhi* ☎ *0522/77–42–41* ⊕ *lepacha.ma/hammam. html* ☞ *50 DH.*

Hammam Ziani. This is a friendly and authentic hammam offering a range of typical services, such as exfoliation and soaping. It also has packages that include massages and algae wraps that come highly recommended. ⊠ *5, rue Abou Rakrak* ☎ *0522/31–96–95* ⊕ *www.hammamziani.ma* ☞ *60 DH.*

SHOPPING CENTERS AND MALLS

FAMILY **Anfa Place.** This mall overlooks the sea opposite the Abdul-Aziz Saud Mosque, right before the Megarama cinema. There is a fair selection of shops—most containing clothing and accessories—but there's also a supermarket plus stores selling music, books, and cosmetics. Right outside, you'll find a host of restaurants and cafés overlooking an accessible stretch of beach. ⊠ *Bd. de la Corniche, Ain Diab* ☎ *0522/95–46–46* ⊕ *www.anfashopping.com.*

FAMILY **Morocco Mall.** At the end of the Corniche, just after the Sidi Abderrahman Islet, sits one of Africa's largest malls. It features all kinds of stores and a sizeable food court. There's also an IMAX theater, a large supermarket, and an adventure playground for kids that includes an ice rink. ⊠ *Corner of Bd. de la Corniche and Bd. de L'Ocean Atlantique, Ain Diab* ☎ *0801/00–12–30* ⊕ *www.moroccomall.net.*

SPORTS AND THE OUTDOORS

BEACH CLUBS

FAMILY **The Tahiti Beach Club.** This is the most polished of the semiprivate clubs found along the Corniche in Ain Diab. Public entry here is 250 DH per person during the week and 400 DH on the weekend. Along with sun and sand, it offers many recreational activities appealing to adults and children alike—including several pools, a trio of top-notch restaurants with ocean views, a spa, a gym, a kids' club, and a surf school. ⊠ *Bd. de la Corniche, Ain Diab* ☎ *0522/79–80–25* ⊕ *www.tahitibeachclub. ma* ☞ *250 DH–400 DH.*

AROUND CASABLANCA

When the clamor and chaos of the city get to you, there's an easy way out. Close to Casablanca, several more diminutive destinations offer relief by way of balmy beaches, relaxed restaurants, and calmer temperaments. Both Mohammedia and Dar Bouaza—each with a distinct, less frenetic atmosphere—are within easy travel distance. These are not touristy towns, but you may well appreciate the contrast. Reaching artsy Azemmour, El Jadida's fortified Cité Portugaise, or the popular strands of El Oualidia takes a bit bigger commitment, yet all are rewarding in their own way.

MOHAMMEDIA

25 km (16 miles) north of Casablanca.

A short drive from Casablanca, Mohammedia and the surrounding area has a long stretch of pretty bays, which draws droves of sunseekers during the summer. It was originally a port town and currently has a delightful harbor and yacht club plus a good choice of fish restaurants, as well as a food market. Charming wooden beach houses line the waterfront. North of town, the coast is good for swimmers, surfers, and sunbathers alike, although currents here can be dangerous.

On Saturday, there is a souk at Al Alia (a southeastern district of Mohammedia) that sells everything from confit camel meat to dentist chairs. It's a grand event for locals, and you can see donkeys, horses, and walkers flocking toward it for miles.

GETTING HERE AND AROUND

Trains from the Casablanca Port station leave every half hour for Mohammedia (18 minutes, 15 DH). A grand taxi from Casablanca costs approximately 10 DH, while a bus will cost you 6 DH.

In Mohammedia, you can take a relatively inexpensive petit taxi, with a minimum fare of 7 DH.

EXPLORING

FAMILY **Plage Les Sablettes.** This long sandy bay attracts swarms of surfers, sunbathers, and families in summer when temperatures can get very high. **Amenities:** food and drink; lifeguards (in summer); parking. **Best for:** sunbathing; surfing; swimming; walking. ✉ *Bd. Hassan II.*

WHERE TO EAT AND STAY

$$ SEAFOOD 🍴 **Restaurant du Parc.** Befitting its name, this restaurant is right on the park, in a 1950s building with a terrace for diners. As is often the case in Mohammedia, the menu bears a distinct fish and seafood theme, so your choices will largely depend on what's been caught that day. **Known for:** well-priced dishes; unpretentious menu; pretty, easy-to-find location. [$] *Average main: 100DH* ✉ *Bd. Zerktouni, on corner, opposite park* ☎ *0523/32–22–11.*

$$$$ SEAFOOD Fodor's Choice ★ 🍴 **Restaurant du Port.** This gastronomic fish restaurant is the most famous place to eat in town. The splendid menu isn't cheap, but it's worth every last dirham because the chef insists on using top-quality ingredients and each dish is crafted with imagination and

sophistication. **Known for:** creative cuisine; friendly, efficient service; great wine list. $ *Average main: 180DH* ⊠ *1, rue du Port* ☏ *0523/32–24–66* ⊕ *www.restoport.ma.*

$$ ⚏ **Hotel Avanti.** The large, rather lavish Hotel Avanti features swish
HOTEL rooms and suites, several restaurants and bars, pools, a spa, and a nightclub. **Pros:** great facilities; some rooms have sea views; excellent location. **Cons:** not for those wanting an intimate ambience; rather expensive for the area; restaurants aren't as inspiring as others nearby. $ *Rooms from: 1300DH* ⊠ *Av. Moulay Youssef* ☏ *0523/30–68–00* ⊕ *www.avantimohammedia.com* ⇨ *156 rooms* ⦿l *Breakfast.*

$$ ⚏ **Sphinx Boutique Hotel.** This enticing boutique hotel, set in a clean-
HOTEL lined 1950s villa, flawlessly balances modern comfort and vintage
Fodor'sChoice elegance. **Pros:** very stylish and comfortable; wonderful garden; chic
★ but friendly atmosphere. **Cons:** some rooms are small; parking can be limited; nearby nightclub can cause noise. $ *Rooms from: 1295DH* ⊠ *Bd. Moulay Youssef, Mohammedia* ☏ *0523/31–00–73* ⊕ *sphinx.ma* ⇨ *17 rooms* ⦿l *Breakfast.*

NIGHTLIFE

Le Roof. The classy bar above the boat-shaped Restaurant du Port regularly draws a fun-loving crowd. DJs make this the chic place to party as the sun sets over the ocean; there's also food available for those in need of a bite. ⊠ *1, rue du Port* ☏ *0523/32–24–66* ⊕ *www.roof.ma* ⊘ *Closed Sun.*

SPORTS AND THE OUTDOORS

FAMILY **Bautilus.** Since Mohammedia is essentially a port town, the thing to do
Fodor'sChoice here is try your hand at boating. It's an ideal way to explore the coast.
★ Beginners and the more experienced alike can choose from a variety of small vessels, including canoes, catamarans, and motorboats. Bautilus is run by Mehdi and Hicham, two passionate sailors who can also arrange sailing excursions, fishing trips, and other on-the-water activities. Sailing lessons start at 250 DH and motorboat trips costs 2,000 DH for a half day or 3,000 DH for a full day. Canoe trips are priced at 250 DH per person for groups of eight or more. ⊠ *Base Nautique de Mohammedia* ☏ *0665/19–69–87, 0645/46–02–28* ⊕ *www.bautilus.com.*

DAR BOUAZZA

20 km (12½ miles) southwest of Casablanca.

This beach town on the outskirts of Casablanca used to be quite small but is expanding quickly, as the swell of villas and apartments proves. A haunt for the White City's expatriate community, it has a curious mix of traditional locals—fishermen, surfers, rural families—plus Americans and Europeans. The expat residents, along with well-off Moroccans looking to relax and get away from the stresses of Casablanca, have spurred an increase in entertainment and leisure activity within Dar Bouazza. Surfing, Jet-skiing, beachside dining with live music (and wine), and spa-going are all options. If you are just looking for a relaxing day at the beach, this is a good choice. You can stop at any of the free public beaches for some fun in the sun.

GETTING HERE AND AROUND

Renting a car is the best option for visiting the area. Head out of Casablanca south on Route d'Azemmour, and take the first right exit down to Plage Oud Merzeq.

Grand taxis from the southern end of Casablanca, in Hay Hassani, can also take you to Dar Bouazza, but specify that you are going to the beach, because some of the taxis don't take the beach road and continue on directly south. The trip costs 10 DH per person.

EXPLORING

FAMILY **La Ferme Pedagogique.** When you need a break from the city bustle, this environmentally friendly farm makes a very pleasant getaway for both adults and children. On-site you can discover organic plants and herbs, as well as visit and look after animals. Food and drinks are available if hunger hits. ✉ *Km 18, Rte. d'Azemmour* ☎ *0540/02–67–17, 0662/41–42–28* 🌐 *www.lafermepedagogique.ma* 🎟 *20 DH.*

FAMILY **Jack Beach.** The most frequented beach in Dar Bouazza is a great place for swimming and surfing in the summer. On the far side, there's a tidal pool area and, when tides are low, the long stretches of soft sand are ideal for strolling and exploring the coast. **Amenities:** food and drink; lifeguards (in summer); parking. **Best for:** surfing; swimming; walking. ✉ *Rte. P3012.*

WHERE TO EAT AND STAY

$$ SEAFOOD FAMILY 🍴 **Sunny Beach.** At Sunny Beach, the menu focuses on fresh fish (think paella and squid) that's cooked to order, with some salads and desserts thrown in for good measure. Kids will be eager to play in the sand, and there are some lounge chairs available for sunbathers and tired parents. **Known for:** family-friendly menu; ideal beachside location; accessible prices. [$] *Average main: 110DH* ✉ *Tamaris 1* ☎ *0661/37–24–72* 🌐 *www.sunnybeachonline.com.*

$$$$ MEDITERRANEAN 🍴 **Les Trois Mâts Chez Joe.** In terms of both gastronomy and comfort, this is probably the best pick among the beach clubs lining this part of the coast. It's open for lunch and dinner, and the menu revolves around seafood with a Mediterranean slant. **Known for:** varied food and drink menu; ideal setting; families welcome. [$] *Average main: 170DH* ✉ *Tamaris I* ☎ *0522/ 33–02–62.*

$$ HOTEL 🏨 **Hotel des Arts.** Though it's not the most charming of hotels, the architecture here is fun and the atmosphere laid-back. **Pros:** ideal location; original design; full-service spa and pools. **Cons:** expensive for the area; service can be slack; themed decor not to all tastes. [$] *Rooms from: 1300DH* ✉ *1120, Jack Beach* ☎ *0522/96–54–50* 🛏 *50 rooms* 🍽 *Breakfast.*

SPORTS AND THE OUTDOORS

SURFING

Glisse School. If you'd like to learn how to surf (or hone existing skills) this school on Jack Beach has excellent instructors—some of whom speak English. The rates are very reasonable, and it's open year-round. A 1½-hour lesson including equipment costs 200 DH. ✉ *Jack Beach* ☎ *0664/46–98–07.*

WATER PARKS

FAMILY **Tamaris Aquaparc.** When it's hot and the children are looking for some thrills, this lavish water park fills the bill. Open from mid-May to mid-September, it's packed full of slides, fountains, and such, and there are places to dine as well. Note that the park gets very busy in summer when sweltering Casablancans look for somewhere to cool off. ⊠ *Km 15, Rte. d'Azemmour* ☎ *0522/96–53–69* ⊕ *www.tamaris-aquaparc. com* ⌨ *160 DH.*

AZEMMOUR

75 km (46 miles) southwest of Casablanca.

Azemmour, situated on both the banks of the Oum Errabi River and the Atlantic Ocean, makes a fantastic weekend or day-trip destination from Casablanca. The charming small town boasts a quintessential Portuguese medina, warm locals, and an artistic influence that gives it a unique flavor. The Portuguese built Azemmour in 1513, and it proudly claims Estavanico, or "Stephan the Black," as a former resident. Estavanico, born in 1500 into slavery, was the first North Africa–born person to arrive in what now is the United States. Traveling with Álvar Núñez Cabeza de Vaca, he was one of just four survivors of the ill-fated Spanish Narvéaz expedition.

GETTING HERE AND AROUND

Train service from Casablanca to Azemmour leaves from l'Oasis station, with trains running about every two hours. With a car, the drive from Casablanca to Azemmour takes about an hour. Buses also run regularly between the two. If you are staying in a riad, take a petit taxi from the train or bus station (about 7 DH) to one of the doors of the Azemmour medina; once there, it's best to call your riad to have an escort lead you from the entrance to the premises. The small medina streets and alleys are a gentle maze, and not easy to navigate alone—but once you've spent some time walking them, you'll get your bearings. What's more, most locals are friendly and will try to help if you become lost.

Bus Contacts CTM. ☎ *0800/09–00–30* ⊕ *www.ctm.ma.*

Train Contacts Office National des Chemins de Fer (*O.N.C.F.*). ☎ *0890/20–30–40* ⊕ *www.oncf.ma.*

EXPLORING

Azemmour's medina is divided into three parts—the Mellah (or Jewish Quarter), the kasbah, and the old medina—and, to appreciate the attractions within it fully, you should arrange for a guide through your riad. While the area retains much of its traditional charm, the influence of local and foreign artists is also visible. Lured by Azemmour's unique lighting, many have chosen to set up shop here; and as you wander the medina streets, their murals are a delightful surprise. It's worth stopping into one of the studios or galleries to see the artists and their work.

Although the new town offers quite a contrast, it warrants a visit as well. Located on the opposite side of the road to the medina, it contains the tomb of Sidi Bouchaib, a saint recognized for his abilities to heal dementia. Only Muslims can enter, but everyone can peep into the initial porch or just admire the architecture outside. From there, wander down through the busy thoroughfare, Boulevard Ahmed Choufani, which is unfrequented by tourists but full of locals. It's flanked by a multitude of hole-in-the-wall shops selling old-school wares, many of which are related to healing and spells. Expect to find anything from leeches and fox tails to animal bones, all used in traditional medicine.

Ahmed el-Amine. Perhaps Azemmour's most renowned resident artist, Ahmed el-Amine has been painting in and around the medina for nearly two decades. He still lives here, working out of this studio. ⊠ *6, Derb el-Hantati* ☎ *0523/35–89–02.*

Galerie Akwas. The medina's original gallery exhibits the work of artists from across the nation. It was founded by Abderrahmane Rahoul, former director of the Ecole Supérieure des Beaux Arts in Casablanca, who is also a well-known and highly respected visual artist himself. ⊠ *4, Bab El Makhzen* ☎ *0661/41–08–31.*

FAMILY **Plage el Haouzia.** Before the Mazagan Beach Resort was built between Azemmour and El Jadida, you could walk along the sand from one community to the other. While that's no longer possible, this is still a stunning strand and one of the cleanest on the coast. There's also a shipwreck that's fun to explore. **Amenities:** food and drink; lifeguards (in summer). **Best for:** sunsets; surfing; swimming; walking. ⊠ *Azemmour.*

WHERE TO STAY

$
B&B/INN
Dar Nadia. There are few lodging choices (and even fewer restaurants) in relatively unspoiled Azzemour; however, there are some evocative options—including this one in the Mellah. **Pros:** a pristine place; homey, relaxed atmosphere; authentic features. **Cons:** can be hard to find; no restaurant (though you can order dinner in advance); Wi-Fi may be a little unreliable. $ *Rooms from: 450DH* ⊠ *3, rue Souika El Malah, Medina* ☎ *0523/35–84–72* ▭ *No credit cards* ⌁ *5 rooms* ❍*| No meals.*

$
HOTEL
Fodor's Choice
★
L'Oum Errabia. This divine guesthouse at the river's edge effortlessly mixes charm and chic. **Pros:** fabulous design and atmosphere; excellent location; wonderful river views. **Cons:** can be a little noisy when busy; can be difficult to find alone; some rooms are rather dark. $ *Rooms from: 800DH* ⊠ *17, impasse Chtouka* ☎ *0523/34–70–71* ⌁ *9 rooms* ❍*| Breakfast.*

$
B&B/INN
Riad 7. Containing just five pretty but compact rooms, this riad gives tradition a twist by focusing on contemporary decor while still highlighting the carefully preserved features of the ancient building it inhabits. **Pros:** centrally located in the old medina; well-restored traditional building; cozy, intimate atmosphere. **Cons:** as is often the case with medina houses, rooms can be a little dark; some rooms are small; lots of stairs. $ *Rooms from: 500DH* ⊠ *2, Derb Chtouka* ☎ *0523/34–73–63* ⊕ *www.riad7.com* ⌁ *5 rooms* ❍*| Breakfast.*

El Jadida's Portuguese cistern was where water was stored when the town was the fortress of Mazagan.

SHOPPING

Mohamed Janati. Besides being one of Azemmour's friendliest faces, the multilingual Mohamed Janati is a skilled weaver. Working at his traditional loom, he's happy to invite you in for tea, a chat, and an introduction to the art of weaving. His rugs, covers, and scarves are absolutely beautiful and sold at reasonable prices. ✉ *229, Derb Eddira, Medina* ☎ *0644/15–99–93.*

SPORTS AND THE OUTDOORS

In addition to water sports like surfing and kayaking, boat trips and fishing excursions along the river can be arranged by the riads. Beaches just south of the city are also beautiful for a stroll or swim.

EL JADIDA

99 km (62 miles) southwest of Casablanca.

El Jadida it best known for its fabulous fortified old town, built by the Portuguese in the 16th century and now a designated UNESCO World Heritage Site. (The name El Jadida actually means "the New" and has alternated more than once with the town's original Portuguese one, Mazagan.) Yet this place has other enticements for tourists, too—including a large sand-rimmed bay and a pretty promenade lined with palm trees and cafés.

GETTING HERE AND AROUND

Train service to El Jadida is limited, and the train station is inconveniently located 4 km (2½ miles) south of town. Buses are fine for trips from Casablanca; frequent ones also come from Safi and Oualidia in the south. In El Jadida, one bus station, Gare Routière, serves all bus companies and grand taxis.

El Jadida has inexpensive metered petit taxis. For local runs, however, it is always advisable to establish an agreed-upon fare before getting in. The going rate for such trips is around 10 DH. The taxi station is next to the bus station. The larger, more-roadworthy grand taxis are available for intercity journeys, like El Jadida to Oualidia (50 DH), as well as for longer trips to Marrakesh (70 DH) or Essaouira (65 DH).

Bus Information CTM. ⊠ *Av. Mohammed V* ☎ *0800/09-00-30* ⊕ *www.ctm.ma.*

Train Information Office National des Chemins de Fer *(O.N.C.F.).* ⊠ *4 km (2½ miles) south of El Jadida* ☎ *2255* ⊕ *www.oncf.ma.*

TIMING AND PRECAUTIONS

Most travelers stay in El Jadida for one or two nights. It's generally considered safe; however, the Cité Portugaise area is poorly lighted at night and the new town has a few seedy bars and clubs. You should exercise caution if visiting after sundown.

EXPLORING

Fodor's Choice
★

Cité Portugaise. El Jadida's main attraction is the atmospheric Cité Portugaise, which was built for military purposes in the early 1500s, overtaken by the Moroccans in 1769, and registered as a UNESCO World Heritage Site in 2004. Impressive (and still imposing) stone walls make it difficult to miss. The Portuguese city was originally a rectangular island with a bastion on each corner, connected to the mainland by a single causeway. Take the entrance on the right where you'll see that the Portuguese street names have been retained. ⊠ *El Jadida.*

Fortress. At the end of Rua da Carreira (Rue Mohammed Al Achemi), you can walk up ramps to the walls of the fortress. Looking down from the heights, you'll see a gate that leads directly onto the sea and, to the right, El Jadida's fishing harbor. ⊠ *Rua da Carreira.*

Jewish cemetery. El Jadida was once home to a very large Jewish population—traces of which are still visible in the city's Mellah, the Jewish quarter of the old medina. If you walk around the walls to the other side of the fortress, you get clear views over the Jewish cemetery. ⊠ *El Jadida.*

Mosque. Beyond the Portuguese Cistern on Rua da Carreira is a fine old mosque, and its original construction makes it one of the focal points of the city. The beautiful white minaret has five sides, all with rounded edges. ⊠ *Rua da Carreira.*

Our Lady of the Assumption. Walking down Rua da Carreira, you'll see on the left an old Portuguese church: Our Lady of the Assumption. Erected in 1628, it's a fine example of late-Gothic Manueline-style architecture. ⊠ *Rua da Carreira.*

Portuguese Cistern. The photogenic Portuguese cistern is where water was stored when El Jadida was still the fortress of Mazagan (some say it originally stored arms). A small amount of water remains to reflect the cistern's gorgeous Gothic arches, a stunning effect. According to local legend, this massive spot wasn't rediscovered until 1916, when a Moroccan Jew stumbled on it in the process of enlarging his shop—whereupon water started gushing in. ⊠ *Rua da Carreira* ☎ *10 DH.*

Sidi Bouzid Beach. This beautiful stretch of sand extends away from El Jadida; you can access it by taking the coastal road about 5 km (3 miles) out of town. It's an ideal place to stroll or watch the sunset. Swimming is great here too, although currents can be strong. **Amenities:** food and drink; lifeguards (in summer); parking. **Best for:** sunsets; swimming; walking. ✉ *El Jadida.*

NEED A BREAK

🍴 **Requin Blue. Right near Sidi Bouzid Beach, the Requin Bleu serves a wide variety of fresh seafood and fish dishes (early risers can also get breakfast or a cup of coffee here). It's conveniently placed and the views are great.** ✉ ***Centre Balnéaire, Sidi Bouzid*** ☎ ***0523/34–80–67*** 🌐 ***www.requinbleu.com.***

4

WHERE TO EAT

$ MOROCCAN

🍴 **Café do Mar.** Spread over several floors, this cute café serves tasty Breton-inspired buckwheat crepes, good quality coffee, and refreshing fresh juices that are just the ticket on hot days. You can spoil yourself with some divine Moroccan pastries, too. **Known for:** indulgent breakfasts; great crepes; pretty location and decor. [$] *Average main: 60DH* ✉ *Cite Portuguaise* ☎ *0523/37–34–00* 🌐 *www.liglesia.com/en/cafedomar.php.*

$$$ MOROCCAN

🍴 **La Capitainerie.** Within the ramparts there isn't much in terms of sit-down dining, save for La Capitainerie, where the menu revolves around seafood with a Moroccan edge. You can order à la carte or choose a fixed-price menu; both change daily. **Known for:** unique setting; brief yet appealing menu; intimate atmosphere. [$] *Average main: 130DH* ✉ *Cite Portuguaise* ☎ *0523/37–34–00.*

$$ SEAFOOD

🍴 **Restaurant du Port.** This old-school fish restaurant, located between the port and ramparts, serves the catch of the day straight out of the water. You can also sit at the bar and dine tapas-style, while enjoying the reasonably priced alcohol selection. **Known for:** simple menu; unpretentious decor; great position. [$] *Average main: 80DH* ✉ *Port d'El Jadida* ☎ *0523/34–25–79* 💳 *No credit cards* 🕒 *No dinner Sun.*

$ SEAFOOD

🍴 **Tchikito.** For fresh fish, an easygoing atmosphere, and low prices, Tchikitos is the way to go. It's a no-frills, no-thrills, easy-on-the-wallet restaurant just outside the medina walls. **Known for:** local ambience; inexpensive prices; homespun service. [$] *Average main: 50DH* ✉ *4, rue Smiha* ☎ *0523/37–18–19* 💳 *No credit cards.*

WHERE TO STAY

$ B&B/INN

🏨 **Dar Al Manar.** This delightful guesthouse just outside of town is an ideal place to unwind. **Pros:** beautiful natural setting; intimate atmosphere; relaxing environment. **Cons:** a little out of town; five rooms can book up fast; no alternative dining options nearby. [$] *Rooms from: 800DH* ✉ *BP 229* ☎ *0523/35–16–45* 🌐 *www.dar-al-manar.com* 🛏 *5 rooms* 🍽 *Breakfast.*

$$ HOTEL
Fodor's Choice ★

🏨 **L'iglesia.** One of Morocco's chicest hotels is partly built within the walls of an old church in the heart of the centuries-old Cité Portugaise. **Pros:** unique interiors; gorgeous building; historical setting. **Cons:** if you stay in the converted church, breakfast is in a different building; expensive for the area; few other restaurant options in the area. [$] *Rooms* *from: 1475DH* ✉ *Eglise Espagnole, Cite Portuguaise* ☎ *0523/37–34–00* 🌐 *www.liglesia.com* 🛏 *15 rooms* 🍴 *Breakfast.*

$$$$ HOTEL FAMILY 🏨 **Mazagan Beach Resort.** Mazagan is a spectacular seaside resort between Azemmour and El Jadida. **Pros:** luxury accommodations; sprawling property; lots of leisure activities. **Cons:** not accessible by public transportation; expensive; very large, so lacks intimacy. [$] *Rooms from: 3000DH* ✉ *16 km (10 miles) northeast of El Jadida* ☎ *0523/38–80–60* 🌐 *www.mazaganbeachresort.com* 🛏 *500 rooms* 🍴 *Breakfast.*

$$ RESORT FAMILY 🏨 **Pullman Mazagan Royal Golf & Spa.** As you'd expect from the Pullman brand, this luxury hotel has large, well-equipped rooms that are decorated in a classy contemporary style. **Pros:** quiet area; good for golf; on the beach. **Cons:** no public transportation; somewhat impersonal; no off-site eateries nearby. [$] *Rooms from: 1250DH* ✉ *Km 7, Rte. de Casablanca* ☎ *0523/37–91–00* 🌐 *www.pullmanhotels.com* 🛏 *127 rooms* 🍴 *Breakfast.*

SPORTS AND THE OUTDOORS

GOLF

Mazagan Golf Club. Designed by South African golfer Gary Player, this is a links course—meaning that it literally links the land with the sea. The 72 par, 18-hole course follows the natural contours of the dunes and delivers panoramic water views. Green fees are 750 DH for 18 holes. ✉ *Mazagan Beach Resort, 16 km (10 miles) northeast of El Jadida* ☎ *0523/38–80–76* 🌐 *www.mazaganbeachresort.com.*

Royal Golf El Jadida. This 18-hole course next to the Atlantic is still worth a visit, even though it is less sophisticated than the nearby one at the Mazagan Beach Resort. Green fees are a modest 370 DH. ✉ *Km 7, Rte. de Casablanca* ☎ *0523/37–91–00.*

EN ROUTE

To leave El Jadida in the direction of El Oualidia, follow signs to Jorf Lasfar. Jorf Lasfar itself is the site of a chemical plant responsible for serious pollution in this region. After this, the coastal road becomes more scenic, passing fertile fields and lagoons. It's also quite an agricultural region and many salt mines are found here.

EL OUALIDIA

175 km (109 miles) southwest of Casablanca, 89 km (55 miles) southwest of El Jadida. From El Jadida, follow sign to Jorf Laser.

This small beach town is famous nationwide for its oysters (if you visit the oyster parks, you can learn how they're cultivated). But what really attracts the large influx of travelers each summer is its bay, which is arguably one of the most picturesque places on Morocco's entire Atlantic coast. The fine sand is gently lapped by a sapphire lagoon, and in the distance white breakers collide beyond the cliffs. The main beach is surrounded by a promontory to the south, a gap where the sea enters the lagoon, an island, and another promontory to the north. Around the corner, a second beach seems wholly untouched, and dunes bearing tufts of grass alternate with little rocky hills.

Sand and sea aside, there aren't many "sights" here. If you have a car, however, the drive south along the coastal road from El Oualidia to Essaouira is a rewarding one with magnificent views—especially in spring, when the wildflowers are out. The town also has a Saturday souk, which is definitely worth a visit.

GETTING HERE AND AROUND

Grands taxis and local buses offer services to Essaouira and El Jadida. Both depart from a stop near the post office on the main road. There is also regular bus service north and south. If you are traveling by car from Marrakesh, follow the road to Safi and take the scenic coast road to Oualidia. If you are driving from El Jadida, follow the coast road down to Oualidia and allow extra time for possible congestion.

Bus Information CTM. ✉ *El Jadida–Safi Rd.* ☎ *0800/09–00–30* 🌐 *www.ctm.ma.*

4

TIMING AND PRECAUTIONS

El Oualidia is a great choice for a stopover on the way north or south, or as a relaxing beach weekend destination.

WHERE TO EAT AND STAY

$$$ SEAFOOD 🍴 **Ostrea II.** The menu at Ostrea II features various types of seafood, but most people come for the oysters—which can be washed down with wine chosen from a respectable list and followed by a classic French dessert. Just after entering town, a sign for the renowned restaurant points right toward the lagoon. **Known for:** fresh oysters cultivated right in front of the restaurant; great views; all-day service. [$] *Average main: 125DH* ✉ *El Oualidia* ☎ *0523/36–63–24.*

$$$ SEAFOOD FAMILY 🍴 **Restaurant à l'Araignée Gourmande.** This unpretentious, family-friendly spot looks out over the beach and lagoon. Not surprisingly, the menu is seafood-oriented (lobster, of course, is the priciest item listed, but it's superb). **Known for:** friendly, no-frills service; moderately priced menu; lovely views plus beach access. [$] *Average main: 125DH* ✉ *Oualidia Plage, Oualidia* ☎ *0523 /36–64–47* 🌐 *www.araignee-gourmande.com.*

$ B&B/INN 🏨 **Dar Beldi.** Located in town, a short car ride from the lagoon, this pretty guesthouse rambles over various levels interspersed with lovely patios and plants. **Pros:** pretty and peaceful; individually decorated rooms; lovely for families. **Cons:** a little far from the beach; some rooms are dark; there's no restaurant (but breakfast is included). [$] *Rooms from: 550DH* ✉ *Douar Moulay Adessalam, Oualidia* ☎ *0523/36–62–88* 🛏 *5 rooms* 🍽 *Breakfast.*

$$ HOTEL 🏨 **L'Hippocampe.** Overlooking the lagoon, this family-run hotel offers clean, functional rooms arranged around a well-kept garden. **Pros:** easy beach access; friendly staff; great for families. **Cons:** rooms aren't particularly inspiring; gets very busy in summer; indoor dining area lacks intimacy. [$] *Rooms from: 1350DH* ✉ *Oualidia Plage* ☎ *0523/36–61–08* 🌐 *www.hippocampeoualidia.com* 🛏 *23 rooms* 🍽 *Breakfast; Some meals.*

$$$$ HOTEL Fodor's Choice ★ 🏨 **La Sultana Oulidia.** Breathtakingly beautiful and discrete, this luxurious little boutique hotel on a secluded corner of Oulidia's lagoon is worth the price if you're in the mood to be truly pampered. **Pros:** beautiful location; luxury facilities and furnishings; flawless service.

Cons: high prices; a little awkward to reach without a car; the atmosphere may be too tranquil for some. [$] *Rooms from: 4400DH* ✉ *3, Parc a huitres* ☎ *0523/36–65–95* 🌐 *www.lasultanahotels.com/oualidia* 🛏 *11 rooms* 🍴 *Breakfast.*

SPORTS AND THE OUTDOORS

SURFING

Gentle waves make Oualidia's lagoon a great place to learn how to surf. Experienced surfers will find waves to their liking on the straightforward Atlantic beaches south of town; one of the better ones is called Mateisha Plage (in the Moroccan dialect) or Tomato Beach.

Surfland. This school runs surfing holidays for both adults and children, with English-speaking instructors and camping accommodations added in. Lessons cost 200 DH (equipment included). Surfers staying elsewhere can join up without a reservation if there's enough space. ✉ *BP 40* ☎ *0523/36–61–10.*

FEZ AND THE MIDDLE ATLAS

with Meknès, Volubilis, and Moulay Idriss

WELCOME TO FEZ AND THE MIDDLE ATLAS

TOP REASONS TO GO

★ **Go back in time:** Fez el-Bali is the world's largest active medieval city and promises a sensorial vacation from modern life.

★ **Indulge your senses in the Meknès food souk:** On Place el-Hedime sample famous olives, aromatic spices, and dried fruit, available in a dizzying array of colors and flavors.

★ **Explore an archaeological gem in Volubilis:** A short trip from Meknès, these well-preserved Roman ruins are considered the most impressive in the country.

★ **Ski the Moroccan Aspen:** Attracting both royalty and the Moroccan elite, the highest peak of the Michlifen ski resort rises to 6,500 feet.

★ **Take an overland adventure:** Two of the most stunning sights in the Middle Atlas are the cascading waterfalls of Ouzoud and the Friouato caves near Taza.

Situated between the mountainous Middle Atlas and valleys of the Rif, Fez and Meknès are rewarding visits with historic monuments, sumptuous palaces, imposing ramparts, and vibrant markets. Fez is by far the more significant destination. Meknès is a calmer city to experience authentic local life, with fewer tourists and hustlers. Side trips to the Roman ruins in Volubilis and sacred village of Moulay Idriss are highly recommended if time permits. The Middle Atlas, the northernmost part of the three Atlas Mountain chains, is a brief surprise on the way to or from the Sahara. Explore provinces like Ifrane, considered "Morocco's Switzerland," Berber cities of Azrou and Sefrou, beautiful forests, picturesque mountain ranges, and the canyons of the Cirque du Djebel Tazzeka near Taza.

1 Fez. Founded in the 8th century on the banks of the Fez River by Moulay Idriss, Fez remains Morocco's grandest and oldest imperial city. Within the medieval stone walls of the medina there are two distinct historic areas: Fez el-Bali (Old Fez) and Fez el-Djedid (New Fez). Farther south, the Ville Nouvelle (New Town) is a modern

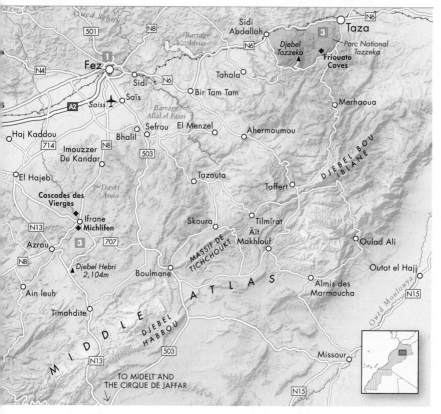

district built in 1912, attracting wealthier residents and strong commercial activity. The city's labyrinthine heart is the medina, enclosing historic minarets, souks, mosques, museums, fountains, and squares that get the well-deserved attention of most visitors throughout the year.

2 Meknès. Founded in the 11th century by the Almoravids, Meknès became an imperial city under the rule of Sultan Moulay Ismail. The city has three distinct areas—the ancient medina with its central Place el-Hedime; the Imperial City, which contains the most impressive monuments; and the Ville Nouvelle (New Town).

3 The Mediterranean Middle Atlas. The northern Middle Atlas begins south and east of Fez and stretches southwest. The Azrou Cedar Forest and the Djebel Tazzeka Massif above Taza are the main attractions in this heavily forested northern zone, along with the ski region near Ifrane.

Updated by
Sarah Gilbert

Designated as UNESCO World Heritage Sites, Fez and Meknès are, respectively, the Arab and Berber capitals of Morocco, ancient centers of learning, culture, and craftsmanship.

Recognized as Morocco's intellectual and spiritual center, Fez has one of the world's oldest universities as well as the largest intact medieval quarters. It is the country's second-largest city (after Casablanca) with a population of approximately 1 million. Meknès, with nearly 850,000 inhabitants, offers a chance to experience all the sights, sounds, and smells of Fez on a slightly smaller, more manageable scale. Both Fez and Meknès still remain two of Morocco's most authentic and fascinating cities, outstanding for their history and culture, and Fez rivals Marrakesh as a top tourist destination and host of international events and festivals.

In between Fez and Marrakesh, the Middle Atlas is a North African arcadia, where rivers, woodlands, and valley grasslands show off Morocco's inland beauty. Snowy cedar forests, ski slopes, and trout streams are not images normally associated with the country, yet the Middle Atlas unfolds like an ersatz alpine fantasy less than an hour from medieval Fez. To remind you that this is still North Africa, Barbary apes scurry around the roadsides, and the traditional *djellaba* (hooded gown) and hijab appear in ski areas.

Most travelers to Morocco can get a glimpse of the Middle Atlas as they whiz between Fez and Marrakesh, or between Meknès and points south. The central highland's Berber villages, secret valleys, scenic woods, dramatically barren landscapes, and hilly plains blanketed with olive groves lie in stark contrast to the exotic imperial cities. For this reason alone, the region is rewarding to discover for its integrity and authenticity.

PLANNING

WHEN TO GO

Busloads of tourists and intense heat tend to suppress the romance of just about anything. Try to visit Fez and Meknès between September and April, before the high season or extreme heat makes it uncomfortable to sightsee. Spring and autumn are really the best time to visit any part of Morocco.

The Middle Atlas is relatively cool year-round, and often snowbound mid-winter with temperatures dropping below 0°C (32°F). For skiing or driving through the snow-filled Michlifen mountain region or Azrou Cedar Forest (occasionally snowed in from January to March, but normally well plowed), come between December and April. April through June is the best time to hike. The high tourist season in the mountains runs mid-March through summer. The most popular festival is the annual Fes Festival of World Sacred Music, currently held in June.

PLANNING YOUR TIME

If you're short of time, Fez should be your priority. The ancient monuments of the medina and the leather tanneries can be explored in one or two days, although you should devote longer to losing yourself in the medieval city's labyrinthine alleyways. A third day could be spent visiting the smaller and more manageable imperial city of Meknès and the impressive Roman ruins of Volubilis. With more time and transport—a rental car or tour—Fez makes the ideal base for day trips to alpine-style Ifrane and the Middle Atlas towns of Sefrou and Azrou. If you really want to experience Berber culture, spend the night in the troglodyte village of Bhalil; or visit the Holy City of Moulay Idriss, just a stone's throw from Volubilis.

GETTING HERE AND AROUND

Most tourists visiting the Middle Atlas set down in Fez, the region's largest city. Traveling within Fez is best done on foot, but taking a petit taxi to points of interest such as the Ville Nouvelle is an inexpensive option. To visit Meknès or Volubilis, take a train, bus, grand taxi (negotiate a price before the journey), or tour. To visit the Middle Atlas, you'll need a car or a tour.

AIR TRAVEL

The new, state-of-the-art Fès-Saïss Airport terminal opened in May 2017 and flights operate regularly from international and domestic destinations, including direct flights from Marrakesh, new in 2017. But you can't fly directly into Fez from the United States; you must connect in Europe or Casablanca. Upon arrival, petits taxis wait outside the airport terminal and train station and carry two to four people. Grands taxis carry six people. Avoid unofficial drivers who hang around the terminals and charge false rates. Taxis should have their meters running. Most drivers request cash payment.

BUS TRAVEL

The CTM is Morocco's best bus company and has service from most major cities to Fez and Meknès. You can reach some destinations in the Middle Atlas by bus, but ultimately, you're going to have to drive or take a taxi or tour.

CAR TRAVEL

The easiest way to tour the well-paved regions in and around Fez and the Middle Atlas is by car. The best map to use is the Michelin Map of Morocco 959; if you can't find this map at home, ask your car-rental company to provide one. A map is a necessity if you plan to venture far from the beaten path. Road signs at major intersections in larger cities are well marked to point you in the right direction. Little white pillars alongside routes indicate distance in kilometers to towns. Traveling farther afield into the Middle Atlas, many secondary roads are unpaved and require a four-wheel-drive vehicle. Through mountain passes, roads can be dangerously narrow, steep, and winding.

TRAIN TRAVEL

Fez and Meknès are served by the ONCF train station that goes east to Oujda, south to Marrakesh, and west to Tangier, Rabat, and Casablanca. Fez and Meknès are also connected by regular local trains, a 45-minute trip.

RESTAURANTS

Every Moroccan city has its own way of preparing the national dishes. *Harira,* the spicy bean-based soup filled with vegetables and meat, may be designated as Fassi (from Fez) or Meknessi (from Meknès) and varies slightly in texture and ingredients. Note that few of the basic medina restaurants in Fez and Meknès are licensed to serve alcohol. Proprietors generally allow oenophiles to bring their own wine, as long as they enjoy it discreetly. Larger hotels and luxury *riads* (renovated guesthouses and villas) have well-stocked bars that serve wine, beer, and cocktails, as do more upscale restaurants.

Most of the Middle Atlas hotels we recommend have fair to excellent restaurants, but venture to stop at small-town crossroads or souks for a homemade bowl of harira for 5 DH or less. Note: some locals may frown upon alcohol of any kind. Be discreet if you carry your own wine or beer. *Dining reviews have been shortened. For full information, visit Fodors.com.*

HOTELS

Hotels in Fez range from the luxurious and the contemporary to more personal, atmospheric riads that offer everything from an Arabian Nights fantasy to authentic traditional living, and more upscale but still boutique versions, such as Palais Amani. Hotels in or near the Fez el-Bali are best, as the medina is probably what you came to see. In Meknès, there is a more limited choice, with a few gems competing at the top end. In the Middle Atlas, the resort of Michlifen Ifrane Suites and Spa draws local elite for its Anglo-European styling. The Middle Atlas offers a selection of good hotels. Some of the inns and auberges off the beaten path should be thought of as shelter rather than full-service hotels, as lodging tends to be unmemorable. *Hotel reviews have been shortened. For full information, visit Fodors.com.*

WHAT IT COSTS IN DIRHAMS				
	$	$$	$$$	$$$$
Restaurants	under 200 DH	200 DH–300 DH	301 DH–400 DH	over 400 DH
Hotels	under 1,200 DH	1,200 DH–1,600 DH	1,601 DH–2,000 DH	over 2,000 DH

Restaurant prices are the average cost of a main course at dinner, or if dinner is not served, at lunch. Hotel prices are the lowest cost of a standard double room in high season.

SAFETY

In general, Fez and Meknès are safe cities. In Fez—less in Meknès—pick-pocketing and unwanted hassle from hustlers and faux guides will be the biggest concern. Harassment from those offering to be tour guides or drivers is best avoided by smiling and firmly saying "no thank you," preferably in French or Arabic. Try not to become visibly agitated, as it could exacerbate the situation.

You can safely explore Fez medina during the day, but ask at your hotel if there are any areas you should avoid after dark. If you get off track, turn around and head back to a more populated area. If you are followed, enter a store, hotel, restaurant, or café and ask for help. At night, poorly lit medina alleyways can be intimidating but are not necessarily unsafe. Often hotels and restaurants will dispatch someone to escort you to your destination.

From December through January, heavy snowfall may cover Middle Atlas roads; however, the snow-removal systems in places such as the Azrou Cedar Forest are relatively good, with cleared driving routes. More remote roads (marked in white on the Michelin map of Morocco) will be difficult to access or completely closed in snowy conditions. Driving off-road or to natural sites such as the Cascades d'Ouzoud in winter, when snowfall can be significant, is not advised.

FEZ

Fez is one of the world's most spectacular city-museums and an exotic medieval labyrinth—mysterious, mesmerizing, and sometimes over-whelming. Passing through one of the *babs* (gates) into Fez el-Bali is like entering a time warp, with only the numerous satellite dishes installed on nearly every roof as a reminder you're in the 21st century, not the 8th. As you maneuver through crowded passages illuminated by shafts of sunlight streaming through thatched roofs of the *kissaria* (covered markets), the cries of *"Balek!"* ("Watch out!") from donkey drivers pushing overloaded mules—overlapped with the cacophony of locals bartering, coppersmiths hammering, and the *muezzin,*the city-wide call to prayer—blend with the strong odors of aromatic spices, curing leather, and smoking grills for an incredible sensorial experience you will never forget.

PLANNING YOUR TIME
FESTIVALS

Fodor'sChoice **Fes Festival of World Sacred Music.** Sponsored by the Foundation of Fez, a
★ nonprofit association working to maintain the city's cultural heritage,
the annual Fes Festival of World Sacred Music focuses on a different
theme each year and has become an international favorite, attracting
some of the world's finest musicians and intellectual scholars for the Fes
Forum roundtable debates. Concerts are held in diverse venues across
the city, from the imposing Bab Al Makina to the beautiful gardens of
the Dar Batha Museum. There are also free concerts, including Sufi
Nights, held daily in a palatial dar. Check the website for festival dates.
⊠ *Fez* ☎ *0535/74–05–35, 0535/74–06–91* ⊕ *www.fesfestival.com.*

GETTING HERE AND AROUND

Fez is an enigmatic, exotic city best explored on foot. Walking beneath
one of the imposing arched babs and into the medina's maze of cobbled
streets stimulates all the senses. Summer months can be unbearably
hot with little air circulation, especially along canopied and crowded
alleyways. The best time to tour is the morning; crowds and temperatures won't be too intense. Nights are cool throughout the year with a
refreshing desert breeze. Remember that Friday is a traditional day of
prayer, and many establishments in the medina are closed.

AIR TRAVEL

The main gateway to the region is Fès-Saïss Airport. Driving to downtown Fez takes about 30 minutes. A taxi will cost around 200 DH; a
local bus from the Ville Nouvelle around 5 DH.

BUS TRAVEL

Hourly CTM buses cover the Fez–Meknès route. The trip takes about
one hour and costs 25 DH. The bus to Marrakesh takes about nine
hours and costs 190 DH. The bus to Casablanca takes around five
hours and costs 100 DH. The bus to Tangier takes around six hours
and costs 125 DH.

Bus Contacts CTM. ⊠ *Pl. Atlas, Ville Nouvelle* ☎ *0653/88–96–21* ⊕ *www.ctm.ma.*

CAR TRAVEL

You will not want a car in Fez. Indeed, a car would probably impede
your ability to negotiate the city. But if you plan to explore the Middle
Atlas region, or if you are beginning a larger trip to Morocco in Fez,
then a car may be appropriate and even necessary.

Rental Cars Avis. ⊠ *Fès-Saïss Airport* ☎ *0535/62–69–69.* **Budget.** ⊠ *Fès-
Saïss Airport* ☎ *0660/17–41–05.* **Hertz.** ⊠ *Fès-Saïss Airport, Ville Nouvelle*
☎ *0535/94–32–62* ⊕ *www.hertz.com.*

TAXI TRAVEL

Grands taxis are large, usually shared taxis (up to six passengers) that
make long-distance runs between cities. This can be faster, more comfortable, and a better value than bus travel. The local petits taxis are
metered, take up to four passengers, and may not leave the city limits.
If the driver refuses to turn on the meter or agree to a reasonable price,
don't hesitate to get out. There is a 50% surcharge after 8 pm.

TRAIN TRAVEL

Trains run between Fez and Meknès each day. They cost from 20 DH and take 45 minutes. There are seven daily trains to Casablanca (five hours, from 110 DH) via Rabat (four hours, from 80 DH). There are five daily trains to Marrakesh (eight hours, from 195 DH). The train to Tangier takes five hours and costs from 105 DH. The Fez train station is on the north side of the Ville Nouvelle, a 10-minute walk from the center of town, and a 10 DH taxi ride from the medina.

Train Information Fez Train Station. ⊠ *Av. des Almohades, Ville Nouvelle* 🕾 *0535/93-03-33.*

GUIDES AND TOURS

There's much to be said in favor of employing a good guide in Fez: you'll be left alone by faux guides and hustlers, and if your guide is good you'll learn much and be able to see more of your surroundings than when having to read and navigate as you move around. On the other hand, getting lost in Fez el-Bali is one of those great travel experiences. Maps of the medina really do work, and there are now numerous signs on medina walls pointing you to important sites, restaurants, and hotels.

The tourist office and your hotel are the best sources for official guides vetted by the ONMT. An official guide costs around 300 DH for a half day and around 500 DH for a full day, more if you include touring regions or special destinations by car.

Cafe Clock Cooking Workshop. At Cafe Clock's one-day cooking workshop you'll uncover the secrets of Moroccan cooking from souk to plate. Fassi cuisine originated in the fondouks where numerous cultures—Andalusian, Indian, and Persian among them—crossed paths, and you'll start by choosing a menu of salad, main course, and dessert. Then shop for ingredients in the souk with one of the café's Moroccan chefs before rustling up everything from tagines to couscous in the kitchen—or on the roof terrace for larger groups—and sitting down to enjoy the fruits of your labor. ⊠ *7, Derb el Magana, Fez el Bali* 🕾 *0535/63-78-55* ⊕ *www.cafeclock.com* 💲 *600 DH.*

The Courtyard Kitchen at Dar Namir. If you want to discover more about modern Moroccan cooking, sign up for a full-day private class with the knowledgeable Tara Stevens, author of the cookbook, *Clock Book*. It's as hands-on as you want it to be; after discussing the menu you'll learn about the use of herbs and spices, age-old cooking techniques, Moroccan wine, and more, as you rustle up five sophisticated dishes that might include traditional bread khobs flavored with wild marjoram, a deconstructed chicken, lemon and olive tagine, and chocolate olive oil cake. Then enjoy the fruits of your labor on the roof terrace, washed down with some of that aforementioned wine. ⊠ *Fez el Bali* ⊕ *www.darnamir.com.*

Craft Draft. Fassi artist Hamza El Fasiki—who comes from a long line of artisans—founded Craft Draft in 2013 to allow people to participate in artisan-led workshops in brass etching, bookbinding, leather embossing and more. Participants learn a practical skill, discover the history behind the art form, and learn about the value of preserving traditional crafts. ⊠ *17, Fondouk Khrashifiyen, R'cif, Fez el Bali* 🕾 *0649/89-41-97* ⊕ *www.craftdraft.org* 💲 *Group workshops from 100 DH per person.*

Culture Vultures Fez. Fez is undoubtedly Morocco's capital of art and crafts, and Culture Vultures leads an interactive small-group tour of the medina workshops of traditional craftsmen—weavers, coppersmiths, tanners, tile makers, and more. As well as gaining an insight into the daily lives of the artisans, you can try your hand at their various crafts. Tours run from Saturday to Thursday with a maximum of six people. They also run artisanal tours in Sefrou. ⊠ *Fez* ☏ *0535/68–33–75* ⊕ *www.culturevulturesfez.org.*

Fodor's Choice
★

Plan-it Morocco. This outfitter offers engaging cultural tours, from unveiling the medina's secrets on the Architecture and Islamic Gardens Tour to culinary adventures on the excellent Souk Tasting Trails tour. Or join a family as they shop for produce in their local souk, pick up bread at their neighborhood *farran* (bakery), then learn how to preserve lemons, make mint tea, and conjure up typical salads and a tagine of your choice in the kitchen of their traditional dar. You'll end by sitting down with the family to share the meal in true Moroccan style. Day trips beyond Fez—take a Roman picnic to Volubilis, barter at the carpet auction in Khenifra, or hike through the Rif Mountains—and longer excursions to the Sahara, the High Atlas, the coast, and all major Moroccan cities are also available. ⊠ *Fez* ☏ *0535/63–87–08* ⊕ *www.plan-it-morocco.com.*

VISITOR INFORMATION

Contacts Fez Tourist Office. ⊠ *Pl. Mohammed V, Ville Nouvelle* ☏ *0535/62–47–69.*

EXPLORING

FEZ EL-BALI

Fez el-Bali is a living medieval city, crafts workshop, and market that has changed little in the past millennium. With no cars allowed and some 1,000 very narrow *derbs* (dead-end alleys), it beckons the walker on an endless and absorbing odyssey. Exploring this honeycomb of ancient alleyways with often chaotic crowds, steep inclines, and pitted cobblestone steps is a challenging adventure. Fez isn't really yours, however, until you've tackled it on your own, become hopelessly lost a few times, and survived to tell the tale.

TOP ATTRACTIONS

Andalusian Mosque. This mosque was built in AD 859 by Mariam, sister of Fatima al-Fihri, who had erected the Kairaouine Mosque on the river's other side two years earlier with inherited family wealth. The gate was built by the Almohads in the 12th century. The grand carved doors on the north entrance, domed Zenet minaret, and detailed cedarwood carvings in the eaves, which bear a striking resemblance to those in the Musée Nejjarine, are the main things to see here, as the mosque itself is set back on a small elevation, making it hard to examine from outside. ⊠ *Rue Nekhaline, Fez el Bali* ☞ *Entrance restricted to Muslims.*

Attarine Medersa. Named for local spice merchants known as *attar*, the Attarine Medersa (Koranic school of the Spice Sellers) was founded by Merinid Sultan Abou Saïd Othman in the 14th century as a students' dormitory attached to the Kairaouine Mosque next door. Its graceful proportions, elegant, geometric carved-cedar ornamentation, and excellent state of preservation make it one of the best representations of Moorish architecture in Fez. ⊠ *Boutouil Kairaouine, Fez el Bali* ⏢ *20 DH.*

Fodor'sChoice **Bab Boujeloud.** Built in 1913 by General Hubert Lyautey, Moroccan
★ commander under the French protectorate, this Moorish-style gate is 1,000 years younger than the rest of the medina. It's considered the principal and most beautiful point of entry into Fez el-Bali. The side facing toward Fez el-Djedid is covered with blue ceramic tiles painted with flowers and calligraphy; the inside is green, the official color of Islam—or of peace, depending on interpretation. ⊠ *Pl. Pacha el-Baghdadi, Fez el Bali.*

Batha Musuem (*Museum of Moroccan Arts*). Housed in Dar Batha, a late-19th-century Andalusian palace built by Moulay el Hassan, the museum of Moroccan Arts has one of Morocco's finest handicrafts collections. The display of pottery, for which Fez is particularly famous, includes rural earthenware crockery and elaborate plates painted with geometrical patterns. Other displays feature embroidery stitched with real gold, astrolabes from the 11th to the 18th century, illuminated Korans, and Berber carpets and kilims. ⊠ *Dar Batha, Pl. de l'Istiqlal, entrance on Mahaj el Methab, Fez el Bali* ☎ *0535/63–41–16* ⏢ *10 DH* ☉ *Closed Tues.*

Borj Nord. Built in 1582 under the command of Saadian sultan Ahmed el Mansour, this former fortress perched above the city guarded and controlled Fez el-Bali. In 1963, a huge collection of weapons originally housed in the Batha Museum was brought to the historic site, creating the interesting display in what is now the national Museum of Arms. Sabers, swords, shields, and armour from the 19th century showcase the history of how arms played a social role in tribal hierarchy. Of importance is the arsenal of sultans Moulay Ismail and Moulay Mohammed Beh Abdellah—the elaborate Berber guns encrusted in enamel, ivory, silver, and precious gems date back to the 17th century. ■TIP→ **Walk up to the crenellated rooftop in late afternoon for a beautiful panoramic view of the city.** ⊠ *Borj Nord, Fez el Bali* ☎ *0535/64–52–41* ⏢ *10 DH* ☉ *Closed Tues.*

Fodor'sChoice **Bou Inania Medersa.** From outside Bab Boujeloud you will see this med-
★ ersa's green-tile tower, generally considered the most beautiful of the Kairaouine University's 14th-century residential colleges. It was built by order of Abou Inan, the first ruler of the Merenid dynasty, which would become the most decisive ruling clan in Fez's development. The main components of the medersa's stunningly intricate decorative artwork are: the green-tile roofing; the cedar eaves and upper patio walls carved in floral and geometrical motifs; the carved-stucco midlevel walls; the ceramic-tile lower walls covered with calligraphy (Kufi script, essentially cursive Arabic) and geometric designs; and, finally, the marble floor. Showing its age, the carved cedar is still dazzling, with each square inch a masterpiece of handcrafted sculpture involving long hours of the kind of concentration required to memorize the Koran. The black belt of ceramic tile around the courtyard bears Arabic script reading "this is a place of learning" and other such exhortatory academic messages. ⊠ *Talâa Kebira, Fez el Bali* ⏢ *20 DH.*

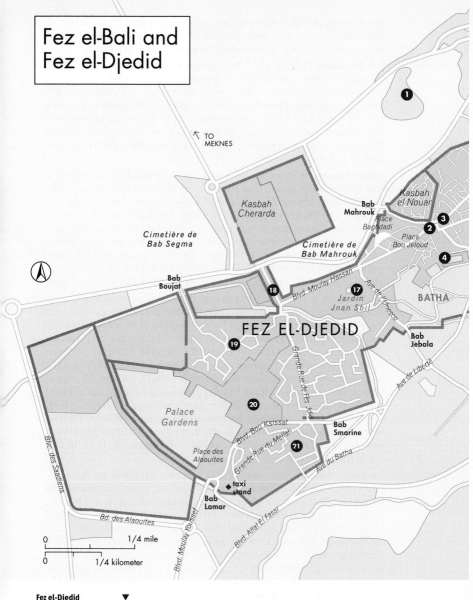

Fez el-Bali and Fez el-Djedid

TO MEKNES

Kasbah Cheranda

Cimetière de Bab Segma

Bab Mahrouk

Kasbah el Nouar

Place Baghdadi

2

3

Place Bou Jeloud

4

Cimetière de Bab Mahrouk

BATHA

Bab Boujat

18

Blvd. Moulay Hassan

17

Jardin Jnan Sbil

Ave. de l'Unesco

FEZ EL-DJEDID

Bab Jebala

19

Grande Rue de Fès-Jdid

Ave. de Liberté

Palace Gardens

20

Blvd. Bou Ksissat

Bab Smarine

Grande Rue du Mellah

21

Ave. du Batha

Place des Alaouites

Place des Alaouites

◆ taxi stand

Bab Lamar

Blvd. des Saadiens

Blvd. Moulay Youssef

Bd. des Alaouites

Blvd. Allal El Fassi

0 _____ 1/4 mile

0 _____ 1/4 kilometer

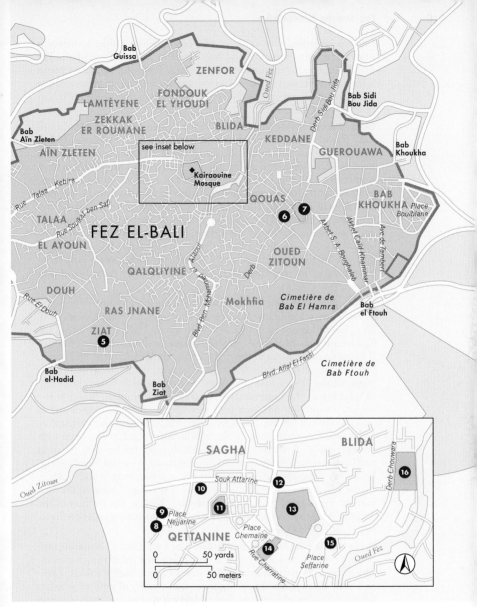

Fontaine Nejjarine. This ceramic-tile, cedar-ceiling public fountain is one of the more beautiful and historic of its kind in Fez el-Bali. The first fountain down from Bab Boujeloud, Fontaine Nejjarine seems a miniature version of the Nejjarine fondouk, with its geometrically decorated tiles and intricately carved cedar eaves overhead. ✉ *Pl. Nejjarine, Fez el Bali.*

Glaoui Palace. Among the medina's many hidden palaces, the extraordinary Dar al Glaoui is one of its most atmospheric. The Pasha of Marrakesh's second home—he ruled over most of southern Morocco in his day—has fallen into disrepair since Morocco's independence from France in 1956, when his power waned. But amid the crumbling ruins, evidence of its former grandeur is visible in the exquisite cedarwood doors, intricate stucco, tiled salons, and the carved wooden balconies that line its patios. The large estate was comprised of 17 buildings and two gardens, with ornate salons, an enormous kitchen, Koranic school, garages, stables, a harem, and a hammam. Abdou—an artist and one of the remaining family members—or his sister will show you some of its treasures. ✉ *1, rue Hamia Douh, Ziat, Fez el Bali* ☎ *0667/36–68–28.*

Kairaouine Mosque. This is considered one of the most important mosques in the Western Muslim world. One look through the main doorway will give you an idea of its immensity. With about 10,760 square feet, the Kairaouine was Morocco's largest mosque until Casablanca's Hassan II Mosque came along in the early 1990s. Built in AD 857 by Fatima, the daughter of a wealthy Kairaouine refugee, the mosque became the home of the West's first university and the world's foremost center of learning at the beginning of the second millennium. Stand at the entrance door's left side for a peek through the dozen horseshoe arches into the *mihrab* (marked by a hanging light). An east-facing alcove or niche used for leading prayer, the mihrab is rounded and covered with an arch designed to project sound back through the building. Lean in and look up to the brightly painted and intricately carved wood ceiling. If you get there just before prayer times, the two huge wooden doors by the entrance will be open, providing a privileged view of the vast interior. For a good view of the courtyard, head to the rooftop of the Attarine Medersa. ⚠ **Only Muslims may enter the mosque.** ✉ *Bou Touil, Fez el Bali* ☎ *0535/64–10–16.*

Musée Nejjarine des Arts et Métiers du Bois. The 14th-century Nejjarine fondouk, or Inn of the Carpenters, is now home to a fascinating museum. The three-story patio displays Morocco's various native woods, 18th- and 19th-century woodworking tools, and a series of antique wooden doors and pieces of furniture. For 10 DH enjoy mint tea on the rooftop terrace with panoramic views over the medina. Don't miss the former jail cell on the ground floor, or the large set of weighing scales, a reminder of the building's original functions—commerce on the ground floor and lodging on the levels above. ■ TIP→ **Check out the palatial, cedar-ceiling public bathrooms, certainly the finest of their kind in Fez.** ✉ *Pl. Nejjarine, Fez el Bali* ☎ *0535/74–05–80* 💰 *20 DH.*

The dye vats of the Terrasse des Tanneurs may be pleasing to the eye, but they are not pleasing to the nose.

Place Seffarine. This wide, triangular souk of the *dinandiers*, or coppersmiths, is a welcome open space, a comfortable break from tight crags and corners. Donkeys and their masters wait for transport work here, and a couple of trees are reminders this was once a fertile valley alongside the Fez River. Copper and brass bowls, plates, and buckets are wrought and hammered over fires around the market's edge, where the smells of soldering irons and donkey droppings permeate the air. Look toward the Kairaouine Mosque at the top of the square to see the Kairaouine University library, which once housed the world's best collection of Islamic literature but is only open to Muslim scholars. ⊠ *Pl. Seffarine, Fez el Bali.*

Sahrij Medersa. Built by the Merenids in the 14th century, one of the medina's finest medersas has been beautifully restored. It's named for the *sahrij* (pool) on which its patio is centered, with rich chocolate-color cedar wall carvings and some of the oldest zellij mosaic tiling in the country. It's still a working school, so head up the narrow steps leading to empty rooms over the central patio and you may hear the chanting of Koranic verses. ⊠ *Andalusian Quarter, Fez el Bali* 🖅 *20 DH.*

Souk el-Henna. This little henna market is one of the medina's most picturesque squares, with a massive, gnarled fig tree in the center and rows of spices, hennas, kohls, and aphrodisiacs for sale in the tiny stalls around the edges. The ceramic shops on the way into the henna souk sell a wide variety of typically blue Fassi pottery. At the square's end is a plaque dedicated to the Maristan Sidi Frej, a medical center and psychiatric and teaching hospital built by the Merenid ruler Youssef Ibn

Yakoub in 1286. Used as a model for the world's first mental hospital—founded in Valencia, Spain, in 1410—the Maristan operated until 1944. ⊠ *Derb Fakharine, Fez el Bali.*

Fodor's Choice
★

Terrasse des Tanneurs. The medieval tanneries are at once beautiful, for their ancient dyeing vats of reds, yellows, and blues, and unforgettable, for the malodorous smell of decaying animal flesh on sheep, goat, cow, and camel skins. The terrace overlooking the dyeing vats is high enough to escape the place's full fetid power and get a spectacular view over the multicolor vats. Absorb both the process and the finished product on Chouara Lablida, just past Rue Mechatine (named for the combs made from animals' horns): numerous stores are filled with loads of leather goods, including coats, bags, and *babouches* (traditional slippers). One of the shopkeepers will hand you a few sprigs of fresh mint to smother the smell and explain what's going on in the tanneries below—how the skins are placed successively in saline solution, quicklime, pigeon droppings, and then any of several natural dyes: poppies for red, turmeric for yellow, saffron for orange, indigo for blue, and mint for green. Barefoot workers in shorts pick up skins from the bottoms of the dyeing vats with their feet, then work them manually. Though this may look like the world's least desirable job, the work is relatively well paid and still in demand for a strong export market. ⊠ *Chouara Lablida, Fez el Bali.*

Zaouia of Moulay Idriss II. Originally built by the Idriss dynasty in the 9th century in honor of the city's founder—just 33 at the time of his death—this *zaouia* (sanctuary) was restored by the Merenid dynasty in the 13th century and has became one of the medina's holiest shrines. Particularly known for his *baraka* (divine protection), Moulay Idriss II had an especially strong cult among women seeking fertility and pilgrims hoping for good luck. The wooden beam at the entrance, about six feet from the ground, was originally placed there to keep Jews, Christians, and donkeys out of the *horm,* the sacred area surrounding the shrine itself. Inside the horm, Moroccans have historically enjoyed official sanctuary—they cannot be arrested if sought by the law. You may be able to catch a glimpse of the saint's tomb at the far right corner through the doorway; look for the fervently faithful burning candles and incense, and the tomb's silk-brocade covering. Note the rough wooden doors themselves, worn smooth with hundreds of years of kissing and caressing the wood for *baraka* (blessing). ⊠ *Bou Touil, on north side of mosque, Fez el Bali* ☞ *Entrance restricted to Muslims.*

WORTH NOTING

Cherratine Medersa. Recent restoration against humidity and other natural aggressions has kept this important historical site intact. Constructed in 1670 by Moulay Rachid, this is one of Fez's two Alaouite medersas. More austere than the 14th-century medersas of the Merenids, the Cherratine is more functional, designed to hold over 200 students. It's interesting primarily as a contrast to the intricate craftsmanship and decorative intent of the Merenid structures. The entry doors beautifully engraved in bronze lead to the *douiras,* narrow residential blocks consisting of a honeycomb of small rooms. ⊠ *Derb Zaouia, Fez el Bali* 🖾 *20 DH.*

FEZ EL-DJEDID

Fez el-Djedid (New Fez) lies southwest of Bab Boujeloud between Fez el-Bali and the Ville Nouvelle. Built after 1273 by the Merenid dynasty as a government seat and stronghold, it remained the administrative center of Morocco until 1912, when Rabat took over the role and diminished this area's visibility and activity. The three distinct segments of Fez el-Djedid consist of the Royal Palace in the west, the Mellah or Jewish Quarter in the south, and Muslim District in the east.

TOP ATTRACTIONS

Bab es Seba. Named for the seven brothers of Moulay Abdellah, who reigned during the 18th century, the Gate of Seven connects two open spaces originally designed for military parades and royal ceremonies, the Petit Méchouar and Vieux Méchouar, now known as Moulay Hassan II Square. It was from this gate that Prince Ferdinand, brother of Duarte, king of Portugal, was hanged head-down for four days in 1437 after being captured during a failed Portuguese invasion of Tangier. ⊠ *Av. Moulay Hassan, Fez el Djedid.*

Dar el-Makhzen. Fez's Royal Palace and gardens are strictly closed to the public, but even from the outside they're an impressive sight. From Place des Alaouites, take a close look at the door's giant brass knockers, made by artisans from Fez el-Bali, as well as the imposing brass doors themselves. Inside are various palaces, 200 acres of gardens, and parade grounds, as well as a medersa founded in 1320. One of the palaces inside, Dar el-Qimma, has intricately engraved and painted ceilings. The street running along the palace's southeast side is Rue Bou Khessissat, one side of which is lined with typically ornate residential facades from the Mellah's edge. ⚠ **Security in this area is high and should be respected. Guards watch visitors carefully.** ⊠ *Fez el Djedid.*

Jardin Jnan Sbil. Gardens play an important role in Moroccan culture, and this gorgeous green space just outside the medina walls is one of the oldest in Fez. Once part of the Royal Palace, it was donated to the city in the 19th century by Sultan Moulay Hassan. Because of its importance, the garden recently underwent four years of restoration to return it to its former splendor, and it reopened to the public in 2011. Now a stroll around its shady pathways, with time to admire its many towering palms, rose bushes, lakes, and fountains, is the perfect escape from the medina's hubbub. ⊠ *Av. Moulay Hassan, Fez el Djedid.*

Mellah. With its characteristically ornate balconies and forged-iron windows, the Mellah was created in the 15th century when the Jews, forced out of the medina in one of Morocco's recurrent pogroms, were removed from their previous ghetto near Bab Guissa and set up as royal financial consultants and buffers between the Merenid rulers and the people. Fez's Jewish community suffered repressive measures until the beginning of the French protectorate in 1912. Faced with an uncertain future after Morocco gained independence in 1956, nearly all of Fez's Jews migrated to Israel, the United States, or Casablanca. ■ TIP→ **Head to the terrace of Danan Synagogue on Rue Der el-Ferah Teati for a panoramic view of the district.** ⊠ *Fez el Djedid* ✛ *Accessible via Place des Alaouites or Bab el-Mellah.*

WORTH NOTING

Moulay Abdellah Quarter. Built by the Merenids as a government seat and a stronghold against their subjects, this area lost its purpose when Rabat became the Moroccan capital under the French protectorate in 1912. Subsequently a red-light district filled with brothels and dance halls, the quarter was closed to foreigners for years. Historic highlights include the vertically green-striped **Moulay Abdellah Mosque** and the **Great Mosque Abu Haq**, built by the Merenid sultan in 1276. ✉ *Fez el Djedid.*

VILLE NOUVELLE

The 20th-century Ville Nouvelle is a modern neighborhood built by the French, with tree-lined avenues, contemporary hotels, fashionable boutiques, and upscale residences. Considerable commercial development is taking place to attract younger, affluent Fassis. There are no outstanding historical sites, but visit this area for newer cafés, restaurants, and lodging.

5

WHERE TO EAT

In the country's culinary capital, foodie pleasures are everywhere: from simple food stalls and cafés to gourmet Moroccan fare in ancient palaces, traditional Moroccan recipes given a contemporary twist by innovative chefs, and French- and Mediterranean-influenced dishes. For something quick and filling, you can always grab a 10 DH bowl of cumin-laced pea or bean soup at one of the many stands and stalls near the medina's main food markets just inside Bab Boujeloud, or take a sightseeing break with a honey-laden pastry and some fresh mint tea. For a heartier meal, there's grilled meat, slow-cooked tagines, and vegetable-topped couscous. Taste Fassi specialties on a fascinating street-food tour, and don't leave without sampling pigeon pastilla, a heavenly combination of sweet and sour flavors. It's often made with chicken nowadays, but the Ruined Garden, in the medina, will cook the authentic dish to order with a day's notice.

FEZ EL-BALI

$$ MOROCCAN

🍴 **L'Amandier.** This fine-dining Moroccan restaurant sits on the top floor of Palais Faraj, with stunning views over the medina, especially romantic at night. The decor is sleek and sophisticated, the service is attentive, and the chef has re-created age-old Fassi recipes. **Known for:** sophisticated Moroccan cuisine; opulent decor. [$] *Average main: 220DH* ✉ *Palais Faraj, Bab Zhiat, Quartier Ziat, Fez el Bali* ☎ *0535/63–53–56* 🌐 *www.palaisfaraj.com/EN/restaurants* 🕓 *No lunch.*

$ ECLECTIC Fodor's Choice ★

🍴 **Cafe Clock.** Set in the heart of the medina, this cross-cultural café is a Fez institution. It's the perfect place to take a sightseeing break with a tea or mocktail, or a bite from the eclectic menu, like the justly famous camel burger; there are vegetarian-friendly options as well. **Known for:** cultural programs; cooking workshops; relaxed vibe. [$] *Average main: 85DH* ✉ *7, Derb el Magana, Fez el Bali* ☎ *0535/63–78–55* 🌐 *www.cafeclock.com.*

$ MOROCCAN

🍴 **Dar Hatim.** They say the best Moroccan food is served at home, and Dar Hatim is the next-best thing. In the convivial, exquisitely tiled dining room of a family home, you can choose from several three-course set menus of traditional Moroccan dishes. **Known for:** home cooking; family dar turned restaurant. [$] *Average main: 190DH* ✉ *19, Derb Ezaouia Fandak Lihoudi, Fez el Bali* ☎ *0535/52–53–23, 0666/52–53–23.*

$$$ MOROCCAN
🍴 **Eden at Palais Amani.** Dining under the stars in this Andalusian-style oasis is a delight, surrounding by citrus trees and next to a twinkling fountain. The chefs take traditional recipes and give them a contemporary presentation, creating a weekly changing three-course dinner using seasonal produce from the market. **Known for:** Morocco meets Mediterranean cuisine; pre- and postdinner cocktails in the rooftop bar. [$] *Average main: 395DH* ✉ *Palais Amani, 12, Derb el Miter, Oued Zhoune, Fez el Bali* ☎ *0535/63–32–09* 🌐 *www.palaisamani.com.*

$ MEDITERRANEAN FAMILY Fodor's Choice ★
🍴 **Fez Café.** This popular bistro-style café-cum-restaurant is set in the delightful oasis of Jardin des Biehn. The daily changing chalkboard menu reflects the Moroccan chef's love of Gallic gastronomy, as he happily mixes Moroccan and French culinary influences, using fresh ingredients from the market and the owners' organic garden. **Known for:** gorgeous garden; vegetarian friendly; serves alcohol. [$] *Average main: 135DH* ✉ *13, Akbat Sbaa, Douh, Fez el Bali* ☎ *0535/63–50–31* 🌐 *www.jardindesbiehn.com/fez-cafe-restaurant* ⏲ *Closed Wed.*

$ MEDITERRANEAN FAMILY
🍴 **Le 44.** Tired of tagines? This light, bright, contemporary riad has been turned into a family- and vegetarian-friendly café-restaurant that serves up pasta dishes, fresh salads, and soups, as well as delicious French desserts like tarte tatin. **Known for:** international flavor; vegetarian options. [$] *Average main: 50DH* ✉ *44, Derb Bensalem, off Talaa Kbira, Fez el Bali* ☎ *0634/70–75–13* ⏲ *Closed Mon.*

$ MOROCCAN
🍴 **Le Kasbah.** Spread over several levels, this good-value restaurant just below Bab Boujeloud offers an entertaining view of the street life below. The menu is standard tourist fare so you're probably better off sticking to a mint tea. **Known for:** great views; local feel. [$] *Average main: 70DH* ✉ *Rue Serrajine, Fez el Bali* ☎ *0535/74–15–33.*

$$$$ MOROCCAN
🍴 **NUR.** Chef Najat Kaanache has returned to her Moroccan roots to open this chic riad-turned-restaurant. The seasonally inspired tasting menu—around eight courses—changes often, reflecting the market finds of the day with a focus on artful presentation and inspired flavor combinations. **Known for:** contemporary Moroccan cuisine in a seasonally inspired tasting menu. [$] *Average main: 700DH* ✉ *7, Zkak Rouah, Fez el Bali* ☎ *0694/27–78–49* 🌐 *www.nur.ma* ⏲ *Closed Mon.*

$$ MEDITERRANEAN Fodor's Choice ★
🍴 **Restaurant Dar Roumana.** One of the city's best eateries is set in the strikingly beautiful courtyard of hotel Dar Roumana. Moroccan chef Youness Toumi has created two- and three-course Mediterranean menus with a Moroccan twist that makes the most of seasonal produce from top local producers. **Known for:** fine dining; beautiful and intimate riad setting; top-notch wine list. [$] *Average main: 275DH* ✉ *Dar Roumana, 30, Derb El Amer, Zkak Roumane, Fez el Bali* ☎ *0535/74–16–37* 🌐 *www.darroumana.com* ⏲ *No lunch. Closed Mon.*

$ MOROCCAN FAMILY Fodor's Choice ★
🍴 **Ruined Garden Restaurant.** This British-run alfresco restaurant, set in the romantic remains of a ruined riad, comes complete with crumbling mosaic floors, fountains, and lush foliage. The à la carte menu and daily specials focus on street food–style dishes prepared using fresh produce from the souk. **Known for:** a sophisticated take on Moroccan street

food; beautiful garden setting. [$] *Average main: 100DH* ✉ *Sidi Ahmed Chaoui, Siaj, Fez el Bali* ☎ *0649/19–14–10* 🌐 *www.ruinedgarden.com* ⏲ *Closed 2nd half July.*

$ MOROCCAN 🍴 **Thami's.** Thami's is the perfect place to enjoy a delicious, well-priced meal with the added bonus of first-rate people-watching at the top of one of the medina's busiest thoroughfares. Thami's has expanded over the years from a single table and four chairs under the shade of a mulberry tree to a full-fledged restaurant. **Known for:** traditional dishes; in the thick of medina life. [$] *Average main: 65DH* ✉ *44, rue Sarrajine, near Bab Boujeloud, at top of Tala'a Sghira, Fez el Bali* ☎ *0660/43–35–05* 💳 *No credit cards.*

VILLE NOUVELLE

$$ MEDITERRANEAN 🍴 **MB Fès.** The menu of this restaurant-lounge features French-influenced fare such as *magret de canard* (duck breast) and sole meunière, and international favorites such as Caesar salad and hamburger, backed up with an impressive wine list. One of the city's most stylish eateries, the minimalist design channels industrial chic with rough-hewn stone walls, slate floors, and floor-to-ceiling windows, complemented by sleek, contemporary furniture. **Known for:** contemporary style; Mediterranean menu. [$] *Average main: 165DH* ✉ *12, rue Ahmed Chaouki, Ville Nouvelle* ☎ *0535/62–27–27* 🌐 *www.mbrestaurantlounge.com.*

WHERE TO STAY

Staying in Fez's medina offers such a unique experience that you're best off choosing a hotel either in or very near medieval Fez el-Bali. Choose an atmospheric riad, boutique hotel, or resort-style hotel. There are also some good new hotels in the Ville Nouvelle. There are no hotels in Fez el-Djedid.

FEZ EL-BALI

$ B&B/INN 🏨 **Dar Arsama.** This tranquil and intimate property has been sensitively restored by its creative, hands-on owners, Violeta from Spain and her Fassi husband, Adil. **Pros:** friendly hosts; delicious food; lovely decor. **Cons:** small property; steep stairs; pedestrian-only access. [$] *Rooms from: 550DH* ✉ *14, Derb Sidi Safi, Fez el Bali* ☎ *0673/22–75–42* 🌐 *www.dar-arsama.com* 🛏 *3 rooms* 🍽 *Breakfast.*

$ B&B/INN FAMILY 🏨 **Dar Finn.** The former offices of the lawyer of the Pasha of Tazi has been restored to its former splendor by a British couple, who have created five rooms and two enormous suites—the Pacha Suite was once his office—large enough for families. **Pros:** plenty of outside space; central location; friendly staff. **Cons:** small property; Wi-Fi patchy in the upstairs rooms; pedestrian-only access. [$] *Rooms from: 936DH* ✉ *27, Zkak Rouah, Chrablyine, Fez el Bali* ☎ *0655/01–89–75, 0535/74–00–04* 🌐 *www.darfinn.com* 🛏 *7 rooms* 🍽 *Breakfast.*

$ B&B/INN Fodor's Choice ★ 🏨 **Dar Roumana.** The House of the Pomegranate is a sumptuously restored residence, with five stunning suites that showcase the work of Fez's famous artisans in their carved cedarwood doors and lofty ceilings, mosaic tile floors, and intricate plasterwork. **Pros:** beautiful decor; great service; excellent restaurant. **Cons:** hard to find (but they have a porter); steep stairs to upper-floor rooms; pedestrian-only access. $ *Rooms from: 856DH* ✉ *30, Derb el Amer, Zkak Roumane, Fez el Bali* ☎ *0535/74–16–37* ⊕ *www.darroumana.com* ⤷ *5 rooms* ¦○¦ *Breakfast.*

$$$
B&B/INN

Le Jardin des Biehn. Attracting a global clientele, this *maison d'hôtes* with a French flavor is a serene experience from the moment you step through the ocher-colored passageway into the luxuriant garden filled with sweet-scented jasmine and roses, olive and citrus trees. **Pros:** eclectic decor; beautiful garden oasis; lovely café restaurant. **Cons:** may be too intimate for some; may get chilly in winter; pedestrian-only access. $ *Rooms from: 1650DH* ✉ *13, Akbat Sbaa, Douh, Fez el Bali* ☎ *0535/74–10–36, 0664/64–76–79* ⊕ *www.jardindesbiehn.com* ⤷ *4 rooms, 5 suites* ¦○¦ *Breakfast.*

$$$$
B&B/INN
Fodor'sChoice
★

Karawan Riad. The nomadic French owners of this contemporary caravansary spent ten years reinventing this palatial 17th-century riad. **Pros:** spacious, beautifully decorated rooms; roof terrace; good restaurant. **Cons:** pedestrian-only access; steep stairs to upper floors; can be hard to find. $ *Rooms from: 2500DH* ✉ *21, Derb Ourbia, Fez el Bali* ☎ *0535/63–78–78* ⊕ *www.karawanriad.com* ⤷ *7 suites* ¦○¦ *Breakfast.*

$$$
HOTEL

La Maison Bleue. Originally the private residence of Sidi Mohammed el Abaddi, a famous judge and astrologer, this 19th-century family home has been renovated and expanded several times over the years, and now it's beginning to fray slightly around the edges. **Pros:** central location; historic building; private balconies. **Cons:** expensive rooms; unreliable service; faded furnishings. $ *Rooms from: 1900DH* ✉ *33, Derb El Mitter, Ain Zliten, Fez el Bali* ☎ *0535/63–60–52* ⊕ *www.maisonbleue.com* ⤷ *18 rooms* ¦○¦ *Breakfast.*

$$$$
HOTEL
Fodor'sChoice
★

Palais Amani. Amid the bustling alleyways near the tanneries and the parking area of Oued Zhoune, Palais Amani is an unexpected oasis of tranquillity and elegance. **Pros:** personalized service; spacious, elegant rooms; elevator. **Cons:** no pool; pedestrian-only access (but close to parking); can be expensive. $ *Rooms from: 2750DH* ✉ *12, Derb el Miter, Oued Zhoune, Fez el Bali* ☎ *0535/63–32–09* ⊕ *www.palaisamani.com* ⤷ *15 rooms* ¦○¦ *Breakfast.*

$$$
HOTEL

Palais Faraj Suites & Spa. Housed in a lavish 19th-century former palace set just outside the medina walls, the 25 suites blend contemporary furnishings with acres of marble, intricately carved cedarwood, ornate zellij tiling, and sparkling chandeliers—the work of a four-year renovation led by experts in Moorish architecture. **Pros:** road access; first-rate facilities; large swimming pool. **Cons:** not in the thick of the medina; not as intimate as a riad; rates can be high. $ *Rooms from: 2000DH* ✉ *Bab Ziat, Quartier Ziat, Fez el Bali* ☎ *0535/63–53–56* ⊕ *www.palaisfaraj.com* ⤷ *25 suites* ¦○¦ *Breakfast.*

$
B&B/INN

Riad Anata. The Belgian owner has given this traditional house a lighter, more contemporary feel while staying true to its Moroccan roots, decorating the five rooms—named after colors—in pale tones, with smooth tadelakt walls and splashes of vibrant color from throws, rugs, and local artwork. **Pros:** personal service; close to taxis and parking; light, bright decor. **Cons:** lacks ornate Moroccan decor; small property; steep stairs. $ *Rooms from: 1155DH* ✉ *Derb El-Hamia, Fez el Bali* ☎ *0535/74–15–37* ⊕ *www.riad-anata.com* ⤷ *5 rooms* ¦○¦ *Breakfast.*

Once the sun sets, Fez begins to come alive with lights.

$$$$ HOTEL 🏨 **Riad Fès - Relais & Châteaux.** For an architecturally refined interpretation of riad living, head to this luxurious hotel: a perfect blend of character, modern convenience, creature comforts, and outstanding service. **Pros:** quiet location; luxurious appointments; sumptuous spa. **Cons:** expensive rates, look for offers; pedestrian-only access; pricey restaurant. [$] *Rooms from: 2100DH* ✉ *5, Derb Ibn Slimane Zerbtana, Fez el Bali* ☎ *0535/74–12–06* 🌐 *www.riadfes.com* 🛏 *44 rooms* 🍴 *Breakfast.*

$ B&B/INN Fodor's Choice ★ 🏨 **Riad Idrissy.** After a meticulous restoration, this delightful British-run riad's triple-height courtyard and five rooms are resplendent with dazzling zellij tiles and ornate stuccowork. **Pros:** charming and attentive staff; access to the Ruined Garden restaurant in the mornings; beautifully decorated. **Cons:** may feel too small and personal for some; steep stairs to upper-floor rooms; pedestrian-only access. [$] *Rooms from: 800DH* ✉ *Derb Idrissy, Fez el Bali* 🌐 *www.riadidrissy.com* 🛏 *5 rooms* 🍴 *Breakfast.*

$$ B&B/INN Fodor's Choice ★ 🏨 **Riad Laaroussa.** Built around a lush courtyard garden—a tranquil oasis from the medina's mayhem right on the doorstep—this 17th-century palace had fallen into disrepair before being rescued and rebuilt by its French-American owners, utilizing the skills of the city's finest craftsmen. **Pros:** swimming pool and courtyard garden; personalized service; central location. **Cons:** intimate property; steep stairs to upper-floor rooms; pedestrian-only access. [$] *Rooms from: 1200DH* ✉ *3, Derb Bechara, Fez el Bali* ☎ *0674/18–76–39* 🌐 *www.riad-laaroussa.com* 🛏 *12 rooms* 🍴 *Breakfast.*

$ B&B/INN 🏨 **Riad Numero 9.** It's just like staying at a friend's house, a friend with impeccable taste that is, and what it lacks in size—there are just three bedrooms set around the courtyard, each on a different level—it more than makes up for in style. **Pros:** perfect for small groups; central location; beautifully decorated. **Cons:** the smallest room is not en suite; windows open onto the courtyard; steep stairs. $ *Rooms from: 1000DH* ✉ *9, Derb Lamsside, Zkak el Ma, Fez el Bali* ⊕ *www.riad9.com* ▭ *No credit cards* ⤳ *3 rooms* ⍾ *Breakfast.*

$

B&B/INN

⌗ **Ryad Mabrouka.** This carefully restored Andalusian town house in the heart of the medina is consistently a pleasure: every detail is polished, from magnificent doors and crafted furnishings to a pretty interior garden with well-maintained pool. **Pros:** central location; good service; terrace. **Cons:** not for families with young children; steep steps; pedestrian-only access. $ *Rooms from: 1000DH* ✉ *25, Derb el Miter, Fez el Bali* ☎ *0535/63–63–45* ⊕ *www.ryadmabrouka.com* ⤳ *8 rooms* ⍾ *Breakfast.*

VILLE NOUVELLE

$$$

HOTEL

⌗ **Barceló Fès Medina.** Despite its name, this contemporary hotel—the Spanish chain's second in Morocco—actually sits in a prime spot at the edge of the Ville Nouvelle, with stellar views over the medina. **Pros:** located between old and new Fez; swimming pool; contemporary design. **Cons:** not in the medina; not as intimate as a riad; lacks an authentic Moroccan feel. $ *Rooms from: 1760DH* ✉ *53, av. Hassan II, Ville Nouvelle* ☎ *0535/94–88–00* ⊕ *www.barcelo.com* ⤳ *134 rooms* ⍾ *Multiple meal plans.*

$$

HOTEL

FAMILY

⌗ **Fes Marriott Hotel Jnan Palace.** Marriott debuted their first Moroccan hotel in the Ville Nouvelle at the beginning of 2017, catering to both leisure and business travelers. **Pros:** spacious rooms; numerous dining options; luxurious pool area. **Cons:** breakfast is expensive; look out for offers; outside the medina; lacks an authentic Moroccan feel. $ *Rooms from: 1200DH* ✉ *8, av. Ahmed Chaouki, Ville Nouvelle* ☎ *0535/94–72–50* ⊕ *www.marriott.com/hotels/travel/fezmc-fes-marriott-hotel-jnan-palace* ⤳ *244 rooms* ⍾ *Breakfast.*

$$$$

HOTEL

⌗ **Hotel Sahrai.** Perched on a hill looking down on the medina, this boldly designed and ultrastylish boutique hotel has brought a new level of contemporary luxury to Fez. Using Taza limestone, marble, wood, metal, and glass, French design guru Christophe Pillet has imitated the layout of the old city. **Pros:** stylish, contemporary decor; choice of restaurants and bars; Givenchy Spa. **Cons:** not for those looking for traditional Moroccan style; can be expensive, check for offers; outside the medina. $ *Rooms from: 2500DH* ✉ *Bab Lghoul, Dhar el Mehraz, Ville Nouvelle* ☎ *0535/94–03–32* ⊕ *www.hotelsahrai.com* ⤳ *50 rooms* ⍾ *Breakfast.*

NIGHTLIFE

The Ville Nouvelle has a more active nightlife in Fez, though many of the best hotel bars are in or near the edge of the medina.

FEZ EL-BALI

BARS

Fodor'sChoice
★

Le Golden Bar. This Art Deco–influenced bar attracts sophisticated locals and visitors as much for the medina views as the creative cocktails. Perched atop the hotel Palais Faraj, with sweeping vistas on three sides, you can sample a well-crafted cocktail, a glass of fine local wine, or beer from a comfortable couch. This intimate spot also hosts live music and DJs on weekend nights. There's also a large alfresco terrace overlooking the jumble of medina rooftops. ■ TIP→ **Get there for sunset to watch the old city turn to gold.** ✉ *Palais Faraj, Bab Ziat, Quartier Ziat, Fez el Bali* ☎ *0661/07–46–99* 🌐 *www.palaisfaraj.com.*

$ MOROCCAN 🍴 **La Mezzanine.** Just a five-minute walk from the medina, this lounge-bar and restaurant is a haven of Fassi cool. It's undergone a modern Moroccan redesign and now the air-conditioned interior is cool white tadelakt with splashes of vivid red. [$] *Average main: 100DH* ✉ *17, Kasbat Chams, Fez el Djedid* ☎ *0611/07–83–36* 💳 *No credit cards* 🕒 *Closed Mon.*

VILLE NOUVELLE

BARS

The Rooftop. Perched on top of the Hotel Sahrai, the equally chic Rooftop bar draws a sophisticated crowd. The indoor-outdoor bar, with its expanse of wood, local stone, and glass, finished off with designer seating and ambient lighting, hosts top DJs on weekends. But the real star of the show is the view over the old city. There are plenty of luxurious alfresco daybeds to lounge on, so grab a creative cocktail and a front-row seat and watch the sun set as the medina fills with twinkling lights. ✉ *Hotel Sahrai, Bab Lghoul, Dhar el Mehraz, Ville Nouvelle* ☎ *0535/94–03–32* 🌐 *www.hotelsahrai.com.*

5

SHOPPING

FEZ EL-BALI

Fez el-Bali is a gigantic souk. Embroidery, pottery, leather goods, rugs and carpets, copper plates, brass pots, silver jewelry, textiles, babouches, and spices are all of exceptional handmade quality and sold at comparatively low prices, considering the craftsmanship that has remained authentic for nearly a thousand years.

CRAFTS

Au Petit Bazar de Bon Accueil. Fassi dealer Mohamed Benabdejlil's store isn't cheap, but it's got an interesting selection of antiques, textiles, and Berber jewelry, which he'll ship worldwide for you. Don't miss the collection upstairs. ✉ *35, Talaa Seghira, Fez el Bali* ☎ *0535/63–37–64.*

Maison de Broderie et de Brocart de Fes. Discover the intricate work of local embroiderers, including beautiful tablecloths and napkins. ✉ *2, Derb Blida, Fez el Bali* ☎ *0535/63–65–46.*

Fodor's Choice ★ **Medin'Art.** The city's first concept store is in the heart of the medina, stocking the work of predominantly Moroccan, or Moroccan-based designers that are breathing new life into ancient crafts. Expect to find butter-soft leather bags from Mouhib, soft scarves from Au Fil de Tanger, T-shirts from Rock da Kasbah, and Km 13's purses and jewelry made from recycled tires. They also have a small store along Talaa Kbira. ■ TIP→ **Fixed prices take the hassle out of haggling, too.** ✉ *19 bis, Zkak lhjarm Talaa Sghira, Fez el Bali* ☎ *617/57–50–79* 🕒 *Closed Fri.*

Continued on page 230

THE AUTHENTICITY OF ARTISANSHIP
Traditional Moroccan Crafts

Shopping in Morocco is an experience you will never forget. In cities like Marrakesh and Fez, the souks are both magical and chaotic, their narrow alleyways overflowing with handcrafted products created using centuries-old techniques.

by Victoria Tang

Open bazaars and medieval markets display the bright colors, bold patterns, and natural materials found throughout Morocco's arts and crafts tradition. Items are proudly made in artisan workshops dating back to ancient times.

Handmade Moroccan arts and crafts demonstrate the influence of Berber, Arab, Andalusian, and European traditions. Using natural resources like copper, wool, silver, wood, clay, and indigenous plants, artisans and their apprentices incorporate symbolic motifs, patterns, and color into wood carvings, textiles, ceramics, jewelry, slippers, clothing, and other decorative arts. Traditional processes from the Middle Ages are still used in many cases and can be observed from start to finish. Be prepared to negotiate a good price for anything you would like to buy: bartering here is expected and considered an art form in itself.

(top left) Ceramic tagines (top right) leather slippers (bottom right) perfume bottles

THE BEST OF MOROCCAN GOODS

Visiting Morocco's souks also gives you the opportunity to view the techniques still used to mass-produce a wide assortment of authentic goods by hand. While prices in Morocco may not be as cheap as they once were, hand-crafted goods can be found at any price point. Even the highest-quality pieces are half of what you'd pay back home.

LEATHER

Moroccan leather, known as *maroquinerie*, has been sought after worldwide. Fez and Marrakesh have extensive working tanneries, producing large quantities of items for export. Sold inexpensively in local markets are bags, belts, luggage, jackets, vests, and beautifully embroidered goat skin ottomans. Leather and suede *babouches* are the ultimate house slippers; myriad colors and styles are available, and they make an inexpensive gift.

SILVER

The most popular silver jewelry in Morocco is crafted by Berbers and Arabs in the southern High Atlas and in the Anti-Atlas Mountains. Taroudant and Tiznit are the most well-known jewelry-producing areas. Desert nomads—Touaregs and Saharaouia—craft silver items for tribal celebrations. Smaller items include fibulas (ornamental clasps to fasten clothing), Touareg "crosses," delicate filigree bracelets, and hands of Fatima (or *khamsa,* meaning five, for the five fingers) that are said to offer protection from the evil eye. There's also a good variety of Moroccan Judaica that includes silver *yads* (Torah pointers), Torah crowns, and menorahs. Silver teapots, serving trays, and decorative pieces capture the essence of Moroccan metalwork with geometric designs and ornate detail.

SPICES

Markets overflow with sacks of common spices used extensively in local cuisine and natural healing treatments. To create tajines and couscous back home, look for cayenne, cumin, turmeric, cinnamon, ginger, paprika, and saffron. Ask shopkeepers to blend *ras el hanout*, an essential mixture of ground aromatic spices including cardamon, nutmeg, and anise used for stews and grilling.

ARGAN OIL

Much valued by the Berbers, argan oil has been used for centuries as an all-purpose salve, a healthy dip for homemade bread, protection for skin and nails, a treatment for scars and acne, a hair conditioner, a skin moisturizer, and even a general cure for aches and pains. With its strong nutty and toasty flavor, argan oil is popularly sold in the food souks of Essaouira, Marrakesh, and Meknès in its purest form for culinary use. The oil is often mixed with other essential oils for beauty and naturopathic treatments.

The Origins of Argan: The oil from the Argania spinosa, a thorny tree that has been growing wild in Morocco for some 25 million years, is a prized commodity. Today, the tree only grows in the triangular belt along Morocco's Atlantic coast from Essaouira down to Tafraoute in the Anti-Atlas Mountains and eastward as far as Taroudant. It takes about 35 kg (77 pounds) of sun-dried nuts to produce one liter of oil.

TEXTILES

For centuries, weaving in Morocco has been an important artisanal tradition to create beauty and spiritual protection. Looms operate in medina workshops, while groups of tribal nomads can be seen weaving by hand on worn carpets in smaller villages. The best buys are multicolored silk-and-gold thread scarves, shawls, and runners, as well as hand-embroidered fabrics used for tablecloths, decorating, and traditional caftans and djellabas.

WOOD

From the forests of the Rif and Middle Atlas, cedar wood is used to create beautiful *mashrabiyya* latticework often found on decorative household chests, doors, and tables. Essaouira is the source of all thuya-wood crafts. Here, only the gnarled burls that grow out of the rare coniferous tree's trunk are used to carve a vast variety of objects, from tiny boxes and picture frames to trays, games, and even furniture often decorated with marquetry in ebony and walnut.

(top) Pressing argan oil in a traditional press
(bottom) argan oil and its source

MOROCCAN POTTERY

 Morocco has earned a reputation as one of the world's best producers of artisanal ceramics. Decorative styles, shapes, and colors vary from city to city, with three major areas producing the best. From platters and cooking vessels to small pots decorated with silver filigree, this authentic craft makes for an inexpensive, high-quality, and practical souvenir.

FEZ

Morocco's most stunning ceramics are the distinctive blue-and-white *Fassi* pieces. Many of the pieces you'll find actually have the word *Fas* (the Arabic pronunciation of Fez) written in Arabic calligraphy and incorporated into geometric designs. Fassi ceramics also come in a beautiful polychrome of teal, yellow, royal blue, and burgundy. Another design

unique to Fez is the simple *mataysha* (tomato flower) design. You'll recognize it by the repetition of a small, four-petal flower design. Fez is also at the forefront of experimental glazes—keep your eyes out for solid-color urns of iridescent chartreuse or airy lemon yellow that would look at home next to a modernist piece by Philippe Starck or Charles Eames.

(top) Blue-and-white Fassi ceramics (left) Moroccan teapot

ASSESSING POTTERY

Look for kiln markings left after the ceramics have been fired. Pottery fired en masse is put in the kiln on its side, so the edges of bowls are often painted after they have been fired. The paint tends to flake off after a while, giving the bowls a more rustic, or antiqued, look.

Another technique for firing en masse is to stack the bowls one on top the other. This allows for the glazing of the entire piece but results in three small marks on both the inside and outside of bowls from the stands on which they were placed. Small touch-ups tend to disrupt the fluidity of the designs, but such blemishes can be used as a bargaining angle to bring down the price.

You can spot an individually fired piece by its lack of any interior faults. Only three small marks can be seen on the underside of the serving dish or bowl, and the designed face should be immaculate. These pieces, often large, intricately glazed serving pieces, are the most expensive that you'll find.

THE ART OF NEGOTIATION

Everywhere in Morocco you will haggle and be hustled by experienced vendors who pounce on you as soon as you blink in their direction. Your best defense is the proper mindset. For your first souk visit, browse rather than buy. Wander the stalls and see what's for sale. Don't enter stores or make eye contact with vendors, or you will certainly be pulled in. You can also visit one of the state-sponsored artisan markets found in most large Moroccan cities, where prices are rather high but fixed.

Once you've found what you want to buy, ask the price (in dirhams). Stick to the price you want to pay. The vendor will claim you are his first customer and never look satisfied. If he won't decrease the price far enough, walk away. Chances are the vendor will run after you, either accepting your best offer or making a reduction.

SAFI

Safi's flourishing pottery industry dates to the 12th century. Produced near the phosphate mines known as Jorf el Asfar (*asfar*, like *safran*, means yellow), because of the local yellow clay, the pottery of Safi has a distinctive mustard color. The potters' elaborate designs and colors rival those of Fez but are in black with curving lines of leaves and flowers, with less emphasis on geometric patterns. The pottery is predominantly overglazed with a greenish blue, though brown, green, and dark reds are also used.

SALÉ

In Salé, potters work on the clay banks of the River Bou Regreg estuary to produce glazed and unglazed wares in classic and contemporary styles, from huge garden urns to delicate dinner sets.

(top) Safi ceramic teapots

MOROCCAN RUGS

 Moroccan rugs vary tremendously in quality and design. There are basically two types: urban (*citadin*) and rural (Berber); each type has endless varieties of shapes, sizes, and patterns. In general, smaller bazaars in the souks carry rural rugs, while larger bazaars and city stores carry a selection of both.

URBAN RUGS

Urban rugs have been woven in Morocco since the 18th century. They have higher knot counts (they're more "finely" woven) than the rural rugs, which technically makes them of higher quality. Urban rugs typically have seven colors and varied patterns including bands of different colors with geometric and floral designs. They are woven by women in cooperatives, Rabat and Salé being the main centers, but also in Meknès, Fez, and Marrakesh.

RURAL CARPETS

Rural carpets, some of which are known as *kilims* (tapestry weave or flat weave) are identified first by region and then by tribe. They are mostly woven by hand in the Middle Atlas (**Azrou** and **Oulmes**) and on the plains around Marrakesh (**Chichaoua**) by women. They're dark red and made of high-quality wool and have bands of intricate geometric designs. A single rug can take weeks or months to complete. No two rugs are ever alike.

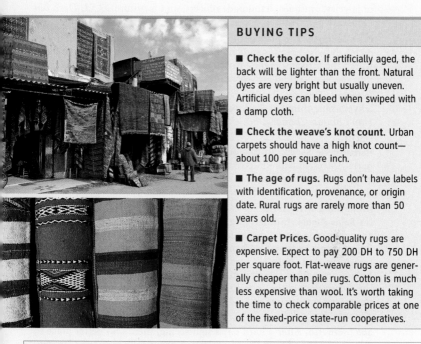

BUYING TIPS

- **Check the color.** If artificially aged, the back will be lighter than the front. Natural dyes are very bright but usually uneven. Artificial dyes can bleed when swiped with a damp cloth.

- **Check the weave's knot count.** Urban carpets should have a high knot count—about 100 per square inch.

- **The age of rugs.** Rugs don't have labels with identification, provenance, or origin date. Rural rugs are rarely more than 50 years old.

- **Carpet Prices.** Good-quality rugs are expensive. Expect to pay 200 DH to 750 DH per square foot. Flat-weave rugs are generally cheaper than pile rugs. Cotton is much less expensive than wool. It's worth taking the time to check comparable prices at one of the fixed-price state-run cooperatives.

OTHER RUG-PRODUCING REGIONS

Middle Atlas rugs are widely available in the town of **Khemisset,** between Meknès and Rabat, where the highly detailed red-striped *zemmour* rugs sell at near wholesale prices. In the mountains north of Fez the women of the **Beni Ouarain** tribe weave rugs with patterns of fine stripes in black and white; they also weave the thick beige pile rugs with cross-hatching that have now become popular with U.S. and European interior designers.

The flat-weave rugs of the High Atlas Mountains (**Aït Ouaourguite,** near Ouarzazate) have a natural background with beige and brown stripes. The wool-pile rugs from this region have alternating soft plush pile with intricate woven motifs—diamonds, zigzags, and tattoo-like motifs in warm tones like mustard-yellow and tomato-red—and are most plentiful in **Taznakht** and the **Tifnout Valley.**

The white, sequined blanket-like rugs displayed on rural roadsides are made in the Middle and High Atlas, and are used both practically and ceremonially, their sequins prized for their reflection of light. Natural dyes are still used for most Berber rugs: orange from henna, blue from indigo, yellow from saffron, and red from the indigenous madder plant.

HAOUZ

The four principal carpet-producing tribes are the **Rehamna, Oulad bou Sbaa, Ahmar** and **Chiadma.** There are two carpet types: reddish-orange monochrome style and the *zarbia,* noted for its enigmatic motifs.

(top left) A modern rug showroom (top right) a rug souk (bottom right) flat-weave kilims

Les Mysteres de Fes. This small store is packed with fascinating pieces of jewelry, antiques, handmade objects, and furniture. ✉ *53, Derb bin Lemssari, Sidi Moussa, Fez el Bali* ☎ *0535/63–61–48.*

Place Seffarine. The picturesque Place Seffarine is the place for all things metal: bowls, boxes, candleholders, and ornate lamps. And you can watch the artisans as they rhythmically hammer the copper and brass into shape outside their workshops. ✉ *Pl. Seffarine, Fez el Bali.*

Terrasse de Tannerie. Shop for butter-soft bags, slippers, and jackets at this labyrinthine shop overlooking the tanneries. Be sure to bargain. ✉ *10, Hay Labilda Chouara, Fez el Bali* ☎ *0535/63–66–25.*

FOOD

Herboristerie Seddik. In this quaint shop, the shelves are stacked with herbs, spices, and all kinds of traditional beauty products such as argan oil, as well as flower extracts and medicinal plants. ✉ *15, Hay Lablida, near Chouara Tannery, Fez el Bali.*

HAMMAMS AND SPAS

Les Bains Amani. Indulge in a luxurious hammam experience at this cross between a traditional hammam and a European-style spa. Les Bain Amani's mosaic-tiled hammam offers a private, romantic, candlelit treatment that, unlike a local hammam, couples can enjoy together. Follow up with a relaxing massage using organic products in one of the treatment rooms. The English-speaking receptionist will explain the treatment beforehand. ✉ *Palais Amani, 12, Derb el Miter, Oued Zhoune, Fez el Bali.*

Fodor's Choice ★   **Spa Laaroussa.** After a hard day's sightseeing, there's no better place to relax and unwind than Riad Laaroussa's beautifully restored 17th-century bathhouse. This private space is covered with dark Carrara marble and, as you steam, you'll be treated to an aromatic body scrub and face mask of *rhassoul* clay, mined in the Atlas mountains. Afterward, indulge in one of the city's best massages with essential oils infused with fragrant orange blossom and jasmine. They treat up to two people (women and/or men) at the same time, and it gets busy, so book in advance. ✉ *3, Derb Bechara, Fez el Bali* ⊕ *www.riadlaaroussa.com.*

METAL

L'Art du Bronze. Hundreds of bronze, copper, and silver objects, antique and new, are sold at affordable prices. ✉ *35, Talaa Sghira, Fez el Bali* ☎ *0535/74–02–77.*

Le Trésor Mirinides. All sorts of jewelry and artisanal Moroccan articles are sold at this friendly shop. ✉ *22, Ain Alou, Fez el Bali* ☎ *0535/63–44–81.*

RUGS

Aux Merveilles du Tapis. Hamid Hakim, proprietor of this carpet shop and brother of a university lecturer in 16th-century English literature, gives an impeccably seasoned and erudite presentation of Moroccan rugs and carpets as well as the architecture and traditional life in a privileged Moroccan residence. This 14th-century medina palace has exquisite ceilings of carved cedar restored and enriched with olive oil. Mr. Hakim's assistants roll and unroll a large selection of rugs with great flair and precision while serving an excellent mint tea. Prices here are steep and tough negotiating is required—don't feel pressured to buy unless you are comfortable with the price. The store is large enough to accept credit cards and ships rugs overseas—and they really do arrive. ⊠ *22, Derb Sebaâ Louyet, near Pl. Seffarine, Fez el Bali* ☎ *0535/63–87–35.*

VILLE NOUVELLE

CRAFTS

Ensemble Artisanal. It's a haul across town on the southeastern edge of the city, but those who make the trek to Ensemble Artisanal will have the rare treat of seeing a cooperative of artisans working on everything from leather to copper to pottery and wood. The Ensemble is also useful if you want to comparison shop: you can get a sense of how the fixed prices here line up with the prices you find in the medina. ■TIP→ **The ironsmith's lanterns here are of a quality you won't easily find in the medina.** ⊠ *Av. Allah ben Abdullah, Ville Nouvelle* ☎ *0535/62–27–04, 0535/62–56–62.*

Les Poteries de Fès. The famous blue-and-white Fassi pottery is made here. You can see how craftsmen mold, glaze, and paint plates, dishes, bowls, and all things ceramic, as well as piece together mosaics with classic zellij tiling. From Bab el-Ftouh it's a 20-minute walk west or a petit taxi ride to the potters' quarters. ⊠ *32, Aïn Nokbi, Ville Nouvelle* ⊕ *Take Rte. N6 Sidi Hrazem* ☎ *0535/76–16–29.*

MEKNÈS

60 km (37 miles) west of Fez, 138 km (85 miles) east of Rabat.

Meknès occupies a plateau overlooking the Bouefekrane River, which divides the medina from the Ville Nouvelle. Meknès's three sets of imposing walls, architectural Royal Granaries, symmetrical Bab Mansour, and spectacular palaces are highlights in this well-preserved imperial city. Less inundated with tourists and more provincial than Fez, Meknès offers a low-key initiation into the Moroccan processes of shopping and bargaining. The pace is slower than Fez and less chaotic. Whether it was post–Moulay Ismail exhaustion or the 1755 earthquake that quieted Meknès down, the result is a pleasant middle ground between the Fez brouhaha and the business-as-usual European ambience of Rabat.

GETTING HERE AND AROUND

AIR TRAVEL

Fès-Saïss Airport serves both Fez and Meknès. The taxi or bus ride from there into Meknès takes about 50 minutes and costs around 330 DH.

BUS TRAVEL

Regular CTM buses cover the Fez–Meknès route hourly. There are buses to Casablanca (around four hours, 90 DH), Tangier (around five hours, 100 DH), and Marrakesh (around eight hours, 180 DH).

Bus Contacts CTM Meknes. ⊠ *Av. des FAR, Ville Nouvelle* ☎ *0535/52-25-83 call center* ⊕ *www.ctm.ma.*

CAR TRAVEL

You don't need (and probably don't want) a car if you are just visiting Fez and Meknès; however, if you want to explore the immediate region of the Middle Atlas, a car (or car and driver) will be crucial since these places can be difficult to reach by bus or grand taxi.

Rental Cars Meknes Car. ✉ *Corner of Av. Hassan II and Rue Safi, Ville Nouvelle* ☎ *0535/51–20–74* ⊕ *meknescar.net.*

TAXI TRAVEL

Grands taxis carry up to six passengers and make long-distance runs between Fez and Meknès. This can be faster, more comfortable, and a better value than bus travel.

Metered petits taxis take up to four passengers, but may not leave the city limits. If the driver refuses to turn on the meter or agree to a reasonable price, do not hesitate to get out. There is usually a 50% surcharge after 8 pm.

TRAIN TRAVEL

The most convenient train station in Meknès is the Rue el-Amir Abdelkader stop close to the administrative center of the city. If you're coming from Tangier, this will be the first stop; from Fez it will be the second. All trains stop at both stations.

PLANNING YOUR TIME

Meknès is a beautifully intact medieval city, easily explored in a short excursion from Fez. From the central Place el-Hedime you can discover the medina's network of small open and covered streets flanked by shops, artisan studios, and food stalls. To see the Imperial City quarter, take a petit taxi or a more atmospheric *calèche* (horse-drawn carriage).

FESTIVALS

Meknès International Animated Film Festival. Meknès's annual international animated film festival (FICAM) takes place each spring at the French Institute. ✉ *Meknès* ⊕ *www.ficam.ma.*

VISITOR INFORMATION

Contacts Meknès Tourist Office. ✉ *27, pl. Administrative, Ville Nouvelle* ☎ *0535/51–60–22.*

EXPLORING

THE IMPERIAL CITY

Fodor'sChoice
★ **Heri el Souani** (*Royal Granaries*). Also known as Dar el-Ma (Water Palace) for the Agdal Basin reservoir beneath, the granaries were one of Moulay Ismail's greatest achievements and are the first place any Meknessi will take you to give you an idea of the second Alaouite sultan's grandiose vision. The Royal Granaries were designed to store grain as feed for the 10,000 horses in the royal stables—not just for a few days or weeks but over a 20-year siege if necessary. Ismail and his engineers counted on three things to keep the granaries cool enough that the grain would never rot: thick walls (12 feet), suspended gardens (a cedar forest was planted on the roof), and an underground reservoir with water ducts under the floors. The

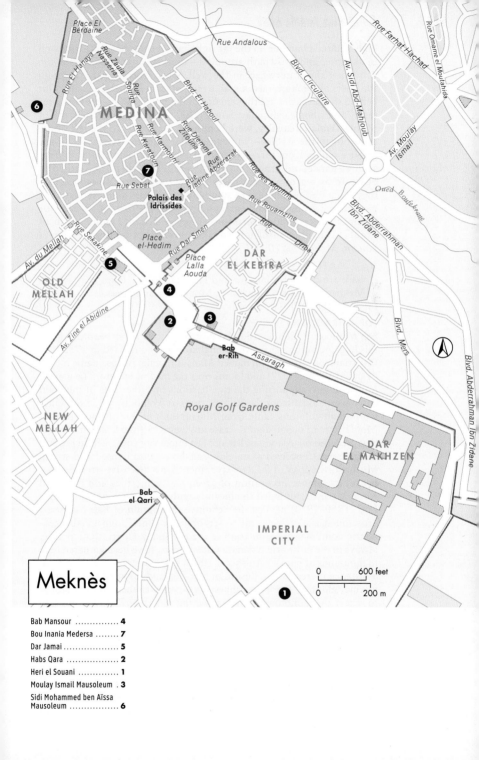

Meknès

high-vaulted chamber on the far right as you enter has a 30-foot well in its center and a towpath around it—donkeys circulated constantly, activating the waterwheel in the well, which forced water through the ducts and maintained a stable temperature in the granaries. Out behind the granaries are the remains of the royal stables, roofless after the 1755 Lisbon earthquake. Some 1,200 purebreds, just one-tenth of Moulay Ismail's cavalry, were kept here. Stand just to the left of the door out to the stables—you can see the stunning symmetry of the stable's pillars from three different perspectives. The granaries have such elegance and grace that they were once called the Cathedral of Grain by a group of Franciscan priests, who were so moved that they requested permission to sing religious chants here. Acoustically perfect, the granaries and surrounding park are now often used for summer concerts and receptions. They're 2 km (1 mile) south of Moulay Ismail's mausoleum, so take a taxi in hot weather. ⊠ *Heri el Souani, Meknès* 🖾 *10 DH.*

BAB MANSOUR AND THE MEDINA

A walk around Bab Mansour and Place el-Hedime takes in nearly all of Meknès's major sites, including Moulay Ismail's mausoleum and the Prison of the Christian Slaves.

TOP ATTRACTIONS

Bab Mansour. Widely considered North Africa's most beautiful gate, this huge horseshoe-shape triumphal arch was completed in 1732 by a Christian convert to Islam named Mansour Laalej (whose name means "victorious renegade") and looms over the medina square. The marble Ionic columns supporting the two bastions on either side of the main entry were taken from the Roman ruins at Volubilis, while the taller Corinthian columns came from Marrakesh's El Badi Palace, part of Moulay Ismail's campaign to erase any vestige of the Saadian dynasty that preceded the Alaouites. Ismail's last important construction project, the gate was conceived as an elaborate homage to himself and strong Muslim orthodoxy of the dynasty rather than a defensive stronghold— hence, its intense decoration of green and white tiles and engraved Koranic panels, all faded significantly with age. French novelist Pierre Loti (1850–1923) penned the definitive description of Bab Mansour: "rose-hued, star-shaped, endless sets of broken lines, unimaginable geometric combinations that confuse the eye like a labyrinthine puzzle, always in the most original and masterly taste, have been gathered here in thousands of bits of varnished earth, in relief or recessed, so that from a distance it creates the illusion of a buffed and textured fabric, glimmering, glinting, a priceless tapestry placed over these ancient stones to relieve the monotony of these towering walls." ⊠ *Rue Dar Smen, in front of the Pl. el-Hedime, Meknès.*

Bou Inania Medersa. Begun by the Merenid sultan Abou el-Hassan and finished by his son Abou Inan between 1350 and 1358, the Meknès version of Fez's residential college of the same name is arguably more beautiful and better preserved than its better-known twin. Starting with the cupola and the enormous bronze doors on the street, virtually every inch of this building is covered with decorative carving or calligraphy. The central fountain is for ablutions before prayer. Head

A horse-drawn calèche is a more relaxing and traditional way to tour Meknès.

upstairs to visit the small rooms that overlook the courtyard. These housed the 60 communal *tolba*, or student reciters. ■ TIP→ The rooftop terrace has one of best panoramic views of Meknès's medina. ⌧ *Rue des Souks es Sebbat, Meknès* ◪ *10 DH.*

Dar Jamai. This 19th-century palace just inside the medina was built by the same family of *viziers* (high government officials) responsible for the Palais Jamaï hotel in Fez. The building itself is exquisite, especially the second-floor carved-cedar ceilings, interior Andalusian garden, and *menzah* (pavilion), which now houses the ethnographic **Museum of Moroccan Art** with an important collection of carpets, jewelry, ceramics, needlework, and woodwork. ■ TIP→ Facing away from Bab Mansour, the ceramics stalls on Place el-Hedime's left side sell oversize tagine pots for as little as 15 DH to 20 DH. ⌧ *Rue Sekkakine, off Pl. el Hedim, Meknès* ◪ *10 DH* ⊙ *Closed Tues.*

Moulay Ismail Mausoleum. One of four sacred sites in Morocco open to non-Muslims (the others are Casablanca's Hassan II, Rabat's Mohammed V Mausoleum, and Rissani's Zaouia of Moulay Ali Sherif), this mausoleum was opened to non-Muslims by King Mohammed V (grandfather of Mohammed VI) in honor of Ismail's ecumenical instincts. An admirer of France's King Louis XIV—who, in turn, considered the sultan an important ally—Moulay Ismail developed close ties with Europe and signed commercial treaties even as he battled to eject the Portuguese from their coastal strongholds at Asilah, Essaouira, and Larache. The mausoleum's site once held Meknès's Palais de Justice (Courthouse), and Moulay Ismail deliberately chose it as his resting place with hopes he would be judged in his own court by his own people. The deep ocher-hue walls inside lead to the sultan's private sanctuary, on the left, heavily decorated with colorful geometric zellij tiling. At the end of the larger inner courtyard, you must remove your shoes to enter the sacred chamber with Moulay Ismail's tomb, surrounded by hand-carved cedar-and-stucco walls, intricate mosaics, and a central fountain. ⊠ *Rue Sarag, near Bab er-Rih, Meknès* ☜ *Free.*

Sidi Mohammed ben Aïssa Mausoleum. Built in 1776 by Sultan Sidi Mohammed ben Abdellah, the *zaouia* of Sidi Mohammed ben Aïssa is the focal point of the legendary Aïssaoua cult, known for such voluntary rituals as swallowing scorpions, broken glass, and poison; eating live sheep; and cutting themselves with knives in prayer-induced trances. Ben Aïssa was one of Morocco's most famous saints. He was said to have made a pact with the animal world and possessed magical powers, such as the ability to transform the leaves of trees into gold and silver coins. Thought to have been a 17th-century contemporary of Moulay Ismail (1646–1727), Ben Aïssa was known as the protector of Moulay Ismail's 50,000-man workforce and persuaded hungry laborers that they were able to eat anything at all, even poisonous plants, glass, or scorpions. Ben Aïssa went on to become the general protector of all his followers. The cult of Aïssa is still around, and has in fact proliferated throughout North Africa to Algeria and beyond. Every year, during Ben Aïssa's *moussem* (pilgrimage) on the eve of the birth of the prophet Mohammed, members of the Aïssaoua fraternity from all over North Africa gather at the shrine. Processions form and parade through Meknès, snakes are charmed, and the saint's followers perform ecstatic dances, often imitating the behavior of certain animals. Although some of the Aïssaoua's more brutal practices have been outlawed, this moussem remains one of Morocco's most fascinating events. ⊠ *Bd. Circulaire s/n, Meknès* ☞ *Entry restricted to Muslims.*

WORTH NOTING

Habs Qara (*Prison of Christian Slaves*). After you pass through Place Lalla Aouda and Bab Filala, the pyramid-shape dome on the right side of the next square is the Koubba al Khayatine (Tailors' Pavilion), named for the seamsters who sewed military uniforms here. Originally known as the Koubbat as-Sufara (Ambassadors' Pavilion), this was where Moulay Ismail received ambassadors from abroad. The stairs to the right of the pavilion entrance lead down to storage chambers originally built as a prison by the Portuguese architect Cara, himself a prisoner who earned his freedom by constructing these immense subterranean slave quarters. Go below to see where the 60,000 slaves (of which 40,000 were reportedly Christian prisoners of war) were shackled to the wall, forced to sleep standing up, and ordered to work on the sultan's laborious building projects. Ambassadors visiting Meknès to negotiate the ransoms and release of their captive countrymen were received in the pavilion above, never suspecting that the prisoners were directly below them. ⊠ *Pl. Lalla Aouda, Meknès* ☜ *10 DH* ☉ *Closed Mon.*

WHERE TO EAT

There are only a few culinary gems in Meknès, but chances are you'll want to sample local delicacies, snack on exotic dried fruits, and savor the ritual sweet pastries and mint tea, purported to be the best in the country. Good cafés and restaurants are scattered in the medina (many near Place el-Hedime). Avenues Mohammed V and Hassan II in the Ville Nouvelle provide a wide choice of Moroccan and French or Mediterranean dishes.

$ MOROCCAN 🍴 **Collier de la Colombe.** A five-minute walk to the left inside Bab Mansour, this graceful medina space with intricate carvings, giant picture windows, and terraces overlooking the Boufekrane River and Ville Nouvelle is a good place to enjoy authentic Moroccan specialties. The menu is classic Moroccan, with highly recommended pastilla (a house specialty), tender grilled lamb, spicy beef brochettes, and mouthwatering fish tagines. **Known for:** great views; good selection of wine and beer. [$] *Average main: 100DH* ✉ *67, rue Driba, via Bab Mansour and P. Lalla Aouda, Ville Nouvelle* ☎ *0535/55–50–41* 🌐 *lecollierdelacolombe.com/?page_id=1653.*

$ MOROCCAN 🍴 **Marhaba.** Fuel up at this canteen-style eatery for outstanding Moroccan cheap eats. Start with freshly made Berber bread and thick *harira* soup. **Known for:** good-value Moroccan dishes; local flavor. [$] *Average main: 20DH* ✉ *23, av. Mohammed V, Meknès* ☎ *0535/52–16–32* 💳 *No credit cards.*

$ FRENCH 🍴 **Le Relais de Paris.** Need a break from couscous? This chain of French restaurants provides some of the best traditional cuisine in town. **Known for:** international menu; lively downstairs bar. [$] *Average main: 170DH* ✉ *46, rue Oqba Ibn Nafia, Ville Nouvelle* ☎ *0535/51–54–88.*

$ MOROCCAN 🍴 **Restaurant Omnia.** Seek out this lovely family-run restaurant in the heart of the medina serving incredibly delicious cuisine with warm smiles in an authentic traditional atmosphere. The selection of Moroccan salads, spicy harira soup, and couscous or tagine are part of a set menu that finishes off with mint tea and honey-laden pastries. **Known for:** family-run restaurant; good-value set menu. [$] *Average main: 95DH* ✉ *8, Derb Ain el Fouki, Quartier Rouamzine, Meknès* ☎ *0535/53–39–38* 💳 *No credit cards.*

WHERE TO STAY

Meknès has not yet attracted the same level of commercial development and active restoration of riads as Fez, although there are an increasing number of places to stay in the medina. For more updated accommodations, there are several decent hotels in the Ville Nouvelle that are reasonably priced and a short walk or taxi ride from the train station.

$ B&B/INN 🏨 **Riad d'Or.** Traditional styling in this basic bed-and-breakfast provides the Moroccan home experience, and visitors on a budget will find decent amenities for the price, including a quality restaurant, clean pool, and panoramic terrace to sunbathe or relax, with great views over the Imperial City. **Pros:** central location near Place el-Hedime; large, well-appointed rooms; small pool. **Cons:** can be noisy; unreliable heat

The souks of Meknès are smaller and easier to navigate than those of Fez.

and air-conditioning; mix of modern and traditional decor. $ *Rooms from: 500DH* ✉ *17, rue Ain el Anboub, at Rue Lalla Alcha Adoula, Hammam Jdid-Bab Issy* ☎ *0535/53–38–71* ⊕ *www.riaddor.com* ⊟ *No credit cards* ⇆ *20 rooms* ⊚ *Breakfast.*

$

B&B/INN

Fodor's Choice

★

⚏ **Riad Felloussia.** Set in the heart of Meknès, between El Hedim square and the medina, the five suites—some of which are split-level, three have air-conditioning—of this lovely riad are full of character, decorated with traditional furniture, Berber rugs, and African art. **Pros:** friendly service; central location; lovely decor. **Cons:** small property; no air-conditioning in some rooms; pedestrian-only access. $ *Rooms from: 480DH* ✉ *23, Derb Hammam Jdid, Bab Aissi, Meknès* ☎ *0535/53–08–40* ⊕ *www. riadfelloussia.com* ⊟ *No credit cards* ⇆ *5 suites* ⊚ *Breakfast.*

$

B&B/INN

⚏ **Ryad Bahia.** This 14th-century family house has been lovingly restored by a couple with years of experience working as Meknès guides and is an impressive anthology of ceramic, rug weaving, and woodworking crafts tucked away on the medina just a few steps from the Dar Jamai museum on Place el-Hedime. **Pros:** medina location; outstanding service; family-friendly atmosphere. **Cons:** long walk from parking lot; no alcohol allowed on premises; small property. $ *Rooms from: 670DH* ✉ *Derb Sekkaya, between Pl. el-Hedime and Bouanania Medersa, just behind Dar Jamai museum, Tiberbarine* ☎ *0535/55–45–41* ⊕ *www. ryad-bahia.com* ⇆ *13 rooms* ⊚ *Breakfast.*

NIGHTLIFE

A somewhat seedy bar and disco scene thrives in the hotels around the train station in the Ville Nouvelle. The bar at **Le Relais de Paris** is a good choice for a quiet drink, or for a livelier scene try the nightclub at **Hotel Rif**, where sometimes you'll hear traditional Gnaoua, sometimes Western folk music.

Summer concerts in the **Heri el-Souani** are favorites of Meknès music lovers. Check with the tourist office for dates and dress warmly—the 12-foot walls built to cool oats and barley chill people as well.

SHOPPING

The diminutive Meknès souk, as with Meknès generally, seems somehow easier to embrace than Fez. Getting lost here is difficult; it just isn't that big. Meknès's merchants and craftsmen can be as exceptional as those in Fez, and what's more, they're easier to negotiate with. Just be prepared, if you try to tell a rug salesman that you're pressed for time, to hear, "Ah, but a person without time is a dead person."

THE SOUKS

Beginning from Place el-Hedime, just past the pottery stands brimming with colorful tagine vessels, a narrow corridor leads into the **Souk Atriya**, the food souk, with a wonderful display of everything from spices to dried fruit to multicolor olives. The **Souk Nejjarine**, the woodworkers' souk, leads into the rug and carpet souk. Farther on in this direction is the **Souk Bezzarine**, a general flea market along the medina walls. Farther up to the right are basket makers, iron smiths, leather workers, and saddle makers, and, near Bab el-Djedid, makers of odd items like tents and musical instruments. The Souk es-Sebat begins a more formal section, where each small section is devoted to a specific craft, beginning with the *babouche* (leather slipper) market. If you are in the market for a carpet, then follow signs to the **Palais des Idrissides**, a wonderful 14th-century palace and carpet emporium.

CRAFTS

Ensemble Artisanal. The government-run Ensemble Artisanal is, as always in Moroccan cities, a good place to watch craftsmen at work and check for fixed-price, quality handcrafted products and prices before beginning to haggle in the souks. ⊠ *Av. Zine el-Abidine, Meknès* ⊘ *Closed Sun.*

Fodor'sChoice **Palais Damasquini.** A specialist in the disappearing art of damascening ★ (inlaying a thread of gold, silver, or copper on a metal surface), the Palais sells jewelry and decorative vases and dishes. ⊠ *11, Koubt Souk Kissaria Lahrir, Meknès* ☎ *0535/53–35–02* ⊘ *Closed Sun.*

FOOD

Souk Atriya. The food souks and *kissaria* (covered market) run along one side of the medina square. A tour through this gastronomic oasis stuffed with all manner of products heaped in elaborately arranged cones and pyramids—prunes, olives, spices, nuts, dates, and sugary pastries in every conceivable shape and color—is a veritable feast for the senses. The variety of olives on display and the painstaking care with which each pyramid of produce has been set out daily is nearly as geometrically enthralling as the decorative designs on the Bab Mansour. Look for the bustling fish stalls for seafood of all kinds straight from the Atlantic, an hour's drive away. ■TIP➔ **The kissaria is a good place to stock up on Moroccan spices and aromatic herbs.** ✉ *Pl. el-Hedime, Meknès.*

SIDE TRIPS FROM FEZ AND MEKNÈS

Volubilis and Moulay Idriss are highly recommended side trips from Fez and Meknès. Volubilis was the Roman Empire's farthest-flung capital, and Moulay Idriss has Morocco's most sacred shrine, the tomb of founding father Moulay Idriss I. Both sites are key to an understanding of Moroccan history. It's possible to see both places in one day, and, if you don't have your own transport, most tours from Meknès or Fez will cover both, although you may not spend as much time in Moulay Idriss as it deserves. If you have to choose between trips to Volubilis and Moulay Idriss, go with the former. The Roman ruins at Volubilis are some of the best archaeological treasures in the country.

Another option is to head over to Oulmès (81 km [50 miles] from Meknès) for an excursion farther into the countryside.

MOULAY IDRISS

23 km (14 miles) north of Meknès, 3 km (2 miles) southeast of Volubilis, 83 km (50 miles) west of Fez.

Moulay Idriss is Morocco's most sacred town, the final resting place of the nation's religious and secular founder, Moulay Idriss I. It is said that five pilgrimages to Moulay Idriss are the spiritual equivalent of one to Mecca, earning it the nickname the poor man's Mecca. Non-Muslims are not allowed inside the tomb at all, and until 2005 were not allowed to spend the night in town. A splash of white against Djebel (Mt.) Zerhoun, the picturesque town tumbles down two hillsides. The pace of life is leisurely, visits are normally hassle-free, and people-watching in the main square offers a view of Moroccan life that hasn't changed for centuries.

Moulay Idriss attracts thousands of pilgrims from all over Morocco to its moussem in late August or early September. Non-Muslims are welcome to attend the secular events, which are a fascinating glimpse into Islamic life and celebrations.

GETTING HERE AND AROUND
Buses (15 DH) leave Meknès for Moulay Idriss every 15 minutes from 6 am until 10 pm. Or take a grand taxi from the Institut Français de Meknès (Rue Ferhat Hachad, between the medina and the Ville Nouvelle) for 10 DH.

TIMING AND PRECAUTIONS
Moulay Idriss is a holy town and requires utmost respect for sacred rituals and customs, so act and dress respectfully. Each Saturday there's a lively local market. During Ramadan, most shops and restaurants are

The moussem in Moulay Idriss draws pilgrims from far and wide in late August or early September.

closed during the day, but you can buy picnic food from the market or eat on the terrace at the hotel Dar Zerhoune. It's thoughtful not to eat and drink on the street during this time.

EXPLORING

Moulay Idriss Medersa. An outstanding historic site from the Merenids, the Moulay Idriss Medersa was built in the 14th century by sultan Abou el Hassan. Hidden in the town's steep and twisting streets, the medersa's striking cylindrical minaret constructed in 1939 is the only one of its kind in Morocco, standing as testimony to Turkish and Arab influences. Originally built with materials from Volubilis, the minaret is decorated with green ceramic tiles bearing inscriptions of the 114 *suras* (chapters) of the Koran. ⊠ *Moulay Idriss Zerhoun* ☞ *Entry restricted to Muslims.*

Sidi Abdellah el Hajjam Terrace. From the Sidi Abdellah el Hajjam Terrace, in the Khiber quarter, you will have the best vantage point to see the holy village of Moulay Idriss and its sacred sanctuaries. The adjoining quarter across the gorge is called Tasga. ⊠ *Moulay Idriss Zerhoun.*

Zaouia of Moulay Idriss I. This important shrine and mausoleum of the Idrissid dynasty's patriarch is off-limits to non-Muslims, marked by a wooden bar so that people bow their head on entering. For a good view, climb to a vantage point overlooking the religious sanctuary—the hike up one of many hills through the town's surrounding alleys is invigorating and a symbolic bow to Morocco's secular and spiritual history. ⊠ *Moulay Idriss Zerhoun.*

WHERE TO EAT AND STAY

The main street through Moulay Idriss (up to the parking area just in front of the mausoleum) has a line of small restaurants serving everything from brochettes of spicy meat to harira. In front, you'll see stands where tagines cook over hot coals for hours until the meat is tender; the kefta tagine is the one to try.

$ MOROCCAN 🍴 **Restaurant at Dar Zerhoune.** This cozy riad—open to guests and nonguests alike—serves home-cooked traditional Moroccan cuisine on the roof terrace with sweeping views over Moulay Idriss, the ruins of Volubilis, and the mountains beyond; there's also an air-conditioned salon. Dishes make the most of fresh, local ingredients; opt for the three-course set lunch or dinner—perhaps the famed Moulay Idriss kefta or a tasty tagine, or opt for something lighter such as Greek salad (made with local cheese) or vegetable soup. **Known for:** a lighter take on traditional dishes; great views. [$] *Average main: 100DH* ✉ *42, Derb Zaouk, Moulay Idriss Zerhoun* ☎ *0535/54–43–71* 🌐 *www.darzerhoune.com.*

$$$$ MOROCCAN Fodor's Choice ★ 🍴 **Restaurant at Scorpion House.** Indulging in a long, leisurely lunch looking down on the sacred city of Moulay Idriss is certainly something to savor, especially when it's served on a terrace at Scorpion House. Enjoy grilled meats, fish, and an array of seasonal Moroccan salads, rounded off with fruit and sweet treats. **Known for:** authentic Moroccan cruise with a contemporary touch; incredible views; beautiful property. [$] *Average main: 600DH* ✉ *54, Drouj El Hafa, Moulay Idriss Zerhoun* ☎ *0655/21–01–72* 🌐 *www.scorpionhouse.com.*

$ B&B/INN Fodor's Choice ★ 🏨 **Dar Zerhoune.** With a prime perch atop a hill, overlooking the tranquil Holy City of Moulay Idriss, this welcoming, Western-owned guesthouse is the perfect place to unwind after the hurly-burly of Fez. **Pros:** friendly staff; roof terrace; free Wi-Fi. **Cons:** quiet town; no TV (but books and board games are available); small property. [$] *Rooms from: 600DH* ✉ *42, Derb Zaouk, Tazga, Moulay Idriss Zerhoun* ☎ *0535/54–43–71* 🌐 *www.darzerhoune.com* 🛏 *6 rooms* 🍽 *Breakfast.*

$$$$ RENTAL 🏨 **Scorpion House.** Set high on a hillside, the Scorpion House is the personal retreat of the owner of Cafe Clock in Fez that's now available as an exclusive holiday rental. **Pros:** beautiful property with stunning views; unique design; exclusive escape. **Cons:** quiet town; pedestrian-only access; high rates. [$] *Rooms from: 3000DH* ✉ *54, Drouj El Hafa, Moulay Idriss Zerhoun* ☎ *0655/21–01–72* 🌐 *www.scorpionhouse.com* 🛏 *3 rooms* 🍽 *Breakfast.*

VOLUBILIS

28 km (17 miles) northwest of Meknès, 88 km (53 miles) northwest of Fez, 3 km (2 miles) west of Moulay Idriss.

Volubilis was the capital of the Roman province of Mauritania (Land of the Moors), Rome's southwesternmost incursion into North Africa. Favored by the confluence of the rivers Khoumane and Fertasse and surrounded by some of Morocco's most fertile plains, this site has probably been inhabited since the Neolithic era.

Volubilis's municipal street plan and distribution of public buildings are remarkably comprehensible examples of Roman urban planning. The floor plans of the individual houses, and especially their incredibly well-preserved mosaic floors depicting mythological scenes, provide a rare connection to the sensibilities of the Roman colonists who lived here 2,000 years ago.

If you prefer to see Volubilis on your own without a guide (less informative but more contemplative), proceed through the entrance, and make a clockwise sweep, starting at the newly built, contemporary visitor center. After crossing the little bridge over the Fertasse River, climb up to the plateau's left edge, and you'll soon come across a Berber skeleton lying beside a sculpture with his head pointed east, a deliberate placement suggesting early Islamization of the Berber populace here.

GETTING HERE AND AROUND

Volubilis is a 30-minute drive north from Meknès, and an hour's drive from Fez. Sometimes marked on road signs as "Oualili," Volubilis is beyond Moulay Idriss on Route N13, which leaves R413 to head northeast 15 km (9 miles) northwest of Meknès. Grands taxis to Volubilis are available from Meknès and Fez for around 200 DH and 400 DH respectively. From Moulay Idriss there are shuttles to Volubilis (5 DH). From Fez, the only regularly scheduled bus connection to Volubilis is via Meknès.

TIMING AND PRECAUTIONS

Volubilis is an expansive site that requires intense walking and sun exposure. Tour earlier in the day or late in the afternoon, wear a hat, and carry a water bottle.

VISITOR INFORMATION

Contacts **Volubilis Visitor Center.** ✉ *Main Gate.*

EXPLORING

Remains of **Roman olive presses** can be seen to the left, evidence of the importance of the olive-oil industry that supported 20,000 inhabitants of this 28-acre city. The first important mosaics are to the right in the **House of Orpheus,** consisting of a dolphin mosaic and one depicting the Orpheus myth in the Tablinum, a back room used as a library and receiving room. Past the public **Baths of Gallienus,** in a room to the right, are a dozen sets of footprints raised slightly above floor level in what was a communal bathroom. The wide-paved street leading up to the **Capitol,** the **Basilica,** and the **Forum** is the **Cardus Maximus,** the main east–west thoroughfare of any Roman town. Across the forum were the market stalls. The **Triumphal Arch,** built in AD 217, destroyed by the 1755 Lisbon earthquake and restored in 1932, is down to the left at the end of **Decumanus Maximus,** the main north–south street. As you look south through the arch, the first building to the left is the **House of the Dog,** named because of an unearthed bronze dog sculpture. The **House of the Knight** has an incomplete but beautifully designed mosaic of Dionysus. Beyond the northernmost gate—the **Tangier Gate**—stands the **Palace of the Gordians,** the residence of the administrators. The best mosaics are found in the **Cortege of Venus.** Look for **Diana Bathing with Nymphs** and the **Abduction of Hylas.**

■TIP→ Volubilis can get very hot, as the ruins offer no shade. Wearing a hat and bringing plenty of water are essential. The ground is uneven and sometimes rocky, so wear your best pair of walking shoes or sneakers. There is a small shady café built around a tree near the car park, for drinks, snacks, and more substantial bites. Entrance to the site is 10 DH and it's open from 8:30 until sunset.

Arch of Caracalla. Rising out of fertile plains and olive groves, the impressive triumphal arch of Volubilis is the center point of the ancient Roman site. Decorated only on the east side, it is supported by marble columns, built by Marcus Aurelius Sebastenus to celebrate the power of Emperor Caracalla. ⊠ *Volubilis.*

Dionysus and the Four Seasons. Along the Decumanus Maximus, the small spaces near the street's edge held shop stalls, while mansions—10 on the left and eight on the right—lined either side. The house of Dionysus and the Four Seasons is about halfway down the Decumanus Maximus; its scene depicting Dionysus discovering Ariadne asleep is one of the site's most spectacular mosaics. ⊠ *Volubilis.*

House of the Bathing Nymphs. Named for its superb floor mosaics portraying a bevy of frolicking nymphs in a surprisingly contemporary, all but animated, artistic fashion, the House of the Bathing Nymphs is on the main street's right side. The penultimate house has a marble bas-relief medallion of Bacchus. As you move back south along the next street below and parallel to the Decumanus Maximus, there is a smaller, shorter row of six houses that are worth exploring. ⊠ *Volubilis.*

House of the Ephebus. The ancient town's greatest mansions and mosaics line the Decumanus Maximus from the town brothel north to the Tangier Gate, which leads out of the enclosure on the uphill end. One of the most famous is the House of the Ephebus, just west of the Triumphal Arch, named for the nude ivy-crowned bronze sculpture discovered here (now on display in Rabat). The *cenacula,* or banquet hall, has colorful mosaics with Bacchic themes. Opposite the House of the Ephebus is the House of the Dog, where a bronze canine statue was discovered in 1916 in one of the rooms off the *triclinium,* a large dining room. ⊠ *Volubilis.*

House of Orpheus. One of the most important houses in the Roman ruins is the House of Orpheus, the largest house in the residential quarter. Three remarkable mosaics depict Orpheus charming animals with his lyre, nine dolphins symbolizing good luck, and Amphitrite in her sea horse–drawn chariot. Head north from here to explore the public Baths of Gallienus and free-standing Corinthian pillars of the Capitol. ⊠ *Volubilis.*

Fodor's Choice ★ **House of Venus.** Volubilis's best set of mosaics, not to be missed, is in the House of Venus. Intact excavations portray a chariot race, a bathing Diana surprised by the hunter Actaeon, and the abduction of Hylas by nymphs—all still easily identifiable. The path back down to the entrance passes the site of the Temple of Saturn, across the riverbed on the left. ⊠ *Volubilis.*

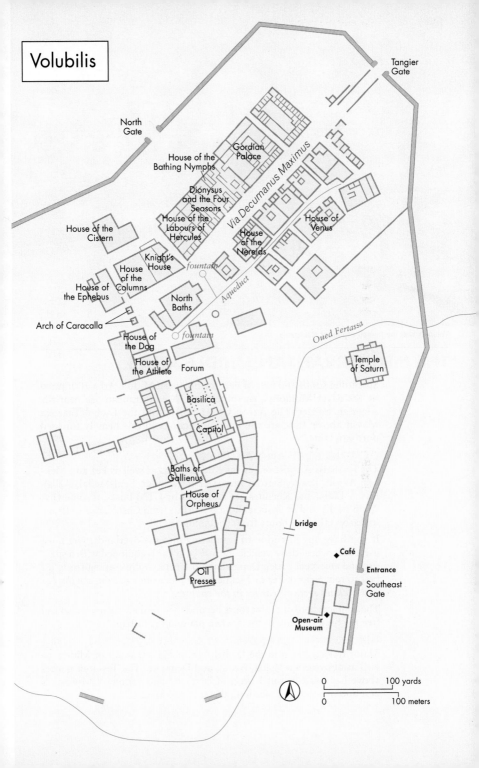

Volubilis

Tangier
Gate

North Gate

Gordian
Palace

House of the
Bathing Nymphs

Via Decumanus Maximus

Dionysus
and the Four
Seasons

House of the
Labours of
Hercules

House of the
Cistern

Knight's
House

House
of the
Columns

fountain

House of
the Ephebus

North
Baths

Aqueduct

House
of the
Nereids

House of
Venus

Arch of Caracalla

House of
the Dog

fountain

House of
the Athlete

Forum

Oued Fertassa

Temple
of Saturn

Basilica

Capitol

Baths of
Gallienus

House of
Orpheus

bridge

◆ Café

Entrance

Oil
Presses

Southeast
Gate

Open-air
Museum ◆

0   100 yards

0   100 meters

Volubilis was the Roman capital of Mauritania.

THE MEDITERRANEAN MIDDLE ATLAS

Spreading south and east of Fez, the northern Middle Atlas is drained by the River Moulouya en route to the Mediterranean Sea near the Algerian border. The Azrou Cedar Forest and the Djebel Tazzeka Massif above Taza are the main attractions in this heavily forested northern zone.

GETTING HERE AND AROUND

The Fès-Saïss Airport serves the Middle Atlas as well as Fez and Meknès. Azrou, Ifrane, Sefrou, Imouzzer du Kandar, Beni-Mellal, Azilal, Kasba Tadla, and Khénifra are all served by CTM buses, if somewhat sporadically and at unsocial hours. The bus from Casablanca to Ifrane to Azrou takes six hours from beginning to end.

If you have any intention of wandering into the overlands, you must use a four-wheel-drive vehicle. Ensure your car is equipped with a spare tire and emergency fuel. Depending on where you're coming from, it's best to rent a car in Fez or Meknès. *(For more information, see the Fez and Meknès sections earlier in the chapter.)*

The contacts here organize tours beyond their immediate towns, so feel free to check out any of these when planning your trip.

HIKING AND TREKKING

Major treks arise from the Djebel Ayachi Massif, south of Midelt, as well as above Beni-Mellal, Azilal, and Demnate. The Tessaout gorges above Lac des Aït-Aadel, west of Demnate, have some of Morocco's best and most spectacular long-distance trekking.

HORSEBACK RIDING

For the equestrian, several stables offer mountain or rural outings on horseback. Try the Centre Equestre et de Randonnée.

Le Centre Equestre et de Randonnées Aïn Amyer. On the outskirts of Fez, Le Centre Equestre et de Randonnées Aïn Amyer has 20 horses in its stables and many of them are the famous Moroccan Barb species, a desert breed with stamina. Depending on the time you have, it's possible to go on a ride of several hours into the countryside. You can also take private classes at the center. ⊠ *Aïn Amyer, Rte. d'Immouzzer, Fez* ✆ *azzmsefer@yahoo.fr.*

FISHING

Morocco, surprisingly, offers trout fishing in the foothills of the High Atlas and in the Azrou Cedar Forest. European brown trout and rainbows, nearly all stocked fish or descendants of repopulated fisheries, thrive in select highland environments. March through May are the prime angling months. Permits and further orientation are available through the Administration des Eaux et Forêts offices in Rabat.

Administration des Eaux et Forêts. ⊠ *605, Rabat-Chellah, Rabat* ☎ *0537/76–00–38, 0537/76–00–41* ⊕ *www.eauxetforets.gov.ma.*

RAFTING

One of the best ways to see Morocco is through the natural beauty of its flowing rivers and dramatic canyons. Morocco Rafting specializes in river-rafting tours. Adventure holidays are available with a range of activities that combine rafting, kayaking, canyoning, and tubing.

Morocco Rafting. This company—open since the late 1990s—specializes in white-water rafting tours on the Ahansei, Oum Er Rbia, Ourika, and Nifiss rivers, along with hot-air ballooning, quad biking, paragliding, and kite surfing. ⊠ *Rue Beni Marine, Marrakesh* ☎ *0661/77–52–51* ⊕ *www.rafting.ma.*

TAZA

120 km (72 miles) east of Fez.

An important capital during the Almohad, Merenid, and early Alaouite dynasties (11th to 16th centuries), Taza was used as a passage into Morocco by the first Moroccan Arabs—the Idrissids—and nearly all successive invaders en route to Fez. Fortified and refortified over the centuries, the city, located in the mountain pass known as the Taza Gap separating the Rif from the Middle Atlas Mountains, is marked by a medina that houses a 14th-century medersa and four mosques.

ESSENTIALS

Bus Contacts Taza CTM Terminal. ⊠ *Pl. de l'Indépendance* ⊕ *www.ctm.ma.*

EXPLORING

First constructed in the 12th century, the haunting city walls have been in various states of renovation. Accessing the main entry point, the Bab er-Rih (Gate of the Wind) leads up to a beautiful panoramic view of the Djebel Tazzeka hills. Through the center of town, walk the main street that connects the medina's four principal mosques—the

Grande Mosquée, the Sidi Azouz mosque, the Mosquée du Marché, and the Andalous Mosque.

Grand Mosque. With its perforated cupola, the Grand Mosque is a historically significant UNESCO World Heritage Site. Dating from the 12th century, the mosque, founded by Sultan Abd el-Moumen, is possibly the oldest Almohad structure in existence and believed to predate the mosque at Tin Mal. Of architectural importance are the mosque's inscribed three-ton chandelier and intricately designed windows and doorways. ■TIP➜ Entrance to the mosque is restricted to Muslims only. ⊠ *Taza* ✛ *Walk toward Bab Er-Rih past medina.*

Souks. Set around the Mosquée du Marché, or Market Mosque, Taza's untouristy souks and the covered stalls of the kissaria are worth exploring. Look out for the shaggy cream-wool rugs with black geometric markings made by the Beni Ourain tribe. ⊠ *Taza.*

WHERE TO STAY

$ 🏨 **Grand Hôtel du Dauphiné.** Though the period charm has diminished, this budget hotel offers clean rooms, shuttered balconies at the front, and agreeable service. **Pros:** very central; close to public transportation; ground-floor café-restaurant. **Cons:** no heat in winter; most rooms don't have en suite bathrooms; old-fashioned decor. Ⓢ *Rooms from: 290DH* ⊠ *Pl. de l'Indépendance, Ville Nouvelle* ☎ *0535/67–35–67* ▤ *No credit cards* ⇆ *26 rooms* ⍾*Breakfast.*

AROUND TAZA

The 123-km (76-mile) loop around the Cirque du Djebel Tazzeka southwest of Taza is one of the most varied and spectacular day trips in the Middle Atlas. Packing a range of diversions from picnicking by the waterfalls of Ras el-Oued to spelunking in the Gouffre du Friouato (Friouato Caves), reaching the summit of the 6,494-foot Djebel Tazzeka, or navigating the gorges of the Oued Zireg, this tour is geared for the serious adventurer. Without stops, the entire multisurface drive takes approximately five hours. The S311 road south from Taza is narrow and serpentine. The Cascades of Ras-El, 10 km (6 miles) south of Taza, is the first stop. The Parc National de Tazzeka has tranquil picnic spots. The right fork on the S311 brings you to the Friouato Caves within the park, while the left path leads out to the lake bed of Dayat Chiker, most impressive in springtime when subterranean waters keep it filled.

Beyond the caves, the road climbs through a pine forest to the village of Bab Bou Idir, abandoned except in summer when the campground and chalets fill with vacationers. After another 8 km (5 miles), the right-hand fork leads 9 km (5½ miles) to the crest of Djebel Tazzeka, 6,494 feet, a tough climb by car or on foot. Your reward is the unique view over the Rif and south to the Middle Atlas.

From Djebel Tazzeka there are another 38 km (23 miles) north along the spectacular Zireg river gorges to Sidi Abdallah des Rhiata, where you can get on the N6 back to Taza or Fez. ■TIP➜ The 7-km (4½-mile) track to the crest of Djebel Tazzeka is a dangerous drive in bad weather.

SEFROU

33 km (20 miles) southeast of Fez, 136 km (84 miles) southwest of Taza.

A miniature Fez at an altitude of 2,900 feet, the small town of Sefrou lies in the fertile valley of the River Agdal. Once known as the Jardin du Maroc, it actually predates Fez and was the first stop on the caravan routes between the Sahara and the Mediterranean coast. It was originally populated by Berber converts to Judaism, who came north from the Tafilalt date palmery and from Algeria in the 13th century. The town remained a nucleus of Jewish life until 1956, when, upon the country's declaration of independence from France, virtually all of the Jewish community fled Morocco.

EXPLORING

Sefrou is a picturesque ancient walled city whose medina is well preserved and worth a visit. With cooler temperatures than nearby Fez, it makes a pleasant summer day trip. Wander around the Mellah quarter, one of the oldest in Morocco, and explore the tranquil medina and the covered souks, where the stalls are set behind bright-green shutters. The town is most noted for its annual Fête des Cerises, or Cherry Festival, that celebrates the yearly harvest in mid-June with food, music, dance, and cultural activities including crowing the Cherry Queen.

OFF THE BEATEN PATH

Bhalil. The small Berber village of Bhalil is an off-the-beaten-track gem, around 5 km (3 miles) from Sefrou. Built across a hillside, the picturesque pastel-color houses that line the narrow, winding streets may appear conventional from the outside, but step inside and you'll discover that many of them are built into the rock face. This design keeps out the scorching summer heat, as well as the icy winter chill, and Bhalil's modern-day troglodytes normally use the cave as a living and dining space. This tranquil village is set at the foot of Djebel Kandar, and it makes a good base for walking, from leisurely rambles to more strenuous all-day hikes. ■TIP➜ You'll often find the women of Bhalil sitting outside their houses sewing intricate djellaba buttons. ✉ *Bhalil.*

OFF THE BEATEN PATH

Culture Vultures and Gallery H'biza. As well as artisanal tours in Fez El-Bali, Culture Vultures, an avant-garde arts and culture organization, runs tours to three ancient fondouks around the main square, visiting everyone from slipper makers to embroiderers. They also run a small, contemporary-art gallery and gift shop housed in the heart of the medina. H'biza translates as "small loaf of bread" and in a Moroccan proverb represents an opportunity not to be turned down. They work with local artists, so pop into their office to see what artists-in-residence and presentations they have coming up. ✉ *Pl. Huddadine* ☎ *0535/68–33–75* ⊕ *culturevulturesfez.org.*

Kef el-Moumen. During the town's famous Cherry Festival, a procession ventures across the Aggai River to the Kef el-Moumen cave containing the prophet Daniel's tomb, a pilgrimage venerated by Jews and Muslims alike. According to legend, seven followers of Daniel slept here for centuries before miraculously resuscitating. ✉ *Sefrou* ☉ *Festival dates vary depending on Ramadan; in 2017 it was held in July.*

Lalla Rekia. West of Sefrou is the ancient fountain of Lalla Rekia, believed to contain miraculous holy water to cure mental illness. Some visitors still bring jugs to the spring to carry away alleged healing benefits from the fount's source. The area is best accessed by rental car or taxi, as public transportation in the area is limited. ✉ *Sefrou.*

WHERE TO STAY

$ B&B/INN Fodor's Choice ★ 🏨 **Dar Kamal Chaoui.** In the tranquil troglodyte village of Bhalil, Kamal and Bea Chaoui have turned their family home into a delightful B&B with four rooms thoughtfully decorated with local touches—perhaps a donkey pannier or an intricately painted wooden door as a headboard—all with handwoven blankets across the beds. **Pros:** charming English and French-speaking owners; interesting village; good walking. **Cons:** quiet area; off the beaten track; small property. [$] *Rooms from: 770DH* ✉ *60, Kaf Rhouni, Bhalil* ☎ *0678/83–83–10* 🌐 *www.kamalchaoui.com* 🛏 *4 rooms* 🍴 *Breakfast.*

IFRANE

25 km (15 miles) southwest of Imouzzer du Kandar, 63 km (39 miles) southwest of Fez.

Built in 1929 during the French protectorate to create a *poche de France* (pocket of France) for expatriate French diplomats, administrators, and business personnel, Ifrane's alpine chalets, contemporary villas, and modern boulevards have become the place to see and be seen for local elite, whose wealth is visibly flaunted with Western designer clothing in European-style cafés and a luxury resort and spa overlooking the Azrou Cedar Forest. Nicknamed "Morocco's Switzerland," Ifrane sits at an altitude of 5,460 feet and is visibly well maintained with manicured gardens, tree-lined streets, and Swiss-style architecture. As a royal mandate, the Al Akhawayn University, an English-language public university with an American curriculum, opened in the mid-1990s and has become one of the country's finest.

ESSENTIALS

Taxis **Ifrane Taxi Stand.** ✉ *Ifrane–Meknès Rd.*

Visitor Information **Délégation du Tourisme d'Ifrane.** ✉ *Av. Mohammed V* ☎ *0535/56–68–21.*

EXPLORING

Known primarily as an upscale ski-resort town, Ifrane is also famous for its cold-water trout fishing and hiking trails around the **Cascades des Vierges** (Waterfall of the Virgins). Zaoula de Ifrane, a small village just north of the city, is home to local artisans. Near the well-photographed stone Atlas lion statue in the center of town, the royal palace of the ruling Alaouite dynasty is still in use by the ruling kingdom and off-limits to the general public, with extraordinarily high security in the area.

WHERE TO EAT AND STAY

$ INTERNATIONAL FAMILY 🍴 **Cafe de Paix.** This modern, family-friendly restaurant–pizzeria–tea salon, is popular with both locals and visitors. The menu offers a range of international dishes, as well as authentic Moroccan tagines and steak

The scenery around Ifrane is almost alpine; it's not uncommon to see sheep grazing on the hillsides.

frites, plus tasty soups, salads, pizzas, and delicious desserts, smoothies, and milk shakes. **Known for:** buzzy café; varied menu. ⓢ *Average main: 70DH* ✉ *Appart Hotel, Av. de la Marche Verte* ☎ *0535/56–66–75* ⊟ *No credit cards.*

$$$$
RESORT
Fodor's Choice
★
🏨 **Michlifen Ifrane Suites and Spa.** Less than an hour south of the world's largest medieval city at Fez, this five-star resort hotel perched atop a hill is a stunningly luxurious retreat near the Michlifen ski slopes that continues to attract wealthy locals. **Pros:** beautiful views; sumptuous suites; spa and sports center. **Cons:** limited public transportation; expensive rates (but check website for offers); quiet area. ⓢ *Rooms from: 2016DH* ✉ *Av. Hassan II* ☎ *0535/86–40–00* ⊕ *www.michlifenifrane. com* ⤶ *71 rooms* ⦿ *Breakfast.*

SPORTS AND THE OUTDOORS
SKIING
Michlifen and Djebel Hebri are the two ski resorts nearest Ifrane and within day-trip range of Fez. If your expectations are modest, a day on the slopes is a pleasant option—there are four trails that are relatively simple. Skis and sleds can be rented at the resorts.

AZROU

17 km (10 miles) southwest of Ifrane, 67 km (40 miles) southeast of Meknès, 78 km (47 miles) southwest of Fez.

Occupying an important junction of routes between the desert and Meknès and between Fez and Marrakesh, Azrou—from the Berber word for "rock"—is a significant ancient Berber capital named for the city's quarry of black volcanic rocks. It was one of Sultan Moulay Ismail's strongholds after he built an imposing fortress here (now in ruins) in 1684. For centuries Azrou remained unknown, a secret mountain town that invading forces never fully located, thanks in part to a cave system designed for concealment and protection. Enjoy the mellow pace and lifestyle of traditional Berber mountain life. The interesting Tuesday souk gets crowded, but the small medina is normally comparatively tranquil. Just before Azrou, the enormous freshwater lake of Dayet Azrou is a popular spot for picnics. You can take a boat out on the water, although swimming is not allowed.

EXPLORING

The heaving Tuesday souk is held in an open area 1½ km (1 mile) to the northeast of the town. It attracts locals from many neighboring towns for its vast selection of local produce, plastic goods, clothes, and more. Place Mohammed V is the tranquil main square, where you'll find several cafés and shops.

Azrou Cedar Forest. The Azrou Cedar Forest is a source of great pride throughout the country. Moroccan cedars, some more than 400 years old, grow to heights of close to 200 feet and cover some 320,000 acres on the slopes of the Middle Atlas, the High Atlas, and the Rif at altitudes between 3,940 and 9,200 feet. Cedar is much coveted by woodworkers, particularly makers of stringed musical instruments. Living among the enormous cedars to the south of Azrou are troops of bold Barbary macaques and birdlife ranging from the redheaded Moroccan woodpecker to owls and eagles. Flora include the large-leaf peony, the scarlet dianthus, and the blue germander, all of which attract butterflies, including the cardinal and the colorful sulfur Cleopatra. You can pick up information, guides, and maps of the forest showing trails and hikes at the Ifrane Tourist Office. ✉ *Azrou.*

Ensemble Artisanale. Azrou's artisan center, just off the P24 to Khénifra (and a mere five-minute walk from Place Mohammed V), is a collection of small crafts shops selling carpets, kilims, stone, and cedar carvings. ✉ *Azrou* 🕒 *Closed Fri.*

Lycée Tarik Ibn Ziad. Seeing a Berber nucleus, the French established the Collège Berbère here in an attempt to train an elite Berber opposition to the urban Arab ruling class; both Arabic and Islam were prohibited. After independence, the movement faded. The Berber college became an Arabic school and was renamed the Lycée Tarik Ibn Ziad. It now teaches a progressive curriculum and hosts international exchange students. ✉ *Bd. Prince Heritier Sidi Mohammed* ☎ *0535/56–24–16.*

WHERE TO STAY

$ HOTEL 🏨 **Palais des Cerisiers.** Situated close to the village center en route to the Azrou Cedar Forest, this pretty, Alpine-style hotel is set in a stone mansion on verdant grounds and well equipped with classic wood furnishings, air-conditioned and centrally heated rooms, serene mountain views, and a large pool. **Pros:** tranquil atmosphere; pool; mountain bikes for exploring. **Cons:** service may be slow; uninspiring decor; rates can be expensive, check website for offers. [$] *Rooms from: 1020DH* ✉ *Rte. Cèdre Gouraud, Hay Ajelabe* ☎ *0535/56–38–30* 🌐 *www.lepalaisdescerisiers.com* 🛏 *20 rooms* 🍴 *Breakfast.*

THE HIGH ATLAS

WELCOME TO THE HIGH ATLAS

TOP REASONS TO GO

★ **Hike North Africa's tallest peak:** Djebel Toubkal, which soars to 13,671 feet, is only a two-day climb. Trekkers can find everything they need at the base of the mountain.

★ **Adrenaline junkies getting their fix:** From mountain biking to skiing to skydiving and hot-air ballooning, outdoor activities in magical surroundings abound. Even just driving through the jaw-dropping mountains can be an adventure, with panoramas you have to see to believe.

★ **Magnificent views in high style:** Some truly first-class hotels have opened their doors to travelers in the High Atlas; the best contribute to the local community.

★ **Berber tradition and culture:** Life in the Atlas has barely altered over hundreds of years. While the arrival of electricity, the Internet, and new roads has brought changes, you'll still find Berber culinary, agricultural, linguistic, and artisanal heritage alive and well.

The two routes over the Tizi-n-Test (Test Pass) and Tizi-n-Tichka (Tichka Pass) are spectacular. For serious trekking, the area around Imlil is the best place to base yourself. There are also less-strenuous walks along many of the dirt roads in the region, for instance along the Agoundis River. Alternatively, visitors can make the hotels around Ouirgane their base, exploring the area on muleback or simply lounging by the pool. The Tin Mal Mosque and the Goundafi Kasbah can easily be reached from Ouirgane on a day trip. The Aït Bougmez Valley is a paradise for gentle exploration. Easy treks through the apple and cherry trees or a medium-grade scramble through the gorges and caves will suit every taste.

1 The Central High Atlas and the Aït Bougmez Valley. Forested with olive groves and live oaks on their lower slopes, the rugged mountains to the south of El-Ksiba and Beni-Mellal offer memorable treks and jeep excursions and form a striking contrast to Azilal's lush Cascades d'Ouzoud and Demnate's natural bridge

at Imi-n-Ifri. The nearby Aït Bougmez Valley is a Berber heartland (it's also known as the valley of happiness) and lies beneath the protective shadow of Mt. M'Goun—Morocco's second-highest peak.

2 Imlil and Ourika Valley. A village between Marrakesh and Mt. Toubkal, Imlil is the center of adventure tourism

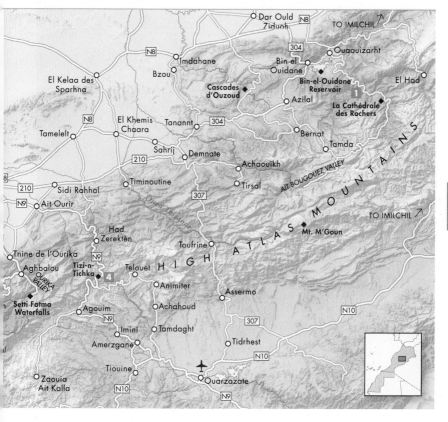

in Morocco. Trekkers en route to the mountain stop here for rest, relaxation, and to breathe in the fresh mountain air so rarely found elsewhere. Through the verdant Ourika Valley, visitors will find a string of charming villages, where you can marvel at the Setti Fatma waterfalls.

3 To Tizi-n-Test. The pass southwest of Marrakesh leads to the trekking center of Ouirgane and on to Taroudant.

4 To Tizi-n-Tichka. Completed in 1936, the Tizi-n-Tichka has recently been widened and improved, but still has lost none of its excitement or the hairpin bends beloved (or feared) by drivers. Though the road is safer and wider than the one over the Tizi-n-Test, it can be a dangerous drive, particularly in winter weather conditions. Still, the views from the pass are like nothing else.

TREKKING IN THE ATLAS

There are few better antidotes to the marvelous mayhem that is Marrakesh than the clear air and amazing vistas offered by the High Atlas Mountains. From gentle strolls through unspoiled Berber villages to full-blown, week-long mountain treks, outfitters can cater to all levels of experience and budget.

Most travelers to the High Atlas associate it with one thing: Djebel Toubkal, North Africa's highest peak, scraping the clouds at 13,671 feet. It is indeed a magnificent sight, and for most of the year it's a relatively easy climb; from late April to early October a strong pair of legs (and boots) will suffice. As the focal point of the range, Djebel Toubkal is very popular in high season, but over its 600-plus-mile length, the High Atlas has over 400 peaks that exceed 10,000 feet, so there are plenty of alternatives. In typical Moroccan style, flexibility is the name of the game. Pretty much any type or length of trek can be organized, from a half-day excursion to lengthy expeditions involving mules and guides. Your level of fitness will determine which you choose.

(above) Two trekkers walking along a river in the Central High Atlas (opposite page, bottom) walking in the Tizi-n-Tichka pass (opposite page, top) a terrace restaurant with a view of the snow-covered Atlas peaks

SAFETY ADVICE

Never walk alone. Always tell someone where you are going, and when you hope to return. Take suitable quantities of food; warm, lightweight clothing; a hat and sunscreen; and a first-aid kit and water-purifying tablets (not bottled water). Most important, wear comfortable boots. Litter and general pollution are a growing problem, so please leave no traces of your visit.

It is generally agreed that the launch point for any foray into the High Atlas is the largest Berber village in the region, Imlil (although it's still quite small). Here, accommodations are both plentiful and cheap, though they can feel a little faded (but they all come with that priceless Berber hospitality).

In the shadow of Djebel Toubkal, Imlil is unprepossessing but has a purposeful bustle, offering all that is necessary for a trek. Everything is for hire: boots (though bring your own if possible), jackets, sleeping bags, crampons, and even a mule, which can carry the loads of four people, including children, over most terrain.

GUIDES

Detailed maps of the region are scarce (and those that exist don't list many of the small villages and passes), but with a guide you shouldn't need one. Imlil is bursting with people willing to lead an expedition. Official guides can be found at the Bureau des Guides et des Accompagnateurs à Imlil, in the main square, or you can ask for a recommendation from your hotel or guesthouse. Official mountain guides undergo rigorous training and take exams within the French mountaineering system. In terms of cost, expect to pay 400 DH to 600 DH per day for a guide, plus more for food and accommodations. If a guide is arranging a trek for you, they

will also arrange the food and accommodations; just be sure to agree on the price beforehand. Mules come in at a very reasonable 150 DH along with their mule driver. It's also expected for you to tip your guide; a standard tip is 100 DH per day for the guide and cook, and 50 DH per person per day for the mule and regular driver.

TREKKING ROUTES

The choice of route will depend upon your level of experience, the season, the length of time, and your budget. The obvious option is to attack Djebel Toubkal—you can be up and down in two days. Head south from Imlil past Sidi Chamarouch and make the easy ascent. Overnight on the mountain in one of two refuges (minimalist lodgings that offer accommodations, showers, food, and hot drinks) at the base of the mountain.

Those with more time and stamina may opt for a circular route, east from Imlil. Over five days, you might visit Tacchedirt, Tizi Likemt (at an impressive 11,663 feet), spend the second night at Azib Lkemt, and the third in Amsouzerte. To the west, Lac d'Ifni (a serene mineral-rich lake) awaits, then back to the one of the refuges before descending to Imlil. Another popular circular route goes up through Tizi Mizk, via Azeeb Tamsoult.

Updated by
Alice Morrison

The High Atlas region is made for outdoor adventures—the perfect antidote to the concentration and animation of Marrakesh. You can hang glide, ski, hot-air balloon, quad bike, and ride mules, but perhaps best of all, you can walk (in the winter, you can even ski).

This is also the heart of Berber mountain culture. so it's the perfect place to experience their hospitality and explore their customs. Or, if trekking isn't your thing, you can relax and wander through the fruit orchards, gorge on fresh peaches and in-season walnuts, and learn about the carpets woven by the women of the region over a cup of hot wild thyme tea.

The High Atlas Mountains rise as a natural fortress between the fertile Haouz Plain around Marrakesh and the deserts of the south. Trapping moisture that blows in from the Atlantic, the mountains pass this bounty along to the land and to the thin rivers that vanish into the southern desert. To reach the mountains, even today's travelers must go through one of the routes guarded by age-old passes: Tizi-n-Test in the west or Tizi-n-Tichka in the east. They benefit from some glorious spots to stay, and the chance to take a quiet look at some intriguing relics of Moroccan history.

PLANNING

WHEN TO GO

The mountains are at their most stunningly beautiful in March and April when the irises are blooming and the cherry trees are flowering. Hiking can be done all year-round, but high season is the spring and fall. Attempting the summits in winter means that you need proper equipment and might encounter weather that will impede your plans, but you will be rewarded with empty mountains and peaceful, snow-filled scenery. Summer here is cooler than in the desert and in Marrakesh, but the sun is still strong and you will need lots of water if you decide to trek.

FESTIVALS

The most famous of festivals in this region is the Imilchil Marriage Festival, held each year in September. Legend has it that a "Romeo and Juliet" story happened here ages ago; since then, an annual festival is held for young people to choose their own partner. Though lately the festival has been attracting more and more tourists, it's still a sight to behold. The Setti Fatma Moussem, held in August, still contains the religious elements of a *moussem* (pilgrimage festival). Foreigners are welcome and will be pulled into the games and entertainment.

PLANNING YOUR TIME

There is so much to see in this region, and since the roads are narrow and serpentine, slopes are steep, and terrain is bumpy, allow plenty of time for getting around. Seven to 10 days is recommended to really see the mountains and to get a good trek in. Start off in either Ourika or Tahannout to get acquainted with the region, while any mountain hike will truly begin in Imlil. The village of Tacchedirt is worth the five-hour trek, as is the more demanding two-day ascent to the great Toubkal. Afterward, explore the route to the pretty village of Ouirgane, and, to complete a circle back in the Marrakesh direction, stop at the barrage of Lalla Takerkoust, a pretty settlement with some pleasant eateries and accommodations.

Alternatively, you can take Route 210 out of Marrakesh, heading toward the Ouzoud Falls, before continuing on to the reservoir Bin el-Ouidane. From here, head back down through Azilal and farther south to the magnificent valley of Aït Bougmez, which can serve as a base for trekking. Whatever you do, definitely don't miss out on getting up to the mountains themselves; even a short, half-day hike on a day trip from Marrakesh is well worth it. Imlil is just a 1½-hour drive from Marrakesh, making a day trip quite doable.

GETTING HERE AND AROUND

Although there's no air travel directly into the High Atlas, getting to the region isn't as difficult as it seems.

AIR TRAVEL

The closest airport is Marrakesh Menara, both to the Central High Atlas regions east of the city and to the areas south of Marrakesh, including the Ourika Valley. Many of the better hotels can arrange direct airport transfers from Marrakesh on your behalf, though this may come at an additional charge.

BUS TRAVEL

You can also hop on a bus from an airport or another major city, but this kind of travel can be time-consuming. If going to areas north and east of Marrakesh, try to avoid the marathon bus that goes from Marrakesh to Fez (via Beni-Mellal); buses run from Beni-Mellal up to Azilal, a common departure point for hiking excursions, departing approximately every three hours between 7 am and 4 pm. Buses also reach destinations in the High Atlas south of Marrakesh.

CAR TRAVEL

Unless you are taking a guided excursion, a car is the best way to explore off-the-beaten path towns at your own pace. If you have any intention of wandering into the hinterland independently, be sure you're driving a four-wheel-drive vehicle, and consider carrying more than one spare tire as well as emergency fuel. It's best to rent a car in Marrakesh and travel on from there. *See the Travel Smart chapter, for more information on rental cars.*

TAXI TRAVEL

You can also take a *grand taxi.* These used to be large, old, yellow Mercedes, but are now being traded in for modern cars (although they are usually still yellow). Prices are per seat, which means you have to wait until the car is filled with passengers to take off, but if you don't want to wait, you can buy up the empty seats or hire the entire car. Be sure to agree on and settle the fare prior to setting off.

SAFETY

The High Atlas is generally very safe and Berbers have a treasured code of hospitality, but travelers should still take precautions. Rural sentiments are quite different from urban ones, so women should dress more conservatively than in larger cities. The biggest safety concern is, of course, for trekkers. You can hike on your own, but you will be safer and learn much more about the local environment if you take a guide. You should not attempt to summit Toubkal or any of the other major summits on your own; those are best done with a large group or with a trained guide.

RESTAURANTS

There are a few excellent restaurants in some of the major hotels, but beyond these, fare is limited mostly to what's available in small hotel restaurants and cafés—mostly tagines. Avoid alcohol except in hotels. In general, drinking won't raise any eyebrows as long as you're among other tourists, but the practice of carrying wine and spirits into the backcountry is not appreciated by villagers. Alcohol is *haram* (forbidden by the Koran), but on a more earthly level it's simply not very socially acceptable. *Restaurant reviews have been shortened. For full information, visit Fodors.com.*

HOTELS

Some more sophisticated hotels in the High Atlas are located in or around Ouirgane, Lalla Takerkoust, and Ourika, which are quickly becoming sought-after refuges from the sometimes excessive stimulation of Morocco's cities. There are a couple of stunning kasbahs around Imlil. Most other lodging in the region consists of inexpensive *gîtes* (backpackers' refuges). Heterosexual couples staying in private homes while trekking will be assumed to be married. It's best not to disabuse your hosts of their assumptions, as it is illegal for a Moroccan and non-Moroccan of opposite sexes to spend the night together if they are not married. If one member of the heterosexual couple is Moroccan, a marriage certificate is likely to be required. *Hotel reviews have been shortened. For full information, visit Fodors.com.*

WHAT IT COSTS IN DIRHAMS				
	$	**$$**	**$$$**	**$$$$**
Restaurants	under 90 DH	90 DH–120 DH	121 DH–150 DH	over 150 DH
Hotels	under 400 DH	400 DH–650 DH	651 DH–1,000 DH	over 1,000 DH

Restaurant prices are the average cost of a main course at dinner or, if dinner is not served, at lunch. Hotel prices are the lowest cost of a standard double room in high season.

WHAT TO WEAR

As weather in this region can be unpredictable, it's best to bring layers. It gets very hot in the summer and very cold in the winter, and you always need something warm for nighttime, regardless of the season. A hat and scarf are vital to protect against the sun. A down jacket, or something equally warm, is necessary for most of the year (note that heating is not a given in guesthouses). Solid footwear, such as boots or sneakers, is important, especially if you're planning on doing a trek. Sandals are socially acceptable and a sturdy, sensible pair can be useful for strolls, although not for demanding hikes. Both women and men should dress conservatively. Women will be better received by locals if they wear longish sleeves, avoiding short skirts and shorts. Both genders should be aware that pants are more practical when mule riding.

TOURS

A good local tour guide will be able to plan with you, and accompany you, on a thorough visit of the region. As well as organizing accommodation and transport (which can be a headache), they'll be able to point you in the right direction of safe and appropriate treks and worthwhile points of interests while supplying all the cultural information you may require. There is also the language advantage; remember that in the mountains, Arabic or a Berber dialect is mostly spoken and a language-savvy guide is an invaluable asset. Be sure to research tour guides and companies in advance as there are some less reputable organizations around. If you are using a guide, ask if they are licensed.

Fodor's Choice **Argan Xtreme Sports.** Owned by the ever-friendly and extremely knowl-
★ edgeable Saif and Samira Kovach, Argan has a great fleet of bikes for on- and off-road bike tours. They offer a variety of tours from Marrakesh into the Atlas, with options for all abilities from family-friendly to professional bikers. Day and multiday excursions are available, and they also do tours in and around Marrakesh. ⊠ *AXS Bicycle Shop, Rue Fatima El Fihria, Marrakesh* ☎ *524/40–02–07 in Morocco, 314/374–20–08 in U.S.* ⊕ *www.argansports.com.*

Pathfinders Treks. This local Berber company offers tours with a focus on showing visitors the real Morocco. All the guides speak excellent English and are specialists in mountain and trekking tours (they also offer tours to the desert). The company is particularly passionate about sustainable tourism and supporting local communities. ⊠ *Douar Tagadirt Ait Ali, Imlil* ☎ *0639/60–74–75* ⊕ *www.pathfinderstreks.com.*

THE CENTRAL HIGH ATLAS AND
THE AÏT BOUGMEZ VALLEY

Deep in the Berber heartland, the Central High Atlas is relatively unscathed by modernity. A large road-building initiative by the Moroccan government means that most areas are accessible, but they retain their wildness and their local traditions The contrast in scenery is quite extraordinary in this area. One minute you will be looking up at a forbidding peak of bare rock, then the next at a patchwork of apple orchards, cut through with silvery streams. Ait Bougmez is the prettiest valley in Morocco with its lush greenery, punctuated by hilltop shrines and ancient granaries. The region's crowning glory is Mt. M'Goun, which stretches up over 13,000 feet, making it the second-highest peak in North Africa.

IMILCHIL

113 km (70 miles) southwest of Midelt, 150 km (93 miles) northeast of Marrakesh.

The joy of a visit to Imilchil is in the journey, but it's also famous for the marriage festival that takes place here every September, when the young people of the community are dressed up in their best and brought together to find everlasting happiness. The surrounding **Plateau des Lacs** (Plateau of the Lakes) includes the lakes of Iseli and Tislit (Fiancé and Fiancée), which were said to be formed by the tears of two star-crossed lovers who then drowned in the lakes they had created. Lac Tislit is 5 km (3 miles) from Imilchil, while Iseli is another 10 km (6 miles) east.

GETTING HERE AND AROUND
Some people will approach Imilchil from Midelt. To reach Imilchil from the west, leave Beni Mellal on Avenue 20 Août Ex (N50), and shortly after take Route Principale 24. Continue on the P3221. After 5 km (3 miles), take the N8 for 44 km (27 miles), then take a right onto the R317 and continue for 119 km (74 miles), arriving at Imilchil after a total of about 170 km (105 miles) and three hours' driving.

CASCADES D'OUZOUD

153 km (95 miles) northeast of Marrakesh.

No trip to the Atlas would be complete without a stop at these impressive falls, which are approachable from the S508 via the 1811. You will most likely hear the roaring water before you get your first glimpse, especially in late spring when the melting snow swells the rivers. The cascades, which are a popular destination for holidaying Moroccan families as well as foreigners, are rarely seen without a rainbow halo. On the way back down, wild Barbary apes play in the trees—avoid feeding them as they can get aggressive. Locals say the apes fall into three categories: those liking olives, those liking tourists, and those disliking both and preferring to hide in holiday season.

There are a number of pop-up snack places at the falls. They are cheap, but may not always be the most reliable in terms of hygiene. There are clean, public toilets in the car park. The colorful boats that sashay

The Berbers

The Berbers, or Imazighen, as they often prefer, are the indigenous people of North Africa, whose regions of occupation stretch from Egypt right across to Morocco and then down into Mauritania and Mali. They make up roughly 40% of the Moroccan population and the Berber language has been adopted as one of the three official state languages. The word "Berber" is thought by many to derive from the Latin word "barbarus" used by the Romans to describe foreigners, especially those from the untamed hinterlands of their empire. The Berber mountain communities were Jewish and Animist until the conquest of Morocco by Islam in the 7th century, and there was a large, residual Jewish population in Morocco until the mid-20th century, when many moved to Israel.

LANGUAGE

There are three main divisions of the Berber language: Taririft in the Rif area; Tamazight in the Mid-Atlas; and Tashlahit in the High Atlas, Anti-Atlas, and Souss. There is no linguistic connection to Arabic, although Moroccan Arabic and the Berber languages have infiltrated each other. They used to be primarily oral languages, but in 2003, the Neo-Tifinagh alphabet was adopted.

THE BERBER WAY

Attention to local sensitivities is much appreciated and often rewarded with the celebrated Berber hospitality. Smiling goes further than anything in creating good will. Dressing modestly is always appreciated. Smoking is an urban phenomenon, so everyone (particularly women) should smoke discreetly. Many High Atlas villagers are outraged that their children behave as beggars by demanding money, pens, or sweets from foreigners; the polite way to refuse is to say, "*Allah esahel,*" which means "God make it easy on you." If you would like to contribute something to these regions, ask your hotel or guide how you can do so through one of the local associations that provide much of the local health care and education in the region. Always be sure to ask permission before you photograph Moroccans.

toward the gushing torrent are really fun to take a ride on, but do be careful. Remember that swimming in the basin carved out of the rock at the base of the falls is strictly forbidden, although you can jump in off the small bridge farther down and swim down to the rockpool.

Downstream, past the Ouzoud falls on the 1811 road, is the Berber hillside village of **Tanaghmelt.** Nicknamed "the Mexican village," the small community is connected by a web of narrow alleyways and semi-underground passages. You may also wish to continue up the 1811 (toward the P24) to see the **river gorges** of the Oued-el-Abid.

GETTING HERE AND AROUND

Around 170 km (105 miles) of good road separate Marrakesh from the Cascades d'Ouzoud, a journey that takes some two to three hours of driving. Leaving Marrakesh, take the Fez road (N8). Continue for around 60 km (37 miles). Turn right toward Azilal (the S508). Approximately 20 km (12 miles) before Azilal, turn left, following signs to Ouzoud.

WHERE TO STAY

$$ HOTEL FAMILY **La Kasbah d'Ouzoud.** Within this traditional Kasbah, you can choose from a mixture of rooms or bungalows dotted around a pool and beautiful gardens. **Pros:** beautiful building; excellent food; lush garden setting. **Cons:** if the phone signal is weak, the credit card machine doesn't work; Wi-Fi can be patchy; rather basic rooms. [$] *Rooms from: 600DH* ✉ *C/R Ait Taguelle, Ouzoud* ☎ *0523/42–92–10* 🌐 *www.kasbahouzoud.com* 🛏 *6 bungalows, 7 rooms* 🍴 *Breakfast.*

$$ HOTEL **Riad Cascades d'Ouzoud.** A haven of beautifully designed spaces, materials, and colors, one of the highlights of this riad is the panoramic roof terrace. **Pros:** a perfect blend of elegance and comfort; welcoming and authentic; amazing location. **Cons:** some rooms on the small side; the walkway in front can get busy with tourists. [$] *Rooms from: 650DH* ✉ *Cascades d'Ouzoud, Ouzoud* ☎ *0523/42–91–73* 🌐 *www.ouzoud.com* 🛏 *9 rooms* 🍴 *Breakfast; All meals; Some meals.*

THE AÏT BOUGMEZ VALLEY

Also known as the valley of happiness, this Atlas valley was basically cut off from the rest of the world until 2001; before then, only a narrow, overgrown track led into the heavenly series of hamlets perched above a river and the richest of flora. Here, slopes dotted with beehives lead down into a grove of walnut and apple trees. The valleys are filled with vegetables and fruit grown using traditional farm techniques; there's not a tractor in sight, only donkeys, simple ploughs, and one seriously hardworking community.

Today, there is an excellent tarmac road that leads to Aït Bougmez. As a result, more visitors come to the area, but it still remains relatively secluded and retains its charm and authenticity. There is a huge variety of terrain in this relatively small area, so there are many options for hikers and bikers. There's of course the challenge of M'Goun mountain for those who want to test themselves, but for the less ambitious, just hiking through the rich fields at the base of the valley and enjoying the pure, refreshing air is a delightful experience.

Almost all houses here continue to be made from the traditional pisé bricks and baked earth, and you'll notice that most have living roofs, since sheaves of grasses are incorporated into the structure. One of the prettiest sights is the poppies peeping from them in spring. Life here is very simple, so don't expect any luxury spa hotels. There are also no restaurants in Aït Bougmez, but you can have a meal in practically any guesthouse with a little advance notice. Of course, you will also be invited in for tea by friendly villagers—be sure to say yes to experience that acclaimed hospitality.

Remember that you are deep in the mountains, and safety is vital. It is easy to get lost. Always travel with a guide, and be aware that much of this terrain is totally deserted for miles and miles on end. In winter, it gets incredibly cold and it's not uncommon to have minor snowstorms.

The Imilchil wedding moussem draws more than just happy couples; livestock vendors are also there in full force.

GETTING HERE AND AROUND

From Marrakesh, expect to spend three and a half hours getting to the Aït Bougmez valley. Leaving Marrakesh on the Route de Fez, take the right turn after 60 km (37 miles) toward Azilal. From Azilal, follow signs to the Aït Bougmez valley. It's a long but bewitchingly beautiful road that calls for careful, unhurried driving through mountain roads that are almost exclusively U-shaped. It's also possible to reach Aït Bougmez by grand taxi from Marrakesh with a change at Azilal. Be aware that the last taxi leaves Azilal around 2 pm in order to make it to Aït Bougmez before nightfall.

EXPLORING

FAMILY **Prehistoric dinosaur footprints.** Kids and adults alike love treading in these giant tracks of both carnivorous and herbivorous dinosaurs that are estimated to be about 185 million years old. There are several dinosaur-footprint sites in the region, but the easiest to find are those in the village of Ibaklliwne. As the road leads into the Aït Bougmez hamlets, it splits in two—this is actually a double valley. Follow the right-hand branch, leading into Tabant, the main village complete with a couple of cement structures, a school, and an administrative building. Follow this track for about 1½ km (1 mile) past the schoolhouses into the village of Ibaklliwne, where you'll find the dinosaur footprints on the hillside. ✉ *Ibaklliwne, Ait Bougmez* 🎫 *Free.*

Sidi Moussa Marabout. A 2½-hour walk from the base of the valley will take you to the steep slope of Sidi Moussa Hill. Here stands a circular earthen building, a shrine to the saint Sidi Moussa (*Moussa* means "Moses" in Arabic), which dates to at least 200 years ago. Sidi Moussa, revered for his skills in curing infertility, was buried here, and his tomb once attracted many visitors, although few still make the pilgrimage. Women thought to have fertility issues would leave a garment at the door and then spend the night inside. For a time the building was used as a collective granary before being restored by the Titmit Village Association. A guardian will serve you a glass of tea and give you a tour (pay him 20 DH minimum or 10 DH per person—all proceeds go to the Association). ⊠ *Ait Bougmez* ✉ *Free; tour, 20 DH.*

WHERE TO STAY

$$$
HOTEL
🍴 **Dar Itrane.** Tucked into the village of Imghlaus, Dar Itrane is an inconspicuous gemstone of a lodge, with little that isn't utterly charming. **Pros:** delightful and helpful staff; delicious homemade food; wonderful views. **Cons:** the smaller beds can be a bit slopey; rooms are basic; can get cold at night. $ *Rooms from: 660DH* ⊠ *Imghlaus Village, Ait Bougmez* ☎ *0523/45–93–12* ⊕ *www.origins-lodge.com* ▭ *No credit cards* ⤳ *17 rooms* |◎| *Some meals.*

$
B&B/INN
FAMILY
🍴 **La Montagne Au Pluriel.** With a fabulous garden, friendly hosts, hot showers, and comfortable beds, this family-owned hotel is one of the most charming choices in the area. **Pros:** gorgeous garden; lots of hot water; friendly and knowledgeable staff. **Cons:** need to go to the roof terrace to get phone signal; can get cold at night; simple accommodations. $ *Rooms from: 150 DHDH* ⊠ *Agouti, Ait Bougmez* ☎ *0661/88–24–34* ⊕ *www.lamontagneaupluriel.com* ⤳ *30 rooms* ▭ *No credit cards.*

$$
HOTEL
FAMILY
🍴 **Touda Ecolodge.** This fantastic lodge occupies a prize position in the valley's deepest village, standing atop a hill with an unbeatable vantage point. **Pros:** magnificent views; well-equipped accommodation; tours and classes can be arranged. **Cons:** the road to get here may be difficult for some vehicles; gets cold at night; phone signal sometimes weak. $ *Rooms from: 600DH* ⊠ *Village Zawiyat Oulmzi, Ait Bougmez* ☎ *0033/683617991 in France, 0662/14–42–85 in Morocco* ⊕ *www. touda.fr* ⤳ *8 rooms* |◎| *All meals.*

SHOPPING

Women's Cooperative of Imghlaus. In the village of Imghlaus, up a dusty slope is a small, unassuming hut where you'd never know that inside was a veritable furor of singing voices and busy fingers. Squashed inside the diminutive hut, about 15 women create exquisite carpets in an organized production line. This cooperative is part of a fair-trade program that ensures the creators get the profits, with no middlemen involved. You can witness the fabrication process from beginning to end: the wool being cleaned, brushed, spun, and then fed through the loom. They'll also show you the natural tints they use: walnut for brown, petals for yellow, and a scarlet root for red. The women work in two shifts and it can take upward of a month to create a large rug. Design is important here; in Aït Bougmez, expect to find a certain motif repeated, and the older women may have this same motif tattooed on their chins or foreheads, an ancient tradition that revealed identity and was seen as beautiful. Prices vary, but expect a minimum of approximately 1,000 DH for a medium-size rug. You can buy directly here, or order online and have it mailed. There are also smaller items for sale. ⊠ *Ait Bougmez* ⊕ *www.theanou.com.*

CLOSE UP

Moroccan Wines

During their occupation of the Maghreb, the Romans exercised their viticulture skills and exploited the climate and the soil, but upon their departure, and with the strengthening of Islam, the grapes literally withered on the vine. Under the French protectorate the vineyards were revived, but fell into state hands once they left in 1956, marking a second decline in production. The French once again took the helm in the 1990s, replacing all the vines and planting them in sand, which maintains the heat and kills phylloxera (the organism that once decimated French vineyards in the 19th century). The harvest is at the end of August and bottling takes place in France. The reds are quite low in tannin, the whites reasonably sharp and benefit from chilling. Wines of note are Médallion and Volubilis (reds and whites), both at the high end of the price range, but don't exclude bargains like the tasty Guerrouane Gris (a slightly orange-colored rosé) or the Président Sémillon Blanc. Look out for Gérard Depardieu Lumiere, a Syrah blend produced from the vineyards of the larger-than-life French actor.

6

SPORTS AND THE OUTDOORS

TREKKING

Hiking in this area is a true joy, thanks to the endless options and a huge variety of terrain in a relatively small area. Treks here are even suitable for families with children older than 11. A trek will give you insight into the valley, mountains, and underground gorges, with stops at villages, secret gorges, and orchards.

Fodor's Choice
★
Epic Morocco. For bespoke, tailor-made tours around Morocco, Epic Morocco is great for trekking through the Aït Bougmez Valley. The company is committed to providing the best possible experiences within the country, taking you off-the-beaten track and into the real Morocco. Whether you're looking for luxury guesthouses or the great outdoors, they do their best to tailor everything to your needs, and they come armed with impressive knowledge of the hiking and biking trails of the country. They also do high-octane adventures like paragliding off Toubkal and rallies across the desert. ⊠ *Residence le Gueliz, Guéliz* ☎ *2081/50–61–31* ⊕ *www.epicmorocco.co.uk.*

IMLIL AND THE OURIKA VALLEY

The village of Imlil is the preeminent jumping-off point for the high country, a vibrant mountain retreat whose existence has been given over to preparing walkers for various climbs around the peaks.

The Ourika Valley is another gateway to the High Atlas peaks, leading out of fuming Marrakesh into the fresh coolness of the mountains. It's a popular place to go for those in need of respite from the clamor and chaos of the city, but who don't want to travel far. Only 20 minutes outside of Marrakesh, it is a haven of green gorges and sparkling yellow wheat fields at the foot of snowcapped mountains. At the very end of the valley is Setti Fatma, a great base for trekkers. It's also where city

families come for the weekend to escape the summer heat, so expect a playful party filled with kids. There are countless cafés and restaurants along the road to Ourika, all filled with Moroccan families out to enjoy the cool mountain air.

You can take a grand taxi from Marrakesh (10 DH to Ourika, 20 DH to Setti Fatma); there are five daily buses (6 DH to Ourika).

IMLIL

64 km (40 miles) southeast of Marrakesh.

The ultimate home base for trekking the High Atlas, you'll find everything you need for your trek here: guides, rooms of varying price and quality, and equipment-rental shops. Imlil is a long strip of a village, built up around the main road. ⚠ Storms may occasionally make the road into town impassable or treks to neighboring settlements impossible. Consider this if you're heading up in rough weather.

GETTING HERE AND AROUND

Rental cars are available from numerous international and local agencies in Marrakesh. You can get to Imlil from Marrakesh by grand taxi for 50 DH per seat or you can rent the whole car for 300 DH. You can also hire a private car and driver, but this will be more expensive at around 900 DH.

TIMING AND PRECAUTIONS

Depending on how adept you are at trekking, you could enjoy hiking for a day or spend an entire week trekking the region. The best time to visit is early or late summer or early fall, but winter is best avoided except for the most avid of outdoors enthusiasts. No matter what the season, it's always recommended to hike with a guide.

Visitor and Tour Information Bureau des Guides. ☒ *Village Center* ☎ *0524/48–56–26.*

EXPLORING

Djebel Toubkal. You can unlock the adventurer inside by scaling this peak, the highest in North Africa. There are several ways to make the ascent, from hikes lasting several days to shorter options. The classic hike is a two or three day round-trip from Imlil. On day one, you hike to the foot of the mountain, which is an eight-hour walk, ascending at a moderate incline. There are two well-equipped refuges to spend the night that offer food and hot showers, as well as a campsite. On day two, you usually get up very early and leave in the dark to get to the first big pass for sunrise, and then push to the top. You can then can either return to the refuge for another night and trek back the next day, or walk straight out back down to Imlil.

The road to Imlil is a left turn off the S501 (the Tizi-n-Test road that leads south from Marrakesh), just after Asni. The 17-km (11-mile) stretch is a spectacular expanse of scrub and cacti, which reaches out to the very foot of Ouanoukrim Massif. ☒ *Imlil.*

WHERE TO EAT

Food can be pretty basic in Imlil (primarily consisting of cafés that provide skewers and tagines), so if you're looking for something more gourmet, you may wish to seek out Kasbah du Toubkal, a 10-minute hike through the town. (There is a reception center on the main street.) The kasbah provides excellent Moroccan dishes to nonguests, in magnificent surroundings. Otherwise, most guesthouses will offer a full, home-cooked meal to nonguests.

$ ✕ **Atlas Toubkal Imlil.** This restaurant located within a riad offers stunning
MOROCCAN   panoramic views from the rooftop terrace, along with delicious and savory food. You'll find all the standard Moroccan dishes here, with a nice selection of well-portioned tagines. **Known for:** good cheap food; kofta (lamb) tagines ; stunning views. Ⓢ *Average main: 80DH* ✉ *Imlil* ✛ *Center of Imlil, just past bridge* ☎ *662/05–82–51* ⊕ *www.riadatlas-toubkal.com* ▭ *No credit cards.*

WHERE TO STAY

Some of Imlil's hotels are right on the main square as you enter the village, but there are plenty more tucked away. Given the rise in popularity for treks in the region, there is now a good choice of hotels catering to a variety of tastes and budgets. They can range from mattresses on the floor of someone's home to opulent suites in luxurious accommodations. A great way to meet locals and see everyday Moroccan life is to stay in a private home for about 100 DH a night per person.

$ ⊡ **Auberge Zaratoustra.** This very pretty auberge is run by a friendly
B&B/INN   couple who offer convivial service and excellent home-cooked cuisine (the couple met in the culinary milieu) with a refined touch. **Pros:** run with care and attention; great food; warm welcome. **Cons:** can be tricky to find; gets quite cold at night; absolutely no frills. Ⓢ *Rooms from: 350DH* ✉ *Imlil* ☎ *0661/74–09–68* ⊕ *www.zaratoustra.com* ▭ *No credit cards* ⇨ *5 rooms, 5 studios* ⦙⦙⦙ *Breakfast; No meals; All meals; Some meals.*

$$ ⊡ **Douar Samra.** This charming, whimsical guesthouse was built from
HOTEL   scratch using traditional methods and materials in the tiny hamlet of
FAMILY   Tamatert, just past Imlil. **Pros:** eclectic design; best food in the Atlas
Fodor'sChoice   Mountains; can help organize guides and treks. **Cons:** can be hard to
★   find; need to order a donkey to transfer your luggage up. Ⓢ *Rooms from: 480* ✉ *Tamatert* ✛ *2 km (1 mile) from parking lot in Imlil. As you climb up, cross river, immediately on right is tiny, rocky track coming down stream's course. Follow this straight up and you come to Douar Samra in about ¼ mile* ☎ *0524/48–40–34, 0636/04–85–59* ⊕ *www.douar-samra.net* ⇨ *8 rooms* ⦙⦙⦙ *All meals.*

$ ⊡ **Hotel and Café Soleil.** This simple, authentic hotel and café is on the
HOTEL   main square of Imlil, and is a big hit with backpackers and trekkers. **Pros:** great local color; hotel can organize treks and tours and will hold luggage for trekkers. **Cons:** basic accommodations. Ⓢ *Rooms from: 300DH* ✉ *Village Square* ☎ *0524/48–56–22, 668/73–11–78* ⊕ *www.hotelsoleilimlil.com* ▭ *No credit cards* ⇨ *18 rooms* ⦙⦙⦙ *Some meals.*

The Kasbah de Toubkal, a luxury hotel, sits high above the village of Imlil.

$$$$
HOTEL
Fodor's Choice
★

⛩ **Kasbah du Toubkal.** Thank your stars that the short trek to this stunning yet simple Kasbah keeps some guests away, so you can gaze over the snowcapped Atlas peaks in peace. **Pros:** very intimate; excellent on-site hammam; hotel can organize tours, including a packed lunch. **Cons:** luxury comes at a price; two-night minimum stay; seclusion might not be to everyone's liking. *$ Rooms from: 1700DH ⊠ Imlil ⊹ Follow main road through Imlil and go right at fork, follow signs up hill, and keep going until you reach top ☎ 0524/48–56–11, 0661/91–85–98 ⊕ www. kasbahdutoubkal.com ⤳ 14 rooms, 3 Berber salons (no en suite facilities), 1 house, 1 dorm* ⦿| *Breakfast.*

$$$$
HOTEL
Fodor's Choice
★

⛩ **Kasbah Tamadot.** Should Hollywood set-makers get to work on a superdeluxe Moroccan mountain retreat, they might come up with something like this; this former villa of a prominent Italian art collector was even restored by Richard Branson himself. **Pros:** complete and absolute luxury; 20% of your breathtaking bill goes to the local Berber community; fantastic pool and spa. **Cons:** far removed from real Morocco; children only allowed certain times of the year; expensive. *$ Rooms from: 5600DH ⊠ Rte. d'Imlil, Asni ⊹ The kasbah is just after Asni on road to Imlil, on left ☎ 877/577–8777 U.S. toll-free, 0524/36–82–00 ⊕ www.virginlimitededition.com/en/ kasbah-tamadot ⤳ 24 rooms including 6 tented Berber-style suites* ⦿| *Breakfast.*

SETTI FATMA

Once you arrive at Setti Fatma, some 65 km (40 miles) from Marrakesh, you'll notice the increase in crowds and, of course, an increase in eating, lodging, and shopping options. But Setti Fatma is typically not the place to relax. It can be a nonstop party atmosphere for local Moroccans, which can be a lot of fun, just as long as you leave your longings for a quiet mountain retreat behind you. One of the main reasons people make their way to Setti Fatma is to visit the seven waterfalls—a two-hour climb from the village center. It's also a great setting-off point for walks into the mountains, where you can explore villages inaccessible by road.

GETTING HERE AND AROUND

A few kilometers along the 2017 from Tnine de l'Ourika, the road forks. Bear left toward Setti Fatma and the full beauty of the Ourika valley awaits you. Walnut trees line the river, which rushes to serve a number of pretty villages leading to Setti Fatma. The tiny village of Aghbalou is especially pretty, and a lovely place to spend a night.

WHERE TO EAT AND STAY

$ MOROCCAN 🍴 **Restaurant-Hotel Azilal.** For only 50 DH, you can get a great meal here consisting of three courses made entirely by the family's mother. Go for a classic Moroccan salad (tomatoes and peppers) and a tagine of your choice and eat on the quaint platform overlooking the river. **Known for:** great home cooking; hearty portions; authentic cuisine. [$] *Average main: 50DH* ✉ *Setti Fatma* ✣ *Near entrance of village on right, with an eating area on opposite side* ☎ *0668/88–37–70* 💳 *No credit cards.*

$ MOROCCAN 🍴 **Timichi.** You need to cross a rickety bridge to get to this restaurant, which buzzes with the hum of local chatter, the sound of the trickling river, and the occasional Berber musician. The menu is predictable, with Moroccan salads, tagines, and a variety of sodas, but it's very tasty and the location is a great vantage point for people-watching. **Known for:** interesting people-watching; tasty tagines; large portions. [$] *Average main: 60DH* ✉ *Setti Fatma* ✣ *At end of village, on left, over last makeshift footbridge* ☎ *0668/94–48–67* 💳 *No credit cards.*

$$ HOTEL FAMILY 🏨 **Auberge Le Maquis.** One of the valley's first lodges, this friendly option guarantees excellent service, good food, and a snug bed for prices that won't break the bank. **Pros:** fantastic welcome; free Wi-Fi throughout; central heating (a rare find in these parts). **Cons:** occasional noise from the road; gets pretty cold at night; not as secluded as some options. [$] *Rooms from: 480DH* ✉ *Km 45, Aghbalou* ☎ *0524/48–45–31* 🌐 *www.le-maquis.com* 🛏 *11 rooms* 🍽 *Breakfast.*

$ B&B/INN 🏨 **La Perle de l'Ourika.** Perched on the edge of a ravine overlooking the river, this guesthouse offers you all the tranquillity you can't find in the center of Setti Fatma. **Pros:** stunning views; peaceful atmosphere; very welcoming owner. **Cons:** pretty basic accommodations; not all rooms have en suite bathrooms; cold at night. [$] *Rooms from: 250DH* ✉ *Setti Fatma, Ourika* ✣ *On left just before you enter main drag of village* ☎ *0682/62–82–50* 🌐 *www.la-perle-d-ourika-guesthouse-ma.book.direct* 🛏 *5 rooms* 🍽 *All meals.*

SHOPPING

Small stands line the road from before Ourika to Setti Fatma, selling crafts, pottery, and the carpets for which the Berbers are so famous. Many of these small stands supply the great boutiques and bazaars of Marrakesh, so if you're in the mood for bargain hunting, you're likely to find a better deal here.

OUKAÏMEDEN

20 km (13 miles) from Imlil.

Although you probably didn't go to Morocco for the snow, if you have a day or two to kill and you enjoy skiing, then a bit of powder isn't out of the question. The ski station at Oukaïmeden is a fun and increasingly popular place to visit, and a good place for novices to get in some practice without the stress of jam-packed slopes. On weekends, the mountains can get a bit crowded with enthusiastic Moroccans, but it is much quieter during the week. If you are a serious skier, then hire a guide and go off-piste; average skiers can just enjoy the novelty of skiing in northern African. The ski season lasts from December until late March.

Hiking and climbing are two other great outdoor pursuits to experience in Oukaïmeden. There are numerous outfitters you can use to organize single day or multiday tours for all levels of ability. There are also lots of fantastic hiking trails in the region; you can explore various routes with a guide or company, or find out information on how to hike on your own at your hotel. There are some lovely short walking trails, but don't go too far without a guide as the mountains can be quite harsh.

GETTING HERE AND AROUND

Transport can be a problem here, as a grand taxi from Marrakesh will drop you off, but might prove unreliable for collection. There is no scheduled bus service. In the busy ski season, you should find shared taxis or even minibuses shuttling between the resort and Marrakesh. Otherwise ask your hotel in Marrakesh to book you a private car and driver or head here on a guided tour.

ESSENTIALS

Guides and Tours Climb Morocco. 🌐 *www.climbmorocco.com.*

TIMING AND PRECAUTIONS

For skiers, Oukaïmeden is often a day trip from Marrakesh. There are a few hotels for those wishing to spend the night. Oukaïmeden, being a resort, is extremely safe. Just be sure to bring warm clothes.

WHERE TO EAT AND STAY

$$ FRENCH FAMILY 🍴 **Chez Juju.** Your best bet for a bit of sophisticated dining in Oukaïmeden, you'll instantly appreciate Juju's yesteryear feel, modeled after alpine-style accommodations. The restaurant has been operating for more than 60 years and serves up distinctly French dishes such as cassoulet and tartiflette, alongside some Moroccan choices like tagines. **Known for:** nice wine menu; cozy, retro atmosphere; standard French cuisine. [$] *Average main: 120DH* ✉ *Village Center* ☎ *0524/31–90–05* 🌐 *www.hotelchezjuju.com.*

$ B&B/INN **Club Alpin Français.** Offering a safe place to sleep for trekkers, skiers, and summer ramblers alike, this very simple and basic dormitory-style accommodation is clean and well run. **Pros:** relaxing and clean; can organize treks. **Cons:** very basic accommodations; not much privacy. *[$] Rooms from: 130DH ✉ Oukaïmeden ✢ On right as you first enter Oukaïmeden ☎ 0524/31–90–36 🌐 www.ffcam.fr 💳 No credit cards 🛏 158 beds (82 dormitory-style and a total of 76 beds in rooms for 4 or 8 people) 🍴 Some meals.*

TO TIZI-N-TEST

To the west of Djebel Toubkal the southern road from Marrakesh through Asni and Ouirgane carves its way through the High Atlas Mountains and offers spectacular views all the way to the Tizi-n-Test pass and beyond. Ouirgane is a great base for trekking and playing in the hills, and has some fantastic lodging options. South of Ouirgane is best done as a road trip, with stops for occasional sights and breathtaking views.

LALLA TAKERKOUST LAKE

Thanks to the abundance of water, the Lalla Takerkoust dam is a good cooling-off point in the region. Fed by the river Oued Nfis, the lake has a shoreline stretching 7 km (4 miles) and offers fabulous views of the High Atlas peaks. It was originally made by the French to ensure the surrounding Houz Plains were watered. There are various activities available such as trekking, horseback riding, and quad biking, as well as water sports (although the ethics of such activities on a reservoir are somewhat questionable). There is also an increasing number of hotels and guesthouses in the area.

GETTING HERE AND AROUND

If you have your own car, take the R203 out of Marrakesh, in the direction of Tahannout and Asni. After around 5 km (3 miles), take the R209, better known as the Route du Barrage, off to the right. Continue until you reach the village of Lalla Takerkoust.

Otherwise, the village can be reached from Marrakesh by bus or grand taxi. The problem with both of these options is that you'll be dropped in the village of Lalla Takerkoust and will need to continue to the lake either on foot or with a local taxi, who will charge at least 100 DH. The easiest option is to ask your hotel for help. Most will organize a taxi transfer for you.

EXPLORING

FAMILY **Lalla Takerkoust Lake.** This reservoir is around 80 years old and a very established feature of the region, built by the French during the protectorate period. The water level fluctuates depending on rainfall and snowmelt, as it is fed from the mountains above. There are a few Jet Skis and paddleboards available to rent and take on the lake, which is not illegal but still questionable, given that this is a working reservoir. Swimming is forbidden since there is no lifeguard, but it's not uncommon to see people taking a dip, especially in the hotter months when temperatures rise. The most popular activity here is simply walking around the lake, which affords lovely views of the region as well as the local birdlife. ⊠ *Lalla Takerkoust.*

WHERE TO STAY

$$$
HOTEL
FAMILY
Jnane Tihihit. Not far from the lake, this paradisiacal farm and guesthouse hides out behind the dusty, unassuming village of Makhfamane. **Pros:** exemplary gardens; total immersion in nature; delicious food. **Cons:** the road to get here is very bumpy; natural pool might not be to everyone's tastes. $ *Rooms from: 890DH* ⊠ *Douar Makhfamane, Lalla Takerkoust* ☎ *0670/96–59–70* ⊕ *www.riad-t.com/jnane-tihihit* ⊅ *15 rooms* ⦿⦿ *Breakfast.*

$$
HOTEL
Le Petit Hotel du Flouka. Set over a series of terraces leading down to the lake, this elegantly refurbished hotel is both relaxing and friendly. **Pros:** congenial ambience; tasteful decor; great views. **Cons:** can get crowded on Sunday; doesn't have a local feel; restaurant can be busy. $ *Rooms from: 550DH* ⊠ *Rte. 203, Lalla Takerkoust* ☎ *664/49–26–60* ⊕ *www.leflouka.com* ⊅ *15 rooms* ⦿⦿ *Breakfast.*

SPORTS AND THE OUTDOORS

HORSEBACK RIDING

FAMILY
Les Cavaliers de L'Atlas. This is a reputable equestrian company that organizes all kinds of horseback excursions in the region. You can take a horse or pony out for anything from two hours to the whole day. It's a great way to discover the area and experience the lake or the nearby Agafay Desert from a different vantage point. Prices range from 400 DH for two hours, 780 DH for a half day, and 980 DH for a whole day, including meal and transfer if needed. ⊠ *Lalla Takerkoust Lake, Lalla Takerkoust* ☎ *0672/84–55–79* ⊕ *www.lescavaliersdelatlas.com.*

OUIRGANE

60 km (37 miles) south of Marrakesh.

Ouirgane is one of Morocco's more luxurious bases for mountain adventures. It doesn't have the highest peaks, but it has a glorious choice of charming hotels and day trips that take in captivating scenery toward the mountainous Tizi-n-Test to the south. You can climb Djebel Toubkal in three days or stay up in the High Atlas for a little longer, safe in the knowledge that you have a snug hotel waiting for you back in Ouirgane. Even if you keep close to town, you can explore the surrounding hills on two "wheels" (foot or bicycle) or four (mule, horse, or quad bike) with ease. In town there's a lively Thursday morning souk. For many, Ouirgane is just a pleasant stop before tackling Tizi-n-Test. But the charming village has a few auberges that make it a good starting point for treks.

GETTING HERE AND AROUND

If you have your own car, Ouirgane is a fairly short drive from Marrakesh. Failing that, a grand taxi costs 25 DH per person from Marrakesh; taxis from Tnine de l'Ourika are available for about 20 DH. The cheapest way is by bus (15 DH), which leaves Marrakesh's Gare Routière five times daily. However, it's easier to make the journey in hired vehicles, often with a hired driver.

EXPLORING

Salt Mines. It is worth negotiating the pot-holed road to the salt mines just off the Amizmiz road (stop at the turning for the Amizmiz road and walk the last part). For centuries, the Berbers have produced salt here but today's relatively low value of the once highly prized natural commodity has greatly endangered the livelihoods of the salt-mining families. ✉ *Ouirgane* ✥ *From Ouirgane, take Amizmiz Rd.* ⏲ *Closed Sat.*

Shrine of Haïm ben Diourne. Site of one of the few Jewish festivals still held in Morocco, this complex contains the tombs of Rabbi Mordekai ben Hamon, Rabbi Abraham ben Hamon, and others. The shrine, known locally both as the "tigimi n Yehudeen" and "marabout Juif" (House of the Jews in Arabic and French, respectively), is a large white structure. The moussem generally happens in May. Tip the gatekeeper after a tour—anything between 5 and 15 DH is fine. ✉ *Ouirgane* ✥ *About 4 km (2½ miles) outside Ouirgane, the shrine is accessible on foot or by mule in less than an hour, or you can drive right up to gate on dirt piste. Turn left after about 1 km (½ mile) at Ouirgane's souk; follow road as it winds through village until you reach pink cubic water tank. Turn right and go to end of road, about 3 km (2 miles).*

WHERE TO EAT AND STAY

$$$ MOROCCAN FAMILY Fodor's Choice ★ 🍴 **Chez Momo.** Nestled in the foothills of the mountains near Ouirgane, at Chez Momo you can sip a cocktail by the small pool or have a barbecued dinner seated on one of the chairs fashioned from tree trunks. It is well worth sampling the Berber cuisine, such as corn or barley couscous or vegetarian tagine, accompanied by homemade tanourt bread with oranges and cinnamon to follow. **Known for:** classic Berber cuisine and style; stunning surroundings. [$] *Average main: 130DH* ✉ *Rte. d'Asni, Km 61 from Marrakesh* ✥ *Dirt road to Chez Momo is roughly 1 km (½ mile) south of bridge over Ouirgane River. Turn right at sign and continue about 164 feet downhill. Turn right again and park among olive trees* ☎ *0524/48–57–04, 0661/58–22–95* 🌐 *www.aubergemomo.com.*

$$$$ FRENCH 🍴 **La Bergerie.** This delightful restaurant and guesthouse combines shaker style with *Little House on the Prairie*. The menu has both excellent French and Moroccan dishes and offers a full bar (something of a rarity in these parts). **Known for:** slow-cooked lamb shank; minimal but still lovely alcohol menu; must-try wild boar. [$] *Average main: 180DH* ✉ *Marigha, Rte. de Taroudant, Km 59, Asni* ☎ *0524/48–57–17, 0661/15–99–06* 🌐 *www.labergerie-maroc.com.*

$$$$ HOTEL 🏨 **Domaine de la Roseraie.** Open for more than 40 years on 60 acres of glorious grounds, La Roseraie is the creation of one of the earliest pioneers of Morocco's hospitality industry. **Pros:** rooms hidden in private natural parkland; great amenities; nice views. **Cons:** quite costly; decor is a bit faded. [$] *Rooms from: 1350DH* ✉ *Rte. de Taroudant, Km 60* ☎ *0524/43–91–28 reservations, 0524/48–56–94 hotel direct* 🌐 *www.laroseraie.ma* 🛏 *42 rooms* 🍽 *All meals.*

SPORTS AND THE OUTDOORS

"Sights" aside, by far the best thing to look at here is the surrounding countryside with its poppies in spring, yellow wheat in early summer, snowcapped mountains in winter, and rushing rivers and glorious, looming hills year-round. You can get out there in so many different ways, and your hotel (or a better-equipped one nearby) is the best way to rent equipment for outdoor activities.

BIKING

You can rent bikes from hotels like La Roseraie or La Bergerie, or you can book a tour with outfitters like Argan Xtreme Sports in Marrakesh.

HORSEBACK RIDING

For horseback riding, La Roseraie is *the* place for the entire region. You can rent horses for local rides or for full-blown tours in the mountains, complete with food and lodging in Atlas villages. Prices start at 200 DH for an hour. As there might be an additional levy elsewhere, it's best to come straight here.

WALKING

Every hotel will be able to fix you up with a walking guide to wander the local hills and rivers, dropping in on the salt mines, the remains of the Jewish settlement, and a Berber house, as you like. It's also only three days on foot (with the help of a mule or two) to the summit of Djebel Toubkal. The route bypasses Imlil altogether, a significant benefit for anyone keen to avoid the trekker base camp.

6

TIZI-N-TEST

The road to Tizi-n-Test is one of Morocco's most glorious mountain drives. The route south from Ouirgane to Tizi-n-Test takes you through the upper Nfis Valley, which was the spiritual heart of the Almohad Empire in the 12th century and later the administrative center of the Goundafi *caids* (local or tribal leaders) in the first half of the 20th century. It's best enjoyed as a day trip by car from Ouirgane, especially as lodging options are seriously basic and few. There are plenty of cafés on the way, however, and a great stop off at Tin Mal Mosque.

The route to Tizi-n-Test clings to the mountainside, sometimes triple-backing on itself to climb the heights in a series of precipitous hairpin bends. It's often only a narrow single lane, with sheer drops, blind corners, and tumbling scree. Expect every bend to reveal a wide and furiously fast Land Rover coming right at you, or worse, a group of children playing soccer. Honk as you round sharp corners, and give way to traffic climbing uphill.

GETTING HERE AND AROUND

To drive the stunning mountain road that winds south toward Tizi-n-Test, you'll need transport. You can pick up a bus (a scary option) or a grand taxi (only slightly better) from Ouirgane. Better to opt drive yourself as then you can take your time and drive within the speed limit. An alternative is to hire a car and driver through your hotel in Marrakesh (or a good hotel around Ouirgane).

The Tin Mal Mosque is one of only two mosques in Morocco that non-Muslims may enter.

EXPLORING

Goundafi Kasbahs. Most of the massive Goundafi Kasbahs, strongholds of the Aït Lahcen family that governed the region until independence in 1956, have long since crumbled away. But just past the small village of Talat-n-Yacoub, look up. A great hulking red Kasbah sits at the top of the hill, amid a scene that is today eerily peaceful, with hawks nesting among the scraps of ornately carved plaster and woodwork still clinging to the massive walls. Built as a counterpart to the original Goundafi redoubt in Tagoundaft, the Kasbah is a compelling testament to the concentration of power in an era said to be governed "tribally." Locals say the hands of slack workers were sealed into the Kasbah's walls during construction. There's usually not a tourist in sight.

It's a rocky, although fairly easy, walk up to it. From the Kasbah you can see the Tin Mal Mosque to the south, across the juncture of the Nfis and Tasaft rivers. Just southeast are the mines of Tasaft. The Ouanoukrim Massif (the group of big mountains at the center of the High Atlas Mountains) dominates the view to the north. ✉ *Above Talat-n-Yacoub, about 40 km (25 miles) south of Ouirgane, Talat-n-Yacoub.*

Tin Mal Mosque. One of only two mosques in the country that non-Muslims may enter (the other is Casablanca's enormous Hassan II mosque), Tin Mal sits proudly in the hills and is well worth a visit. Built by Ibn Tumart, the first Almohad, its austere walls in the obscure valley of the Nfis formed the cradle of a formidable superstate and was the birthplace and spiritual capital of the 12th-century Almohad empire. Today the original walls stand firm, enclosing a serene area with row after row of pale brick arches, on a huge scale built to impress. **TIP→ Admission to the mosque is free, but tip the guardian anything between 5 DH and 20 DH and he'll show you around and explain a little of the history.** ✉ *Tin Mal* ✥ *The signposted turnoff for mosque is about 4 km (2½ miles) south of Talat-n-Yacoub. Turn right, cross bridge, and follow path up other side of valley.*

Tizi-n-Test. The Tizi-n-Test pass climbs up to a staggering 6,889 feet and provides extraordinary views to the north toward the mountain peaks and south toward the Souss valleys. It's a hair-raising road trip calling for low gears and snail-like speeds, but the views are worth every second. ✉ *76 km (47 miles) southwest of Ouirgane.*

WHERE TO EAT AND STAY

$ CAFÉ 🍴 **La Haute Vue.** This small café right at the summit of Tizi-n-Test is the perfect place to take in the astounding view with some Berber biscuits and mint tea on beautiful wrought-iron chairs made by the owner's son. It's also a good spot to stop along the road and wander up the hills. **Known for:** homemade biscuits; sublime views; ironwork furniture. [$] *Average main: 60DH* ✉ *Tizi-n-Test summit, 6,889 feet* ☎ *0661/40–01–91* 💳 *No credit cards.*

$$ B&B/INN 🏨 **Dar El Mouahidines.** A very nice garden and a decent restaurant make this plain but functional hotel a nice place to stay near Tizi-n-Test. **Pros:** only hotel between Tin Mal and the Tizi-n-Test pass; great start-off point for Adrar n'Iger. **Cons:** very simple accommodations; cold at night. [$] *Rooms from: 400DH* ✉ *Douar Tassouakt, Tin Mal* ✥ *8 km (5 miles) past Ijoukak on main road to Taroudant* ☎ *0676/25–34–52* 🛏 *8 rooms* 🍽 *Some meals.*

TO TIZI-N-TICHKA

The scenery around the Tichka Pass is peaceful and more low-key than the rest of the High Atlas. It's soothing and stunning in equal measure, a good bet for stimulating walks and a relaxing hotel stay. If you're just passing through en route to the southern oases, the vista from the Tichka road itself is amazing—especially in spring—and the Glaoui Kasbah at Telouet is worth a look.

TIZI-N-TICHKA

110 km (68 miles) southeast of Marrakesh.

Winding its way southeast toward the desert, the Tichka Pass is another exercise in road-trip drama. Although the road is generally well maintained and wide enough for traffic to pass—and lacks the vertiginous twists of the Tizi-n-Test—it still deserves respect. Especially in winter, take warm clothes with you, as the temperature at the pass itself can seem another latitude entirely from the balmy sun of Marrakesh. **TIP→ Sometimes gas can be difficult to find, particularly unleaded, so fill up before you hit the mountains. There's a station at the town of Aït Ourir, on the main road to Ouarzazate.**

6

The road out of Marrakesh leads abruptly into the countryside, to quiet olive groves and desultory villages consisting of little more than a *hanut* (convenience store) and a roadside mechanic. You'll pass the R'mat River, the Oued Zat, and the Hotel Hardi. From here the road begins to rise, winding through fields that are either green with barley and wheat or brown with their stalks. At Km 55 you'll encounter the Hotel Dar Oudar in Touama. In springtime magnificent red poppies dot the surrounding fields.

On the way up into the hills, look for men and boys, often standing in the middle of the road, waving shiny bits of rock. These are magnificent pieces of quartz taken from the mountains that they sell for as little as 20 DH. On your left at Km 124 from Marrakesh you'll see the **Palais-n-Tichka,** a sort of Wal-Mart for these shiny minerals, as well as other souvenirs. It's also a good restroom stop.

The road begins to climb noticeably, winding through forests and some of the region's lusher hillsides. A broad valley opens up to your left, revealing red earth and luminously green gardens. At Km 67 stands Mohammad Noukrati's Auberge Toufliht. From Toufliht there is little between you and the Tichka Pass but dusty villages, shepherds, and rock. You might find a decent orange juice, trinket, or weather-beaten carpet in villages like Taddert, but you'll probably feel pulled toward the pass. The scenery is rather barren, and as the naked rock of the mountains begins to emerge from beneath the flora, the walls of the canyon grow steeper and more enclosing.

Around Km 105 you'll see several waterfalls across the canyon. The trail down is precipitous but easy enough to follow; just park at the forlorn-looking refuge and the Café Tichka at Km 108. The trail winds to the left of the big hill, then cuts to the right and drops down to the falls after a short walk of half an hour or so. The Tichka Pass is farther along, at 7,413 feet above sea level. Depending on the season and the weather, the trip over the pass can take you from African heat to European gloom and back.

NEED A BREAK

🍴 La Maison Berbère. This rest stop has made more of an effort than most of the others on this route, with a high-ceiling and traditionally decorated salon permeated by the unmistakable smell of real coffee. Take a late breakfast or a tagine on the terrace at the back, overlooking a small garden and poppy-dotted fields. ✉ ***5 km (3 miles) before Taddert, Rte. de Ouarzazate*** ☎ ***0524/37–14–67.***

WHERE TO EAT AND STAY

$ MOROCCAN

🍴 **Dar Oudar.** More a restaurant with rooms than an out-and-out hotel, this is a good stop-off point before the climb to the Tichka Pass. The kitchen is justifiably proud of its reputation and makes delicious french fries, as well as tagines and grills. **Known for:** best french fries in the Atlas; tasty kefta brochettes; starting point for the climb up the Tichka Pass. [$] *Average main: 60DH* ✉ *Rte. de Ouarzazate, Km 56* ☎ *0524/48–47–72* 🌐 *www.daroudar.moonfruit.fr* 💳 *No credit cards.*

$$ HOTEL Fodor's Choice ★ **I Rocha.** Hidden on a promontory above Tizirine, a small Berber town, this is one of the best lodges in the region. **Pros:** lovely terrace; sparkling rooms; hotel can arrange cooking courses, trekking, or stargazing by telescope. **Cons:** wine prices are very inflated; not all rooms have true double beds. [$] *Rooms from: 550DH* ✉ *Tizirine* ⊕ *Take signposted left at Tizirine (also called Douar Tisselday), halfway down main road that runs from Tizi-n-Tichka to Ouarzazate. Follow steep dirt track for 500 feet* ☎ *0667/73–70–02, 0666/38–72–11* 🌐 *www.irocha.com* 💳 *No credit cards* 🛏 *7 rooms* 🍴 *All meals.*

TELOUET

116 km (72 miles) southeast of Marrakesh, 20 km (12 miles) east of P31.

The main reason for visiting this otherwise unremarkable village is to see the incredible kasbah of the Glaouis (which is sometimes referred to simply as "Kasbah Telouet"). Built in the 19th century, the kasbah is now in near ruin, but the interior still hints of the luxury that once was.

It was from Telouet that the powerful Glaoui family controlled the caravan route over the mountains into Marrakesh. Although the Goundafi and Mtougi caids also held important High Atlas passes, by 1901 the Glaoui were on the rise. The legend goes that the Glaoui brothers saved the life of Sultan Moulay el-Hassan during a snowstorm, and in gratitude he gave them a collection of first-rate artillery. They then used it to subdue all their rivals, and were positioned to bargain when the French arrived on the political scene. The French couldn't have been pleased with the prospect of subduing the vast, wild regions of southern Morocco tribe by tribe. Thus the French-Glaoui alliance benefited both parties, with Mandani el-Glaoui ruling as Grand Vizier and his brother Tuhami serving as pasha of Marrakesh.

6

GETTING HERE AND AROUND

Getting to Telouet isn't always easy. The best way, aside from with a tour group, is to take a grand taxi from Marrakesh or drive yourself.

TIMING AND PRECAUTIONS

The kasbah itself takes no more than three hours to explore. Take care, as parts of it are beginning to crumble.

EXPLORING

Kasbah Telouet. A formerly luxurious testament to the wealth of the Glaoui family, Kasbah Telouet is now in ruins, but is still a beauty to explore. About five minutes south of Tizi-n-Tichka is the turnoff for the Glaoui Kasbah at Telouet. The road is paved but narrow, and winds from juniper-studded slopes down through a landscape of low eroding hills and the Assif-n-Tissent (Salt River). In spring, barley fields soften the effect, but for much of the year the scene is rather bleak.

Parking for the kasbah is down a short dirt road across from the nearby auberge Chez Ahmed. Entry is free, but you should tip the parking attendant and the guardian of the gate. Inside, walking through dusty courtyards that rise to towering mud walls, you'll pass through a series of gates and big doors, many threatening to fall from their hinges. Different parts are open at different times, perhaps according to the whims of the guard. Most of the kasbah looks ravished, as most of the useful or interesting bits had been carried off when the Glaoui reign came to its abrupt end in 1956. This sense of decay is interrupted when you get upstairs: here, from painted wood shutters and delicately carved plaster arabesques to exquisitely set tile and broad marble floors, you get a taste of the sumptuousness the Glaoui once enjoyed. Because it was built in the 20th century, ancient motifs are combined with kitschy contemporary elements, such as traditionally carved plaster shades for the electric lights. The roof has expansive views. ⊠ *Telouet*.

WHERE TO EAT AND STAY

$
AFRICAN

✕ **Chez Ahmed.** A small but clean café and guesthouse is located next door to the Kasbah Telouet parking lot. Owner Ahmed is highly knowledgeable of Glaoui history, and he can organize tours of the surrounding area. **Known for:** knowledgeable and welcoming host; good but basic food; history tours offered. $ *Average main: 70DH* ⊠ *Telouet* ☎ *0524/89–07–17* ▭ *No credit cards.*

$$$$
HOTEL
Fodor's Choice
★

🖫 **Domaine Malika.** This small boutique hotel would not be out of place in one of the world's hippest capitals: how wonderful, then, that it is here in the High Atlas. **Pros:** light-hearted, tasteful, and unique decor; hotel will organize tours, airport transfers, and cooking lessons; beautiful hammam, pool, and olive grove. **Cons:** the place is very small, so book ahead; expensive for the area. $ *Rooms from: 1500DH* ⊠ *Ouirgane* ⊹ *From Marrakesh, take Taroudant road in direction "Tahnanaoute." Before Ouirgane, in Douar of Maghira, turn right toward Amizmiz. The hotel is 500 meters ahead on left* ☎ *0524/48–59–21* ⊕ *www.domaine-malika.com* ⊘ *Closed early Dec.* ⤺ *7 rooms* ⦿ *Breakfast.*

$$$$
HOTEL
Fodor's Choice
★

🖫 **Kasbah Bab Ourika.** This luxurious retreat is a delightful example of how to build a near-perfect romantic getaway that's eco-friendly to boot. **Pros:** gorgeous ambience that's hard to top; staff can arrange activities and treks in the area; eco-friendly and gives back to the community. **Cons:** the road to the kasbah is bumpy; very expensive; doesn't give a sense of true local culture. $ *Rooms from: 1500DH* ⊠ *Kasbah Bab Ourika, Ourika Valley Atlas Mountains, Route de l'Ourika* ☎ *0668/74–95–47, 0661/63–42–34* ⊕ *www.kasbahbabourika.com* ⤺ *30 rooms* ⦿ *Breakfast.*

$$$$
HOTEL

🖫 **Widiane Suites and Spa.** If you want to splurge and leave the bare Berber guesthouses behind for some true spa luxury, look no further than Widiane. **Pros:** the place to go to treat yourself; the hotel can arrange a wide variety of activities in the area. **Cons:** opulence on this scale jars somewhat with the rural simplicity of surroundings; quite pricey. $ *Rooms from: 2250DH* ⊠ *Chemin du Lac de Ben El Ouidane, Bin el Ouidane* ☎ *0523/44–27–76* ⊕ *www.widiane.net* ⤺ *31 rooms* ⦿ *Some meals.*

THE GREAT
OASIS VALLEYS

WELCOME TO THE GREAT OASIS VALLEYS

TOP REASONS TO GO

★ **Desert dreams:** Live out those Lawrence of Arabia fantasies by sleeping on dunes under the stars.

★ **Dadès Gorge:** Follow mountain trails through some of Morocco's most beautiful scenery.

★ **Kasbah trail:** Marvel at and stay in ancient strongholds that dot the landscape.

★ **Morocco's Hollywood:** Spot celebs in Ouarzazate, home to visiting film crews.

★ **Flower power:** Visit the Valley of Roses in spring to see endless specimens in the wild.

The Great Oasis Valleys cover a huge area, in a sort of lopsided horseshoe from Ouarzazate (the largest town in the north-west corner), east past the magnificent Dadès and Todra gorges on the northern road, south to the dunes at Merzouga, and looping back west on the southern road through the Drâa Valley to Zagora, M'hamid, and the great expanse of desert that reaches all the way across Erg Chigaga to Foum Zguid. To miss any of these roads would be to miss some of Morocco's most characteristic immensity— wide-open spaces and tundra-like desolation.

1 Ouarzazate. Ouarzazate (pronounced wah-zaz-zatt) is a natural crossroads for exploring southern Morocco. The town has a wide range of accommodations as well as a few sights that can fill up a day. Most important, Ouarzazate has excellent road connections, putting the entire region within reach.

2 The Dadès and Todra Gorges. These sister canyons, located within about two hours' drive from each other northeast of Ouarzazate, have been carved into the rocks over millennia by the snowmelt waters of the High Atlas. Trekking and mountain biking are favorite activities for tourists.

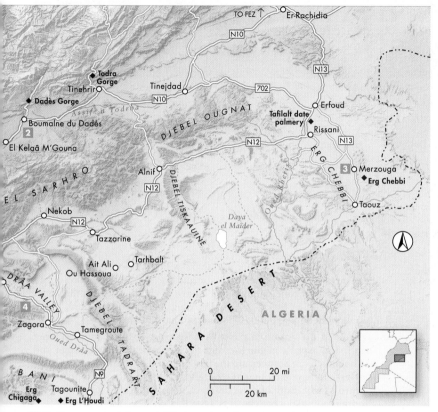

7

3 **To Merzouga and the Dunes.** If you opt to visit the south of Morocco, then it's almost criminal not to at least spend a night in the Sahara. The village of Merzouga is readily accessible by road, and the dunes of Erg Chebbi can be reached on foot or by camel.

4 **The Drâa Valley.** This fertile valley—extending along the shores of Morocco's longest river from Agdz, through Zagora as far as M'hamid—offers one of the most colorful and diverse landscapes in the kingdom. For those heading into the dunes at Erg Chigaga, Zagora is your last contact with modern services such as banks, pharmacies, and gas stations.

Updated by
Alice Morrison

Morocco without the Sahara is like Switzerland without the Alps, and a desert sojourn is fundamental to an understanding of the country. After you've seen the Atlas Mountains, followed by palmeries and kasbahs, a trip down to the desert may seem a long way to go to reach nothing, and some Moroccans and travelers will warn you against it. Don't listen to them.

The void you encounter in the Sahara will remind you why prophets and sages sought the desert to purge and purify themselves. Unless you have oodles of time, though, you'll have to choose between the dunes of Erg Chebbi at Merzouga and Erg Chigaga beyond M'hamid, which are separated by 450 km (279 miles) of hard driving.

Of course, a vacation in the valleys isn't just about sublime Saharan sand. The asphalt might end and the desert begin at Merzouga and M'hamid, but in between are the oases flanked by the Todra and Dadès gorges—sister grand canyons separating the High Atlas from the Djebel Sarhro Massif. Both of these dramatic gorges appeal to hikers, and the Todra is a hot spot for climbers as well.

Permeating it all is a palpable sense of history. Once, the caravan routes from sub-Saharan Africa to Europe passed through Morocco's Great Oasis Valleys, with their cargoes of gold, salt, and slaves. From the Drâa Valley came the Saadian royal dynasty that ruled from the mid-12th to mid-17th century, and from the Ziz Valley and the Tafilalt Oasis rose the Alaouite dynasty, which relieved the Saadians in 1669 and which still rules (in the person of King Mohammed VI) in 21st-century Morocco.

PLANNING

WHEN TO GO

You'll pay lower off-season rates and encounter fewer convoys of tourists if you travel the oasis routes in early December or mid-January through early March. High season begins in mid-March but doesn't fully kick in until April or Easter (whichever comes first). The Christmas and New Year period is also popular; if you want to visit a desert camp then, it's wise to book at least two months ahead. Summer is extremely hot in the desert and some hotels close during July and August, especially if this coincides with the holy month of Ramadan. If you plan to visit the Sahara in summer, traveling east via the Dadès and Todra gorges to Merzouga is slightly easier since the shaded depths of the canyons offer some respite from the sun.

PLANNING YOUR TIME

Doing the entire Great Oasis Valleys circuit is a serious undertaking, and you might miss the best parts for all the whirlwind traveling. So it's important to set priorities and carefully plan your itinerary. You could easily spend 14 days exploring. Allow at least five to seven if you want to include hiking time and a trip into the Sahara; then decide which dunes you want to discover—Erg Chebbi or Erg Chigaga.

From Ouarzazate, allot a minimum of two days to reach Erg Chebbi, traveling east through the Todra Gorge and Dadès Valley to Merzouga (this allows for an overnight stop in the Todra Gorge en route). On the return leg you can circle along the southern flanks of the Djebel Sarhro, passing via traditional villages like Nekob, into the Drâa Valley before arriving in Ouarzazate again.

Reaching Erg Chigaga from Ouarzazate requires a 4x4 vehicle and at least two days of driving (this again allows for an overnight stop). Head south through the Drâa Valley, admiring Agdz and Zagora en route to M'hamid; then continue off-road for about 50 km (31 miles) to the dunes. Returning to Ouarzazate, drive the route in reverse or loop back via Foum Zguid.

GETTING HERE AND AROUND

The most convenient arrival and departure points for touring this vast region are the towns of Ouarzazate (if you're traveling from Marrakesh and the Atlantic coast) or Er-Rachidia (if you're traveling from Fez, Meknès, or the Mediterranean coast). Given a choice, opt for Ouarzazate, as it is an interesting town in its own right. Ouarzazate is a key transport hub for forays into the Dadès and Todra gorges, the Drâa Valley, and the desert regions beyond Zagora. Er-Rachidia is itself of little interest to travelers.

AIR TRAVEL

Royal Air Maroc (⊕ *www.royalairmaroc.com*) serves Ouarzazate's Taourirt International Airport, offering direct flights daily from Casablanca and multiple ones per week from Paris. The airline also connects Casablanca with Er-Rachidia thrice weekly and Zagora twice weekly. Petits taxis (local taxis) provide ground transport from these airports; however, if you need to catch an early return flight, it's best to arrange transportation back to the airport through your hotel the night before.

BUS TRAVEL

Bus is the main mode of public transport south of Marrakesh. Compagnie du Transports au Maroc (locally known as CTM) and Supratours buses run to Ouarzazate, through the Drâa Valley, and down to Zagora and M'hamid.

CAR TRAVEL

The only practical way to tour the Great Oasis Valleys is by car. Being surrounded by gorgeous, largely unexplored hinterlands—like the Todra or Dadès gorges—without being able to explore safely and comfortably defeats the purpose of coming down here. Driving the oasis roads requires full attention and certain safety precautions: make sure you have enough fuel, slow down when cresting hills, expect everything from camels to herds of sheep to appear in the road, expect oncoming traffic to come down the middle of the road, and be prepared to come to a full stop if forced to the right and faced with a pothole or other obstacle. Additionally, consider buying a local sim and a data scratch card for your smart phone as Google Maps will be your friend. That said, there is a big road-building program in Morocco, so new roads may not be on your map. Also, many towns and villages have no signs, so you may have to stop and ask exactly where you are. Moroccans get around by asking directions; don't be afraid to do the same. If you haven't rented a car someplace else, you can rent one on arrival in Ouarzazate. Consider getting a 4x4: it's not essential but definitely makes life easier in some places.

Rental Cars Europcar. ⊠ *Av. Mohammed V, Pl. 3 Mars, Ouarzazate* ☏ *0524/88–20–35* ⊕ *www.europcar.ma.* **Hertz.** ⊠ *35, av. Mohammed V, Ouarzazate* ☏ *0524/88–20–84* ⊕ *www.hertz.com.* **Tafoukt Cars.** ⊠ *88, rue Er-Rachidia, Ouarzazate* ☏ *0524/88–26–90.*

WHAT TO DO

Hikes, treks, dune-buggying, rock-climbing, and even camel safaris can be the active highlights of any trip through the southern oases, dunes, or gorges, but it's also pretty exciting to just sit still in the cool of an oasis or within the ancient walls of a kasbah. The main roads through the region are all paved, making most places accessible in a rental car or taxi; a 4x4 will be required for venturing across country between the two gorges or into the desert on any road marked as a *piste* (an unpaved backcountry road). In both the Dadès and Todra gorges it is well worth giving yourself time to hike; employ the services of a local guide who knows the area intimately and can provide more spectacular perspectives on the canyons and local life. The Todra Gorge is also prime territory for rock climbers, but it is advisable to bring your own gear. Serious trekking adventures through the M'Goun Massif (above the Dadès Valley) or around Djebel Sarhro, south of Tinerhir, are by far the best way to see this largely untouched Moroccan backcountry but these should be booked through an expert company such as Epic Morocco. For exploring the desert either at Merzouga or M'hamid it is best to travel by camel, or if budget allows by 4x4. Wonderful multiday camel treks can take you through the lower reaches of the Drâa Valley oasis and into the dunes.

SAFETY

You shouldn't have problems traveling this part of Morocco, but always exercise caution if going into remote areas.

Be prepared to be followed by local kids who may want to engage you in conversation. Rather than money (which just encourages begging), give them items such as pens or pencils. If they are selling homemade handicrafts, then of course give them a few dirhams for their efforts.

■ TIP➡ Where possible, make sure you engage a qualified guide through one of the official Bureaus de Guides or with a specialist company—this is especially important when trekking in the desert or mountains.

RESTAURANTS

In the rural areas outside of Ouarzazate there are virtually no restaurants, just weathered streetside cafés with basic bathroom facilities (bring your own toilet paper!). These local spots can be great; just ask about the meal of the day, rather than look at the menu. Otherwise, lunch stops, complete with decent bathroom facilities, are best found in the hotels and auberges listed. For evening meals it is best to book your accommodation with half board. The fare you'll be served along the southern oases routes tends to be hearty and simple. *Harira* (a tomato and lentil soup) is more than welcome as night sets in and temperatures plunge. *Mechoui* (roast lamb) is a standard feast—if you can order it far enough in advance. Some of the best lamb and vegetable tagines in Morocco are simmered over tiny camp stoves in random corners and campsites down here. You may want to keep a bottle of wine in the car or in a day pack, as many restaurants (even in hotels) don't serve alcohol, but have no problem with customers bringing their own. Always ask first, though, as some places object. *Dining reviews have been shortened. For full information, visit Fodors.com.*

HOTELS

Hotels on the southern oasis routes generally range from mediocre to primitive, with several charming spots, simple but lovely gites (self-catering homes), and a few luxury establishments thrown in. This is not the place for major chains. Come with the idea that running water and a warm place to sleep are all you really need, and accept anything above that as icing on the cake. Bedding down outdoors on hotel terraces is common (and cheap) in summer, as are accommodations in *khaimas* (Berber nomad tents). The night sky is so stunning here that spending at least one night *à la belle étoile* (beneath the stars) seems almost mandatory. Any of the desert hotels and guesthouses in Merzouga or M'hamid will be able to arrange an unforgettable night under canvas, along with the necessary camel or 4x4 vehicle to get there. Basic bivouac camps, costing around 250 DH per person per night, typically have mattresses on the floor of large Berber tents and a shared bathroom block. Luxury tented camps—featuring private safari-style tents with Berber rugs, plush furnishings, and en suite chemical toilets—fulfill the Arabian Nights "glamping" fantasy; rates start at around 1,500 DH per person. Whatever you choose, bear in mind that many lodgings in remote areas still don't accept credit cards; double check the terms of payment and be sure to have sufficient cash on hand if required. *Hotel reviews have been shortened. For full information, visit Fodors.com.*

WHAT IT COSTS IN DIRHAMS				
	$	$$	$$$	$$$$
Restaurants	under 70 DH	70 DH–100 DH	101 DH–150 DH	over 150 DH
Hotels	under 450 DH	450 DH–700 DH	701 DH–1,000 DH	over 1,000 DH

Restaurant prices are the average cost of a main course at dinner, or if dinner is not served, at lunch. Hotel prices are the lowest cost of a standard double room in high season.

FESTIVALS

Each year villages here host a number of *moussems* (festivals) that are linked to the religious or agricultural calendar. These usually feature feasting, dancing, traditional music, and possibly a wonderful display of horsemanship called a fantasia. The downside is that they often don't have specific dates, so encountering one is largely a matter of luck. That said, there are a few festivals you can largely rely on: the **Rose Festival** of Kelaâ M'Gouna (Dadès Valley) in early May; the **International Nomads Festival** in M'hamid el Ghizlane (Drâa Valley) in mid-March; and the **Erfoud Date Festival** (Ziz Valley) in October. Check with the local tourist office or a nearby hotel for the exact dates about a month ahead of your visit.

OUARZAZATE

204 km (127 miles) southeast of Marrakesh, 300 km (186 miles) south-west of Erfoud.

An isolated military outpost during the years of the French protectorate, Ouarzazate—which means "no noise" in the Berber Tamazigh language—long lived up to its name. Today, however, the town is Morocco's Hollywood, and moviemakers can regularly be found setting up shop in this sprawling desert crossroads with wide, palm-fringed boulevards. Brad Pitt, Penélope Cruz, Angelina Jolie, Samuel L. Jackson, Cate Blanchett, and many more have graced Ouarzazate's suites and streets; and a film school here provides training in the cinema arts for Moroccan and international students. Yet despite the Tinseltown vibe and huge, publicly accessible film sets, Ouarzazate retains a laid-back atmosphere, making it a great place to sit at a sidewalk café, sip a café noir, and spot visiting celebs—or at least have a chat with the locals, who'll happily recount their experience working as an on-set extra (at its peak in the late 1990s, the movie industry provided casual work for almost half of the local population). Not surprisingly, though, the main attraction is still the cinematic surrounding terrain that made Ouarzazate a mainstay for filmmakers in the first place: namely, the red-glowing kasbah at Aït Ben Haddou; the snowcapped High Atlas and the Sahara, with tremendous canyons, gorges, and lunar-like steppes in between.

GETTING HERE AND AROUND

The center of Ouarzazate is easily explored on foot. Avenue Mohammed V, the main street, runs from east to west with shops, cafés, banks, pharmacies, and tour agencies all along its length. Most hotels are near the Kasbah Taourirt; however, a cluster of boutique guesthouses dot the outlying palm groves, across the bridge in the direction of Zagora. If you're staying at the latter—or visiting the film studios—you'll need to rent a car or rely on cabs.

AIR TRAVEL

There are daily flights to Ouarzazate's Taourirt International Airport from Casablanca and twice-weekly ones from Paris. The airport is 3 km (2 miles) from the town center and can be reached by petits taxis.

BUS TRAVEL

Ouarzazate is well served by buses from Marrakesh (4 hours), Agadir (8½ hours), Casablanca (8½ hours), Taliouine (3½ hours), Taroudant (5 hours), Tinerhir (5 hours), Er-Rachidia (6 hours), Erfoud (7 hours), Zagora (4½ hours), and M'hamid (7 hours). CTM buses run from the eastern end of Avenue Mohammed V. Supratours buses run from the western end of Avenue Mohammed V. Other public buses run from the *gare routière* (bus station) about 2 km (1 mile) from the town center, just off the N9 route to Marrakesh. Shared *grands taxis* (long-distance taxis) will also bring you here from Marrakesh, Er-Rachidia, Agadir, and Zagora; these can be hired for private day excursions, too.

Bus Contacts CTM Ouarzazate. ⊠ *Av. Mohammed V, next to main post office at east end* ☎ *0524/88–24–27* ⊕ *www.ctm.ma.* **Supratours.** ⊠ *Av. Mohammed V* ☎ *0524/89–07–96* ⊕ *www.oncf.ma.*

GUIDES AND TOURS

Many travel agents and tour companies in Ouarzazate offer day excursions as well as longer outings that might include nights in the Dadès and Todra gorges or Saharan camping and camel trekking. You'll find them along Avenue Mohammed V, in Place el-Mouahidine, and frequently attached to hotels—just be sure to ask exactly what is being included in price (e.g., 4x4, driver, guide, meals, hotels, camel trip). Visitors who'd rather do a DIY driving tour will find car rental agencies along Avenue Mohammed V, too. ∎TIP→ **If you book a desert tour in advance, you'll avoid being hassled by touts when you reach Merzouga or M'hamid.**

Cherg Expeditions. Private day trips through the valleys and gorges or into the mountains to discover amethysts are led by Cherg Expeditions. You can sign on for multiday desert tours, too. Nearby destinations include the Fint Oasis and the kasbahs at Aït Ben Haddou. ⊠ *2, pl. el Mouahidine* ☎ *0524/88–79–08, 0661/24–31–47* ⊕ *www.cherg.com.*

Zbar Travel. Well-priced tours and excursions throughout southern Morocco are offered by Zbar Travel, a respected English-speaking agency with a second office in M'hamid. ⊠ *12, pl. Al Mouahadine* ☎ *0668/51–72–80* ⊕ *www.zbartravel.com.*

7

TIMING AND PRECAUTIONS

For those traveling to the desert, this is an important town for stocking up on cash and purchasing essentials like maps, batteries, and other supplies. If you're heading south to M'hamid, it's also the last town where you will find a supermarket selling wine, beer, and liquor.

EXPLORING

Atlas Studios. If you're looking for things to do in Ouarzazate, visit Atlas Studios—Morocco's most famous studios—next to the Hotel Oscar. Guided tours start every 45 minutes, and the price is discounted if you're a guest of the hotel. It isn't Disney World, but you do get a sense of just how many productions have rolled through town—including Hollywood blockbusters like *The Mummy* and *Gladiator,* and classics films like *Cleopatra* and *Lawrence of Arabia.* ■ TIP→ **Ask for Mohammed Brad Pitt as your tour guide.**

For another angle on the Ouarzazate film industry, check out the rather grand-looking kasbah off to the right just out of town on the way to Skoura. One enterprising local producer, frustrated by the increasingly expensive charges being levied on film crews wanting to film around real kasbahs, decided to build his own and undercut the competition. ✉ *Tamassint, Rte. de Marrakesh, Km 5, next to Hotel Oscar* ☎ *0524/88–22–23* 🌐 *www.studiosatlas.com* 🎟 *50 DH.*

Fint Oasis. About 20 km (12 miles) outside of town, heading south via Tarmigte, the picturesque Fint Oasis is a popular destination for day-trippers. The track leading to it is rough but can be handled in a standard vehicle if you drive with extreme care. Head off-road toward the dark, rocky escarpment and the track eventually meets the river, where palm trees spring into view. You can walk through Berber villages along the riverbed and stop for a simple lunch at one of the few local auberges. ■ TIP→ **Many agencies in Ouarzazate can arrange half- or full-day guided visits to the oasis.** ✉ *Tarmigte.*

Kasbah Taourirt. Once a Glaoui palace, the Kasbah Taourirt is the oldest and finest building in Ouarzazate. This rambling edifice was built of *pisé* (a sun-dried mixture of mud and clay) in the late 19th century by the so-called Lords of the Atlas. ■ TIP→ **It is worth hiring a guide at the entrance to take you around for about 100 DH.** ✉ *Av. Mohammed V* 🎟 *20 DH.*

WHERE TO EAT

$$ FRENCH 🍴 **Accord Majeure.** Popular with tourists and expats, Accord Majeure is a friendly French-style bistro that serves consistently good French and non-Moroccan food and Moroccan wines. The menu focuses mostly on classic dishes like beef bourguignonne, but there are also interesting culinary detours—such as Thai curry, Italian pasta, and fresh seafood (a rarity in this part of the country). **Known for:** Moroccan wines; French food; outdoor terrace. [$] *Average main: 100DH* ✉ *Quartier Mansour Eddahbi, (opposite Le Berbère Palace hotel)* ☎ *0524/88–24–73* 🌐 *www.restaurant-accord-majeur.com* ⏲ *Closed Sun.*

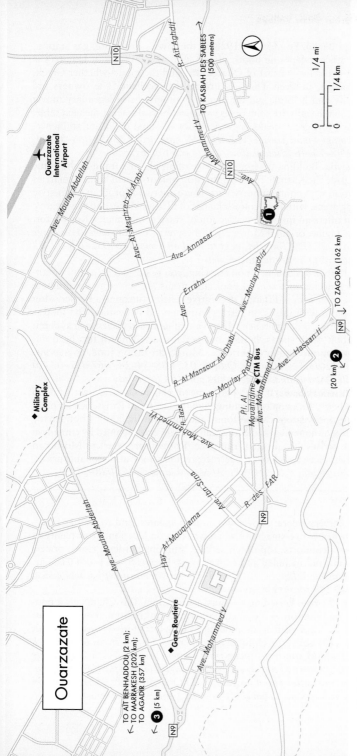

Ouarzazate

Ouarzazate International Airport

◆ Military Complex

Ave. Moulay Abdellah

Ave. Moulay Abdellah

Ave. Al-Maghreb Al-Arabi

Ave. Annasar

Ave. Erraha

Ave.

R. Al Mansour Ad-Dhabi

Ave. Moulay Rachid

Ave. Moulay Rachid

Ave. Mohammed VI

Ave. Mohammed VI

R. Mohammed Taza

Ave. Ibn Sina

Hay. Al Mouqauama

R. des. FAR

Pl. Al Mouahidine ◆ **CTM Bus**
Ave. Mohammed V

Ave. Hassan II

R. Aït Aghdif

Ave. Mohammed V

→ TO KASBAH DES SABLES
(500 meters)

N10

N10

N10

N9 ↓ TO ZAGORA (162 km)

N9

N9

↓ [20 km] ②

◆ **Gare Routière**

← TO AÏT BENHADDOU (2 km);
TO MARRAKESH (202 km);
↓ TO AGADIR (357 km)

③ [5 km]

0 —— 1/4 mi
0 —— 1/4 km

Atlas Studios **3**
Fint Oasis **2**
Kasbah Taourirt **1**

$$
INTERNATIONAL
Fodor'sChoice
★

✕ **Chez Dimitri.** Founded in 1928 as the town's first store, gas station, post office, telephone booth, dance hall, and restaurant, Dimitri's is the fun and lively heart of Ouarzazate, and the food—whether Greek, Moroccan, or even Thai—is invariably excellent. The owners are friendly and helpful, and the signed photographs of legendary movie stars on the walls are sometimes enhanced by real stars at the next table. **Known for:** great steaks; signed photos of stars; night-out ambience. $ *Average main: 100DH* ⊠ *22, av. Mohammed V* ☎ *0524/88-33-44, 0524/88-73-46* ⊕ *www.dimitri-restaurant-ouarzazate.com.*

$$
MOROCCAN

✕ **Douyria.** Building up from the base of an old pisé (mud-built) home alongside the Kasbah Touarirt, this *douyria*, or "small house," marries tradition with contemporary flair. There are two Moroccan salon-style dining areas, with bold color schemes of lilac and lime, and the creative menu offers an interesting selection of starters and mains. **Known for:** camel tagine; original Moroccan dishes; terrace with views. $ *Average main: 100DH* ⊠ *Taourirt, next to Kasbah Touarirt* ☎ *0524/88-52-88* ⊕ *www.restaurant-ouarzazate.net.*

$$$
INTERNATIONAL

✕ **La Kasbah des Sables.** Upon entering, you're greeted by a wall of lanterns reflected in a central pool, and meals are served in six intimate areas, each with a different decorative scheme (imagine a Berber salon or a patio with tables on terraces surrounded by water). The food is imaginative, mixing French-Moroccan influences in dishes such as confit of rabbit, with spices, honey, and peach sauce. **Known for:** beautiful decor; unique dining experience; Moroccan fusion food. $ *Average main: 120DH* ⊠ *Hay Ait Qdif* ☎ *0524/88-54-28, 0673/52-07-20 mobile* ⊕ *www.lakasbahdessables.com* ⊗ *Closed July.*

$
CAFÉ

✕ **Patisserie Habouss.** If you've got time to relax in Ouarzazate, there's no place better for people-watching than the terrace of Patisserie Habouss. Locals and visitors can be found indulging in its famous homemade gâteaux or honey-soaked Moroccan pastries accompanied by cinnamon coffee or freshly squeezed fruit juice. **Known for:** excellent Moroccan pastries; nice views from the terrace; regional food at reasonable prices. $ *Average main: 40DH* ⊠ *Pl. Al Mouahidine* ☎ *0524/88-26-99.*

WHERE TO STAY

$$$$
HOTEL
Fodor'sChoice
★

▦ **Le Berbère Palace.** Movie stars and magnates tend to stay at Ouarzazate's only five-star hotel when working on location. **Pros:** plenty of creature comforts; top-notch service; stunning gardens. **Cons:** pricey; breakfast not included and expensive. $ *Rooms from: 1700DH* ⊠ *Av. Al Mansour Eddahbi* ☎ *0524/88-31-05* ⊕ *www.hotel-berberepalace. com* ⇆ *249 rooms* ⦿ *No meals.*

$$
B&B/INN

▦ **Dar Chamaa.** Poised on the outskirts of town, Dar Chamaa is a boutique riad that offers a contemporary take on traditional design. **Pros:** good service; stylish accommodations with lots of mod-cons. **Cons:** out of the city; not very helpful management. $ *Rooms from: 650DH* ⊠ *8 km (5 miles) south of Ouarzazate center, Tajda* ✛ *From Ouarzazate center, follow road to Zagora across bridge and then turn left into palm groves (just after Hotel les Jardins de Ouarzazate)* ☎ *0524/85-49-54* ⊕ *www.darchamaa.com* ⇆ *18 rooms, 2 suites* ⦿ *Breakfast.*

The busy Atlas Studios is one of the top attractions in Ouarzazate.

$$$$ **Dar Kamar.** For anyone seduced by tales of Glaoui wealth and influ-
B&B/INN   ence, this 17th-century pasha's courthouse has magisterial appeal. **Pros:**
beautiful interiors; doting service. **Cons:** cheaper rooms (3rd category)
get little daylight. $ *Rooms from: 880DH* ✉ *45, Kasbah Taourirt*
☎ *0524/88–87–33* ⊕ *www.darkamar.com* ⇥ *14 rooms* ⦿ *Breakfast.*

$ **Hotel Marmar.** What it lacks in amenities and decor this no-frills
HOTEL   hotel more than makes up for in affordability and location near the
bus stops in the center of town. **Pros:** central location; cheap rooms;
some rooms have a/c and heat. **Cons:** no frills; not all staff speak English; can be noisy. $ *Rooms from: 200DH* ✉ *19, av. Moulay Abdellah*
☎ *0524/88–88–87* ⊕ *www.hotel-marmar.com* ⇥ *200 rooms* ⦿ *Breakfast* ▭ *No credit cards.*

$$ **Riad Dar Barbara.** Run by an English-Moroccan couple, this guest-
B&B/INN   house in a residential neighborhood on the outskirts of Ouarzazate has
huge rooms with traditional decor, air-conditioning and heating, and en
suite bathrooms. **Pros:** friendly English-speaking staff; spacious rooms;
air-conditioning and heating. **Cons:** outside of town; bathrooms need
updating; no pool. $ *Rooms from: 500DH* ✉ *8 km (5 miles) south
of Ouarzazate, Tajda* ☎ *0524/85–49–30* ⊕ *www.riaddarbarbara.com*
▭ *No credit cards* ⇥ *8 rooms* ⦿ *Breakfast.*

SHOPPING

Labyrinthe du Sud. You'll discover a treasure trove of antiques, car-
pets, Touareg and Berber jewelry, and trinkets at Labyrinthe du Sud.
Credit cards are accepted. ✉ *Rte. de la Kasbah des Cigognes, Tajda*
☎ *0524/85–42–43* ⊕ *www.labyrinthe-sud.jimdo.com.*

SPORTS AND THE OUTDOORS

FOUR-WHEELING

Quads Aventures. You can rent quad bikes from Quads Aventures at the entrance to Atlas Studios, on the main Marrakesh road. They're good for day trips to the natural and historic wonders that have become backdrops to blockbuster films, including the kasbah at Aït Ben Haddou and a plateau used in *Gladiator.* The outfitter also rents canoes, great for the sparkling lake just southeast of town. Two hours of quad-biking costs 450 DH per person with reductions for groups. ⊠ *Km 5, Rte. de Marrakech, next to entrance to Atlas Studios* ☎ *0524/88–40–24* ⊕ *www.quadsaventures.com.*

AÏT BEN HADDOU

30 km (19 miles) northwest of Ouarzazate.

The *ksar* (fortified village) at Aït Ben Haddou is something of a celebrity itself. This group of earth-built kasbahs and homes hidden behind defensive high walls has come to fame (and fortune) as a backdrop for many films, including David Lean's *Lawrence of Arabia,* Ridley Scott's *Gladiator,* and as Astapor, the slave city in *Game of Thrones.* Of course, it hasn't always been a film set. It got going in the 11th century as a stop-off on the old caravan routes, with salt heading one way and ivory and gold heading back the other. Strewn across the hillside and surrounded by flowering almond trees in early spring, the red-pisé towers of the village fortress resemble a sprawling, dark-red sand castle. Crenellated and topped with an ancient granary store, it's one of the most sumptu-ous sights in the Atlas. The ksar is a UNESCO World Heritage Site.

GETTING HERE AND AROUND

The village is easily reached by road. There are very few buses to Aït Ben Haddou, so if you don't have a car the best and cheapest option is to charter a grand taxi in Ouarzazate. On arrival, you'll find two main entrances to the kasbah. The first, by the hotel-restaurant La Kasbah, has ample safe parking and you can cross the riverbed via stepping-stones. Farther down the road is the second entry point opposite the Riad Maktoub. Here you can leave your car at the side of the road and then take a short stroll to a footbridge across the river to the kasbah.

WHERE TO EAT

There are a few café-restaurants on the roadside close to the parking areas of Aït Ben Haddou. However, you should avoid those with all the tour buses parked outside, as quality is invariably poor. Lodgings like Riad Maktoub or Ksar Ighnda, listed below, offer reliable alterna-tives—both are open to the general public for lunch or dinner. Choose a smaller establishment, where you will find locals eating their lunch or sipping a coffee.

WHERE TO STAY

$

B&B/INN

☉ **Auberge Ayouze.** This restored pisé home maintains an aura of authen-ticity thanks to typical architectural features, like carved Berber motifs and ceilings woven from reeds and date palms. **Pros:** great value; authen-tic setting. **Cons:** no pool; not much English spoken; only two rooms have heating and air-conditioning. $ *Rooms from: 310DH* ✉ *Douar Asfalou, 2 km (1 mile) north of Aït Ben Haddou* ☎ *0524/88–37–57* 🌐 *www.auberge-ayouze.com* 🛏 *6 rooms* 🍴 *Breakfast.*

$$$ B&B/INN 🏨 **Kasbah Ellouze.** Next to the old kasbah of Tamdaght, the rustic Kasbah Ellouze (Kasbah of Almonds) is brimming with character. **Pros:** kasbah setting; helpful staff; great food. **Cons:** rooms are dark and cold in winter; hot water not always reliable. $ *Rooms from: 980DH* ✉ *5 km (3 miles) north of Aït Ben Haddou on P1506, Tamdaght* ☎ *0524/89–04–59* 🌐 *www.kasbahellouze.com* 💳 *No credit cards* 🕓 *Closed June and July* 🛏 *13 rooms* 🍴 *Breakfast.*

$$$ HOTEL 🏨 **Ksar Ighnda.** The most upmarket accommodation in the village, Ksar Ighnda stands on the grounds of an old mud-built *ksar*—though only the original olive trees remain in the garden near the pool. **Pros:** spacious gardens and common areas. **Cons:** standard rooms are small; restaurant serves average-quality meals and meager breakfasts. $ *Rooms from: 1000DH* ✉ *Douar Asfalou, 2 km (1 mile) east of Aït Ben Haddou* ☎ *0524/88–76–44* 🌐 *www.ksar.ighnda.net* 🛏 *50 rooms* 🍴 *Breakfast.*

$$ B&B/INN 🏨 **Riad Caravane.** Influenced by the fashionable interiors of Marrakesh's hip riads, Riad Caravane has stylish rooms, a roof terrace looking out to the kasbah, and a small dipping pool. **Pros:** chic design; village atmosphere. **Cons:** some rooms are small; hard to find. $ *Rooms from: 650DH* ✉ *Aït Ben Haddou* ☎ *0524/89–09–16* 🌐 *www.riad-caravane.com* 🛏 *8 rooms* 🍴 *Breakfast.*

7

SKOURA

50 km (31 miles) southwest of El Kelaâ M'Gouna, 42 km (26 miles) northeast of Ouarzazate.

Surprisingly lush and abrupt as it springs from the tawny landscape, Skoura deserves a lingering look for its kasbahs and its rich concentration of date palm, olive, fig, and almond trees. Pathways tunnel through the vegetation from one kasbah to another within this fertile island—a true oasis, perhaps the most intensely verdant in Morocco. ■ **TIP→ Skoura is such a magical place, that if you're on a grand tour of the Great Oasis Valleys, think about basing yourself here (for at least two days) rather than Ouarzazate.**

With so many grand deep-orange-hue kasbahs in Skoura, a tour of the Palmery is compulsory. The main kasbah route through Skoura is approached from a point just over 2 km (1 mile) past the town center toward Ouarzazate. The 18th-century **Kasbah Aït Ben Moro** is the first fortress on the right (now restored and converted to a hotel); you can leave your car at the hotel, which will happily arrange for a local guide to walk you through the Palmery, past the Sidi Aïssa *marabout* (shrine to a learned holy man). Alternatively, continue along the main road for a few hundred meters till you find the Museum of Skoura. By the Amerhidil River is the tremendous **Kasbah Amerhidil,** the largest kasbah in Skoura and one of the largest in Morocco. The partially renovated edifice is open to the public.

Down the (usually bone-dry) river is another kasbah, **Dar Aït Sidi el-Mati,** while back near the Ouarzazate road is the **Kasbah el-Kabbaba,** the last of the four fortresses on this loop. North of Skoura, on Route 6829

The Kasbah Amerhidil is the largest in Skoura.

through Aït-Souss, are two other kasbahs: **Dar Lahsoune,** a former Glaoui residence, and, a few minutes farther north, the **Kasbah Aït Ben Abou,** the second largest in Skoura after the Amerhidil.

EXPLORING

Museum of Skoura. Constructed and entirely funded by schoolteacher Abdelmoula el Moudahab, this small but fascinating private museum houses a collection of traditional Berber costumes, artifacts, manuscripts, and antiques belonging to several generations of local families. Abdelmoula, who speaks good English, can explain tribal differences and describe the various types of kasbahs and holy shrines found in the Skoura region. ✉ *Douar Ihzgane* ☎ *0524/85–23–68* 🎟 *20 DH.*

WHERE TO STAY

$$ B&B/INN 🏨 **Chez Talout.** A rustic farmhouse about 7 km (4½ miles) outside Skoura, Chez Talout is worth the trek for its warm welcome, wonderful food, and roof-terrace views across the palmery to Skoura's kasbahs. **Pros:** excellent cuisine; lovely pool; lush rural setting. **Cons:** well off the beaten track. [$] *Rooms from: 600DH* ✉ *7 km (4½ miles) southwest of Skoura, Ouled Aarbia* ✣ *7 km (4½ miles) before Skoura if coming from Ouarzazate, turn left off main road just after Idelssane* ☎ *0662/49–82–83* 🌐 *www.cheztalout.com/en* 💳 *No credit cards* 🛏 *15 rooms* 🍴 *Breakfast.*

$$$$ HOTEL Fodor's Choice ★ 🏨 **Dar Ahlam.** A restored 19th-century kasbah, Dar Ahlam, "the House of Dreams," is one of Morocco's most exclusive and sumptuous hideaways and with its epic desert setting, impeccable service, and intimate more-house-than-hotel feel, you may never want to wake up. **Pros:** epitome of luxury; fairy-tale desert setting; magical meals at your whim and location changes nightly. **Cons:** pricey; remote location; reservations limited

and must be made far in advance. [$] *Rooms from: 13530DH* ✉ *Kasbah Madihi, Skoura Palmery* ☎ *0524/85–22–39* 🌐 *www.darahlam.com* 🕒 *Closed Aug.* 🛏 *13 rooms, 1 villa* 🍴 *All-inclusive.*

$$$ B&B/INN FAMILY 🏨 **Les Jardins de Skoura.** Styling itself as a *"maison de repos,"* this restored farmhouse casts such a spell over guests that many of them find it difficult to leave, staying on for days in its warm, lazy embrace. **Pros:** idyllic surroundings; excellent facilities; hospitable host. **Cons:** hard to cross the river if there is heavy rain. [$] *Rooms from: 880DH* ✉ *Skoura Palmery* ✣ *2 km (1 mile) before Skoura (from direction of Ouarzazate), and after passing Kasbah Aït Ben Moro follow yellow arrow signs for left turn, additional 4 km (2½ miles) of track to get to house* ☎ *0524/85–23–24* 🌐 *www.lesjardinsdeskoura.com* 💳 *No credit cards* 🕒 *Closed July* 🛏 *8 rooms* 🍴 *Breakfast.*

$$$ HOTEL FAMILY Fodor's Choice ★ 🏨 **L'Ma Lodge.** Set in the heart of the Palmery amid lush gardens (the owners planted 2,500 different plants), L'Ma Lodge is an exquisite escape from modern life. **Pros:** wonderful rooms; delicious food; a haven of tranquillity. **Cons:** there are only seven rooms so book early. [$] *Rooms from: 900DH* ✉ *Douar Oued Ali Khamsa* ✣ *At end of village, turn left and then right opposite gendarmerie. After 3 km (2 miles), turn right at sign and follow white arrows* ☎ *0524/85–22–81, 0666/64–79–08 mobile* 🌐 *www.lmalodge.com* 🛏 *7 rooms* 🍴 *Some meals.*

SPORTS AND THE OUTDOORS

BICYCLE TOURS

Alfalfa Bicycle Tours. Bicycling round the Palmery with a local guide is a delightful experience, allowing the ability to cover quite a bit of ground and to interact with locals who will be delighted to see you on a bike. Toufiq, the owner of Alfalfa, is knowledgeable and friendly. Bike tours are 80 DH for a half day or 120 DH if your legs feel up to a full day. ✉ *Skoura* ✣ *Center of Skoura near Banque Populaire* ☎ *0611/72–30–05* ✉ *tmousaoui0@gmail.com.*

HORSEBACK RIDING

Skoura Equestrian Centre. This well-run spot just outside of town offers professional English-speaking riding instruction, as well as horseback excursions around the kasbahs of Skoura oasis; expect to pay 300 DH for two hours or 500 DH for a full day with picnic lunch. The center is managed by Sport-Travel Maroc in Marrakech. You can also ask your hotel to book for you. Book in advance. ✉ *2 km (1 mile) north of Skoura on road to Toundout* ☎ *0524/43–99–69* 🌐 *www.sporttravel-maroc.com.*

THE DADÈS AND TODRA GORGES

The drive through Morocco's smaller versions of the Grand Canyon is stunning, and the area merits several days' exploration. The Dadès Gorge is frequented more by independent travelers than tours, while the Todra is much more about mass-organized tourism. So many buses stop at the most beautiful point that you almost forget it's supposed to be beautiful. If you avoid lunchtime (when all the tour buses disgorge), and venture on, there are some great walks and lovely spots where you can feel much more alone. For multiday hikes or serious day trekking it may be best to pre-arrange through one of the recommended experienced agencies or guides. For day or partial-day hikes, you can usually book a guide through your hotel.

THE DADÈS GORGE

Boumalne du Dadès is 53 km (33 miles) southwest of Tinerhir, 116 km (72 miles) northeast of Ouarzazate.

Snaking its way up from Boumalne du Dadès, the narrow roadway that is gradually swallowed up by the gorge is captivating. Along the route you'll see sprawling, emerald-green valleys and classic kasbahs set against a backdrop of surreal wind-sculpted, geological formations. The immensity of the gorge itself is a humbling reminder of our own vulnerability to the forces of nature and time. The switchback road helter-skelters to the end of the tarmac at Msemrir, but (in good weather) you can loop across to Todra Gorge in a 4x4 vehicle or continue northward on a rocky piste to Imilchil. The scenery of the Dadès Gorge is astounding, and if you can break away on foot to explore further, you will encounter Berber nomad families living in caves and rocky crags carved into the mountainside.

GETTING HERE AND AROUND

The easiest access point for the Dadès Gorge is the town of Boumalne du Dadès, which is linked to Ouarzazate in the west and Er-Rachidia in the east by the N10. CTM buses frequent this route, providing transportation to and from Boumalne du Dadès. The road through the gorge itself is mostly paved. Traveling beyond Msemrir requires a four-wheel-drive vehicle, and even then only if conditions are right. The piste routes can be treacherous, especially during the rainy season between December and February. If you do not have your own transport, grands taxis from Boumalne du Dadès will take you on the scenic drive.

Bus Contacts CTM. ✉ *Av. Mohammed V, Boumalne du Dades* ⊕ *www.ctm.ma.*

TIMING AND PRECAUTIONS

The Dadès Gorge is beautiful all year. In summer the steep canyon walls and rushing rivers are refreshing after the heat of the desert. In winter, however, the region gets considerable rainfall that makes the pistes impassable. Always ensure you have a full tank of gas, a spare tire, and plenty of water if embarking on cross-country routes.

VISITOR INFORMATION

Contacts Bureau des Guides a Boumalne du Dadès. ✉ *Av. Mohammed V, just after bridge on left (if coming from Dadès Gorge), next to WafaBank, Boumalne du Dades* ☎ *0667/59–32–92.*

EXPLORING

The town of **Boumalne du Dadès** marks the southern entrance to the Dadès Gorge, which is even more beautiful—longer, wider, and more varied—than its sister, the Todra Gorge. The 63 km (39 miles) of the Dadès Gorge, from Boumalne through Aït Ali and on to Msemrir, are paved and approachable in any kind of vehicle. Beyond that are some great rocky mountain roads for four-wheel-drive vehicles with good clearance. Boumalne itself is only of moderate interest, though the central market square is a good vantage point for a perusal of local life. The shops Artisanale de Boumalne and Maison Aït Atta merit a browse for their local products at local prices, particularly rosewood carvings and rosewater.

The lower Dadès Gorge and the Dadès River, which flows through it, are lined with thick vegetation. While the Todra has its lush date palmery, the Dadès has figs, almonds, Atlas pistachio, and carob trees. A series of kasbahs and *ksour* (plural of *ksar,* or fortified house) give way to Berber villages such as Aït Youl, Aït Arbi, Aït Ali, Aït Oudinar, and Aït Toukhsine—*aït* meaning "of the family" in the Tamazight Berber language.

Two kilometers (1 mile) up the road from Boumalne is the **Glaoui Kasbah,** once part of the empire of the infamous pasha of Marrakesh, T'hami el-Glaoui. The ksour at **Aït Arbi** are tucked neatly into the surrounding volcanic rock 3 km (2 miles) farther on from Glaoui Kasbah.

Ten kilometers (6 miles) from Aït Arbi is the village of Aït Sidi Boubker in the **Tamlalt Valley,** mostly known for the bizarre red rock formations called "Les Doigts de Singes" (or "Monkey's Fingers") after their curiously organic shapes carved by water and wind. A little further beyond them are more sculpted rocks known as the "Valley of Human Bodies," where local legend says that lost travelers died of hunger and were transformed into rocks. After Aït Oudinar, where most of the lodging options are clustered, the road crosses a bridge and gets substantially more exciting and empty, and the valley narrows dramatically, opening up around the corner into some of the most stunning views in the Dadès. Six kilometers (4 miles) north of the bridge, the **Hôtel la Kasbah de la Vallée** has basic accommodations, a restaurant, and a licensed bar. A few kilometers from here, a staggering series of hairpin bends descend into the belly of the camera-ready canyon.

Aït Hammou, the next village, is 5 km (3 miles) past the Kasbah de la Vallée. It makes a good base camp for walking north to vantage points over the Dadès River or, to the east, to a well-known cave with stalactites (ask the Hôtel la Kasbah de la Vallée for directions). At the top of the gorges is **Msemrir,** a village of red-clay pisé ksour that has a café with guest rooms. To go farther from Msemrir, you'll need four-wheel drive to follow the road (R704) that leads north over the High Atlas through Tilmi, the Tizi-n-Ouano, and Agoudal to Imilchil and eventually up to Route P24 (N8), the Marrakesh–Fez road. The road east from Msemrir climbs the difficult Route 3444, always bearing right, to another gorgetop town, Tamtattouchte. It makes for a great off-road drive.

WHERE TO EAT

Like other rural locales, the Dadès Gorge has few dining options, but lunch is served at most of the small auberges and hotels: as long as you turn up between midday and 3 pm, when the tagines are bubbling, you should be able to find a table. Chez Pierre and Dar Jnan Tiouira *(see below)* are particularly noted for their excellent food.

7

CLOSE UP

The Sahara Desert

Life's truly picture-perfect moments come few and far between: a sea of sand dunes, shimmering gray, yellow, orange, and red throughout the day, is one of them. The Sahara is the most beautiful, enigmatic, and awe-inspiring natural wonder that you can experience in Morocco—but if at all possible, don't rush through the experience. Spend some time getting to know the people and their unique outlook on life as well.

Should you have time for it, an expedition into the deeper desert provides a glimpse into a forgotten world. You may enter the desert by camel or jeep, but you will be able to sleep in a traditional bedouin tent or something even more comfortable and luxurious. But it is not all about ancient worlds—you may even have the opportunity to snowboard down the dunes.

POINTS OF ENTRY

The two main desert destinations in Morocco are very different— Merzouga lies nine hours' drive due east of Ouarzazate via the Dadès and Ziz valleys; M'hamid is five hours' drive south of Ouarzazate via the Drâa Valley.

From Fez, **Merzouga** is the most convenient overnight desert stop. The onward route then takes you through the Todra and Dadès gorges before reaching Ouarzazate. The dunes near Merzouga, called Erg Chebbi, have sand piled high like a fancy hairdo, and you can dip your toe in as you like. The desert is easily accessible by road right to the edge of the golden sands. Here you can spend a night very happily in an oasis bivouac camp, sleeping under the stars, and another back in Merzouga at an auberge or luxury hotel with majestic dune views.

M'hamid is the best entry point for the more adventurous and is the easiest place to reach if you are coming from Marrakesh. The paved road ends in the village, and beyond there's nothing but desert scrub, stony paths, and soft dunes. Erg Chigaga is the star attraction, some 50 km (31 miles) distant from the village. The sands go on for miles, and excursions by 4x4, camel, or a combination of both can be for as long or short as you like. Typically, a one-night trip by camel from M'hamid gets you to nearby Erg L'Houdi (The Dunes of the Jews); four days round-trip gets you to Erg Ezahaar (The Screaming Dunes), and five days gets you to the highest dunes in the region, Erg Chigaga.

Erg Chigaga can be reached by desert piste (unsealed dirt road) in a 4x4 in around three hours, so an overnight getaway is possible. Alternatively, a two-day camel trek from M'hamid will get you to Erg Chigaga, and you can book a 4x4 vehicle to bring you back the next day. Bivouacs in Erg Chigaga range from simple, nomad-style shared camps to super-deluxe private encampments.

WHAT SHOULD YOU KNOW?

Temperatures can reach 55°C (131°F) in June, July, and August. If you must go in summer, take sunset camel rides into the dunes, spend the night, and head back at dawn. The best (and busiest) time is between March and early May. October to February is nice, too, although it can be very cold at night from December through February.

The desert is unforgiving, and the inexperienced can easily become the expired. You must never attempt to visit the desert without an experienced guide. If you arrive in Merzouga or M'hamid without having prebooked a guided tour, make sure your guide is legitimate; the best thing is to book through one of the recommended local companies. The best way to avoid hassles is to make all arrangements in advance and arrange pick-up if you don't have your own transportation, or a roadside meeting if you do.

The impressive Erg Chebbi, near Merzouga, are more amenable to a quick in/out overnight, but they are a full 10-hour drive from Fez or two full days hard driving from Marrakesh. Erg Chebbi is very impressive, and solitary spots can be found on the fringes, with a good range of basic-to-deluxe accommodations. Southwest of M'hamid, however, you have eye-popping dunes that stretch for miles, including the Erg Chigaga. Ideally, allow at least two days (by camel) to get there from M'hamid, but a round-trip from Marrakesh is possible in three days with a 4x4.

Most tour operators, hotels, and auberges have their own permanent tented camps (bivouacs) hidden among the oases and dunes. Tents are usually good for between two and four people, but you can generally have a tent to yourself if traveling alone. If you want to keep the stars within eyeshot all night, you can also just sleep on a blanket on the sand. Most fixed camps have a restaurant tent (some serving alcohol), separate toilets, and washing facilities of some kind. In Merzouga and M'hamid, at the edge of the desert, there are also traditional auberges and plusher hotels of varying grades of luxury (some even have swimming pools).

WHAT TO DO IN THE DESERT

You might think there's not much to do in the desert, but when there are no shops, no electricity, and no running water, just getting by becomes wonderfully time-consuming. You can cook bread in the sand; count stars and identify constellations until the sky caves in; climb to the crest of the dunes at sunset; and learn Berber drumming by the campfire. Camel trips are de rigueur and in Erg Chebbi, near Merzouga, they rarely last more than three hours, with dinner generally waiting for you at your chosen bivouac camp. Beyond M'hamid, farther south, there's a much greater range of desert terrain to explore. Away from the fixed camps, the experience of camping sauvage, with just a nomad guide and camel for company, gives a fantastic insight into the real desert way of life. For thrill-seekers there are quad bikes and buggies for desert safaris, or you can try your skills at boarding down the high dunes. Alternatively, just take it easy and watch the changing moods, colors, and textures of the dunes all day long.

7

WHERE TO STAY

$
B&B/INN
⌂ **Auberge des Peupliers.** An ideal base for anyone craving simple Berber hospitality, Auberge des Peupliers has cozy accommodations with distinctive clay sinks, electric heating, and en suite showers; newer rooms include traditional features (like carved motifs) and face out across the gorge. **Pros:** friendly, helpful service. **Cons:** older rooms look shabby. $ *Rooms from: 30DH* ✉ *Ait Ouffi, 27 km (17 miles) north of Boumalne Dadès, Rte. de Dadès Gorge, Boumalne du Dades* ☎ *0524/83–17–48* ▭ *No credit cards* ⇱ *12 rooms* ⦿ *Some meals.*

$$
B&B/INN
⌂ **Chez Pierre.** Clinging to the rocky face of the Dadès Gorge, this guesthouse is a wonderful place to both eat and stay in the area. **Pros:** beautiful situation; great service and decor; fantastic food. **Cons:** property and rooms accessed via steep stairways. $ *Rooms from: 550DH* ✉ *27 km (17 miles) north of Boumalne du Dadès, Rte. de Dadès Gorge, Boumalne du Dades* ☎ *0524/83–02–67* ⊕ *www.chezpierre.org* ⇱ *9 rooms* ⦿ *Breakfast.*

$$$$
B&B/INN
⌂ **Dar Jnan Tiouira.** This kasbah and family-run guesthouse marries the traditional craftsmanship of the surrounding Berber tribes with the modern amenities discerning visitors expect. **Pros:** fabulous location; great food; luxurious rooms. **Cons:** steep ramps and stairs throughout; staff not always on hand. $ *Rooms from: 1300DH* ✉ *22 km (13½ miles) north from Boumalne, Rte. de Dadès Gorge, Aït Ouffi* ☎ *0667/35–18–60* ⊕ *www.darjnantiouira.com* ▭ *No credit cards* ⇱ *10 rooms* ⦿ *Some meals.*

$
HOTEL
Fodor'sChoice
★
⌂ **Ecobio Riad.** Clinging to the cliff face, the views from this new eco-friendly riad are fabulously dizzying while rooms are are decorated in the pale colors of the bleached-out desert, using all natural, local materials, with homespun bedspreads and pristine en suites. **Pros:** lovely views; pretty rooms; environmentally aware. **Cons:** on the road but isolated. $ *Rooms from: 300DH* ✉ *Douar Ait ibrirne, Boumalne du Dades* ☎ *0661/24–83–37* ⊕ *www.ecobioriad.com* ⇱ *6 rooms* ⦿ *Breakfast.*

$$$$
HOTEL
FAMILY
⌂ **Hotel Xaluca Dadès.** Part of the Grup Xaluca chain, this vast hotel offers high-quality accommodation in a region that generally lacks luxury. **Pros:** spacious, airy lounges; plenty of family amenities. **Cons:** located at edge of Boumalne, far from the gorge; ugly architecture; popular with tour groups. $ *Rooms from: 1000DH* ✉ *Rte. de Er-Rachidia, Boumalne du Dades* ☎ *0524/83–00–60* ⊕ *www.xaluca.com* ⇱ *106 rooms* ⦿ *Breakfast.*

SPORTS AND THE OUTDOORS

Mohamed Amgom. An experienced local Berber guide, Mohamed Amgom offers treks in the Dadès Valley for 400 DH per day. He can also organize four-wheel-drive vehicles for excursions throughout the Dadès and Todra gorges. ☎ *0666/59–41–42.*

THE TODRA GORGE

194 km (121 miles) northwest of Rissani, 184 km (114 miles) northeast of Ouarzazate.

The towering limestone stacks of the Todra Gorge are breathtakingly beautiful, as is the winding route upward from Tinerhir, which leads you there through delightful groves of date palm, pomegranate, fig, and olive trees. The namesake river that carved the gorge also feeds vegetation, forming the Todra Oasis—Morocco's highest—cradled in the southern slopes of the High Atlas. This whole mountainous area is the heartland of the Aït Atta tribe of Berbers, who have inhabited the region for centuries. Today it's also a top spot for trekking and rock climbing. Local hotels can organize guided hikes lasting several hours or several days. Mountaineers, ascending from the oasis to the steep cliffs of the gorge above, will also find plenty to keep them occupied, including several technical climbs for the experienced and some newer sections marked out for novices. Although hotels here may be able to offer you a guide and climbing equipment, the quality and condition of the latter cannot be vouched for, so bring your own or sign on for an organized tour run by a reputable outfitter.

GETTING HERE AND AROUND

The town of Tinerhir (also spelled "Tinghir"), on the main N10 route from Ouarzazate and Er-Rachidia, is the most convenient access point for visiting the Todra Gorge. Long-distance buses travel here from Agadir, Casablanca, Marrakesh, Fez, Meknès, and Rabat. Buses also arrive from Ouarzazate (five hours), Er-Rachidia (three hours), and Erfoud (four hours); most stop on Avenue Mohammed V, on the northern side of the main square.

To reach the gorge, take route R703 (3445) north toward Tamtattouchte, and follow the riverbed upward for about 15 km (9 miles). If you don't have your own vehicle, you can catch a grand taxi to take you up through the Todra palmery as far as the Todra Gorge; the 30-minute drive should cost about 30 DH per person. There are also minibuses that transport locals to the villages above the Todra Gorge; you can ask to be dropped off on the way through.

Bus Contacts CTM Tinerhir. ⊠ *Av. Hassan II, next to main square, Tinerhir* ☎ *0524/83–43–79* ⊕ *www.ctm.ma.*

TIMING

The steep sides of the gorge can often mean that the route through the gorge itself is in shade, but the effect of angled sunlight shifting across the rock face during the day creates a sublime canvas of red and orange. Mid- to late afternoon is the best time to visit.

EXPLORING

The 15-km (9-mile) drive up from Tinerhir to the beginning of the Todra Gorge will take you through lush but slender palmeries, sometimes no wider than 100 feet from cliff to cliff. An inn and a café await near the spring, but you're better off not stopping, as the site itself isn't remarkable, and the concentration of hustlers and overhelpful children is dense.

The 66-foot-wide entrance to the Todra Gorge, with its roaring clear stream and its 1,000-foot-high rock walls stretching 325 feet back on either side, is the most stunning feature of the whole canyon, though the upper reaches aren't far behind. The farther off the beaten path you get, the more rewarding the scenery; a walk or drive up through the gorge on paved roads to Tamtattouchte is particularly recommended. There are some marked trails leading from Le Festival hotel.

From the thin palmery along the bottom, the walls of the Todra Gorge remain close and high for some 18 km (11 miles). Eagles nest in the Todra, along with *choughs* (red-beaked rooks), rock doves, and blue rock thrushes.

Museum of the Oasis. This small but ambitious community-oriented spot is well worth a stop if you're driving east from Tinerhir toward Merzouga. Housed in the 19th-century ksar of El Khorbat, it contains old maps, photos, antiques, and exhibits that document the traditional lifestyle of the southern oasis, with proceeds going to development and educational projects in the village. You can also buy locally made items at the craft workshop, and then enjoy a meal or spend a night in the atmospheric El Khorbat guesthouse ($$)—both are part of the same tourism initiative. ⊠ *48 km (31 miles) east of Tinerhir, Tinejdad* ☎ *0535/88–03–55* ⊕ *www.elkhorbat.com* 🖾 *20 DH.*

La Source des Poissons Sacrés (Springs of the Sacred Fish), about halfway to the beginning of the gorge, is so named for the miracle performed by a sage, said to have struck a rock once to produce a gushing spring, and twice to produce fish. Today the sacred source is frequented by young Berber women who are experiencing difficulties in conceiving children. (It is rumored that bathing in the water has about an 80% success rate.) You can also stop here to camp and have a refreshing drink.

WHERE TO STAY

$

B&B/INN

🔲 **Auberge Baddou.** This small hotel is a worthy choice for budget accommodations at the far northern end of the Todra Gorge. **Pros:** spotless rooms; friendly service. **Cons:** rather isolated in unattractive village; cheaper rooms have shared bathrooms; central heating is an extra 150 DH per night in winter. $ *Rooms from: 400DH* ⊠ *Aït Hani, 29 km (18 miles) north of Tinerhir, Tamtatouchtte* ☎ *0672/52–13–89* ⊕ *auberge-baddou-todra.com* 🖃 *No credit cards* 🗗 *18 rooms* ⦿| *Some meals.*

$$

B&B/INN

🔲 **Dar Ayour.** This pretty guesthouse sits at the edge of the river amid fig trees, olives, and date palms with the walls of the Todra Gorge towering above. **Pros:** peaceful setting; small outdoor swimming pool. **Cons:** some rooms very small; bathrooms are basic. $ *Rooms from: 600DH* ⊠ *Km 17, Rte. des Gorges de Todra, Douar Tizgui, Tinerhir* ☎ *0524/89–52–71* ⊕ *www.darayour.com* 🗗 *18 rooms* ⦿| *Some meals.*

$$

B&B/INN

FAMILY

Fodor's Choice

★

🔲 **Le Festival.** Made from the same mountain rock that surrounds it, this quirky eco-hotel is owned and operated by the charming Addi Sror, who speaks excellent English. **Pros:** dramatic isolation; great meals; environmentally sensitive. **Cons:** castle and cave rooms are about 200 DH–300 DH extra per night; few in-house amenities; three rooms in main house share a bathroom. $ *Rooms from: 700DH* ⊠ *Rte. de Todra Gorge, 5 km (3 miles) north of Todra Gorge, 12 km (7 miles) south of Tamtattouchte, Tinerhir* ☎ *0661/26–72–51* ⊕ *www.aubergelefestival-todragorge.com* 🖃 *No credit cards* 🗗 *15 rooms* ⦿| *Some meals.*

TO MERZOUGA AND THE DUNES

This particular southeastern corner holds some of Morocco's greatest sights, principally the Sahara's picture-perfect undulating dunes near Merzouga, and the Tafilalt date palmery. Now that the road to Merzouga is completely paved, you can drive straight there without stopping.

EN ROUTE

Approaching Erfoud from the direction of Tinejdad, you can't help but notice the hundreds of holes that start appearing along both sides of the road about 27 km (17 miles) before you reach town. Although they resemble giant molehills, the holes are actually wells called *khettara*. Part of an ancient Persian-designed irrigation system, which was first brought to Morocco by the Arabs in the 12th century, these wells access water from the natural water table, channeling it through underground canals to different palm groves. On the left-hand side of the road, as sand dunes begin to pile up, look for the ones dug to irrigate the Tafilalt Oasis back in the 14th century. Local guide **Said Ouatou,** who can be found in a Bedouin tent beside the road (also on the left), will explain the science and history. ■ TIP→ Be careful if you have young children: the edges of the wells can crumble.

ERFOUD

81 km (50 miles) south of Er-Rachidia, 300 km (186 miles) northeast of Ouarzazate.

Any expedition to Erg Chebbi will entail passing through—or possibly spending a night in—Erfoud. Formerly a French administrative outpost and Foreign Legion stronghold, this frontier town on the Algerian border has a definite Wild West (in this case, Wild South) feel to it. Practical-minded travelers will be interested in the grid of low, dusty red buildings that house banks, shops, and other amenities.

The military fortress at Borj-Est, just across the Ziz to the east, provides the best possible view over the date palmery, the desert, and Erfoud from its altitude of 3,067 feet above sea level. Near the Borj-Est are quarries famous for their black marble, one of Erfoud's principal products; this luxurious solid is surprisingly rich in petrified marine fossils.

GETTING HERE AND AROUND

Erfoud sits at the southern end of the Ziz Oasis. From the north, the only way here is the N13 via Er-Rachidia. From Ouarzazate, take the N10 and turn onto the R702 just after the village of Tinejdad. This direct route avoids Er-Rachidia.

Buses to Erfoud depart from Er-Rachidia (1½ hours), Fez (11 hours), Rissani (1½ hours), and Tinerhir (4 hours). From Er-Rachidia you can take buses to Ouarzazate, Marrakesh, Midelt, and Meknès.

Bus Contacts CTM Erfoud. ✉ *Complex Commerciale, Av. Mohammed V* ☎ *0535/57–68–86* ⊕ *www.ctm.ma.*

TIMING AND PRECAUTIONS

The biggest annual event is the Erfoud Date Festival, which coincides with the date harvest in October (the exact days vary from year to year). As with all the Moroccan Sahara regions, the best way to avoid excessive heat is to visit between February and May or September and November.

EXPLORING

FAMILY **Tahiri Museum of Morocco.** Midway between Erfoud and Rissani, this private museum is hard to miss—just look for the giant replica dinosaurs standing outside. Take a peek inside at the interesting, well-presented collection curated by Moroccan paleontologist Brahim Tahari; it includes fossils, bones, minerals, flints, crystals, and assorted oddities. ■ **TIP→ There's a shop attached if you want to purchase your own bit of prehistory.** ✉ *Km 17, Rte. de Rissani* 🎫 *Free, donations welcome.*

WHERE TO EAT AND STAY

When hunger hits, your best option is to head to one of the hotels listed below. That said, there are a few simple eateries along the main street in the town center.

$$ MOROCCAN 🍴 **Pizzeria-Restaurant des Dunes.** If you're craving pizza, try this tourist-friendly spot just opposite the gas station as you enter Erfoud from the direction of Er-Rachidia. It serves standard pies plus a local variation on the theme called *madfouna tafilalt* (aka Berber pizza), which is a baked flat bread stuffed with meat. **Known for:** pizza; terrace. [$] *Average main: 80DH* ✉ *Av. Moulay Isamil* ☎ *0535/57–67–93* 🌐 *www.restaurantdesdunes.com* 💳 *No credit cards.*

$$ HOTEL 🏨 **Hotel Kasbah Tizimi.** This faux 1960s kasbah is popular with package-tour operators, but it's a decent midrange place for independent travelers to stop on the way to or from the desert as well. **Pros:** reasonable prices; nice pool and patio area. **Cons:** filled with tour groups; substandard bathrooms. [$] *Rooms from: 700DH* ✉ *Rte. de Jorf* ☎ *0535/57–61–79* 🛏 *78 rooms* 🍽 *Breakfast.*

$$$$ HOTEL 🏨 **Kasbah Xaluca.** In a desert town that lacks any character-filled boutique accommodations, the rambling Kasbah Xaluca is the best choice available and offers a sense of authenticity combined with luxury facilities. **Pros:** pretty pool area; attentive service; all the modern conveniences. **Cons:** distance from dunes; full of tour groups. [$] *Rooms from: 1000DH* ✉ *5 km (3 miles) north of Erfoud, on road to Er-Rachidia, Maadid* ☎ *0535/57–84–50* 🌐 *www.xaluca.com* 🛏 *110 rooms, 24 suites, 8 bungalows* 🍽 *Breakfast.*

SHOPPING

No trip to Erfoud is complete without a visit to one of the many marble and fossil workshops. This section of desert was once a rich seabed filled with many types of marine creatures that no longer exist. Trilobites, urchins, ammonites, and other fossils are abundant in the local stone, and huge slabs are quarried, dissected, polished, and shaped here to create all manner of objects from tabletops to pendants. Most of the workshops give demonstrations as well as exhibit the finished articles.

Fossiles d'Erfoud. This fossil showroom, workshop, and factory has English-speaking owners who are happy to show individuals and groups around the facilities. The showroom has just about every object you might imagine could be made from fossils, and there are plenty of un-"improved" fossils to go around as well. Credit cards are accepted and international shipping can be arranged. ✉ *107, av. Moulay Ismail* ☎ *0535/57–60–20* ⊕ *www.fossilesderfoud.com.*

MERZOUGA

53 km (33 miles) southeast of Erfoud, 134 km (83 miles) southeast of Er-Rachidia.

Merzouga has an ever-expanding strip of hotels and guesthouses, with options ranging from simple to sublime. The village's main draw, though, is the easy access it offers to Erg Chebbi, and its magnificent dunes. A dawn or dusk trip to the dunes has become a classic Moroccan adventure, and is worth the effort. A series of café-restaurant-hotels overlooks Erg Chebbi, and most run camel excursions to the top as well as to oases where you can spend the night in permanent bivouacs. Many tour operators now offer exclusive and luxurious camps tucked in dunes away from the crowds—picture tents kitted out with woven carpets, antiques, lanterns, four-poster beds strewn with rose petals, and en suite washing facilities. You can also expect chilled champagne and fine dining by candlelight, but be prepared—paradise doesn't come cheap! ■TIP➔ If you have some extra time it is worth taking a day trip to the colorful local market at Rissani and the ruins of the once-great city of Sijilmassa—now just a few remaining walls but with a great sense of history.

GETTING HERE AND AROUND

The N13 from Erfoud goes straight to Merzouga. Minibuses and grands taxis bring tourists from Rissani and Erfoud.

GUIDES AND TOURS

Once in Merzouga you get around either by foot, dune buggy, camel, or 4x4. If you haven't come on an organized tour, the hotel or guesthouse you choose will be able to make arrangements for you, using their own local guides and bivouac camps.

Berber Space Morocco. Berber Space Morocco is an all-round activity-based tour company that can offer you everything from camel treks, 4x4 adventures, and dune buggy races to more sedate cycling tours and visits to the dunes and oases. It was set up by the young and entrepreneurial Hassan, who prides himself on his Berber heritage and on knowing everything—they call him Hassan Google. ☎ *0670/13–76–63, 0662/47–57–17* ⊕ *www.berberspacemorocco.com.*

Omar Berhi Camel Trekking. Omar grew up in the desert south of Merzouga and now lives near the dunes in the village of Hassi Labied. He leads one- to three-night camel treks into the Erg Chebbi dunes, charging around 400 DH per person per night, which includes parking and a hot shower when you get back. ✉ *Hassi Labied* ☎ *0641/87–67–17* ⊕ *www.cameltrekking.com.*

Your Morocco Tour. This U.S.-Moroccan agency can organize tours from Marrakesh or Fez that include a night spent at its luxury bivouac in the dunes of Merzouga. The price (about 1,800 DH per person with dinner, breakfast, drinks, and the camel trek) is built into the cost of a longer tour package. ✉ *Merzouga* ☎ *0662/34–48–16* 🌐 *www.your-morocco-tour.com.*

TIMING AND PRECAUTIONS

In summer, prepare for the extreme daytime heat by bringing sunglasses, sunblock, and plenty of bottled water. In winter, the nights can be viciously cold, so pack extra layers if camping out. **■ TIP→ The fine sand of the Sahara will find its way into everything. Carry zip-top plastic bags for keeping items sand-free, especially electronic equipment and cosmetics.**

EXPLORING

Dayet Srji. Near the dunes, this seasonal salt lake is a surprising sight—sometimes you see pink flamingos in early spring. ✉ *Merzouga.*

Fodor's Choice ★ **Erg Chebbi.** In most cases your hotel is your best bet for an organized tour of Erg Chebbi. Every auberge near the dunes is there because it's a prime jumping-off point for a sunrise or sunset journey, either on foot or by camel. Most auberges have their own permanent bivouac in the dunes, often not far from others but generally fairly well concealed—which lets you pretend no one else is around even if they are. Most bivouac areas are organized into series of small tents for couples and larger groups, so you don't have to share with everyone. If you want to be utterly private, make sure your auberge doesn't share a tented site with any other, or ask to camp in the dunes on your own. ✉ *Merzouga.*

WHERE TO STAY

There are nearly 100 guesthouses and hotels to choose from in the area, but the best are north of Merzouga in the desert village Hassi Labied; these also benefit from being closest to the towering sands. All will be able to arrange a night's stay in a bivouac camp, and you can usually return to the hotel for a shower the morning after.

$$ B&B/INN 🏨 **Kasbah Mohayut.** A mud-built auberge in the Saharan tradition, Kasbah Mohayut has comfortable, air-conditioned rooms that are decorated in the local style (think tiled floors, date-palm ceiling, wrought-iron beds, and colorful rugs); there are also spacious family suites with huge king-size beds, a salon, and a private terrace looking out to the dunes. **Pros:** right beside the dunes; pretty pool. **Cons:** this part of dunes is often busy with other tourists. [$] *Rooms from: 600DH* ✉ *1½ km (1 mile) south of Hassi Labied, Hassi Labied* ☎ *0666/03–91–85* 🌐 *www.hotelmohayut.com* 🛏 *26 rooms* 🍴 *Some meals.*

$$ B&B/INN 🏨 **Ksar Sania Eco-Lodge.** At the edge of the Sahara, this unique French-owned eco-lodge lets guests bed down in handsome, hexagonal bungalows that are built from straw-covered mud; the rooms are very spacious and stylish, with tasteful furnishings, rich colors, and traditional ceilings. **Pros:** highly original concept; environmentally friendly. **Cons:** service can be slack. [$] *Rooms from: 640DH* ✉ *2 km (1 mile) south of Merzouga* ☎ *0661/35–99–10* 🌐 *www.auberge-ksarsania-merzouga.com* 💳 *No credit cards* ⏲ *Closed during Ramadan when it falls in summer* 🛏 *15 rooms, 5 huts* 🍴 *Some meals.*

$$$$ HOTEL **Riad Cafe Du Sud.** An exclusive retreat of just four individually designed rooms set in a fabulous location on the dunes, the Riad Cafe Du Sud provides traditional, simple, and calm desert living with all the luxuries of the modern world such as plentiful hot water and a strong shower. **Pros:** individually designed rooms; exclusivity. **Cons:** few rooms so reservations should be made in advance; pricey. [$] *Rooms from: 1500DH* ✉ *BP 120 Ksar Merzouga* ☎ *0670/76–11–06* 🌐 *www.riadcafedusud.com* 🛏 *4 rooms* 🍴 *Breakfast.*

$$$ B&B/INN **Riad Madu.** Opened in 2013 by the Annam brothers from Merzouga, Riad Madu is a cut above the other Saharan inns dotting the edge of the Erg Chebbi dunes, showcasing the brothers' experience in the European tourism and hospitality sectors—good English is spoken, guests are greeted warmly, and attention to detail is evident throughout. **Pros:** enthusiastic staff; half-board meal plan available; attention to detail. **Cons:** other desert hotels nearby. [$] *Rooms from: 870DH* ✉ *5 km (3 miles) north of Merzouga, Hassi Labied* ☎ *0535/57–87–40* 🌐 *www.riadmadu.com* 💳 *No credit cards* 🛏 *12 rooms* 🍴 *Breakfast.*

$$ B&B/INN **Sahara Garden Kasbah & Bivouac.** Situated far from the madding crowd at the northern tip of Erg Chebbi, Sahara Garden has 10 perfectly comfortable guest rooms in the main building—but the adjacent eco-oriented bivouac is a bigger draw. **Pros:** stunning location; deluxe camping. **Cons:** difficult to find. [$] *Rooms from: 500DH* ✉ *17 km (10½ miles) north of Merzouga, Hassi Labied* ✥ *Follow signs to Hotel Yasmina* ☎ *0670/18–13–94* 🌐 *www.sahara-garden.com* 🛏 *10 rooms, 6 deluxe tents, 30 standard tents* 🍴 *Some meals.*

$$$$ ALL-INCLUSIVE Fodor's Choice ★ **Sahara Stars Camp.** True to its name, this new camp in the dunes offers stunning, unimpeded view of the stars, enjoyed from luxurious tents with hot power showers, plush beds, elegant decor, and lovely touches like flowers scattered on the bed and pom-pommed hats to guard against the sun. **Pros:** luxury tents; great food; a secluded location. **Cons:** only accessible by camel or quad. [$] *Rooms from: 2000DH* ✉ *Ras El Erg Chebbi* ☎ *0662/47–57–17, 0661/87–47–53* 🌐 *www.saharastarscamp.com* 🛏 *6 rooms* 🍴 *All meals.*

SPORTS AND THE OUTDOORS

Mouhou (Quad) Tours. Mouhou Tours offer quad biking across the dunes or around the town of Merzouga. Phone ahead to organize a pick up from your hotel. ☎ *0637/39–06–58* 🌐 *www.mouhoutours.com.*

DJEBEL SARHRO AND NEKOB

95 km (59 miles) east of Agdz, 165 km (103 miles) southwest of Rissani.

If you pick the southern oasis route, don't miss the chance to stay in Nekob, Morocco's most kasbah-filled village. Locals have come up with all sorts of reasons for why there are 45 of them. The amusing and believable theory is that members of a rich extended family settled here in the 18th and 19th centuries and quickly set to work trying to out-build and out-impress each other. There's little in the way of showing off in the village today. The children are wild and the place a little untouched for the moment.

Visitors can pick up handcrafted carpets and head scarves made by local women at the weekly Sunday souk, or simply sit back, stare over the palmery, and savor the experience. If you're looking for a more active alternative, the trekking potential north of town stretches as far as Boumalne du Dadès, 150 km (93 miles) away and on the northern oasis route. It's a five-day hike to Tagdift or Iknioun.

GETTING HERE AND AROUND

Nekob lies on the southern oasis route between Agdz and Rissani, skirting the southern slopes of the Djebel Sarhro. Minibuses and grands taxis travel here from Rissani, Zagora, and Ouarzazate.

Exploring the mountain ranges and peaks of Djebel Sarhro requires a four-wheel-drive vehicle.

■ TIP→ Walking in the Sarhro is a wonderful experience but to get the most out of it book with a specialist company before you arrive. Epic Morocco offers migration walks with the nomads in season.

EXPLORING

Djebel Sarhro Massif. The wonderfully panoramic oasis Route 6956/R108 (which becomes 3454/N12 after Tazzarine) is one of the safest, fastest, least crowded roads in Morocco, and it offers unparalleled views up into the Djebel Sarhro Massif and all the way over to the Tafilalt date palmery. Count on four hours for the 233-km (140-mile) trip from Route P31/N9 (the Ouarzazate–Zagora road) to Rissani, in the date palmery. ⊠ *Nekob.*

NEED A BREAK

✕ **Auberge Kasbah Meteorites.** Morocco is a magnet for fossil fans, and much of the activity centers around the town of Alnif, on Route 3454/N12 between Rissani and Tazzarine. About 13 km (8 miles) west of Alnif is Auberge Kasbah Meteorites where you can enjoy a simple lunch, a dip in the immaculate pool, and a two- to three-hour excursion with a guide who'll show you the best place to hunt for fossils and ancient stone carvings. **Known for:** good local food; a chance to hunt for fossils. ⊠ *Ksar Tiguima, 13 km (8 miles) west of Alnif, Nekob* 🕾 *0661/70–26–30* ⊕ *www.kasbahmeteorites.com.*

WHERE TO STAY

$$$
B&B/INN
FAMILY

Kasbah Hotel Aït Omar. The premier address in the village of Nekob, this old family kasbah has been lovingly restored to high specifications. **Pros:** very comfortable; great service; environmentally friendly ethic. **Cons:** awkward, steep stairways. $ *Rooms from: 900DH* ⊠ *Nekob* 🕾 *0524/83–99–81* ⊕ *www.hotel-aitomar.de* ▭ *No credit cards* ☉ *Closed July and Aug.* ⤙*4 rooms, 10 apartments* ♚*Breakfast.*

$$$
B&B/INN

Kasbah Imdoukal. This gorgeous Moroccan-owned kasbah sits in the heart of the village. **Pros:** in the center of Nekob; plenty of atmosphere. **Cons:** prices are a bit high. $ *Rooms from: 790DH* ⊠ *Douar N'Kob, Nekob* 🕾 *0524/83–97–98* ⊕ *www.kasbahimdoukal.com* ▭ *No credit cards* ⤙*18 rooms, 2 suites* ♚*Breakfast.*

$$
HOTEL

Riad Auberge Ouadjou. This pleasant, friendly hotel is a no-frills option with a manager who can speak English (with a British or American accent as required) and rooms that are simple, cool, and clean. **Pros:**

clean, simple rooms; swimming pool; Berber tent (added fee). **Cons:** basic. [$] *Rooms from: 500* ✥ *On left as you leave town on road to Agdz* ☎ *0524/83–93–14* 🌐 *www.ouadjou.com* 🛏 *6 rooms, 4 tents* 🍴 *Some meals* 💳 *No credit cards.*

THE DRÂA VALLEY

Morocco's longest river, the Drâa once flowed all the way to the Atlantic Ocean just north of Tan-Tan, some 960 km (597 miles) from its source above Ouarzazate. With the sole exception of a fluke flood in 1989—the only time in recent memory that the Drâa completed its course—the river disappears in the Sahara southwest of M'hamid, some 240 km (150 miles) from its headwaters. The Drâa Valley and its palmery continue nearly unbroken from Agdz through Zagora to M'hamid, forming one of Morocco's most memorable tours.

As wild as you may have found certain parts of Morocco thus far, the trip down to the Sahara will seem more so, something like steady progress into a biblical epic. The plains south of Ouarzazate give way to 120 km (75 miles) of date palmeries and oases along the Drâa River, and between Agdz and Zagora more than two-dozen kasbahs and ksour line both sides. The occasional market town offers a chance to mingle with the diverse peoples you'll see walking along the road in black shawls. Though most of the inhabitants are in fact Berbers, the Drâa Valley is also home to Arabs, small communities of Jews or the Mellahs they once inhabited, and numerous Haratin (descendants of slaves brought into Morocco from sub-Saharan Africa along the caravan routes that facilitated salt, gold, and slave trading.

After Zagora and Tamegroute, the road narrows as the Tinfou Dunes rise to the east and, farther south, a maze of jeep tracks leads out to Erg L'Houdi (Dune of the Jew). Finally, in M'hamid el Ghizlane (Plain of the Gazelles), with sand drifting across the road and the Drâa long since gone underground, there is a definite sense of closure—the end of the road.

AGDZ

69 km (43 miles) southeast of Ouarzazate.

Agdz, at the junction of the Drâa and Tamsift rivers, marks the beginning of the Drâa palmery. A sleepy market town and administrative center, Agdz (pronounced *ah*-ga-dez) has little to offer at first glance other than the 5,022-foot peak Djebel Kissane and the Kasbah Dar el-Glaoui. But in the palm groves at the edge of town you'll discover some gorgeous boutique hotels and mini-kasbahs; these make an ideal base for a day or two of hiking and exploring. This is an ideal place to wander through the palmery and get to understand a little about how agriculture works in an oasis. There is also a center specializing in building from natural materials such as clay. From Agdz south to M'hamid, the P31/N9 road follows the river closely except for a 30-km (19-mile) section between the Tinfou Dunes and Tagounite.

GETTING HERE AND AROUND
Agdz is served by buses and grands taxis traveling between Ouarzazate and Zagora. The trip takes approximately two hours from either town.

TIMING AND PRECAUTIONS
A great time to visit is in October when the date harvest is in full swing but it is wonderful at any time of the year. The market is stacked with boxes of the most delicious and succulent varieties. ■ TIP→ **Schistosomiasis, a parasite, has been reported in the Drâa River, so don't be tempted to swim or even wade across.**

EXPLORING

Cascades du Drâa. Look for the turnoff to the Cascades du Drâa (also known as the Cascades de Tizgui) on the left, 30 km (19 miles) south of Ouarzazate and 10 km (6 miles) before Agdz. Over thousands of years, the water has carved out natural pools that are ideal for a refreshing dip. The waterfalls are not huge—not on the scale of Ouzoud—but if you want to see palm trees, figs, and oleander flowers springing from the rocks, and dip your toes (or all of you) in cold water, they are still worth a detour. ⊠ *Agdz.*

OFF THE
BEATEN
PATH

Ksar Igdâoun. The truncated pyramidal towers and bastions of the Ksar Igdâoun are visible 15 km (9 miles) past the turnoff onto Route 6956/R108 to Tazzarine. There used to be three gates to the ksar: one for Jews; one for other people who lived nearby; and one for the local governor. ⊠ *Agdz* 🏛 *10 DH.*

Tamnougalt. Lining virtually the entire Drâa Valley from Agdz to Zagora are some two dozen ksour and kasbahs on both sides of the river. Perhaps the most amazing ksour in this region are at Tamnougalt, 6 km (4 miles) south of Agdz—the second group of red-pisé fortifications on the left. The resident Berber tribe, the Mezguita, governed its own independent republic from here until the late 18th century; the crenellated battlements and bastions were a necessary defense against desert nomads. For a deeper understanding of the tribe's traditional way of life, peruse the displays of farming and household implements in Tamnougalt's Kasbah des Caids du Mezguita museum. Occupying a restored 16th-century edifice, it is run by Hassan Aït el Caid (a descendant of the original caids who controlled the trade caravans passing through the region). Hassan can also take you on a walking tour through the village and the oasis, and explain the local Berber tribes and their origins en route. Donkey treks and picnics can be arranged as well. ⊠ *Tamnougalt* ☎ *0667/34–56–02* ⊕ *www.kasbah-des-caids.com* 🏛 *Museum 20 DH.*

WHERE TO EAT AND STAY
If you're passing though at lunchtime, the town has a slim selection of cafés; alternately you can continue on to Chez Yacob *(see below)*, located south toward Zagora in the village of Tamnougalt.

$ ✕ **Agdz Café Restaurant.** Located at the edge of town as you arrive from
MOROCCAN the direction of Ouarzazate, this terrace café with easy parking outside
FAMILY is a good place to stop for lunch or a drink. It serves hearty tagines, brochettes, salads, and other snacks; the clean restrooms are an added bonus. **Known for:** hearty tagines; clean restrooms (bring your own paper). 💲 *Average main: 60DH* ⊠ *Agdz* ▭ *No credit cards.*

$$$ B&B/INN **Bab el Oued.** Six freestanding rooms await guests at this handsome eco-lodge. **Pros:** beautiful location; environmentally sensitive. **Cons:** food quality inconsistent; dark, poorly lit rooms. [$] *Rooms from: 825DH* ✉ *Tamnougalt* ☎ *0660/18–84–84, 0619/40–28–32* 🌐 *www.babeloued-maroc.com* 💳 *No credit cards* 🛏 *2 rooms, 4 suites* 🍴 *Breakfast.*

$$ B&B/INN **Chez Yacob.** This kasbah has been renovated to retain all its traditional charm including thick pisé walls pierced with tiny windows screened with *moucharabia* (carved wood latticework), and a central courtyard. **Pros:** rooms face onto courtyard; great views over palmery; en suite bathrooms and a/c. **Cons:** very little parking; can be crowded at lunch time ; small windows. [$] *Rooms from: 600DH* ✉ *6 km (4 miles) from Agdz on route to Zagora* ☎ *0524/84–33–94* 🌐 *www.lavalleedu-draa.com* 💳 *No credit cards* 🛏 *9 rooms* 🍴 *Some meals.*

$$ B&B/INN **Dar Amazir.** Enter this warm and intimate guesthouse through two Berber doors that lead into a courtyard with a swimming pool and the sound of birdsong. **Pros:** lovely pool; good food; good Wi-Fi. [$] *Rooms from: 620DH* ✉ *Aslim* ✥ *After taxi rank in town in main square, take first left and follow that road down* ☎ *0665/46–63–39* 🌐 *www.daramazir.com* 🛏 *8 rooms* 🍴 *Breakfast* 💳 *No credit cards.*

$$$$ B&B/INN FAMILY Fodor's Choice ★ **Kasbah Azul.** The aptly named "House of Peace" is tucked away in the palm groves outside Agdz. **Pros:** arty vibe; great for kids. **Cons:** books up quickly. [$] *Rooms from: 1155DH* ✉ *2½ km (1½ miles) north of Agdz, Douar Asslim* ☎ *0524/84–39–31* 🌐 *www.kasbahazul.com* ⏲ *Closed during Ramadan (call ahead)* 🛏 *7 rooms* 🍴 *Breakfast.*

7

TINZOULINE

59 km (37 miles) southeast of Agdz, 130 km (81 miles) southeast of Ouarzazate.

Tinzouline holds an important weekly souk. If you're here on a Monday, take this opportunity to shop and make contact with the many peoples of this southern Moroccan region where Berber, Arab, Jewish, and Haratin communities have coexisted for centuries. The Tinzouline ksour are clustered around a majestic kasbah in the middle of an oasis that includes several villages. Tinzouline is also one of the most important prehistoric sites in pre-Saharan North Africa: from the ksour a 7-km (4½-mile) gravel path leads west of town to cave engravings depicting mounted hunters. These drawings are attributed to Iron Age Libyo-Berbers, lending further substance to the theory that Morocco's first inhabitants, the Berbers, may have originally come from Central Asia via central and eastern Africa.

ZAGORA

95 km (59 miles) southeast of Agdz, 170 km (106 miles) southeast of Ouarzazate.

Zagora is—and does feel like—the boundary between the Sahara and what some writers and travelers have referred to as "reality." After Zagora, time and distance are measured in camel days: a famous painted sign at the end of town (near the impressive new Zagora Province offices) features a camel and reads, "Tombouctu 52 Days"—that is, "52 days by camel." M'hamid, 97 km (60 miles) farther south, marks the actual end of the paved road and the beginning of the open desert, but Zagora is where the sensation of being in the desert kicks in.

On your way out of town, heading across the bridge signposted toward M'hamid, you'll find the town of Amezrou, and in it, the fascinating **Kasbah des Juifs** (Kasbah of the Jews).

GETTING HERE AND AROUND

Zagora is easily reached by the main road from M'hamid and Ouarzazate. Buses and grands taxis navigate this route. The town's CTM bus station is on the main street. Zagora itself is easy to explore on foot or by inexpensive petit taxi. Numerous local tour agencies offer camel trips, oasis treks, and desert camping.

Bus Contacts CTM Zagora. ⊠ *37, bd. Mohammed V* ☎ *0524/84–73–27* ⊕ *www.ctm.ma.*

GUIDES AND TOURS

Fodor'sChoice
★

Caravane du Sud. This family-run agency specializes in the desert regions and villages around Zagora. Local guides with an eco-tourism ethos lead 4x4 and camel tours. You can get the best out of a tour by discussing it beforehand in some detail and letting them know what you really want to do. Service is excellent. ⊠ *Zagora* ☎ *0524/84–75–69, 0661/87–68–74* ⊕ *www.caravanesud.com.*

Tombouctour. Long-established Tombouctour organizes tours throughout Morocco; the local office in Zagora will set up overnight excursions or desert safaris for travelers turning up at its door. ⊠ *79, av. Mohammed V* ☎ *0524/84–82–07* ⊕ *www.tombouctour.com.*

EXPLORING

Amezrou. Three km (2 miles) south of Zagora, Amezrou is famous for its Jewish silversmiths, who made decorative jewelry in this small village until the creation of the Israeli State in 1948, when all but 30,000 of Morocco's 300,000 Jews left for Israel. Berber craftsmen continue the tradition in the Mellah here. It's a worthwhile stop if you don't mind the clamor of children eager to be hired as your guide. You may also be able to find some interesting Jewish antiques if you ask. ⊠ *Zagora.*

Djebel Zagora. The town's promontory, capped by an 11th-century Almoravid fortress, is an excellent sunset vantage point—it overlooks the Drâa palmery with the distant Djebel Sarhro Massif to the north and the Tinfou Dunes to the south. Djebel Zagora is reached via the first left turn south of the Kasbah Asmaa hotel; there's also a twisting footpath up the 3,195-foot mountain from the hotel itself. ⊠ *Zagora.*

Ksar Tissergate Museum. Deep within the evocative alleys of the Ksar Tissergate—a 17th-century fortified village—this fascinating museum displays local costumes, agricultural implements, domestic utensils, jewelry, and other artifacts. Unlike most museums in southern Morocco, exhibits here have explanations in English. You access it through the Kasbah Ziwana and they can supply you with a guide for a small tip. ⊠ *Next to Kasbah Ziwana, 8 km (5 miles) from Zagora on road to Ouarzazate, Tissergate* ☎ *0667/69–06–02* ⊕ *kasbah-ziwana-zagora.com* 🎫 *20 DH.*

The magnificent dunes at Erg Chebbi are just outside of Merzouga.

WHERE TO EAT AND STAY

$ MOROCCAN 🍴 **Le Dromadaire Gourmand.** Having hung up his *sheshe* (turban) after years of guiding tourists through the desert, Mustapha el Mekki has established one of the most popular eateries in Zagora. It serves regional specialties such as tagine *de mariage* (a slow-cooked casserole of beef with apricots, prunes, and almonds) and a Drâa Valley vegetable soup. **Known for:** classic tagines and other Moroccan dishes; BYOB policy; lovely sidewalk terrace. [$] *Average main: 70DH* ✉ *Av. Mohammed V, near TOTAL gas station* ☎ *0661/34–83–94* 🌐 *www.dromadaire-gourmand.com* 💳 *No credit cards.*

$$$$ B&B/INN Fodor's Choice ★ 🏨 **Azalai Desert Lodge.** Hidden within the Drâa Valley oasis, the Azalai Desert Lodge is a luxurious retreat with secluded gardens, creative cuisine, and an interior that has been featured in several prestigious design magazines. **Pros:** luxury at the edge of the desert; beautiful decor. **Cons:** remote location. [$] *Rooms from: 1450DH* ✉ *7 km (4 miles) north of Zagora, Tissergate* 🌐 *www.azalaidesertlodge.com* 💳 *No credit cards* 🕓 *Closed July and Aug.* 🛏 *8 rooms* 🍽 *Some meals.*

$$$ HOTEL 🏨 **Casa Juan.** A delightful and original hotel set in the small village of Ait Isoul, Casa Juan offers the best of both worlds here: the palmery and the desert, splendid in their green and gold. **Pros:** between the desert and the palmery; original rooms full of interesting things. **Cons:** off the beaten track. [$] *Rooms from: 900DH* ✉ *Aït Isfoul, Tagounite* ✣ *70 km (43 miles) from Zagora on N9* ☎ *0661/ 74–37–10* 🌐 *www.casajuansahara.com* 🛏 *6 rooms, tents available* 🍽 *Breakfast* 💳 *No credit cards.*

$$ B&B/INN FAMILY 🏨 **Kasbah Sirocco.** A popular pit stop on the way to the desert, Kasbah Sirocco has clean, functional rooms; all have air-conditioning, and most have views of the relaxed pool terrace. **Pros:** great pool; full range of

services. **Cons:** can be noisy. [$] *Rooms from: 660DH* ✉ *2 km (1 mile) southeast of Zagora on road to M'hamid, Amezrou* ☎ *0524/84–61–25* 🌐 *www.kasbah-sirocco.com* 🛏 *20 rooms* 🍴 *Breakfast.*

$$ B&B/INN 🏨 **Kasbah Ziwana.** If you're fed up with faux kasbahs, then here's the real deal. **Pros:** comfortable rooms in a genuine kasbah; next door to the museum. **Cons:** lack of natural light; few amenities. [$] *Rooms from: 660DH* ✉ *Ksar Tissergate, 8 km (5 miles) from Zagora on road to Ouarzazate, Tissergate* ☎ *0667/69–06–02* 🌐 *www.kasbah-ziwana-zagora.com* 💳 *No credit cards* 🛏 *13 rooms* 🍴 *Some meals.*

$$$ B&B/INN 🏨 **Riad Dar Sofian.** Originally built as a family home, this rambling three-story riad is full of over-the-top Moroccan decor, with stucco plasterwork, colorful mosaic tiling, ornate ceilings, and antique furnishings competing for attention. **Pros:** lots of creature comforts; Wi-Fi; lovely pool. **Cons:** mismatched decor; no elevator. [$] *Rooms from: 900DH* ✉ *Amezrou* ☎ *0524/84–73–19* 🌐 *www.riaddarsofian.com* 🛏 *10 rooms* 🍴 *Breakfast.*

M'HAMID

68 km (42 miles) south of Tinfou, 97 km (60 miles) south of Zagora, 260 km (161 miles) southeast of Ouarzazate, 395 km (245 miles) southwest of Rissani.

Properly known as M'hamid el-Ghizlane, or Plain of the Gazelles, M'hamid neatly marks the end of Morocco's Great Oasis Valleys and the end of the asphalt road. It was once an outpost for the camel corps of the French Foreign Legion, and a large military barracks reminds visitors that the Algerian border is not far away. Looking at modern M'hamid—a one-street village with overeager tour companies hustling for business—you may wonder what's worth defending, but consider the obvious upside. The Sahara awaits at the end of the main street, making this a vital departure point for desert forays, most notably to Morocco's highest dunes at Erg Chigaga, 50 km (31 miles) west.

In the palm groves just before M'hamid, the outlying villages of Ouled Driss and Bounou have interesting kasbahs that can be visited. A short hop across the dried riverbed of the Drâa, next to M'hamid's mosque, takes you toward the site of the original village, some 2 km (1 mile) away, where a 17th-century Jewish-built kasbah is still inhabited by the local Haratin population.

The sand drifting like snow across the road (despite the placement of palm-frond sand breaks and fences), the immensity of the horizon, plus the patient gait of camels combine to produce a palpable change in the sense of time and space at this final Drâa oasis. The ocean of dunes 7 km (4½ miles) beyond M'hamid will satisfy any craving for some real Saharan scenery.

GETTING HERE AND AROUND

Buses arrive here twice daily from Marrakesh via Zagora and Ouarzazate. Grands taxis and minibuses also make the journey to and from Zagora.

KSOUR AND KASBAHS

Ksour (plural for *ksar*) are fortified villages with houses, granaries, cemeteries (both Jewish and Muslim), hammams, and shops. Kasbahs are fortified castles belonging to a single family and often contain their own granaries, wells, and places for prayer. Moroccan ksour and kasbahs are all built of *pisé*, a sun-dried mixture of mud and clay. The Erfoud–Ouarzazate road through the Dadès Valley is billed as the "Route of the Thousand Kasbahs," with village after village of fortified pisé structures, many decorated with carved and painted geometrical patterns (the more intricate the motif, the wealthier the owner). The kasbahs served the caravan trains that passed along this trans-Saharan trade route. Camel trains loaded with salt or gold were targets for bandits so staying in a fortified village made sense. The merchants preempted what is now the tourist trade. The Drâa Valley is also rimmed with kasbahs and ksour for the length of the Agdz–Zagora road. Highlights of the Dadès route are the Kasbah Amerhidil, at the Skoura oasis, and the Aït Ben Haddou kasbahs, near Ouarzazate; showstoppers in the Drâa Valley include the 16th-century ksour at Tamnougalt, just south of Agdz, and the 17th-century Ksar Tissergate, just north of Zagora—both now feature interesting museums. Increasingly, these historic structures are being restored and converted into guesthouses. Staying in one that achieves the perfect balance is an unforgettable experience.

GUIDES AND TOURS

Arriving in M'hamid without having already reserved accommodation or excursions can be intimidating due to fiercely competing touts. That said, there are several local agencies to choose from if you want to trek or take a 4x4 expedition deeper into the dunes and surrounding desert.

Caravan of Dreams. Run by Ali Laghfiri, who grew up in the village of M'hamid, this German-Moroccan outfit offers camel treks and 4x4 excursions to a picturesque camp in the Erg Lehoudi dunes. Cooking and drumming lessons at the camp can also be arranged. ⊠ *Village center, Mhamid* ☎ *0670/02–00–33* ⊕ *www.caravane-de-reve.com.*

FAMILY **Sahara Services.** This full-service travel agency offers camel treks to the nearby dunes of Erg Lehoudi and 4x4 trips to a luxury bivouac in Erg Chigaga from its office in M'hamid. The agency also specializes in family-friendly trips. ⊠ *Village Center, Mhamid* ☎ *0661/77–67–66* ⊕ *www.saharaservices.info.*

Zbar Travel. The local office of Zbar Travel serves as a launchpad for sand-boarding adventures, camel treks, and 4x4 outings. The agency also has a very comfortable bivouac camp in the dunes of Erg Chigaga. ⊠ *Main St., next to Hotel El Ghizlane, on right as you enter village, Mhamid* ☎ *0668/51–72–80* ⊕ *www.zbartravel.com.*

TIMING AND PRECAUTIONS

M'hamid has a Monday souk that's famous for the occasional appearance of nomadic, trans-Saharan traders of the Reguibat tribe. Much chronicled by writer Paul Bowles, these ebony-skinned fellows habitually wear the indigo sheish, a linen cloth wrapped around the head and face for protection from the elements. The dye from the fabric runs, tingeing the men's faces blue and leading to their nickname, the "Blue Men." Don't expect too much in the way of merchandise, though; the souk has lost much of its appeal in recent years. Noteworthy annual events include the International Nomads Festival, staged in mid-March to promote understanding of the nomadic traditions of the Moroccan Sahara; and a world music festival called Taragalte, which takes place in the nearby dunes in November. ■TIP→ **Many hotels and desert camps close during July and August due to the unbearable heat.**

EXPLORING

Fodor'sChoice
★

Erg Chigaga. The splendid Erg Chigaga dunes are the principal reason why visitors make the trek south to M'hamid. Wild, remote, and largely unspoiled, they're only accessible by heading west out of the village on 50 km (31 miles) of dusty and stony pistes. The journey takes three hours in a 4x4 vehicle or three days on a camel, though hurried jet-setters bound for Erg Chigaga's luxury bivouac camps sometimes come by helicopter direct from Marrakesh. Morocco's highest dunes, rising almost 1,000 feet, are approached by crossing smaller dunes, *hammada* (rocky Martian-like terrain), and flat expanses, which are sometimes flooded in winter. A few nomadic families still live in the region, herding their camels and goats through the pasture, which can be surprisingly lush. ⊠ *50 km (31 miles) west of M'hamid, Mhamid.*

Ksebt el-Allouj. The ruins of the ksar Ksebt el-Allouj, dating from the Saadian dynasty, lie across the Drâa riverbed on the other side from the village from M'hamid, about 2 km (1 mile) from the town center. The ksar is uninhabited and is interesting to explore. ⊠ *Mhamid.*

WHERE TO STAY

$$$
HOTEL
FAMILY

Chez le Pacha. One of a string of kasbah-style hotels in palm groves as you approach M'hamid, Chez le Pacha is a well-run establishment that offers a lot at a reasonable price. **Pros:** stylish accommodations; helpful staff. **Cons:** the half-board plan is compulsory. $ *Rooms from: 800DH* ⊠ *Bounou, 5 km (3 miles) north of M'hamid, Ouled Driss, Mhamid* ☎ *0524/84–86–96* ⊕ *www.chezlepacha.com* ↙ *16 rooms, 10 huts* |○| *Some meals.*

$$$$
HOTEL

Kasbah Azalay. The only luxurious lodging actually in the village of M'hamid is this Spanish-owned kasbah hotel at the edge of the palmery. **Pros:** plenty of creature comforts; magnificent pool and spa. **Cons:** lack of communal terraces or salons for socializing; often empty. $ *Rooms from: 1100DH* ⊠ *M'hamid el Ghizlane, Mhamid* ☎ *0524/84–80–96* ⊕ *www.kasbahazalay.com* ↙ *43 rooms* |○| *Breakfast.*

$$
B&B/INN

Le Drom' Blanc. Hidden in the palm groves of Bounou, this guesthouse has simple en suite rooms set around a central patio, plus nomad-style tents and self-contained pisé bungalows in the garden. **Pros:** secluded location in palm groves; one wheelchair-accessible room. **Cons:** rooms are very dark; not much English spoken. $ *Rooms from: 580DH* ⊠ *Bounou, 5 km (3 miles) north of M'hamid, Ouled Driss, Mhamid* ☎ *0524/84–68–52* ⊕ *www.ledromblanc.com* ↙ *4 rooms, 6 tents, 3 bungalows* |○| *Breakfast.*

AGADIR AND THE SOUTHERN ATLANTIC COAST

with Essaouira and the Anti-Atlas

WELCOME TO AGADIR AND THE SOUTHERN ATLANTIC COAST

TOP REASONS TO GO

★ **Catch a wave:** The magnificent Atlantic coastline draws hundreds of surfers and other water-sports fanatics every year to ride its huge breaks and test their wits against the winds.

★ **Satisfying seafood:** Whether you are haggling down by Essaouira port for your own fish or enjoying the day's catch at an upscale restaurant in Agadir's marina, both cities are a seafood-lover's paradise.

★ **Family fun:** Donkey and camel rides, swimming pools, and ice-cream stalls make Agadir heaven for children, while stylish resort hotels serve up every luxury Mom and Dad could possibly want.

★ **Walking in the Anti-Atlas:** Enjoy the spectacular scenery around Tafraoute and the pretty villages of the Ammeln Valley, without another tourist in sight.

★ **Taroudant:** Explore the authentically Moroccan walled city with its strong crafts tradition, fascinating souks, and some lovely boutique hotels.

Morocco's southern coastal towns might be just a few hours from bustling Marrakesh, but their laid-back vibe makes you feel you're a world away. Moroccans and Europeans flock to this region in summer for the sea breeze, the sandy beaches, the luxurious resorts, or the numerous festivals that ensure that there's always music in the air. This is also argan country: otherwise known as "Morocco gold," this tree's oil is changing the economic prospects of local women and the beauty regimes of women across the world.

1 Agadir. Agadir is essentially a large, regional trading city fronted by Morocco's premier beach resort. Long popular with European sun worshippers and tourists, visitors spend most of their time on the sweeping sandy beach at the south end where there are a number of all-inclusive and five-star resort hotels. You can find some less crowded local beaches to the north and south; the Souss Massa National Park is also nearby.

2 Essaouira. Essaouira is quieter and more emblematically Moroccan than Agadir, though it's becoming more popular, with bus tours coming for the day from Marrakesh or Agadir. The beach stretches for miles in a curving bay with an almost constant breeze great for water sports, but most visitors are attracted by the car-free medina and the busy port with its fresh-fish restaurants.

3 The Souss Valley and Anti-Atlas. The region around the Anti-Atlas Mountains, comprising Taroudant, Tafraoute, and Tiznit, is relatively undiscovered by tourists, attracting nature lovers, walkers, and climbers instead. It's easily reached from family-friendly Agadir, providing a completely different kind of travel experience.

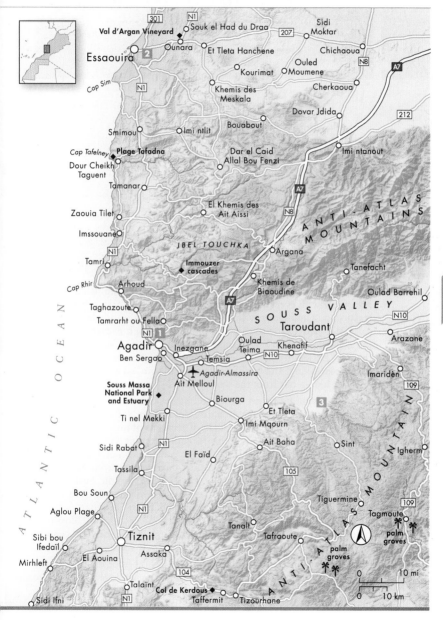

301 N1
Val d'Argan Vineyard ♦ Souk el Had du Draa
Sidi
Moktar
207
Ounara Et Tleta Hanchene
Chichaoua
Essaouira 2
N8
A7
Kourimat Ouled
Moumene
Cap Sim N1
Khemis des
Meskala
Cherkaoua
212
Dovar Jdida
Smimou Imi ntlit
Bouabout
Cap Tafelney
Plage Tafadna
Dar el Caid
Allal Bou Fenzi
Imi ntanout
Dour Cheikh
Taguent
Tamanar
El Khemis des
Ait Aissi
ANTI-ATLAS
MOUNTAINS
Zaouia Tilet
N8
Imssouane
JBEL TOUCHKA
A7
Tamri N1
Immouzer
cascades
Argana
Tanefacht
Cap Rhir
Arhoud
Khemis de
Biaoudine
Oulad Barrehil
A7
SOUSS VALLEY
N10
Taghazoute
Tamrarht ou Fella
Taroudant
Arazane
Agadir N1 1
Oulad
Teima
Khenafif
Ben Sergao Inezgane
N10
Temsia
Imariden
Agadir-Almassira
109
Souss Massa
National Park
and Estuary
Ait Melloul
Biourga
3
Et Tleta
Ti nel Mekki
Imi Mqourn
Sidi Rabat N1
Ait Baha
Sint
Igherm
El Faïd
105
Tassila
Bou Soun
Tiguermine
109
Aglou Plage N1
Tagmoute
palm
groves
Tanalt
Sibi bou
Ifedaïl
Tiznit
Tafraoute
palm
groves
Mirhleft El Aouina
Assaka
104
Sidi Ifni Talaïnt
N1
Col de Kerdous ♦
Taffermit Tizourhane

0   10 mi
0   10 km

8

ATLANTIC OCEAN

Updated by
Jane Folliott

While they're both on the coast and have beaches that people rave about, Essaouira and Agadir couldn't be more different. A hippie hangout whose secret travelers refused to reveal for years, Essaouira is only now coming into the limelight as a mainstream destination, but it nevertheless retains its slightly "other" ambience. Windy beaches attract watersports enthusiasts rather than sunseekers, and riad-hotels cater to independent travelers.

Agadir, on the other hand, was made for mass tourism. It's a modern resort city with every kind of singing, dancing, and casino-betting distraction on hand along with long stretches of hot, sandy beaches, and calm seas perfect for sunbathing families. Both, however, have lively ports worth seeing in action and superb fresh fish and seafood. Between the two are less frequented spots good for surfing, windsurfing, kitesurfing, kayaking, and bodyboarding, or, for the less active, sunbathing and just hiding out from the world a little.

For those wanting to get closer to nature, head inland southeast of Agadir, and you'll find fruit orchards, argan trees, saffron crocus fields, pretty painted villages, and kasbahs. The plains of the Souss Valley and the jagged Anti-Atlas Mountains provide stunning vistas with plenty of scope for adventure. The picturesque walled town of Taroudant has historic sights and markets that attract day-trippers from Agadir, but it is also a great base for exploring and trekking into the Anti-Atlas or western High Atlas mountains. A very worthwhile circuit from Taroudant will include the towns of Tafraoute and Tiznit. Tafraoute is famed for its scenic backdrop of towering granite boulders, almond blossoms, blue-painted rocks, and nearby rock carvings, while the 19th-century walled town of Tiznit is famed for its silversmiths and jewelry souk.

Whether your interests involve holing up in luxury or diving into the surf, this coastal area offers a great deal. For nature lovers and culture vultures there are ancient medinas, kasbahs, pretty villages, and wilderness all within easy reach.

PLANNING

WHEN TO GO

Unlike inland destinations that get too hot in summer, high season for the coast is July and August, with peaks at Christmas, New Year's Day, and June. The best months for visiting may be September and October, when it's off-season but still warm. Summer tends to be busy with vacationing Moroccan families; spring in Agadir is the main season for vacationers and families from abroad. Surfers and water-sports fans come year-round, although winter and early spring are by far the best times for surf.

In the Souss Valley, spring is the most spectacular time to visit, when almond trees and wildflowers are in bloom, the harvest is near, and the weather is sunny but not too hot. Fall temperatures are moderate, but landscapes are a bit drabber after the summer harvest. As long as rains don't wash out the roads, winter is pleasant as well—it is particularly popular for climbers in the mountains. Coastal areas are mild, although inland temperatures can be cold and heated rooms hard to find. If you must come in summer, stick to the coast: even an hour inland, in Taroudant, the July and August heat is unbearable in all but the nighttime hours.

PLANNING YOUR TIME

Most visitors to the region fly into Agadir or reach Essaouira from Marrakesh, but there are now a few direct flights to Essaouira from Europe. Both cities easily warrant more than just a day trip, so it's worth booking at least a couple of nights in a local riad. You can decide to stick to just one city, but many people decide to hit up both while in the area. From Agadir, the Anti-Atlas region is easily accessible in day excursions or with an overnight stay in Tafraoute or Taroudant. These trips can be arranged with a rental car or through one of the many local travel agencies. The area further south of Agadir, where the desert meets the ocean, is beautiful, and has a fascinating and turbulent history of occupation and independence, but requires a longer trip as distances are great and public transport very limited. If you are fortunate to be traveling to any of the region's towns during a festival, book accommodations well in advance.

GETTING HERE AND AROUND

AIR TRAVEL

The key international air hub in the region is Agadir, although visitors based in Essaouira may fly in to Marrakesh or Essaouira itself. Agadir's Al Massira Airport is 35 km (21 miles) east of town. *Grands taxis* (large shared taxis for up to six passengers) to downtown Agadir are a fixed price of 200 DH, but many drivers expect you to haggle. There is also a shuttle bus (4 DH) every 30 minutes from the airport to nearby Inezgane (13 km [8 miles] southeast of Agadir), where several bus services and grands taxis provide connections to other southern destinations as well as to the main bus station in Agadir. Otherwise, your hotel will usually be happy to arrange your airport transfer.

8

Essaouira's Mogador Airport has several flights a week direct from the United Kingdom and some European cities. The airport is 16 km (10 miles) south of the town. There are no regular buses or shuttles from the airport, but grands taxis to Essaouira cost 150 DH, and your hotel can usually arrange transfers.

BUS TRAVEL

There is frequent bus service offered by both CTM and Supratours connecting to Essaouira, Marrakesh, and Casablanca, as well as grands taxis that travel between cities.

CAR TRAVEL

A freeway now connects Marrakesh and Agadir and has cut travel times considerably; the journey takes approximately three hours. Explorations of the area around Taroudant and Tafraoute can be done as side trips from Agadir. If you don't want to drive yourself, one of the most enjoyable ways to cover this broad area is to organize a tour through one of several agencies based in Agadir. You can rent a car in either Agadir or Essaouira if you want to explore the region at your own pace.

SAFETY

Essaouira and Agadir are quite safe, with almost no violent crime. Lone female travelers will feel more comfortable in these towns than in some other parts of Morocco. Travelers should keep an eye on their personal belongings, however, as pickpockets are common, especially during festival time when the streets are jam-packed.

RESTAURANTS

All along the coast you can get great grilled or battered fresh fish and seafood that's inexpensive and tasty at any time of day. For a better fish experience, go to a restaurant and try fish tagine or skewered and marinated fish brochettes. International cuisine is also readily available in both Agadir and Essaouira. *Dining reviews have been shortened. For full information, visit Fodors.com.*

HOTELS

You'll find a full range of options, from small budget hotels to Agadir's five-star behemoths. In Essaouira, many old traditional family homes, or *riads,* have been restored and converted to beautiful guesthouses. In summer it's best to reserve rooms in advance, and for the more upscale boutiques, you may have to book several months in advance whatever the time of year. There's also an increasing number of rental apartments in Essaouira and "apartment hotels" in Agadir; both offer self-catering options.

The Souss has some choice small hotels ranging from simple *auberges* (inns) and restored riads to former palaces and country retreats. *Hotel reviews have been shortened. For full information, visit Fodors.com*

WHAT IT COSTS IN DIRHAMS				
	$	$$	$$$	$$$$
Restaurants	under 70 DH	70 DH–90 DH	91 DH–110 DH	over 110 DH
Hotels	under 450 DH	450 DH–700 DH	701 DH–1,000 DH	over 1,000 DH

Restaurant prices are the average cost of a main course at dinner or, if dinner is not served, at lunch. Hotel prices are the lowest cost of a standard double room in high season.

FESTIVALS

Agadir and Essaouira are music hot spots, so it is no surprise that both cities host popular music festivals. Held in July, Agadir's Festival Timitar celebrates native Berber music, while Essaouira's world-famous Gnaoua and World Music Festival, held each June, hosts international musicians as well as native ones. Various towns around the Anti-Atlas have developed festivals to celebrate aspects of local culture, including in Taroudant (focusing on traditional music every June); Tafraoute (celebrating the almond blossom in February and local music and culture in August); and Tiznit (honoring the traditional silversmiths in August).

AGADIR

8

270 km (168 miles) southwest of Marrakesh, 460 km (285 miles) south of Casablanca.

Agadir is, above all else, a holiday resort, so don't hope for a medina, a souk, or a kasbah (although it does have all three, after a fashion). Think sun, sea, and sand. These are what it does best, as hundreds of thousands of visitors each year can testify.

There's no reason to begrudge the city its tourist aspirations. Razed by an earthquake in 1960 that killed 15,000 people in 13 seconds, Agadir had to be entirely rebuilt. Today it's a thoroughly modern city where travelers don't think twice about showing considerable skin, and Moroccans benefit from the growing number of jobs.

There's a reason why this popular European package vacation destination is overrun with enormous, characterless beachfront hotels. The beach, all 10 km (6 miles) of it, is dreamy. A 450-yard-wide strip, it bends in an elegant crescent along the bay, and is covered with fine-grain sand. The beach is sheltered and safe for swimming, making it perfect for families. Farther north, where small villages stand behind some of the best waves in the world, is a surfers' paradise.

Even if you have no interest in surfing, jet-skiing, golf, tennis, or horseback riding down the beach, you can treat Agadir as a modern bubble in which to kick back. It's equipped with familiar pleasurable pursuits—eating, drinking, and relaxing next to the ocean—and modern amenities such as car-rental agencies and ATMs. It isn't quite Europe, but neither is it quite Morocco.

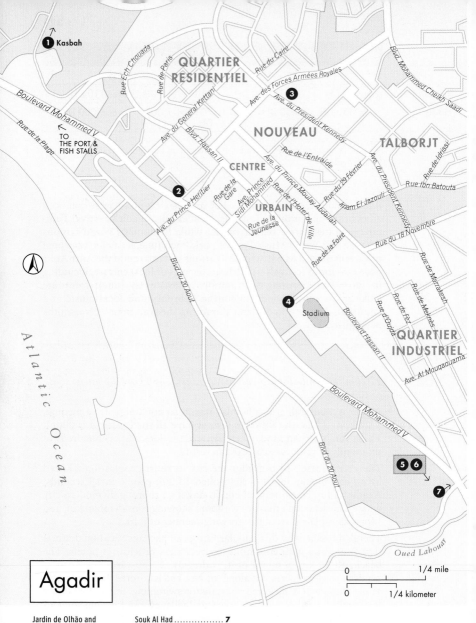

Agadir

GETTING HERE AND AROUND

Most travelers fly directly into Agadir's Al Massira airport. Although there are no direct flights from North America, connections from Casablanca and European airports are easy. Inexpensive buses are easy ways to get here from Essaouira, Marrakesh, and beyond. If all else fails, grands taxis can take you just about anywhere for the right price.

Once in Agadir, you'll find that downtown is easily navigable on foot, although you may prefer to taxi in from your hotel. The city's orange petits taxis are easy to flag down. Agadir also has many car-rental agencies, including Hertz and Avis.

Bus Contacts CTM. ⊠ *Gare Routiere Municipale, Bd. Al Akkad* ☎ *0528/82–53–41* ⊕ *www.ctm.ma.* **Supratours.** ⊠ *Gare Routiere Municipale, Bd. Al Akkad* ☎ *0528/22–40–10* ⊕ *www.supratours.ma.*

Rental Car Contacts Avis. ⊠ *Bungalow Hotel Marhaba, Av. Mohammed V* ☎ *0528/82–14–14 downtown, 0528/83–92–44 airport* ⊕ *www.avis.com.* **Dan Car.** ⊠ *Av. Mohammed V* ☎ *0528/84–46–00.* **Europcar.** ⊠ *Av. Mohammed V* ☎ *0528/84–02–03 downtown, 0528/83–90–66 airport* ⊕ *www.europcar.com.* **Exotik Cars.** ⊠ *5, av. Général Kettani,* ✛ *Next to Hotel Aferni* ☎ *0528/84–11–42* ⊕ *www.exotikcars.net.* **Hertz.** ⊠ *Bungalow Marhaba, Av. Mohammed V* ☎ *0528/84–09–39 downtown, 0528/83–90–71 airport* ⊕ *www.hertz.com.*

GUIDES AND TOURS

Complete Tours. This English-run operation based in Agadir with offices in Marrakesh and Casablanca can put together your whole trip, including hotels, excursions, and meals—everything, in fact, but the flight. ⊠ *Immeuble Oumlil, 26, bd. Hassan II* ☎ *0528/82–34–01* ⊕ *www. complete-tours.com.*

Massira Travel. This agency offers a range of trips with an English-speaking guide all over Morocco, including to Essaouira, Marrakesh, Imouzzer, Tafraoute, Tiznit, and farther afield. ⊠ *25, bd. du 20 Août* ☎ *0528/84–77–13.*

VISITOR INFORMATION

You can pick up a copy of the bilingual French–English *Agadir Tour Guide* magazine or the French-only *Agadir Premiere Le Mag* in many shops and restaurants. Both offer a better idea of what's on than a trip to the local tourism delegation.

EXPLORING

For those looking for a more comprehensive tour of town, a ridiculous yet amusing way to see the town is with the Petit Train, a small white tram with three carriages pulled by a motorcar at the front. It leaves every 40 minutes (9:15 am until 6 pm) from the kiosk at the base of Vallée des Oiseaux on Boulevard 20 Août. It's as touristy as a Hawaiian shirt, but kids love it and it's a great way to get off your feet. Tickets cost 18 DH, and the ride lasts 35 minutes.

FAMILY **Jardin de Olhão and Musée de la Mémoire.** Located in the heart of the city, this garden (also called Jardin du Portugal) offers a pleasant, cool green retreat from the heat of the sun. Built in tribute to Agadir's "twin" city in Portugal, Olhão, it features architecture that recalls that of the Moors of southern Spain. Two pavilions attached to the garden house the Musée de la Mémoire, a moving exhibition of photos and writings documenting the earthquake of February 29,1960, which devastated the city. ⊠ *Av. President Kennedy, Talborjt* ⊠ *Museum 10 DH, playground 5 DH.*

FAMILY **Kasbah (Agadir Oufella).** High up on the hill to the northwest that looks over Agadir is the old kasbah. This was the main site of Agadir until an earthquake razed the city in 1960, creating the opportunity for the development of modern Agadir, which stands today to the south. There is nothing to see of the former city, but the breathtaking views, especially at sunset, make the trip worthwhile. There is no public transport and the road is steep, so arrange your trip up and down before beginning the ascent.

Emblazoned on the side of the hill below the kasbah are three Arabic words that keep guard over Agadir at all times. Their meaning? God, country, and the king. By day they're a patchwork of huge white stones against the green grass. By night they're lighted up powerfully against the dark. The huge hill is really a burial mound, covering the old medina and the impromptu graves of those who died in the earthquake. ⊠ *Agadir.*

FAMILY **La Medina d'Agadir.** This combination ethnological museum and bazaar is the dream of Moroccan-born Italian decorator-architect Coco Polizzi, who wanted to replace the medina Agadir lost to the 1960 earthquake with a new one on his own land. Located in Ben Sergao, a few miles south of Agadir, on the Inezgane road, the remarkable 13-acre project was completed in 2007 by hundreds of Moroccan craftsmen following centuries-old techniques. Each stone is laid by hand, and the buildings are made of earth, rock from the Souss, slate from the High Atlas, and local woods such as thuya and eucalyptus. Decorations follow both Berber and Saharan motifs. You can find a few mosaic craftsmen, painters, jewelers, metalworkers, and carpenters in workshop nooks throughout the medina. The medina also houses a restaurant, shops, and even an amphitheater. ⊠ *La Medina d'Agadir, Bensergao* ☎ *0528/28–02–53* ⊠ *40 DH* ☉ *Closed during Eid el Adha* ☞ *Grands taxis from Agadir cost around 100 DH round-trip.*

Fodor's Choice **Musée Municipale du Patrimoine Amazighe.** Agadir's municipal museum
★ celebrates the Berber Amazigh heritage of the region with collections of photography, jewelry, artifacts, and local handicrafts, as well as temporary exhibits. It's worth a visit to learn about the symbolism seen in Berber carpet and jewelry, and about the *Igouder* (plural of *agadir*, a communal granary) of the local villages. If you're lucky, there may be an English-speaking intern on hand to guide you around. ⊠ *Passage Ait Souss, Av. Hassan II* ☎ *0528/82–16–32* ⊠ *10 DH* ☉ *Closed Sun.*

FAMILY **Souk Al Had.** In the northeastern corner of the city is a daily bazaar selling souvenirs, household goods, and the produce of the fertile Souss plains. You'll need to bargain hard. ⊠ *Av. Abderrahim Bouabid* ☉ *Closed Mon.*

Agadir is Morocco's top resort destination, with more all-inclusive beach resorts than any other place in the country.

Souss Massa National Park. The Souss Massa National Park lies around 60 km (37 miles) south of Agadir and is a breeding ground for a number of indigenous and migratory bird species, including the bald ibis. There are also captive-breeding programs for four threatened North African antelope and gazelle species, as well as for ostriches, which were previously extinct in Morocco since 1945.

Tours are available within the park, which also contains a number of guesthouses and other accommodation options. Many of these support sustainable tourism and offer bird- and animal-watching excursions. ⊠ *Parc National de Souss Massa* ☎ *0528/33–38–80.*

FAMILY **Vallée des Oiseaux** (*Valley of the Birds*). It's not so much a valley as a pleasure garden connecting Avenue Hassan II to the beach. It not only has birds, but also monkeys, fountains, and lovely green surroundings. Very popular with Moroccan families and young couples as well as tourists, it makes for a pleasant stroll between downtown and the beachfront. ⊠ *Bd. du 20 Août.*

BEACHES

AGADIR

FAMILY **Agadir Beach.** The beach here swings around a crescent from southeast to northwest. You're more likely to find a quiet spot if you wander south, although be careful to avoid the private beaches of the resorts. The most crowded areas, frequented year-round by families and locals, are to the north. Along the flanking thoroughfare, known as the Corniche (promenade), you'll find cafés, bars, and restaurants. At the very northern end is the swanky marina development where private yachts are moored. The promenade comes alive at dusk, when families and youngsters take their evening walks, but as night falls, it can become a little sketchy. Nonetheless, from the shelter of a café terrace, it's still a good spot to stop and watch the world go by. The northern tip is also the place to rent a Jet Ski, catamaran, or surf equipment. **Amenities:** food and drink; water sports. **Best for:** sunset. ⊠ *Agadir.*

NORTH OF AGADIR

Taghazout. This is the area to visit if you want to tackle some of Morocco's best surfing. You probably won't be alone, either. In summer the beaches north of Agadir on the Essaouira road—especially those in the rapidly expanding Taghazout area—are crammed with Moroccan families (who often camp there). Catering to their needs is a range of cafés, hostels, and rental apartments. While Taghazout village still feels like a rough-and-ready surfers' frontier town, the area just south, called Taghazout Bay, is being developed with luxury and family resorts in the hopes of attracting a more upmarket clientele. **Amenities:** food and drink; water sports. **Best for:** surfing; swimming; sunset. ⊠ *Taghazoute.*

CAP RHIR

Cap Rhir. During most of the year, a few stray Western surfers seek out waves around the bend from the lighthouse at Cap Rhir. There are no facilities, so it's ideal for those seeking a quiet sunset. You may come across a bald ibis in the area north of the lighthouse, which is said to be one of their nesting sites. **Amenities:** none. **Best for:** solitude; sunset. ⊠ *Cap Rhir.*

OFF THE BEATEN PATH

Imouzzer Cascades. If you are looking for a more isolated and less developed excursion away from the beach, from Aourir (12 km [7 miles] north of Agadir), take the paved road 50 km (31 miles) up into the Ida Outanane Mountains to the waterfalls here, near Immouzer des Ida Outanane. Check with locals—the waterfalls are often dry when the region is experiencing drought. On your way you'll pass through the palm gorge of Paradise Valley, where the rocky riverbank welcomes picnicking Moroccan families and foreigners alike. The Berber souk in Immouzer is on Thursday and is a great place to buy local honey. The many opportunities for walking and hiking make this an ideal day excursion from Agadir. ⊠ *Agadir.*

WHERE TO EAT

Neon signs throughout Agadir lure you in to sample not so much the delights of Moroccan cuisine as the woes of fast food and international menus. Nevertheless, many of these restaurants have good locations along the beachfront or in the town center.

Agadir is famous for its fish and seafood, as well as its lively deep-sea fishing port (Morocco's busiest) where you can eat lunch at the stalls. Each stall offers nearly identical food, including squid, prawns, sole, lobster, and whiting, and for nearly identical prices. So walk around and pick what you'd like; the better-organized stalls have chalkboards listing the catch of the day and the price. Frequented by locals and travelers alike, it's a great bet for cheap and fun eats and now shares space with Morocco's swankiest marina, which is also becoming a culinary hot spot.

All major hotels have both Moroccan and Continental restaurants, which has led to the sad demise of many well-established local restaurants, but there are many sophisticated new eateries springing up around the marina. Downtown there is a good selection of Italian, French, Thai, and even Japanese and Indian restaurants.

$$$$ SPANISH 🍴 **Les Blancs.** At the edge of Agadir's trendy Marina district, Les Blancs is a shiny, white, modernist retreat serving colorful Spanish paellas, including black squid ink rice, green rice with veggies, and red king prawns. In addition to the contemporary indoor dining room, an informal bar-cum-restaurant with boardwalk-style flooring and huge windows overlooks the bay, as does the outdoor terrace with woven seagrass umbrellas. **Known for:** Spanish-style tapas; sea view. [$] *Average main: 180DH* ✉ *Marina* ☎ *0528/82–83–68.*

$ CAFÉ 🍴 **Boulangerie Pâtisserie Tafarnout.** This popular bakery in the center of town serves a wide range of breads, cakes, and traditional Moroccan pastries for breakfast, lunch, or a light snack. Highlights include buttery croissants, indulgent cakes, savory panini and sandwiches, as well as good strong coffee. **Known for:** selection of artisan breads; indulgent pastries and cakes. [$] *Average main: 40 DH* ✉ *Av. Hassan II* ☎ *0528/84–44–50.*

$$ STEAKHOUSE 🍴 **Camel's.** Fantastic camel tagines remain the highlight of the largely international menu at this beachside restaurant, as the name suggests. Like its neighbors, it caters to all audiences with candlelit tables, flat-screen TVs, live music, and a wine list. **Known for:** camel tagine; paella; jambalaya chicken. [$] *Average main: 90DH* ✉ *Bd. Tawada (Rue de la Plage)* ☎ *0528/82–85–60.*

$$$ BARBECUE 🍴 **Chez Mimi la Brochette.** This popular seaside institution brings a little style to the strip at the northern end of the beach. Everything is grilled over a wood fire, and you can get great fish, including lobster and prawns. **Known for:** grilled brochettes; seafood, including lobster. [$] *Average main: 100DH* ✉ *Promenade Tawada (Rue de la Plage), Corniche d'Agadir* ☎ *0528/84–03–87* ⏲ *No dinner Fri. No lunch Sat.*

$$$ EUROPEAN 🍴 **L'Eden.** The French-style cuisine here draws mainly from what's fished fresh out of the sea each morning but changes regularly according to the chef's suggestion. The restaurant's panoramic views of the beach and the sea are an added plus, as is the great-value lunch menu. **Known for:** good value lunch menu; fresh seafood; beach views. [$] *Average main: 100DH* ✉ *6, Front de Mer* ☎ *0528/84–85–96.*

$$ BRITISH 🍴 **English Pub.** Just when you thought you couldn't get Yorkshire pudding in Morocco, you come across this street-side bar, café, and restaurant. You can also get a full English breakfast of sausage, bacon, eggs, and beans, and, of course, fish-and-chips. **Known for:** British food; televised football; karaoke. [$] *Average main: 80DH* ✉ *Bd. du 20 Août* ☎ *0528/84–73–90.*

$ FAST FOOD Fodor's Choice ★ 🍴 **Le 116.** This small but buzzy salad-and-crepe bar offers great-value healthy snacks and small meals, including DIY salads (in three sizes), quiches, and panini. It attracts local office workers, foreign residents, and tourists for its healthy food, excellent Italian espresso, and fresh juices and smoothies. **Known for:** make your own salads; lots of vegetarian options. [$] *Average main: 40DH* ✉ *116, av. des F.A.R.* ☎ *0528/82–03–12* 💳 *No credit cards* ⏲ *Closed Sun. and during Ramadan.*

8

$$$ MOROCCAN Fodor's Choice ★

🍴 **Le P'tit Dôme.** This chic eatery claims an impressive menu of Moroccan specialties and local seafood, with a large Moroccan and French wine list (Champagne included) to boot. Sit on the terrace or in the chic black-and-white dining room. **Known for:** good value fixed menus; quality Moroccan food. [$] *Average main: 100DH* ✉ *20, bd. Août* ☎ *0528/84–08–05.*

$$$$ MEDITERRANEAN Fodor's Choice ★

🍴 **Pure Passion.** The passion in the name of this sophisticated restaurant is for Mediterranean-style food made from fresh, local produce. This means lots of seafood and pasta dishes, but also steak and stunning desserts. **Known for:** seafood; desserts; attentive staff. [$] *Average main: 190DH* ✉ *Marina* ☎ *0528/84–01–20* 🌐 *www.purepassion.ma.*

$$$$ SEAFOOD

🍴 **La Scala.** La Scala has rapidly gained a reputation as one of Agadir's finest fish restaurants. Here you can enjoy excellent quality seafood including lobster and John Dory; there's also a tasty duck breast for those who prefer meat. **Known for:** seafood; good service. [$] *Average main: 200DH* ✉ *Rue de l'Oued Souss, Complexe Tamelt* ☎ *0528/84–67–73* 🌐 *www.lascala-agadir.com.*

$ PIZZA

🍴 **La Siciliana.** With a broad menu of pizzas, homemade pasta, and Italian desserts, this Moroccan-run Italian eatery is a favorite among locals amid the string of Italian restaurants that line Avenue Hassan II. They can also deliver, should you crave a quiet night in, but they don't serve alcohol. **Known for:** best pizza in town; homemade pasta. [$] *Average main: 70DH* ✉ *65–67, av. Hassan II, near Vallée des Oiseaux* ☎ *0528/82–09–73* ⏲ *Closed during Ramadan.*

WHERE TO STAY

Besides a couple of boutique guesthouses, you can forget riad-style intimacy in Agadir; your choices are mainly executive-style functionality or giant beachfront complexes that cater primarily to European package tours. As a general rule the luxury (and price) increases as you move southward down the beach, where five-star resort complexes are still being built.

The hotels along Boulevard du 20 Août leading onto Chemin des Dunes have so many amenities and restaurants that you'll feel no need to leave their beachside complexes. Indeed, more and more hotels are becoming all-inclusive. Be wary of these, however, as they don't guarantee fine dining and many local experts think they will lead to a slip in standards. If you just need a bed while passing through Agadir, there are less expensive, basic hotels in the center of town, north of the beach. There's also a lively trade in "*résidences,*" self-catering apartments that you can rent by the night. These even have communal hotel facilities such as swimming pools and are an affordable option for families.

$$$$ RESORT

🏨 **Atlantic Palace.** If you think you're entering a royal residence when approaching this place, you're not far from the truth; it's owned by a Moroccan royal cousin. **Pros:** relaxing spa and great facilities; beautiful pool; larger than average rooms. **Cons:** some rooms could do with an update; bar is expensive compared to downtown; service from staff not always up to five-star standards. [$] *Rooms from: 1500DH* ✉ *Rue Oued Souss, Secteur Touristique* ☎ *0528/82–41–46* 🌐 *www.atlanticpalace.com* 🛏 *329 rooms* 🍽 *Multiple meal plans.*

$$$$ RESORT FAMILY **ClubHotel Riu Tikida Dunas.** One of three Riu resorts on the beachfront, this one gives you value for your money as all-inclusive options go (drinks are also included). **Pros:** pretty pools; large gardens; beachfront location. **Cons:** very busy with package tour groups; minimum five-night stay; 40-minute walk from city center. [$] *Rooms from: 2500DH* ✉ *Chemin des Dunes* ☎ *0528/84–90–90* 🌐 *www.riu.com* 🛏 *406 rooms* 🍴 *All-inclusive.*

$$$$ B&B/INN Fodor's Choice ★ **Dar Maktoub.** Set on the edge of the Souss-Massa National Park, within easy reach of Agadir, Dar Maktoub is a gorgeous boutique hotel with a beautiful garden. **Pros:** stellar service in an intimate location; close to golf courses and nature reserve; large gardens and pool. **Cons:** a taxi or rented car required to reach Agadir; not wheelchair accessible; no other restaurants nearby. [$] *Rooms from: 1045DH* ✉ *Av. Moulay Ali Cherif, Inezgane* ☎ *0661/37–63–44* 🌐 *www.darmaktoub.com* 🛏 *10 rooms* 🍴 *Some meals.*

$$ HOTEL **Hotel Aferni.** This reasonably priced hotel in the town center has clean and modern rooms with large bathrooms and occasional balconies. **Pros:** central location near restaurants; swimming pool; rooms clean with large bathrooms. **Cons:** Wi-Fi can be intermittent; very small garden next to pool; roadside rooms can be noisy. [$] *Rooms from: 550DH* ✉ *Av. General Kettani* ☎ *0528/84–07–30* 🌐 *www.hotelaferni-agadir.com* 🛏 *45 rooms* 🍴 *Some meals.*

$ HOTEL **Hotel El Bahia.** If you're not desperate for beach views and don't mind a 20-minute walk to get there, then El Bahia is a central and good-value option. **Pros:** inexpensive rates; clean rooms; close to local markets and restaurants. **Cons:** few amenities; no restaurant; some rooms have shared bathroom. [$] *Rooms from: 320DH* ✉ *Rue el Mehdi Ibn Toumert, Talborjt* ☎ *0528/82–39–54* 💳 *No credit cards* 🛏 *27 rooms* 🍴 *Breakfast.*

$$ HOTEL **Hotel Kamal.** If you don't need to be near the beach, this is an affordable option in downtown Agadir. **Pros:** clean and neat; all rooms have a bath; parking on-site. **Cons:** no restaurant, but there are plenty nearby; roadside rooms noisy; can be busy with groups. [$] *Rooms from: 465DH* ✉ *Bd. Hassan II* ☎ *0528/84–28–17* 🌐 *www.hotel-kamal.com* 🛏 *128 rooms* 🍴 *Breakfast.*

$$$ HOTEL **Mogador Al Madina.** Part of the Moroccan Mogador Hotels & Resorts chain, this complex, set back from the beach, lacks the wide-open vistas of other resorts but is slightly quieter. **Pros:** friendly and helpful staff; close to beach; generous breakfast. **Cons:** overpriced; no real views; no Wi-Fi in rooms. [$] *Rooms from: 980DH* ✉ *Bd. du 20 Août* ☎ *0528/29–80–00* 🌐 *www.mogadorhotels.com* 🛏 *232 rooms* 🍴 *Some meals.*

$ HOTEL **La Petite Suède.** While the name is a little baffling (it means "small Sweden"), this is an inexpensive hotel run by a Moroccan family. **Pros:** very affordable; friendly staff; close to beach. **Cons:** drab and old fashioned design; few facilities; Wi-Fi can be intermittent. [$] *Rooms from: 350DH* ✉ *Corner of Av. Hassan II and Av. General Kettani* ☎ *0528/84–07–79* 🌐 *www.petitesuede.com* 💳 *No credit cards* 🛏 *24 rooms* 🍴 *Breakfast.*

$$$ RENTAL FAMILY **Résidence Yasmina.** Common areas at this self-catering complex have impressive hand-painted tiles and trickling fountains, but the older apartments are outdated and shabby. **Pros:** two pools; balconies with great views; central location. **Cons:** shabby decor in old wing;

Western Sahara

In 1975 more than 350,000 unarmed Moroccans walked south in the Green March, taking possession from the Spanish of what are now officially known as Morocco's Southern Provinces (though internationally known as the Western Sahara). Since 1975, conflict between the Polisario (Saharan separatists) and the Moroccan military has been sporadic, and a referendum to determine the province's political future has been postponed numerous times. There is currently a ceasefire, and the U.N. has a large presence in the big cities. Foreign visitors to the area are likely to be surfers or here on business, as Morocco is encouraging significant investments in the area. The main attraction for the traveler, aside from the journey to the middle of nowhere, is a chance to set foot in the Sahara, as the cities are new and charmless, food and wine scarce, and the military presence pervasive. However, there are several towns worth visiting before crossing the disputed border.

At the time of writing, tourists with Moroccan entry stamps were free to travel to the Southern Provinces. However, the situation is politically charged, so check before you head this far south and be prepared for numerous police checkpoints. These are usually amicable, but it could be worth it to prepare a form with your vital information printed in French, especially if you don't speak the language (which has replaced the Spanish of the colonial era).

THE TOWNS

Guelmim is known as the Gateway to the Sahara, and the ensuing drive south to Tan-Tan—along which the landscape turns ever more arid and desertlike—illustrates why. It's an easy trip (107 km [66 miles] south of Tiznit), shooting through empty stretches of flat *hamada* (stony desert) broken only by the occasional village or café and one gas station. Although you're likely to catch your first glimpse of large camel herds here, the town doesn't have much to entertain a tourist, and even the exotic-sounding camel market is little more than an average weekly souk.

As you approach **Tan-Tan** (125 km [78 miles] south of Guelmim), you may think you're seeing a giant mirage. Fear not, for your eyes do not deceive you: there really are two enormous kissing camels forming an archway over the road into town. Carved out of stone in the 1970s, these affectionate creatures are one of Tan-Tan's chief claims to fame and the subjects of many a Western Sahara postcard. Tan-Tan's main significance (beyond the kissing camels) is that it was the official starting point for the Green March of 1975. The southern end of Boulevard Mohammed V is Tan-Tan's main square, Place de la Marche Verte (Green March Square). This is the main transportation hub for taxis and cars headed back to Guelmim and on to Laayoune. The town makes a logical stop on a trip farther south, and is a passable choice for an overnight stay, although some tourists report unfriendly locals. The beach here, Tan-Tan Plage, is popular with surfers.

At 150 km (93 miles) south of Tan-Tan, the modest fishing village of **Akhfenir** has the first gas station, cafés, and stores on the coastal route after Tan-Tan. Footpaths down to a gorgeous beach make Akhfenir a good place for an en-route swimming stop. At 85 km (53 miles) south of Akhfenir, you'll find the largest of the few coastal towns on this route and the last before the disputed border. **Tarfaya** offers panoramic ocean views, excellent seafood, and a nice place to explore before the road turns inland.

Laayoune, the former capital of the Spanish Sahara, has thrived under Moroccan rule. A calm and easy place to navigate, Laayoune (115 km [71 miles] south of Tarfaya) makes the best base for trips around the Western Sahara. It's quite impressive to look around at surrounding dunes and landscape and contemplate the very existence of a town this size in the middle of the Sahara Desert. Moroccan investment is pouring into the town to capitalize on the benefits of deep-sea fishing, and any Moroccans one encounters are as likely to be from elsewhere, drawn here by construction work, fishing, and government subsidies.

Smara's central site has long been an important Saharan caravan stop, but most of the fun, it must be said, is in getting here. Once you *are* in Smara, however, the remains of the Palace Ma el-Ainin make a great stopping point. There is a guardian who will be happy to show you around, if you can find him.

Dakhla is the last frontier for most travelers to the Western Sahara, as there is little else south of here until you reach the Mauritanian border. Dakhla's main attractions are its superb beaches and the surrounding cliff, and it's become a magnet for kite-surfers. As a result, many guesthouses and surf companies are setting up in Dakhla to meet the growing demand from this market. Two well-established outfits that also have bases in Essaouira are Ocean Vagabond ⊕ *www.oceanvagabond. com* and Kite Morocco ⊕ *www. kitemorocco.com.* In recent years, the Moroccan government has invested heavily in infrastructure development in the town, and since 2006 Dakhla has celebrated the meeting of ocean and desert with the annual Dakhla Festival ⊕ *www.dakhla-festival.com* held in February.

GETTING HERE AND AROUND
Unless arriving by plane, be prepared for a long journey to reach this region. The CTM ⊕ *www.ctm.ma* and Supratours ⊕ *www.supratours. ma* buslines operate services most days from major cities to Laayoune (13 hours from Casablanca, 10 hours from Marrakesh, 8 hours from Agadir) and to Dakhla (20 hours from Casablanca, 17 hours from Marrakesh, 14 hours from Agadir). The national airline, Royal Air Maroc, operates flights from Casablanca to both Laayoune and Dakhla. This is probably the most convenient and hassle-free way to approach this less-developed province.

8

elevator only goes to fifth floor (of six); can be noise from road at night. $ *Rooms from: 800DH* ✉ *Rue de la Jeunesse, off Av. Hassan II* ☎ *0528/84–26–60* 🌐 *www.residence-yasmina.com* 🛏 *114 apartments* 🍴 *No meals.*

$$$$ B&B/INN Fodor's Choice ★ **Riad Villa Blanche.** An elegant boutique hotel—the first of its kind in Agadir—Riad Villa Blanche feels as though it has been plucked from the chicest Marrakesh address and dropped at the edge of the ocean. **Pros:** beautiful decor; intimate scale; excellent service. **Cons:** surrounded by large hotel resorts; far from main tourist beach or downtown; the bar can be noisy at night. $ *Rooms from: 1900DH* ✉ *No. 50 Cité Founty, Baie des Palmiers, Sonaba* ☎ *0528/21–13–13* 🌐 *www.riadvillablanche.com* 🛏 *28 rooms* 🍴 *All meals.*

$$$$ RESORT **Sofitel Agadir Royal Bay Resort.** One of two Sofitel brand hotels in Agadir, this branch manages to provide both privacy and intimacy on a grand scale. **Pros:** excellent amenities; comfortable rooms; direct beach access. **Cons:** starting to feel a little dated; very expensive; can be busy with large groups. $ *Rooms from: 2000DH* ✉ *Cité Founty P4, Baie des Palmiers, Bensergao* ☎ *0528/84–92–00* 🌐 *www.sofitel.com* 🛏 *273 rooms* 🍴 *Some meals.*

$$$$ RESORT Fodor's Choice ★ **Sofitel Agadir Thalassa Sea & Spa.** If luxury is important to you, or total relaxation and detox, this Sofitel branch in Agadir is for you. **Pros:** heated pool; great health and fitness facilities; direct beach access. **Cons:** corridors are rather dark; rooms are open plan to the bathroom; far from town center and main tourist beach. $ *Rooms from: 2300DH* ✉ *Baie des Palmiers, Secteur Touristique, Cité Founty P5* ☎ *0528/38–80–00* 🌐 *www.sofitel.com* 🛏 *173 rooms* 🍴 *Multiple meal plans.*

$$$ HOTEL **Le Tivoli.** Only 500 yards from the beach, the "Blue Sea Le Tivoli" is a less expensive option than many of the Agadir behemoths. **Pros:** light and airy rooms; large, clean pool; close to beach. **Cons:** uninspiring buffet meals; noisy pool area; outdated design. $ *Rooms from: 950DH* ✉ *Bd. du 20 Août, Secteur Touristique* ☎ *0528/84–76–40* 🌐 *www.hotelletivoli.com* 🛏 *280 rooms* 🍴 *Some meals.*

NIGHTLIFE

For many in Agadir, nightlife constitutes a stroll along the waterfront and a coffee with friends. But with its relaxed mores, Agadir can be a clubbing hot spot, particularly for young people looking to cut loose. Many places don't get going until after midnight, but the beachfront is always busy earlier on, with diners and drinkers making the most of the beach environment. Although Agadir lacks the class of Marrakesh, a number of places, mostly based in the resort hotels, are putting up some decent competition.

Be warned: nighttime also attracts many prostitutes, some underage, who throng the cheap bars. The authorities aren't afraid to imprison foreigners who patronize them. Hotel clubs tend to have a more exclusive patronage; in general, the more expensive the drinks, the fancier the clientele. Many bars and clubs close during the Muslim holy month of Ramadan.

BARS AND CLUBS

Actor's. Part of the Royal Atlas Hotel, Actor's attracts a young crowd with its playlist of Western dance, house, and R&B music, often with well-known Moroccan and Arab hits toward the end of the night. *Shisha* (a hookah water pipe) is also available. ⊠ *Royal Atlas Hotel, 20, av. Aout* ☎ *0528/29–40–40* 💲 *200 DH.*

Papagayo. A long-standing favorite is Papagayo, attached to the Rui Tikida Beach resort, which attracts international DJs pumping out fairly mainstream tunes. ⊠ *Hotel Riu Tikida Beach, Chemin des Dunes* ☎ *0528/84–54–00* 💲 *100 DH.*

So Lounge. The chicest and best nightclub is without doubt So, which charges a hefty admission price for nonguests of the Sofitel. Located on two levels, there's live music every night, a chic restaurant, and three bars, including exclusive champagne and vodka bars. It's so trendy you could scream, or simply dance the night—and morning—away. ⊠ *Sofitel Agadir Royal Bay Resort Hotel, Baie des Palmiers* ☎ *0528/82–00–88* 💲 *300 DH.*

Zanzibar. Those looking for postdinner, preclub drinks with a touch of East African colonial elegance should stop by Zanzibar at the Riu Tikida Beach Resort. ⊠ *Hotel Riu Tikida Beach, Chemin des Dunes* ☎ *0528/84–54–00.*

CASINOS

Casino Atlantic. Part of the Atlantic Palace Hotel, Casino Atlantic is the long player of the bunch, with 16 gaming tables offering blackjack, roulette, poker, and 200 slot machines going all afternoon, night, and early morning. ⊠ *Atlantic Palace Hotel, Secteur Balnéaire et Touristique* ☎ *0528/84–33–66* ⊕ *www.casinoagadir.com.*

Casino Le Mirage. This casino is part of Les Jardins d'Agadir Club Hotel and has blackjack, poker, roulette, and slot machines. ⊠ *Les Jardins d'Agadir, Secteur Touristique Et Balneaire* ☎ *0528/84–87–77.*

Casino Shem's. This long-standing favorite offers poker, blackjack, slot-machines, and great sea views. ⊠ *Bd. Mohammed V* ☎ *0528/82–11–11* ⊕ *www.shemscasino.fr.*

8

SHOPPING

Baz'Art Salam. This store offers a wide range of quality Moroccan-made items at fixed prices near the Lebanese mosque. The selection features modern twists on classic crafts such as Fez leather bags, glazed ceramics, oversized candles, and Sens de Marrakech cosmetics. The shop is owned by two brothers who speak excellent English and are happy to advise on purchases without being pushy. ⊠ *124–126, av. des F.A.R.,* ☎ *0528/82–45–53.*

L'Echappee Belle Etape Berbere (l'Atelier d'Izza). This charming gift shop, located in Talborjt, stocks an extensive range of handcrafted gifts, baskets, clothing, homemade jams, upcycled craft items, home furnishings, and jewelry. It's a real treasure trove, and the owner, "Izza," always welcomes with a smile. ⊠ *7, rue Mohamed Boufous, Talborjt* ☎ *0678/74–22–27* ⊙ *Closed Sun. and Mon.*

La Fabrique. Find leather goods and designer-label fashions here. This is not the kind of place where a bit of haggling will halve the price, so be ready to pay higher prices. ⊠ *91, av. Hassan II* ☎ *0528/84–61–76.*

Fodor's Choice ★ **Kasbat Souss.** Established by an association of local artisans, this complex of more than 60 shops a short distance outside town sells leather products, woodwork, jewelry, pottery, candles, sculpture, embroidery, and argan oil. It's a relaxed place to wander and browse without any of the usual souk hassle, and prices are reasonable. There's also a small café at the center. You can take a taxi from downtown Agadir for around 50 DH. ⊠ *Rte. d' Inzegane Km 5, Bensergao* ⊹ *Just after Palais Royale* ☎ *0528/28–19–43.*

Madd. This boutique jewelry store entices you with 18-carat gold from behind a warm wooden exterior. There's another branch in the new Marina development at the north end of Agadir beach. ⊠ *38–40, av. Hassan II* ☎ *0528/84–05–92.*

Palais du Sud. For an emporium of carpets, ceramics, leather, lanterns, and ornate boxes, visit Palais du Sud. Behind the golden doors, all goods have price tags, which makes buying hassle-free. ⊠ *Rue de la Foire, north of Av. Hassan II* ☎ *0528/84–35–00* ⊕ *www.palaisdusud. com* ⊙ *Closed Sun.*

SPAS

Diar Argan. This spa offers a range of treatments such as massages, manicures, and pedicures, as well as argan oil products, the so-called Berber gold, available for purchase. A two-hour massage with argan oil costs 330 DH. ⊠ *104, Immeuble Iguenoiane, bd. Mohammed V* ☎ *0528/82–84–86* ⊕ *www.diarargan.com.*

Le Spa Villa Blanche. Seven kinds of exotic massages using Western and Eastern techniques and essential oils are offered in the sumptuous, candlelit spa of Riad Villa Blanche. You can choose from a Sahara hot-sand massage, an "apres-souk" massage, or an energizing massage with argan oil and lemon. ⊠ *Riad Villa Blanche, Baie des Palmiers Secteur, 50 Cité Founty, Sonaba* ☎ *0528/21–13–13.*

SPORTS AND THE OUTDOORS

GOLF

Golf de L'Océan. The newest of the golf courses along Agadir's coast, the Golf de L'Océan, designed by Belt Collins, is part of the Atlantic Palace Hotel resort and is open to both resort guests and nonresidents. Regular minibus shuttles run from the Atlantic Palace Hotel. ⊠ *Bensergao* ☎ *0528/27–35–42* ⊕ *www.golfdelocean.com* ⊠ *400 DH for 9 holes, 250 DH for golf cart, 100 DH for caddy; 700 DH for 18 holes, 400 DH for golf cart, 150 DH for caddy* ⅃. *Desert course 9 holes, 3128 yards, par 36. Garden course 9 holes, 3126 yards, par 36. Dunes course 9 holes, 2949 yards, par 35.*

Golf du Soleil. This American-style, championship course was designed in a classic style amid a eucalyptus forest and has several challenging obstacles. Guests of any of the three Tikida resorts in Agadir receive a discount and shuttle bus service to and from the hotels. ⊠ *Chemin des Dunes, Bensergao* ☎ *0528/33–73–30* ⊕ *www.tikidagolfpalace.com* 🚌 *420 DH for 9 holes, 250 DH for golf cart, 70 DH for caddy; 700 DH for 18 holes, 400 DH for golf cart, 100 DH for caddy* ⅄. *Championship course 18 holes, 6057 yards, par 72. Tikida course 18 holes, 6535 yards, par 72.*

Golf Les Dunes. This American-style golf course is 10 km (6 miles) from central Agadir. The 27-hole course runs over hilly, thickly wooded countryside. There are free shuttles operating from various hotels in town. ■ TIP→ **It is advisable to play in the afternoon, as mornings can be busy with guests from the hotel that owns the golf club.** ⊠ *Chemin Oued Souss* ☎ *0528/83–46–90* ⊕ *www.golflesdunesagadir.com* 🚌 *500 DH for 9 holes, 300 DH for golf cart, 80 DH for caddy; 700 DH for 18 holes, 400 DH for cart, 120 DH for caddy* ⅄. *Eucalyptus course 9 holes, 3416 yards, par 36. Oued course 9 holes, 3358 yards, par 36. Tamaris course 9 holes, 3472 yards, par 36.*

Royal Golf Club. Established in 1952 by a Scotsman, the Royal Golf Club is Agadir's oldest. One of the smaller courses in Agadir, covering more than 30 acres with English-style Bermuda 419 and Cucuyo grass, it is 12 km (7 miles) from Agadir on the road to Aït Melloul. ⊠ *Km 12, Rte. Aït Melloul* ☎ *0528/24–85–51* ⊕ *www.royalgolfagadir.com* 🚌 *200 DH for 9 holes; 280 DH for 18 holes; 200 DH for golf cart; 50 DH for caddy* ⅄. *9 holes, 2932 yards, par 36.*

JET-SKIING

Club Royal de Jet-Ski. At the north end of Agadir beach, near the marina entrance, you'll find Jet Skis for hire. The honorary president of the Club Royal de Jet Ski is actually Moroccon King Mohammed VI, although it's unlikely you'll find him here. ⊠ *Agadir.*

SURFING

Surf dudes the world over rate Morocco's southern Atlantic coast one of the world's best places to catch waves. There has recently been something of a surfer boom in the region. Today there are countless surf schools, many run by foreigners who came to surf and then simply couldn't tear themselves away. Many surf shops and schools are based in Taghazoute, 22 km (14 miles) north of Agadir. From there, instructors will take clients to local bays and points according to wind and tides.

Original Surf Morocco. A professional, Moroccan-owned outfit, Original Surf Morocco is based in Tamraght, a village famous for its bananas and beaches, about 16 km (9 miles) to the north of Agadir. With more than 10 years of experience, it offers surfing lessons and accommodations in a so-called surf house. ⊠ *Tamraght* ☎ *0528/31–58–37* ⊕ *www.originalsurfmorocco.com.*

Surf Town Morocco. This surf school and guesthouse is 16 km (9 miles) north of Agadir in Tamraght. English-speaking instructors can take you to local surfing points like Boiler, Killer Point, and Devil's Rock. Board hire is 100 DH a day and the type of instruction depends on the experience of the surfer and the length of time chosen. Inexpensive accommodations are also available with half-board. ⊠ *Tamraght* ☎ *0664/47–81–76* ⊕ *www.surftownmorocco.com.*

8

ESSAOUIRA

171 km (103 miles) north of Agadir.

Once Morocco's main trading port and a stronghold of Jewish culture, Essaouira became famed as a hippie hangout for surfers and expat artists in the 20th century. These days Essaouira offers its cool breezes and relaxed atmosphere to a broader range of visitors. The windy city remains a favorite destination for its picturesque fishing harbor, medina walls, blue shutters, twisting *derbs* (alleyways), and sea, sand, and surf.

Essaouira pretty much has a nine-month high season, from mid-March until early November, with extra peaks around Christmas, New Year's, and the hugely popular Gnaoua and World Music Festival in June. More hotels and guesthouses have opened in recent years, including a five-star resort and golf course south of the town in Diabat, but the town remains peaceful in its laid-back bustle—an enticing blend of fishing port, historical medina, and seaside haven.

EN ROUTE The coastal stretch between Sidi Ifni and Essaouira presents the most spectacular drive anywhere in Morocco. The northern half of the trip from Agadir on the P8/N1 road to Essaouira is particularly stunning. A drive is pleasant in itself, but you can stop and relax at several turn-offs from the main road both north and south of Agadir. Unspoiled beaches lie just 10 km (6 miles) north of Sidi Ifni; the only travelers who find the unmarked dirt road come in campers during the summer months.

GETTING HERE AND AROUND

Essaouira's airport is served by only a handful of European budget airlines, so the easiest and most common way to get to Essaouira is by bus. There is no train service and little parking space for private cars, but road connections are good, and buses can get you efficiently and easily to and from Agadir, Casablanca, and Marrakesh. The drive from Marrakesh or Agadir to Essaouira takes about three hours, with bus companies Supratours and CTM operating several daily services. Grands taxis are also an option.

The medina of Essaouira is compact, pedestrian-friendly, and easily walkable. Outside the walls, the local petits taxis are blue and have a fixed price of 7 DH during the day and 8 DH after 8 pm. A journey to Diabat costs 30 DH to 50 DH. You can hail the taxis on the street or pick them up at taxi stands outside the main medina gates.

Several local travel agents can arrange day trips and longer tours in a minibus or 4x4.

Bus Contacts CTM Essaouira. ⊠ *Pl. 11 Janvier, Quartier Borj, Ville Nouvelle* ☏ *0524/78–47–64* ⊕ *www.ctm.ma.* **Supratours.** ⊠ *South Bastion, Medina* ⊕ *Across from Borj Bab Marrakech* ☏ *0524/47–53–17* ⊕ *www.supratours.ma.*

Rental Cars Chaaba Cars. ⊠ *7.01, rue Mae El Aaynine, Lotissement 4* ☏ *0600/05–15–30* ⊕ *www.chaabacar.com.* **El Ghazwa Car.** ⊠ *501, av. Al Aqaba, Lot 4,* ☏ *0524/78–48–41, 0661/66–18–41.*

TOURS

Fikra Travel. Based out of Essaouira and Ouarzazate, Fikra Travel offers personalized tours of Morocco, specializing in the south and desert regions. It will tailor tours to suit your traveling needs and often deals with small groups and families traveling by 4x4, but can also offer routes by bus, camel, or even donkey. ⊠ *Tresor Kafila Shop, Rue Laalouj, Medina* ☎ *0662/82–55–46* ⊕ *www.fikratravel.com.*

Morocco Made Easy. A specialist in tailor-made holidays in Morocco, Australian-born founder Jane Folliott has over 15 years' experience working and living in Morocco. Based in Essaouira, this company can arrange a broad range of trips for individuals, families, and small groups, from day excursions to longer cultural and historical journeys throughout the country. Itineraries can be designed to suit your budget, level of comfort, and sense of adventure. ⊠ *Quartier Erraounak* ☎ *0666/40–95–48.*

PLANNING YOUR TIME

Weekend visitors to Essaouira often leave wishing they had more time. If you can, plan to spend several days in this relaxing seaside town. The most popular time to visit is summer, but the best time is September when both tourist numbers and winds drop. Although the temperature is tolerable year-round, this is Africa's windy city, so don't expect to swim before May or after September.

FESTIVALS

Essaouira hosts three major festivals each year: Le Printemps Musical des Alizés, a classical and chamber music festival held in April; Gnaoua and World Music Festival, a mix of jazz, rock, pop, and world music held in June; and Le Festival des Andalousies Atlantiques, which showcases Arabo-Andalusian music and flamenco at the end of October.

FodorsChoice ★ **Gnaoua and World Music Festival.** Essaouira is always packed over the third weekend of June, as tens of thousands of people from all over the world come to enjoy the annual four-day Gnaoua and World Music Festival. It's one of the best times to listen to traditional Gnaoua musicians. These descendants of African slaves established brotherhoods across Morocco and are healers and mystics as well as musicians. Among their troupes of metal castanet (*krakab*) players, bass lute (*gimbri*) players, and drummers, they have mediums and clairvoyants who perform wild, spellbinding acts. ■ TIP→ **If you plan to visit the festival, make sure you reserve accommodations at least three months in advance as hotels and guesthouses will be full.** ⊠ *Essaouira* ⊕ *www. festival-gnaoua.net.*

VISITOR INFORMATION

Contacts Delegation Provincial de Tourisme. ⊠ *10, rue du Caire, Medina* ☎ *0524/78–35–32.*

EXPLORING

Dar Souiri. Home to the active Essaouira-Mogador Association, Dar Souiri is the hub of cultural life in Essaouira. Check the notice board outside the door for information on upcoming festivals, concerts, film screenings, and other cultural events. Inside, the building is an excellent example of 18th-century Mogador architecture and houses an art gallery and a library. Free Wi-Fi is also available. ✉ *2, rue de Caire, Medina* ☎ *0524/47–52–68* ⊕ *www.essaouiramogador.org* ⊗ *Closed Sun.*

■▬▬▬
NEED A
BREAK

✕ **Patisserie Chez Driss.** This local institution off the main square dates back to 1929. Prices are very reasonable, so you can start your day with great coffee and breakfasts; you can also take your pick from the French and Moroccan pastries baked fresh every day. ✉ *9, rue el Hajjali* ☎ *0524/47–27–93.*

Medina. This isn't so much a sight as the very essence of Essaouira, where you are most likely to stay, eat, shop, and wander. The medina was designed by French architect Théodore Cornut in the late 18th century, on the instructions of Sidi Mohammed Ben Abdullah, who wanted to create a new town and port to rival Agadir and demonstrate Morocco's outward focus. Cornut built the kasbah and the Sultan invited prominent Jewish traders to settle here. Mogador (as it was then known) soon thrived.

The medina is now a UNESCO World Heritage Site and efforts are underway to restore some of the key buildings of Mogador's heyday, namely the Simon Attia synagogue and the Danish consulate. The former Portuguese consulate and church are also earmarked for restoration. All feature the colonnaded ground floor and rooms off internal walkways on the higher levels that are typical of the era.

From the kasbah, heading northwest, pass through the Mellah Kdim (old Mellah) before finally reaching the Mellah proper. It was in this latter area that less affluent Jews settled. Following the end of the French Protectorate and the creation of the state of Israel, most of Mogador's Jews left and the area became home to poorer urban families and squatters in the ruined shells of former Jewish town houses. The area is under redevelopment, so many buildings have been demolished. Two original synagogues can be visited: Synagogue Slat Lkahal and Haïm Pinto Synagogue. The area is best avoided after dark. ■ TIP➜ As you approach the Mellah, look for the Star of David carved in stone above doorways. ✉ *Medina.*

North Bastion and Medina Skala. The distinctive outlines of the medina *skala* and its citadel (the North Bastion) frame the waves dramatically at sunset. The bastion once held emergency supplies of fresh water and the large circle of stones in the center marks what was known as a call-point, or alarm system, to warn of approaching invaders. Guards would warn of danger by stomping on the resonant circle. ■ TIP➜ If you stand in the middle of the circle and stomp your foot or yell, you'll hear the echo ring far. ✉ *Essaouira.*

Fodor's Choice
★

Port of Essaouira. Built in 1769 in the reign of Sidi Mohammed Ben Abdellah by an Englishman who had converted to Islam, Essaouira's port is still going strong in the southwest corner of town, and it's the one must-see sight for any traveler coming here. Trawlers and other boats bob along the quay, and middlemen and independent sailors sell the daily catch of sardines, calamari, and skate from small dockside tables. You'll be selling yourself short if you don't have a meal of the freshest fish imaginable at one of the shoreside grill restaurants. As Moroccan ports go, it's also one of the most beautiful, not to mention accessible and tourist-friendly. ⊠ *Essaouira.*

Port Skala. Essaouira has two principal *skala* (fortified bastions), with fabulous cannons: the medina skala and the port skala. Each was a strategic maritime defense point. Unlike the straight-edged Moorish constructions in other Moroccan cities, the ramparts in Essaouira are triangular, so the insider looking out has a broader field of vision than the enemy peering in. Orson Welles filmed scenes of his film *Othello* from the tower of the port skala, picking up a magnificent panorama of town, port, and bay all in one that can still be seen today. ■TIP→ **The entrance fee is worth it to get the picture-postcard view of the medina through a round opening in the wall.** ⊠ *Medina* 🔓 *10 DH; free for Muslims on Fri.*

Sidi Mohammed Ben Abdellah Ethnological Museum. The stunning former French-colonial town hall holds this smartly arranged collection of items from everyday and ritual life in and around the Essaouira area. Current exhibits include items related to the China tea trade in anticipation of the construction of a tea museum. The permanent collection includes musical instruments of both Gnaoua and Sufi sects; displays of regional carpet styles and wood-carving techniques and motifs; and examples of Muslim, Jewish, and rural Ishelhin Berber rites and dress. ⊠ *7, rue Laalouj, Medina* ☎ *0524/47–23–00* 🔓 *10 DH* ☽ *Closed Tues.*

NEED A BREAK

✕ **Gelateria Dolcefreddo.** Come here for the best coffee and the best ice cream in town; its location on the main square is also great for people-watching. **Known for: homemade gelato; variety of coffee; people-watching.** ⊠ *Pl. Moulay Hassan* ☎ *0663/57–19–28.*

South Bastion. The South Bastion, also known as the Bastion Bab Marrakech, is a carefully restored element of the original fortified medina walls. Managed by the local Delegation of the Culture Ministry, it is open to the public when exhibitions and events take place, like the annual Gnaoua and World Music Festival. The flat roof offers a view over the rooftops to the beach and is often the backdrop to concerts and other performances. The area in front of the bastion (now a parking lot) was the site of the town's original Muslim cemetery. ⊠ *Bab Marrakech, Medina.*

OFF THE BEATEN PATH

Val d'Argan Vineyard. Just outside Ounagha, about 35½ km (22 miles) from Essaouira, is Morocco's first organic vineyard. Established by Charles Melia, an experienced winemaker of the Rhône valley in France, it covers 128 acres, 100 of which are under cultivation. The vineyard produces a selection of ranges and labels featuring red, white, rosé, and—typical in Morocco—*vin gris* (gray) wines. Many of the wines here are commonly featured on wine lists in Essaouira and Marrakesh restaurants. Tours and tastings can be arranged in French, English, or Arabic, and there is a restaurant on-site with a panoramic view of the vineyard and olive trees. ✉ *Domaine du Val d'Argan, Ounagha* ☎ *0524/78–34–67* ⊕ *www.valdargan.com.*

BEACHES

Diabat Beach. Essaouira's beach is fine for an early-morning jog or a late-afternoon game of soccer, but serious sunbathers typically head south to quiet Diabat. Walking along the beach, cross over the mouth of the river and continue past the Borj el Baroud, a former Portuguese fortification. To your left, a few miles south of town nestled in eucalyptus fields, you'll see the ruins of the so-called Sultan's Palace. This building is said to have inspired Jimi Hendrix to write "Castles in the Sand," although he actually released the track a couple of years before his visit to this village, which has been trading on his name ever since. On a windy day the only escape is behind the Borj at low tide. **Amenities:** none. **Best for:** solitude; sunset. ✉ *Essaouira* ✛ *A petit taxi can take you to rotary at edge of town (from which point you can walk to beach via unpaved road) or into village of Diabat (via new Sofitel Golf complex).*

FAMILY **Essaouira Bay.** Essaouira's main beach is a sweep of sand along the bay that has provided shelter to seafarers from Atlantic storms since antiquity. Although temperatures are moderate all year and the sun is nearly always shining, the wind is consistently strong, making sunbathing or swimming less attractive than farther south in Agadir. Nonetheless, sun-bed rentals are relatively inexpensive or even free if you eat at one of the cafés at the southern end of the beach.

The wind comes from the north and creates three main areas. The most northerly part, tucked up into the armpit of the port, has wind that comes in gusts. Just south of this the wind strengthens, with fewer gusts. Farther south are the steady, strong trade winds the town is known for, and that make it a mecca for wind- and kite surfers. The range of areas makes the bay perfect for every level of water-sports enthusiast.

The surrounding islets, the Iles de Mogador, are home to nine bird species, including the endangered Eleanora's falcon. They are closed to visitors during breeding season (April to October), but otherwise you can get a boat trip from the port, with boats leaving morning and afternoon depending on weather conditions. **Amenities:** food and drink; lifeguards (summer only); toilets; parking (10 DH); water sports. **Best for:** sunset; swimming; walking; windsurfing. ✉ *Essaouira.*

Sidi Kaouki. The tranquil beach village of Sidi Kaouki is often touted as an alternative to Essaouira's beach and is a destination of choice for younger backpackers, surfers, and windsurfers, which should give you an idea of the typical wind velocity and wave size. It doesn't have the amenities of its larger neighbor, but the "Town" consists of a number of guesthouses, a couple of shops, and some small restaurants all serving the same standard tourist menus. It's easy to rent mountain bikes, quad bikes, or ponies for a jaunt along the beach toward Ouassane (the

Essaouira's medina was built by a French architect to house Jewish merchants and create the country's foremost trading port.

village to the north) or Sidi M'barek (with a waterfall and wide sandy beach) to the south. ■TIP→ **For the energetic, it's possible to walk along the beach and over a cliff from Essaouira to Sidi Kaouki—about 13 miles one way. Walking in the opposite direction (against the wind) is not recommended. Amenities:** food and drink; parking (5 DH–10 DH per day in summer); toilets; water sports. **Best for:** surfing; sunset; walking. ⊠ *Sidi Kaouki* ✣ *Sidi Kaouki is 27 km (17 miles) southwest of Diabat. Turnoff is 15 km (9 miles) south of Diabat on Agadir road. No. 2 Lima bus goes to Sidi Kaouki.*

OFF THE BEATEN PATH

Numerous paved roads jut off the road to Agadir heading toward the beaches along the coast, including the fishing and camping site at **Plage Tafadna**, 37 km (23 miles) south of the Sidi Kaouki turnoff. Farther south, **Imssouane**, a fishing village on a peninsula just inside the border between Essaouira and Agadir provinces, is a popular spot for locals and backpackers who want to find total seclusion. There are two beaches here—one for surfing and a calmer one that's perfect for families. Accessibility to the beaches and the locals' experience of foreign visitors lessen as you move south until you head beyond Cap Rhir and the increasingly developed beaches north of Agadir.

WHERE TO EAT

There are some great restaurants in Essaouira. From port catches grilled in front of you to inventive and expensive fish dishes in the swankiest restaurants, seafood tends to headline menus when the surf permits. A must-do experience is lunch or dinner in one of the seafood grills near the port: feast on charcoal-grilled sardines, calamari, red snapper, sea bass, whiting, and shrimp (crab is usually too dry) from among the array of stalls, and experience the color and bustle of the port. You choose your fish, then establish a price based on weight. The later in the day, the lower you'll be able to negotiate the price, but as Essaouira can be very windy, enjoying lunch alfresco in the sun makes much more sense than a breezy dinner. This is a great place to go if you are tiring of tagine. You could also take a stroll along Avenue L'Istiqlal (known by locals as "Haddada"), or better still Avenue Mohammed el-Quori (known by locals as "Souk Waka"). Here you'll be able to pack an exotic picnic of salty battered fish, potato patties, stuffed sardines in fresh Moroccan bread, almonds and peanuts, fruit, and sticky Maghrebian sweets.

In addition, there are also lots of traditional Moroccan options and excellent examples of French, Italian, and even Asian food.

$$$$
ECLECTIC
✕ **Caravane Café.** This renovated riad filled with the artwork and collections of its host, artist Didier Spindler, offers an imaginative menu that is a fusion of Moroccan, European, and Asian flavors. The decor is an eclectic mix of Buddha statues, pop art, and palm trees. **Known for:** fusion of Moroccan, European, and Asian flavors; nightly entertainment. Ⓢ *Average main: 160DH* ✉ *2 bis, rue Cadi Ayad, Medina* ☎ *0524/78–31–11* ☾ *Closed Mon.*

$
EUROPEAN
✕ **Chez Françoise.** There's a daily range of bites, including quiches, salads, and the occasional crepe, at this nice little lunch place that's great for vegetarians. With only two rows of four small tables set beneath the artwork of owner Francoise's husband, it makes a good stop for afternoon tea. **Known for:** many vegetarian options; light meals made with fresh local produce. Ⓢ *Average main: 60DH* ✉ *1, rue Houmane el Fetouaki* ☎ *0631/55–90–24* ▬ *No credit cards* ☾ *Closed Sat. No dinner.*

$$$$
ECLECTIC
✕ **Dar Caravane.** Set in beautiful gardens, Dar Caravane is a great choice for lunch and to escape the winds at the beach with a day by the pool. Like its sister restaurant (Caravane Café) in the town center, the menu fuses world flavors reflecting the travels of the owners, Didier and Jean-Paul. **Known for:** beautiful gardens and pool; fusion of flavors from Morocco, Asia, and Europe. Ⓢ *Average main: 150DH* ✉ *Rte. d'Agadir Km 1* ☎ *0524/78–48–04.*

$
MOROCCAN
✕ **Dar Mounia.** This unpretentious Moroccan restaurant in the heart of the medina is spacious and cool. Hidden among the extensive menu of couscous, tagine, and pastilla variations are a few refreshing surprises. **Known for:** central location; simple, tasty food at a reasonable price. Ⓢ *Average main: 70DH* ✉ *2, rue Laalouj, Medina* ☎ *0524/47–29–88* ⊕ *www.dar-mounia.com* ▬ *No credit cards.*

$$
MOROCCAN
✕ **La Découverte.** Owner and chef Frederique employs only locals and uses ingredients from local farmers and co-ops to implement her slow-food philosophy. Using traditional recipes and always with the greatest respect for the heritage and provenance of her dishes, she and sous-chef Khadija create a menu of authentic salads, mains, and desserts plus daily specials. **Known for:** home-style cooking; fresh local produce. Ⓢ *Average main: 80DH* ✉ *Rue Houmman el Fatouaki* ☎ *0524/47–31–58* ⊕ *www.essaouira-ladecouverte.com* ▬ *No credit cards* ☾ *Closed Sat.*

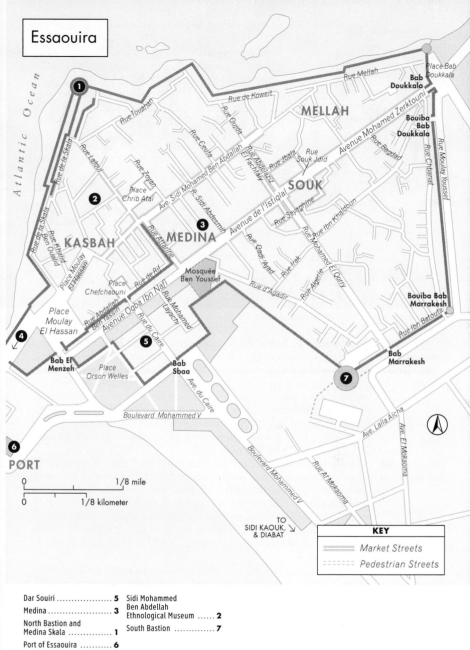

Essaouira

Atlantic Ocean

MELLAH

Rue Mellah
Rue de Koweit
Rue de la Skala
Rue Touahen
Rue Latouli
Rue Zayan
Rue Ceuta
Rue Ouida
Place Chrib Atai
Ave. Sidi Mohamed Ben Abdallah
R. Sidi Abdesmih
Rue Abdelaziz El Fachtaly
Rue Jbala
Rue Souk Jdid

Place Bab Doukkala
Bab Doukkala
Bouiba Bab Doukkala
Avenue Mohamed Zerktouni
Rue Bagdad
Rue Chbanat
Rue Moulay Youssef

SOUK

KASBAH
Rue Khalid Ben Oualid
Place Moulay El Hassan
Place Chefchaouni
MEDINA
Rue Attarine
Avenue de l'Istiqlal
Rue Sayaghine
Rue Mohamed El Qorry
Rue Ibn Khaldoun
Rue Qadi Ayad
Rue Irak
Rue Algerie
Rue d'Agadir

Place Abdallah Ben Yassin
Avenue Oqba Ibn Nafi
Mosquée Ben Youssef
Rue de Rif
Rue Mohamed Lavachi
Rue du Caire

Place Moulay El Hassan
Bab El Menzeh
Place Orson Welles
Bab Sbaa
Ave. du Caire

Bouiba Bab Marrakesh
Rue Ibn Batourla
Bab Marrakesh

Boulevard Mohammed V

PORT

0 ———— 1/8 mile
0 ———— 1/8 kilometer

Boulevard Mohammed V
Rue El Mokaoma
Ave. Lalla Aicha
Ave. El Mokaoma

TO
SIDI KAOUK,
& DIABAT

KEY
━━━━ Market Streets
┄┄┄┄ Pedestrian Streets

The Essaouira medina is a UNESCO World Heritage Site.

$$$$ MEDITERRANEAN Fodor's Choice ★ 🍴 **La Fromagerie.** A few miles outside town on the edge of thuya and olive groves, owner Abderrazak welcomes you warmly to his artisanal cheesery and open-air restaurant. Enjoy a fixed-menu lunch of salads topped with local goat-and-sheep-milk cheeses, followed by (for non-vegetarians) a *mechoui* (lamb spit roast), and wine to complement. **Known for:** different cheeses made on the premises; pretty countryside setting; large portions. [$] *Average main: 225DH* ✉ *Rte. de Safi, Douar Larabe* ✣ *1 km (½ mile) after rotary on Essaouira-Marrakesh road* ☎ *0666/23–35–34* 💳 *No credit cards.*

$$$ MOROCCAN 🍴 **La Licorne.** This Moroccan restaurant offers a selection of tagines with flavor combinations you don't often find, such as tagine of beef with honey and dried fruits or saffron chicken with almonds. It also has an excellent selection of seafood dishes and desserts. **Known for:** experimental Moroccan cuisine; extensive selection of Moroccan and foreign wines. [$] *Average main: 95DH* ✉ *26, rue de la Scala* ☎ *0524/47–36–26* 🌐 *www.restaurant-lalicorne-essaouira.com* 💳 *No credit cards* 🕒 *Closed Mon. No lunch.*

$$ MEDITERRANEAN 🍴 **Loft.** This cozy, chic café and restaurant offers a small, seasonal menu of fresh local produce, seafood, and a few surprises such as a mille-feuille of eggplant and goat cheese. After your meal, try a spiced coffee or Berber tea. **Known for:** arty, bohemian decor; regularly changing menu; spiced coffee. [$] *Average main: 70DH* ✉ *5, rue Hajjali, Medina* ✣ *In alley behind clocktower square* ☎ *0524/78–44–62* 💳 *No credit cards* 🕒 *Closed Tues.*

$$$ MOROCCAN 🍴 **Le Mogadorien.** Often overlooked in favor of the smaller lounge-style restaurants farther along the street, Le Mogadorien has a similar menu but a lot more style. The decor reflects Essaouira's Berber, Arab, Jewish,

and Christian heritage, giving you a choice of low-slung Moroccan salon seats or regular chairs and tables. **Known for:** hearty portions; vegetarian options. [$] *Average main: 110DH* ✉ *7, pl. Chefchaouni* ⊕ *In clocktower square* ☎ *0524/47–49–50.*

$$$$ MOROCCAN 🍴 **Le Patio.** This French-run restaurant offers Moroccan cooking with a twist; for example, fish tagines are made with pears, apples, or prunes. The small tables are set around a large starry lantern, and the deep-red walls, white muslin, and candles create a romantic atmosphere, although it's a little too dark for gazing into each other's eyes. **Known for:** romantic setting; large menu. [$] *Average main: 120DH* ✉ *28 bis, rue Moulay Rachid* ☎ *0524/47–41–66* ⏲ *No lunch.*

$ EUROPEAN 🍴 **Platinum.** A few blocks east of the beach, this is one of the city's best cafés. The excellent salads, pasta, pizza, and meat and fish dishes are served all day, while breakfasts come in European or Moroccan style. **Known for:** variety of fresh salads; large selection of pizzas; modern airy space with shaded outdoor terrace. [$] *Average main: 50DH* ✉ *Av. Lalla Amina, Quartier des Dunes* ☎ *0524/78–50–91* 💳 *No credit cards.*

$$ MOROCCAN 🍴 **Safran.** In a sunny spot in the cobbled old grain market, Safran offers a range of grilled fish, à la carte lunches and suppers, freshly made juices, and much more. A great location for an alfresco meal or just a coffee, if you sit here long enough, you'll see plenty of Essaouira's musical and acrobatic street entertainers. **Known for:** open-air dining; a wide selection of fixed menus or à la carte. [$] *Average main: 70DH* ✉ *116, pl. Marché aux Grains, Medina* ☎ *0600/60–50–31* ⏲ *No dinner in winter.*

$$ ITALIAN Fodor's Choice ★ 🍴 **Silvestro.** A long-standing favorite among locals, expats, and tourists, this authentic Italian restaurant serves the best crispy pizzas in the medina, straight from a wood-fired oven. The menu also features home-cooked pasta dishes. **Known for:** authentic Italian food; wood-fired pizza; large portions. [$] *Average main: 80DH* ✉ *70, rue Laalouj, Medina* ☎ *0524/47–35–55* ⏲ *Closed during Ramadan.*

$$$$ SEAFOOD 🍴 **La Table by Madada.** In a former warehouse of the sultan's Jewish traders, this is one of three Madada brand businesses in Essaouira. The restaurant and bar offers fresh seafood prepared imaginatively and according to the seasons. **Known for:** fresh seafood, including lobster pastilla; live music entertainment on weekends. [$] *Average main: 165DH* ✉ *7, rue Youssef el Fassi, Medina* ☎ *0524/47–21–06* 🌐 *www.latablemadada.com* ⏲ *No lunch.*

$$$$ MEDITERRANEAN Fodor's Choice ★ 🍴 **Taros.** This restaurant and bar is the "place to be" in the evenings. It's named after the wind that blows off the sea, which you can feel firsthand with cocktails on the terrific rooftop terrace with views of the port. **Known for:** rooftop terrace bar; nightly music. [$] *Average main: 160DH* ✉ *Pl. Moulay Hassan, at Rue de la Skala, Medina* ☎ *0524/47–64–07.*

$ VEGETARIAN 🍴 **La Triskala.** This vegetarian restaurant near the ramparts creates a cozy atmosphere, with quirky design and simple, tasty, seasonal food such as the falafel platter, sardine ball tagine, and stuffed eggplant. The chocolate gâteau is pretty amazing, too. **Known for:** vegetarian food; quirky design with cozy corners and secret mezzanine areas for dining; home-style cooking. [$] *Average main: 65DH* ✉ *58 bis, rue Touahen, Medina* ☎ *0524/47–63–71* 💳 *No credit cards.*

8

$$$$ MODERN EUROPEAN Fodor's Choice ★ 🍴 **Umia.** This chic restaurant tucked away along the skala is a real treat. The daily changing menu—prepared in an open kitchen—blends seasonal and local ingredients with French *savoir faire*. The airy restaurant draws in a clientele of expats and tourists with its muted dove grays, glossy white furniture, and quirky art touches, such as a gorgeous Gnaoua mural. **Known for:** fresh local produce; menu changes daily; chic minimalist decor. [$] *Average main: 120DH* ✉ *26, rue de la Skala, Medina* ☎ *0524/78–33–95.*

$ ITALIAN 🍴 **Vague Bleue.** One of Essaouira's best-kept secrets, this little hole-in-the-wall restaurant never fails to impress. Manager Brahim offers freshly prepared Italian mains (fish, chicken, and pasta), all served with a trio of salads and two juices to start. **Known for:** simple tasty food; great value. [$] *Average main: 50DH* ✉ *2, rue Sidi Ali Ben Abdullah, Medina* ☎ *0611/28–37–91* ▭ *No credit cards* 🕒 *Closed Fri.*

$ VEGETARIAN 🍴 **Yoo.** This vegetarian snack café in the old grain market square serves a limited menu of vegetarian sandwiches, focaccia, and homemade frozen yogurt with a variety of toppings, as well as a great selection of fresh juices. Enjoy with entertainment by local wandering minstrels. **Known for:** frozen yogurt; simple vegetarian food. [$] *Average main: 50DH* ✉ *Pl. Marche aux Grains, Av. Mohamed Zerktouni, Medina* ☎ *0630/71–74–96* 🕒 *Closed Jan.* ▭ *No credit cards.*

COOKING CLASSES

Many riads offer cookery classes or demonstrations, but the two best places in Essaouira to learn about Moroccan cuisine are L'Atelier de Madada, a modern designed cooking school; and Khadija's Kuzina, where you cook in a local home.

Fodor's Choice ★ **L'Atelier by Madada.** This is the best cooking school in town. Here you'll get an authentic, step-by-step introduction to Moroccan cuisine. Chef Mouna shares the secrets of generations of Moroccan housewives with simultaneous English translation. The first to reserve each day gets to choose from a range of menus, including tagines, pastilla, couscous, and traditional cooked salads. Classes last around four hours and include a tour of the spice souk where the meal's ingredients come from. A glass of wine costs extra. ✉ *Rue Mohamed Ben Massoud, Medina* ☎ *0700/18–90–17* 🌐 *www.lateliermadada.com.*

Fodor's Choice ★ **Khadija's Kuzina.** For an authentic, home-cooking experience in Moroccan cuisine, stop into Khadija and Hussein's home, where you will learn how to prepare several typical dishes, including salads, tagines, couscous, and pastilla. Afterward, sit together with the family to enjoy the fruits of your labors. You may often join other travelers, and the first to reserve picks the menu. It's also possible to arrange a special class on Moroccan pastries. ✉ *Av. Allal al Fassi, Quartier Bouhaira* ✣ *Opposite Pharmacie Bouhaira* ☎ *0613/98–58–90, 0670/07–12–32.*

WHERE TO STAY

The riad mania spread to Essaouira just a few years ago and is still going strong, although many of the first foreign riad renovators have now built villas in the countryside where the winds and humidity are lower. Rooms are generally less opulent and less expensive than those in Marrakesh, but you'll find plenty of charm and elegance. There are also plenty of even less expensive hotels, but fewer of the seriously budget hippie hangouts of yesteryear.

For hotels with swimming pools you'll have only one expensive option within the medina: L'Heure Bleue Palais. Other beachfront hotels with pools are fine if you have a large family, and may offer shelter on windier days, but the beach is never very far away on foot.

Another option is to rent an apartment, by the night or by the week. There's a wide range of options, from spartan bedrooms with showers that don't work, to an entire super-styled riad. Renting is often a better deal than staying in a hotel, especially if you're with a group. Rooms book up quickly, especially in summer, so reserve (sometimes months) ahead. **■ TIP→ You can only take a car as far as a medina gate, so you'll have to heave your luggage to that dear little out-of-the-way spot down 10 twisting alleys yourself. The best option? Pick up a carossa (a small cart on wheels) from the parking lot outside one of the gates and pay the owner and cart wheeler 20 DH for his trouble.**

$$ B&B/INN **Dar Liouba.** This is actually two properties combined and remodeled to ensure the atrium and bedrooms are flooded with light. **Pros:** more light than most riads; warm welcome; rooftop sea views. **Cons:** can be difficult to find; lots of stairs; rooms on lower floors can be noisy from the street below. [$] *Rooms from: 650DH* ✉ *28, Impasse Moulay Ismail, Medina* ☎ *0677/54–32–84* 🌐 *www.darliouba.eu* 🛏 *9 rooms* 🍴 *Some meals.*

$$$$ B&B/INN **Dar Maya.** With only five rooms but plenty of communal spaces, every inch of Dar Maya is designed to perfection, creating the boutique hotel Essaouira has been waiting for. **Pros:** intimate and chic; attentive English-speaking staff; ocean views. **Cons:** rooms are often booked up; quite expensive; owners have dogs that roam the house. [$] *Rooms from: 1595DH* ✉ *33, rue Oujda, Medina* ☎ *0524/78–56–87* 🌐 *www.riaddarmaya.com* 🛏 *5 rooms* 🍴 *Some meals.*

$$$$ HOTEL Fodor's Choice ★ **Heure Bleue Palais.** Enjoy ample space and amenities like nowhere else in the medina at Essaouira's most prestigious lodging, a meticulously designed property with colonial ambience in cream, granite, and dark wood. **Pros:** more space than you'd think possible in the medina; the only pool inside the medina walls; beautiful architecture. **Cons:** not the typical Moroccan decor some might expect; by far the most expensive rates in the medina; noise from the billiards room and bar can reverberate up to the rooms. [$] *Rooms from: 1980DH* ✉ *2, rue Ibn Batouta, Medina* ☎ *0524/78–34–34* 🌐 *www.relaischateaux.com/heurebleue* 🛏 *33 rooms* 🍴 *Multiple meal plans.*

$$$$ HOTEL **Hotel Atlas Essaouira and Spa.** The Hotel Atlas provides beachfront five-star service with all the facilities you would expect from the Moroccon brand. **Pros:** private beach; delicious restaurant; plenty of facilities.

Cons: corporate feel; lacks charm; popular with big groups. [$] *Rooms from: 1400DH* ✉ *Bd. Mohammed V* ☎ *0524/47–99–99* 🌐 *www.hotelatlasessaouira.com* 🛏 *156 rooms* 🍴 *Some meals.*

$$$$ B&B/INN 🏨 **Madada Mogador.** Stylized, elegant, and designed to perfection, Madada Mogador is perfectly poised just within the medina walls to ensure easy access and ocean views from most rooms. **Pros:** attentive staff; cool lounge spaces; chic design features. **Cons:** confusing shared entrance with hotel next door; two-night minimum stay; small common areas. [$] *Rooms from: 1485DH* ✉ *5, rue Youssef el Fassi, Medina* ☎ *0524/47–55–12* 🌐 *www.madada.com* 🛏 *7 rooms* 🍴 *Breakfast.*

$$ B&B/INN FAMILY 🏨 **Maison du Sud.** Enter through a traditional, heavy, stone arch off a busy medina street, and find the cool interior of this long-established, Moroccan-run inn, made of two large town houses. **Pros:** great central location in the medina; triple and quadruple rooms available; substantial breakfast. **Cons:** some rooms feel cramped; can fill up with groups; can be dark. [$] *Rooms from: 540DH* ✉ *29, av. Sidi Mohammed Ben Abdellah, Medina* ☎ *0524/47–41–41* 🌐 *www.riad-maisondusud.com* 🛏 *24 rooms* 🍴 *Some meals.*

$$$$ HOTEL FAMILY 🏨 **Le Medina Essaouira Hotel Thalassa Sea & Spa MGallery by Sofitel.** The closest to the medina of the city's two beachfront five-star hotels, the property has a location and facilities that are second to none. **Pros:** large pool; private beach; great spa; good access for those with reduced mobility. **Cons:** lacks Moroccan charm beyond the lobby; popular with large groups; service can be lacking given its five-star status. [$] *Rooms from: 1300DH* ✉ *Bd. Mohammed V* ☎ *0525/07–25–26* 🌐 *www.sofitel.com* 🛏 *117 rooms* 🍴 *Some meals.*

$$$ HOTEL 🏨 **Riad Al Madina.** This beautiful 18th-century riad is wrapped around a stone courtyard where you'll find a trickling fountain. **Pros:** sun-filled rooms and patio; in-house hammam; central location. **Cons:** can feel very crowded; rooms can be cramped; gets busy with groups. [$] *Rooms from: 880DH* ✉ *9, rue Attarine, Medina* ☎ *0524/47–59–07* 🌐 *www.riadalmadina.com* 🛏 *54 rooms* 🍴 *Some meals.*

$$$ B&B/INN 🏨 **Riad Baladin.** The personal attention from the manager is a highlight here and starts with a welcome briefing and introduction to the best-kept secrets of the medina. **Pros:** larger and lighter rooms than most riads; personalized service; quiet cul-de-sac location. **Cons:** cash only; no meals other than breakfast; confusing stairways can make it difficult to find your room. [$] *Rooms from: 810DH* ✉ *9, rue Sidi Magdoul, Medina* ☎ *0524/47–30–94* 🌐 *www.riadbaladin.com* 💳 *No credit cards* 🛏 *10 rooms* 🍴 *Breakfast.*

$$ B&B/INN 🏨 **Riad Chakir.** This colorful and friendly budget riad is actually made up of three neighboring houses. **Pros:** great value and location; friendly, English-speaking staff; lovely roof terrace. **Cons:** some rooms cramped; more homey comfort than boutique chic; used by a major adventure travel company so often full. [$] *Rooms from: 385DH* ✉ *13, rue Malek Ben Morhal, off Av. Istiqlal, Medina* ☎ *0524/47–33–09* 🌐 *www.riad-chakir.com* 🛏 *20 rooms* 🍴 *Breakfast.*

$$$$ B&B/INN 🏨 **Riad Chbanate.** This former 18th-century *caid*'s (local official's) residence has been transformed into a boutique hotel flooded with light. **Pros:** gorgeous rooftop suite with 360-degree views of the city;

beautifully decorated rooms; modern architecture with some traditional elements. **Cons:** some rooms have open-plan bathrooms, which are not to everyone's taste; not suitable for people with limited mobility; the street to the hotel can be dark at night. $ *Rooms from: 1430DH* ✉ *179, rue Chbanate, Medina* ☎ *0524/78–33–34* ⊕ *www.riadchbanate. com* ➲ *8 rooms* †○† *Some meals.*

$$
B&B/INN

⛾ **Riad Kafila.** Located right on the medina walls, Riad Kafila has some of the best direct ocean views in the city. **Pros:** bright salon with stunning ocean views; homey ambience; impressive hospitality. **Cons:** the windows of the sea-view rooms are too high for an actual view; no air-conditioning; not suitable for people with limited mobility. $ *Rooms from: 650DH* ✉ *4 bis, rue Yamen, Medina* ☎ *0524/78–32–75* ⊕ *www. riadkafila.com* ➲ *7 rooms* †○† *Some meals.*

$$$
HOTEL

⛾ **Riad Mimouna.** Tight against the northern side of the medina walls, this riad sits over the water's edge, letting you have the raging sea all to yourself. **Pros:** ocean views; central heating in winter; traditional architectural features. **Cons:** some rooms too weather-beaten; atmosphere more like a hotel than an intimate riad; patchy Wi-Fi. $ *Rooms from: 850DH* ✉ *62, rue d'Oujda, Sandillon, Medina* ☎ *0524/78–57–54* ⊕ *www.riad-mimouna.com* ➲ *33 rooms* †○† *Some meals.*

$$$$
RESORT

⛾ **Sofitel Essaouira Mogador Golf & Spa.** If you're done with the cutesy but crowded scene of the medina and yearn for space and views as far as the eye can see, this Sofitel is for you. **Pros:** heaps of facilities including three pools, four restaurants, a hammam, and kids' club; extensive gardens; sea views. **Cons:** far from the medina and the free shuttle stops at 6 pm; the beach is a 20-minute walk away; some parts of the hotel look run down. $ *Rooms from: 1500DH* ✉ *Domaine de Mogador, Diabat* ☎ *0524/47–94–00* ⊕ *www.sofitel.com* ➲ *175 rooms* †○† *Multiple meal plans.*

$$$$
B&B/INN

⛾ **Villa de l'Ô.** The Essaouira location of this small regional chain exudes sophistication, with its wood-paneled library, colonial-style decor, sleek roof terrace, and sweeping views of the whole beach. **Pros:** conveniently located and easily accessible; fabulous roof terrace; pool access at the sister hotel outside the medina. **Cons:** this kind of service gets pricey; parts of the hotel are looking a little tired; some rooms can be cold in winter. $ *Rooms from: 1200DH* ✉ *3, rue Mohamed Ben Messaoud, Medina* ☎ *0524/47–63–75* ⊕ *www.villadelo.com* ➲ *12 rooms* †○† *Breakfast.*

$$$$
HOTEL

⛾ **Villa Maroc.** Embodying much of what international travelers seek in a Moroccan hotel, the intimate Villa Maroc is delightfully decorated to epitomize a "traditional" Moroccan style that never really was. **Pros:** great service; sizable rooms; on-site hammam. **Cons:** when busy, a minimum stay may be required; half-board bookings preferred; not suitable for people with limited mobility. $ *Rooms from: 1400DH* ✉ *10, rue Abdellah Ben Yassine, Medina* ☎ *0524/47–31–47* ⊕ *www.villa-maroc. com* ➲ *21 rooms* †○† *Some meals.*

APARTMENT RENTAL AGENCIES

Arriving in the city's outskirts, you'll see men dangling keys by the side of the road, hoping to rent you an apartment. It's best to go through official agents, however.

8

Castles in the Sand. British interior designer Emma Wilson rents out two medina townhouses. Dar Beida, the "White House," is one of Essaouira's most sumptuous addresses. The villa is filled with hip furnishings and decor from the 1950s and 1960s. Cool 21st-century perks include iPod speakers and wireless Internet. The other villa, Dar Emma, has more traditional ambience. ⊠ *Essaouira* ☎ *0667/96–53–86 in Morocco* ⊕ *www.castlesinthesand.com.*

Jack's Apartments. Several beautiful old medina studios, apartments, riads, and penthouses are available for rent. Each is serviced daily, and all are fully equipped with towels, sheets, blankets, soap, and a hair dryer. In addition, Jack's team can provide breakfast and other meals delivered to your door. ⊠ *1, pl. Moulay Hassan, Medina* ☎ *0524/47–55–38* ⊕ *www.jackapartments.com.*

NIGHTLIFE

Most Essaouira residents consider nightlife to involve simply hanging out at a café on the main square, but should you fancy partying into the night after dinner, there are a few options.

Le Chrysalis. By far the most appealing of Essaouira's nightclubs, every night at Le Chrysalis has a band playing an eclectic set of covers of popular Western tunes, as well as Moroccan and West African favorites. The drinks aren't cheap, but the atmosphere is lively and the place pulls in a range of tourists, locals, and expats of varying ages. ⊠ *Complexe Bin Laswar, next to Bab Sbaa* ☎ *0524/47–26–63, 0666/45–00–93* ⊕ *www.lechrysalis-essaouira.com.*

Loubou's. At the younger end of the scene, Loubou's is loud and smoky with a DJ pumping out dance music while customers suck on water pipes in chairs around the dance floor. Admission is typically free unless a guest DJ has been flown in for the night. ⊠ *Complexe Bin Al Aswar, next to Bab Sbaa* ☎ *0524/78–48–72.*

So Lounge. Modeled after its successful older sister in Agadir, the So Lounge at the Sofitel in Diabat is the height of sophistication. A cocktail bar and restaurant overlooks the main bar, stage, and dance area; live music is played every night except Monday. Admission is free, but it's recommended that diners book a table. ⊠ *Sofitel Essaouira Mogador Golf & Spa, Domaine de Mogador, Diabat* ☎ *0524/47–94–00* ⊕ *www.sofitel.com.*

SHOPPING

Essaouira is a great shopping destination. Although the range may be more limited than in Marrakesh or Fez, the vendors are a lot more relaxed and starting prices are often reasonable.

Essaouira is famed as an artisan center expert in marquetry and inlay. Boxes, platters, and picture frames made of local thuya wood make excellent gifts, and the wood-carvers' souk below the skala is a popular place to purchase them. A hard, local wood that shines up to almost plastic perfection, thuya is sculpted for both artistic and practical use. Almost-life-size statues and sculptures sit alongside boxes, bowls, and chess sets. Scan a number of stores to see whether you prefer the even-toned thuya branch inlaid with mother-of-pearl or walnut or one with swirling root designs. To get a bulk price, buy a bunch of items from a craftsman who specializes in them.

The main areas for purchasing local crafts and souvenirs are Rue Sidi Mohammed Ben Abdullah, Derb Laalouj, and along the skala. Colorful, woven baskets hang from herbalists' stores in the spice souk and Place Marché aux Grains across the road. While the bazaars, tended by turbaned men of the South, will sell antique (and faux-antique) silver jewelry, locals tend to buy new items from the jewelry souk off Avenue L'Istiqlal. Dive into the small, shady alleyways off the main areas to find more treasures such as carpets, cushion covers, up-cycled antiques from ruined Jewish houses, jewelry and punched metal, and goatskin lamps.

Essaouira is also home to a number of expat artists and craftspeople. Many restaurants and boutique stores sell their work in glass cabinets at fixed prices.

ANTIQUES

Galérie Aida. For tasteful used pewter platters, goblets, and ceramic teapots, as well as new and used English and French books, check the Galérie Aida, underneath the ramparts. There is also a large selection of antique daggers. The gallery's owner, Joseph Sebag, one of Essaouira's last remaining Jewish residents, is knowledgeable about the city's Jewish history. ⊠ *2, rue de la Skala, Medina* ☎ *0524/47–62–90.*

Galerie Boutique Elizir. If you are into retro and vintage furnishing and decor, find three floors of them at this gallery that showcases the collections of Abdelatif, who ran a restaurant of the same name in this space. Explore this treasure trove to discover furniture, artwork, clothing, and decorative objects, both Moroccan and European, from bygone decades. ⊠ *Av. de l'Istiqlal, Medina* ☎ *0524/47–21–03.*

Galerie Jama. Tucked away at the end of the street, Galerie Jama seems more museum than shop. You can browse among wooden doors, mosaic vases, vintage Berber rugs, and all sorts of wonderful odds and ends. Get ready to negotiate if you see something you like. ⊠ *22, rue Ibn Rochd, Medina* ☎ *0670/01–64–29* ⊕ *www.galeriejama.com.*

ARGAN OIL AND SPICES

Au Petit Bonhomme de la Chance. Habiba Ajaoui was the first female shopkeeper in the Essaouira medina and she's always happy to pass the time chatting with clients (in Arabic, French, or English) over a cup of steaming tea. She sells spices and argan and cactus-seed oils at reasonable prices and can get you everything you need for the hammam. She also has a large repertoire of henna tattoo designs, which are priced according to their complexity. ⊠ *30, rue Laalouj, Medina* ☎ *0666/01–45–02.*

Chez Makki. The five Makki brothers have taken over their father's herbalist business and turned it into an empire. Several of the shops on Place Marché aux Grains and in the spice souk across the road are run by them. They know their stuff and are happy to explain which spices are used in which recipes and the difference between real and fake saffron over a pot of royal tea. They also sell a range of solid perfumes, argan-oil products, and ceramics. ⊠ *221, Souk Laghzal, Spice Market, Medina* ☎ *0524/47–30–90.*

8

BERBER GOLD: ARGAN OIL

The Moroccan argan forest, which stretches from Essaouira down past Agadir and along the Souss Valley to the Anti-Atlas, is unique, as there is nowhere else in the world where the tree grows so well. As you travel across the region, you will see the short, spiny trees in fields and on hillsides.

In recent years, as the aesthetic properties of argan oil have been widely publicized, the Moroccan government has developed a strategy to support the creation of women's co-ops to extract and market the oil, as well as to preserve the unique biosphere and protect against overuse. As prices have risen, argan oil has become known as "Berber gold," with leading beauty brands including it in their products and famous television chefs developing recipes to include it.

The difference between cosmetic and culinary oils is that the latter is the result of grinding the almonds found inside the argan nut after toasting, while cosmetic oil is ground directly.

Without a doubt, the argan boom has brought much-needed employment opportunities to rural areas, particularly for women. However, many establishments that claim to operate on cooperative principles (especially those on main tourist thoroughfares) often do not. Also, many co-ops that tout "bio" or "organic" branding may use nuts that have not been sprayed with pesticides, but few have actually been able to secure organic certification.

When buying argan oil, try to buy from a genuine cooperative to ensure you get the real deal and that your money helps rural women. The UCFA is a union created with aid from foreign development agencies to help professionalize and support women's argan co-ops. They have a list of their members online at ⊕ *www.cooperative-argane.com.*

If your concern is the oil being 100% organic, it may be that the production is less hands-on and more mechanized than in rural co-ops. The oils produced at Sidi Yassine outside Essaouira are widely exported and therefore rigorously certified. You can buy them at Histoire de Filles. ⊕ *www.sidiyassine.com*

A great souvenir is *amlou,* a paste made from toasted almonds or peanuts, argan oil, and local honey. Often called "Berber Nutella," it tastes more like a kind of nut butter.

ART GALLERIES

There are many galleries in the medina displaying contemporary Moroccan and expatriate mixed-media productions. These are also often exhibited at Dar Souiri or in the South Bastion at Bab Marrakech.

Espace Othello Gallerie d'Art. Named after Orson Welles's *Othello,* which was shot in town, this gallery exhibits local and international artists and antiques. Look out for Scottish artist Caroline Fulton's work, which features indigenous Moroccan animals in rural and medina settings. ⊠ *9, rue Mohammed Layachi, Medina* ☎ *0524/47-50-95* ⊙ *Closed Mon.*

Galerie d'Art Damgaard. Danish collector Frederic Damgaard is credited with bringing the *naïve* art of Essaouira to an international audience. His Galerie d'Art Damgaard, across from the clock tower, has well-curated displays of work by Essaouira painters and sculptors and is also a great place to pick up souvenir books on local art and culture. ✉ *Av. Oqba Ibn Nafiaa, Medina* ☎ *0524/78–44–46.*

Yellow Workshop. Danish artist Sanne Busk, who has made Essaouira her home, specializes in collage art made with hand-painted paper. Her husband, Hassan, is a master *guembri* (traditional Gnaoua stringed instrument) maker and crafts unusually decorated wood instruments. Their work is showcased in this gallery, along with workshops and demonstrations. ✉ *Rue Mohamed Diouri, Medina* ☎ *0697/40–25–43 Sanne, 0660/31–36–05 Hassan* ⊕ *www.yellowworkshop.com.*

HAMMAMS AND SPAS
If you want an authentic hammam experience, collect the necessary soap, scrub mitt, and other products from a spice shop such as Au Petit Bonhomme de la Chance and prepare to get down and dirty with the locals. If you prefer something a little more refined, head to a spa; there are plenty in hotels and around the medina. The following hammams and spas are open to all (even nonguests, if in a hotel).

PUBLIC HAMMAMS
Hammam Pabst. Located in the Mellah, this is one of the oldest hammams in Essaouira. Now brightly painted, it has a plaque indicating that Orson Welles once used it as a location during the filming of *Othello*. Because of this, it's popular with tourists and the ladies who are on hand to scrub and massage clients can get a little greedy. Check on the door for the most up-to-date male/female opening hours. ✉ *Rue Annasr, Medina* ☎ *10 DH (massage or scrub extra).*

Hammam Sidi Abdelsmih. On the street of the same name, this women-only hammam is open all day until midnight. For just 50 DH, you can get a great scrub-down by one of the local ladies. If your male partner wants the same, he should head over the Hammam Bolisi in Rue Dar Dheb, near Maison du Sud. Don't forget to bring a towel and a spare pair of underwear (because you wear one pair inside). ✉ *Rue Sidi Abdelsmih, Medina.*

HOTEL HAMMAMS
Hotel Riad Al Madina. This popular riad has a rather good hammam that nonguests can use. A 30-minute scrub with argan oil, roses, sugar, and salt costs 200 DH. ✉ *9, rue Attarine, Medina* ☎ *0524/47–59–07* ⊕ *www.riadalmadina.com* ☎ *Treatments 70 DH–400 DH.*

Villa Maroc. The first riad guesthouse in Essaouira has a private "Oriental Spa" hammam open to nonguests and offers a range of treatment packages, including massages for children. A traditional scrub with black soap and a scrub mitt plus a *ghassoul* (therapeutic mud) wrap and a 10-minute massage costs 600 DH per person. Forty-five-minute massages with argan oil cost upward of 320 DH. ✉ *10, rue Abdellah Ben Yassine, Medina* ☎ *0524/47–31–47* ⊕ *www.villa-maroc.com.*

8

DID YOU KNOW?

Essaouira (originally called Mogador) is one of Morocco's best port towns to visit. A walk along the ramparts and a seafood dinner at one of the many local restaurants are two must-dos of any visit.

SPAS

Azur Spa. A wide range of treatments are available at this spa—including aromatic massage, reflexology, seaweed baths, and exfoliation—but it's the beautiful, black-marble hammam that remains the star attraction. Fluffy robes, slippers, and black soap are provided, as is herbal tea after your treatments. A traditional hammam with scrub costs 200 DH and a relaxing one-hour massage, 350 DH. Men, women, and couples can use the hammam together. ⊠ *15, rue Khalid ben Walid, Medina* ☎ *0524/78–57–94* ⊕ *www.azur-spa-essaouira.com.*

Bio Spa Esthétique. This spa and hammam offers great value in a clean and welcoming setting in the heart of the medina. The package deals frequently include an argan-oil scrub or massage. A simple hammam scrub is 130 DH while a 1½-hour package that includes an argan scrub, face scrub and mask, and back massage is 300 DH. ⊠ *9, rue Irak, Medina* ☎ *0524/78–46–88.*

Heure Bleue Palais. Located at Bab Marrakech in the medina, this palatial riad hotel has a hammam plus treatment and massage rooms open to nonguests who book in advance (book either one or two days ahead). A full list of packages and treatments is on the website. ⊠ *2, rue Ibn Batouta, Bab Marrakesh, Medina* ☎ *0524/78–34–34* ⊕ *www. heure-bleue.com.*

Le Medina Essaouira Hotel Thalassa Sea & Spa by MGallery by Sofitel. Situated on the seafront, with ocean views from the relaxation lounge, this has to be the best-equipped spa in town. It specializes in thalassotherapy with water jet showers, hydrating baths, massages, and aqua gym workouts. There's also a gym, hammam, hair salon, heated outdoor pool, and sun deck as well as a whole menu of beauty treatments. ⊠ *Bd. Mohammed V, Medina* ☎ *0524/47–90–00* ⊕ *www.thalassa.com.*

CRAFTS AND JEWELRY

Basma. Hafida welcomes all her customers with a smile and offers a keenly curated selection of Morocco-made jewelry, leather bags, shoes, small paintings, and other decorative items. ⊠ *20 bis, rue Skala* ☎ *0524/78–34–66.*

La Fibule Berbère. Amid dozens of other Ali Baba–cave-style shops in the Essaouira medina, La Fibule Berbère is one of the oldest and one of the few that accepts credit cards. The shop displays stunning ethnic jewelry, such as huge silver pendants, *fibules* (clasps for attaching pendants and closing shawls), and bulky necklaces made in the Berber and Toureg styles. ⊠ *51–53, rue Attarine, Medina* ☎ *0524/47–62–55, 0661/06–97–74* ⊕ *www.fibuleberbere-essaouira.com.*

Histoire de Filles. Essaouira's only concept store is located near Bab Sbaa and offers a range of clothing, jewelry, accessories, organic argan oil, and small decorative items. Products are designed locally by Moroccan and international designers. This is the closest you'll get in Essaouira to the modern design stores of Marrakesh. ⊠ *1, rue Mohamed Ben Messaoud, Medina* ☎ *0524/78–51–93.*

Mashi Mushki. Shopping at the Mashi Mushki store in Essaouira gives you the chance to support locals, as a percentage of the profits goes to the Project 91 charity, which helps young Souiris (natives of Essaouira)

ESSAOUIRA'S LOCAL MARKETS

If you don't mind getting up early to catch the action, your hotel or a local tour operator will be happy to arrange a visit to a local market (although all are also accessible by local bus or grand taxi). The highlight is Had Draa on a Sunday, where the earliest risers are rewarded with a view of camel trading. Cattle, donkeys, horses, sheep, and goats are also traded, the latter often taking a direct route to the on-site abattoir. This is a farmers' market in the true sense; it's unlikely you'll find many souvenirs to buy between the animal feed, fresh vegetables, cobblers, and vendors of plastic sheeting, but it is a fascinating insight into rural Moroccan life. Other smaller markets are on Wednesday (Ida Ougourd), Thursday (Meskala), Saturday (Akermoud), and Sunday (Smimou). Rural Moroccans are often conservative, so please dress accordingly and cover thighs and shoulders to avoid unwanted attention. The markets are very picturesque, but local people may be offended if you photograph them without asking and may say no if you do.

to improve their lives through job training and other activities. Some of the items are made in the neighborhood or by co-ops, which also benefits locals. Pick up craft items with a conscience. While you're there, leave your unwanted clothes at the thrift shop across the street. ⊠ *91, rue Chbanat, Medina* ⊕ *www.dar91.com.*

Trésor Kafila Shop. This shop offers a range of handmade items from all over Morocco and the Sahara, including mirrors, jewelry, leather bags, and small pieces of furniture. The kettle is always on and you'll eventually be invited to join in for a cup of sweet mint tea to seal your deal. ⊠ *86, rue Laalouj, Medina* ☎ *0662/82-55-46.*

WOODWORK

Thuya furniture is as unavoidable on the streets of Essaouira as in-line skaters in Malibu Beach. Try to buy from the artisans, as this is the only way they can make a decent return on their ancient craft. The cheap boxes you see in the tourist shops have passed through so many middlemen that the craftsman ends up with nearly nothing. If you want to find nontouristy workshops off the main streets, take a right onto Rue Khalid Ibn el-Walid, just off Place Moulay Hassan, to seek out the thuya cooperative called Coopérative Artisanale des Marqueteurs.

Fodor's Choice ★ **Coopérative Artisanale des Marqueteurs.** Walk through a nondescript passageway into a classic 19th-century riad and you'll find the Coopérative Artisanale des Marqueteurs, whose members have been turning out finely decorated boxes, ornaments, tables, and other furniture since 1948. Everything has a tag with the artisan's code number and reasonable fixed prices. At the end of the month, the craftsmen collect their income and a small proportion goes to the upkeep of the building and the running of the co-op. You won't find tour groups here as there is no commission for guides, making it a tranquil place to stop and admire decades of craftsmanship. ⊠ *6, rue Khalid Ibn el Walid, off Pl. Moulay Hassan, Medina* ☎ *0524/47-56-76.*

SPORTS AND THE OUTDOORS

CYCLING

Mogador2Roues. Bikes here rent for 120 DH per day for personal use, while guided tours of three to four hours along local trails run 350 DH per person, with cheaper rates for larger groups. Motorscooters are also available for exploration farther afield. ⊠ *22, rue Al Attarine, Medina* ✛ *Opposite Hotel Souiri* ☏ *0671/01–82–52, 0668/19–53–68.*

FOUR-WHEELING

Sahara Quad. This company organizes quad-bike excursions including pickup from your hotel to their starting point. Rentals are offered for as little as one hour to as long as three days; a popular circuit takes in Diabat and Cap Sim, south of Essaouira, returning through the thuya cedar forests. A two-hour circuit for two riders costs approximately 660 DH. ⊠ *355, Lot Eraounak* ☏ *0673/44–95–41.*

GOLF

Golf de Mogador. The 18-hole golf course at Diabat, designed by Gary Player, is an integral part of the same resort that includes the Sofitel hotel. Surrounded by sand dunes, the course rolls down toward the sea and sits among forests of eucalyptus and thuya. Lessons are available and there are discounts for Sofitel guests. ⊠ *Domaine de Mogador, Diabat* ☏ *0525/08–10–10* 🖬 *475 DH for 9 holes, 200 DH for golf cart, 100 DH for caddy; 750 DH for 18 holes, 350 DH for golf cart, 120 DH for caddy* 🏌*. 18 holes, 7227 yards, par 72.*

HIKING

Ecotourisme et Randonnées. Owner Edouard is a former forester from France and is fanatical about sustainable tourism. His colleague, Ottman, can take you on a number of walking circuits around the local countryside, where he will explain flora, fauna, and local culture and customs in English. You can also eat with a local family during the tour. They will organize trips to the local vineyard as well as to a Berber market. Make your reservation at La Découverte restaurant in the medina. ⊠ *8 bis, rue Houmman el Fatouaki, Medina* ☏ *0615/76–21–31* ⊕ *www.essaouira-randonnees.com.*

HORSEBACK AND CAMEL RIDING

Fodor's Choice **Ranch de Diabat.** This is a long-standing family-run business that can
★ organize horse-riding and camel trips from a ranch in Diabat. A camel or horseback ride costs from 150 DH per hour, while a half-day camel trip with lunch starts at 450 DH. Horseback riding lessons and trail rides of several days can be organized for groups. They also have an activity center with dune buggies and quad bikes for hire. ⊠ *Ranch Diabat, Diabat* ☏ *0524/47–63–82* ⊕ *www.ranchdediabat.com.*

Zouina Cheval. This company organizes horseback riding excursions on Diabat beach and in the countryside around Essaouira, with treks from one hour to a full day for beginners and experienced riders alike. Longer multiday treks with camping for groups and camel trips are also possible. Prices start from around 160 DH per hour and 600 DH for a full day with a picnic lunch. ⊠ *Diabat* ☏ *0669/80–71–01* ⊕ *www. zouina-cheval.com.*

The beaches south of Essaouira are among Morocco's top surfing spots.

WATER SPORTS

If you are a water-sports enthusiast, it is important to understand where the wind and wave conditions are best for each sport. In Essaouira Bay and farther south to Sidi Kaouki, you will most often find kitesurfing. When the wind gets going, windsurfers come out in Essaouira and to the north at Moulay Bouzerktoun. Only beginner surfers attempt anything around Essaouira; the best breaks for experienced surfers are much farther south, between Imssouane and Agadir.

FAMILY
Fodor's Choice
★

Explora. A professional Moroccan-English company offers a wide range of water sports with qualified instruction at prices considerably cheaper than the nearest competition. The company can also arrange your accommodation and many other outdoor activities such as horseback riding, quad-biking, camel treks, and mountain biking. Kitesurfing lessons start at 660 DH for two hours. The company has its activity base on the southern end of the beach (at Avenue Mohammed V near junction with Route d'Agadir) and also a supplies shop in the medina. ⊠ *12, av. Istiqlal, Medina* ☎ *0611/47–51–88* ⊕ *explorawatersports.com.*

Ion Club - Ocean Vagabond. This joint venture with Ocean Vagabond is the biggest outfit in town. It prides itself on the quality of its equipment and its multidisciplinary and multilingual instruction. Factor this into the cost of courses, which are pricier than elsewhere along the bay: two hours of kitesurfing instruction costs 825 DH in a group, while a private lesson is double that price. The more experienced can rent everything they need to explore the coast: boards, a kit, and even roof racks. ⊠ *Plage, at southern end of beach, Quartier des Dunes* ☎ *0524/78–39–34* ⊕ *www.oceanvagabond.com.*

Magic Fun. After 10 years on the Essaouira seafront, Magic Fun has moved to a base farther north at Moulay Bouzerktoun. Here, the multilingual owner specializes in windsurfing and paddleboarding while his wife runs a café with sheltered views of the sea. Because of the wind conditions here, they don't cater to beginners, but concentrate instead on improving skills. They can pick you up for no extra charge from Essaouira, and offer a lounge area and basic rooms for those who don't want to travel back the same day. ⊠ *Moulay Bouzerktoun* ☎ *0661/10–37–77* ⊕ *www.magicfunafrika.com.*

THE SOUSS VALLEY AND ANTI-ATLAS

Few venture this far south in Morocco, but those who do are rewarded with a real insight into the life and culture at the edge of the great Sahara. The Moroccan southwest combines glorious beaches, arid mountains flanked by lush palm groves, hillsides scattered with spiny argan and Barbary fig cactus, and olive, almond, and orange orchards. The region's character is strongly flavored by its Tashelhit-speaking Berbers, who inhabited these mountains and plains before Arabs ever set foot in Morocco, giving the region a distinctively rural atmosphere.

East and south of Agadir you leave the world of beach vacations and enter Berber country. Scenic drives take you past hills covered with barley and almond trees, palm groves, kasbahs, and the Anti-Atlas Mountains themselves. In town, poke around the monuments and souks of Taroudant or shop for Morocco's finest silver in Tiznit. Keep in mind the towns are not the attraction in the region; people come here to commune with nature, admire the vistas, and get away from it all.

TAROUDANT

85 km (51 miles) east of Agadir, 223 km (138 miles) southwest of Marrakesh.

Known as the "Grandmother of Marrakesh," Taroudant is often promoted as an alternative destination to that other former Saadian capital, but these labels are misleading and deny Taroudant its essence. The Taroudant medina walls were built in the 16th century to defend the capital and are almost entirely complete. Today, they encircle a spacious, fully functional Moroccan market town serving a large rural hinterland where tourism plays only a limited role in the local economy. People in Taroudant are less jaded than in more tourist-focused areas and are happy to chat with visitors as they go about their daily business. You're more likely to see an artisan at one of the markets upcycling something for use on a farm than creating a trinket for a tourist.

People, customs, and the Arabic and Tashelhit Berber languages mix in this town of around 60,000 inhabitants. The town's relaxed feel, the easy interaction with locals, inexpensive dining, and a couple of guesthouse gems make Taroudant an ideal base for exploring the Souss Valley and the western High Atlas.

Some of Taroudant's fortified walls are 900 years old.

GETTING HERE AND AROUND
The principal road routes to Taroudant are easily navigable and well signposted. The N10 runs east from Agadir and leads eventually to Taliouine, Tazenakht, and Ouarzazate. There are also scheduled buses from Agadir (1½ hours), Ouarzazate (5 hours), Casablanca (10 hours), Rabat (13 hours), and Marrakesh (6½ hours). Efficient and comfortable CTM buses leave from the gare routière outside Bab Zorgane on the southern side of the medina.

Once you arrive in the city, everything is within walking distance.

Bus Contact CTM. ✉ *Gare Routière, Bab Zorgane, just inside city walls* ☎ *0528/85-38-58* ⊕ *www.ctm.ma.*

Rental Cars Malja Cars. ✉ *Bab Targhount, Mbarek Oussalem* ☎ *0528/55-17-42.*

GUIDES AND TOURS
Moulay Brahim Bouchra. For a guided tour of the city, Moulay Brahim Bouchra has encyclopedic knowledge of Taroudant and speaks English very well. Tour from 150 DH for a half day. ✉ *Taroudant* ☎ *0662/19-24-63* ✉ *From 125 DH.*

TIMING AND PRECAUTIONS
Taroudant attracts visitors all year-round thanks to its favorable climate, although it can get very hot in summer. Most visitors stay a night or two to explore the local region while en route to another destination such as Tafraoute or Ouarzazate.

EXPLORING

Whatever you do in the late afternoon, don't miss the sight of colorfully dressed Roudani (Taroudant native) women lined up against the ramparts near the hospital like birds on a ledge, socializing in the cool hours before sunset. Sunset tours of the ramparts aboard a *calèche* (horse-drawn carriage) are available; the driver may expect you to haggle for your fare—around 70 DH per hour is about right.

City Walls. The city walls of Taroudant are unique in their completeness and for the fact that the new city has not yet encroached upon them, making them not only easily visible but also approachable. There are five main entry points into the city (from the northwest, going clockwise): Bab el Kasbah, Bab Zorgan, Bab Targhount, Bab Ouled Bounouna, and Bab el Khemis. There is only one place where you can climb up stairs onto the ramparts for a view across the town, at Bab el Kasbah. The best way to see the ramparts is at sunset in a *calèche* (horse and trap) as the setting sun casts a golden glow over the walls, and local women come out in their bright costumes to chat in the cooler air. ⊠ *Taroudant.*

Dar Baroud. Diagonally across from Bab Sedra, across Avenue Moulay Rachid and with the hospital on your right, is the Dar Baroud, once a French ammunition-storage facility. This high-walled building is closed to the public—and is locally rumored to be haunted—but stand back on the sidewalk opposite and you can admire its delicate carved stone walls from the exterior. ⊠ *Taroudant.*

Kasbah. In the northeast side of the city, you'll find the kasbah, or the former king's quarter. It was built by Alouite leader Moulay Ismail in the 17th century—some of the pasha's palace remains intact and has been converted into a hotel (Palais Salam, which you can visit for a drink or meal). On Avenue Moulay Rachid, with the main gate (Bab el Kasbah) behind you, you'll see a smaller gate (Bab Sedra) on the right, which is the old entrance into the kasbah quarter. Inside the walls is a typical medina residential area with little left of any original structures apart from the gates. The area in front of the hotel is now a public park and a great place for watching the evening promenade. ⊠ *Taroudant.*

FAMILY
Fodor's Choice
★

Palais Claudio Bravo. Chilean artist Claudio Bravo came to Morocco in 1972 and built this palatial home with stunning gardens and stables 10 km (6 miles) outside Taroudant. Following his death in 2011, the estate was transformed into a museum showcasing his art and collections, including works by friends like Picasso. The palace is divided into several pavilions connected by inner courtyards and covered walkways, while inside the guest rooms, salons, and Bravo's private rooms and studios are paintings, sculptures, and artifacts, including Roman and North African ceramics. Wander through the gardens full of exotic plants to the large water basin, and rest in the shade of a pavilion with a cup of tea and views of the Atlas Mountains. A full guided tour takes two to three hours, but it's possible to do an unguided visit of the gardens. The hefty entry fee includes transportation by horse carriage from the entrance to the main building. ■TIP➜ You must reserve in advance to visit. You can also reserve for lunch or dinner (expect to pay 400 DH–500 DH per person). ⊠ *Rte. de Tamaloukt, Agwidir*

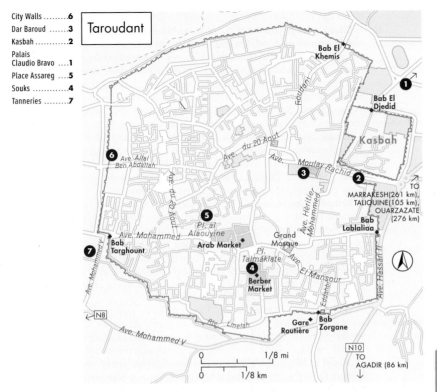

☎ 0691/24–21–61, 0661/96–81–21 ✉ *Guided tour 200 DH, gardens only 100 DH* ☾ *Closed Mon.*

Place Assareg. This plaza sits between the two main souks (the so-called Arab and Berber markets) and serves as the center of life in Taroudant. Although not as lively as Marrakesh's Place Djemâa el-Fna, you still may be able to see performers on the square in the late afternoon. Be sure to join the locals in taking a mint tea on a café terrace and watching the scene unfold. ✉ *Taroudant.*

Souks. In the city itself, the municipal market (also referred to as the Berber souk) sells spices, dried fruits, and other household essentials. In an open-air area to the east, you'll find men upcycling plastics and tires into saddles, water troughs, and panniers for donkeys. The older, so-called Arab market is the better one for souvenirs, and here you can pick up local terra-cotta, brass, and copper items, along with leather sandals, rugs, jewelry, and the standard attire of the Moroccan housewife: fleece pajamas. ✉ *Taroudant.*

Tanneries. Just outside Bab Taghount, you'll find the gifted artisans of Taroudant's tanneries. You can see them working the leather firsthand (not always a pleasant olfactory experience) and can then purchase locally made leather goods such as bags, poufs, sandals, and decorations. ✉ *Taroudant.*

WHERE TO EAT

$$ MOROCCAN

🍴 **Chez Nada.** If you want to stick within the city walls for some no-hassle Moroccan food, you can't go wrong at this father-and-son joint established in 1950. The menu features standards such as couscous, harira, and pigeon pastilla (order in advance). **Known for:** pigeon and chicken pastilla; hearty portions of couscous. [$] *Average main: 90DH* ✉ *Rue Moulay el Rachid* ☎ *0528/85–17–26* 💳 *No credit cards.*

$$$ MEDITERRANEAN Fodor's Choice ★

🍴 **Dar Zitoune.** Set among gorgeous gardens and featuring a menu of local produce, Dar Zitoune is worth the visit from Taroudant. Serving a refined Mediterranean-style menu, it's a favorite with locals as well as with passing tour groups. **Known for:** extensive Mediterranean-style menu; large gardens with fruit trees and flowering plants. [$] *Average main: 100DH* ✉ *Boutarialt el Barrania, 2 km (1 mile) south of Taroudant* ☎ *0528/55–11–41* 🌐 *www.darzitoune.com.*

$$ MOROCCAN FAMILY

🍴 **Restaurant Jnane Soussia.** This outdoor restaurant is a long-standing favorite for Moroccan families, offering great food and lots of space. Traditional cuisine is served under a *caidal* (white canvas) tent around two small swimming pools, in a garden full of orange, fig, and papaya trees and flowers. **Known for:** mechoui (traditional roasted lamb); large gardens full of trees and flowering plants; swimming pool for children. [$] *Average main: 80DH* ✉ *Just outside Bab Zorgan, on right side of road as you head west* ☎ *0528/85–49–80.*

$$$$ MOROCCAN Fodor's Choice ★

🍴 **Riad Maryam.** Taroudant's oldest family-run riad prides itself on its restaurant for good reason. While Habib greets the guests, his wife Latifa works wonders in the kitchen to produce a spread of salads, pastilla, tagines, or couscous fit for a king, not to mention the best *pastilla du lait* (a dessert of fine, crispy phyllo pastry layered with pastry crème) in town. **Known for:** a feast of traditional Moroccan cuisine; homemade pastilla du lait. [$] *Average main: 200DH* ✉ *140, Derb Maalem Mohamed, Bab Targhount* ☎ *0666/12–72–85* 🌐 *www.riadmaryam.com* 💳 *No credit cards.*

WHERE TO STAY

$$$$ RESORT

🏨 **Dar al Hossoun.** This luxury boutique hotel is a true eco-lodge, located in the countryside 8 km (5 miles) from Taroudant. **Pros:** luxury in a countryside setting; individually designed and decorated rooms; attentive service from staff. **Cons:** located 5 miles from town; can be difficult to find; no other restaurants nearby. [$] *Rooms from: 1300DH* ✉ *Qartier Hossoun, Sidi Mbark* ✥ *Off Amskroud–Agadir Rd.* ☎ *0528/85–34–76* 🌐 *www.alhossoun.com* 🛏 *16 rooms* 🍽 *Some meals.*

$$ B&B/INN

🏨 **Dar Dzahra.** Tucked away south of the main square, Dar Dzahra is full of surprises. **Pros:** very central; great pool; triple and family rooms offered. **Cons:** easy to get lost on the way there; only basic amenities in rooms; no air-conditioning. [$] *Rooms from: 550DH* ✉ *73, Derb Akka* ☎ *0528/85–10–85* 🌐 *www.dzahra.com* 💳 *No credit cards* 🛏 *10 rooms* 🍽 *Some meals.*

$$$ B&B/INN FAMILY

🏨 **Dar Zahia.** This unique guesthouse, hidden behind an unassuming door at the end of an alley, is an oasis in this bustling city. **Pros:** local Berber flavor; beautifully designed; a quiet and calm oasis. **Cons:** a little difficult to find; bathrooms are shared; staff doesn't speak much English. [$] *Rooms from: 935DH* ✉ *175, Derb Chrif* ☎ *0528/85–08–01* 🌐 *www.darzahia.com* 🛏 *4 rooms* 🍽 *Some meals* 💳 *No credit cards.*

$$$$
HOTEL
Fodor's Choice
★

Dar Zitoune. Located just outside Taroudant, Dar Zitoune is a wonderful retreat from the bustling town. **Pros:** large gardens full of fruit trees and flowering plants; three swimming pools; generous breakfast. **Cons:** a mile from old city; can be busy with groups coming for lunch; often fully booked. $ *Rooms from: 1200DH* ✉ *Boutarial El Berrania, on road to Agadir Airport, 2 km (1 mile) from town* ☎ *0528/55–11–41* ⊕ *www.darzitoune.com* ❐ *32 rooms* ❑ *Multiple meal plans.*

$$
B&B/INN
FAMILY

La Maison Anglaise. This English-speaking, family-friendly guesthouse, which doubles as a cultural center, has been certified by Green Key for its sustainable operations and environmental responsibility. **Pros:** very eco-friendly; extensive activity program; staff are very welcoming. **Cons:** not all rooms have air-conditioning or an en suite bathroom; often booked up in advance; a little difficult to find. $ *Rooms from: 600DH* ✉ *422, Derb Aferdou* ☎ *0661/23–66–27 in Morocco, 01239/61–54–99 in U.K.* ⊕ *cecu.co.uk* ⊟ *No credit cards* ❐ *9 rooms* ❑ *Some meals.*

$$$
B&B/INN
Fodor's Choice
★

Le Palais Oumensour. This luxurious boutique hotel in the heart of Taroudant's medina has been beautifully renovated from an old riad. **Pros:** great location; good value; beautiful architecture. **Cons:** often fully booked; no credit cards accepted; front rooms over the alley can be noisy. $ *Rooms from: 990DH* ✉ *Borj Oumensour* ☎ *0528/55–02–15* ⊕ *www.palaisoumensour.com* ⊟ *No credit cards* ❐ *11 rooms* ❑ *Some meals.*

$$$
HOTEL

Palais Salam. This 18th-century pasha's palace hotel has seen better days, welcoming ambassadors and aristocracy, but still retains a sense of the grand, starting with the giant courtyard at the center and exotic gardens. **Pros:** large gardens and terraces; easy access by car; located at an entrance to the old town. **Cons:** some areas and rooms rundown; can be full of large bus groups; bar can be noisy at night. $ *Rooms from: 850DH* ✉ *Av. Moulay Ismail, outside ramparts* ☎ *0528/55–02–01* ❐ *142 rooms* ❑ *Some meals.*

$$
B&B/INN
FAMILY
Fodor's Choice
★

Riad Maryam. This is Taroudant's oldest family-run riad, inside an authentic Moroccan townhouse dating from the early 19th century and with many period features. **Pros:** quiet and calm; one of the best dining options in town; you are made to feel at home. **Cons:** kitsch room decor; can be noisy when booked out for meals; no parking nearby. $ *Rooms from: 500DH* ✉ *140, Derb Maalem Mohamed, Bab Targhount* ☎ *0666/12–72–85* ⊕ *www.riadmaryam.com* ❐ *6 rooms* ❑ *Some meals* ⊟ *No credit cards.*

$$$
B&B/INN
FAMILY

Riad Tafilag. In a typical Moroccan neighborhood, Riad Tafilag is the kind of place you could stay for a week. **Pros:** complete relaxation in boutique style; good value; attentive staff. **Cons:** a little difficult to find; lots of stairs; communal areas cluttered with craft and gift items for sale. $ *Rooms from: 715DH* ✉ *31, Derb Taffellagt* ☎ *0528/85–06–07* ⊕ *www.riad-tafilag.com* ❐ *9 rooms* ❑ *Some meals.*

SHOPPING

Taroudant is famous for leather: there are 200 shops in Taroudant dedicated to sandals alone. A walk down even the quietest of streets will feature the incessant tap-tapping of cordwainers at work. Other local products include saffron and lavender, sold by the ounce in herbal stores. The locally pressed olive and argan oils are nationally renowned; ask the herbalists if they can get you a liter. You can also pick up antique jewelry in Taroudant from local Muslim and Jewish Berber tribes.

Antiquaire Haut Atlas. For serious collectors, Antiquaire Haut Atlas has one of the best collections of Berber jewelry in southern Morocco, some of it dating from the 17th and 18th centuries. Even if you're not in the market for a trinket, wandering around the dusty rooms of carpets, candlesticks, and charms makes for a diverting half hour. And if you *are* in the market, Mr. Houssaine accepts all major credit cards and is open every day. ✉ *61, Souk el Kabir* ☎ *0528/85-21-45.*

Sculpteur De Pierre. Here's the best place to go for sculpture, both for quality and range of workmanship. Craftsman Larbi El Hare uses marble, limestone, and alabaster. Small stone masks start at 60 DH. He also makes some of the best mint tea in town, brewed by his erstwhile team of draftsmen polishers. He's been here a while, so ask in the Grande Marché if you can't find his shop. ✉ *Fondouk el Hare, 29, Rahba Kedima, near soap souk* ☎ *0668/80-78-35.*

TAFRAOUTE

152 km (94 miles) southeast of Agadir.

Tafraoute is a pretty and quiet regional market and administrative center, nestled at the bottom of a valley. Usually overlooked by groups, it's a great base for exploring an area rich in natural beauty and overflowing with walks, many of which can be undertaken without bumping into another tourist. It is also a base for those wishing to experience some of Morocco's best rock climbing. Although the dizzying mountains around Tafraoute may prove forbidding to cyclists or light hikers, half-day excursions can take you to prehistoric rock carvings, the Ammeln Valley, or the villages off the main road to Tiznit. It's also worth planning a day's excursion to the Aït Mansour gorges to the south of town, where you'll find a lush, verdant palm grove. The region around Tafraoute is a great place to visit some spectacular *agadirs*—hilltop granaries perched at the top of sheer cliffs. They include those at Amtoudi, Tasguint, and Ikouka.

GETTING HERE AND AROUND

The R105 is a spectacular road running over mountains from Agadir to Tafraoute via Aït Baha. You can pick up this road coming from Taroudant to Tafraoute or travel via the alternative Igherm road. There are buses to Tafraoute from Aït Baha (2 hours), Agadir via Tiznit (5 hours), Marrakesh (10 hours), and Casablanca (14 hours). There are also grands taxis from Tiznit.

Once in Tafraoute, if you don't have a rental car, your best bet is to travel on foot or by bicycle.

TIMING AND PRECAUTIONS

This region can get extremely hot in summer. Climbers prefer to come in winter and spring, when almond blossoms cover the hillsides. Walkers and trekkers following less obvious routes should hire a local guide, or if you want to include Tafraoute as part of a longer Souss Valley tour, then it's worth going through one of the many agencies based in Agadir.

EXPLORING

Ammeln Valley. The Ammeln Valley is becoming a magnet not only for climbers, but also for nature-lovers and hikers. A walk in the valley might start at the village of Oumesnat, where the **Maison Traditionelle** is well worth a visit. ■TIP→ **Wear sturdy shoes for the short walk from the car park.** At the museum in a traditional Berber house, the caretakers will happily explain the old ways of the Anti-Atlas, introducing you to domestic implements, the tea ceremony, and the local women's embroidered black wrap, the *tamelheft*. Express your appreciation for the tour by tipping generously. From Oumesnat you can follow paths to the neighboring villages. **Taghdicte** makes a good base for ambitious Anti-Atlas climbers. ⊠ *Tafraoute.*

Gazelle Rock Carving. The prehistoric gazelle rock carving just 2 km (1 mile) south of Tafraoute is an easy walk or bike ride from town. The sparse etching has been retouched, but it's still interesting and gives you an idea about how long these desolate mountains have sustained human cultures. To get here, follow signs to "Tazka" from behind Hôtel Les Amandiers; go through the village to the palm and argan fields beyond. You may find offers to guide you from local children: if you accept, then be sure to thank them with a small gift, such as a pen or toy, but avoid giving money. Although everyone calls it a gazelle, locals in the know will tell you that the celebrated rock carving just out of town is in fact of a *mouflon* (wild sheep). Those energetic enough can visit more cave paintings at Ukas, south of the town of Souk Had Issi, 50 km (31 miles) southeast of Tafraoute. ⊠ *Tafraoute.*

Painted Rocks. A slightly bizarre tourist attraction, the Painted Rocks outside Tafraoute (follow signs) is most dramatically experienced in late afternoon, when the hillsides stacked with massive round boulders turn a rich mustard hue before sunset. Belgian artist Jean Veran painted a cluster of these natural curiosities in varying shades of blue in 1984 and they have been retouched ever since. Checking out amateur copies is as much fun as looking at the originals. On quieter days, it's also a great place to spot local geckos, lizards, and squirrels. The route to the rocks is now paved, making access easier than ever. ⊠ *Tafraoute.*

Palm Groves of Aït Mansour. The palm groves of the Aït Mansour Gorge southeast of Tafraoute deserve a full day's excursion, although you could take the road as a scenic (and longer) route to Tiznit.

About 2 km (1 mile) southwest out of town, you'll see the so-called Napoleon's hat of massive boulders on your right. Occasionally, you'll see foreign climbers here, with their incongruously high-tech rock-climbing gear. Continue past the pretty village of Aguerd Oudad. When the road forks, the right one going to the Painted Rocks, take the left branch. A winding paved road takes you higher into the Anti-Atlas Mountains. The views are spectacular and the scenery changes as the road rises and then descends again, crossing a riverbed, which—even when dry—betrays the presence of underground water by the cactus and oleander growing in them. Twenty kilometers (12 miles) out of Tafraoute, turn right toward Aït Mansour.

8

After another 14 km (9 miles) of winding descent, you reach the palm groves. Suddenly, water, shade, and greenery are abundant, and you may find an open shop happy to serve you a sweet mint tea or soda. The lone goatherds of the peaks are replaced here by shrouded women, either transporting on their backs palm-frond baskets of dates supported by ropes around their foreheads or walking to Timguilcht to visit its important saint's shrine. Continue on the piste to Souk Had Issi, whose busy market is held on Sunday. From there the piste loops back to Tafraoute, or you can take a lower road to connect to Tiznit over the dramatic Col de Kerdous. ⊠ *Tafraoute.*

WHERE TO EAT

$ ✕ **La Kasbah.** The menu here is classic tourist fare (omelets, tagines,
MOROCCAN soups, and salads), but the quality is excellent. Try the vegetarian tagines; with prunes, nuts, and plenty of veggies; or the house specialty, *Kalia*, a Saharan dish of thinly sliced beef and vegetables. **Known for:** authentic local cuisine at local prices; vegetarian tagine. $ *Average main: 70DH* ⊠ *Rte. Imiane (R107), on right as you leave town* ☎ *0672/30–39–09* ▭ *No credit cards.*

$$ ✕ **Restaurant L'Etoile du Sud.** Since 1968 the "Star of the South" has been
MOROCCAN serving couscous and tagines in a red-velvet dining room or under a huge red-and-green velvet caidal tent. The harira is hearty and satisfying after a long day's drive, and there is plenty of parking. **Known for:** central location; hearty servings. $ *Average main: 90DH* ⊠ *Av. Hassan II, next to post office* ☎ *0528/80–00–38* ▭ *No credit cards.*

$ ✕ **Restaurant Marrakech.** Haute cuisine it isn't, but the tagines here
MOROCCAN are fresh and cheap and appreciated by many locals. The cool, freshsqueezed juices make this a nice spot to catch your breath and get out of the sun. **Known for:** good value; popularity with locals as well as tourists. $ *Average main: 50DH* ⊠ *Av. Hassan II, in center of town* ☎ *0663/22–92–50* ▭ *No credit cards.*

WHERE TO STAY

$$ ⬚ **Auberge Kasbah Chez Amaliya.** Nestled among the mountains and
B&B/INN occasional almond blossoms of the Ammeln Valley, Chez Amaliya is a
FAMILY great base for hikers, climbers, and the less active. **Pros:** vivacious host
Fodor's Choice will make you feel right at home; great views; large pool and terrace
★ with sunloungers. **Cons:** outside the city center; can be full of tour groups; Wi-Fi can be limited in rooms. $ *Rooms from: 500DH* ⊠ *Valley d'Ammeln, signposted off R105 as you approach from Aït Baha* ☎ *0528/80–00–65* ⊕ *www.chezamaliya.com* ⇆ *18 rooms* ⦿ *Some meals.*

$$$ ⬚ **El Malara.** This modern, kasbah-style guesthouse offers comfortable
B&B/INN accommodation in a quiet rural setting outside Tafraoute. **Pros:** very welcoming hosts and staff; an interesting menu that fuses Moroccan and Mediterranean flavors; large, clean swimming pool. **Cons:** 6 km (4 miles) outside town; Wi-Fi is intermittent; no restaurants nearby. $ *Rooms from: 720DH* ⊠ *Afela Ouaday* ⊹ *6 km (4 miles) out of Tafraoute on Tiznit-Tahala road (R104)* ☎ *0658/18–18–36* ⊕ *www. elmalara.com* ☾ *Closed July* ⇆ *7 rooms* ⦿ *Some meals* ▭ *No credit cards.*

Tafraoute, in a quiet valley, is often overlooked by the larger tour groups, but offers beautiful walks in the surrounding countryside.

$$ HOTEL **Hôtel Les Amandiers.** This former officers' mess of the French Protectorate is a piece of Moroccan postcolonial history as well as a hotel that dominates the town, providing panoramic views of the mountains that surround it. **Pros:** great views; has a bar; good-size pool. **Cons:** parts of the hotel still have a slightly institutional feel; service can be slow; Wi-Fi only works in reception area. [$] *Rooms from: 510DH* ✉ *Town center* ☎ *0528/80–00–88* 🌐 *www.hotel-lesamandiers.com* 🛏 *60 rooms* 🍴 *Some meals.*

$ HOTEL **Hotel Salama.** A favorite with groups and right in the center of town, the Salama overlooks the busy area around the market, where old men sell dates and local women bring their homemade argan oil. **Pros:** central location; nice views; on-site parking. **Cons:** rooms overlooking the market can be noisy; rooms quite basic; no Wi-Fi in rooms. [$] *Rooms from: 372DH* ✉ *Town center* ☎ *0528/80–00–26* 🌐 *www.hotelsalama.com* 💳 *No credit cards* 🛏 *37 rooms* 🍴 *Some meals.*

SHOPPING

Tafraoute's market is held on Tuesday and Wednesday and often has a good selection of woven palm-frond baskets, argan oil, and *amalou* (almond and argan paste). Tafraoute is the place to come for mountain *babouches* (slippers). These are different from the slip-on varieties found in the souks of Marrakesh and Fez, as they are specially made with a heel covering to aid mountain walking. Take note of Berber babouche color-coding: yellow for men, red for women, pompoms for unmarried girls, and spangled designs only for special occasions. The traditional local women's dress is a large black piece of fabric with braiding or embroidery at the edges. These can easily be converted into soft furnishings such as table cloths or curtains.

Maison du Troc. With a great range of carpets and other artisanal goods, this place is worth a visit if you feel the need for souvenirs. Although the area isn't well-known for carpet making, Mohammed and his team are happy to explain the different types of rugs from various regions. ⊠ *Rte. Imiane* ☎ *0528/80–00–35.*

Maison Touareg. Not to be confused with the excellent Maison Traditionelle museum, the Maison Touareg is a bazaar, carrying a nice selection of regional Berber carpets. ⊠ *Rte. de l'Hotel Les Amandiers, Av. Mohammed V* ☎ *0528/80–02–10* ⊕ *www.maisontouareg.com.*

TIZNIT

100 km (62 miles) west of Tafraoute, 98 km (61 miles) south of Agadir.

Typically a lunch stop en route to somewhere else, Tiznit is not a popular destination for tourists. But it is a great base for exploring the surrounding area and for those who dislike the high-rise, beach-resort feel of Agadir. The restaurant scene isn't great, but a couple of smaller guesthouses have emerged in recent years that serve excellent homemade cuisine. The big draw of Tiznit is its reputation as Morocco's silver center. Otherwise it has few sights, and even the ones it does have are currently under restoration as of this writing.

GETTING HERE AND AROUND

Tiznit is well signposted if traveling by road, with the N1 bringing you from Agadir, or the R104 from Tafraoute. Several daily buses arrive from Sidi Ifni (1½ hours), Agadir (2 hours), and Tafraoute (2 hours). The bus station is a 15-minute walk along Boulevard Mohamed Hafidi from the medina entrance at Bab Jdid. The CTM office is located at the bus station. There are also grands taxis from Agadir.

Tiznit is a compact city and everything within the medina walls is within walking distance. Bikes can be hired on the Méchouar Square or from certain riads.

TIMING AND PRECAUTIONS

Tiznit makes for an easy day trip from Agadir or for a break in an exploration of the Anti-Atlas and southern Morocco region. In summer it gets extremely hot and it may be more pleasant to stay on the coast at Aglou Plage or Agadir.

EXPLORING

Grande Mosquée (*Great Mosque*). The minaret of the Grande Mosquée is the oldest example of a Saharan–style minaret in Morocco, an architectural feature more commonly seen in Niger and Mali. Perches poke out from all sides, making it look like someone forgot to take out the scaffolding after it was completed. These perches are said to assist the dead in their ascent to paradise. ⊠ *Tiznit.*

Lalla Zninia Spring. Near the Grand Mosquée, the Lalla Zninia Spring (also known as the Source Bleue) is touted as Tiznit's main sight. In the evenings, the pool is lit up, while locals take in the night air in the adjacent square. The spring honors the saint after whom Tiznit is named. There are several legends relating to this woman. One has it that she was a shepherd girl who brought her flocks to this spot and smelled the then-undiscovered spring below; her sheep dug (if you can imagine sheep digging) until they found the water, and the town was born. Another story talks of a repentant prostitute who later became a saint. In any case, to catch a glimpse of her tomb on afternoons when devotees visit, follow the prison wall and turn left on the first narrow neighborhood street; the tomb is behind a green-painted door on your left. ✉ *Tiznit.*

Méchouar. The main square, the Méchouar, is the heart of town and was once a military parade ground. Nowadays it has become a car park with a clutch of cheap hotels and cafés around it. Down a side street off the main square (heading in the direction of the ramparts) you'll find a smaller square lined with orange trees, where locals buy from the mint, date, and dried-thyme vendors whose carts are parked between the rows of clothing and housewares. Off the square, you'll find the town's main souks. ✉ *Pl. el Méchouar.*

WHERE TO EAT AND STAY

$$ MOROCCAN 🍴 **À l'Ombre du Figuier.** Behind a small blue door in an unusually buttressed wall, this quaint restaurant welcomes with a fig tree-shaded courtyard (hence the name) and Moroccan dishes, including a fish tagine, spiced chicken, beef brochettes, couscous, and pastilla. The menu changes regularly, as everything is freshly made. **Known for:** fresh local produce; large portions at reasonable prices; strong Wi-Fi. [$] *Average main: 75DH* ✉ *22, passage Akchouch, dit "Métro" Idzakri* ✥ *From Pl. Mechouar, take passage marked "entree 4" to Gallery Riad Akchouch and look for signs* ☎ *0528/86–12–04* 💳 *No credit cards.*

$ MOROCCAN 🍴 **Riad Le Lieu.** Popular among the guests of local riads and hotels, Riad Le Lieu is a beacon in the otherwise dismal dining scene of Tiznit. In a part of the former palace next door, chef Jihad prepares a range of Moroccan specialties, which are served on the patio and terraces. **Known for:** rabbit and camel tagines; pretty vine-covered patio. [$] *Average main: 65DH* ✉ *273, impasse Issaoui, Rue Imzilen, Pl. Mechouar* ☎ *0528/60–00–19* 🌐 *www.riadlelieu.com* 💳 *No credit cards.*

$$$$ HOTEL 🏨 **Hotel Idou Tiznit.** This large four-star hotel caters primarily to the business market but is the only option in town for accommodation other than a small guesthouse. **Pros:** full range of facilities, including a pool; helpful staff; located at the entrance of the old town. **Cons:** can get busy with large groups; feels a bit sterile; the bar can get noisy at night. [$] *Rooms from: 1100DH* ✉ *Av. Hassan II* ☎ *0528/60–03–33* 🛏 *93 rooms* 🍽 *Multiple meal plans.*

$$$ B&B/INN Fodor's Choice ★ 🏨 **Riad Janoub.** The design of this luxury riad, hidden behind nondescript walls in the medina, was inspired by the Andalusian and Moorish architecture of grand old residences. **Pros:** stunning Moorish architecture; a little bit of luxury at a great price; easily accessed by car. **Cons:** the dining room is cramped; swimming pool is unheated; can be noisy when pool is busy. [$] *Rooms from: 825DH* ✉ *193, rue de la Grande Mosquee, Quartier Tafrgant* ☎ *0528/60–27–26* 🌐 *www.riadjanoub.com* 🛏 *7 rooms* 🍽 *Some meals.*

$$ B&B/INN 🏨 **Tigmi Kenza.** This chic, sophisticated riad near Place Mechouar infuses a modern flavor to traditional Moroccan architectural techniques. **Pros:** stylish contemporary design; spacious rooms; lovely roof terrace. **Cons:**

lunch and dinner not available; no air-conditioning; Wi-Fi only in reception. [$] *Rooms from: 500DH* ✉ *30, rue al Mourabitine, Hay Idzekri* ☎ *0528/60–03–62* 🛏 *7 rooms* 🍴 *Breakfast* 💳 *No credit cards.*

SHOPPING

Tiznit has earned a reputation as *the* place to buy silver jewelry in Morocco, and the local market has responded accordingly. The silver markets of Tiznit sell more—and better—silver per square foot than any other market in Morocco. Some vendors also sell handwoven cream-color blankets, traded by local women for a few pieces of new silver. Merchants cater increasingly to Western tastes and wallets. Many shops around the main square are really wholesalers, trading their silver all over Morocco and abroad, so don't expect any encounters with the artisans. Most items are produced in the home, so tourists are unlikely to see any actual production and the shops advertising it are unlikely to be manufacturing real silver jewelry.

Bijouterie Aziz. This low-pressure jewelry store sells Saharan and Berber silver jewelry. ✉ *5, Souk Joutia* ☎ *0668/69–77–47.*

Coin des Berberes. Located next to the Lalla Znina Spring, this large jewelry shop showcases new and old Berber jewelry, as well as artisans at work. Also for sale are carpets, pottery, and other Moroccan crafts. ✉ *4, rue de la Source Bleue* ☎ *0528/60–16–17.*

Trésor du Sud. Away from the souk, Trésor du Sud has an enormous showroom of high-quality handcrafted Berber jewelry. In addition, the workshops allow you to see the silversmiths in action. Carpets and other Moroccan crafts are also for sale. This is not the cheapest jewelry showroom in town, but you can pay with a credit card. ✉ *Bab al-Khemis* ☎ *0528/86–47–89* 🌐 *www.tresordusud.com.*

MOROCCAN ARABIC VOCABULARY

Most Moroccans are multilingual. The country's official languages are modern standard Arabic and French; most Moroccans speak Moroccan Arabic dialect, with many city dwellers also speaking French. Since the time of the French protectorate, French has been taught to schoolchildren (not all children) starting in the first grade, resulting in several French-language newspapers, magazines, and TV shows. Spanish enters the mix in northern Morocco, and several Berber tongues are spoken in the south as well as the north. In the medinas and souks of big cities, you may find merchants who can bargain in just about any language, including English, German, Japanese, and Swedish.

A rudimentary knowledge of French and, especially, Arabic will get you far in Morocco. If you're more comfortable with French, by all means use it in the major cities; in smaller cities, villages, and the mountains, it's best to attempt some Moroccan Arabic. Arabic is always a good choice, as Moroccans will go out of their way to accommodate the foreigner who attempts to learn their national language. Some letters in Arabic do not have English equivalents. When you see "gh" at the start of a word in this vocabulary, pronounce it like a French "r," lightly gargled at the back of the throat. If unsure, stick to a "g" sound.

ENGLISH	ARABIC	PRONUNCIATION

GREETINGS & BASICS

ENGLISH	ARABIC	PRONUNCIATION
Hello/Peace upon you.	Salaam ou alaikum.	sa-**lahm** oo allah-ee-**koom**
(Reply:)		
Hello/And peace upon you.	Wa alaikum salaam.	wa allay-koom sa-**lahm**
Good-bye	Bislamma.	bess-**lah**-ma
Mr./Sir	Si	see
Mrs./Madam/Miss	Lalla	lah-la
How are you? Fine, thank you.	Labass, alhamdul'Illah	la-**bahs**, al-**hahm**-doo-lee-**lah**
(No harm?) (No harm, praise be to God.)	Labass	la-**bahs**
Pleased to meet you.	Mitsharafin.	mitsh-arra-**fayn**
Yes/No	Namm/La	nahm/lah
Please	Afek	**ah**-feck
Thank you	Baraka Allahu fik	**ba**-ra-kah **la**-hoo **feek**
You're welcome.	Allah yubarak fik.	ahl-lah yoo-**bah**-rak feek

ENGLISH	ARABIC	PRONUNCIATION
God willing	insh'Allah	in- **shah**-ahl-lah
Excuse me./I'm sorry (masc.).	Smahali.	**sma**-hah-li
Excuse me./I'm sorry (fem.).	Smahailia.	sma-high- **lee**-ah

DAYS

Today	el yum	el yom
Yesterday	imbarah	im-ber-ah
Tomorrow	ghadaa	gha-dah
Sunday	el had	el had
Monday	tneen	t'neen
Tuesday	thlat	tlet
Wednesday	larbaa	lar-bah
Thursday	el khamis	el kha-mees
Friday	el jemaa	el j'mah
Saturday	sebt	es-sebt

NUMBERS

1	wahad	**wa**-hed
2	jouj	jewj
3	thlata	**tlet**-ta
4	rbaa	ar- **bah**
5	khamsa	**khem**-sah
6	sta	stah
7	sbaa	se- **bah**
8	taminia	ta- **min**-ee-ya
9	tseud	tsood
10	aachra	**ah**-she-ra
11	hadash	ha- **dahsh**
12	tanash	ta- **nahsh**
20	aacherine	ah- **chreen**
50	khamsine	khum- **seen**
100	milla	**mee**-yah
200	millatein	mee-ya **tayn**

ENGLISH	ARABIC	PRONUNCIATION

USEFUL PHRASES

ENGLISH	ARABIC	PRONUNCIATION
Do you speak English?	Ouesh tat tkelem belinglisia?	**wesh** tet te- **kel**-lem **blin**-gliz- **ee**-yah?
I don't understand.	Ma fahemtsh.	ma- **f'emtch.**
I don't know.	Ma naarf.	ma- **nahr**-ef.
I'm lost.	Ana tilift.	ahna t'-lift.
I am American (masc.).	Ana amriqui.	ahna am-ree-kee.
I am American (fem.).	Ana amriqiya.	ahna am- **ree**-kee-yah.
I am British.	Ana inglisi.	anna in-ge- **lee**-zee.
What is this?	Shnou hada?	**shnoo** ha-da?
Where is ... ?	Fein ... ?	fayn ... ?
the train station	mahatat el tren	ma-ha- **tat** eh-tren
the city bus station	mahatat tobis	**ma-ha**-tat **toh**-beese
the intracity bus station	mahatat al cairan	**ma**-ha-tat al-kah-ee-rahn
the airport	el l'aéroport	el lehr-oh-por
the hotel	el l'hôtel	el l'oh- **teel**
the café	l'khaoua	al-kah- **hou**-wah
the restaurant	el restaurant	el rest-oh- **rahn**
the telephone	tilifoon	**til-lee**-foon
the hospital	el l'hôpital	el l'oh-bee-tahl
the post office	l'bosta	**al**-bost- **a**
the restroom	w.c.	**vay**-say
the pharmacy	pharmacien	far- **ma-cienn**
the bank	l'banca	**al** bann- **ka**
the embassy	sifara	see-far- **ra**
I would like a room.	Bghit bit.	**bgheet**-beet.
I would like to buy ...	Bghit nechri ...	bgheet-nesh- **ree** ...
cigarettes	garro	**gahr**-oh
a city map	kharretta del medina	kha- **ray**-ta del m' **dee**-nah
a road map	kharretta del bled	kha- **ray**-ta del blad
How much is it?	Bi sha hal hada?	**bshal hah**-da?

ENGLISH	ARABIC	PRONUNCIATION
It's expensive.	Ghaliya.	**gha**-lee-ya.
A little	Shwiya	**shwee**-ya
A lot	Bizzaf	bzzef
Enough	Baraka	**ba**-rah-ka
I am ill. (masc.)	Ana marid.	ah-na ma- **reed.**
I am ill. (fem.)	Ana marida.	**ah**-na ma- **reed**-ah.
I need a doctor.	Bghit doctor.	bgheet dok- **tohr.**
I have a problem.	Aandi mouchkila.	**ahn**-dee moosh- **kee**-la.
left	lessar	**lis**-sar
right	leemen	**lee**-men
Help!	Awni!	**aow**-nee!
Fire!	Laafiya!	**lah**-fee-ya!
Caution!/Look out!	Aindek!	**aann**-deck!

DINING

I would like ...	bghit ...	bgheet ...
water	l'ma	l'mah
bread	l'khobz	l'khobz
vegetables	khoudra	**khu**-dra
meat	l'hamm	l'hahm
fruits	l'fawakeh	el fah- **weh**-kee
cakes	l'haloua	el **hahl**-oo-wa
tea	atay	**ah**-tay
coffee	kahoua	**kah**-wa
a fork	forchette	for- **shet**
a spoon	maalka	**mahl**-ka
a knife	mousse	moose

TRAVEL SMART
MOROCCO

GETTING HERE AND AROUND

▮ AIR TRAVEL

Morocco is served by major airlines from North America, the Middle East, and Europe. Consider flying if traveling long distances within Morocco. For example, to concentrate on the southern oasis valleys, land in Casablanca, take a connecting flight to Ouarzazate, and rent a car. Domestic carriers may require reconfirmation to hold your seat, so remember to place this call ahead of time, or ask your hotel to do it for you; a call to the airline also suffices. The national airline, Royal Air Maroc, flies to more than 80 destinations worldwide and within Morocco. Look for special offers and last-minute promotions on the airline's website.

AIRPORTS

Although Rabat is the capital, it is Casablanca's Mohammed V Airport (CMN) that serves as the main entry point for nonstop flights from the United States. From here, U.S. travelers can easily connect to other destinations throughout the country on frequent domestic flights. They can also reach Morocco easily through European hubs like London, Paris, Amsterdam, Madrid, and Frankfurt. A number of airlines offer regularly scheduled direct flights to major destinations like Marrakesh (RAK), Agadir (AGA), Fez (FEZ), Ouarzazate (OZZ), Rabat (RBA), and Tangier (TNG). Other airports with regularly scheduled domestic or international service include Al Hoceima (AHU), Dakhla (VIL), Essaouira (ESU), Fez Ifrane (GMFI), Laayoune (EUN), Oujda (OUD), Nador (NDR), and Tetouan (TTU).

Airport Information Moroccan Airport Authority. ☎ 080/1000-224 ⊕ www.onda.ma.

GROUND TRANSPORTATION

Office National des Chemins de Fer, the national rail company, has a station directly under Casablanca's Mohammed V Airport. Trains come and go between 6:30 am and 11 pm and make travel to and from the airport easy and hassle-free. The ride to the city takes 30 minutes. Taxis are always available outside arrivals at the Casablanca airport; official fares to the city and other destinations are posted on a board at the taxi stand. It costs approximately 250 DH. Many hotels offer a transfer service to/from the airport.

Contacts Office National des Chemins de Fer. ☎ 2255 ⊕ www.oncf.ma.

FLIGHTS

Royal Air Maroc and other major carriers and budget airlines offer daily direct or one-stop flights to Agadir, Casablanca, Fez, Marrakesh, Rabat, and Tangier from nearly all western European countries. Discount airlines such as Air Arabia, EasyJet, and Ryanair fly to many of the major cities. ⚠ **Be aware that certain flights between Casablanca and the United States have been affected by a ban on laptops in the cabin, a measure enforced by U.S. Homeland Security. Check airline and USHS websites for further information.**

▮ BOAT TRAVEL

If traveling from Spain, take a ferry across the Strait of Gibraltar. There are several options from Algeciras, Tarifa, and Gibraltar, with the most popular crossing from Algeciras to Tangier. Algeciras to Ceuta (Spanish territory inside mainland Morocco, *Sebta* in Moroccan Arabic) is a popular and shorter route. High-speed ferries make the trip in 30 to 40 minutes. Unfortunately, disembarking in Tangier can be a less than relaxing way to enter Morocco. You're likely to be greeted by hawkers and harassers, who won't cease to bother you until you've parted company with some money, or at best suffered some verbal abuse. If you do find yourself hassled by bogus peddlers or officials asking for a bribe, rest assured, there is no need to hand over any extra cash if you have a boat ticket, no matter what you are told. Always buy a ticket from an official source as there are many tricksters at the ports.

Information Southern Ferries Ltd. ☏ 0844/815-7785 in U.K. ⊕ www.southernferries.co.uk. **Trasmediterránia.** ☏ 902/45-46-45 in Spain ⊕ www.trasmediterranea.es.

▌ BUS TRAVEL

For cities not served by trains (mainly those in the south), buses are a good alternative. They're relatively frequent, and seats are usually available.

Compagnie de Transports Marocains (CTM), a national bus company, runs trips to most areas in the country and guarantees your seat and luggage service. They also offer online booking. These buses stop at designated CTM stops (which are not necessarily in the regular bus station) and for bathroom breaks, but be sure to stay near the bus, as they have been known to leave quickly, stranding people without their luggage in unfamiliar places.

Another major bus company, Supratours, is connected to Morocco's national rail service. It offers comfortable service to major cities as an extension of the rail network and can offer through ticketing on buses whose departure times are coordinated with the arrival of trains.

There are a number of smaller bus companies, called "souk buses." They're a way to get to really rural areas not served by larger companies. They are not always comfortable or clean or fast, but they can be hailed in every village they pass through. A number of smaller companies are now operating new buses with modern conveniences such as Wi-Fi and a/c on competitive routes like those in and out of Rabat and Casablanca; overnight travel is also an option. If possible, shell out the few extra dirhams for the punctual and pleasant CTM or Supratours buses unless you're going to out-of-the-way places.

In each city the bus station—known as the *gare routière*—is generally near the edge of town. Some cities have separate CTM or Supratours stations. Make sure you're at the right one! Ignore the posted departure times on the walls—they're seldom up to date. Ask at the ticket booth when the next bus leaves to your chosen destination. There's nothing wrong with checking out a bus before you buy your ticket, as some are dilapidated and uncomfortable. The *greeson* will sell you a ticket, take you to the bus, and put your luggage underneath (you should tip a few dirhams for this).

Buy tickets at the bus station prior to departure (ideally a day ahead of time but tickets often only go on sale an hour before departure); payment is by cash only. Tickets are only sold for the seats available, so once you have a ticket you have a seat. Other than tickets, there are no reservations. Children up to age four travel free. Car seats and bassinets are not available for children.

FARES

Fares are very cheap; it's about 160 DH on CTM or Supratours for the three-hour journey from Marrakesh to Essaouira. Expect to pay no more than 10 DH per piece of luggage. Additionally, most CTM (and some Supratours) stations have inexpensive luggage storage facilities.

Bus Information CTM. ✉ *Km 13.5 Rte. de Casa-RabatSidi Bernoussi, Casablanca* ☏ 0800/09-00-30 ⊕ www.ctm.ma. **Supratours.** ☏ 0537/73-10-61, 0537/73-10-64 ⊕ www.supratours.ma/en.

▌ CAR TRAVEL

A car is not necessary if your trip is confined to major cities, but sometimes it's the best and only way to explore Morocco's mountainous areas, small coastal towns, and rural areas such as the Middle or High Atlas.

Driving in Morocco is relatively easy and a fantastic way to see the country. Roads are generally in good shape, and mile markers and road signs are easy to read (they're always written in Arabic and French). Remember that small mountain villages are still only reached by *piste* (gravel path), and that these rough roads can damage a smaller car. Bear in mind that traffic becomes more erratic during the holy month of Ramadan and no matter what time of year, you are likely to be approached at red lights or even on village roads with pleas to buy tissues, chewing gum, and souvenirs, or simply for any loose change. When you're driving on open country roads, *grand taxi* drivers tend to drive down the white lines, so anticipate them coming round a bend!

Hiring a car and driver is an excellent but more expensive way to really get into the crevices of the country and to tap into local knowledge and connections. Drivers also serve as protectors from potential faux guides and tourist scams. Be warned, however, that they themselves are often looking for commissions and might steer you toward particular carpet sellers and tourist shops. Be sure to negotiate an acceptable price before you take off. Expect to pay at minimum between 1,500 DH to 2,000 DH for a private tour per day, with prices higher depending on itinerary. Drivers must be licensed and official, so be sure to ask for credentials to avoid any unpleasantness down the road.

BOOKING YOUR TRIP

The cars most commonly available in Morocco are small European sedans, such as Renaults, Peugeots, and Fiats. ■TIP→ **Rental cars are nearly always stick shift.** Expect to pay at least 450 DH a day for these. Many companies also rent four-wheel-drive vehicles, a boon for touring the Atlas Mountains and oasis valleys; expect to pay from 1,400 DH per day for a standard SUV, more for something at the top of the range. A 20% VAT (value-added tax) is levied on rental rates. Companies will often let you rent for the day or by the kilometer. And, although they are now obligatory, you may have trouble finding child seats for rental cars if you're traveling with young children.

Note that you can negotiate the rental of a *grand taxi* with a driver just about anywhere in Morocco for no more than the cost of a rental car from a major agency. Normally you negotiate an inclusive price for a given itinerary. The advantage is that you don't have to navigate; the disadvantage is that the driver may have his own ideas about where you should go and will probably not speak English. For less haggling, local tour operators can furnish vehicles with multilingual drivers at a fairly high daily package rate.

The best place to rent a car is at Casablanca's airport, as the rental market is very competitive here—most of the cars are new, and discounts are often negotiable. Local companies give a lower price than the international agencies (even after the latter's "discounts"). Most recommended agencies have offices at Casablanca's airport and branches in the city itself, as well in Rabat, Marrakesh, and Fez. To get the best deal, book through a travel agent or a comparison website like ⊕ *www.rentalcars.com.*

Rental Agencies Europcar. ☎ *0522/53-91-61 Casablanca-Mohammed V Airport, 0535/62-65-45 Fez-Saiss Airport, 0524/43-77-18 Marrakesh-Menara Airport, 0539/39-32-73 Tangier Ibn Battouta Airport, 0539/94-19-38 Tangier Maritime Port* ⊕ *www.europcar.com.* **Sixt Car.** ☎ *0522/53-66-15* ⊕ *www.sixt.com.* **Thrifty Car.** ☎ *0522/54-00-22* ⊕ *www.thrifty.com.*

GASOLINE

Gas is readily available, if relatively expensive. The gas that most cars use is known as *super,* the lower-octane variety as *essence.* Unleaded fuel (*sans plomb*) is widely available but not currently necessary for local cars; it costs around 10 DH a liter.

Diesel fuel (*diesel*or *gasoil*) is significantly cheaper. Most gas stations provide full service; tipping is optional, but if you do tip, the standard amount is 2 DH. Only a few stations take credit cards. Most gas stations have restrooms and some have cafés, with Afriquia stations generally regarded as the best.

PARKING

When parking in the city, make sure that you're in a parking zone or the authorities will put a locking device on one of your wheels. If you are unlucky enough to have your wheel clamped, look out for the clamper, who will most likely be lurking nearby. A payment of 50 dirhams is usually all it takes for him to remove the locking device.

When you park, give the *gardien*a small tip (2 DH–5 DH) upon leaving. Many parking attendants are actually watching your car while you park it in a public street. This is their source of income and it's not worth haggling over a few cents. Some larger cities have introduced the European system of prepaid tickets from a machine, valid for a certain duration.

ROAD CONDITIONS

Road conditions are generally very good and the network of toll highways (*autoroutes*) has expanded in recent years. There are nine autoroutes. These radiate mainly out of Casablanca, Rabat, Marrakesh, and Fez, and reach as far north as Tangier, Tetouan, and Oujda. South from Casablanca you can reach Marrakesh and Agadir. These autoroutes are much safer than the lesser roads. There are periodic tollbooths charging from 5 DH to 20 DH. Make sure that you carry loose change in coins as booths generally do not accept credit cards.

On rural roads expect the occasional flock of sheep or herd of goats to cross the road at inopportune times. In the south you'll see road signs warning of periodic camel crossings as well. In the mountains, side-pointing arrows designate curves in the road. However, be aware that some

dangerous curves come unannounced. In the countryside you're more likely to encounter potholes, narrow roads, and speeding taxi drivers.

Night driving outside city centers requires extreme caution. Many roads are not lit. Beware of inadequate or unfamiliar lighting at night, particularly on trucks—it's not uncommon for trucks to have red lights in the front or white lights in the rear. Ubiquitous ancient mopeds rarely have working lights or reflectors—same goes for donkey and mule carts, bicycles, and pedestrians. Many drivers think nothing of driving on the opposite side of the road or reversing at high speed along busy roads. Taxis pull up without notice to the side of the road.

ROADSIDE EMERGENCIES

In case of an accident on the road, dial 177 outside cities and 19 in urban areas for police and 122 from a mobile phone. For firemen and emergency medical services, dial 15. As emergency numbers in Morocco may not be answered quickly, it's wise to hail help from passersby and/or street police if possible. Even in the most rural areas, someone will appear to assist a stranded traveler. When available, it's also more effective to summon a taxi to reach medical help instead of relying on ambulance service.

RULES OF THE ROAD

Traffic moves on the right side of the road, as in the United States and most of Europe. There are two main rules in Morocco: the first is, "priority to the right," an old French rule meaning that in traffic circles you must yield to traffic entering from the right; the second is, "every man for himself." Any car that is ahead of you—even by an inch—considers itself to have priority.

You must carry your car registration and insurance certificate at all times (these documents are always supplied with rental cars). Morocco's speed limits, enforced by radar, are 120 kph (75 mph) on autoroutes and from 40 or 60 kph (25 or 37 mph) in towns. Commonly enforced penalties include speeding, not stopping at a stop sign, and running a red light. On the spot fines are payable to the issuing officer, or your driver's license may be confiscated. Always ask for the fine "ticket" as this reduces the risk of corruption.

It is mandatory to wear seat belts for both drivers and passengers. Failure to do so will result in a hefty fine. Talking on cell phones while driving is also illegal, even though most Moroccans do it.

▌ TAXI TRAVEL

Moroccan taxis take two forms: *petits taxis,* small taxis that travel within city limits, and *grands taxis,* large taxis that travel between cities. Grands drivers usually wait until the taxi is full before departing.

Taxis are color-coded according to city—in Casablanca and Fez they're red, in Rabat they're blue, in Marrakesh they're beige, and so on. Petits taxis can be hailed anywhere and take a maximum of three passengers. The fare is metered and not expensive: usually 5 DH to 30 DH for a short or medium-length trip. Taxis often pick up additional passengers en route, so if you can't find an empty cab, try hailing a taxi with one or two passengers already; the driver should run a separate meter for each passenger. Passengers traveling together pay one fare.

Grands taxis travel fixed routes between cities and in the country. Two passengers can squeeze in front with the driver, and four sit, very cramped, in the back. Don't expect air-conditioning, a luxurious interior, or even fully functioning windows, although the old Mercedes diehard taxis are slowly being replaced by modern minivans, which are less nostalgic but much more comfortable. Fares for these shared rides are inexpensive, sometimes as little as 5 DH per person for a short trip. You can also buy several seats for comfort or charter a grand taxi for trips between cities, but you need to negotiate a price in advance.

▌ TRAIN TRAVEL

If sticking mainly to the four imperial cities—Fez, Meknès, Rabat, and Marrakesh—you're best off taking the train and using petits taxis. Morocco's punctual rail system, run by the Office National des Chemins de Fer, mostly serves the north. From Casablanca and Rabat the network runs east via Meknès and Fez to Oujda, north to Tangier, and south to Marrakesh. Supratours buses link trains with Tetouan, Nador, Essaouira, and Agadir, and you can buy through tickets covering both segments before departing.

Trains are divided into first class (*première classe*) and second class (*deuxième classe*). First class is a very good buy compared to its counterpart in Europe, but second class is comfortable, too. Long-distance trains seat six people to a compartment in first class, eight to a compartment in second class. A first-class ticket guarantees a reserved seat; it's worth the extra money, especially during busy periods.

Fares are relatively inexpensive compared to Europe. A first-class ticket from Casablanca to Fez costs 174 DH. You can buy train tickets at any station up to six days in advance or online. Purchasing your ticket on the train is pricier and can only be done in cash. Children travel free up until the age of 4. Ages 4 to 14 are charged a children's fare, which is generally a little over 50% of the adult fare.

Information Office National des Chemins de Fer. ☎ *2255 24-hr information line* ⊕ *www.oncf.ma.*

▌ TRAM TRAVEL

Both Casablanca and Rabat now have sparkling-new tram services, which have taken the burden off the urban buses and taxis and lessened some of the traffic crush. Tickets are easy to purchase on platforms, and announcements and destinations are provided in French and English.

ESSENTIALS

▪ ACCOMMODATIONS

Accommodations in Morocco range from opulent to extremely sparse, with everything in between. Hotels can be on a par with those of Europe and the United States, but five-star comforts begin to disappear the farther off the beaten path you venture. Hotels lack amenities particularly in smaller towns and villages, but these hotels often make up for a lack of luxury with genuine charm, hospitality, character, and location.

RIADS

Book a room in or rent an entire well-furnished *riad* (a traditional town house with interior courtyard or garden) in the medinas of the most visited cities, such as Fez, Marrakesh, and Essaouira. This is a unique opportunity to experience traditional Moroccan architecture and live like wealthy families of old. Most riads are available on popular booking engines such as booking.com or Tripadvisor. Another option is Marrakech Medina Booking, which offers riads and villas for rent in Marrakesh, Essaouira, Ouarzazate, and Fez. Moroccan Villas is a British company that offers villa and riad rentals with properties in Marrakesh and Oualidia.

Riad Rentals Marrakech Medina Booking. ✉ *Rue Dar el Bacha, Medina* ☎ *0526/10–04–93* ⊕ *www.marrakech-medina.com.* **Moroccan Villas.** ✉ *2 Villiers Ct., 40 Upper Mulgrave Rd., Cheam* ☎ *0207/060–5414 in U.K.* ⊕ *www.moroccanvillas.com.*

HOTELS

Hotels are classified by the Moroccan government with one to five stars, plus an added category for five-star luxury hotels. In hotels with three or more stars, all rooms have private bathrooms, and there is an on-site bar. Air-conditioning is common in three-star hotels in Fez and Marrakesh and in all five-star hotels. Standards do vary, though; it's possible to find a nice two-star hotel or, occasionally,

a four-star hotel without hot water. In the same vein, hotels that are outside the star system altogether ("unclassified") can be satisfactory.

High season in Morocco is generally from mid-December to mid-January and mid-March to mid-April. Early June, before the intense summer heat settles in, is also considered high season. In the Atlas region, January and February attract many visitors for winter sports. In the Sahara, September through November are the most popular months. Many properties charge peak-season rates for your entire stay even if travel dates straddle peak and nonpeak seasons. As with everything in Morocco, hotel rates may be negotiable; always ask if there are specials.

Most hotels in Morocco now accept email requests for reservations and even small riads and guesthouses are usually listed on popular hotel-booking engines.

▪ COMMUNICATIONS

INTERNET

Internet use has exploded in Morocco, and cybercafés are everywhere, even in the smaller towns. On average they charge 10 DH to 20 DH an hour. Wi-Fi is widely available in hotels and cafés, so it's easy to keep in touch with friends and family with a laptop, tablet, or smartphone.

Take the same security precautions you would anywhere with your electronics, and always use a surge protector.

PHONES

The country code for Morocco is 212. There are nine digits in local numbers, starting with "0." The area codes are as follows: Agadir, 0528; Casablanca, 0522; Settat and El Jadida, 0523; Marrakesh, 0524; Fez and Meknès, 0535; Oujda, 0536; Rabat, 0537; Tangier, 0539; Taroudant, 0528; Tetouan, 0539. Mobile phones (numbers starting 06) are now far more widespread than landlines and many Moroccans have two numbers. When dialing a Moroccan number from overseas, drop the initial 0 from the area code. To call locally, within the area code, just dial the number (local numbers are six digits).

For international calls from Morocco, dial 00 followed by the country code. Country codes: United States and Canada, 1; United Kingdom, 44; Australia, 61; New Zealand, 64. Note that when calling from out-of-country into Morocco you always drop the "0," and the number becomes nine digits.

CALLING WITHIN MOROCCO

Public phones are located on the street, and you must purchase a *telecarte*, or phone card, to use them. They come in denominations from 10 DH to 100 DH. You insert the card and then place your local or international call.

Téléboutiques are everywhere in Morocco. These little shops have individual coin-operated phones. You feed the machine with dirhams to make local calls. You can also make international calls by calling directory assistance or calling directly.

Access directory assistance by dialing 160 from anywhere in the country. Many operators speak English, and all speak French.

CALLING OUTSIDE MOROCCO

To call the United States directly from Morocco, dial 001, then the area code and phone number. Calls from Morocco are expensive, but rates are cut by 20% if you call after midnight. The cheapest option in direct international dialing is from a public phone, using a telecarte.

AT&T has a local access number for making international calls, which is useful if you already have a calling card.

Contacts AT&T Direct Access. ☎ *00/211–0011 in Morocco.*

MOBILE PHONES

GSM mobile phones with international roaming capability work well in the cities and along major communication routes. 4G is widespread, but roaming fees can be steep, especially for data, so use Wi-Fi

whenever possible. It's almost always cheaper to send a text message than to make a call, since text messages have a very low set fee (often less than $0.25).

Alternatively, if you just want to make local calls, you can buy a new SIM card in Morocco with a prepaid service plan (note that your provider will have to unlock your phone to use a different SIM card). You'll then have a local number and can make local calls at local rates. Morocco currently has three mobile-phone companies, Inwi, Maroc Telecom, and Orange. All offer prepaid calling cards and phone sales. A simple phone costs as little as 100 DH. If you're spending more than a few weeks in the country or traveling in remote spots, these are indispensable.

■TIP➡ **You will need your passport to buy a SIM card, even just a pay-as-you-go one.**

Contacts Cellular Abroad. ☎ *800/287–5072 within U.S., 310/862–7100 outside U.S.* ⊕ *www.cellularabroad.com.* **Mobal.** ☎ *888/888–9162 sales* ⊕ *www.mobalrental.com.* **Planet Fone.** ☎ *888/988–4777* ⊕ *www.planetfone.com.*

■ CUSTOMS AND DUTIES

Customs duties are very high in Morocco, and many items are subject to taxes that can total 80%. The following may be imported without duty: 150 ml of perfume, 250 ml of eau de toilette, 1 liter of spirits, 1 bottle of wine, 200 cigarettes or 25 cigars or 250 grams of tobacco. Large electronic items will be taxed if they are found in your luggage. It's always easier to take things in person instead of having them sent and cleared through customs at the post office, where even the smallest items will be taxed.

The importation and exportation of Moroccan dirhams is strictly forbidden and it's not possible to exchange more than 1,000 DH outside Morocco. There is no limit for how much foreign currency you import; however, when leaving Morocco, you are limited to changing back only 50% of the amount you exchanged at the beginning of your vacation. This transaction will be questioned at the Bureau de Change in airports, hotels, and banks, often with the specific demand to see verification of any currency transactions made during your stay. Keep all currency exchange receipts on hand, or you may have more dirhams on hand than you can legally leave the country with.

Information Government of Morocco Customs Administration. ☎ *080/100–7000* ⊕ *www.douane.gov.ma.*

■ EATING OUT

Moroccan cuisine is delectable. Dining establishments range from outdoor food stalls to elegant and disproportionately expensive restaurants, with prices approaching those of Europe. Simpler, cheaper restaurants abound. Between cities, roadside restaurants commonly offer delicious tagines, couscous, or grilled kebabs with bread and salad; on the coast, charcoal-grilled or fried fish is an excellent buy, and you can often choose your meal from the daily catch. Marrakesh and Fez are the places for wonderful Moroccan feasts in fairy-tale surroundings, and Casablanca has a lively and diverse dining scene. The listed restaurants represent the best in each price range and cuisine type.

MEALS AND MEALTIMES

Moroccan hotels normally serve a Continental breakfast (*petit déjeuner continental*), often included in the room rate. If not, you can buy an equivalent meal at any of numerous cafés at a much lower price. The more expensive hotels have elaborate buffets. Hotel breakfasts are usually served from 7 to 10 or 10:30. Lunch, typically the most leisurely meal of the day, is served between noon and 2:30. Hotels and restaurants begin dinner service at 7:30, though crowds are on the thin side until 8:30 or 9. In a Moroccan home you probably won't sit down to eat until 9 or 10 pm. Restaurants stay open later in the more cosmopolitan city centers.

Lunch (*déjeuner*) in Morocco tends to be a large meal, as in France. A typical lunch menu consists of salad, a main course with meat and vegetables, and fruit. In restaurants this is generally available à la carte. On Friday the traditional lunch meal is a heaping bowl of couscous topped with meats and vegetables in a light *bouillon*.

At home, people tend to have afternoon mint tea, then a light supper, often with soup. Dinner (*diner* in French) in international restaurants is generally à la carte; you may select as light or heavy a meal as you like. Many of the fancier Moroccan restaurants serve prix-fixe feasts, with at least three courses and sometimes upward of five. If you're a vegetarian or have other dietary concerns, state this when you make a reservation; many restaurants will prepare special dishes with advance notice.

Lunch and dinner are often served communal-style, on one big platter. Moroccans use their right hands to sop up the juices in these dishes with bread. Bread is used as an all-purpose utensil to pull up little pieces of vegetables and meat. In restaurants bread will always be offered in a basket. Utensils will be offered to foreigners. All restaurants, no matter how basic, have sinks for washing hands before and after your meal.

Unless otherwise noted, the restaurants listed *in this guide* are open daily for lunch and dinner.

Sunday is the most common day for restaurant closings.

During Ramadan, everything changes. Many cafés and nearly all restaurants are closed during the day; the *ftour* (as it's known in Morocco, also known as *iftar*) or "break fast," is served precisely at sunset. Many people stay up for an additional meal, the *suhour,* before sunrise. Hotels and tourist-oriented restaurants continue to serve meals to non-Muslim guests as usual, but don't be surprised if there's a slight break in service at sunset when the staff have their meal.

PAYING

For price charts deciphering the price categories of restaurants and hotels, see "Planning" at the beginning of each chapter. Only the pricier restaurants take credit cards; MasterCard and Visa are the most widely accepted. Outside the largest cities you'll rarely be able to use your credit card.

RESERVATIONS AND DRESS

Reservations are generally a good idea at more popular spots, but might not be possible at places on the cheaper end of the scale: we mention them only when they're essential or not accepted. Book as far ahead as possible, and reconfirm as soon as you arrive. Jacket and tie are never required.

WINES, BEER, AND SPIRITS

Although alcohol is forbidden by Islam, Morocco produces red, white, rosé, and *gris* wines in the Meknès vicinity, as well as near Essaouira, and the national beer is Flag Special; Heineken is produced under license in Casablanca. More expensive restaurants and some hotels and bars aimed at tourists are licensed to serve alcohol. Supermarkets like Carrefour and Acima sell alcohol to foreigners with proper identification (except during Ramadan, when liquor sections are usually closed). Bottle shops in small towns also sell beer and spirits.

■ ELECTRICITY

To use electric-powered equipment purchased in the United States or Canada, bring a converter and adapter, though many electronics these days are dual-voltage; check your AC adapter to see if yours is. The electrical current in Morocco is 220 volts, 50 cycles alternating current (AC); wall outlets take the two-pin plug found in Continental Europe. Power surges do occur.

■ EMERGENCIES

Although pharmacies maintain normal hours, a system is in place that ensures that one is always open. You'll find a schedule of late-closing pharmacies posted on the pharmacy door or the adjacent wall. Pharmacies are easy to spot, just look for the neon-green crescent-moon symbol.

■ HEALTH

Although Moroccan water is generally safe to drink (in cities at least), it's better to drink only bottled water and canned or bottled soft drinks to be on the safe side. Look for the blue-and-white labels of Morocco's most popular bottled mineral water, called Sidi Ali. Try to resist the temptation to add ice to room-temperature beverages. Use reasonable precautions and eat only fully cooked foods, but if you have problems, mild cases of diarrhea may respond to Imodium (known generically as Loperamide) or Pepto-Bismol. Be sure to drink plenty of fluids; if you can't keep fluids down, seek medical help immediately.

In summer, heatstroke and dehydration are big risks to travelers and Moroccans alike. Be sure to drink plenty of water and rest in the shade any chance you get. If you do get dehydrated, pharmacies sell rehydration salts called Biosel.

■ TIP→ **Sunscreen is widely available in pharmacies, supermarkets, and specialty cosmetic stores but is outrageously expensive. Pack your own.**

Note that scorpions, snakes, and biting insects live in the desert regions. These rarely pose a problem, but it wouldn't hurt to shake out your shoes in the morning. Dog bites pose the risk of rabies; always get a rabies vaccination at the earliest possible opportunity if you are bitten. Many medinas have a huge street cat population. Avoid petting these cute critters that weave in and out of narrow passageways, feeding on refuse.

Medical care is available but varies in quality. The larger cities have excellent private clinics. The rest of the country depends on government-run smaller clinics and dispensaries. The cost of medical care is relatively low—an office consultation and exam will cost between 250 DH and 500 DH depending on the level of specialty. While medical facilities can be quite adequate in urban areas, particularly in private clinics, English-speaking medical help is rare except in very large cities.

OVER-THE-COUNTER REMEDIES

Nearly all medicines, including antibiotics and painkillers, are available over the counter at Moroccan pharmacies. Aspirin is sold as Aspro; ibuprofen is sold as Analgyl, Algantyl, or Tabalon. Acetaminophen, the generic equivalent of Tylenol, is sold as Doliprane and is widely available.

∎ HOURS OF OPERATION

Moroccan banks are open Monday to Thursday 8:30 to noon and 2 to 4. On Friday, the day of prayer, they close slightly earlier in the morning and open a little later in the afternoon. Post offices are open Monday to Thursday 8:30 to noon and 2:30 to 6:30, Friday from 8:30 to 11:30 and 3 to 6:30. Government offices have similar schedules.

Museums are generally open 9 to noon and 2:30 to 6. Standard pharmacy hours are 8:30 to 12:30 and 3 to 9:30. Your hotel can help you locate which pharmacies are open around the clock. Shops are typically open every day from about 9 to 1 and from 3 or 4 to 7.

Remember that during Ramadan the above schedules change, often with later opening times or the midday closing omitted. On Friday many businesses close down for the day or for the noon prayer (and may not reopen afterward).

HOLIDAYS

The two most important religious holidays in Morocco are Aïd el-Fitr, which marks the end of the month-long Ramadan fast, and Aïd el-Adha or Aïd el-Kebir, the sheep-sacrifice feast commemorating the prophet Ibrahim's absolution from the obligation to sacrifice his son. Both are two-day festivals during which all offices, banks, and museums are closed. The other religious holiday is the one-day Aïd el-Mouloud, commemorating the birthday of the prophet Mohammed.

Ramadan (which lasts around 30 days and becomes progressively earlier by 12 days each year) is not a holiday per se, but it does change the pace of life. Because the Muslim calendar is lunar, the dates for Ramadan and other religious holidays shift each year, so check ahead.

The most important political holiday is Aïd el-Arch, or Throne Day (July 30), which commemorates the coronation of King Mohammed VI. Morocco's other holidays are as follows: January 1, New Year's Day; January 11, anniversary of the proclamation of Moroccan independence; May 1, Labor Day; August 14, Oued ed-Dahab, otherwise known as Allegiance Day; August 20, anniversary of the revolution of the king and the people (against the French); August 21, Youth Day; November 6, commemoration of the Green March, Morocco's claim on the Western Sahara in 1975; November 18, Independence Day.

∎ MAIL

Post offices are available everywhere and visible by their yellow signs. Outgoing airmail is reliable. Note that if you mail letters at the main sorting office of any city (usually situated on Avenue Mohammed V), they will arrive several days sooner than if you mail them from elsewhere. Airmail letters to North America take between 5 and 14 days. A 20-gram airmail letter or postcard costs about 15 DH to mail to the United States.

SHIPPING PACKAGES

Sending packages out of the country is easy enough. Go to the *Colis Postaux* (parcel post office; one in each town), where you can also buy boxes. You'll need to fill in some forms and show the package to customs officials before wrapping it. Airmail parcels reach North America in about two weeks, Europe in about 10 days. DHL offers a special rate for handicraft items shipped overseas, and some carpet stores can arrange shipping, though this can double the price of your purchase. The international Amana Service at the Post Office takes three to five days from Morocco to Europe. UPS operates only in Casablanca. FedEx has locations in Agadir, Casablanca, Fez, Marrakesh, Rabat, and Tangier.

Express Services DHL. ☎ *0537/77–99–35 Rabat, 0522/32–15–31 Casablanca ⊕ www. dhl-ma.com.* **FedEx.** ✉ *298, bd. Mohammed V, Casablanca* ☎ *0522/45–80–41 branch number ⊕ www.fedex.com/ma.* **UPS.** ✉ *Immeuble Oasis Sq. , Quartier Oasis Sq., Casablanca* ☎ *0520/31–13–11 ⊕ www.ups.com.*

■ MONEY

Most costs in Morocco are low compared to both North America and Europe. Fruit and vegetables, public transportation, and labor are very cheap. (Cars, gasoline, and electronic goods, on the other hand, are relatively pricey.) Sample costs are in U.S. dollars.

Meal in cheap restaurant, $10–$18; meal in expensive restaurant, $25–$60; 1.5 liters of bottled water, $0.60; cup of coffee, $0.90; museum admission, $1–$2; liter of gasoline, $1.10; short taxi ride, $1–$2. Prices here are given for adults; reduced fees are usually available for children and large groups, but not students or senior citizens.

Because the dirham's value fluctuates, some upscale hotels, tour operators, and activity specialists geared toward tourists publish their prices in euros, but accept dirhams (these places also usually take credit cards).

ATMS AND BANKS

You'll usually get a better rate of exchange at an ATM than you will at a currency-exchange office, hotel, or even international bank, even accounting for the fees your bank may charge. Reliable ATMs are attached to banks in major cities, and there's one in the arrivals hall at Casablanca's airport. BMCE and Wafabank belong to the Cirrus and Plus networks.

CREDIT CARDS

Inform your credit-card company before you travel, especially if you're going abroad and don't travel internationally very often. Otherwise, the credit-card company might put a hold on your card, owing to unusual activity—not a fun thing to try to resolve halfway through your trip. Record all your credit card numbers and keep them in a safe place in case something goes wrong.

Although it's usually cheaper (and safer) to use a credit card for large purchases (so you can cancel payments or be reimbursed if there's a problem), note that some credit card companies and the banks that issue them add substantial percentages to foreign transactions, whether in foreign currency or not.

Credit cards are accepted at many hotels, upscale restaurants, and more expensive souvenir shops, but there's usually a surcharge to cover their bank fees.

CURRENCY AND EXCHANGE

The national currency is the dirham (DH), which is divided into 100 centimes. There are bills for 20, 50, 100, and 200 DH, and coins for 1, 5, and 10 DH and 5, 10, and 20 centimes. As a foreign tourist, you may never see the centime coins. You might hear some people refer to centimes as francs; others count money in rials, which are equivalent to 5 centimes each. A million is a million centimes, or 10,000 DH. There is usually more than one style of banknote in circulation at any time.

The exchange rate for the U.S. dollar is the same at all banks, including those at the airport; wait until you get to Morocco to get your dirhams as they are not available outside the country. For larger amounts, it may be possible to negotiate your rate at a Bureau de Change. You can change dirhams back into U.S. dollars or euros at the airport upon departure, as long as you've kept the exchange receipts from your time of entry. The limit for this transaction is 50% of what you converted over the duration of your stay.

PACKING

The average temperature in Morocco is 63°F (17°C), with minimums around 45°F (7°C) in winter (colder in the mountains) to above 80°F (27°C) in summer (and significantly hotter in the desert). Unless you visit in the sweltering heat of August or a biting cold snap in January, you'll most likely need to pack for a range of temperatures. It's especially important not to underestimate how incredibly cold it gets in the mountains, where indoor heating is scarce. If you expect to hike and camp, pack all your gear, including a 0°F sleeping bag. The Atlantic coast is cooled by fresh breezes, even during the summer months.

Crucial items to bring to Morocco include sunscreen, walking shoes, and, for women, a large shawl or scarf (to be wrapped around your head or arms for respect or your shoulders for warmth), a French and/or Moroccan Arabic phrase book (in the countryside many people will not speak French or potentially even Arabic).

Don't expect to find soap, washcloths, or towels in budget hotels, nor toilet paper in most bathrooms; it's smart to pack your own, including tissues, hand sanitizer, and pocket-size baby wipes for convenient hygiene. Tampons are rarely found in Morocco, so it is best to pack those, too.

Casual clothes are fine in Morocco; there's no need to bring formal apparel. Everywhere but the beach, however, you'll need to wear trousers or long skirts rather than shorts; tank tops, short skirts, and midriff-baring shirts should not be worn.

PASSPORTS

U.S. citizens with a valid passport can enter Morocco and stay up to 90 days without a visa.

RESTROOMS

It's customary to tip the attendant in a public toilet 1 DH. Be warned that many public toilets are Turkish-style squatters. It's prudent to carry hand sanitizer, a small bar of soap, and a cotton bandana for drying your hands when traveling around the country. ■TIP→ **Always carry your own toilet paper or tissues—while easy to find in stores, only hotels can be relied on to have well-maintained bathrooms.**

SAFETY

Morocco is a relatively safe destination. Violent crime is rare. People who pester you to hire them as guides in places like Marrakesh and Fez are a nuisance but not a threat to your safety. Pickpocketing, however, can be a problem. In souks, open markets, and other crowded areas, carry your backpack or purse in front of you. Cell phones, cameras, and other portable electronics are big sellers on the black market and should be kept out of sight whenever possible. Bags and valuables can be snatched by thieves on mopeds. Keep an eye on your belongings at crowded beaches, as it is not unheard of for roving gangs to make off with your stuff while you are swimming.

Morocco, along with its neighbors, has experienced social unrest and international terrorism over the past few years, just like its North African and European neighbors. The country has, however, been widely praised for its handling of these issues, and foreign governments frequently accord Morocco a lower security (i.e., a higher safety) rating than its neighbors.

Female travelers—and especially single female travelers—sometimes worry about treatment on the streets of Morocco. There really isn't anything to worry about; you'll most likely be leered at, spoken to, and sometimes followed for a block. Women walking alone are targeted by vendors hoping to make a sale. This attention, while irritating, isn't threatening. Don't take it personally; Moroccan women endure it, as well. The best way to handle it is to walk purposefully, avoid eye contact, and completely ignore men pestering you. If they don't let up, a firm reprimand with the Arabic "*hashuma*" ("shame"), or the French "*Laissez-moi tranquille*" ("Leave me alone") should do the trick. If this still doesn't work, look for a local police officer or head into a restaurant or museum.

Contacts U.S. Embassy. ⊠ *Km 5.7, Av. Mohamed VI, Souissi* ☎ *0537/63–72–00 Rabat* ⊕ *ma.usembassy.gov.*

TAXES

City, local, government, and tourism taxes range between 10 DH and 40 DH at all lodgings. There are no airport taxes above those originally levied on the ticket price. The VAT (called TVA in Morocco) is generally 20% and not refundable.

TIME

Morocco observes Greenwich Mean Time year-round (five hours ahead of Eastern Standard Time), so for most of the year it's on the same clock as the United Kingdom: five hours ahead of New York and one hour behind Continental Europe. Morocco observes Daylight Saving Time during the same period as Continental Europe, except when Ramadan is in summer, when the country temporarily goes back into Winter Time, which is two hours behind Continental Europe or four hours ahead of New York.

THE FODORS.COM CONNECTION

Before your trip, be sure to check out what other travelers are saying in travel talk forums at ⊕ *www.fodors.com.*

TIPPING

Tipping in Morocco is always appreciated. There are no hard-and-fast rules concerning how much and when to do it. Waiters in proper restaurants are always tipped up to 10% of the bill. In taxis, you can round up to the nearest 5 DH (for example, if the meter says 12 DH, pay 15 DH). At informal cafés the tip is normally 1 DH or 2 DH per person in the dining party. Porters, hotel or otherwise, will appreciate 5 DH or 10 DH. It's customary to give small tips of 1 DH or 2 DH to people such as parking, baggage, and restroom attendants. When in doubt, you can't go wrong by tipping. It is considered normal by Muslims to give money to beggars should they ask for it. Most, but not all, are deserving of a small coin or two.

VISITOR INFORMATION

The Moroccan National Tourist Office maintains Visit Morocco, a website in eight languages, including English. The tourist office also has Much Morocco, a website aimed specifically at English-speaking markets.

Contacts Moroccan National Tourist Office. ⊠ *Angle Rue Oued Al Makhazine/Rue Zalaga-BP, Agdal* ☎ *0537/67–40–13 in Morocco, 212/221–1583 in U.S.* ⊕ *www.visitmorocco.com; www.muchmorocco.com.*

INDEX

PHOTO CREDITS

Front cover: ugurhan/iStockphoto [Description: Golden door in Fez, Morocco]. 1, Anibaltrejo I Dreamstime.com. 2-3, cdrin / Shutterstock. 4, Edelweiss086 I Dreamstime.com. 5 (top), Bogdanwanko I Dreamstime.com. 5 (bottom), Saiko3p I Dreamstime.com. 6 (top left), Rudolf Tepfenhart/ Shutterstock. 6 (top right), Jan Wlodarczyk / Alamy. 6 (bottom right), Icon72 I Dreamstime.com. 6 (bottom left), Prochasson Frederic / Alamy. 7 (top), Ccharleson I Dreamstime.com. 7 (bottom), Anibaltrejo I Dreamstime.com. 8 (top left), Simonhack I Dreamstime.com. 8 (top right), Independent Picture Service / Alamy. 8 (bottom right), Kasto80 I Dreamstime.com. 8 (bottom left), Karim Tibari. 9 (top), Benhammad I Dreamstime.com. 9 (bottom), Sabinoparente I Dreamstime.com. 10, Witr I Dreamstime.com. 11 (top), Witr I Dreamstime.com. 11 (bottom), Boggy I Dreamstime.com. 13, Lorna Piche/iStockphoto. **Chapter 1: Experience Morocco:** 16-17, Prometheus72 / Shutterstock. 36, Terrance Klassen / age fotostock. 37 (top), JD Dallet / age fotostock. 37 (bottom), Vladimir Melnik/ iStockphoto. 38 (left), Ray Hems/iStockphoto. 38 (top right), Attila JANDI/Shutterstock. 38 (bottom right), Uploadalt/Wikimedia Commons. 39 (top left), WitR/Shutterstock. 39 (bottom left), Graham Lawrence / age fotostock. 39 (right), John Copland/Shutterstock. 40 (left), Philippe Michel / age fotostock. 40 (top right), Jerzy Strzelecki/Wikimedia Commons. 40 (bottom right), Anthon Jackson/ Shutterstock. 41 (left), Public domain. 41 (top right), Henry Zbyszynski/Flickr, [CC BY 2.0]. 41 (bottom right), Holger Mette/iStockphoto. 42 (left), Wendy Connett / age fotostock. 42 (right), Jaroslaw Grudzinski/Shutterstock. 43 (left), Juan Monino/iStockphoto. 43 (right), OPIS/Shutterstock. **Chapter 2: Marrakesh:** 45, Cleaper I Dreamstime.com. 48, Diego Grandi/Shutterstock. 58, Mashaku/Shutterstock. 63, PetePhippTravelshots / age fotostock. 72, Tony Worpole / Alamy. 78, La Mamounia. 96, jean-pierre lescourre / age fotostock. **Chapter 3: Tangier and the Mediterranean:** 109, Alvaro Leiva / age fotostock. 112, Holger Mette/iStockphoto. 121, roberthardiing / Alamy. 122, Peter Erik Forsberg / age fotostock. 131, Aguaviva/Shutterstock. 137 and 144, Alvaro Leiva / age fotostock. **Chapter 4: Rabat and Casablanca:** 147, Ian Cumming / age fotostock. 150, Witold Ryka/iStockphoto. 157, Graham Lawrence / age fotostock. 164, JD Dallet/age fotostock. 175, Javier Gil / age fotostock. 182, Graham Lawrence / age fotostock. 191, Vladimir Melnik/Shutterstock. **Chapter 5: Fez and the Middle Atlas:** 197, Javier Larrea / age fotostock. 200, Dallas Events Inc/Shutterstock. 211, Javier Larrea / age fotostock. 212, Mlenny Photography/iStockphoto. 219, Alessen84 I Dreamstime.com. 222 (top), Lorna Piche/iStockphoto. 222 (bottom), Rechitan Sorin/Shutterstock. 223 (top), Gautier Willaume/Shutterstock. 223 (center), Walter Bibikow/age fotostock. 223 (bottom), chiakto/Shutterstock. 224 (left), stefano pensotti/age fotostock. 224 (top right), ventdusud/Shutterstock. 224 (bottom right), Philip Lange/Shutterstock. 225 (top left), David Ooms/Flickr, [CC BY 2.0]. 225 (bottom left), David Romero Corral/iStockphoto. 225 (top right), Tom Fakler/iStockphoto. 225 (bottom right), Luisa Puccini/ Shutterstock. 226 (top), Juan Carlos Muñoz / age fotostock. 226 (center), Philip Lange/Shutterstock. 226 (bottom), chiakto/Shutterstock. 227, Walter Bibikow / age fotostock. 228 (top), Jon Purcell / age fotostock. 228 (bottom), robert van beets/iStockphoto. 229 (top), Philip Lange / Shutterstock.com. 229 (bottom), narvikk/iStockphoto. 235, Bjanka Kadic / age fotostock. 238, JD Dallet/age fotostock. 241, Christophe Boisvieux / age fotostock. 246, Ray Hems/iStockphoto. 251, Peky/Shutterstock. **Chapter 6: The High Atlas:** 253, Kay Maeritz / age fotostock. 256, Ronald Naar / age fotostock. 257 (top), Alan Keohane/www.kasbahdutoubkal.com. 257 (bottom), DAVID HOLT/Flickr, [CC BY SA 2.0]. 258, Alan Keohane/www.kasbahdutoubkal.com. 265, SUETONE Emilio / age fotostock. 268, PATRICK FORGET/age fotostock. 271, Alan Keohane/www.kasbahdutoubkal.com.. 278, Agostinho Gonçalves/Shutterstock. **Chapter 7: The Great Oasis Valleys:** 283, Peter Adams Photography Ltd / Alamy. 286, Sander Huiberts/iStockphoto. 295, Heeb Christian / age fotostock. 298, FRILET Patrick / age fotostock. 312-313, Jan Wlodarczyk / Alamy. 319, Carles Fortuny/Shutterstock. **Chapter 8: Agadir and The Southern Atlantic Coast:** 323, Egmont Strigl / age fotostock. 326, Ruslan Kalnitsky/Shutterstock. 333, Czekma13 I Dreamstime.com. 349, Philippe Michel / age fotostock. 352, Egmont Strigl /age fotostock. 362-363, Egmont Strigl / age fotostock. 367, Explora Essaouira. 369, Witold Ryka/ iStockphoto. 377, Peter Adams / age fotostock. **Back cover, from left to right:** Byvalet I Dreamstime. com; alex saberi/Shutterstock; Rechitan Sorin/Shutterstock. **Spine:** globe666 / Shutterstock. **About Our Writers:** All photos are courtesy of the writer except for the following: Sarah Gilbert, courtesy of Ruth Cohen.

NOTES

NOTES

NOTES

NOTES

NOTES

NOTES

NOTES

ABOUT OUR WRITERS

Rachel Blech is a travel writer and former broadcaster for Irish radio and RTÉ Radio based in Marrakesh. While making a radio documentary for Essaouira's Gnawa Music Festival in 2006, she met Saharoui nomads from southern Morocco who invited her to visit their local festival and experience their way of life. Since then, she has juggled projects between Ireland and Morocco and now lives mainly in Marrakesh, organizing cultural tours to the southern oases and desert regions. Her company, SheherazadVentures, is run in partnership with the nomadic family she met on that first visit. Rachel also writes for *Footprint* and *Time Out* and has been published in *EasyJet* inflight magazine and *Travelspeak* magazine. She updated the Marrakesh chapter this edition.

Freelance writer **Jane Folliott** updated the Agadir and the Southern Atlantic Coast chapter this edition.

More than a decade ago, **Olivia Gunning Bennani** left London's journalism world and headed to Morocco for a six-month trip. Since then she's been writing about her expeditions through the country and beyond, covering everything from family treks through the Atlas peaks atop a mule to the prolific verdure of the Honey Route and Paradise Valley. She lives in Casablanca with her husband and two young children. For this edition, she updated the Rabat and Casablanca chapter.

Sarah Gilbert is a freelance writer and photographer who calls London home when she's not traveling for numerous magazines, newspapers, and websites such as *Condé Nast Traveller* (UK), *Wanderlust, The Guardian,* and *The Independent.* She fell in love with Morocco in 2002 and has returned many times. A former resident of Fez and honorary Fassi, Sarah finds its history, culture, and people endlessly fascinating. She updated the Fez and the Middle Atlas and Tangier and the Mediterranean chapters this edition.

An adventurer living in Morocco, **Alice Morrison** first came to the country to run the fabled Marathon Des Sables in 2014, and liked it so much she decided to stay. Since then, she has traveled all over Morocco, but says her heart is split between the desert and the mountains. In 2017, her first television series aired on the BBC; it followed her journey along the old salt roads from Tangier all the way to Timbuktu in Mali. She has also completed the first trek from the highest point of North Africa, Mount Toubkal, straight across the Atlas Mountains to Agadir on the Atlantic Ocean. She is also the author of *Morocco to Mali: An Arabian Adventure.* She updated the High Atlas and Great Oasis Valleys chapters this edition.

In 2012, **Lynn Sheppard** left a career in government and diplomacy to pursue her dream of living in Morocco. She has lived in the United Kingdom, Belgium, Germany, and Japan, worked across Europe, Asia, and Africa, and speaks six languages, but it was Essaouira, on Morocco's Atlantic coast, that captured her heart when she first visited in 2001. She's now lived there for more than two years, supporting local nonprofits on project management, fund-raising, and social media, as well as writing for her ⊕ *www.maroc-o-phile.com* blog. Lynn updated Experience and Travel Smart chapters this edition.